struggled with Marx, and through a process of critique have appropriated some, though certainly not all, of his productive insights. Few today would consider themselves orthodox Durkheimians, but for those whose perspectives are fundamentally derived from his, I hope this work adds to the understanding of societal integration and disintegration and of the massive change in social forms that he perceived. My other intellectual debts have largely, I think, been indicated in the text.

On a more personal level, a number of individuals provided invaluable comments on all or part of various drafts of the manuscript, some of them years before this project even looked like it would turn into a book: Chris Bell, Eric Bermann, Helene Boyd, Robert Coles, Roy Edgley, Andrew Hahn, Carol Holden, Alfred Kellam, Harold Korn, Lucian Pye, Joel Migdal, J. Christopher Perry, Roy Rappaport, Kay Saakvitne, Russell Smith, Susan Suckling, Marc Westen, Sheldon White, Lewis Wurgaft, Robert Zajonc, and three anonymous reviewers. Susan Allen-Mills at Cambridge University Press has been invaluable in her advice, critical suggestions, and support for the project. Janis Bolster and Amit Shah at Cambridge worked diligently at production and copyediting. To these people I owe much of the book's coherence, and the foolishness that remains is of my own doing.

I would like to extend special thanks to two people whose help and encouragement I could not have done without: to my wife Marcia, who suffered through many a dinner-time discussion about subjects like totems and teddy-bears, and whose uncanny habit of asking questions like, "How do you know what an infant is thinking?" at precisely those moments when I had begun to take myself too seriously has helped keep me honest; and to Marie Jahoda, a wonderful friend, mentor, and sparring partner, whose respect for ideas is equalled only by her respect for people.

SELF AND SOCIETY

Self and Society

NARCISSISM, COLLECTIVISM, AND THE DEVELOPMENT OF MORALS

DREW WESTEN
University of Michigan

The right of the
University of Cambridge
to print and sell
all manner of books
was granted by
Henry VIII in 1534.
The University has printed
and published continuously
since 1584.

CAMBRIDGE UNIVERSITY PRESS
Cambridge
New York   New Rochelle   Melbourne   Sydney

Published by the Press Syndicate of the University of Cambridge
The Pitt Building, Trumpington Street, Cambridge CB2 1RP
32 East 57th Street, New York, NY 10022, USA
10 Stamford Road, Oakleigh, Melbourne 3166, Australia

First published 1985
Reprinted 1987, 1988 (twice)

Printed in the United States of America

Library of Congress Cataloging in Publication Data
Westen, Drew, 1959–
Self and society.
Bibliography: p.
1. Personality and culture. 2. Self. 3. Moral
development. 4. Narcissism. 5. Collectivism.
I. Title.
BF698.9.C8W47 1985 302.5 84–28478
ISBN 0 521 30171 8 hard covers
ISBN 0 521 31770 3 paperback

TO MARCIA

Contents

vii

Contents

Contents

ix

Preface

> Society must be studied in the individual and the individual in society; those who desire to treat politics and morals apart from one another will never understand either.
>
> Rousseau

Two hundred years after Rousseau wrote these words, the social sciences relate to one another like the three rings of a circus: their activities are largely independent, though an occasional tightrope walker straddles the boundaries in defiance of the frightful distance between himself and solid ground. The purpose of this book is to provide a safety net, so that momentary stumbles do not prove fatal or debilitating.

Many problems confront theorists who attempt to reconcile psychological with sociocultural variables, the greatest of which is the integration of different levels of analysis. The easiest – and the most fallacious – method of simultaneously examining personality processes and sociocultural phenomena is reductionism, i.e., considering one set as dependent, and the other as independent variables. A truly integrated approach, in contrast, must be able to treat both individual and social variables as dependent and independent and to reassemble the data in some coherent fashion. Such is the aim of this project.

The book proposes a theory of personality, a social theory, and a theory about the interrelation of the two. Not only analytically, but stylistically, such a crossing of traditionally distinct disciplinary boundaries presents problems that I have been only partially successful in resolving. The analysis of psychological data, for example, is written with the intent both to suggest to psychologists a new way of viewing personality and psychological development, and to explicate for nonprofessional readers the personality theory. A similar situation occurs in sections of the book that are anthropological, sociological, or philosophical. The problem lies in creating exposition that is neither too elementary, and therefore redundant for the specialist, nor overwhelming for the "visiting professional" from

xi

another field. In some cases I have tried to write on two levels, choosing words that convey meanings for those who know the nuances of the discipline as well as for those who do not. In many cases I am sure to have succeeded both in boring the expert and bewildering the alien. As to the former, I can only beg the reader's indulgence. For the latter I have tried to cite copiously from the literatures that have informed my views.

I am not, in this book, producing any new data. We have plenty of "evidence" in the social sciences; the problem is that we have difficulty deciding what it is that our evidence documents. If "science progresses," it does so through an interaction between inquiring minds, empirical observations, and previous theories. We do not advance our knowledge through the dogged collection of statistically significant but scientifically and socially insignificant trivialities; empirical observation is useless if it cannot corroborate, disconfirm, or otherwise provide insight into theoretical perspectives or practical applications that are not, themselves, trivial. Pouring "facts" into "science" is like pouring sand onto the beach: no matter how much we accumulate, knowledge will always slip through our fingers. Yet the equal and opposite danger is that we create deductive havens for our homeless minds, that our quest for cognitive order is prepotent over our interest in reality. The contrast between these two modes of inquiry seems to loom as large in twentieth century social science as it did in the philosophical skirmishes between Locke and Descartes (if not in arguments between Plato and Aristotle), and the preferences of researchers for one style or another probably rest as much upon temperament as upon substantive issues.

In this book the reader will participate in a dialogue with both "facts" and "theories." Perhaps we would sometimes do well to treat facts as theories, since all observations are theoretically tinged, and theories as facts, since past and current theories present themselves as social facts with which every new generation of researchers must reckon. The arguments presented here will rely upon empirical data, whether from the clinic, the laboratory, or the field, as well as critical analyses of the theories and concepts of thinkers whose footprints indelibly mark the psychological, sociological, and anthropological paths to be traversed. Our current understanding is a partial function of both our own observations (and those of others) and of paradigms lost:[1] one person's, generation's, or tradition's conceptualizations uniformly arise in relation both to "objective reality" and to previous thought. The approaches we develop must always be viewed in context of the approaches we shed. Intellectual advances are moulting seasons, and in the moments of transitional bareness, we must

---

[1] My apologies to whoever first used this phrase.

examine both the stimuli impinging upon us and our previous coats if we aspire to brighter plumage.

The book consists of three parts. Part I, "A Theory of Personality," proposes a view of the structure, dynamics, and development of personality that draws upon a wide spectrum of theories and data, including psychoanalysis (particularly ego psychology and object relations theory), cognitive social learning theory, existential psychology, systems theory, attribution research, social cognition research, moral psychology, and ethology. Chapter 1 provides a brief review of competing traditions in personality theory. Chapter 2, entitled, "Emotion: A Missing Link Between Psychodynamic and Cognitive-Behavioral Psychology?" offers a theory of emotion that serves as a conceptual bridge between aspects of the two most sophisticated and seemingly irreconcilable contemporary approaches to personality. Chapter 3 proposes a model of the structure and dynamics of personality, and Chapter 4 focuses on the development of personality, narcissism, and moral judgment. It argues that the development of ego processes, narcissism, and moral beliefs are intertwined and attempts to show how the child moves from an initial reconciliation of self and other in which only his own needs are important, to a later position in which morality is defined by significant others, to a possible synthesis in which the individual creates her or his own idiosyncratic view of the ideal relation of self and other. The final section of the chapter discusses the relevance of the perspective proposed here both for future research and for clinical practice.

Part II, "A Theory of Culture," leaves the individual level of analysis and starts afresh with an examination of the development of social theory in sociology and anthropology in Chapter 5. The aim of Part II is to elaborate a theory of sociocultural structure and change that brings together ideas and data from such diverse thinkers and perspectives as Marx, Durkheim, functionalism, structuralism, ecological anthropology, symbolic anthropology, and systems theory. Chapter 6 provides a structural model which examines the dialectic between ideals and social structure and shows how culture mediates between conflicting needs of collectivities and individuals. Chapter 7 proposes a theory of the evolution of collectivism and morality at the societal level, focusing on the way in which a collectivism that ascribes value and power to the group is being overturned in favor of a conception that gives primacy to the individual.

Part III, "Personality and Culture: A Synthesis," integrates the models enunciated in Parts I and II. Chapter 8, "Culture and Personality: Dying Species or Vigorous Hybrid?" critically reviews the literature which has attempted to understand the relation between culture and personality and argues that a key flaw in much of this literature is the assumption that one can develop a model that bridges the two levels of analysis without first developing sophisticated (and interlocking) theories at each level. In other words, the only way to begin to comprehend the interrelation of personality and culture is to develop, first, an adequate theory of personality which can deal with such issues as the motivation and dynamics of normal and pathological functioning, and second, an adequate theory of culture which can aid in the understanding of sociocultural dynamics in times of both relative stability and relative change. Chapter 9 discusses the relation between sociocultural and personality structure and dynamics. Chapter 10 examines the question of "primitive mentality" and explores the relation between collective representations and individual psychology in preindustrial societies. After a discussion of the concepts of "modernization" and "development," Chapter 11, on "The Psychodynamics of Modernization," points to two psychological changes that consistently correlate with various processes of modernization: a heightened emphasis of self and a breakdown of accepted and internalized structures of authority. These changes are related systematically to the theories of personality structure and development of Part I and sociocultural structure and development of Part II, and several aspects of modernization are delineated which produce these effects. A central thesis of this book is that greater emphasis of self is an inherent aspect of modernization, not primarily a by-product of capitalism, colonialism, or social change in general; and that the greater self-emphasis that arises with the processes of modernization constitutes a moral revolution. Chapter 12 explores the psychological impact of the breakdown in shared systems of belief that occurs in periods of rapid social change and shows how the theory developed here can elucidate a concrete case by reanalyzing data from Java on events surrounding a funeral in the midst of social upheaval. Chapter 13 is entitled, "Breakdown and Recovery: Paradigmatic Processes in Personal Identity and Cultural Integration." It examines six seemingly unrelated phenomena – Kuhnian scientific revolutions, cultural revitalization movements, personal religious experiences, identity crises and reformations, brainwashing, and rites of passage – and demonstrates that they share a common pattern that provides insight into the relation between individual identity and cultural integration. The concluding chapter draws from a wide array of independent empirical studies, with the intent of demonstrating that modernization produces a type of self-oriented personality which correlates with an emerging cultural shift in moral orientation from a belief in the legitimate primacy of the group to a belief in the sovereignty of the individual.

Some readers may already be taken aback by the abstract and theoretical nature of this enterprise. The reader may be uneasy not only with such a heavy dosage of theory, but she or he may also find unsettling "grand theories," of which this is undoubtedly one. My justification for presenting an abstract theory – and an exceedingly broad one, at that – is that we simply cannot and do not operate without such frameworks. The alternative to devising new and better theories is not to work without them but to accept old and faltering ones. The anthropologist who examines a ritual and determines that it fulfills a socially necessary purpose is making an extraordinary assumption – that groups or societies have collective "needs" that somehow become translated into concrete acts – which is essentially functionalist and presupposes functionalist *theory*. The sociologist who makes a statistical study of income distribution while consciously eschewing social theory does not realize that he is tacitly accepting a positivist-empiricist philosophy of science which sees the "observable facts" as the essence of science, and social science as modeled on the natural science paradigm. Not only may such a researcher be taking for granted such highly abstract concepts as "socioeconomic status," but he is committing himself to a view that sees meaning as secondary to – if not entirely outside the parameters of – the study of human beings. This is a very *theoretical* view which asserts that important social facts can be expressed statistically, a perspective which without doubt requires strong and explicit justification. To assume, further, that one can fruitfully examine income distribution without simultaneously examining class relations is implicitly to take a theoretical position against Marxist sociology, which asserts that one cannot understand the former without examining the latter. The psychologist who studies "self-esteem" as an isolated personality variable has chosen his object of study because of implicit beliefs and assumptions about personality that lead him to believe that people's judgments of self-esteem are somehow psychologically significant.

As soon as one crosses disciplinary boundaries, the importance of attending to covert assumptions multiplies. The difficulty in developing a broad interdisciplinary theory that is not naive, reductionistic, or simply absurd is enormous, and has discouraged many from undertaking the task. Yet the absence of an explicit theory bridging individual and sociocultural levels of analysis does not imply the absence of implicit theory. Researchers in all disciplines use poorly articulated grand theories all the time. The foundation of many anthropological analyses of decision making in preindustrial societies is an unexamined rationalistic psychological theory that few who study personality would accept. The implicit sociological theory of dominant models of cognition in psychology is of individual information processors separately encoding and retrieving information about the world, themselves, and the other information processors with whom they come in contact.

The point of all this is that to reject explicit theory is to demonstrate not a noble agnosticism, but a profound naivete about the nature of thought as well as social science. People cannot perceive the world without conceptual frameworks, and as people are both the subject and object of social study, the elaboration of these schemata is indispensable. To provide a broad theoretical framework is not dishonestly to pretend omniscience; to the contrary, it is to be intellectually honest in enunciating one's perspective, which would otherwise remain penumbral and unexamined, and to suggest that this model would be useful for others to use.

One final word about the nature of the constructs proposed here requires brief mention. "Reality" is not directly recorded in scientific concepts. As Kuhn, among others, has emphasized, psychological, sociological, and cultural factors intervene in the "scientific" attempt to describe our universe. If this is true regarding such topics as the nature of planetary motion, in which we can take a somewhat disinterested perspective, one would certainly expect to find such factors operating in relation to the object of thought in which we have the most stake: ourselves.

In proposing a set of constructs (such as "culture ideal," "internal narcissism," and a number of others), I am in one sense suggesting that these concepts denote real objects and, in another, claiming them to be only of heuristic value. In contending that a person may experience guilt when he compares aspects of his "self-system" with aspects of his "ego ideal" (Chapter 3), I am obviously not arguing that one can see sections of the brain roped off and marked accordingly. What I am saying is that the discrepancy between a self-image and an affect-laden moral goal is a real discrepancy that is more easily understood by postulating psychic "structures," defined as constellations of functionally related processes. In this sense I clearly differ from structuralist theories in social science that view structures as real in some physical sense. Perhaps the most one can say about concepts in the social sciences is that they somehow reflect both the object and the observer, that they point to real phenomena in an imperfect way because of the needs and imperfections of the observer. Science, Sphinxlike, lies somewhere between humanity and nature, and since *human* nature is the object of social scientific inquiry, then social science is to be found somewhere between mind and humankind.

By way of acknowledgment, my three greatest intellectual debts are to Freud, Marx, and Durkheim. The orthodox Freudian who reads this book may fear that I have emasculated Freud's theory, that by abandoning energy concepts and the id I have murdered the primal father and now intend to devour him. The orthodox Marxist who scans these pages may similarly brand me a bourgeois apologist or (if charitable) a misguided sufferer of false consciousness, having cast aside economic determinism, faith in a radical proletariat, and an exclusive emphasis on class as an analytical (if not a political) tool. One who reads more closely, I hope, will see that I have not castrated psychoanalytic notions but have tried to work through them to arrive at a fuller understanding; and that I have, indeed,

I A Theory of Personality

1 Personality Theory: The Three Faces of Psyche

IN AN ARTICLE on contemporary personality psychology in a recent edition of the *Annual Review of Psychology*, Ravenna Helson and Valory Mitchell note:

> Personality psychology has sometimes been seen as the domain of a little group of rational technicians who specialize in criticizing each other's measure of the insignificant, then conclude that the existence of the obvious is doubtful, then doubt whether the study of personality is worthwhile. (1978, pp. 579-80)

As psychologists since Freud have known, jokes and delusions all contain some grain of truth, and as psychologists for over a decade have known, the above quotation is neither entirely a joke nor wholly a delusion.

Personality psychology is a splintered field, for some time in the throes of a move away from global theorizing, emphasizing instead the development of second- and third-order theories and empirical research. In a rather ironic sense, psychology has always had multiple personalities: the first major theorist, Freud, had little influence on academic psychology (especially in America) until around the time of his death; and shortly thereafter the universities produced their first really comprehensive theory of personality, Skinnerian behaviorism, which split the discipline into two mutually hostile camps.[1] From the behaviorist matrix have emerged cognitive social learning approaches that focus on cognitive processes, the interaction between personality variables and specific situations, and socially mediated learning. In the 1950s a "third force" in personality theory arose, which includes existential and humanistic psychology. Research in personality psychology also includes a number of other empirical approaches, collectively known as trait psychology, which attempt the delineation and measurement of various dimensions of personality (e.g., intro-

---

[1] Unfortunately, the first law of academidynamics states that every simplification is an oversimplification: the twain of Freudian psychoanalysis and pre-Skinnerian (Hullian) behaviorism did, in fact, meet at Yale in the 1940s (see, for example, Miller and Dollard, 1941).

3

version/extroversion, perceived locus of control, Machiavellianism). In contrast to these more atomistic, trait-centered approaches, psychodynamic, cognitive-behavioral, and humanistic/existential psychology constitute the three major traditions which attempt to provide an overall, comprehensive picture of the structure and development of human mental life. To understand the current state of personality theory thus requires a brief, if overly schematic, presentation of the basic tenets and development of these three approaches.

Psychoanalysis and Its Discontents

Philosophers have speculated about the nature of personality at least since Plato's tripartite division of the soul into a rational, an appetitive, and a spirited part, but not until Freud did personality theory begin to scale the walls of the Platonic cave. Freud's first model of the mind appeared in his *Interpretation of Dreams* (1900), a work which he considered to include "the most valuable of all the discoveries it has been my good fortune to make" (p. xxxii). In it he proposed, contrary to the prevailing wisdom, that much of mental life is unconscious, and that the meaning of every dream lies in unconscious, infantile wishes. The theory he proposed, known as his topographic model, distinguishes three systems within the mind: the conscious, the preconscious, and the unconscious.

The conscious is the region of the mind of which we are immediately aware and is responsible for motor activity. The preconscious includes those thoughts that are accessible to consciousness but are not, at the moment, conscious (e.g., one's telephone number). The preconscious and the unconscious are both *descriptively* unconscious; i.e., the contents of these systems are not conscious. The difference between them is that, whereas the contents of the preconscious can become conscious at any time, the contents of the system "unconscious" are inaccessible to consciousness because they are repressed (e.g., one's ex-lover's telephone number). The contents of the unconscious are nonverbal and generally infantile. The unconscious is not organized according to the principles of rational thought; contradictory thoughts and impulses can exist side by side, and Kantian categories of time and causality are foreign to it.

The unconscious is the psychic reservoir of instinctual energies, and it knows only one kind of thought: the wish. This unorganized, illogical, wishful mode of thought Freud calls "primary process" thinking. Primary process thought pays no heed, and in fact has no access, to reality. It operates solely on the basis of the "pleasure principle," seeking pleasure and avoiding pain in the most expedient fashion. The preconscious, in contrast, utilizes rational, logical, "secondary process" thinking and is guided by the "reality principle," no longer accepting mechanisms such

4

as hallucination as valid modes of gratification. Somewhere between the conscious and the unconscious lies a censor responsible for repressing impulses from the unconscious that are unacceptable to the preconscious. Thus, the reality principle holds the pleasure principle in check because gratification of unconscious desires in the real world would ultimately lead to unpleasurable results. Unfulfilled unconscious wishes – and infantile sexual wishes, in particular – continue to clamor for satisfaction, and dreams, like neuroses, psychoses, and phenomena such as slips of the tongue (Freud, 1901) allow these wishes to be gratified in some form. Unlike the preconscious, the unconscious is thus *dynamic,* or energizing. Psychic conflict, a phenomenon to which Freud drew special attention, is conceived as a battle between the conscious/preconscious and the repressed unconscious.

Central to Freud's conceptualization of the psyche is the notion of drive or instinct. As countless intellectual historians and commentators on Freud's thought have noted, Freud derived his concept of drive (*Treib*) from the German physicalist tradition of Helmholtz and Brücke, his "scientific ideal father imagoes" (Holt, 1976, p. 163). Psychic energy is no different from any other type of energy in the natural world and thus obeys natural laws. Freud relied upon a drive-discharge model that proposes that psychic excitation builds up and seeks discharge. He based this view on a hydraulic metaphor that most closely resembles the accumulation of urine in the bladder (Holt, 1976). It is hydraulic also in the sense of a closed hydraulic system in physics, such that a fixed quantity of water can be converted into steam and reconverted into the same amount of water; psychic energy is fixed in quantity but can be transformed in various ways. An instinct, according to Freud, has a source (a body organ), an aim (some form of discharge), an object (e.g., a person), and an intensity.

Alongside this quantitative approach to drives, which views instinct as a quantity of excitation, is a dualistic, qualitative view which developed throughout Freud's career. (For an excellent article tracing the development of Freud's instinct theory, see Bibring, 1941.) Freud originally conceived of two instincts, sexual instincts and ego instincts, and in this he was undoubtedly influenced by Darwin's evolutionary theory and Schopenhauer's philosophy (and its offspring), both of which emphasized the conflict between the good of the species (and its need for procreation) and the good of the individual (the classical notion of self-interest). Freud paid attention primarily to the sexual instinct, which he denoted by the term "libido." The first major change in this theory occurred when his study of narcissism (1914) led him to believe that part of the desire for self-preservation stems from libidinal attachment to (or "cathexis" of) the ego. Gradually the role of aggression became more prominent in Freud's thinking, and eventually he shifted from a dualism of ego and sexual instincts to a dualism of sexual and aggressive instincts (1920). He maintained that view for the rest of his career, enlarging the theory to suggest that libido and aggression are psychic manifestations of a ubiquitous, cosmic conflict between Eros and Thanatos, life and death. In this later view, the instinct for self-preservation is conceived as a component of the erotic instinct.

While his instinct theory was always dualistic, Freud's preoccupation throughout his career was with the vicissitudes of libido. In his developmental or "genetic" model, first enunciated in 1905, Freud proposed a series of stages in the development of the libidinal drive. These stages are viewed as *psychosexual:* they are seen as stages in the development of personality, not just phases in the "organization" of libido. Thus, the ontogeny of the psyche and of the sexual drive are intertwined. Each stage is associated with a particular location on the body, or "erogenous zone." In the first phase, the oral phase, sexual gratification relates to the mouth, as hunger is a prime issue for the infant. The second, or anal stage, occurs around the age of two. During this period, conflicts over toilet training are paramount, and a conflict ensues between compliance and defiance.

The third phase is the phallic phase, and masturbatory activity begins to move to the genitals as the child discovers a new and powerful source of excitation. This is the period in which the child must come to terms with the Oedipus complex, and according to Freud, the way in which the child resolves this trauma is decisive for later personality development. The Oedipal age boy desires to "have" his mother in an exclusive relationship, and he sees his father as a powerful rival, as well as a loved object. He fears that his father will castrate him for his desires (the "castration complex"), so he relinquishes his Oedipal wishes – or rather, represses them – and identifies with his father. The girl in the Oedipal period must come to terms with her physical inferiority (lack of a penis); she blames her mother for this deprivation and turns to her father as a primary love object. In both the male and the female, matters are more complicated than this because, in fact, both boys and girls desire to some extent the same-sex parent (the "negative Oedipus complex").

The phallic phase (roughly ages three to six) is followed by a "latency" period, in which the child licks his Oedipal wounds (so to speak) and diverts his sexual aims to self-development and the acquisition of culture ("sublimation" of libido). With the emergence of adolescence, Oedipal issues resurface, repressions break down, and the serenity of the latency years dissolves. If all goes well, the child reaches the fourth and final, or genital stage. In this stage, pregenital libidinal desires (oral, anal, and phallic) become integrated with, and subordinate to the desire for heterosexual genital sex. In less than optimal development, a developmental arrest or "fixation" may occur at a particular stage, or a failure to consolidate development at one level may lead to a "regression" to a previous one. In actuality, no one entirely transcends any of the stages. The result of a fixation or regression may be a particular character or personality organization. The oral character, for example, is needy and dependent, always trying to "take things in;" the anal character may be stingy and "withholding."

Freud maintained his drive-instinct and developmental models throughout his career, but he became dissatisfied with the topographic view by 1920 (the same year that he proposed the antinomy of sex and aggression). Three years later he began to advocate a new model, which came to be known as his structural model (1923), which received perhaps its best articulation in his *New Introductory Lectures* (1933) and the *Outline of Psycho-analysis* (1939). The structural model distinguishes three psychic "structures" or "institutions:" the id, the ego, and the superego. The id is conceived as the reservoir of the libidinal and aggressive drives, and like its conceptual predecessor, the unconscious, it is characterized as operating by the pleasure principle and utilizing primary process thought. The ego is the self-interested, executive institution of the psyche, which is under the sway of the reality principle and utilizes secondary process thought. It is responsible for perception, cognition, and motor activity, and when threatened by dangerous stimuli from within and without, it uses various "mechanisms of defense," such as repression, regression, reaction-formation (turning a desire into its opposite, e.g., "sour grapes"), and projection (ascribing one's own forbidden wishes or attributes to some external "object")[1] to protect itself.

The ego must reconcile its three masters: the id, reality, and the superego. The superego is the psychic representative of morality which the individual internalizes from parents and society. Although Freud seems never entirely to have given up the topographic model (it appears again in his last work in 1939), he developed the structural model because of his observation that many of the processes he had ascribed to the preconscious (such as repression) were, in fact, carried out unconsciously and were not accessible to consciousness. Thus, in the structural model, intrapsychic conflict occurs between the three structures; it is no longer seen as a conflict between consciousness and the unconscious.[2]

The Freudian theory of personality is powerful and complex, and while it tends to receive scant coverage in academic psychology departments in the United States in particular, it continues to be a mainstay of clinical

---

[1] "Objects," in psychoanalytic parlance, are psychic representations of things, people, ideas, etc., to which libido may become attached, although the term is often used to refer to the actual external reality rather than its internal representation.

[2] For the reader unacquainted with Freud, the following would provide a fairly balanced, historical view of his work: Freud, 1900, 1905, 1912, 1933, 1939. For excellent secondary material, see Arlow and Brenner, 1964; Jahoda, 1977; and Hall and Lindzey, 1978.

practice in psychology, psychiatry, and psychiatric social work. Every modern personality theorist has perforce had to engage in dialogue with Freud, whether as revisionist or adversary, and the rationalistic, nonemotive bent of much of current thinking in personality psychology reflects the problems encountered by any personality theorist who fails to grapple adequately with Freud's work. While Freud's influence on theories of personality has been nearly universal, one can isolate five "psychodynamic" traditions to which psychoanalysis has given rise.

The first offspring of psychoanalysis were its early revisionists, Adler (see 1929, 1969) and Jung (1971), who, like most critics of the orthodox Freudian position, do not find Freud's instinct theory compelling. Adler focused on the will to power, as opposed to the drive for sex, and he emphasized the importance of feelings of inferiority on personality development. Jung developed a complex and often mystical psychodynamic view which propounded the complementarity of various psychic processes and structures (such as unconscious and conscious, feeling and thinking, male and female parts of the psyche) and asserted that all human beings share a "collective unconscious" with which they must bring their lives into harmony.

The second psychodynamic tradition emphasized the social aspects of personality and the influence of culture on personality formation. Writers such as Fromm (1955), Horney (1937, 1950), and Sullivan (1953) argued that Freud failed to recognize the role of cultural and historical factors on the formation of personality, and Erik Erikson (1963, 1968), one of a handful of psychoanalysts whose work has entered mainstream (academic) psychology, has attempted to bring psychoanalytic theory closer to an understanding of the role of the "historical moment."

The third tradition is a development within psychoanalysis known as ego psychology. Whereas Freud concentrated largely on the id and only relatively late in his career began to focus on the ego, ego psychologists maintain that the ego, with its function of adaptation to reality, is central to the understanding of personality. Following Anna Freud (1936), ego psychologists have focused on the adaptive and maladaptive mechanisms of defense used by the ego, and following Hartmann (1939), they have examined "conflict-free" spheres of ego functioning, such as cognition and perception. This latter interest has brought psychoanalytic thought into some communication with academic psychology, though relatively few psychologists straddle that fence. The fourth tradition, also within psychoanalysis, is the object relations school. This approach concentrates on the internal "object world" of the individual, on her or his mental representations of social reality. In recent years, ego-psychological and object-relational approaches have begun to converge in the work of theorists such as Kernberg (1976).

8

The final tradition derived from psychoanalysis is less a school of thought than a rubric or a set of clinicians and writers which one can loosely label "eclectic." A vast number of mental health professionals would place themselves in this category, and in large part one could say that eclectic psychodynamic psychologists find psychodynamic approaches (i.e., approaches which examine feelings, internal meanings, defenses, etc.) compelling, yet they reject Freudian theory as a general model of mental life.

Skinnerian Behaviorism and the Response to Its Stimulus

The second major theory of the psyche is behaviorism, and B.F. Skinner's version is the most comprehensive and has been the most influential. Skinnerian behaviorism rests upon an entirely different epistemology than psychodynamic approaches. It is a radical empiricism, which views internal mental states as intersubjectively unverifiable and outside the parameters of scientific investigation. Whereas psychoanalysis relies upon data from the clinic or the couch, Skinner's source of data is the laboratory, and rats, pigeons, and humans are his subjects. Skinner's viewpoint developed from the earlier behaviorist views of Pavlov (1927) and Watson (1925). His thought is a reaction against Cartesian dualism, with its separation of mind and body; introspective psychology, with its emphasis on subjective experience; and psychoanalysis.

Skinner is interested in behavior, as opposed to internal behavioral dispositions. Anathema to Skinner is the search for a psychic "deep structure," "latent content," or "metapsychology" lurking beneath observable behavior. For the behaviorist, psychology is the study of behavior and its relation to the environment, and the purpose of psychology is the prediction and control of human behavior. Skinner would not, in fact, speak of "personality" at all; for him, behavior is the result of conditioning.

Fundamentally, he distinguishes between "respondent conditioning" (the classical conditioning pioneered by Pavlov) and "operant conditioning." Respondent conditioning is the psychology of reflexes. An unconditioned stimulus (e.g., food) is paired (presented) with a conditioned stimulus (e.g., a bell), so that when an organism (e.g., a dog) responds to one, it responds to the other; in this manner the animal comes to associate the two stimuli and to respond to the conditioned stimulus in the same manner as it would respond to the unconditioned stimulus (e.g., by salivating). To give a human example, if a woman left her panties by the bed whenever she and her lover engaged in sexual activity, her lover may become aroused whenever he sees her panties. The response elicited by the unconditioned stimulus (such as arousal when the man sees his lover) is a "reflex," and the relationship between conditioned stimulus and response is a "conditioned reflex."

9

Only a small percentage of human behavior is reflex, so Skinner developed the concept of operant conditioning. Whereas the stimulus in respondent conditioning temporally precedes the response, in operant conditioning the response comes before the payoff, which is called the "reinforcer." An operant is a class of behaviors emitted rather than elicited. When an operant is reinforced, the frequency of its occurrence rises. For example, if a pigeon happens to peck at a target and is rewarded with food, the probability that it will do so again increases. Pecking is an operant that is reinforced by food. If the pigeon is continually rewarded (reinforced), it will continue that action. The probability of a response (operant) is not dependent only upon rate of reinforcement: it depends, as well, upon the state of the organism, i.e., whether deprivation or satiation prevails. For example, if a pigeon is not hungry, the likelihood that it will keep pecking is reduced. In more Skinnerian parlance, one would not say that a pigeon is "hungry," only that it has not been reinforced recently with food. The crucial factor in predicting the pigeon's actions (operant behavior) is its "history of reinforcement"; by examining its feeding record and its prior reinforcement for pecking responses, one could predict the probability of its pecking at the target. When a reinforced behavior is no longer rewarded, it undergoes "extinction," which means that the response gradually disappears from the organism's repertoire of behavior.

A reinforcer is any stimulus that strengthens a behavioral response (i.e., increases the chance of its occurrence). A positive reinforcer is a stimulus which, when presented, strengthens the response. A negative reinforcer is one which, when *removed*, strengthens a response. Punishment, like negative reinforcement, involves an aversive stimulus, but a punishing stimulus is one which, when presented, *weakens* a response. For example, the food given to the pigeon pecking at the target constitutes positive reinforcement. If the pigeon had been rewarded instead by the removal of a loud sound, negative reinforcement would have been involved. If the pigeon had pecked at the experimenter, one would suspect that punishment would be the relevant principle.

Skinner adds another important case, that of "operant discrimination." In this type of learning, the operant is not emitted randomly as in operant conditioning (until being reinforced). Instead, a given stimulus increases the probability that the operant will be emitted. For example, the pigeon may learn that when a light comes on, the probability is greater that it will be reinforced for pecking. This form of conditioning is something of a hybrid between respondent and operant conditioning. Skinner summarizes the three forms of conditioning:

> (1) Certain events—like the color and taste of ripe fruit—tend to occur together. Respondent conditioning is the corresponding effect upon behavior. (2) Certain activities of the organism effect certain changes in the

environment. Operant conditioning is the corresponding effect on behavior. (3) Certain events are occasions upon which certain actions effect certain changes in the environment. Operant discrimination is the corresponding effect upon behavior. (1953, p. 125)[1]

Skinnerian behaviorism generated voluminous research in the 1950s and 1960s, particularly in America. Indeed, that many universities refer to the disciplines which study human beings as the "behavioral sciences" is largely a tribute to Skinner's enormous influence. Nevertheless, few today would accept a radical behaviorism as a theory (or alternative to the notion) of personality. (For an excellent summary of contemporary behaviorist thought, see Bolles, 1975.) The reasons for this cannot be explored here, though the reader should be aware that the difficulty in predicting a single pecking behavior of a pigeon outside of very special controlled conditions has never been overcome, which lends little hope for the idea of a behaviorist account of complex human behaviors, especially over time. Perhaps the acid test for a Skinnerian behaviorist would be the following scenario. Imagine a professor of behaviorist psychology lying in a hospital bed, paralyzed by a stroke. He is thinking, however, and realizes if he can think but cannot speak or act, he is nevertheless capable of knowledge and thought, despite his physical debility. He suddenly realizes that his view of personality must be wrong, and he longs to tell his students, but he is incapable of speech. At such a moment, is the professor still a behaviorist?

The seeds of the destruction of a radical behaviorism were sown in the late 1940s when researchers within the behaviorist paradigm began to discover latent learning. Tolman (1948) found that rats were actually learning about mazes even when they were not being reinforced. Tolman discovered that rats familiar with a maze could run it faster than unfamiliar rats when reinforced for the first time. What became clear was that the rats were forming cognitive maps of their environment, even before being reinforced.

The "cognitive revolution" in psychology in the 1960s and 1970s produced a serious challenge to orthodox behaviorism. Computer models of information processing suggested a metaphor for psychologists interested in human information storage and retrieval, and this new approach required the examination of "internal" mental connections and processes, thus challenging Skinner's antimentalist epistemology. Of course, Piaget had been talking of schemas, structures, and the mental operations which transform them for forty years, but the quest for a science of the observable had cast a shadow over many of Piaget's efforts, especially in behaviorist American psychology.

---

[1] The presentation of Skinner's views here is derived primarily from Skinner, 1953, 1971, 1974.

This interest in cognitive processes combined with an emphasis on the importance of social reinforcement and social life in general to produce from the behaviorist matrix a new perspective which, in the hands of some of its more cognitively oriented adherents, borders on a "fourth force" in personality psychology. This approach is cognitive social learning theory, most closely associated with the work of Mischel (1968, 1973, 1979), Bandura (1969, 1977a, b), and Rotter (1966). Recently Cantor and Kihlstrom (1982) have been working toward what they call a "cognitive theory of personality."

Cognitive social learning theory asserts that behavior is cognitively and socially mediated. Whereas behaviorism posits the automatic connection of stimulus and response, social learning theory contends that mediating between stimulus and response is an active, thinking individual. The response to a stimulus is dependent upon the way the person interprets and comprehends it. Thus, if a person develops an expectation or "expectancy" (Rotter, 1954) that a given course of action will be rewarding, he will pursue it, even if objective stimulus conditions suggest otherwise. A person can also gain cognitive control over his own behavior by self-reinforcing certain courses of action or deliberately altering his thoughts about a stimulus. For example, Mischel and his colleagues (Mischel, 1984; Mischel and Moore, 1980) have for several years been studying the way children learn to delay gratification by distracting themselves or thinking about the more neutral aspects of the rewards they will receive if they can wait (e.g., thinking about marshmallows as fluffy white clouds instead of as chewy, tasty treats).

According to social learning theorists, much of behavior is socially mediated. Bandura (1967, 1977a) has examined the ways in which learning can occur through such processes as vicarious reinforcement (learning through others' mistakes) and "modeling" (imitation) of the behavior of others. Other researchers with a cognitive social orientation (e.g., Swann and Read, 1981; Cantor and Kihlstrom, 1982) have stressed the importance of social cognition in personality processes. In so doing, they have added something very central to the study of personality, namely an empirically grounded emphasis on information processing. The most significant problem with current social cognitive approaches to personality is that they tend to provide a model of a motiveless *homo academicus* whose only dynamic motivations are knowledge and competence. *Homo academicus* has fully evolved (and hopefully will quickly become extinct) in Little's (1983) conception of "personal projects." Little proposes that people's aims can be likened to the academic's development of research projects and quest for a long curriculum vitae. His model of the development of "personal projects" thus includes stages of project inception, planning, action, and termination, and he even includes substages of "funding" and "publication." Jung was surely right when he said that every psychology is the personal confession of the psychologist.

Much of the literature on social cognition and its relation to personality lacks an understanding of the dynamic role of emotion or motivation. In presenting what they hope will blossom into a new theory of personality, Cantor and Kihlstrom (1982) define personality psychology as the field that studies "the distinctive patterns of thought, behavior, and experience that characterize the individual's unique adjustment to his or her life situation" (1982, p. 142). Notably absent from this definition is any mention of motives or emotions. Cantor and Kihlstrom contend that the structure and dynamics of personality are equivalent to the structure and dynamics of cognition, particularly social cognition. Similarly, Markus (1983) sees self-concepts (cognitions about the self) as capable of motivating action, and Meichenbaum, Butler, and Joseph (in press) view cognitive structures as motivating. With a few very notable exceptions (e.g., Zajonc, 1980; Taylor and Crocker, 1981; Clark and Isen, 1982), social cognition research has viewed emotion as something that somehow gets "attached" to a cognitive representation of a stimulus. This is not surprising, since emotion has itself been appended or "attached" to information processing models based on a computer analogy.

In contrast to psychodynamic psychologists, many cognitive social learning theorists have disagreed with the search for underlying, generalized motives, dispositions, character types, or traits. Mischel (1968) issued a broadside attack on psychodynamic and trait psychology, pointing to the failure of empirical research to support the belief in underlying traits or motives with consistent behavioral results. Instead, in keeping with his behaviorist roots, he argued that the causes of behavior are in large measure situational, that if a person uniformly acts in a way which, for example, the psychoanalyst would call "obsessive," this is because the individual's environment must uniformly be evoking "obsessive" responses. Mischel emphasized the extent to which people behave differently in different situations, and he argued against the exclusive search for generalized personality characteristics.

Mischel reviewed an immense amount of data, largely from trait psychology, and found that, while intelligence and phenomena related to cognitive abilities and aims showed considerable temporal and cross-situational consistency, the correlation between various questionnaire-based personality measures and actual behaviors was typically around .2 or .3. He argued that correlations of that magnitude do not support the notion of unitary traits producing similar behavior over time and across a wide variety of domains.

Mischel's 1968 critique sent shock waves through the field of personality psychology which still reverberate almost two decades later. He pointed

13

out, with considerable justification, that psychoanalysis and trait psychology systematically downplay the importance of situations in determining everyday responses. Further, he underscored the dangers of trying to predict behavior on the basis of inferences about personality, especially irrespective of concrete knowledge about relevant situational variables.

While Mischel's critique thus had considerable merit, it was problematic in a number of respects that are gradually becoming apparent. The first is a misunderstanding of the aims of psychodynamic psychology, which he unceremoniously lumped together with trait psychology.[1] In so doing he ignored a significant difference in the content and epistemology of psychodynamic versus either trait or behaviorist psychology. Mischel mistakenly attributed to psychodynamic psychology the behaviorist epistemology, which sees the aim of psychological knowledge as the prediction and control of human behavior. The psychoanalyst or psychodynamic clinician, however, is not particularly interested in predicting behaviors; she or he is interested in understanding the structure and dynamics of a person's inner experience. While the theory focuses on inner life, when a psychodynamic clinician is trying to predict behavior he is every bit the interactionist as the cognitive social learning theorist. When a clinician is confronted with a patient who is sounding potentially suicidal, he does not ask himself, "Is this person a suicidal personality?" or, "Is this person high on the S-scale?" Rather, he tries to get a sense of what precipitated the crisis, what the person is thinking and feeling, what the idiosyncratic meaning of suicide to the particular patient is, whether the patient has a convenient means of suicide at his disposal, whether the person has attempted suicide before, what kind of social supports the patient has, etc.

Mischel is indeed right in warning against spending much of one's time labeling one's fellows as oral, anal, or phallic characters, and he is equally correct in pointing to the lack of a theory of situational influence on behavior in psychoanalysis. Freud was not, however, an experimental psychologist interested in predicting variance; if he had been, Mischel would certainly be correct in noting that psychoanalysis is inadequate since individual differences in personality typically account for less than ten percent of the variance on most experimental tasks. Mischel has conflated two questions: first, do some stable patterns of personality exist; and secondly, are these useful in prediction.[2] The answer to the first is unequivocally yes.

---

[1] Mischel (1968, 1973b) frequently cites problems with trait studies as refutations of psychoanalysis.

[2] The confusion of these two questions in part stems from a failure to separate the issue of whether stable patterns exist from the issue of whether they can be measured. Human beings are such flexible creatures that even enduring personality processes are unlikely to express themselves in all or most situations, so one can neither expect underlying processes to be easily measured, nor can one conclude that the absence of an alleged indicator of an enduring process in a particular situation is evidence of its nonexistence. There is obviously

The answer to the second is more qualified: certain personality variables can be useful for prediction in some domains, but they should be used in conjunction with other variables.

A second problem with Mischel's critique is an ambiguity about what he proposes in place of a predominant emphasis on personality variables. Mischel believes his argument was misconstrued as a call for a radical situationism, but he was responsible for creating some of the ambiguity himself. While at some points he clearly stated that he had no intention of denying the existence of personality variables (1968, p.38), in the same book he wrote that "the concept of personality traits as broad response predispositions is thus untenable" (p. 146), and, "The empirically established behavioral consistencies, however, do not seem large enough to warrant the belief in very broadly generalized personality traits" (p. 43). Five years later (1973a, b) Mischel argued that even expectancies are relatively specific, not generalized as Rotter (1966) had proposed.

In this regard, Mischel's view has been amply falsified. Block and Block (1980) have demonstrated considerable consistency across behaviors, situations, time, and self-reports as well as teachers' and parents' reports on personality dimensions they call "ego-resiliency" and "ego-control." Even researchers with theoretical positions closely allied with Mischel's have come to speak of generalized "attributional styles" (e.g., Seligman et al., 1979), and Mischel himself now acknowledges at least temporal stability of many personality processes (Mischel, 1979). He has recently (1984) even suggested that if one averages out situations, one will indeed find individual differences in dimensions such as the tendency to act aggressively, a position that is certainly compatible with a psychodynamic approach.

Cognitive social learning theorists have escaped the problems of situationism (i.e., situational determinism) by becoming interactionists, arguing that behavior is a function of person-situation interaction. At an empirical level, in terms of prediction of behavior, this makes obvious sense. At a theoretical level, I have difficulty seeing how it tells us anything we did not already know. Certainly Freud would not have argued that his patients free-associated on the couch because their personality made them do so, or

a very difficult methodological question here, of how to distinguish between a falsification of a hypothesis, an invalidation of a measure, and a falsification of a subhypothesis that a phenomenon should express itself in a particular situation. To demonstrate, as Mischel clearly has, that people are remarkably flexible in tailoring their responses to situations does not prove that they have no enduring or global intentions, fantasies, ways of seeing things, or ways of protecting themselves against painful emotions. A tendency to behave relatively flexibly or inflexibly in certain situations may itself be an enduring personality disposition. As will be argued in Chapter 3, one can profitably look at motives, schemas, and affect-regulation mechanisms as hierarchical organizations with some relatively specific and some relatively global aspects.

that the associations they produced were not influenced by his presence. Transference itself involves a person-situation interaction: a patient may bring with him a tendency toward projecting certain kinds of material onto therapists, teachers, etc., but he will not generally have a transference to a rock.

Humanistic and Existential Psychology

The "third force" in personality theory includes a wide array of theories and theorists. One can trace its lineage to the humanism of the Renaissance, if not to the Protagoran maxim that "man is the measure of all things." Humanistic psychology emphasizes the experiencing individual and her or his subjective world and is in part an outgrowth of European phenomenology.

Humanistic psychology is also a reaction against psychoanalysis and behaviorism, primarily on two counts. First, both psychoanalysis and Skinnerian behaviorism can be construed as reductionistic, mechanistic, and deterministic. For the psychoanalyst, mental life largely depends upon the vicissitudes of libido and aggression, and no mental act is a chance occurrence. For the behaviorist, mental life per se is nonexistent or irrelevant: behavior is a function of stimuli and reinforcement, and any sense of purposive behavior in human beings is illusory. The humanistic psychologist, in contrast, posits an active, creative self unencumbered by, or acting freely within the parameters of, natural laws. Secondly, both psychoanalysis and behaviorism frequently attribute greater knowledge to a skilled observer than to the person himself. The psychoanalyst uses her knowledge about the nature of psychic conflict and development to assess a patient's character, defensive structure, and underlying conflictual issues, and she aims in treatment to help the patient accept and utilize these and other insights to help him come to terms with the roots of his neurosis. The behaviorist changes people's actions by altering contingencies of reinforcement. The humanistic psychologist avers that the patient is the only one with privileged access to his own psyche, which means that an individual is the ultimate authority on himself.

Humanistic psychology is thus, in a sense, extremely individualistic, substituting private meanings for public meanings. One could argue that humanistic psychology has tried to do to psychoanalysis and behaviorism what the Protestant Reformation did to Catholicism: external mediation is rejected, and the individual is viewed as the ultimate authority on his own life; the person must interpret for himself the rules of his existence. Where such ardent individualism resides, existentialism cannot be far away, and indeed, humanistic and existential psychology are closely allied. Many existential psychologists have drawn inspiration from the philosophy of

Sartre. A Sartrian might respond to cognitive social learning theory, for example, by arguing that it may in many cases be descriptively correct, but that even descriptively it fails to account for true autonomy, and prescriptively it is a recipe for conformity, inauthenticity, and "being-for-others" as opposed to "being-for-oneself." The major existentialist psychologists include Binswanger (1958, 1963), Boss (1977), Frankl (1959), Laing (1959), and May (1953) (and one could make a case for Fromm here as well). Despite their differences, the existential psychologists all stress the importance of subjective experience and "meaning;" the dangers of losing touch with one's own inner self or feelings; and the hazards of conceiving of oneself as thinglike, as (in Sartrian terms) a "thing-in-itself," rather than as a changing, forming, creative source of will and action. This emphasis on flexibility and openness to experience is characteristic of most humanistic psychology, especially that of Rogers (1959, 1961) and, to a lesser extent, Maslow (1954, 1962).

The most widely used humanistic/existential theory of personality is Rogers' "person-centered" approach (1959, 1961). The theory is neither complicated nor particularly comprehensive, though it has served as a useful way of organizing clinical data for counselors who do short-term crisis intervention, or work with students for very brief periods in university counseling centers.

Rogers' view is predicated on a Rousseauean conception of human beings as basically good but corrupted by circumstance. Rogers contends that a person has a true self which is often distorted by the desire to gain the positive regard of other people. As a child develops, she learns that in order to be loved, she must meet certain standards; she later internalizes these "conditions of worth" and consequently distorts herself still further. Low self-esteem, according to Rogers, results from a discrepancy between self and ideal self. Such a discrepancy may cause the person to close off many areas of her experience that are not congruent with her concept of herself or her ideal self.

Rogers' primary motivational construct is the "actualizing tendency," which Rogers defines rather amorphously as the tendency of the organism to enhance and maintain itself (1959). Included in this tendency are motives to survive, to be open to experience, and to express one's true self, though as Robert Kegan has pointed out, this construct sheds "more warmth than light" (1982, p. 6). Opposing the actualizing tendency are the needs for "positive regard" from others, and the need for positive self-regard, which often requires distortion of the self to meet imposed standards. A healthy person should be able to actualize himself while simultaneously regarding himself highly.

The line of demarcation between humanistic/existential psychology and the other two traditions of personality theorizing is not always entirely distinct. While humanistic/existential psychology largely developed in antithesis to psychoanalysis, many of its proponents began as psychoanalysts, and currently the interests of the two have begun to converge in certain areas, notably in the (often ambiguous) concept of the "self." Cognitive-behavioral researchers are also showing interest in issues of the self (see, e.g., the volume edited by Wegner and Vallacher, 1980), and like humanistic psychologists, they are largely concerned with the individual's current cognitions and experiences.

Theories Past and Present

This review of the three traditions of personality theory is hardly comprehensive, though hopefully it has provided some insight into the history and current status of the field. (For a fuller account, see Mischel, 1976; Hall and Lindzey, 1978; and Pervin, 1978). Despite areas of convergence, the three approaches to personality largely exist in isolation from one another, with, for example, social cognition researchers ignoring fifty years of rich theoretical work by psychoanalytic object relations theorists (for reviews of object relations theory, see Guntrip, 1971; Greenberg and Mitchell, 1983), and object relations theorists largely ignoring a growing body of very relevant empirical data on the development of children's understanding of the social world (see Shantz, 1975; Selman, 1980). Psychodynamic psychology has offered the most sophisticated account of the depths of psychic functioning, and it has proven the most clinically useful in understanding the interrelation of thought, feeling, desire, fantasy, and behavior. Its mechanistic drive theory has, however, sometimes led psychoanalytic theorists below the depths of the psyche and into the caverns of unfalsifiable fantasy or clearly falsified dogma. Cognitive social learning theory, which has incorporated the behaviorist understanding of conditioning within a cognitive framework, has provided the most thorough understanding to date of the learning of everyday behaviors and strategies of adaptation. It has, however, been tremendously limited by a reluctance to examine unconscious processes, a failure to recognize the extent to which behaviors may hold symbolic significance (i.e., stand for something else) and thus be performed as symbolically transformed responses to seemingly unrelated motives, and a relative inattention to emotion. Humanistic and existential theories, while generally less comprehensive, have contributed to our understanding of the importance of a sense of meaning to existence and of the painful condition in which structures of meaning disintegrate and the person must face himself and the world without his accustomed set of values, self-concepts, routines, and blinders.

As noted earlier, global theorizing in personality is largely out of vogue. The intricacies, difficulties, and inconsistencies within and between the various approaches have for years led to a "back to the facts" movement which views high level theorizing as a distortion, if not a distraction. No theoretician would deny, of course, that the higher the level of abstraction, the less resemblance to reality. Max Weber (1949) spoke to this issue in a seminal tract on the philosophy of social science[1] in the early decades of this century. The problem for the social scientist is that she or he can never get back to unmediated facts, and the failure to articulate high level models by no means indicates the absence of generalizations and assumptions at the greatest level of abstraction. As Hall and Lindzey note in their text on personality,

> There is no such thing as "no theory;" consequently, the moment we attempt to forget about theory "for the present" we are really using implicit, personally determined and perhaps inconsistent assumptions concerning behavior and these unidentified assumptions will determine what will be studied and how. (1978, pp. 16-17)

The pitfalls of research outside the context of a larger conception of personality are amply illustrated by the history of social psychology.[2] That cognitive dissonance (the idea that if a person holds two discrepant beliefs he will be motivated to change one) received "more widespread attention from personality and social psychologists during the decade of the sixties than any other contemporary statement about human behavior" (Bem, 1972, p. 15) is the kind of academic aberration that could be avoided if psychologists were to operate within some framework, rather than to test, willy-nilly, whatever hypothesis happens to occur to them (and to hold the potential of attracting research funds).

Personality psychologists have been working over the last thirty years with two vastly different and incompatible notions of what personality psychology is and must do, and the failure to distinguish the two has had a significant and deleterious impact on the field. The first view assumes that the aim of personality theory is to provide an integrated view of the way an individual human being thinks, feels, and acts. This view sees personality theory as the branch of psychological theory that tries to integrate psychological knowledge across the various subdisciplines and to provide a general framework through which any psychologist may begin to form specific hypotheses. A personality theory in this view is a broad schema or gestalt through which information about people is processed. It is at once nomothetic and idiographic: the aim is both to provide general principles of mental functioning and to be able to apply these principles to explore the concrete experience of a given individual. This is the conception of

[1] I use the term "social science" in this book in deference to convenience and common usage, rather than to express any convictions about the proper methods of social inquiry.
[2] The reluctance to rely upon theory was, however, motivated in part by the absence of a theory of personality that was simultaneously empirically testable and sophisticated.

19

personality theory which has in many ways been forgotten (though some, such as Cantor and Kihlstrom, 1982, have fortunately tried to revive it), and it implicitly rests on the assumption commonly held by cognitive psychologists (and post-Popperian philosophers of science) that reality is so multifaceted that a person – including a psychologist – must have schemas or paradigms into which information is assimilated.

The second view assumes that the aim of personality theory is to examine individual differences on various psychological dimensions. This is the perspective implicitly accepted by trait psychologists, and it is an atomistic one that does not attempt integration of psychological knowledge aimed at a general theory of mind and/or action. The researcher committed to this set of assumptions is de facto committed to a trait approach because the aim is to find certain personality dimensions (e.g., need for achievement, locus of control, field dependence), develop empirical measures of them, and examine individual differences on these dimensions. This is an entirely different enterprise than the quest for a broad schema or paradigm of human mental life or behavior. It is also an enterprise Mischel rightly attacks because its adherents almost by definition rule out of consideration the interaction of aspects of personality with environmental stimuli, instead focusing solely on individual differences.

The aim of the following three chapters is to develop a theory of personality in the first sense, i.e., a schema through which to view human mental life and behavior. My intention is to present a theory sufficiently broad as to accommodate relevant current clinical and research findings and techniques, yet sufficiently cohesive and circumscribed as not to consist of a hodgepodge of ideas from epistemologically inconsistent perspectives or a descriptive listing of research and citations mislabeled as theory. I am well aware of both the Scylla of grab-bag eclecticism and the Charybdis of myopic adherence to a limited paradigm, and in being self-consciously eclectic I have been careful to bear in mind that the primary aim is synthesis, not a summation of truncated theses and antitheses. Though I have undoubtedly failed in navigating entirely safe passage between Scylla and Charybdis, I hope the reader will find that the tattered vessel that emerges can nevertheless remain afloat.[1]

The discussion will proceed as follows. Chapter 2, entitled, "Emotion: A Missing Link between Psychodynamic and Cognitive-Behavioral Psychology?" will present a theory of emotion that is both a cornerstone of the personality theory developed here and a link between approaches that have hitherto seemed largely incompatible in both content and epistemol-

[1] It is regrettable that limitations of space prevent the kind of comprehensive critique of previous theories that would help justify embarking upon this difficult voyage. I will, however, try to point out along the way the problems encountered by other theorists who have sailed these waters, and I hope to do so more systematically at a later date.

20

ogy. Chapter 3 will present a theory of psychic structure and dynamics, integrating a theory of motivation with an analysis of "ego processes" of cognition and regulation of emotion. Chapter 4 will provide a model of the development of personality and moral judgment, arguing that the two are inseparable. It will examine developmental models of narcissism and object relations, moral judgment, and ego processes, and will provide an alternative conceptualization that integrates various approaches and proposes a stage beyond "superego" morality or the morality of social learning. It will also suggest some advantages, both in conceptual terms and in terms of opening new avenues for research, of utilizing this framework.

2 Emotion: A Missing Link between Psychodynamic and Cognitive-Behavioral Psychology?

OVER THREE DECADES have passed since the pioneering efforts by Dollard and Miller (1950) to effect a rapprochement between behaviorist and psychodynamic psychology. Since that time, the two psychologies have largely gone their separate ways (though one may find an occasional joint communique in which the two camps pursue a limited detente in order to address common problems; see Wachtel, 1977, 1982). The Hullian learning theory that inspired Dollard and Miller gave way to Skinnerian behaviorism, which in turn appears to be passing the behaviorist torch (an aversive stimulus to the psychodynamically inclined) to cognitive social learning theory.

The significance of this latter development for integrative work cannot be overstated because the movement from a focus on behavior to thought in mainstream psychology has altered, if in unforeseen ways, the hiatus between the content and epistemology of academic and psychodynamic psychology. The gulf between an interest in observable behavior versus mental operations which previously existed was an insurmountable barrier between the two psychologies. Freudians argued that one could never understand behavior without looking at mental processes and structures, and behaviorists argued that such processes and structures are either nonexistent or irrelevant to a scientific psychology. When the cognitive revolution in psychology lifted the taboo on cognitive operations, associational networks, and the like, it was just a matter of time before an interest in another set of "internal" processes, those relating to emotion, would arise. Now that academic psychologists have begun thinking about the relation between affect and associational networks, and talking about cognitive representations with emotions attached, the divergence between cognitive-behavioral and psychodynamic psychology in terms of object of study and beliefs about the importance and validity of examining mental processes has begun to diminish. This is not, of course, to deny the obvious fact that the two psychologies diverge far more than they converge, and that any attempt simply to "put them together" would prove hopeless. My aim in this chapter is to show how a theory of affect can bridge crucial aspects of the two psychologies and allow one to reinterpret and bring together a wide range of observed phenomena.

The nature and functions of affect[1] have never been clearly delineated in either psychodynamic or cognitive-behavioral psychology. With Skinner, the behaviorists scrupulously followed the methodological assumptions inherited from British empiricism which mandated a focus strictly on the observable. In so doing they jettisoned perhaps the main psychological tenet common to the empiricist tradition from Hobbes onward, that human beings are essentially creatures motivated by the desire for pleasure and the avoidance of pain. In Skinner's hands, pleasure and pain became unverifiable and thus expendable concepts, to be replaced by the more observable (and tautological) "reinforcement." Emotions are intellectual outcasts which have no place in Skinnerian behaviorist thought; when discussed, they are viewed primarily as physiological patterns accompanying responses. One would, however, expect to ascribe greater functional significance to such a salient psychological faculty as emotion. Other behaviorists (e.g., Mowrer, 1960; Wolpe, 1974; Solomon, 1980) have accorded affect a far more significant role. After the cognitive revolution in psychology, social learning theorists placed a thinking organism between stimulus and response, yet, true to the rationalist bent inherited from empiricism, they failed to let this organism *feel*.

Affect has a rather checkered history in psychoanalysis. One normally thinks of psychoanalysis as a psychological approach that has thoroughly examined the nature of human emotional experience, but this is far more accurate at the level of clinical than theoretical understanding. Affect theory in psychoanalysis has remained problematic because it has been unable to detach itself from drive theory. Psychoanalytic theory asserts that all motivation stems from the libidinal and aggressive drives, but one can think of many instances in which emotions or anticipated emotions can be motivating even when they are in no way connected with these hypothesized drives. A simple example is when a person comes into work on time to avoid the upsetting circumstance of being fired.

Psychoanalysts often use the terms "affect" and "drive" interchangeably, as when they say that a person who was enjoying another's company was motivated by the sexual drive, or that a furious person was manifesting the aggressive drive. One can certainly make a case that this confusion permeated Freud's thinking, for example, on aggression. To say that anger is a basic emotion experienced by all people, and that direct aggression is a behavioral response sometimes elicited by anger, does not imply that hu-

---

[1] I use the terms "affect" and "emotion" interchangeably, in accordance with what is rapidly becoming standard usage in the literature.

23

man beings have a drive toward aggression (or, at Freud's most metaphysical, death). This would be analogous to claiming that since anxiety is a biologically rooted emotion that often elicits the behavioral response of taking valium, then human beings must have a drive for ingesting anxiolitic medication. To argue that anger, and consequently aggression, has biological roots does not imply that anger is always waiting under the surface, seeking discharge. Otherwise one must be willing to say that *all* emotions are really drives pressing for discharge, giving us at least eight or nine basic drives, which are always waiting for an opportune moment to lurch into consciousness and steal the virtue of maiden reason. This is a thoroughly Platonic view of the "passions," but as will be argued shortly, it is not an acceptable one. It does, however, point to the very significant relationship between emotion and motivation.

The present chapter will assert that a general theory of emotion can provide a bridge between psychodynamic and cognitive-behavioral analysis. It will argue for the centrality of affect in mediating between stimulus and response as well as in motivating defenses. Stimuli, it will contend, never themselves reinforce responses: what makes a behavior more or less likely to occur is its link to an affect or affectlike experience of localized sensory pleasure or pain. A person can deal with a painful affect in a number of ways, including direct action (which the behaviorist emphasizes) and defense (emphasized by the psychoanalyst). The link between the two psychologies is an approach informed by systems theory that views affect as a feedback mechanism which, consciously and unconsciously, activates control mechanisms designed to attain or maintain various set-goals or ideal states. The person may manage affect through either behavioral interventions or internal mental operations.

Counter-Conditioning Behaviorism to Respond to Emotions

Most theorists of affect posit that an emotion has three components: a physiological state, a subjective feeling, and a behavioral expression. Behaviorist theory tends to view emotions as epiphenomena of the conditioning process, though Mowrer (1960) and Wolpe (1974), among others, have emphasized the role of feelings in conditioning. As Gray (1979) notes, ". . . the emotions are usually treated within learning theory as states that are elicited by unconditioned instrumentally reinforcing stimuli or by stimuli that have been associated (by classical conditioning) with such unconditioned reinforcing stimuli" (p. 307). The central question raised by this view relates to the function of affect. Certainly one can see how the cry of an infant expressing her pain or hunger will be reinforced, but how could the subjective feeling be reinforced? The feeling is not pleasant, and the cry without the feeling would be equally effective in eliciting caretaking behavior. Is the feeling superfluous, and if so, how did it evolve?

The problem stems from the notion of reinforcement. To say that a particular behavior has been reinforced is to observe that it is more likely to recur. In a classic Skinnerian experiment, one would say that when the pigeon produces an appropriate pecking behavior, it is reinforced by a pellet of food. That formulation, I will argue, is incorrect. Stimuli can never reinforce responses. The intervening variable that results in reinforcement is an emotion or proto-affective positive or negative sensory experience. What accounts for the pigeon's increased likelihood of producing the pecking behavior is that the behavior has become associated with a pleasurable taste or a reduction of hunger. That the pigeon could be equally conditioned through electrical stimulation of the brain suggests that what has reinforced the behavior is not the presentation of a stimulus but the emergence or diminution of a *feeling*. Whether the feeling is as localized and concrete as hunger pangs or a pin prick, or as diffuse as anxiety, it nevertheless serves the same function: the reinforcement or discouragement (punishment) of behavior.

While some students of emotion exclude sensory experiences of pleasure and pain from the category of affect, others find such distinctions arbitrary (Scott, 1980, p. 53). One need not enter that fray to point out that, despite their neurophysiological differences, sensory-based feelings and other emotions serve the same function: the selection of behavior through reinforcement and punishment. Whether a person escapes an electric shock because it hurts or because he is scared that it will endanger his life (or both), the escape behavior is being "reinforced."

Evidence of the effects of emotion on conditioning is ample. For example, Latane and Schachter (cited in Schachter and Singer, 1964) found that rats injected with epinephrine were markedly superior in avoidance learning to rats receiving a placebo. The rats in the experimental condition avoided shocks nearly three times as often as the rats in the control group. One could account for these results by hypothesizing the role of emotion on learning. Similarly, animal research has consistently demonstrated that antianxiety drugs alter certain forms of learning. In particular, these medications "impair the animal's ability to withhold responses in anticipation of punishment," which cannot be accounted for simply by an analgesic effect (Gray, pp.308-9). This suggests that anxiety may be important in the punishment and extinction of certain behavioral responses.

The notion of "stimulus-response" pairings is actually a shorthand for a process mediated by affect. A conditioning experiment in which a dog is rendered immobile while being subjected to electric shocks provides a good illustration. If a conditioned stimulus is presented which has occurred consistently a few seconds before the shocks, the dog will experience anxiety or terror upon presentation of the conditioned stimulus. The behaviorist would say that the dog has come to associate the conditioned stimulus with an aversive stimulus, the shock. More cognitively oriented learning theorists (e.g., Bolles, 1975) would assert that the conditioned stimulus is a predictive cue (or as Pavlov would say, a "signal") that alerts the dog of the impending shock. This is no doubt true, but the shock would be of only marginal significance to the dog if it did not produce a painful feeling. In this example the dog may have been inhibited in forming a stimulus-response pairing (i.e., a mental connection) by being restrained, but it has clearly come to associate the stimulus with an affect[1] (cf. the "two-factor theory" of avoidance learning, Mowrer, 1947; Rescorla and Solomon, 1967). Any response the dog may subsequently produce when free which allows it to flee when presented with the conditioned stimulus will be reinforced because it is associated with eliminating an aversive *affect* (i.e., it is negatively reinforced). Eventually the response may be produced automatically upon presentation of the stimulus, so that the affect is no longer even necessary in eliciting the response. This should not obscure the point that what has reinforced the behavior is its association with elimination of a noxious emotional state.

There is no such thing as an "aversive stimulus"; aversion is a characteristic of the organism, not the stimulus. A stimulus would not be reinforcing were it not associated with an affect. In espousing a radical empiricism, Skinnerian behaviorists mistakenly imputed to stimuli characteristics of organisms. This was necessarily so, given the attempt to avoid examination of subjective experience and the assumption of an animal passively responding to its environment. The parallel empiricist view of cognition was rejected by psychologists because it failed to recognize the extent to which individuals actively order their experience, though a similar understanding of the organism's role in interpreting the affective consequences of a stimulus that determine its significance in conditioning is still forthcoming in the literature rooted in behaviorism.

The theoretical failure to attribute aversion to the organism has practical consequences when cognitive-behavioral techniques are applied to humans. Cognitive-behavioral clinicians routinely assume that what would feel good to themselves will be experienced the same way by their patients. Goldfried and Robins (1979, p. 64) provide an example of their therapeutic work in which the therapist is trying to help the patient see that he is making progress. If one makes rationalistic assumptions about what every person will experience as positive (in this case, assuming that hearing of

---

[1] For simplicity, from this point forward I will include localized sensations of pleasure and pain under the term "affect" or "emotion."

one's progress might spur one to consolidate changes), then this makes sense, and certainly in many cases it does. As soon as one begins to think phenomenologically, however, instead of thinking of reward and aversion as residing in stimuli, then matters get more complex. A patient who is torturing herself psychologically for various misdeeds will experience progress as an "aversive stimulus" because it threatens to block her penitence. Such patients – and they are no small minority among people in treatment for depression – frequently bolt therapy as soon as they find themselves improving.[1]

Similarly, a woman treated for a chronic problem with self-esteem despite "objective" success at various pursuits was telling her therapist how her mentors were sure to discover her defectiveness in an upcoming task. At that point her therapist innocently volunteered that in reality she was obviously quite competent, and that they therefore should look at her sense of defectiveness. She became very angry with him, and what emerged from examining her anger was that any time she receives a compliment about her ability, attractiveness, or whatever, she becomes angry at the person for rubbing her nose in what to her appears to be a clear and unalterable inferiority.

Even in research using animals as subjects, learning theorists have begun to move away from straight stimulus-response models to models that view cognition as a mediating process. Earlier behaviorists, attempting to avoid mentalistic explanations, postulated an automatic connection of stimulus and response without intervening cognitive processes. This strict empiricist approach culminated in Skinner's move away from theoretical explanations of learning mechanisms to more strictly empirical generalizations and a preoccupation in the field with procedures as opposed to theory. A significant problem with this focus on method and observation is that it excludes from discussion most of the interesting questions, such as *why* the rat presses the bar when bar-pressing is associated with a bright light or food pellet.

Modern behaviorists have reappropriated Tolman's (1951) emphasis on the way organisms perceive stimulus events and on the "expectancies" they form of how stimuli will be associated with one another and with their behaviors (Seligman and Johnston, 1973; Bolles, 1972, 1975). Bolles, for example, argues that learning "consists of the acquisition of information about the environment, rather than the attachment of particular responses to particular stimuli . . . ." (1975, pp. 202-3). This emphasis on cognitive mediation in conditioning is essential to integrating behaviorist research with contemporary developments in cognitive psychology, but it

---

[1] Wachtel (1977, pp. 248-9) has similarly argued against the attempt to describe praise and punishment "objectively."

fails to account for motivation. Without a reinforcement mechanism, Bolles cannot explain why the rat presses the bar rather than philosophizes about the probability of association between bar-pressing and food once it has learned to expect that bar-pressing produces food on a particular schedule of reinforcement.

Animals, including humans, form cognitive associations between stimuli and affects, stimuli and behavior, and behavior and affects, just as they form associations between one stimulus and another (as in classical conditioning and most cognition). These associations do not impel them to act. Skinner experimented with starving rats, and if he had used fat, sated rats, he would have discovered different laws of learning. Rats with full stomachs will not press bars often for food, even though they have largely the same structure of cognitive associations in their heads as when they are hungry. Acquisition of information occurs continuously in animals and humans whether they are hungry or not (though the particular information acquired in part depends upon affective state), but the pursuit of various goals is, while *mediated* by information, never *motivated* by information.

The difference becomes clear when one distinguishes two ways in which the term "reinforcement" has been used. In traditional behaviorist usage, reinforcement means the strengthening of a connection between two events. In operant conditioning, the connection between a stimulus and a response is allegedly strengthened. In this form of conditioning reinforcement is synonymous with reward. Pecking at a target, for example, is reinforced (rewarded) with food. Reinforcement is not, however, synonymous with reward in other contexts. Research on conditioned fear reactions (summarized in Bolles, 1975) has demonstrated that an animal can be conditioned to experience fear in the presence of a stimulus by repeatedly pairing the stimulus with a fear-inducing or painful stimulus (such as a shock). Systematic desensitization procedures used by behavioral therapists attempt to break the association between the conditioned stimulus and the fear. Bandura argues that one way to do this is to provide "repeated nonreinforced exposure to threatening events" (1969, p. 304). By "nonreinforced" he means that a cognitive connection is not strengthened. To reinforce the connection between fear and the stimulus would not, in this case, mean that one would reward the fear reaction. Reinforcement in this case would be punishing, whereas punishment is the opposite of reinforcement in operant conditioning. Similarly, in describing Garcia's well-known research (see Garcia and Koelling, 1966) in which a particular taste becomes associated with a punishment, so that an animal comes to avoid drinking water with that flavor, Bolles summarizes one interpretation of the results: "There is a stimulus, the taste of food; there is a response, drinking; and the connection between them is weakened by the negative consequences, the illness, that follows some time later" (1975, p. 174).

From the standpoint of behavior, the connection between the taste and the response is indeed weakened, but from a cognitive standpoint, the association between the stimulus and the consequences of the response is strengthened; i.e., the animal learns even *more* clearly that the drinking response should be avoided in the presence of this taste. Behavioral extinction in this case occurs simultaneously with cognitive reinforcement, which is, using the standard behaviorist language, a contradiction in terms. One can clarify the matter by suggesting that the *weakening* of the behavioral connection between the taste and the drinking response is a consequence of the *strengthened* connection between drinking and a set of consequences that the organism does not like. The connection between drinking and illness is a cognitive association. The weakened "connection" between drinking and taste is not a cognitive association; it is a behavioral response motivated by affect. The cognitive connection is informational; the behavioral "connection" is motivated. Cognitive connections are strengthened or "reinforced" simply by observation and assimilation of information (as in the classical principle of "contiguity"). Response tendencies are strengthened or "reinforced" by their affective consequences.

Moving from behaviorism and animal learning to contemporary social learning theory and human learning, one finds a similar inattention to the critical role of affect. Social learning theorists came to recognize that people can anticipate the effects of their behavior, which led Rotter (1966), for example, to apply the concept of expectancy to human learning and behavior. Yet what is not clear in Rotter's model is that many expectancies that influence behavior involve in part the prediction of the *affective* consequences of a behavior. When a person predicts that if she steals a car she will go to jail, a crucial factor that determines whether or not she will steal the car is her affective response or anticipated affective response to going to jail. If she views going to jail as positive or neutral, the threat of imprisonment will not deter her action. The idea that people can be motivated by cognition is rampant in psychology and stems from the philosophical view of the "rational man" who acts according to the mandates of reason. I will argue throughout Part I that this view, espoused by philosophers since Plato, rests upon a false conception of the relationship between reason and desire, which poses "reason as guide." Reason (cognition, in psychological parlance), however, can only provide means, not ends.[1]

---

[1] This is not to say that something like "intrinsic motivation" (Hunt, 1965) may not motivate the acquisition of knowledge, or that one cannot speak of a *primarily* "conflict-free ego sphere" (Hartmann, 1939). Perhaps the main anomaly that turned psychologists from radical behaviorism toward more cognitive approaches is evidence of learning without reinforcement. Human beings are equipped with an expanded neocortex that allows for complex cognitive processing, and evolutionarily one would expect selection of an organism that processes information and seeks understanding in advance of pressing need to

29

Affects, then, are selection mechanisms that select behavior. In the case of operant conditioning, the individual learns through trial and error how to maximize positive, and minimize negative affect. By using expectancies and simple forethought, the person may perform this trial and error process in thought instead of in action. Once one recognizes that learning can occur in the absence of behavior, one opens the door to the possibility that various forms of "internal behavior" – mental processes – can be reinforced by affect, which leads to a discussion of affect in psychodynamic psychology.

Psychodynamic Psychology: Defenses Can Be Reinforced

Psychoanalytic affect theory resembles the Freudian id: contradictory ideas coexist and alternately clamor for attention. Affect theory in psychoanalysis shares another characteristic with the id: it appears to pay little attention to temporal factors. Freud's early and more mature conceptualizations of emotion both tend to appear in psychoanalytic writings, though a few analysts (see, for example, Brenner, 1974; Plutchik, 1980a, b) have attempted to bring together a general psychoanalytic approach to affect.

Rapaport (1953) has distinguished three periods in Freud's understanding of emotion. Originally Freud viewed affect as a quantity of mental energy attached to various memories which fuels behavior. His second theory viewed affects as avenues of drive discharge into the interior of the body. In this view, emotions are safety valves for discharging instinctual energy. In his final theory, which he developed in terms of anxiety, anxiety serves as a "signal for the avoidance of a danger-situation" (Freud, 1926, p. 64). In this model defense mechanisms, notably repression, arise in response to anxiety, whereas previously Freud had understood anxiety as a by-product of unfulfilled libido. Most psychoanalysts would accept Anna Freud's (1936) position that defenses arise in response to affects and drives, while others (e.g., Plutchik, 1980a, p. 24) conceive of defenses as attempted resolutions of conflicts among drives, emotions, and reality. I will shortly attempt to show that defenses arise *only* in response to emotions, and that the notion of defenses against drives or reality is mistaken.

In *Inhibitions, Symptoms and Anxiety* (1926), in which he developed the concept of anxiety as signal, Freud remarked in passing that repression "is, fundamentally, an attempt at flight" (p. 79). The behaviorist views

know about particular aspects of the environment. While this form of "cognitive motivation" is no doubt significant (though one wonders even here about the extent to which affective factors such as interest or intellectual excitement motivate even the "coldest" cognitive acts), what is being argued against is the prevalent assumption that cognition can motivate action beyond this sphere. As will be demonstrated shortly, motivational statements phrased in cognitive terms generally leave implicit a significant affective component that provides the impetus to act; the basic motivational structures will need to be reconceptualized as cognitive-affective schemas.

flight as a natural response to an "aversive stimulus," i.e., to a painful affect. Could repression and flight serve the same function?

Piaget (1970) conceived of thought as *interiorized action* (cf. Vygotsky, 1978), i.e., as mental behavior that is often more efficient than the carrying out of an actual behavior. By the beginning of Piaget's preoperational stage, the infant is no longer stimulus-bound and can perform various behaviors in her head instead of in the world. Precisely at the same time one begins to see the operation of various mechanisms of affect-modulation and defense — interiorized actions, so to speak — which the child may use in place of action. When one examines the nature of defenses, one finds that they perform precisely the same function as behaviors: the maximization of pleasurable, and minimization of unpleasurable emotions. Affects are selection mechanisms that select not only behaviors but defenses. A defense that does not eliminate a negative affect will not continue to be used (or will be supplanted by another defense), just as a behavior that fails to eliminate the aversive feeling associated with a stimulus will not tend to recur.

Another way to state this relationship between affect and defense is in terms of reinforcement theory. A defense that minimizes a negative affect or maximizes a pleasurable one will be reinforced, i.e., will be made more likely to occur again. To use a simple, everyday example, if a student cheats on an examination and experiences guilt, he may reduce the guilt by rationalization, telling himself that he was only getting the grade he would have deserved if he had studied. The function of the rationalization is to reduce the guilt, and this reduction makes all the more likely that the student will rationalize the next time he faces a similar situation, as well as providing him with good cause to maintain his cheating rationalization as long as the cheating issue is on his mind. In other words, the "internal behavior" of rationalization has been "reinforced." To give a clinical example, a patient whose alcoholic father left the family when the patient was eight years old developed a fantasied image of himself as a self-made man molded without help from his father. He saw himself as his mother's son, and before entering treatment in his late twenties refused to acknowledge any contribution his father had made to his development. In discussing this during one session he unintentionally remarked, "I'm not my father's son." This total repudiation served several functions. In terms of positive reinforcement, it allowed him to gratify aggressive wishes towards his father and to maximize enjoyment of an Oedipal fantasy that his father had never even been in the family. In terms of negative reinforcement, it allowed him to escape the feeling of having been rejected and abandoned by his father by turning it around and doing the rejecting himself. By repudiating identification with his father he was also escaping fears of becoming like him. (Dollard and Miller [1950] similarly argued for the role of anxiety-reduction in motivating defenses, and Wachtel [1977] has elaborated the implications of that position for integrating behavioral and psychoanalytic treatments in a remarkably open-minded and challenging book).

Just as performing mental experiments in one's head is more efficient than constantly performing them in reality, utilizing defense mechanisms can save one from performing behaviors that are inefficient or potentially damaging. Nina Bull, for example, sees biting of the lip and clenching of the jaw and fists as ways a child learns to control his or her tendencies to behave aggressively (1951). A more efficient way of handling aggression is to interiorize this inhibition completely by, for example, choking off the affect entirely. This is not only more efficient, but it may be more adaptive since expression of anger in many cultures and families can result in punishment or disapproval. Clinically, the phenomenon that led Freud to postulate an instinct for aggression was the extent to which his patients handled anger by suppressing it in various ways, and every clinician since Freud's time has dealt with numerous patients, perhaps the majority, who are thoroughly convinced that anger is illegitimate and must be contained at all costs.

The conflict between expression and suppression of emotion or impulse is precisely the type of situation behaviorists have been unable to elucidate because of their relative inattention to psychic conflict. In behavioral terms, if two mutually exclusive, competing behaviors have been reinforced, the operant with the greater reinforcement value (or, one might say, affective valence) will be produced. At some point, punishing a rat for a behavior previously rewarded will eliminate the operant from the rat's behavioral repertoire. In approach-avoidance conflicts, the animal has two options, approach and avoidance. (Dollard and Miller, 1950, who were influenced by psychoanalysis, offered other alternatives similar to some to be discussed here.)

In human beings, however, the capacity for symbolic and higher level cognitive transformations allows for a third possibility that psychodynamic psychologists call a "compromise-formation." For example, in Milgram's famous obedience experiments, in which subjects believed they were delivering severe shocks to someone in another room, one of the subjects captured on film found himself torn between the desire to obey and the anxiety and fear provoked by hurting another person. His response was a compromise which reconciled the conflicting affects: he shocked the person (obedience) while shaking his head (as if to say, "No, I am not doing this"). This is a fairly trivial example of a compromise-formation, and to take the analysis any further (and to systematize the link between psychodynamic and cognitive-behavioral psychology) requires presentation of a model of emotion informed by systems theory.

Emotion: A Missing Link

Systems Theory and the Integration of Two Relatively Closed Systems

Over a century ago Darwin (1872) pointed out that emotional expression serves as a signal to other animals. The cry of a baby human or chimpanzee, for example, is a signal to its mother or caretaker that it is in distress. What students of affect have less generally recognized (with the exception of Tomkins, 1960) is that affect is a signal to the animal itself, and that this signal is analogous to feedback in systems theory. The general feedback function of proto-affective states such as hunger is well known. When homeostasis or some "set-goal" of satiety is disturbed, stomach contractions, glucose levels, and a variety of other processes produce a feedback mechanism subjectively experienced as hunger, which activates "control mechanisms" such as searching for, and ingesting food, which restore the system to homeostasis. The general model is best exemplified by a thermostat that regulates heat. A person sets the temperature to seventy degrees (a "set-goal" or ideal state), and when the temperature falls too far below the set-goal, feedback arises which activates control mechanisms (the heating system) to bring the temperature back to the ideal state.

In human beings, emotion is a primary feedback mechanism which alerts the person that various set-goals are or are not being achieved.[1] A discrepancy between ideal state (set-goal) and perceived/cognized reality results in a negative affect which motivates the person to take some form of corrective action. Such actions may take three forms: behavior, coping, and defense mechanisms. Behaviors are motor activities which have effects in the external world. Coping mechanisms are intrapsychic responses which are primarily conscious, or largely under conscious control. Defenses are primarily intrapsychic responses which are unconscious and rely for their efficacy on their inaccessibility to consciousness. Obviously, behavior, coping, and defense form a continuum, rather than being entirely discrete categories of control mechanisms.[2] All three classes of response are control mechanisms that arise either to modulate negative affect or to attain or maintain positive affect.

Several theorists have, in one form or another, pointed to similar phenomena. Menninger et al. (1963) have connected the Freudian view of

---

[1] As will be argued shortly, many of these set-goals are biological and innate, rather than cognized and learned, as when pain receptors in the skin alert the brain to potential tissue damage.
[2] The distinction between them is in some ways arbitrary. Many view behaviors as coping mechanisms and avoid speaking of defenses at all. Behavior may serve an adaptive function (often referred to as "coping"), or it may be used defensively, i.e., to fulfill a purpose that is unconscious and cannot easily be made conscious.

signal anxiety with the notion of feedback, and Lazarus and his coworkers (1981, 1982) have elaborated the process through which stress activates various coping mechanisms, as will be discussed in a later section of this chapter. Plutchik and his colleagues (1980a, b) have offered a psychodynamic approach that views defenses as responses to affect, and Bowlby (1969, 1973) has developed a systems approach to emotion which he has related to attachment theory. Klein (1967) has attempted to bring together cognitive and dynamic processes with his concept of "peremptory motivation." On a perceptual level, Hunt (1965) has argued that incongruity between expectation and perception can result in a phenomenon he calls "intrinsic motivation." Scheier and Carver (1982), following Powers (1973), have utilized control systems theory to understand behavior.

In psychodynamic terms, the approach to be developed here suggests that an individual may deal with an affect such as guilt by a direct behavior (e.g., confession), a coping strategy (e.g., selective inattention, by focusing on something unrelated to the guilt), or a defense (e.g., denying that one really committed the guilt-inducing act). In more behavioristic terms, various behaviors, coping strategies, and defenses are reinforced through their association with positive affects or reduction of aversive affects. In the above example the various control mechanisms are negatively reinforced, i.e., made more likely because they reduce a painful emotion.

The model presented thus far, of course, only describes certain relatively simple conditioning processes. The model becomes slightly more complex when one recognizes that people develop anticipatory affect mechanisms that allow them to assess the likely affective consequences of a given course of action. The student may predict that if he cheats, he will experience guilt, which may deter him from cheating or motivate him to develop a rationalization even before he cheats. These anticipatory mechanisms may be entirely cognitive, in that the person predicts the outcome and his or her affective reaction to it; or the (cognitive) prediction of the outcome may itself provoke an affect, which then serves to condition the person's future response.

A number of experimental studies support the notion of behavioral and mental control mechanisms activated by affective signals. Pettijohn, Wong, Ebert, and Scott (1977) studied separation distress vocalization in dogs, which serves to alert the mother of the puppy's distress. In terms of the model developed above, distress vocalization is a behavioral control mechanism activated by a negative affect. That it was the affect which activated the distress vocalization is demonstrated by the fact the administration of imipramine, an antidepressant, eliminated the distress response. This suggests that once the feedback mechanism (distress) was eliminated, the control mechanism (vocalization) was no longer motivated. The purpose of

34

distress vocalization is to attain a set-goal of proximity to a mothering object. When unmedicated puppies were reunited with their mothers, distress vocalization ceased. Other stimuli, such as food and toys, failed to reduce the distress cries because they did not eliminate the "perceptual-evaluative mismatch" (Holt, 1976) between the set-goal and perceived/cognized reality.

Similar findings occur with human subjects with even more complex emotions. Darley and Latane (1968) found empathic distress, evidenced by trembling hands and sweaty palms, among subjects who believed they were hearing someone have an epileptic seizure. In other words, the hiatus between a set-goal of generalized welfare of others and the perceived distress of another person produced a painful affect. The experimenters found that subjects who responded behaviorally to this response showed reduced signs of distress, clearly suggesting that the behavioral control mechanism elicited by the distress signal reduced the negative affect.

Several studies (Freedman, Wallington, and Bless, 1967; Regan, 1971; and Regan, Williams, and Sparling, 1972) have demonstrated that adults who are led to believe that they have harmed someone and consequently experience guilt show an increased tendency to help others (even people unrelated to the alleged misdeed). One may hypothesize that the feedback signal of guilt activates a number of altruistic behavioral control mechanisms which probably had previously been associated with guilt-reduction.

This form of flight as distress-reduction mechanism can be carried out internally. A number of experimental studies have shown that instructing subjects to view a victim in a detached way reduces empathic distress (Stotland, Sherman, and Shaver, 1971; Aderman, Brehm, and Rosenthal, 1974). Researchers interested in the social psychology of war (e.g., Kelman and Lawrence, 1972) have discussed dehumanization of the enemy as a way of making killing psychologically tolerable, and Bandura and Rosenthal (1966) observed that some individuals avoid empathic distress through various cognitive mechanisms (i.e., internal "behaviors") such as thinking about something else. Quite similar is the commonplace experience of avoiding crying during a touching scene in a movie or play by staring at the exit sign or some other neutral stimulus, or avoiding discomfort during an injection or minor medical intervention by looking the other way or thinking of something pleasant.

Cognitive dissonance can be viewed as a specific case of the more general mechanism described here. The theory of cognitive dissonance as enunciated by Festinger (1957) states that if a person holds two contradictory beliefs or performs a behavior that seemingly disconfirms a belief, he is motivated by an unpleasant tension akin to anxiety to alter his cognitions. In terms of the model proposed here, the anxiety motivates cognitive activity (and often cognitive distortion) to eliminate the cognitive conflict and hence the arousal. While Bem (1972) and others have reinterpreted some of the original evidence for dissonance theory in nonmotivational terms, a large body of research suggests that, indeed, dissonance reduction can be motivated by unpleasant arousal (Wicklund and Frey, 1981).

The desire to minimize negative, and maximize positive emotion can affect both specific thought contents and more general information processing strategies (see Bruner, 1947, for the influence of conditioning on perception). For example, empirical research suggests that people bend their expectations to fit their desires in predicting outcomes in political races (Granberg and Brent, 1983). In other words, people gain anticipatory pleasure and avoid the anticipatory distress caused by a discrepancy between desired and expected results by biasing their expectations and thus minimizing the discrepancy. A more pervasive bias in information processing is the tendency to recall pleasant information more easily than unpleasant (Clark and Isen, 1982), which could readily be conditioned in the manner described here.

A plethora of evidence suggests that it is the perceived discrepancy between set-goal and reality that produces an affect and ultimately a behavioral or mental response. Rubinstein, Shaver, and Peplau (1982) found that loneliness was not associated as much with any objective conditions as with the *perception* of a discrepancy between actual life and desired life. Weiner et al. (1972) studied attributional biases in individuals who were either high or low on need for achievement. Those who had a high need for achievement tended to attribute success to their own ability and effort, and failure to a lack of effort, whereas those whose achievement needs were not so strong did not evidence this self-serving bias. While the difference between the two groups may stem in part from generalized expectancies for personal control for the group high in need achievement, an equally likely, and complementary explanation is that people with high goals for themselves are more likely to rationalize their failures than those with lower goals because the discrepancy is likely to be larger and the affect more intense. Similarly, studies of people prone to depression report that many impose very high standards upon themselves and devalue their accomplishments (Rehm, 1977; Kanfer and Hagerman, 1980), which creates a doubly high mismatch between ideals and perceived reality and exacerbates depression.

Studies on the processes necessary to delay gratification can be reinterpreted in this light. The work of Mischel and his colleagues (see Mischel, 1979, 1984) on delay of gratification in children documents the impact of focus of attention and cognitive transformations on frustration and impulse control. Children who are told to focus on the "hot," consummatory features of a reward such as a marshmallow (attending to its anticipated taste and chewiness) find delay much more frustrating than those who are directed to attend to "cold," nonarousing features or to some other distracting thought, and the former group routinely opt for lesser but immediate rewards because they simply cannot wait.

From the perspective of the model being proposed here, attention to "hot" aspects of the reward makes the set-goal (eating the marshmallow) much more salient and thus intensifies frustration caused by a mismatch between the ideal state and cognized reality. The frustration, in turn, activates the control mechanism of reaching for a reward. Attention to "cold" aspects, in contrast, renders the desirable part of the set-goal less salient, hence attenuating arousal. Focusing on irrelevant, distracting thoughts minimizes awareness of both set-goal and perceived state and thus also results in decreased frustration and correspondingly high ability to delay gratification.

Several studies have similarly shown that instructing children to think "happy" thoughts produces greater delay or persistence behavior in temptation experiments than either providing no instructions or the direction to think sad thoughts (Masters and Santrock, 1976; Moore, Clyburn, and Underwood, 1976). One could hypothesize that thinking happy thoughts directs attention away from the aversive affect caused by delay and thus renders the response of seeking immediate gratification less compelling.

Duval and Wicklund's "self-awareness" theory (1972; Wicklund, 1975) proposes that focusing attention on oneself makes discrepancies between current behavior and behavioral standards more salient, resulting in an aversive affective state that can in turn lead to altered behavior. This theory has been consistently confirmed across several behavioral domains (see Greenberg, 1980; Scheier and Carver, 1982). For example, Scheier, Fenigstein, and Buss (1974) found that subjects gave electrical shocks to women in a learning experiment less when their attention was self-directed. Kanfer's model of self-regulation (1980) similarly points to the importance of self-monitoring as a precursor to recognition of discrepancies between standards and behavior, though like most cognitive-behavioral accounts, Kanfer's does not acknowledge the extent to which lack of self-monitoring can be defensively motivated in order to minimize aversive affect.

A study by Bandura (1983) most clearly documents the relation between set-goals, cognized state, emotion, and response. Subjects performed a strenuous activity and received either behavioral goals and feedback on their performance, goals alone, feedback alone, or neither goals nor feedback. Those in the condition with both goals (for improvement over baseline performance) and information on actual performance responded with heightened performance, unlike the other groups. Goals alone initially boosted performance but did not continue to do so. These results support the model proposed here. The subjects who received both standards and information about current performance experienced a discrepancy which resulted in a tension state as well as a probable anticipation of positive affect upon goal attainment. The affect or affects in turn motivated heightened effort. Neither performance feedback nor goals alone produced increased effort because neither created a mismatch between ideal state and cognized reality. The goals alone condition produced a temporary increase in effort because it heightened salience of a standard, but it did not produce a sustained effort because subjects were unaware of any discrepancy between goal and attainment.[1]

Bandura argues that a discrepancy between standards and performance is motivating only if the person believes he is capable of meeting the standard; otherwise, the person is likely to become discouraged and relinquish all effort. To test this hypothesis he had subjects fill out a questionnaire to assess their expectancies of self-efficacy in improving performance, and he found that those who were given high standards to meet and expected success heightened their performance, whereas those with low efficacy expectations who were nonetheless dissatisfied with their performance vis-à-vis high standards responded as poorly as those who had high efficacy expectancies but no goals.

This study nicely shows how a behavioral response to affective feedback generated by a mismatch between a set-goal and cognized reality will be selected only if the person expects that he can produce an adequate response. What Bandura does not offer is an analysis of what the person might do if he expects that he cannot produce an adequate response. The model proposed in the present chapter suggests that the person may turn to intrapsychic "behavior," i.e., coping or defensive responses, when adaptive behavior seems too difficult or painful. Further, it proposes that the mechanism which evokes a response of the latter sort is precisely the same as that which elicits a behavioral response, namely an affect generated by the discrepancy between set-goal and cognized reality. In Bandura's experiment the subject in the goal plus performance data condition was limited in his ability to distort his perceptions since he was told precisely how well he was doing. In everyday life, standards and performance are often considerably more ambiguous, allowing the person to distort his perception of either or both, and hence to reduce the discrepancy between them. In the experiment the subject's defensive options were considerably constrained, though he could relieve his distress by, for example, displacing his disgruntlement at himself onto the experimenter or basking in the knowledge, upon debriefing, that the experiment had been rigged.

---

[1] In actuality, a similar experiment could have been arranged so that this condition resulted in higher performance than the goals plus performance condition by setting very low standards. In that case, knowledge of performance would lead to minimal discrepancy and hence minimal effort, whereas subjects who received goals but no performance data might assume a necessary level of performance higher than actually required to meet the goal.

Considerable experimental evidence thus supports the model of affect as feedback. Two extended examples will help in developing the model as well as showing its relevance to real life situations. The first is grieving related to object loss. (For an excellent review article, see Averill, 1979.) Following Bowlby (1961), most theorists point to roughly three phases of the grieving process (similar to Kubler-Ross's stages of reaction to dying, 1969). The first is a stage of protest, yearning, and denial of the loss. Parkes (1970) has observed several responses common in this stage, including preoccupation with memories of, searching for, and imagining the presence of the lost love object. The second stage is a period of disorganization and depression, often alloyed with anger. In the third and final stage, the person "works through" the loss, detaching himself from the lost object and finding meaning again in a world without the person who is gone.

The grieving process can be understood in terms of the model developed here as a "reequilibration"[1] process that involves the alteration of a number of set-goals. Grieving involves an extremely painful affective signal that can be broken down into several components. First, following Bowlby (1969, 1973), one can argue that the grieving individual has established a set-goal for proximity to the loved object, and the loss of the object provokes a painful feedback signal caused by the discrepancy between the desired state and the perceived state.

A second source of painful emotion derives from what Hoffman (1978) has called an "empathic distress response." An empathic distress response is an aversive affect that can result from the discrepancy between some desired state of welfare of an object (or class of objects) and perceived/cognized reality. A person may thus experience distress upon object loss both for "selfish" reasons (loss of proximity to the object) and for less selfish reasons (feeling sorry for the person who has died).

A third source of distress resulting from the loss of a loved one may involve other ramifications of the death, such as financial losses that provoke an anticipated discrepancy between a set-goal of standard of living and perceived reality. A fourth is the loss of a role and set of interactional norms related to the lost person. Loss of a spouse, for example, eliminates a number of interactional patterns that had become routinized and therefore required little attention and anxiety. The loss may result in a breakdown of routinized behavior patterns, which results in anxiety; this anxiety may be especially debilitating since it occurs at the same time as distress caused directly by the loss. This aspect of grief

---

[1] I put "reequilibration" within quotation marks because I think the notion of homeostasis or equilibrium is a slightly inappropriate biological metaphor when applied to the psychology of emotions, which is why I chose to speak of set-goals, ideal states, and mismatches instead of equilibria.

distress may become far more problematic if the deceased person was a significant part of the survivor's identity, so that loss of the object is tantamount to loss of sense of self or a part of self. Fear of loss of self or fear of mortality may also be evoked by the death of a loved one, particularly someone one's own age.

A fifth contributor to grief is what social exchange theorists refer to as a loss of reinforcement, especially social reinforcement (Lazarus, 1968; Lewinsohn, Weinstein, and Shaw, 1969). The survivor is accustomed to receiving various forms of positive reinforcement (i.e., positive affect) from the lost person (e.g., hugging, praise), which will no longer be available. This is similar to the behaviorists' notion of "frustrative nonreward," in which an accustomed reward is not forthcoming, a situation that is essentially equivalent to punishment (Gray, 1979). The idea of "social reinforcement," however, is, like its parent concept of reinforcement, tautological and in need of further explanation. One must determine *which* aspect of the interpersonal interaction is pleasurable ("reinforcing") and *why* it is pleasurable. For example, praise from the other person may contribute to self-esteem, which can be conceived as the comparison between ideal self (in psychoanalytic parlance, superego and ego ideal) and self-image, as will be elaborated in the next chapter.

A final source of anguish upon loss is guilt, which may arise secondarily as a response to other affects or may be involved from the start. Obviously, guilt is especially likely to arise if the survivor was somehow responsible for the loss of the object. Yet guilt is often present despite the survivor's innocence in regard to the death. Clinically, one frequently finds patients with guilt feelings about a dead person toward whom they harbored death wishes at some point in time. By an omnipotence of thought, which may be quite split off from the rest of adult consciousness, the person has equated the thought and the deed. Similarly, a person may guiltily chastise herself for failing to accede to this or that wish of the person before he died. In both cases guilt is a feedback mechanism produced by a discrepancy between self-image and ideals about what she (the survivor) should be or how she should have acted.

Loss may thus invoke a set of painful affective reactions. In fact, any one of these components may spark others. This may occur in one of two ways. First, related emotions may be closely connected in an associational network, so that elicitation of one makes more likely the activation of others. This presupposes that affects, like cognitions, may be represented in associational networks. Experimental studies of cognitive processes have amply demonstrated that activation of a concept primes related concepts (Anderson and Bower, 1973; Collins and Loftus, 1975; Anderson, 1976; Brown, 1979), and considerable evidence suggests that affective processes may act similarly. Positive and negative feeling states, for example, have been shown to facilitate mood-congruent memories (Bower, 1981; Clark and Isen, 1982).

Secondly, object loss is such a painful and disruptive event that it is likely to evoke the kind of global, relatively undifferentiated negative affect that many psychodynamic theorists have postulated as characteristic of early emotion before the person has learned to understand and modulate affect. Thus, the response to loss may be an intense negative emotion that feels like sadness, anger, shame, and guilt all rolled into one.

The person's response to the emotions created by a loss may, at least at first, be equally global and primitive. In the first stage of grief, the person uses various mechanisms designed to negate the loss. Bowlby (1961) emphasizes protest behavior common among primates including humans in the early stages of separation. Distress cries and other protest behavior may originally arise ontogenetically as reflexes, but they generally become reinforced because of their usefulness in quelling separation distress (by signaling the loved object to appear). When the loved one dies, these routinized behaviors are invoked, though in reality to no avail. They are produced not only because they were previously reinforced when the object was alive, which gives the person the illusion that perhaps they may work again, but also because they have been associated with reduction of distress in the past and thus may aid somewhat in distress reduction even if their actual utility is minimal (i.e., they are "secondary reinforcers" responsible for something like a placebo effect).

Calling out for a dead loved one, however, is not particularly adaptive (and except for its placebo value, will not be reinforced). It is one of a class of responses in the early stages of grief which can be conceived as forms of denial. Various "internal" and "external" behaviors (i.e., defensive, coping, and behavioral strategies) may be utilized to deny the object loss. For example, outright denial ("I know she is not dead") is a common response, which Kubler-Ross (1969) argues is the first stage of the process of dealing with death. Similarly, people in the early stages of grief often hallucinate the presence of the dead person or see the person in lifelike dreams (see Rees, 1975). In both cases the person is trying to deny the loss by imagining the presence of the object. Preoccupation with the dead person's memory is also a way of keeping the person psychologically alive. The reason for this preoccupation is betrayed by the popular expression that a person is "alive in my memory."

In terms of the model developed here, the function of all of these strategies is the same: to decrease the disparity between an ideal (set-goal) and cognized reality by distorting the perception/cognition. The result is a reduction in the distress signal. Pictorially, one can represent the situation as in Figure 1.

In other words, the discrepancy between the ideal of the lost object not

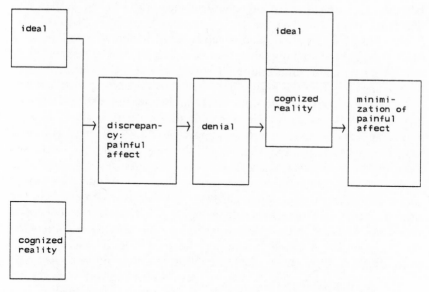

Figure 1

being lost and the perceived/cognized reality of the death creates a painful affect. This affect in turn activates a defense mechanism, denial, which minimizes the ideal/cognition discrepancy by altering the cognition in the direction of the ideal state. This, in turn, reduces the painful emotion, which consequently reinforces the denial.

The choice of such a reality-distorting defense as denial (or hallucination of the loved one's presence) in the early stages of grief attests to the intensity of the affect and the pressing need to modulate it. As will be argued in Chapter 3, defenses and coping strategies may be arranged hierarchically in descending order of "marginal utility." If, for example, selective inattention can relieve the distress, it will more likely be used by most people because it is less disruptive and maladaptive than defenses such as denial (or in the extreme case, hallucination). In many forms of psychopathology, however, and particularly in character disorders, various low level defenses are routinely used, even when the emotion does not seem particularly poignant. Part of defense analysis in psychodynamic psychotherapy involves – my fears of castration by psychoanalysts for saying this, aside – the counterconditioning of dysfunctional defenses. By calling attention to the defense and its source in a particular conflict, the therapist is inhibiting the capacity of the defense to continue warding off painful affects, which renders it more likely to undergo "extinction" (i.e., it is no longer reinforced). From this perspective, it is not surprising that psychoanalysts have found that defense analysis and conflict analysis are frequently inseparable (Brenner, 1975). Similarly, calling attention to deleterious side effects of the defense inhibits its use by attaching various negative affects to the use of the defense itself. This is not, of course, all that defense analysis entails, though the significance of counterconditioning should not be overlooked.

Ultimately the "grief-work" must result in detachment and reorganization. In terms of the model presented here, this means that "working-through" an attachment so that distress and defense are no longer operative involves reducing the set-goal/cognized reality discrepancy (which will be called, slightly amending Holt's [1976] term, a *cognitive-evaluative mismatch*) by reducing the set-goal. Only by experiencing the pain and undergoing the process of grieving can the person reach the point at which he no longer needs the loved one. Unresolved grief, with all its clinical manifestations, involves the attempt to deny the significance of the loss by defensively refusing to rework the set-goal (often by avoiding thinking about the mismatch). This view is in fundamental agreement with Freud's hypothesis that the function of the grieving process is gradually to "decathect" the object, i.e., to reduce the set-goal and thus eliminate the requirement that one can only be happy if the lost person could be alive. Precisely how this occurs, and why it appears to take at least six months to a year, is unclear. The ideal probably never disappears entirely, though it may become reduced enough so that, for example, a photograph of the deceased individual can bring a smile or satisfy whatever cravings for the person remain. Evidence that, in fact, grieving involves the reduction of a set-goal is provided by cases reported by Lindemann (1944) of women who prematurely grieved their husbands who were away at war. When the husbands returned, the wives rejected them because the wives simply did not want them anymore. Separation from their husbands no longer caused these women distress because they had altered their set-goals regarding their husbands. Normally, anticipation of a death is psychologically useful because it allows gradual, rather than sudden alteration of important set-goals (for empirical evidence, see Ball, 1977).

The model, as presented so far, still minimizes the extent to which processing occurs between the initial feedback signal and the ultimate "internal" or "external" response. Another example will illustrate the ways in which the model can incorporate a wider range of phenomena. Suppose a young, unmarried woman in our culture discovers that she is pregnant and is very upset. Schematically, one can represent the situation as in Figure 2.

The discrepancy between her ideal state and cognized reality produced a painful affect. For simplicity, we will ignore the various components of this affective state relating to issues of how the baby would affect her life and simply focus on one component: guilt. This feedback signal activates

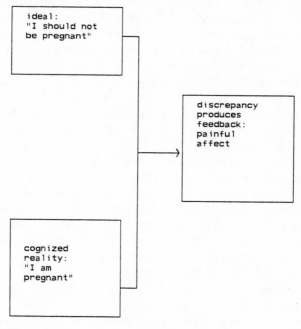

Figure 2

many conscious and unconscious anticipated responses, i.e., ideas about how to deal with the situation. The guilt may be so severe that it immediately activates defenses such as repression or denial, which prevent her from even considering other possibilities.[1] Such a response may be an isolated psychological event, or it may represent an aspect of an "hysterical style" (Shapiro, 1965), which means a tendency to deal with affects in precisely this way, by repression or denial. One may suspect that the tendency of the person with this character style not to think out alternatives in various situations results in part from the constriction of anticipatory problem solving caused by ready use of such defensive procedures. The impulsiveness attributed to hysterical characters, which forces them to act on their impulses without much thought, can be considered as an aspect of the same phenomenon: affects are managed quickly with immediate internal or external responses, with little time allowed for the consideration of alternatives. The global cognitive style and minimal attention to anomalous details characteristic of people with this character style may result in part from the inability to tolerate the anxiety of cognitive ambi-

[1] Lest this example seem farfetched, I should perhaps mention that counselors in university settings, in particular, frequently encounter women who continue to deny their pregnancy for months despite obvious physical manifestations.

guity. Indeed, experimental evidence demonstrates that antianxiety drugs tend to reduce fear of novelty (Gray, 1979), which suggests that cognitive ambiguity (i.e., confronting stimuli which are not easily assimilable) produces a form of anxiety (see also Pribram, 1980). One would thus not be surprised to find that people who cannot tolerate negative affective signals also might tend to defend against recognizing anomalous aspects of reality.[1]

Returning to the example, while denying the situation (i.e., "the rabbit was lying") may be one response considered in order to manage the guilt, it is a fairly low level response, and unless it is characterologically routinized, other alternatives will probably be considered first. For example, two obvious options to consider in this situation are having an abortion and having the baby. Suppose that the woman is devoutly religious and believes that abortion is murder. When she (consciously or unconsciously) anticipates abortion, a new affective situation comes into play. She anticipates a behavior, having an abortion, but this deviates markedly from her ideal, which says that women who have abortions are murderers. This discrepancy between anticipated reality and ideal precipitates another affective signal of guilt. Thus, the strategy of relieving her guilt at being pregnant by having an abortion may be successful in relieving the initial guilt at being pregnant, but it is unsuccessful because it leads to a second guilt at allegedly being a murderer. This anticipated response is thus rejected.

The second option open to her, having the baby, fails to alleviate her original guilt about being an unwed mother, and her anticipation of the consequences of having the child may only intensify the guilt. This anticipation may also evoke other negative anticipatory affects, such as shame at being viewed by her family or community as a scarlet woman. The response of having the baby must, consequently, also be rejected. Initially, then, her response may be denial because neither of her other options proves acceptable. One may represent the situation pictorially, as in Figure 3.

As this example clearly shows, when various behavioral strategies cannot diminish the affective signal, the person may resort to a defense mechanism to alleviate the distress. Lest this example appear too rationalistic, it should be stressed again that often the strength of the emotion may be so

---

[1] The notion that cognitive ambiguity results in anxiety has received support from a number of independent areas of investigation. Kuhn (1970) considers the recognition of anomalous data and consequent unease in a scientific community as the motivation behind scientific revolutions and ultimately paradigm shifts. Similarly, anthropologist Mary Douglas (1966) has explained various cultural beliefs in taboo and consequent purification rituals as responses to cognitive ambiguity. This is another example in which what looks on the surface like "cognitive motivation" has a salient affective component. Anyone who has devoted considerable thought to a subject or discipline knows the anxiety produced by recognition that one's way of understanding important phenomena needs to be abandoned, perhaps in favor of a view as yet unformulated. Intellectual anxiety is anxiety nonetheless.

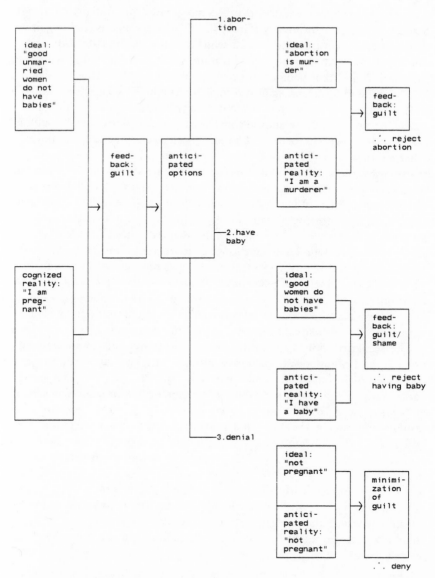

Figure 3

severe as to shut off the search for nondefensive alternatives, or the person may be characterologically prone routinely to use defenses that are far from optimal. In this light, one aim of psychotherapy is to break vicious feedback loops in which an affect consistently evokes a single defense or set of defenses, constricting the search for more adaptive alternatives.

Even the above analysis, however, is quite oversimplified. First, affective consequences of anticipated responses may themselves be managed with various behavioral and defensive strategies, and these factors are often weighed in the balance. For example, the guilt created by having an abortion could be managed by rationalization: "In my case, this is not really murder because . . ." This rationalization would bring the anticipated reality back into line with the ideal, thus reducing the cognitive-evaluative mismatch and with it, the guilt. In this manner the woman may minimize the negative affect caused by her pregnancy by combining a behavior (having an abortion) with a defense (rationalization).[1]

Secondly, most actions are far more complex because they involve compromise-formations that simultaneously answer to conflicting affects. If, for example, the woman considers having the baby, she may be torn between the anticipated shame and guilt on the one hand, and the potential joy of having a child, on the other. The resulting strategy that maximizes positive, and minimizes negative emotion[2] may be a compromise: have the baby, but arrange to have her sister adopt it. By so doing, she reduces the shame and guilt of rearing a child as an unwed mother, while still gaining the pleasure of participating in the child's life as an aunt. Psychoanalysts generally look at phenomena such as symptoms as compromise-formations, though the principle is the same in everyday examples such as this: synthesize competing thoughts or behaviors to resolve conflicting mismatches.

Indeed, the selection of responses to mismatches is a far less mechanistic process than I have described it thus far. While people do develop routinized control mechanisms (e.g., the defense mechanisms described by Anna Freud, 1936), much of the time they are far more creative in tailoring

---

[1] One should not assume that a single cognitive-evaluative mismatch will always evoke a single response. Even without activating a second mismatch (as occurred in the above example), one mismatch may result in multiple responses, as when a grieving person both denies the death and calls the hospital for confirmation. Fleming, Baum, and Singer (1984) have similarly pointed out in relation to stress research that different strategies may be used to cope with a single stressor, as when a person who has been informed that he has a disease consults a specialist as well as alters his lifestyle (p. 945). Multiple set-goals may also prompt a single response, as when a student enrolls in college both because he wants his parents' approval and because he wants an education or heightened job prospects. A single response may be elicited by conflicting set-goals as well, as in a compromise-formation. What one considers a single response is, of course, to some extent arbitrary since any response may be partitioned into its component subresponses (cf. Sternberg's analysis of cognitive tasks, 1979).

[2] In reality, people differ in the extent to which they prefer maximizing pleasure or minimizing pain. Those with a lower threshold for painful emotions, for example, will be less concerned with maximizing pleasure than managing negative affect. The failure to recognize these differences has, incidentally, influenced political philosophy in the work of John Rawls (1971), who attempts to demonstrate that a rational society would naturally pursue a "maximin" rule aimed at minimizing the discomfort of the most disadvantaged.

responses to particular situations. Responses are less mechanistic in another sense: people frequently tolerate painful emotions, often at the service of other set-goals or ideals. Many times no response is appropriate or optimal, and a person must simply experience the unpleasant affect. The pregnant woman in the above example may keep the child and tolerate the shame and guilt because she cannot see any other way to fulfill what she sees as moral obligations. At other times the person may determine that the set-goal is inappropriate or must be abandoned, and this is by no means always defensive. The pregnancy, for example, may force the woman to reconsider some of her beliefs and ultimately to change some of her moral set-goals. One of the major sources of change in psychotherapy is the recognition and abandonment of dysfunctional set-goals developed in childhood, and as will be argued in Part III, the abandonment of old set-goals is a basic component of many forms of social change.

A third complication, which should be immediately apparent, is that people do not always accurately predict the response that optimizes affect in their "felicific calculus." The woman who decides to give her baby to her sister may later discover that, in her anticipation, she had mistakenly minimized the pain she would feel when the baby called her sister "mama." She may have done so for defensive reasons, but she also may simply have made a cognitive error. Defensively, she may have been so concerned to relieve the immediate distress that she sacrificed her future happiness. Cognitively, the ability to predict the affective consequences of actions involves complicated sets of processes that the individual only gradually develops. This ability constitutes what psychoanalysts (following Anna Freud, 1973) would call a "developmental line," which would be a ripe area for study by developmentalists and social cognition researchers.

A fourth possibility is that the woman may defend against her initial guilt with other emotions. She may, for example, get angry at the man who got her pregnant. This may not, of course, be defensive; she may have every reason to be angry at him. Yet anger can often be a more comfortable emotion than guilt, and if she can turn her conscious attention to her anger, she may not consciously experience the guilt, or she may defensively misinterpret the guilt feelings as part of her anger at her lover. (The issue of consciousness of affect will be addressed shortly.) One may suspect that a similar process occurs in grieving, when, as Kubler-Ross reports, many people pass through a period of anger at doctors, friends, God, etc., which effectively reduces their consciousness of depression.

Various behaviors may also be elicited to produce competing affects such as joy or sexual pleasure to divert attention from negative affects. "Binging" or compulsive eating, for example, may provide the person with a stimulus usually associated with pleasure which can overshadow guilt or

48

depression. Overzealous sexual behavior, such as compulsive masturbation or promiscuity, may also produce pleasurable sensations that direct attention away from affects such as anxiety, although the sexual behavior may then come to be associated with the anxiety itself, leading to secondary dysfunctions.

Finally, the anticipatory thoughts themselves can provoke negative affects and defensive operations, often before they even become conscious. The pregnant woman in the example above may become so guilt-ridden by even the thought of aborting the child that she represses the idea. One patient whose father was physically abusive, and who responds to "evil" thoughts with guilt and depression, denies having wished to kill her father, though she can remember wishing that something might happen to him that would be beyond her control. Clearly at some point she must have fantasized about killing her father, but her ideas about what "good girls" should and should not even *think* caused her to deny this wish and thus avoid the guilt. What was left of the wish was a fantasy of the same goal—her father's death—without the causal attribution that evoked the guilt. When he does die, however, she will probably unconsciously connect her wish with his death and suffer the emotional consequences. This discussion raises the critical question of the relation between wishes and affects, which allows one to consider the issue of whether or not affect theory can supersede drive theory as an explanation of human motivation.[1]

Wishes and Affects: Where Drive Was, There Shall Affect Be

Earlier it was claimed, though without justification, that defenses arise only in relation to affects or anticipation of affects, and never to "drives" or "reality" (or, for that matter, to "ideas"). I hope now to demonstrate that not only are defenses motivated by affect, but that one can dispense with the concept of drive entirely, while losing nothing in explanatory power. The advantage of shifting from drive to affect as an explanatory concept is twofold. First, it allows one to escape the interminable difficulties of Freudian instinct theory, and to explain, with a single model, both the more primitive impulses so richly explored in psychoanalytic writings, and the "adaptive," everyday behaviors described by cognitive social learning theorists. Secondly, a shift from drive to affect brings theoretical discourse much closer to the level of psychological experience and clinical practice. I have never seen a drive activated or reactivated in a clinical hour, but I have often seen people experiencing rage, fear, sadness, envy, anxiety, joy, love, lust, pride, or curiosity. As a psychotherapist one pays closest attention to fantasies, thoughts, and behaviors that seem to be the

---

[1] By "motivation" I mean the impetus for action, i.e., that which "energizes" the system.

most highly charged emotionally, and clinical practice could surely be enriched by theory that hovers closer to the level of concrete experience.

The easiest step in the argument is to show that defenses are never direct responses to reality without affective mediation. This is analogous to the earlier contention that cognitively mediated operant conditioning never proceeds without the involvement of affect. The notion of defense against "reality" originated in Freud's famous statement that the ego serves three masters: the id, the superego, and reality. Reality, however, can never motivate a defense (or behavior) unless in some way it is (1) perceived, and (2) conflicts with an ideal state. If one of my set-goals did not involve self-preservation, the "reality" of an approaching train would not compel me to leave the tracks (nor would it lead me to deny the presence of the train if I were tied to the tracks). If I am affectively indifferent, reality is motivationally of no consequence. An attempt by the CIA to invade Nicaragua by proxy presents itself as the same "reality" to a conservative American as it does to me, though it may be cognized in different ways. It provokes my anger and not the conservative's because we share neither similar ideals about the aims of U.S. foreign policy or the welfare of Nicaragua, nor beliefs about the discrepancy between stated national goals and actual policy. Similarly, a person never defends against an "idea" (e.g., "the sky is blue") unless the idea conflicts with some ideal state (e.g., "the sky is falling," and for various reasons I wish it would not).

The second step in the argument is to distinguish between emotions and wishes. Diffuse anxiety is a paradigm case of an affect without perceived connection to its source, though the argument to be developed here is that *all* affects initially exist without a causal attribution. An experiment by Maslach (1978) using hypnosis provides a pure case of affect initially unconnected to a causal attribution. Maslach presented subjects with a hypnotic suggestion which resulted in an aroused affective state akin to anxiety (increased breathing, racing heart, sweaty palms, and sinking feeling in the stomach). The experimenter also gave one group of subjects a suggestion for posthypnotic amnesia. Subjects who were uninformed as to the real cause of their arousal (through posthypnotic suggestion) attributed their aroused condition to various sources, including performance anxiety, worries about upcoming final exams, etc. A control group who were not given the suggestion for amnesia did not similarly search for erroneous reasons for their emotional state (cf. Schachter and Singer's notion of evaluative need, 1962), and did not find the aroused state aversive.

While this experiment involves a special situation, hypnosis, it may suggest that, however affect becomes aroused, its causes can only be assessed post facto, and these attributions may be erroneous. In other words, the subjects in Maslach's study experienced an emotion the cause of which they could not explain, and they proceeded, using available information about the situation and themselves, to find a cause. I will argue that this is not, in fact, an exception based on an altered state of consciousness, but that the attribution of the cause of an emotion (and the development of strategies to alleviate or maintain it) *always* follows the cognitively unencumbered affective signal.

What is being suggested, *pace* Kant, is that there is no noumenal realm of psychological cause and effect to which the individual is privy. The actual cause of any emotion is a nonexperiential process which the individual can only *infer* from his past history and current situational factors. The attribution of cause of affect is always probabilistic. In some cases we may be relatively certain of the source of our affect since the emotion appears directly following a stimulus or thought. If, for example, a doctor tells me I have cancer and I suddenly experience terror, I would be a shrewd gambler to bet that the information had something to do with my emotion. In other cases, however, causal attributions are not so clear. If I wake up in the morning feeling anxious, the closest I may be able to come to discovering the reason is to speculate that I must have had a bad dream. Rather than these being different cases with different principles, both the cancer example and the dream example involve probabilistic attribution of causes, though the former may have a lower "intuitive p-value." (The ability to discriminate between causal attributions with differing degrees of certainty may constitute another developmental line; see Nisbett and Wilson's discussion of the conditions that give rise to subjective certainty about mental processes, 1977, p. 255).

What I am essentially arguing is that we should apply Hume's critique of empiricism to inner experience. Hume observed that causality entails a psychological inference, not a direct transcription of nature. He argued that we can never actually perceive cause and effect relationships: all we can observe is the *constant conjunction* of two events A and B, and if A consistently precedes B, we make the psychological – and probabilistic – inference that A is causally related to B.

Similarly in the realm of affect, imputations of cause always involve inference, and quite often that inference is incorrect, as in Maslach's hypnosis study. Attribution research in social psychology has documented extensively the phenomenon of causal misattribution of emotion (for reviews of relevant literature see Zillman, 1978; Pennebaker, 1980; Harvey and Weary, 1981). For example, in an experiment by Dutton and Aron (1974) an attractive woman approached male subjects on one of two bridges and asked them to fill out a questionnaire regarding some pictures. One bridge was a very high, wobbly suspension bridge likely to evoke fear; the other was safe and sturdy, only a few feet above water. Dutton and Aron hypothesized that the subjects on the first bridge would be much more aroused and would attribute their arousal as sexual. The investigators found that not only did subjects on the frightening bridge see significantly more sexual themes in the pictures, but fifty percent of them subsequently telephoned the woman (she had given them her phone number and offered to let them know the results), whereas only ten percent of those on the safe bridge availed themselves of her offer. Thus, not only did the subjects on the scary bridge misinterpret their arousal, but they misinterpreted its cause (bridge versus woman) as well.

Nisbett and Bellows (cited in Nisbett and Wilson, 1977) presented subjects with a lengthy application portfolio of an alleged job applicant and asked them to make a number of judgments, including, for example, how much they liked her. Subjects also rated the extent to which they believed their opinions were influenced by a number of experimentally manipulated factors (e.g., the applicant was either described or not described as attractive, or the subjects were told that they would meet the applicant or that they would meet a different applicant). The subjects' beliefs about what influenced their judgments were by and large incorrect, and the correlation between believed causality and actual measured causality as to the subjects' feelings about the applicant (liking or disliking) were rather strongly negative. In other words, subjects were incorrectly inferring the cause of their affective judgments. Their inferences were, however, strongly correlated (.89 for the liking judgment) with inferences of subjects who were simply asked questions such as how much they expected that physical attractiveness would influence their liking of a person. Nisbett and Bellows concluded that the subjects who rated the applicant were basing causal attributions of their judgments on the same intuitive and culturally constructed implicit causal theories used by observers, rather than on the observation of the actual cause of their preferences.

As often as not, people develop causal misattributions for defensive reasons. If, for example, I am feeling angry at my mother, and I hold an ideal which tells me that good people do not have such feelings toward their mothers, I may defensively stifle the affect. In this case, the defense is to eliminate the feedback signal itself because the signal has been defined as morally reprehensible. Alternatively, I may continue to experience the affect but deliberately misattribute its cause, concluding that I am angry at one of my students. The poor student will suffer, of course, but students are often easier targets of anger than mothers. (This is not, I should add, my philosophy of education.) The defense mechanism of displacement, then, involves the (unconsciously) deliberate causal misattribution of affect. Indeed, many defenses would not be effective if not allied with such a misattribution. Experimental evidence of the use of misattribution to eliminate aversive feeling states is provided in a study by Schwartz and Clore (1983). Subjects in bad moods could be induced to experience greater life

52

satisfaction by misattributing mood to external, transient factors, while subjects in good moods were not affected by misattribution manipulations.

This causal analysis, in which the person tries to discover the source of her emotional states, often contributes to the individual's choice of responses to the affect. (For experimental demonstrations of the impact of attributions on responses, see Dienstbier et al., 1975; Zillman, 1978, pp. 362-3; Harvey and Weary, 1981, pp. 108-9). If, for example, I believe that I am anxious because I have waited several months to hear from a reviewer on a book I have written, I may call the publisher to allay my anxiety. If the behavior eliminates the affect, I will conclude that I was right, and if not, I may conclude otherwise. This, of course, is bad intuitive science: something other than the original cause can sometimes quell a negative affect (just as one can reason from false premises to veridical conclusions). More to the point, my belief in the attribution is likely to render it at least somewhat effective because of the placebo/secondary reinforcement effect described earlier. This effect may then further "reinforce" the belief and its attendant response, so that I may further associate it with distress reduction.

Suppose, however, that I call the publisher and she is on vacation. Now my anxiety has intensified because, even though the actual cognitive-evaluative mismatch that created my anxiety may have been the budding recognition that I have accumulated a year's worth of psychiatric charts to fill out on my patients and I have very limited time, my erroneous causal attribution has created a new set-goal which is not being achieved, namely, talking to the publisher. Thus, what began as an anticipated behavioral response to an affect has become a *wish*. A wish can be defined as a cognitive-affective schema that arises in response to an affect. A wish includes an anticipatory affect tied to a projected response; in other words, a person expects a positive affect and/or reduction of a negative affect if reality fulfills the set-goal or desired state. Unlike an affect, a wish necessarily is a wish *for* something and thus includes a cognition (a representation of a stimulus or response) as well as an affect. A wish inherently involves the recognition that one does not have what one desires; we do not wish for what we already have. Schematically, the development of a wish can be represented as in Figure 4.

As should be clear, a wish may thus become an affect-eliciting structure comparable to a cognitive-evaluative mismatch, which can similarly produce negative emotions when unfulfilled. The wish itself may also provide some positive affect in its fantasy function: by imagining what the desired state would be like to attain, one may experience a partial anticipatory affect, and the hope that the wish could someday be fulfilled may also produce some pleasurable emotion.

Wishes are a mixed blessing because a person may fear them or feel

53

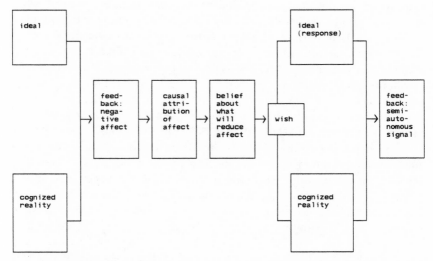

Figure 4

guilty about them. The patient who repressed her death wishes toward her father probably both feared allowing the wish to remain conscious, because that made the probability higher that she might actually act on it (which would be even more distressing), and felt guilty about even having the wish in the first place. Repressed wishes such as these exert an enormous influence on human behavior, and they can be especially dysfunctional because they may rely upon belief systems or schemas that have long since been abandoned but remain operative in these repressed pockets of belief/feeling. Clinically, one confronts "archaic" wishes of this kind frequently, which involve egocentric, often magical thinking characteristic of the period at which the wish was repressed. My patient who believed that her father's death would somehow eliminate her problems still holds onto that belief and its attendant wish, despite the adult reality that she no longer lives at home. Similarly, another patient whose father would never show her any affection as a child holds an almost magical belief about what would happen if she could do something that would make him take notice. Many of her actions as an adult reflect this wish to please her father, even though her father is no longer realistically in the picture. Essentially, what has occurred in these cases is that a schema developed in childhood to which intense affect has been connected has survived largely intact despite years of cognitive development. Frustration or satisfaction of repressed wishes such as this tends to produce emotions and resulting behaviors the cause of which the individual is unaware.

The reader who is not a clinician or whose orientation is not primarily psychodynamic may doubt the existence of such repressed pockets of experience, particularly if she or he is conversant in contemporary information processing models of cognition that do not allow for split-off schemas or trains of association rendered inaccessible by dynamic factors. I will later call upon experimental research to document the existence of these phenomena, but for now I will give two simple examples from everyday life that reveal similar properties. The first is the common experience of people as they move into adulthood of meeting an adult, such as a teacher, whom they knew as a child. In that situation people will frequently use the teacher's surname, even though they are normally not in the habit of referring to other adults as "Mister" or "Missus." Essentially, what has happened is that an old cognitive-linguistic construction has been evoked after years of disuse and has not yet been reworked under current principles of functioning. Readers who are inclined to see this as just an empty linguistic artifact of no real significance should reflect upon similar experiences of their own. Those who do so will probably recall both the childhood awe toward the adult or teacher that was at least temporarily evoked along with the formality of the name, as well as the discomfort of the period of readjustment in which they tried to rework the archaic schema to fit with their current ways of understanding and feeling toward other adults. The same phenomenon often occurs when people try to learn to deal with their parents as adults, except that the transition is usually more gradual, and many more schemas remain developmentally primitive.

A second situation in which one can observe pockets of material relatively unchanged by cognitive development is the recall of long-forgotten affect-laden memories. I recently remembered an incident in which my family had brought home a new pet and foolishly left it for a few minutes in a car on a hot day, resulting in a terrified, overheated animal. Though at the time I had been concerned for the animal, shortly thereafter I "tagged" the incident as a funny memory since the animal had, not surprisingly, behaved quite strangely for the next few minutes. Recalling the event as an adult, I was aghast, and guiltily revised my childhood estimation of its humorousness. This is an example of a childhood affective assessment which, because it had never come to my conscious attention as an adult, had never been reworked. Many incidents of this sort not only fail to reach consciousness but are deliberately kept from consciousness – i.e., are repressed – because they are painful or anxiety-provoking. The episode, the affect, and the repression all remain governed by childhood assumptions because they cannot consciously be reworked, and they may be evoked and motivate action in adulthood without the person's awareness. This was precisely the phenomenon that led Freud to the psychoanalytic method of interpretation and treatment.

Returning to wishes, a wish, then, involves an anticipatory affect attached to a cognitive representation of a stimulus, behavior, or situation. As such, it requires as a prerequisite representational intelligence. One cannot wish for something until one can store and retrieve a representation of it. One must thus reject Freud's hypothesis in *The Interpretation of Dreams* (1900) that primary process thought, supposedly characteristic of infancy, is essentially wishful thought. The whole notion of "instinctual wishes" present from birth not only presupposes the doctrine of innate ideas (for a philosophical review of thought on innate ideas since Plato, see Edgley, 1970), for which one can muster little firm evidence (at any point in the lifespan), but it is especially problematic given that object permanence does not emerge until the second half of the first year of life[1] (cf. Izard's contention, 1979, that what he calls cognitive-affective structures do not emerge until the last quarter of the first year of life; see also Kagan, 1976, pp. 69-70). The psychoanalytic concept of drive derivatives that somehow "represent" the instincts in psychic life is a confused one, which does not account well for the relation between innate predispositions and the acquisition of complex motives through learning.

If one eliminates these notions of drive, drive derivatives, and instinctual wishes, how can one account for motivation? The argument here is that, while as psychologists we may develop hypothetical constructs about the aims of human behavior, the primary cause of internal and external responses is affect. A case that would seem at first glance to be problematic from this viewpoint is attachment behavior, which the psychoanalyst would claim must be examined in terms of drive theory, and the behaviorist might explain (available primate evidence to the contrary) in terms of secondary reinforcement (i.e, the caretaker is valued because she is a source of food).

One can, however, integrate a theory of attachment into the model of affect proposed here without resorting to a theory of drive that founders on the mind-body problem (i.e., how can a drive be both somatic and psychical?). One can hardly doubt, given evidence from both human infants and other primates, that attachment is a need that is essentially wired into the organism. Given the extended infancy characteristic of the higher primates, such a need would have proven very adaptive and would likely have been preserved through natural selection. The only real question is how one can conceptualize this need as a source of motivation without assuming that the infant has in its mind a primordial image of a mother whom it is driven to pursue in reality and fantasy.

One can avoid the difficulty by defining this "need for attachment" in terms of the various set-goals involved. One may suppose that an early

---

[1] Primary process thought appears to resemble preoperational thought, rather than sensorimotor intelligence.

set-goal in relation to primary caretakers involves, as Bowlby (1969) suggests, proximity. When the child of fourteen months looks around and sees that his mother is absent, he experiences intense distress and may search for her or start to cry to implore her to return. Looking from the outside in, we may conclude that attachment behavior is genetically determined and formulate a hypothetical construct of the need to attach. Looking from the inside out, however, the baby simply learns that when his caretaker disappears he finds himself in distress, and when she is with him he feels much better. What "drives" the infant is thus his desire to minimize his distress and maximize his pleasure. From a motivational point of view, one need not turn to instinct theory to explain his relationship to his caretaker. (Another way of stating this, more in accord with psychoanalytic theory, would be to view affect as the "psychic representative of the drives." Even if one wishes to speak this way, however, one must move away from a drive-discharge, tension-release motivational theory and toward a theory of emotion and its biological foundations that makes greater psychological and evolutionary sense.)

Again, none of this is to suggest that the infant lacks various genetically based reflexes such as rooting and sucking which facilitate attachment, or that certain innate releasing mechanisms, as the ethologists call them (Tinbergen, 1951; Hinde, 1970), may not participate in the process. In early infancy, for example, neonates begin to express special interest in stimuli resembling human faces, which makes evolutionary sense in terms of bonding and attachment. Psychologically speaking, the infant does not hear a voice within itself (a "representation of an instinct") that impels it to seek human faces. Rather, the baby's brain is genetically wired so that the infant experiences a pleasurable affect in response to stimuli resembling a face and will thus come to associate these stimuli with the affect.[1] This association, not a drive, accounts at the motivational level for the infant's behavior. (This way of looking at motivation basically takes the best from psychoanalytic and behaviorist understanding of motivation: with the behaviorist, it recognizes the role of conditioning in even the earliest learning, yet with the psychoanalyst, it suggests that we need to examine *why* certain behaviors are "reinforcing" or "reinforced.")

Later, of course, the young child may recognize his own wish to be near

---

[1] That largely preprogrammed biological events (occurring along a relatively fixed maturational timetable) could influence behavior through their impact on emotion is fully in keeping with what is known about the impact of tissue states on subjective experience. Cabinac (cited in Garcia, Hawkins, and Rusiniak, 1974) has shown that whether a warm stimulus is experienced as pleasant or unpleasant depends on the person's internal temperature; if the temperature is high, for example, warmth will be aversive. Regarding feeding behavior, Garcia and his colleagues have demonstrated that "homeostatic states monitored by internal receptors produce changes in the incentive values of external stimuli sensed by the peripheral receptors, and guide feeding behavior (1974, p. 831).

his caretaker, and if he grows up to be a psychologist, he may develop even more complex theories about the sources of his motivation. Wishes all necessarily include intuitive theories of motivation: the young child's recognition of his desire to be with his primary caregivers results from his recognition that he is in distress if they are absent. He has essentially put together a theory to explain his own feelings and behavior. Wishes, then, are ontogenetically later acquisitions than affects because they require representational intelligence.

The individual thus, as an "intuitive scientist" or "intuitive psychologist" (Ross, 1977), must come to learn about his own motivation, and much of psychotherapy involves helping the person develop better theories about what he really wants. These intuitive theories tend to be distorted because they form part of the person's self-concept and are therefore, like other aspects of self-concept, frequently tested against various ideals. The recognition, for example, that one is a selfish person in many people would conflict with internalized altruistic standards and consequently produce guilt and diminished self-esteem. As in the example of the woman with death wishes toward her father, disavowing the wishes also serves to inhibit acting on them. In fact, her guilt and fears about her anger toward her father were so unacceptable to her that she fed the anger at him back into her own guilt at her aggressive desires toward him and on more than one occasion had committed very self-destructive acts. The anger she felt toward her father was readily turned inward – i.e., the cause of the anger was deliberately misattributed – because it could fuel her already existing anger at herself for her aggressive desires. Indeed, the self-destructive acts provide an excellent example of a compromise-formation. They expressed her guilt about her angry feelings and aggressive desires, and they also represented a defensive misattribution of the cause of her anger – i.e., a displacement – onto herself. They also served another function, which she later articulated, as an attempt to get someone (in large measure her father and various substitutes for him) to show that he cares. That she chose an act which harmed herself to try to elicit his caring is not surprising, given that he abused her when she was a child, which was in large part the only kind of attention she received from him. She also had, as a teenager, provoked his aggression toward her, and the self-destructive acts were thus part of a pattern that involved repressed childhood beliefs and feelings about how to elicit caring and the relationship between affection and abuse.

A person comes to know his own motivation through four sources. The first is by observing his own affects and their links to certain stimuli or events. If, for example, I feel angry and upset every time a certain woman walks into the room, I come to believe that I dislike her. Secondly, a person learns about his own motivations by experiencing his conscious wishes. If I think to myself, "I would like to eat an ice cream cone," that informs me about my motivation. Thirdly, as Bem (1972) stresses, a person also learns about his motivation from observing himself behave. Finally, other people often label a person's emotional state, which provides additional information about one's emotions and wishes. This, too, is another central facet of psychotherapy. By observing to the patient how he looks emotionally, or what, by his actions, he appears to be feeling, the therapist can facilitate the patient's recognition of, and exploration of his feelings and their causes.

Thus far I have described wishes and cognitive-evaluative mismatches as if they were unitary structures at a single level of generality. In reality that is not the case, and since wishes and mismatches are cognitive-affective schemas, a brief look at schemas and the nature of hierarchical categorization in cognitive psychology might prove useful in fleshing out the model.

The notion of "schema" was first developed by Bartlett (1932) and Piaget (1926) and refers to a pattern of thought or gestalt into which one assimilates information and through which one reconstructs previously stored information through memory. As Taylor and Crocker have pointed out, a schema "can be thought of as a pyramidal structure, hierarchically organized with more abstract or general information at the top categories and more specific information nested within the general categories" (1981, p. 92). Components of the schema are connected to other schemas and their subcomponents through networks of association. A person's schema of men, for example, might include categories of older men and younger men, and at the lowest level of categorization would be representations of specific men, such as father. The lowest levels, as they are the most concrete, are likely to have the richest webs of associations with other schemas (Taylor and Crocker, 1981). Information may be processed through the schema (i.e., the schema may be "activated") from the top down (from the more general to the specific) from the bottom up (from specific instances to more abstract categories), or laterally through a network of associations (Collins and Loftus, 1975; Taylor and Crocker, 1981).

Recent research has suggested that affect-laden schemas may, at least in some respects, follow similar principles. Gordon and Holyoak (1983) found that positive affect developed through repeated exposure to a set of stimuli generalized to previously unseen stimuli along lines predictable from a hierarchical model of schemas. Relying upon Zajonc's (1968) demonstration that mere exposure to a stimulus leads to increased liking of it, they constructed one experiment in which subjects were repeatedly exposed to letter strings constructed on the basis of a complex rule system and found that positive affect generalized toward previously unseen letter strings that followed the same rule. In a second experiment, subjects who were exposed to complex visual patterns created by distorting common forms manifested an orderly gradient of affective generalization to previously unseen patterns at varying levels of distortion from the pattern. In other words, the closer the stimulus was to a pattern "tagged" with positive affect, the more the subject liked the stimulus.

Fiske (1982) has observed a similar phenomenon, which she calls "schema-triggered affect," in experiments on categorization in social cognition. According to Fiske, when features of a stimulus match characteristics of a prototypical member of a social category (called a "prototype;" see Rosch, 1978; Cantor and Mischel, 1979), the affect associated with the category will be activated. In other words, abstract schematic categories have emotions attached, so that presentation of a member of the category will elicit category-based affect. Victims of stereotypes as well as researchers who have studied stereotypes have, of course, known this for decades: a member of a minority group may find that people dislike him simply because he is a member of a disliked category. In a series of experiments, Fiske demonstrated that the greater the number of features that a person shares with the prototypic member of a category, the more likely is schema-based affect to be triggered, and that the degree of affect varies with degree of association (i.e., number of shared attributes).

Just as cognitive-affective schemas of this sort appear to follow a number of principles similar to those described by cognitive psychologists, one has good reason to believe that the same is true of the cognitive-affective schemas described here, namely wishes and cognitive-evaluative mismatches. Set-goals are arranged hierarchically, which means that people have both relatively generalized and relatively specific motives. A person may have a generalized wish to be liked, which includes subcategories of wishing to be liked by particular classes of people (peers, subordinates, authorities, etc.). At the lowest level would be the desire for the affection of particular people. One principle guiding the activation of the wish with a new acquaintance is the extent to which the acquaintance or the situation fits the prototypical features of the schema.

Many people, for example, go through life primarily interested in affiliation with members of the same sex, so that the wish to be liked is differentially activated with different person-categories. This suggests that within the structure of a generalized wish, categories may receive differential emotional weighting. This weighting may often be a compromise-formation, representing the most satisfactory solution one has been able to achieve to a conflict between a related wish and some impediment to it (such as another wish). A man who is primarily interested in friendship with other men and disinterested in forming ties with women may be compromising a homosexual wish with strong prohibitions against it. In such a case he is sublimating his sexual impulse into an acceptable form and receiving substitute gratification, albeit not as much as he would receive if he could engage in homosexual relations without the conflict. Given the dense associative connections (i.e., the similarity) between interpersonal attraction and sexual attraction, male friendships are likely to trigger a good part of the positive affect associated with the real wish, in much the manner described in the studies by Fiske and Gordon and Holyoak which found a gradient of affect generalization varying by degree of association.

Many set-goals can be seen to be organized hierarchically. For example, as will be elaborated in Chapter 3, a person may have a broad schematic network constituting an "ideal self," which may include categories relating to moral behavior, physical attractiveness, intelligence, and the like. At the lowest level of generalization are standards in concrete situations. Perceived discrepancy between ideals and performance in a concrete instance may evoke minimal distress if it does not activate a superordinate category (e.g., of physical attractiveness) or closely related lateral associations. A blemish on the face one morning may be slightly disconcerting, but it does not necessarily lead to a crisis of self-esteem.

It may do so, however, if it activates several associatively connected cognitive-evaluative mismatches (instances in which one has appeared defective) or triggers a generalized mismatch between ideals of bodily attractiveness and body-image, which could in turn trigger related categories (e.g., competence) or even a generalized mismatch between ideal self and self-concept. This kind of snowballing effect frequently occurs in people who are acutely or characterologically depressed, whose awareness of a small misdeed often evokes a littany of supporting instances or a general conclusion that they are simply bad or defective people. The emotional consequence is often disgust, shame, guilt, or despair. From a "mental processing" perspective,[1] one can understand part of this snowball effect in terms of the activation of intersecting primed associations or "nodes" in an associational network: memories of related instances will be activated along associative lines in "episodic memory" (Tulving, 1972), and memories of both instances and categories related to whatever emotion the person is experiencing will be activated because they are affectively associated (through what one might call "affective memory"). The result is that memories and categories of self as bad or inadequate will be doubly primed and hence more likely to become conscious (or at least the affect associated with them is likely to reach awareness).

This mental processing explanation should not be considered to the

---

[1] I use the term "mental processing" here, as opposed to "cognitive processing" or "information processing," to underscore the fact that this processing is affective as well as strictly cognitive or "informational." The notion of information processing came from a "cold" computer metaphor that is becoming increasingly less helpful as academic psychology moves toward an understanding of the dynamics of affect.

exclusion of a more dynamic explanation because this kind of snowballing is so intensely painful that, were dynamic factors not involved, one would expect it to be conditioned away. In other words, over time, the person would learn to use all kinds of defensive affect-regulation processes to prevent activation of associated instances and superordinate categories. Frequently, however, people who are depressed and feel worthless or guilty do not believe that they deserve to feel better, and by punishing themselves through self-sabotage, physical masochism, or depression may alleviate some of the guilt or shame that produced their depression or self-loathing in the first place. To give a very simplified example, a student who cheats on an examination and feels guilty may punish himself to alleviate the guilt. What better form of penitence could one devise than mental self-flagellation, such as reminding himself of all the other ways in which he is defective?

Snowballing can occur not only from the "bottom up," as described thus far, but also from the top down. A person who experiences a mismatch between moral ideals and perceived behavior and considers himself morally despicable may then begin to find other faults with himself, such as inadequate intelligence. Activation of the "intelligence" mismatch may then elicit memories of specific instances in which he behaved stupidly. In a superb series of studies, Bower (1981) has demonstrated the tendency to recall information stored under the same affective category as current emotional state.

Just as wishes and cognitive-evaluative mismatches can be arranged hierarchically, so can the responses they evoke. Behaviors and coping mechanisms were earlier described as if they were unitary and specific. That, too, was a temporary simplification. A single wish – particularly if it is a relatively generalized one – is likely to evoke complex and sometimes long term behaviors and plans which may themselves become autonomous set-goals. These complex responses, which are also often hierarchically organized, have been discussed by a number of psychologists under different labels such as "plans" (Miller, Gallanter, and Pribram, 1960), "skills" (Bruner, 1971), "program controls" (Powers, 1973), "scripts" (Schank and Abelson, 1977; Abelson, 1981), and "tasks" (McFall, 1982).

At the level of cognitive problem-solving, Sternberg (1979) has separated out various tasks, subtasks, and component processes involved in reasoning skills. McFall (1982) has generalized the "task" notion, through applying it in particular to the dubious and value-laden concept of "social skills." He argues that tasks are hierarchically organized. Nested within a task such as "finding a spouse," he contends, are smaller tasks such as meeting potential mates, dating, and developing an intimate relationship. These tasks, in turn, consist of subtasks such as going to parties, etc.

Schank and Abelson (1977) offer a more sophisticated approach in their concept of "scripts." A script is a schema consisting of knowledge about stereotyped event sequences. Scripts both permit comprehension of social events and organize action. According to Schank and Abelson, scripts are often routinized and do not necessarily require conscious attention. For example, one completes the steps required to dine at a restaurant (sitting down, reading the menu, etc.) without consciously planning each step (Abelson, 1981). Scripts consist of subtasks that are often temporally sequenced; in one's restaurant script reading the menu will be performed before paying the bill. The script concept is particularly useful in its description of the impact of environmental factors on scripted knowledge. While some scripts prescribe specific behaviors and allow few options, others permit wide latitude in choosing behaviors to fulfill various subtasks. Though much of this is unconscious, a person is likely to attend consciously to script-related behavior when the scripted sequence is impeded (e.g., the waiter announces that the cook has gone home).

Powers (1973) also emphasizes the impact of environmental feedback (or rather, the person's perception of it) on ongoing behavior at various levels of tasks and subtasks, from the general goal or standard down to specific motor movements. While most of these models of plans, tasks, scripts, and the like note the impact of environmental feedback, few have concentrated on the motivational sources that activate these schemas or action-sequences or on the role of emotion in motivating the overcoming of obstacles to fulfillment of subtasks that would threaten achievement of the set-goal. Much of the time, of course, cognitive feedback is sufficient to motivate the person to respond to environmental contingencies or to alter maladaptive subtask strategies. If I become aware that I have forgotten to include an idea I meant to discuss in a manuscript, I can simply go back to the appropriate place in the text and insert it. This process is relatively affect-free, unless, of course, I am not using a word-processor and have to have the whole thing retyped, which could create cognitive-evaluative mismatches about wasting time, having to pay a typist, etc.

Yet if, instead, in trying to insert the missing concept I discover that it is fallacious, that no other idea will suffice, and that my entire thesis is consequently incorrect, I will suddenly come to see the extent to which the subtask of inserting a concept – as a component of the global task of writing the book – was ultimately affect-driven. The result of nonfulfillment of this set-goal would be a painful affective state accompanied by cognitions ("there goes tenure") about whatever wishes drove me to write the book. A significant problem with most previous descriptions of plans, tasks, and related concepts is the assumption of rational actors in pursuit of realistic goals for reasons of which they are by and large aware. To the contrary, most long-term projects and commitments are multiply determined. My intention to write a book, for example, may stem from all kinds of wishes, from the eminently reasonable, such as enhancing knowledge or furthering my career, to the eminently perverse and unconscious, such as outdoing a sibling or fulfilling infantile exhibitionist impulses.[1]

Wishes and cognitive-evaluative mismatches may not only produce specific responses or chains of responses, but they may affect cognitive processing more generally. As Klein (1967) argues in a discussion of motivated ideas, persistent goals and concerns influence the information to which a person selectively attends, even when the particular set-goal is not consciously salient; the person will focus upon and seek information relevant to unfulfilled wishes (see also Bruner and Klein, 1960). Similarly, enduring cognitive-affective schemas that motivate action will prompt formation of what Rapaport (1957) has called "cognitive organizations," by which he means enduring cognitive tools or methods of problem solving. Further, cognitive constructions that begin as defenses may become schemas through which information is processed, achieving what Allport (1937) called functional autonomy, so that the person may perceive reality in a distorted way without continued dynamic motivation.

Much of the analysis provided thus far has presupposed that various wishes and emotions may be operative without being conscious. Clinically, this is an indispensable assumption. When a patient appears in therapy with a briefcase and on more than one occasion during the hour jokes that it looks like it could contain a bomb, one begins to sense an affect, even though the patient may be quite convinced that she is not feeling any anger. The following section will present evidence in support of the notion of unconscious emotion.

The Case for Unconscious Emotion: Must We Feel What We Think We Feel?

Social psychologists have long recognized, at least implicitly, that various emotional dispositions may exist even when they are not conscious. Attitude theory presupposes such a view: attitudes are defined as including an affect as well as a belief (and a behavioral tendency), and since a person holds many attitudes that may not be conscious at every moment, various affective dispositions must be stored and remain unconscious at any given time. Psychoanalysts go further in claiming that not only do human beings store affective dispositions, but that feelings which are unconscious at a particular moment may nevertheless be influencing behavior.

Before turning to experimental evidence supporting the notion of unconscious affect, I would like to present two arguments in its favor. First,

---

[1] Of course, the latter two are totally fictitious and hypothetical; my motives for writing this book are entirely noble.

in terms of efficiency and adaptation, consciousness as a prerequisite to affective experience would be severely constraining, and a creature which could select responses unconsciously on the basis of affect would be far more likely to survive. When a person asks me where I would like to go for dinner tonight, I do not consciously run through a list of every restaurant in town and experience an affect related to it. This would be an impossibly cumbersome process, and as research suggests that similar search processes occur unconsciously regarding strictly cognitive phenomena (Sternberg, 1975), the likelihood is high that the same could be true regarding cognitive-affective processes. An extraordinary number of stimuli (including thoughts as well as perceptions) impinge upon the individual every second, far exceeding the capacity of conscious processing. Does it take too great a leap of imagination to suggest that, given the affective implications of many of these stimuli, affective processing – which may influence behavior – can occur outside of consciousness as well?

A simple behavior such as driving a car fairly responsibly (remaining on the proper side of the road, etc.) provides a good illustration. A person's decision not to drive on the wrong side of the road when other cars are approaching stems from her wish to stay alive and a fear that if she switches sides of the road she may find the affective consequences quite disturbing.[1] If, in fact, the person drives on the correct side of the road in order not to be injured, must one suppose that feelings about self-preservation and death must preoccupy her consciousness? Constant conscious attention to the affective sources of one's motivation is neither necessary nor possible. One is thus led to consider the possibility of unconscious emotion.

The second argument for unconscious affect stems from an examination of unconscious cognitive processing. Given that activation of a concept or memory primes associated ideas which, though unconscious, are now more likely to become conscious (cf. the Freudian preconscious), and that emotions appear to be represented in associational networks, then one has good reason to suppose that emotions, once primed, can also be preconscious (see Clark and Isen, 1982, pp. 86-7). This raises the question of whether such preconscious affect can influence conscious thought or behavior.

Similarly, Shevrin and Dickman (1980) have shown quite convincingly, through an analysis of experimental research on selective attention, cortical evoked potentials, and subliminal perception, that academic psychol-

---

[1] This may be an erroneous assumption since dead people tend not to experience emotions. This is, I suppose, one of those "laws of human behavior" that empiricists are always talking about, though one could see a dead person's indifference to affect as an effective mechanism of defense (perhaps against rigor mortis). The reader skeptical of the case I am making for unconscious affect will no doubt be gratified to find that I do not intend to extend the argument to postmortem emotion.

ogy has come to accept and rely upon the idea that a great deal of information processing occurs unconsciously. Selective attention researchers (see Kahnemann, 1973) would be unable to understand how particular stimuli are selected for conscious attention without examining selection processes that occur outside of awareness. That a person attends to a particular stimulus and not another depends upon various preconscious selection mechanisms. Indeed, the truism that a person pays attention to things in which he is interested may imply unconscious emotion, given that many affect theorists consider interest itself an emotion.

In any case, if one accepts the view that selective attention to stimuli relies upon processes that lie outside of awareness, then one cannot reject a priori the possibility that the unconscious processing involved in selective attention involves affect that is not conscious, or further, that people may selectively attend to their emotions, which implies a stage of preconscious affect. Everyone has experienced occasions upon which he did not see something he "did not want to see" because to do so would have been painful. In terms of selective attention, this suggests that the preconscious anticipation of a painful emotion arising from perception of the stimulus was responsible for directing attention away from it. One must thus at the very least concede that cognitive anticipation of affect can occur unconsciously.

One may be compelled to go further, however, in speculating that attention to affects does not involve an entirely different process than attention to the perceived stimuli to which selective attention researchers have selectively attended. This may be most obvious in the case of proto-affective sensory pleasure-pain experiences that are neurally not so different from other perceptual processes to which the individual selectively attends. What may be less obvious, but nonetheless true, is that preconscious processing is involved in selective attention to emotion, which implies that the emotion passes through a period in which it is outside of conscious awareness. If this is true, two further possibilities arise: first, that the emotion can influence responses before it even becomes conscious, and secondly, that some emotional reactions may never become conscious, despite their motivational significance.

Experimental evidence from several quarters suggests not only that emotions can exist outside of awareness, but also that unconscious emotions can influence behavior. In terms of selective attention, Broadbent (1977) has found that neutral words are more easily perceived than unpleasant words. The differential perception can only be explained in terms of the unconscious processing of the affect-laden words.

A second line of evidence supporting the notion of unconscious affect comes from hypnosis research. As several investigators have noted, physiological indicators of pain generally persist despite hypnotic analgesia (Evans and Paul, 1970; Hilgard, 1979). In other words, while the subject may not consciously experience pain, the affect does not appear to be eliminated. One way to make sense of this finding is to hypothesize that hypnotic suggestion to eliminate pain results in suppression of, or selective inattention to the affective signal, rather than its elimination.

The finding that Hilgard (1979) describes as the "hidden observer" phenomenon is relevant in this context. Hilgard hypnotized subjects so that they would report pain only through writing. The writing was automatized so that it would not require conscious attention, and the subject was given a suggestion of analgesia, making him unaware of any pain. The subject's hand was then immersed in cold water to produce pain. At the conscious level, the analgesia was effective: highly hypnotizable subjects reported no pain. The interesting finding was that the automatic writing estimates of the magnitude of pain outside of the subject's awareness steadily increased as the hand remained immersed, which is precisely the pattern that occurs without hypnotic analgesia. The magnitude of pain recorded by writing, while approaching that of unhypnotized subjects, remained slightly lower.

One can draw two inferences from these results. First, while conscious experience of pain may be eliminated with hypnosis, unconscious affect can persist. Secondly, consciousness of pain probably performs a feedback function (perhaps mediated, as Izard, 1977, would argue, through perception of one's facial expressions and behavior) which amplifies the affect, so that inhibiting consciousness of the affect through hypnotic suggestion reduces its intensity but does not altogether eliminate it.

Incidentally, one could account, from a cognitive-behavioral perspective, for the reinforcement of the tendency to behave for reasons deliberately kept outside of conscious control. A child may learn quite early that he is less likely to be punished for misdeeds deemed unintentional by those around him. Given that the ability to dissemble convincingly must develop gradually, the child may learn that acting without awareness himself of his intentions or affects may prove even more effective. (For a sociobiological argument about the evolution of deception and self-deception, see Trivers, 1971.) Affects serve a dual signal function: they provide feedback both to the individual (through subjective–conscious and unconscious–experience) and to relevant others (through emotional expression). Learning to divorce these two feedback functions, so that one may feel one thing and show another, must be a difficult developmental process (see Ekman's discussion of emotional "display rules," 1982). The child eventually learns that he can escape responsibility for his intentions and affects by remaining consciously unaware of them and inhibiting their expression. The failure to inhibit the conscious feeling will often evoke the expression, and as Izard has argued (and some experimental evidence supports his position; see Laird, 1974), the expression tends to evoke the feeling, so that optimal deception involves the suppression of both. When the child has mastered this art of deception and begins to escape penalties for his actions, this response is reinforced.

A third line of evidence regarding unconscious motivation comes, if unwittingly, from conditioning experiments and behavior therapy. If, as has been argued earlier, conditioning is mediated by affect, then conditioning that occurs without conscious connection of affects with stimuli or responses must involve unconscious processing of emotion. Recent evidence suggests that heart rates can be conditioned in two-day-old infants (Crowell et al., 1976), and one can hardly assume that the infant is making conscious connections.

In a recent study, Weinberg, Gold, and Sternberg (1984) conditioned a Pavlovian fear response in anesthetized rats by injecting them with epinephrine. Noise paired with a shock presented while the rats were unconscious produced a fear response ten days later. Affective processing thus occurred without consciousness. Garcia and Rusiniak (1980) found that conditioning can occur without consciousness, which documents the unconscious registration of affect. The investigators conditioned taste aversion to a conditioned stimulus (presented while the animal was conscious) by pairing it with a nausea-inducing stimulus administered while the animal was anesthetized. This suggests that the nausea was experienced, or at least encoded, without consciousness.

Hutchins and Reynold (cited in Leventhal and Everhart, 1978) similarly found that memory traces of painful affect could be discovered in dental patients who had been anesthetized with nitrous oxide, but not with novocaine. Leventhal and Everhart drew the conclusion from this study that whereas novocaine blocks neural conduction entirely, "nitrous oxide blocks consciousness of pain but does not block the conduction of signals and the formation of traces (schemata) in the central nervous system . . ." (p. 281). An interesting follow-up to this experiment would have been to measure physiological and self-reported indexes of stress in patients anesthetized with novocaine and nitrous oxide upon their next visit to the dentist. One would expect greater stress among the nitrous oxide group.

Various findings of behavior therapists can be reanalyzed as evidence of unconscious emotion. Genital plethysmography is a technique used to measure sexual arousal that, in the male, allows a direct quantification of degree of erection. Behavior therapists who had formerly believed that they had eliminated homosexuality in male patients have found, upon examining plethysmographic data, that they had simply suppressed the response without eliminating arousal (McConaghy, 1976; Freund, 1977).

Whether or not the patients had any residual consciousness of arousal is unclear.

Rachman (1978) has described as "desynchrony" the process by which behavioral, physiological, and subjective fear experience fail to covary. A plethora of behaviorist research suggests that a person may suppress a behavior or conscious experience of an emotion, without eliminating the physiological indicators of affect. Fenz and Epstein (1967) studied parachute jumpers and found that, for experienced jumpers, physiological measures of fear increased steadily throughout the jump, while subjective measures showed a period of decreased fear shortly after the jump began. One may argue for some kind of temporal lag between the two indicators, though a more convincing explanation would propose that the fear activated various coping or defensive procedures which, at least temporarily, reduced the conscious experience of emotion.

A fourth set of data on unconscious emotion includes other studies that demonstrate marked differences between self-reports and physiological or behavioral indicators of emotion. Asendorpf and Scherer (1983) compared heart rate, facial expressions, and self-reports of "repressors" and nonrepressors (as determined by questionnaire) during an anxiety-provoking task and found a statistically significant difference between the two groups: only the repressors showed a discrepancy between low self-reported anxiety and heart rate and facially expressed anxiety.

Zillman (1978) has studied a phenomenon he calls "excitation transfer," in which a person acts on physiological arousal despite his unconsciousness of it. Zillman distinguished three phases of arousal after subjects performed strenuous exercise. In the first, immediately after activity, the subjects were aware of their arousal and attributed it to the exercise. In the second, subjectively experienced and observable indicators of arousal (e.g., heavy breathing) disappeared, but physiological arousal did not. Finally, in the third phase, physiological arousal returned to baseline. Zillman presented subjects in each of these phases with an anger-arousing stimulus in one experiment and an "erotic stimulus" in another. He reasoned that during phase one, subjects would attribute much of their arousal correctly to exercise and would thus be less prone to aggression and would report less sexual excitement. In phase two, when they were still aroused but unaware of it, they would attribute all of their arousal when provoked or sexually stimulated to the stimulus and would respond with increased aggression or sexual excitement. In phase three, with decreased arousal, their responses would be less intense. The results confirmed Zillman's predictions, which suggests first, as noted earlier, that people can misinterpret the causes of their emotions and act on the misattributions, and secondly, that unconscious arousal can motivate behavior. In a related series of experiments, Berkowitz (1978) found that subjects

69

who were aroused by exercise and frustrated by a confederate of the experimenter exhibited more aggression toward the confederate even though they were not aware of feeling angry.

A final source of evidence that supports the existence of unconscious emotion is research on cortical evoked potentials (electrical activity in the brain) and subliminal perception. Kostandov and Arzumanov (cited in Shevrin and Dickman, 1980) found significant differences in amplitude of evoked potentials in response to emotionally neutral versus emotion-laden words presented subliminally, which suggests unconscious affective processing. Heinemann and Emrich (1981) presented subjects with neutral and emotion-laden words flashed on a screen with gradually increasing intensity, so that originally the words could not be seen at all. Emotional words evoked significantly greater alpha rhythms than neutral words even before the subject reported seeing anything. In other words, the emotional content of the words was unconsciously recognized, and emotional and neutral words were differentially processed outside of awareness. Similarly, Silverman (1976) has found, in a series of experiments, differences in various responses after subliminal presentation of stimuli which, according to psychoanalytic theory, are "conflictual," as opposed to those which are benign (although some researchers have had trouble replicating his results). Again, affective processing appears to occur outside of conscious awareness.

In a dichotic listening experiment (presenting simultaneous auditory input into both ears), Wilson (1975) found unconscious affective learning. Subjects who were instructed to attend to a human voice in one channel reported no knowledge of tone sequences presented in the other. They were unable to discriminate new sequences from sequences that had been repeated as many as five times in the unattended channel, but they exhibited significantly greater liking toward the latter (the "mere exposure" or familiarity effect). In other words, they developed affective preferences while consciously unaware that they had heard anything.

The weight of evidence from selective attention experiments, studies using hypnosis, conditioning and behavior modification research, studies comparing self-reports with physiological and behavioral measures of emotion, and research using evoked potentials and subliminal perception suggests that emotional experience is not synonymous with conscious emotion, counter to the assumptions of the vast majority of emotion theories. Processing of affect can occur unconsciously, and indeed, an organism that could respond only to the affective implications of stimuli receiving conscious attention would be at a severe evolutionary disadvantage. What remains unclear is whether, and in what ways, conscious and unconscious emotions differ, and whether affective processing can occur independently of some kind of affective arousal.

Affective Arousal and Management: A General Model

Thus far I have argued for a significant role of affect in motivating behavior, contending that situations and knowledge of situations rarely *directly* cause behavior. This should not be taken to mean that situational factors or cognition do not significantly influence behavior; rather, reality and cognition determine behavior primarily through their interaction with emotion. Human beings continuously process information and develop knowledge about themselves and their environment, and this cognitive activity is in no sense secondary to, or derivative of their affective judgments. Knowledge alone, however, does not motivate action. Nor does affect typically determine action without cognitive judgments and expectancies. While for clarity I have rigidly distinguished affect from cognition, it should be evident that thoughts and feelings are components of the same psyche, and that cognitive-evaluative mismatches are as thoroughly cognitive as they are affective.

Cognition influences behavior primarily in three ways, which can be readily distinguished using the model offered here. First, to the extent that cognitive-evaluative mismatches produce affects that motivate behavior, cognitions about the current status (fulfillment or nonfulfillment) of set-goals will obviously greatly influence behavioral outcome. If a person believes he has attained his goal, he will not experience an unpleasant emotion and will thus not be motivated to alter his present course of action. Beliefs ranging from the relatively specific to the relatively global (e.g., "nobody likes me") will affect behavior in this way.

Secondly, set-goals themselves are in part cognitive, including representations of specific and general desired outcomes. Attributions about what will make one happy in part determine set-goals, as do cognitions about what other people want or what makes other people happy. The set-goals we pursue are thus influenced by cognitively mediated conditioning and social learning (modeling, vicarious reinforcement, direct tutelage, exhortation, etc.; see Bandura, 1977a).

A third cognitive influence on behavior is on the "output" side: beliefs about reality in the form of expected outcomes and beliefs about one's capacities influence the strategies a person uses to escape painful emotions and produce pleasant ones (see Bandura, 1977b). Again, both generalized and specific expectancies are of importance in influencing behavior. For example, unrealistically low global self-efficacy expectations will inhibit effective action, much as a specific belief that a particular person is untrustworthy will prevent one from seeking that person's help in a specific situation.

Just as the proposed model does not downplay the role of cognition in behavior, it equally does not ignore "reality" or situational variables. If a student fails an examination and is upset by it, he is likely to take an action such as speaking to the professor. One is apt in such a case to say that his behavior is motivated by the stimulus or situation of flunking the test, but that is not, strictly speaking, correct. If the student had no set-goals about academic performance, he would not be disturbed by this "stimulus" and would therefore not act. What accounts for his behavior is an affect produced by a discrepancy between a wished-for state and cognized reality. No doubt reality has a significant causal role in behavior by influencing cognized states, but its influence is always mediated by both cognition and affect.

Similarly, when one observes that football players uniformly behave aggressively while on the playing field, one will obviously be more successful in explaining their aggressiveness by paying attention to the requirements of the game than by invoking drives (though certainly one should not ignore the fact that smashing people around seems to be a favorite pastime of men in most, if not all cultures in one form or another). A social scientist interested in explaining aggression in football games would obviously do well to focus primarily at a level of analysis other than intrapsychic dynamics. Yet in explaining a specific action of a given player one must ask why he is obeying "situational demands," in this case why he is hitting so hard, and one is likely to find a combination of set-goals involved, such as desire to win, desire to please the coach and fans, fulfillment of culturally defined masculine ideal self-images, displaced hostility, and the like. Simply because one does not find significant individual differences on a variable does not imply an unmediated situational effect. If human beings did not all find the idea of death unsettling, one would not observe that the "situation" of a fire in a theater provokes a fairly standard set of responses.

If most people act similarly in a situation one has reason to believe that they may have similar motivations, not that the situation determined their behavior without being mediated by "person variables." An absence of individual differences does not imply an absence of psychological causality: one must be careful to distinguish statistical causes, which are useful in explaining variance and making predictions, from efficient causes. The role of situations must always be understood in the context of the cognitive-affective schemas that motivate behavior.

The aim of this chapter has been to develop a theory of affect, relying in part upon ideas from systems theory, which may aid in effecting a rapprochement between psychodynamic and cognitive-behavioral psychology. While presenting this theory of affect as feedback, with its various implica-

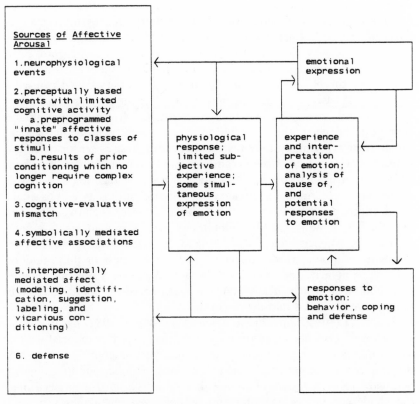

Figure 5. Arousal and management of emotion

tions, the chapter has focused upon a particular form of affective arousal, which involves a mismatch between an ideal state and cognized reality.[1] In fact, emotions may arise in a number of ways, though the feedback function and consequent regulation of the emotion through behavior, coping, and defense mechanisms remain the same. A general model of the arousal and management of emotion is diagrammed in Figure 5.

The model delineates six sources of emotional arousal. The first involves biological or neurophysiological events. A classic example is Schachter and Singer's (1962) celebrated study, in which subjects injected with epinephrine showed significantly greater emotional arousal than placebo controls (though cognitive factors appeared to exert some influence upon the emotional experience). A less artificial example occurs, one might

---

[1] Wishes can probably be conceived as a subtype of cognitive-evaluative mismatches.

hypothesize, in the case of physiochemically based affective disorders which have been attributed to various neurotransmitter dysfunctions (Baldessarini, 1977; Cooper, Bloom, and Roth, 1978).[1]

The second way emotion can be aroused entails far less cognitive processing than the cognitive-evaluative mismatches and wishes discussed throughout this chapter (listed as the third source for emotional arousal on Figure 5). This second source of emotion involves the production of affects from primarily perceptual events (though one may fruitfully conceptualize cognition and perception as lying on a continuum of processing activity rather than as being entirely discrete processes, just as sensory pleasure-pain experiences and emotion can be viewed as a continuum of feeling). This class of events may be subdivided into two categories. The first includes what ethologists call innate releasing mechanisms as well as similar rapid affective responses to stimuli without extensive cognitive processing described by Zajonc (1980). Stimuli such as the human face, as noted earlier, tend to elicit interest and liking in the first quarter year of life, and the evidence points in the direction of the innateness of this emotional reaction. Similarly, the cry of a baby appears to be a noxious stimulus across cultures, which suggests that the experienced irritation produced by the cry may be wired into the organism.

Zajonc (1980; Zajonc, Pietromonaco, and Bargh, 1982) has marshaled considerable evidence demonstrating that affect may be produced without substantial cognitive processing. Taking as a starting point his research on the connection between familiarity and liking, Zajonc found through experiments using a variety of stimuli that subjects tended to prefer stimuli they had seen before to unfamiliar stimuli even when they were consciously unaware of the familiarity. Zajonc concluded that "preferences need no inferences," i.e., that affective discriminations may arise prior to cognitive discriminations. In a later paper (Zajonc, 1984), he has attempted to pin down the neuroanatomical basis for these relatively quick, perceptually based emotions.

[1] Though many psychiatric researchers tend to equate "endogenous" depression of this sort with "genetically determined" depression, this may not be true in all cases. Simply because a depression responds to antidepressant medication (which is often taken as proof of its biological basis) does not imply its genetic roots or its autonomy from psychological processes. The evidence from dogs presented earlier (Scott, 1979) showed that imipramine eliminated distress in dogs separated from their mothers, just as it relieves distress in depressed humans. While obviously the response of the puppies to imipramine relies upon biochemistry (as do all mental acts), the psychological cause of their distress was apparent. Similarly, experiments with monkeys separated from their mothers has found that some of the monkeys develop abnormal EEG patterns. We are as yet as helpless as Descartes in understanding how psychical causes produce physiological changes (and especially structural changes in the brain that could account for an abnormal EEG). In regard to the class of biological sources of emotion, however, one may suspect that physiological imbalances in catecholamines and the like may at some point attain autonomy from their psychological roots even in cases where the original problem was primarily psychological.

Zajonc's evidence is irrefutable, though one should note that perceptually based emotions may rely upon prior cognitive and affective processes and states. For example, seeing a familiar stimulus in its usual context may evoke positive affect, whereas seeing it where it does not belong may induce the opposite. A student of mine (who I have every reason to assume does not dislike me) generally responded with a smile upon seeing me when she walked into class. When she once saw me at her dormitory, however, I was an anomalous stimulus to assimilate into her "dorm schema:" I did not "belong" there, and her perception of me produced a startle-reaction that she interpreted negatively. I hope that accounts for her reaction since she shrieked, somewhat automatically, "Oh no! Not here!"

In all probability presentation of a stimulus such as another person may evoke a hierarchical set of responses somewhat akin to a decision tree. The individual's initial reaction to the person may be a quick judgment of familiarity, which results, given other state-related factors, in either liking or disliking, though usually the former. If familiar, the next question may be whether this is a person about whom the individual has previously come to feel positively or negatively. The hypothesis that these are two consecutive processes could be fairly readily tested with reaction-time experiments and is suggested by anecdotal evidence. A certain individual whom I frequently encounter in town is an especially noxious stimulus to me, though to my dismay, my first reaction upon seeing him is always a smile. I quickly remind myself that I dislike him, which wipes the smile off my face. To his apparent dismay, he, too, appears unable to suppress an initial smile of familiarity. Before I thought about this in terms of Zajonc's work, I had begun to wonder if, in fact, I do not dislike this fellow so much after all, though I am pleased now to recognize this as an erroneous reading of my own facial expression and am once again free to detest him.

As this example suggests, relatively rapid, perceptually based emotional reactions may arise in another way, when a stimulus once became paired, often through higher level cognitive processes, with an affect. Cognitively mediated classical conditioning may produce a fairly instantaneous affective response to a conditioned stimulus, so that cognitive processes no longer intervene. In fact, this is far more efficient and adaptive than having to recalculate the affective consequences of a given stimulus or response every time it becomes relevant.[1] If a person discovers that every time she

---

[1] The model presented here may help to elucidate a number of points of contention in the literature on affect and its arousal best exemplified by the running argument between Zajonc (1980, 1984) and Lazarus (1982) in the *American Psychologist* regarding the role of cognition in arousing emotion. Zajonc has taken the stand that emotions can occur without cognitions, whereas Lazarus contends that inferences always precede preferences. Lazarus is no doubt correct in claiming that cognitive evaluations similar to the cognitive-evaluative mismatches described here are responsible for many, if not most, emotions in

has lunch with a certain colleague she finds herself left with a diminished sense of self-esteem (caused by a cognitive-evaluative mismatch between aspects of her ideal self and perceived self), she may come to feel upset every time this colleague approaches. One need not assume that this anticipation of diminished self-esteem and its connection to the stimulus occurs either consciously or unconsciously every time the colleague approaches. Rather, the connection between stimulus and affect has been routinized so that the cognitive term can be left out altogether.[1] One can readily see how these routinized affective responses can become dysfunctional. The original cognitive-evaluative mismatch that produced the association between the stimulus and affect which is now routinized may no longer be relevant, in which case the affective response is an atavism that can be quite maladaptive. Two people may come to dislike each other while in competition with each other for a job and later find themselves working together. The aversion may remain even though its initial cause is no longer present. Another function of psychotherapy, both psychodynamic and cognitive-behavioral, is to deroutinize affective responses that are no longer appropriate. Both psychodynamic and behavioral treatment of phobias attempt to do precisely this, though in very different ways (see Wachtel, 1977).

Affective arousal may ensue from a fourth source, symbolically mediated affective associations. A particular stimulus (whether a thought, perception, or even an affect) may "set off" an association that is affect-laden[2] (cf. Clark and Isen, 1982). A network of associations may be primed in this manner but not reach the threshold of consciousness (or, as will be demonstrated shortly, deliberately kept out of consciousness). This cognitive-affective "set" or activated network may nonetheless influence thought, feeling, and behavior.

Psychoanalysis since its inception has elegantly described the rich, emotionally laden webs of meaning lying behind conscious thoughts and feel-

---

human beings. Yet Zajonc is on equally firm ground in arguing for the existence of perceptually based affective reactions such as those described above. Zajonc (1984) is also correct in pointing out that Lazarus's definition of emotion as a process involving cognitive appraisal essentially attempts to define the controversy away. Part of the problem in reconciling their two viewpoints is semantic: Lazarus considers any process involved in the creation of an emotion cognitive, whereas Zajonc more sharply distinguishes between cognition and perception and pays less attention to unconscious processing. The discussion that follows will, hopefully, shed additional light on this controversy.

[1] The behavioral response may also become habitual, so that the affective term can be left out as well, with the person responding before he even experiences (conscious and probably unconscious) arousal. See Zillman, 1978, p. 346.

[2] This can underlie phenomena psychodynamic clinicians include under the rubric of "transference." Elsewhere (Westen, 1984d), I have explored the mental processing components of transference reactions and have distinguished several distinct psychodynamic and social-cognitive processes usually labeled as "transference."

ings, and it has argued that one idea in an associational network can come to stand for another, so that behaviors and thoughts can take on symbolic meaning. Perhaps the greatest deficit in cognitive social learning approaches is the failure to accept the existence of, let alone account for, such symbolic phenomena. With the development of cognitive psychology, it has become possible to examine the component dynamic-cognitive processes responsible for the type of symbolic transformations described at a more global level by psychoanalysis.

A couple of brief examples should make clear what the phenomenon in question is and how one might be able to begin to explain it. A fairly simple example is a commonplace occurrence in psychotherapy, when a patient dreams of having sexual relations with someone who seems quite similar in certain respects to the therapist. A patient of mine, for example, once related a dream in which she was left alone on an island with a man whose face was unfamiliar but who happened to be about my size, have dark hair and a mustache, and seem fairly sensitive. The patient was a married woman who has little tolerance for her own fantasies or impulses, and she was entirely unaware that she was describing someone like me. Was it merely an unverifiable flight of psychoanalytic fancy (or egocentrism) to assume that she was telling me something about her relationship with me? It behooves one who proposes such symbolic transformations to demonstrate the mechanisms through which they can occur, and in a moment I hope to do that.

Another example will pose the issue perhaps more dramatically. The patient was a woman referred for projective testing who had shown clear signs of gender identity confusion and difficulty developing a comfortable sexual orientation. On a Rorschach (ink blot) card that people typically see as two animals climbing up a rock or tree, the patient saw two "slimy beavers." With my perverse psychodynamically trained mind I, of course, recognized that "beaver" is a disparaging American slang term for vagina, and that her response of "slimy beavers" probably betrayed feelings about female sexuality. When queried as to why the beavers looked slimy, she could provide no clear answer and speculated that they probably looked slimy because they were a bit fuzzy. Her next response lent further credence to the dynamic interpretation of the beaver percept: she noted that the blot also looked like "a woman's crotch." When questioned, she evidenced no awareness of the connection between the two responses.

In the examples of the dream and the slimy beaver, an unconscious wish (being alone with me) or an affect-laden thought (female sexuality as disgusting) has expressed itself in a symbolic derivative, or to put it another way, one node in an associative network has become conscious in place of another. An understanding of the interaction of cognitive and dynamic processes can help elucidate the mechanisms involved in this transformation.[1]

Experimental research has clearly demonstrated that activation of one concept (or affect) in a network primes associated concepts or nodes, making them more likely to become conscious (Collins and Loftus, 1975). For example, studies by Meyer and Schvaneveldt (1971; Meyer, 1973) document that information can be retrieved faster from memory if related information has recently been accessed. The investigators found that subjects who were asked to classify letter strings either as words or nonwords could identify words faster if they had just made a similar discrimination regarding a semantically related word.

An unconscious network of associations can thus influence thought and behavior (evidenced in shorter reaction times). This has been demonstrated more dramatically in a superb series of experiments by Motley on the experimental elicitation of "Freudian slips" (1980). Motley and Baars (1976) have developed a method for eliciting verbal slips by briefly presenting a word pair tachistoscopically, preceded, by a fraction of a second, by a word pair aimed at interfering with correct verbal articulation. For example, the word pair "best rose" is briefly flashed a tenth of a second before the target pair "red bowl." A buzzer then sounds, signaling the subject to produce verbally the word pair he has just seen. He will frequently respond in such a case with a slip such as "bed roll." This technique has been shown to elicit spoonerisms in roughly thirty percent of the target word pairs attempted by the subject.

In a first experiment, Motley (1980) demonstrated that spoonerisms could be induced at a higher frequency by presenting interference word pairs semantically related to the expected slip. For example, to produce the spoonerism "mad bug" from the target pair, "bad mug," Motley presented the interference pair "angry insect" or "irate wasp." In a second study, he showed that spoonerisms could be increased significantly if congruent with the subject's "cognitive set" (actually, cognitive-affective set). Subjects in one condition were led to believe that they would be receiving random electrical shocks during the experiment, while subjects in a second condition were induced to activate a "sex set" through the behavior and provoc-

---

[1] One of my aims in this discussion is to demonstrate the existence of psychodynamic processes by a slightly different method than that used by the small group of experimentally oriented psychoanalytic psychologists (Rapaport, Klein, Holt, and their students) whose fascinating work has attempted to study complex dynamic events directly in the laboratory (e.g., Shevrin's exciting programme of research, some of which is reported in Shevrin [1980], which uses neurophysiological measures to document dynamic processes). An alternative method, used here, is to separate complex dynamic events into their component cognitive and affective processes, to use experimental data to demonstrate the existence of these processes, and to argue for their interaction in ways that make sense of the much more complex, naturally occurring processes observed in everyday life and clinical practice.

ative attire of a seductive female experimenter. Subjects in the first experimental condition produced significantly greater electricity-related spoonerisms (e.g., "shad bock" became "bad shock"), while subjects in the the the sex-related condition produced significantly more sexual slips (e.g., "lood gegs" became "good legs"). In a third experiment Motley showed that subjects characterologically high on sexual anxiety (as evidenced on a relevant personality inventory) had a significantly higher rate of sexual spoonerisms.

Motley's research nicely demonstrates the effect of cognitive-affective associational networks and conflictual issues on behavior, in this case production of speech. In order to account for the types of phenomena illustrated by the transference dream and the slimy beaver, one must further demonstrate, first, that people may not be aware of the activation of various networks, and secondly, that they may block from awareness particular thoughts in a network even while a network is "active."

Nisbett and Wilson (1977), as noted earlier, have shown that conscious awareness of "higher mental processes" is often incorrect, and that reporting of cognitive processing, when it is correct, is the result of implicit causal theories, not introspection. They have demonstrated this directly regarding people's knowledge of the evocation of associational networks. Subjects memorized word pairs that were expected to influence subsequent responses. For example, memorizing the pair "ocean-moon" was expected to make more likely the response of "Tide" when subjects were later asked to name a laundry detergent, and in fact this expectation was confirmed. When asked why they named Tide, however, the subjects offered speculations such as, "My mother uses Tide," or "I like the Tide box."

If knowledge of an activated network may be unconscious, the likelihood is high that knowledge of a specific node in the network, even the node responsible for priming the associations, may escape conscious awareness. A wonderful experiment years ago by Maier (1931) documents precisely that. Maier hung two cords from the ceiling of a laboratory strewn with all kinds of artifacts. The subject's task was to find a way to tie the two cords together even though the cords were too far apart to reach one while holding the other. The hardest solution to imagine, which most subjects could not spontaneously produce, was to tie a weight to one cord and swing it so one could grab it while holding the other. Maier found that if he nonchalantly put one of the cords in motion, within a minute many subjects figured out the solution, though they were generally totally unaware of the role of his cue. From the present perspective the most pertinent answer a subject (in this case, a psychology professor) gave to explain how he had come upon the solution was the following: "Having exhausted everything else, the next thing was to swing it. I thought of the situation of swinging across a river. I had imagery of monkeys swinging from trees." This subject was thus aware of the activation of a web of associations (swinging monkeys, etc.), but he was unaware of the particular node in the network that sparked the associations.

Similarly, the woman who saw the slimy beaver was unaware of the network of associations that had been evoked, which was evident in her failure to recognize an obvious connection between beaver and crotch. That the beaver and crotch percepts were activated was largely a cognitive (or, more precisely, schematic) phenomenon: enduring wishes, concerns, concepts, fears, and mismatches — in a word, cognitive-affective schemas — focus attention, shape perception, and influence memory, which is why projective testing can be so useful. In this particular case one need not turn to metaphors of a bubbling unconscious, with dynamic issues pushing to reach the surface, to explain what is basically a cognitive phenomenon, the guiding of perception by active schemas (on schemas as guides to perception, see Neisser, 1976).

One should not, however, rule out dynamic hypotheses as to why this woman seemed unaware of her sense of female sexuality as slimy and disgusting. She may well have done so because to acknowledge this schema would be painful (particularly in light of her feminist ideals). One reason for suspecting a defense here is her lack of recognition of the meanings of beaver and of its relation to the temporally contiguous response about the woman's crotch. Cognitive failures of this sort may well be strictly cognitive, unmotivated acts; however, with affectively charged perceptions, thoughts, wishes, and cognitive-evaluative mismatches, lack of awareness of a particular concept or schematic network may be dynamically motivated. In the case of my patient's dream, for example, various thoughts and feelings in the therapy situation evoked a sexual wish toward me. To acknowledge the wish, however, would be painful because it would, in her mind, threaten her tenuous marriage and set her up for perceived rejection. The result was that the wish was repressed, and its exclusion from consciousness was negatively reinforced by the prevention of a painful affect.

Repression of a single wish, however, may not keep from consciousness associated thoughts, feelings, and wishes, or it may be less able to do so during altered states of consciousness. The extent of repression is likely to be determined by a trial-and-error conditioning process: if repressing a single "node" is not hedonically adequate, wider repression will be necessary (as, perhaps, in the case of very traumatic experiences which may be dissociated totally from consciousness; see Klein, 1967, p. 119). As argued earlier, however, a person may be characterologically predisposed to defensive overkill, and one suspects that the ability to defend more flexibly is an aspect of the maturation of affect-regulation abilities.

In the case of the sexual dream, most of the whole complex of associations around the patient's sexual wish appeared to have been unconscious, but a symbolic transformation of the wish reached consciousness following an altered state, namely dreaming. Despite its unconsciousness, the wish-complex remained active, and, in the dream, related associations to a wish for an exclusive relationship with me (e.g., being alone on an island with a mustached man) appeared while the actual wish was repressed. Fantasied experience of the relationship with the unknown man likely activated some of the positive affect associated with fulfillment of the real wish (through the mechanisms described by Fiske, 1982, and Gordon and Holyoak, 1983) while repression of the actual content of the wish prevented (or at least diminished) experience of associated displeasure (cf. Dollard and Miller [1950] on learning mechanisms involved in displacement).

More typical in human life (and in psychotherapy) is the repression of a specific node without conscious obliteration of the entire network. The result is that thoughts, fantasies, emotions, and behaviors connected with the repressed thought or wish will become conscious or will infiltrate other thoughts and actions as in Motley's demonstration of the influence of cognitive-affective set on verbal productions. This is precisely what is meant by a compromise-formation. The patient who joked with me about the bomb in her briefcase was attaching an unacceptable wish, to hurt me because she was furious, onto an acceptable idea, a joke about a bomb. She thus avoided the negative consequences of her wish while gaining pleasure through enjoying an attenuated wish of blowing me up and feeling satisfaction at expressing her anger.[1]

Because one wish or thought can stand for another, a therapist whose theoretical position leads him to accept his patients' claims and goals at face value is making a tremendous mistake. Mischel, for example, exhorts therapists to confine themselves to "client-defined problematic behavior" so that patients "might achieve help with the behaviors of concern rather than be given insights of dubious validity into their hypothetical origins or symptomatic significance" (1979, p.743). While his warning to therapists who too often allow their theories to determine their observations is well taken, his assumption that patients always know or can talk about what is causing their distress is unfounded. Indeed, the decision to seek therapeutic help is often a compromise-formation shaped by many motives, and the person may, through the cognitively and affectively mediated conditioning described in this chapter, achieve maximum satisfaction by seeking help but repressing his real concerns. The problem with accepting the patient's initial complaint as the focus of treatment is particularly evident in univer-

---

[1] The reader unaccustomed to this way of thinking may suspect that the inference of her anger from a simple joke is rather farfetched. These kinds of inferences must always, of course, be made cautiously, though in this case it was borne out when the patient skipped the following two sessions and subsequently told me that she could not face me because she was angry.

sity mental health settings, where a student will sometimes come in with concerns about his study habits, and the therapist will gradually discover, if he probes deeply enough, that the person is having trouble studying because he is severely depressed, preoccupied with suicidal thoughts, or distracted by active fantasies of murdering someone.

As Motley's experiment on sex anxiety and spoonerisms demonstrates, a person's thought and behavior may be influenced not only by momentarily activated networks, but also by chronically "activated" concerns. The person may thus readily assimilate and attend to stimuli that fit in with broad schemas about, for example, interpersonal relations ("women are all dangerous and to be avoided"), or he may pursue specific and generalized wishes of which he is unaware (being sadistic to women who are under his authority).

Returning to the general model of affective arousal and management, a fifth source of affect may be called interpersonally mediated affect. The "contagion" effect in crowds (see Le Bon, 1895) is one example, as are culturally defined taboos. Taboos are classes of events which the individual has learned from her culture to pair with certain negative emotions. The phenomena social learning theorists call "modeling" and psychodynamic psychologists call "identification" also fall into this category (the relation between these two concepts will be explored in Chapter 4), as people can learn affective responses from those around them. The "attitudes" studied by social psychologists are often examples of this form of affect-production. Hypnotic suggestion also falls into this class, as does labeling, in which someone tells an individual that she looks angry or sad or whatever, and this interpersonal feedback influences her actual emotional state. Vicarious conditioning, in which the person comes to associate an affect with a stimulus or response by observing someone else's trial and error, is also included here. In actuality, symbolically mediated affective associations and interpersonally mediated affect are ultimately reduced to either automatized perceptually based affective arousal or cognitively based arousal. Classes of events either become associated with affects and provoke immediate perception-based affects, or they become wishes or set-goals which may arouse affects when they are fulfilled or frustrated.

A final source of affect is defensively motivated arousal, in which the person activates one emotion to avoid experiencing a more dysphoric one. This often occurs in the grieving process (see Kubler-Ross, 1969) when the person avoids facing his own or someone else's death or impending death by becoming furious at doctors, the dying person, or others. Adorno et al. (1950) argue that hatred of minority groups may stem from projection of one's own rejected impulses or self-images onto the despised group. Reaction-formation is a defense in which a person turns one affect into its opposite, as when, for example, he feels warmth toward someone who has just done him wrong.

These six sources of emotional arousal produce, one can hypothesize, an initial emotional experience that includes a physiological state, an unconscious feeling, and often an emotional expression. As is shown in Figure 5, this may lead to an immediate cognitively unmediated response (behavior, coping strategy, or defense) and/or to conscious and unconscious processing of the emotion. The latter involves interpretation of the affect and its causes, as well as conscious and unconscious anticipations of possible responses. This may lead, in turn, to further emotional expression resulting from the cognitively based interpretation of the affect, as well as to various behavioral, coping, or defensive operations to manage the emotion.

As can be seen from Figure 5, the path from affective arousal to ultimate responses is not unidirectional. At each step, various activities feed back into the previous sets of processes. For example, behavioral, coping, and defensive responses, once activated, often alter the situation that originally produced the affect. The child who experiences a cognitive-evaluative mismatch between need for mother and perceived absence of her may respond by crying, which hastens her return; her return eliminates the discrepancy between set-goal and cognized reality and hence, the affect. Self-observation of emotional expression influences interpretation of emotional state, which then alters emotional arousal itself.

This model may prove useful in a number of ways, one of which is to clarify thinking about cognitive-affective interactions. A significant problem in the affect literature, which has by and large escaped notice (though see Zillman, 1978), stems from a confounding of the initial cognitive/perceptual activity which may be involved in arousing an affect and the secondary cognitive processes that result in its interpretation and attribution of cause. The issue arose with and was obscured by Schachter and Singer's (1962) famous study. The experimenters were interested in how cognitions channel emotions once the (physiological part of the) emotion already exists. (In actuality they were studying the influence of cognitions given a tendency for emotional arousal which could be activated cognitively.) By injecting subjects with epinephrine they were trying to produce emotional arousal directly. Subjects found themselves with a physiologically aroused state that required explanation and interpretation, just as Maslach's (1979) hypnotized subjects had to look for a cause for their arousal.

In everyday life, people seldom find themselves aroused by injections of epinephrine. Rather, the physiological arousal they perceive is generally a reaction to some perceived or cognized event that either automatically triggers an affect or evokes it because of its divergence from an ideal state.

In other words, the cognitive activity examined by Schachter and Singer is ordinarily a *second* cognitive process that was not involved in originally causing the emotion. This secondary cognitive activity reflects the person's effort as an "intuitive scientist" to make sense of an emotion with which he is now presented as a fait accompli.

The problems that have occurred because of the failure to distinguish between the two cognitive/perceptual processes, the first of which produces the affect and the second, which attempts to make sense of the feeling once it has been produced, are not limited to theoretical confusions. Indeed, an entire clinical approach, used especially in the treatment of depression, rests upon this confusion. Beck (1976) has proposed a cognitive theory of depression which essentially views it as a disorder of thinking. He argues (Kovacs and Beck, 1979) that "the depressive's"[1] negative bias in viewing himself, his situation, and his future results from selective attention to negative cognitions; Beck does not consider that *affect* must be involved in channelling attention to these thoughts. In other words, the criterion for letting a thought into consciousness for these people is an affective one: the thought must be unpleasant, if not self-deprecatory. Beck's own analysis suggests that it is affect which is selecting cognitions, not cognitions which produce affects.

The difficulty with Beck's approach is that the beliefs the depressed person produces for the cognitive therapist are essentially rationalizations of an affective state which are simply probabilistic, like all attributions of cause of affect. In other words, while some original cognitive-evaluative mismatch may have produced the depressed feeling, the individual, as argued earlier, has no access to it. The person finds himself depressed and begins to develop theories to explain it; the individual starts to lament that the future is bleak or that he is stupid. These beliefs may be the same ones that originally evoked the depression, or they may not. Often they are not, and a conscious understanding of the real reasons is not immediately accessible to the person for both cognitive and defensive reasons (i.e., the person is making causal attributions poorly because he is not thinking well and/or because he is defensively distorting his beliefs). Beck assumes that "one's cognitions, attitudes, values, and the like are accessible to introspection . . ." (p. 419). While a person may be aware of his theories about the causes of his emotions (and even this may not be true), Beck mistakenly

---

[1] I will refer to "the depressive" or "the phobic" against my better judgment in deference to the need for conciseness and to stylistic conventions in academic research on psychopathology. This type of terminology fosters the kind of "us-them" thinking characteristic of much of academic work on psychopathology. We are all sometimes depressed for neurotic reasons or irrationally afraid of something, and psychoanalysis, while it lacks a language for describing normalcy, has amply shown that neurosis is not something that other people have. My use of quotation marks around words such as "the depressive" is thus a compromise-formation reflecting my desire to write concisely and my wish not to be misunderstood.

concludes that this is the same as saying that the person is aware of the *actual* causes of his emotions. As Nisbett and Wilson have made so clear, we often "tell more than we can know" about our internal processes (1977). Cognitive therapy is effective in altering a person's speculations about why he feels the way he does, but it may not alter the underlying causes of the emotion which still remain operative.

The argument against Beck here is not simply another standard psychodynamic attack on therapies that get at "symptoms" as opposed to "causes." A comparison of Beck's cognitive therapy with Maslach's study of emotional arousal produced by hypnosis will suggest that cognitive therapy has difficulty eliminating the symptom, which is an affect, not a set of secondary cognitions recruited by the affect. As described earlier, Maslach hypnotized subjects to experience an unpleasant state of arousal, and under a suggestion of amnesia, the subjects began to produce all kinds of explanations for their arousal, such as fear about impending final exams. The cognitive therapist would now step in and prove to the person that the exams are not frightening after all, which may result in some arousal reduction through a placebo effect and selective inattention to the affect but would quite miss the point and leave the arousal untouched.

A significant problem with most cognitive approaches to psychotherapy (e.g., Meichenbaum, 1977; Meichenbaum, Butler, and Joseph, in press) is the assumption that if one simply helps a patient build a new web of consciously accessible associations, the old ones will go away. We do not, unfortunately, know under what circumstances the building of new schemas will halt processing of information through old ones, but we do know that as a general rule this assumption is invalid. As shown earlier, latent associational networks influence both behavior and conscious thoughts and feelings, and helping a patient keep conflicts and depressing cognitive-evaluative mismatches from consciousness may simply bolster a defense that has proven inadequate.

When cognitive therapy reduces the underlying depression, it does so in two ways. First, by exploring the patient's explanations for his depression, the therapy may touch upon the actual causes. In this sense it differs little from psychodynamic psychotherapy. Psychodynamic therapists have always focused on the way distorted perceptions of reality influence mood and behavior, though Beck's perspective nicely calls attention to these more cognitive roots of psychopathology, whereas psychoanalytic theory stresses conflicts. What a psychodynamic approach elucidates and Beck's does not is why a person would hold mistaken beliefs that clearly cause emotional distress. The attribution and social cognition literatures are full of studies documenting self-serving biases in attribution (see Greenwald, 1980), and a tendency to see one's future as bleak and oneself as worthless and incompetent would certainly be extinguished were it strictly a cognitive error. A person does not insist, contrary to reality, that he is unlovable and incapable of sustaining an intimate relationship and consequently isolate himself because he has somehow acquired a mistaken belief about himself. To see oneself as unlovable – and therefore, as in many cases, deliberately to make oneself unlovable – must be less painful than to try to be loved and experience rejection, or to succeed in love when one has internalized set-goals that forbid it.

Human beings are creatures who try to minimize pain, and when one sees a person who appears to draw it upon himself through self-punitive cognitions or behaviors, one should suspect that at some point in his life he decided that his current path is less painful than the route that seems more "adaptive" to those around him. One function of a psychotherapist is to help the person rethink a maladaptive decision that may once have seemed reasonable but is now routinized, unconsciously operating, and wreaking havoc on his emotional life. My own limited clinical experience with characterologic depressions suggests that the attendant self-denial and masochism tend to serve the functions of guarding against future pain by minimizing expectations, mastering fear of punishment by inflicting it and thereby controlling it oneself, gaining satisfaction through identification with a parent who was seen as abusive, or garnering a paradoxical sense of moral self-worth by seeing oneself as a sinner who recognizes and punishes his own sinfulness.

Cognitive therapy may reduce depression in a second way, by diverting conscious attention from the depressive affect and the cognitions it recruits (and replacing them in part with affectively-charged learned beliefs about the potential success of the therapist's ministrations). The resulting diminution of negative affect would be similar to that found in Hilgard's hidden observer experiments. Hilgard, it will be remembered, found that automatized writing which monitored "covert pain" reported far more pain than was consciously recognized by the subjects, but slightly less than that reported by unhypnotized controls. I argued that this was because conscious attention amplifies affective feedback. One would thus expect that, whatever its effects on conscious emotion, cognitive therapy would produce a minor diminution in unconsciously experienced depression.

Available evidence, cited by Beck himself, supports precisely this hypothesis. Using a sample of 218 patients, Beck (1967) found that depressed patients dreamed significantly more than nondepressed controls about being ugly, rejected, abandoned, or about similar depressive themes. A study by Hauri (1976) found that such themes persisted in the dreams of "remitted" depressives, though one cannot directly compare the results to see if the remitted depressives showed slightly fewer depressive themes. Beck concluded from this research that "cognitive disturbance may be long-term and persist even after symptomatic improvement" (p. 430). One would suspect that if one followed longitudinally a group of depressives treated with cognitive therapy for tendency to suicide, one would find that they attempt suicide somewhat less often than untreated depressives but significantly more than nondepressed controls.

In summary, cognitive therapy rests upon the confusion of an initial perceptual/cognitive-evaluative process which accounts for the depression, and a second cognitive process which interprets and attributes causes to it. While such therapy may sometimes influence the underlying affect or decrease conscious awareness of it, it fails to eliminate the feeling and its underlying cognitive-affective schemas – with, one would expect, unfortunate behavioral consequences – because it ignores unconscious affective processes and mistakes cognitive causal attribution for actual cause. The depressed affect essentially recruits causal explanations, which the therapist systematically shatters, leaving the affect largely untouched.[1] This is not to discount the importance of the strictly cognitive processes that perpetuate depression, such as negatively biased schemas. Rather, it is to say that such schemas are unlikely to persist without dynamic motivation. Even when depression stems primarily from learned beliefs about one's worthlessness or incompetence, as when a child learns in school that he is not academically talented despite internalized set-goals for academic success, the persistent tendency to ignore disconfirming instances (e.g., in which he is competent) cannot be explained solely in terms of biased self-schemas. As anyone who knows or has worked with characterologically depressed people can attest, individuals with this kind of character structure or who are prone to self-denigration do not simply fail to perceive their successes; they work hard to discount them and forget them, and the active quality of the distortion betrays its defensive nature. This defense frequently serves the function of preventing an upward revision of set-goals that the person fears could not be fulfilled. The child who persistently fails in school may gradually reduce his pain by lowering his standards. (For empirical evidence, see Dweck and Gilliard, 1975). Subsequent intermittent successes may be threatening – and therefore need to be defended against – because they evoke the old set-goals or suggest that the

---

[1] One wonders if the separation of an initial perceptual/cognitive process from a secondary cognitive process may not have a bearing upon the argument between Zajonc and Lazarus. That a subject can experience liking toward a nonsense syllable with which, unknown to him, he is familiar, may be one more instance in which an affect is produced nonexperientially and only subsequently receives probabilistic causal attribution. Had Zajonc asked subjects why they thought they preferred the familiar syllables, he probably would have received the same kinds of erroneous causal attributions that Maslach encountered in her hypnotized subjects. Subjects probably would have pointed to esthetic features which, from past experience, might have been a good guess of the cause of their feeling, but a guess nonetheless. In other words, a subliminal perceptual/cognitive process produced a feeling of liking or disliking which the subject would then, using a *second* cognitive process, attempt to interpret and explain.

person revise his set-goals upward, which seems to him a recipe for misery, given his beliefs about his abilities. Cognitive interventions may be very useful in this situation to confront anachronistic competence expectancies that make the defense necessary.

The model advanced here can be applied to many other phenomena and theoretical perspectives. One example, which follows from the last, is Bandura's discussion of self-efficacy (1977b, 1982). Bandura argues that self-efficacy expectancies significantly influence behavior, and that many pathological phenomena, such as phobias, can be explained in terms of erroneous appraisals of self-efficacy. A person's generalized and specific self-efficacy expectancies enter into the model of affect and its regulation developed here at two points. First, efficacy appraisals in part determine the responses a person uses to deal with emotions. For example, if a person wishes to become a lawyer but does not believe he can handle the work, he may decide instead to become a politician. Secondly, not only are appraisals of efficacy important in choosing behavioral control mechanisms, but they are also compared against set-goals of efficacy (components of ideal self) and thus influence self-esteem. Someone with a generalized expectancy that he cannot accomplish anything is bound to think poorly of himself regardless of his behavior and to become depressed, apathetic, or frustrated and angry.

Here Bandura's analysis of self-efficacy dovetails with Seligman's discussion of the relationship between learned helplessness and depression (Seligman, 1975; Abramson et al., 1978), which can also profitably be examined in the context of the proposed theory of affect. Following Bandura (1977b), Seligman's reconceptualization of his original helplessness model (Abramson et al., 1978) distinguishes the effects of low outcome expectancies (expectations of the outcome of a given action) from low efficacy expectancies (expectations of one's ability to perform the behavior) in producing depression. Both can be usefully viewed in terms of set-goals and cognitive-evaluative mismatches: a chronic mismatch between an important set-goal and an outcome expectancy that augurs continued frustration is likely to result in depression, just as a mismatch between an ideal self-image as efficacious and a chronic sense of one's own ineptitude leads to diminished self-esteem and consequent depression. This view of the causes of some forms of depression is not altogether different from psychodynamic notions, though the latter tend to stress conflict between set-goals rather than simple inability to achieve single set-goals.

Seligman's model of learned helplessness, like Bandura's model of self-efficacy, tends to overstate the importance of the person's sense of control or efficacy as opposed to expectations of results. In trying to explain phobias in terms of the efficacy construct, Bandura contends that "phobics" will not approach the phobic object because of a low efficacy expectancy; i.e., they do not believe they can do it. If one asks someone with a dog phobia, however, why he refuses to go near a dog, he will probably respond that he is afraid, not that he lacks the efficacy to walk forward. His efficacy expectancy is his belief about whether or not he can overcome his fear, and if the fear disappears, his efficacy expectancy is likely to change. The crucial causal factor is thus the fear.

One can see this more clearly by examining the set-goals involved in the phobic person's attempt to overcome his aversion. He has two conflicting set-goals when he is sitting in Bandura's office: a desire to be free from terror, and a desire to overcome his phobia. Ideally, the same behavior could fulfill both (fearlessly approaching the dog), but in reality the two goals are conflicting. As the subject/client/patient attempts to meet the set-goal of overcoming his phobia by moving toward the dog, his desire for freedom from fear is disturbed, activating the control mechanism of avoidance, which conflicts with the control mechanism (walking toward the dog) that was activated by the other set-goal. This, in turn, confirms him in his belief that he lacks the efficacy to overcome his phobia. As the fear decreases, however, the conflict between set-goals subsides, and the person has little difficulty imagining himself approaching the dog. In other words, the behavior of approaching the animal does, indeed, depend on the person's expectation that he can overcome his fear, but this expectation depends in large measure upon the intensity of the fear he must overcome. It is thus the outcome (fear), not the sense of low self-efficacy, that primarily maintains the phobic behavior (although there are likely to be some cases in which efficacy expectations outlive affect expectations).

The same problem is endemic to Seligman's model. Nowhere has clear evidence been produced to show that people who lack control but are rewarded generously (i.e., good outcome, bad efficacy or helplessness) will be terribly depressed; available evidence on noncontingent positive reinforcement largely suggests otherwise (Miller and Norman, 1979). If a person has a set-goal (e.g., to be wealthy) and the goal is being met, he is not likely to be depressed. If, however, a cognitive-evaluative mismatch arises, the person will become upset and eventually depressed if the discrepancy remains. The ability to control the mismatch could eliminate the depression by allowing fulfillment of the set-goal, but nonattainment of the goal (i.e., lack of desired outcome), not sense of helplessness, has produced the depression.

In terms of the theory offered in this chapter, when a person experiences a mismatch between set-goal and cognized reality, he is motivated by affect to reduce the discrepancy. Whether or not he chooses a given behavior depends on his expectation of his ability to carry it out (efficacy expectancy) and his expectation of whether or not it will eliminate the mismatch (outcome expectancy). Depression results from chronic nonfulfillment of a highly valued set-goal, not from efficacy expectancies about specific behaviors. Whether the person becomes depressed thus depends on whether the set-goal is attained, either through his own effort *or* through some external circumstances.

To put this another way, Bandura fails to distinguish between behavior-outcome expectancies (Mischel, 1973) and other outcome expectancies. A behavior-outcome expectancy is an expectation about whether a behavior can be expected to produce a given result. An outcome expectancy regarding a set-goal is an expectation about whether a set-goal will be met, either through one's own efforts or some other means. A person who wishes to be wealthy may have a high outcome expectancy because his name is Rockefeller, even though he may be thoroughly convinced that the outcome of any action he takes will only make him poorer. He is thus likely to take no action and simply enjoy his inheritance, unless being a successful entrepreneur is one of his highly charged set-goals. Behavior-outcome expectancies influence emotional state only to the extent that they affect outcome expectancies relating to set-goals. It is not primarily the helplessness that produces depression when one is helpless to prevent an aversive outcome; it is the aversive outcome. This is why Seligman's theory is helpless (so to speak) in explaining the etiology of depressions related to grief, guilt, or a sense of emptiness.

Helplessness or low self-efficacy *can* lead directly to depression if personal ability to effect changes in one's life is a valued set-goal, e.g., as an aspect of ideal self. In that case, a mismatch between desired competence or control and cognized reality produces lowered self-esteem. Neither Bandura nor Seligman has carefully separated efficacy as a set-goal from efficacy as an influence on selection of behavioral responses to other set-goals. If a person wants to be a lawyer and does not believe himself efficacious enough to go to Harvard Law School, he can meet the set-goal of becoming a lawyer by going to another school and will thus avoid depression. If, however, being able to get into Harvard is pivotal for his sense of himself as intelligent, competent, or efficacious, then the mismatch between desire to be intelligent enough to get into Harvard and the reality of not being able to do so will produce lowered self-esteem.[1]

A final area in which the present theory diverges from the learned helplessness model is in Seligman's description of a "depressive attributional style," in which the person attributes failure to internal, global, and stable personality characteristics instead of to situations, bad luck, lack of

---

[1] It is perhaps no accident that theories stressing the role of a sense of personal efficacy in determining mood and self-esteem would emerge in a Western industrial society, where so much of self-worth is dependent upon achievement, or that the preponderance of Seligman's examples are of students and professors, two groups whose esteem is especially dependent upon judgments of ability.

effort, etc. Seligman proposes that this attributional style leads to depression, but, like Beck, he does not explain why a person would develop such a masochistic way of processing information. While this style may result in part from learned attitudes toward the self as unworthy, inadequate, etc., it is likely to be maintained as well for dynamic reasons, such as to punish oneself for those attributes.

Stress, Coping, and Affect

In recent years a burgeoning literature has arisen on stress, and the theory of affect presented here can be used to reinterpret and integrate contemporary models of stress and coping. The concept of stress originally developed in biology with Selye's (1936) observation of a generalized adaptation syndrome (GAS) that emerged in response to physical or psychological threats. The stress concept was later appropriated by sociologists (particularly those who focus on role strain, e.g., Pearlin and Schooler, 1978) and psychologists. The two most sophisticated theories of stress and coping from a psychological perspective are those of Richard Lazarus (1981) and Norma Haan (1977).

According to Lazarus (1981) and his colleagues, stress resides in the transaction between person and situation and entails a person's perception that demands on her tax or exceed her available psychosocial resources. Lazarus's model proposes an interplay between cognitive appraisals and coping mechanisms. An individual makes a primary appraisal of a situation, in which she decides whether it is irrelevant to her, benign/positive, or stressful. Stress may be of three types: harm or loss; threat, by which is meant anticipated harm; or challenge, which represents an opportunity for growth.

Once the person has made this primary appraisal, she makes a secondary appraisal, which is an evaluation of her options. Secondary appraisal is characterized by conscious or unconscious consideration of the various coping strategies available. Lazarus differentiates four modes of coping: information seeking, direct action, inhibition of action, and intrapsychic processes. He postulates that people are continuously reappraising situations, and points out that coping (for example, with the death of a loved one) is a constellation of many actions and intrapsychic events, not a single act or personality trait.

Lazarus is an excellent theoretician, and his model of stress and coping has much to recommend it, not the least of which is the methodology it has inspired. Lazarus emphasizes the importance of naturalistic observation and is averse to attempts to measure coping which rely strictly on self-reports or which are overly rationalistic (e.g., those that deny the importance of defensive processes). His general model resembles one aspect of the model proposed here, namely the concept of cognitive-evaluative mismatch. Primary appraisal is analogous to the recognition of a discrepancy between a set-goal and reality, and secondary appraisal resembles the decision analysis described here through which the person chooses behavioral or intrapsychic responses.

I would argue that the present model can subsume Lazarus's analysis of stress and coping, and that the stress concept as used by Lazarus is less useful than the present approach. Lazarus's perspective as it stands is problematic in several respects. First, the relationship between stress and emotion is unclear. Lazarus argues that when a "person construes an encounter as damaging, threatening or challenging, we speak of psychological stress; when it is evaluated as positive, a positively toned emotional state usually accompanies or follows it" (1981, p. 10). He further goes on to contend that coping mechanisms respond to stress. What is unclear in this formulation is how stress leads to coping. Stress is a construct, not a feeling or motive. If one is focusing on the subjective experience that motivates action, one must examine a persons's feelings, of which "stress" is not one (unless one wants to view stress as synonymous with anxiety, in which case it is one emotion among many that motivate action).

This raises a second issue, regarding the utility of lumping together a number of motivational phenomena under the rubric of stress. According to Lazarus, people cope in order to "survive and flourish" (1981, p. 10), to establish a state of "well-being" (p. 25), to "invest their lives with useful personal meanings" (Lazarus and DeLongis, 1983, p.250), and to serve "adaptation" (Holroyd and Lazarus, 1982, p. 25). These terms are all quite vague and do not specify what the person is hoping to attain or maintain in a given encounter. What may be more useful is to examine the specific set-goals that lie behind cognitive-evaluative mismatches and wishes which account for motivation. A person whose wife has just died is not only suffering from "stress" produced by a threat to his "well-being;" he is experiencing a particular emotion (sadness, perhaps alloyed with anger) in response to disturbance of several set-goals. One can speak of this, of course, as a breakdown in his sense of well-being, but one can go much further by identifying the particular emotion, the particular set-goal being threatened, and the responses chosen to ameliorate the discrepancy between set-goal and cognized reality.

A third problem with a model that links stress to coping (instead of affect to coping) is that it prevents one from examining a person's differential response to different emotions. Objectively, retirement and object loss can both be significant stressors, but a person who rests his identity more on his occupation than his relationships is likely to respond to work-related set-goals with more dysfunctional defenses or coping mechanisms than someone whose identity is more interpersonally defined. Similarly, people differ on their tolerance for various emotional states; some cannot tolerate anger, while others find anxiety insufferable.

Plutchik (1980a), in fact, has argued that different affects evoke different defenses, though his approach is somewhat mechanistic, postulating a one-to-one correspondence between emotions and defenses. (For example, he argues for a relationship between fear and repression, yet one can just as easily cope with fear through reaction-formation, i.e., through defensive bravado.) Nevertheless, Plutchik's point is a good one, that different emotions may activate different clusters of responses, and to the extent that one speaks simply of stress evoking responses, one will be unable to examine this phenomenon.

Another major model of psychological stress and its management is that proposed by Haan (1977, 1982). In contrast to the work of Lazarus, one finds in Haan's writings explicit links to Freudian notions of conflict and defense. Haan has attempted in her theory of stress to integrate Piagetian concepts with psychoanalytic clinical understanding. She argues, with justification, that psychoanalysis (even in its more ego-psychological moments) fails to account for the more rational, adaptive, problem-solving aspects of human life.

She points to three modes of response to stress: coping, defense, and fragmentation. Coping entails conscious, rational, reality-directed action, whereas defense presupposes distortion of reality and circumvention of adequate problem-solving. With fragmentation, the person proves unequal to the challenges of life and retreats from intersubjective reality (1977, p. 34). Haan summarizes her view of these three processes in a pithy formula: "The person will cope if he can, defend if he must, and fragment if he is forced . . ."(p. 34).

According to Haan, coping, defense, and fragmentation are ego processes used to help the person maintain a consistent view of self (p. 33). She attempts to provide a taxonomy of ego processes, arguing that each of several basic processes has a coping, defensive, and fragmentive mode. For example, the generic process of "sensitivity" is related to the coping mechanism of empathy, the defense mechanism of projection, and the fragmented process of delusion.

Perhaps the most significant achievement of Haan's model is its attempt to integrate valuable contributions of psychoanalysis into an understanding of the more reality-oriented aspects of human psychological functioning. Haan has also attempted to recast the notion of "ego" in more process-oriented language, which is a welcome corrective to metapsychological accounts in psychoanalytic writings that can sometimes overly concretize psychic "structures" or "institutions."

Nevertheless, Haan's approach has weaknesses that can be avoided with the perspective offered here. First, her constructs regarding motivation and the activation of ego processes are inadequate. At her most general, Haan claims that the three modes of ego processes are used to solve "general problems of living" (p. 37). Elsewhere she refers to them as "strategies of problem resolution with respect to the self, to others, and to the world and its essential social logic and immutable physical structure" (p. 48). Motivational constructs such as these are not particularly helpful, and one can gain both theoretically and methodologically by specifying relevant set-goals determinative of action.

At other points Haan contends that people cope, defend, and fragment strictly for the purpose of "attaining and maintaining a consistent sense of self" (p. 33). This is clearly one important purpose of such mechanisms, but it is not the only aim of human endeavor. People defend, for example, against loss and against cognitions that are difficult to assimilate into existing schemas, and they cope in order to achieve ends such as the protection of significant others, which are not primarily concerned with the maintenance of a consistent self-concept. The breakdown of self is clearly one form of cognitive-evaluative mismatch, but it is only one of many.

Secondly, in moving away from psychoanalysis, Haan has cast off one of the most significant aspects of psychodynamic theory: the understanding of process in terms of function. This is perhaps most clear in her attempt to develop a descriptive taxonomy of ego processes. To take the example of the generic process of "sensitivity," Haan classifies empathy, projection, and delusion as modes of sensitivity because, one may suppose, each represents a way of understanding other people and their motivations. This is certainly one way of classifying these phenomena descriptively, but it obscures the dramatically different functions of these allegedly related processes. The function of empathy is to help one understand and relate to another person. The function of projection is to protect oneself from a painful emotion associated with recognition of a dreaded aspect of self. Delusions may serve a variety of functions, such as self-aggrandizement, or they may result from neurophysiological dysfunction. Losing sight of the function of different defenses or coping mechanisms renders these concepts less useful in understanding human mental life.

A third problem is Haan's misappropriation of the Piagetian concepts of equilibrium, assimilation, and accommodation. She often uses them, as did Piaget, to mask unclear thinking. For example:

> The view of ego to be developed here is that it is exclusively processes, specifically the ceaseless acts of people assimilating new information about themselves and their environments and accommodating to these assimilations by constructing actions that attain and re-attain an unremitting series of dynamic equilibriums. (P. 33)

It is difficult to see how one can truly integrate such a cognitive view of ego processes with dynamic processes of conflict and defense. The defense mechanism of repression, for example, militates against both assimilation *and* accommodation: painful information is not assimilated into existing schemas (or is made difficult to retrieve); nor do prevailing schemas accommodate to the information. Perhaps more importantly, the unassimilability of repressed ideation (or cognitions defensively rejected in any other way, such as projection or reaction-formation) does not stem from the type of cognitive discrepancy described by Piaget as likely to evoke accommodations. To the contrary, defensive processes arise because of a discrepancy between an affect-laden ideal state and cognized reality. Similarly, when Haan writes of fragmentation as an "accommodation to stress" (p. 49), she is shifting to the everyday, non-Piagetian meaning of accommodation. Certainly cognitive transformations, including both assimilations and accommodations, occur with all defensive processes, but one cannot reduce the latter to the former.

I would contend that the theory of arousal and regulation of emotion proposed here can explain the data supporting the models of Haan and Lazarus and can thus integrate an understanding of the processes described as stress and coping into a general theory of personality. Perhaps it would not be unwise to go one step further and argue that, as a psychological construct, the notion of stress should be abandoned in favor of attention to specific emotions unless it can point to phenomena that cannot be explained in terms of affect. Levitt (1980) discovered in reviewing relevant literature that the word "stress" is constantly used in connection with emotion. Indeed, it is difficult to find a psychological stress theorist who does not equate or conflate the two. Goldberger and Breznitz (1982), for example, define stress as "all that is unpleasant, noxious, or excessively demanding" (p. xi). Pearlin and Schooler (1978), in an empirical study of coping processes in a sample of 2300 people, "rely on the reported experience of emotional upset as our indicator of stress . . ." (p. 4). Spielberger (1979) and Endler (1980) both tie stress to anxiety, though one has difficulty reconciling such a move with the recognition that loss may be stressful even though it primarily involves sadness as opposed to anxiety. In all of these cases stress is used synonymously with unpleasant affect of one type or another, and it is not clear what is to be gained by introducing the stress concept. The concept should, at the very least, be narrowed to refer only to a cumulative tension that influences mood state, and should be seen as evoking psychological and physiological responses only to the extent that these responses cannot be explained by specific affects or combinations of affects.

In sum, the concept of stress as a psychological phenomenon, unless significantly narrowed, obscures efforts to distinguish reactions to different emotions. The notion of coping is nevertheless valuable, as one type of control mechanism used to "optimize" emotion. The stress and coping

95

approaches of Lazarus and Haan are useful in both their empirical and theoretical contributions and can be profitably integrated into a model of emotion and its management.

Conclusion

The theory of affect proposed here is clearly crude and underdeveloped. It is, for example, less useful in understanding pleasurable affects than unpleasurable ones, and it does not explain many aesthetic emotions. It also does not offer a systematic theory of persistent mood states, nor does it clearly distinguish between affective processing and affective arousal. The emotion of anger may require some additional principles, since it at times appears to be a positive emotion, as when a person enjoys righteous indignation, while at other times it is very unpleasant. Nevertheless, the theory offers an analysis of the function and consequences of emotion that may serve as a bridge between contemporary psychodynamic psychology and current cognitive and social learning approaches to personality derived from behaviorism. It argues that we must abandon the basically passive conception of human nature endemic to behaviorism (and its intellectual ancestor, British empiricism) which views behavior as a response to stimuli. Stimuli themselves can never exert influence upon behavior without perceptual/cognitive and affective mediation, and the view that reinforcement depends upon properties of the stimulus instead of upon the person's affective reaction to it must be abandoned.

It argues, further, that psychoanalytic drive theory, with its importation of biological metaphors, energy concepts, and the like to psychological discourse is conceptually neither adequate nor necessary. Emotions, produced (and interpreted) through various biological, perceptual, and cognitive processes, are a primary source of human motivation. What is thus excised from psychodynamic and cognitive-behavioral psychology can be replaced by an approach informed by systems theory which views emotion as a feedback signal responsible for motivating various behavioral, coping, and defensive procedures.

The cognitive revolution in psychology has brought together a number of perspectives and focused attention on the intricacies of human thinking. Perhaps we will need an "affective revolution" to remind us that human beings are creatures who not only think but, unlike computers, also feel, wish, and sometimes seek help.

3 The Structure and Dynamics of Personality

THE THEORY OF affect proposed here is not in itself a complete theory of either motivation or psychodynamics. Such a theory must include an explication of the enduring configurations of motives (i.e., of set-goals, mismatches, and other cognitive-affective schemas), as well as an examination of the way an individual carries out these motives in an environmental context and resolves conflicts between various wishes, ideals, mismatches, prohibitions, and affects.

I will now propose such a model and in so doing will utilize the metaphor of psychic "structure." Different theorists in the social sciences have used this term, and in order to avoid ambiguity I will define "structure" at the outset as referring to *constellations of functionally related processes.* This view is probably closest to the psychoanalytic notion of structure embodied in Freud's structural model, though I have defined the term as above to avoid the kind of reification of structures that has plagued psychoanalytic theory. As many writers, both within and without psychoanalysis have pointed out, psychic structures are repeatedly concretized in psychoanalytic literature, often treated as organs instead of constructs.

Though some of his disciples have carried this practice to extremes (reifying drives as well), Freud was often guilty of this himself, which has caused a popular misconception that Freud posited a set of homunculi within the brain. Psychoanalytic writers often speak of "the ego" as experiencing anxiety or depression, when it is the person, not the ego, who is anxious or depressed (see Mendelson's [1974] criticism of Bibring's otherwise excellent paper on depression, 1953). Reification is not, however, inherent in a structural approach. When I speak of "ego ideal" as a structure, as I will do shortly, I refer to a set of processes which serve similar functions. These processes are clustered together in the model because of their similarity and the heuristic value of ordering them this way; they could be classified quite differently, though I do not believe it would be as useful to do so.

97

Self-Needs and Other-Needs

Abraham Maslow, a humanistic psychologist, argues that "the basic human needs are organized in a hierarchy of relative prepotency" (1954, p.83). The lowest level on Maslow's hierarchy is that of the physiological needs. The individual originally desires food, warmth, air, and other biologically determined requisites for existence. Once the person has sated these demands, his desires broaden. The second level of Maslow's hierarchy consists of safety needs. The safety needs include shelter and protection, and Maslow hypothesizes that the infant's desire for an omnipotent parent stems from these needs. When the individual feels relatively safe, he begins to desire love; he seeks affection and a sense of belonging. Maslow asserts that the frustration of love needs is the origin of most psychopathology in contemporary society. Once the individual has attained this level, he seeks esteem, including the impulse for mastery and the esteem of others.

At the pinnacle of Maslow's hierarchy is the need for self-actualization, the realization of the person's full human potential. Explaining that a sated need is no longer a real need, Maslow contends that the appearance of any chronic need other than self-actualization represents sickness. In *Toward a Psychology of Being* (1962) Maslow distinguishes deficiency needs (largely the first four levels of need on his hierarchy) from growth needs (primarily self-actualization). A healthy society, he claims, is one that fosters self-actualization of its members (1954, p. 105), freeing them from constant vigilance of their deficiency needs. Calling for a new psychology for self-actualizers, Maslow contends that self-actualizers demonstrate an absence of psychic conflict. "In these people," he asserts, "the id, the ego, and the superego are collaborative and synergic; they do not war with each other nor are their interests in basic disagreement as they are in neurotic people" (1954, p. 233).

Maslow's model is optimistic, and while it suggests a way of viewing motivation which is novel and rich, it suffers from its extreme sanguinity because it fails to account for conflict in any meaningful way. Crucially, it does not distinguish between "egoistic" needs and social needs. For example, as will be suggested later, the desires for self-esteem and the esteem of others are related but can become independent; the two, in fact, often conflict. Further, while security needs logically follow physiological needs, love needs and esteem needs do not necessarily appear in any sequence or in relation to physiological or security needs. From a psychoanalytic or even a cognitive perspective (Piaget and Inhelder, 1969), only in the newborn are social and self needs continuous since the neonate cannot distinguish self from other; in Freudian terms, ego-libido and object-libido are synonymous only in infancy (or psychosis; see Freud, 1914). Like Freud's model, Maslow's confounds the development of needs (in Freud's case, psychosexual) with the development of personality. Maslow's theory of motivation is somewhat less reductionistic, though not clinically helpful.

A reanalysis of the concept of the hierarchical nature of needs suggests a more useful formulation, reconciling Freudian, Maslowian, and systems theoretical paradigms. Put simply, one can distinguish two distinct clusters of motives: *self-needs*[1] and *other-needs*. "Needs" here refer to motivational structures, i.e., constellations of related cognitive-affective schemas which are motivating.

The self-needs are arranged hierarchically. Similar to Maslow's model, the lowest level of individual need consists of the *physical needs*, including the tendency to seek physical pleasure and avoid pain and the desire for self-preservation. Once the physical needs have been sated, the individual seeks *security* and *comfort*. The third level of self-needs consists of desires for *mastery, competence,* or *play*.[2] (For an interesting developmental model of competence needs, see White, 1960.)

Each of these needs encompasses a number of set-goals, and the quality and intensity of discrepancy between set-goal and cognized reality is in part determined by level of need. The individual achieves an "equilibrium" or "homeostasis" (i.e., tension within tolerable limits between set-goal and perceived state) with respect to a set-goal and may become aware of the relevant "need" only when a cognitive-evaluative mismatch arises, leading to behavioral, coping, or defense mechanisms. If, for example, a two-year-old has attained a certain level of security, the desire for security may no longer impinge upon his consciousness. His attention turns to other matters, often relating to higher levels of need such as play or mastery. If the child suddenly perceives his security as threatened, this cognitive-evaluative mismatch will take precedence over any higher level desires or enjoyments. Where seconds before the toddler was confidently exploring his environment, now he recoils for protection (cf. Ainsworth, 1979). In actuality, rarely does one achieve total satisfaction of a need. Instead, the person or

---

[1] I reluctantly use the word "self" inconsistently here, not referring to the whole person, as it is used in all other contexts in the book. It is used here in juxtaposition to "other" (self versus other), referring to needs that are primarily nonsocial. A logical alternative would be to speak of "egoistic" needs instead of "self-needs," but since the term "ego" will later be introduced, this would be equally problematic.

[2] One might argue that a synthesis of the needs for play and mastery creates a need for what one might call creativity broadly defined, which is somewhat akin to Maslow's self-actualization (though without the teleological implications). One need not be competent at something to "play" with it, nor need one be able creatively to play with something to be competent at it. In other words, with creativity not only has the individual learned to master aspects of reality, but she has developed the capacity – and the desire – to create them. Creativity in this sense, like the German idealist philosophers' "objectification," allows the individual to project herself upon her environment, to create a subjective reality that others recognized as objectively real.

organism establishes various set-goals and tolerates a cognitive-evaluative mismatch within certain limits. (The ability to tolerate certain degrees of "disequilibrium" constitutes another developmental line, one amenable to empirical study.)

Each level of need contains many elements and becomes, in the course of development, related to numerous set-goals. Desires for food and sleep, for example, are needs at the physical level, and each has subcomponents that are in part elaborated by culture and experience. What constitutes an adequate source of nutrition, for example, varies by culture and individual, and a person will evolve set-goals and wishes regarding different kinds of foods. To speak of a hierarchy of needs is not to say that, in some mechanistic way, lower level needs are always prepotent over higher level ones. In certain instances, this relation no longer holds, though it is generally the case. Studies of starving prisoners in World War II and simulations of that situation (Franklin et al., 1948; Bruch, 1973, pp. 266–7) have shown that starving people become preoccupied with food above all else and often develop detailed rituals around anything relating to food. Observers have noted a similar pattern of behavior among anorexics, who may also be physiologically starving (Bruch, 1973).

The notion of hierarchically organized needs receives empirical support from a variety of quarters. White (1959) reviews evidence in both animals and humans showing that exploration and mastery produce satisfaction irreducible to fulfillment of physiological needs, and that, in fact, such behaviors typically arise when physiological tensions are at low ebb. What Hunt (1965) and others have described as "intrinsic motivation," particularly the pursuit of understanding and mastery of reality without apparent "extrinsic" reward (often prompted, as Hunt argues, by novelty or a simple discrepancy between cognitive expectations and current perceptions or thoughts), may be conceived as an aspect of the need for mastery, which becomes operative in the absence of pressing physiological needs or threats to security (for a review of relevant literature on "intrinsic motivation," see deCharms and Muir, 1978.) In a study of preschoolers, Singer and his colleagues (Singer, 1979) similarly found that imaginativeness of play showed strong inverse correlations with fear and fatigue, suggesting that unfulfilled lower level needs (or powerful negative affect states of any sort) inhibit activation of play motives. Studies of exploratory behavior in infants corroborate the notion of security as a prerequisite to activation of exploratory or mastery needs. Carr, Dabbs, and Carr (1975) found that eighteen- to thirty-month-olds spent more time playing when they could see their mothers (which, one might hypothesize, provides a sense of security).

The self-needs constitute one set of motivational processes in humans, i.e., one motivational structure. A second set involves social needs which will be called other-needs. John Bowlby (1969; see also Sroufe and Waters,

100

1977; Ainsworth, 1979) documents the innateness of the need for attachment, hypothesizing its evolutionary basis in a desire for proximity to the mother for protection. Bowlby, an ethologist and psychoanalyst, points to similar behavior in the higher primates, and the notion that primates including our own species inherently seek attachments has become widely accepted throughout much of psychology. Questions abound, however, about the nature and existence of critical periods for attachment and other psychological processes (see, for example, Kagan, 1976). The other-needs are a cluster of motives which differentiate out of an original need for attachment that includes various set-goals involving physical touch, proximity to caretakers, etc. From this original matrix emerge set-goals for love, social approval, social aspects of sexuality, friendship, and the like. This notion is in some respects similar to Sullivan's description of the development of various socially oriented dynamisms (1953).

This theory of need differs from the Freudian notion of libido in a number of important ways, such as the absence of a tension-release drive theory and the separation of sensual needs for pleasurable excitation, social needs, and sexual needs. Rather than viewing love as an epiphenomenon of the sexual drive, this approach sees love, sexual intimacy, and the desire for various forms of social contact as motives that are not isomorphic but relate to similar affects that may at times be evoked simultaneously.[1] The psychoanalytic model confounds sex, attachment, and love. To say that an infant's clinging to his mother or father is in any sense sexual is a perversion (so to speak) of the term "sexuality," though certainly many aspects of infantile experience are *sensual* (i.e., physically pleasurable), and oral satisfactions may become linked to sexual fantasies and impulses. The Freudian would respond that sexuality is a broad term, and that attachment is a form of libidinal investment. When one pins him down as to the difference between an adult sexual relationship and a

---

[1] Other-needs other than attachment may have some genetically based components, though at this point this is largely speculation. Maternal behaviors, for example, have been hormonally manipulated in rats (see Rosenblatt, 1969; Moltz et al., 1970), though one must obviously be very cautious in generalizing to humans. Robert Trivers (1971) examines and compares the evolution of "reciprocal altruism" in fish, birds, and humans and concludes that symbiotic cleaning in fish, warning calls in birds, and altruistic behavior in humans are evolutionarily adaptive and could have been produced by natural selection. In another article (Trivers and Hare, 1976) he suggests that altruistic behavior is dependent upon degree of relatedness of the helper to the helped, and he provides evidence from the social insects. E.O. Wilson, a founder of sociobiology, similarly proposes a genetic basis for altruistic behavior in *On Human Nature* (1978). The book, his intellectual offspring, is currently enjoying notable reproductive success. Darwin (1895) himself posits a "social instinct." While sociobiology is a nascent field, and neither its methods nor its findings are as yet approaching solidification, psychology must certainly consider the animal roots of human behavior and the significance of selection pressures on human development. For a rich and reasoned essay along these line by a psychologist with broad knowledge and keen insight, see Campbell, 1975.

friendship, he will explain that the latter is a de-sexualized version of the former. But what does sex mean in this latter sense of "de-sexualiza-tion?" It means *genital,* i.e., sexual in the everyday sense of the term. The Freudian system escapes difficulties such as this by shifting meanings of sexuality. If one views an infant's relation to her mother and a woman's relation to her lover as manifestations of the same impulse, the only differentiation one can make is zonal, i.e., genital versus oral. Yet are the desires for closeness to the mother and adult intimacy and genital satis-faction really isomorphic? If so, masturbation must involve attachment to, or love of one's genitals. Surely the essence of masturbation is not love of the genitals; one does not love or feel attached to a zone as one loves or feels attached to a person. The qualitative difference between sexual love and friendship is obscured by labeling any favorable disposi-tion toward anything as "libidinal." (One finds this problem particularly salient in Kernberg's equation of libido with pleasurable, and aggression with unpleasurable affect, 1976.)

Other-needs include both the individual's own social motives and repre-sentations of the needs of others which have become motivating as set-goals. Other-needs are obviously thoroughly related to a person's percep-tions of the social world, including both generalized cognitions of social rules and others' behavior and specific schemas or object-representations. The work of a number of psychological schools is relevant to an under-standing of other-needs. One of the most astute observers of the vicissi-tudes of this set of needs (which he assumes to be the whole personality) is Harry Stack Sullivan, whose *Interpersonal Theory of Psychiatry* (1953) contains many provocative ideas, such as that of the "chumship" (p. 227). Also relevant here are the writings of the object relations school of psycho-analysis (for a superb review, see Greenberg and Mitchell, 1983). On a more cognitive level, social cognition researchers have been exploring people's perceptions of other people, perspective-taking abilities, under-standing of social causality, and the like, in various experimental and quasi-experimental situations (see Cantor and Kihlstrom, 1982, for an excellent review of the major lines of social cognition research and their relation to personality). That object relations theorists and social cognition researchers do not read each other's work is a pity, since both have been approaching the same topic in different ways and each could benefit greatly from an acquaintance with the other.

The other-needs include affiliation, attachment, love, jealousy, and other social motives. Other-needs may be taken by the individual as ends in themselves, or they may be utilized as means to other ends (e.g., becom-ing friends with someone because he holds some power and can be useful; compare the notion of narcissistic object relations in psychoanalytic litera-ture). Similarly, self-needs may be seen as either means or ends. Mastery, for example, may be a goal in itself or a means of eliciting esteem from an individual or group. Sexual desires have both self-need (physical gratification) and other-need (intimacy) components.

Both self-needs and other-needs have their bases in innate tendencies, but this is not to suggest that they are genetically determined and unrelated to experience and culture. To postulate a "gene" for mastery or even security would probably be unfounded; to suggest a genetic basis for physical needs, including self-preservation, would not. Similarly, that a "gene" for love exists is doubtful, but that attachment behavior spontaneously arises in a wide variety of primates and is fostered by a number of genetically programmed responses (such as smiling in the infant) is empirically verifiable. The argument here is that genetic proclivities give rise to clusters of set-goals and affects which are developed and interpreted through socialization and experience.

The separation of constellations of set-goals into self-needs and other-needs is in many respects arbitrary, though it is useful in distinguishing motives aimed at adaptation, survival, and personal satisfaction and growth from motives that are more strictly social. These constructs are flexible in that they can accommodate new research and theories about the evolution of biological constraints and proclivities to experience certain events as positive or negative (see, e.g., behaviorist literature on phobias and "preparedness"; Seligman, 1972) or to produce certain adaptive responses (e.g., Bolles's discussion of species-specific defense reactions, 1970).

Ego Processes: Ego Real and Ego Ideal

Self-needs and other-needs, then, constitute two sources of motivation. Three other psychic structures, the ego real, ego ideal, and an integrating function between them, form a composite *ego* which is the basis of personality. The *ego real* corresponds in many ways to notions of the ego prevalent in current psychoanalytic ego psychology (see White, 1963; Blanck and Blanck, 1974; Loevinger, 1976). The ego real as used here represents the processes responsible for motor activity, selection of control mechanisms, "adjustment to reality," etc. More systemically, one can attribute to the ego real two functions: perception/cognition and the regulation of emotion. These functions will be explored in greater detail below.

The *ego ideal* is a set of functions involved in imparting meaning on existence and providing ideals. It consists of a constellation of ideal self-representations, general and specific moral rules, and values and ideals that comprise a "meaning-system" or a way of imposing value on the existence of oneself, significant others, and one's life. The set of ideal self-representations, which one may collectively call the "ideal self," represents an accretion of learned and self-generated standards, and significant

103

aspects of it may come to be hierarchically organized. The ideal self is a cognitive-affective schema or set of schemas which consists of various conscious and unconscious ideals, rules, and identifications that are connected through networks of associations and may be activated "laterally" or "vertically." Similarly, moral rules may be organized hierarchically into general principles and subprinciples or may be primarily accumulated and activated as concrete injunctions. The same is true of the values which provide the person with a vision of how things should be and what in life is worthwhile. Ideal self-representations, moral standards, and meaning-imparting values are obviously thoroughly interconnected: ideals about one's own behavior are likely to relate to broader values, though the more ontogenetically primitive and concrete (and often unconscious) the ideals, the less they will relate to broader values and aspirations.

The composite structure of the ego ideal, comprised of these substructures, can be viewed in two ways: as the center of morality and as an immortality-system. To understand its first function, as the center of morality, an examination of the concept of the ego ideal as developed by Freud is useful. Freud originally proposed the concept of ego ideal in his classic article, "On Narcissism" (1914), an essay which signaled an incipient move toward the structural model. According to Freud, when an ego forms in infancy, all libido becomes attached to it, creating a narcissistic state in which the child ascribes perfection and omnipotence to himself. Gradually, for reasons which Freud at this point did not give (although he later invoked the Oedipus complex as an explanation), the child must transfer his original narcissism to an ideal ego or "ego ideal" developed in response to parental injunctions:

> The narcissism seems to be now displaced on to this new ideal ego, which, like the infantile ego, deems itself the possessor of all perfections . . . That which he projects ahead of him as his ideal is merely the substitute for the lost narcissism of his childhood – the time when he was his own ideal. (1914, p. 74)

In *Group Psychology and the Analysis of the Ego* (1921) Freud delineates four functions of the ego ideal: "self-observation, the moral conscience, the censorship of dreams, and the chief influence in repression" (p. 42). In *The Ego and the Id* (1923), Freud's first enunciation of the structural model, he develops the notion of the superego as synonymous with the ego ideal. The ego ideal is there described as the "heir of the Oedipus complex" (p. 26), an internal representation of a seemingly omnipotent external authority. Freud describes the superego in Lecture XXXI of the *New Introductory Lectures* (1933) in terms very similar to his earlier description of the ego ideal in his work on group psychology (cited above), although he leaves somewhat unclear the relation between ego ideal and superego. He allots to the superego three functions: "of self-observation, of conscience, and of (maintaining) the ideal" (p. 66). At another point in the same lecture, he refers to the superego as the "vehicle of the ego ideal by which the ego measures itself . . ." (p. 65). In his final work, the *Outline of Psycho-Analysis* (1939), Freud speaks of the superego but not at all of the ego ideal, suggesting that he finally subsumed the ego ideal into the superego.

Freud's concept of the ego ideal, then, fluctuated throughout his career, eventually being superseded by his notion of the superego. A number of psychoanalytic writers have remained unsatisfied with this position and have attempted to resolve some of the ambiguities involved in Freud's conception of the ego ideal and its relationship to superego and ego. Nunberg (1932) is the first in a long line of authors utilizing the formula, "To differentiate between the two structures is really impossible, but . . ." Though generally confusing references to the ego ideal still appear in psychoanalytic writing, the term has largely fallen into disuse.

In relation to the model of the ego ideal to be developed here, which bears enough resemblance to its Freudian precursor to justify the same name, the importance of Freud's concept of the ego ideal/superego is his view of the ego ideal as the psychic "seat" of morality. As will be argued in the next chapter, however, the Freudian notion of the ego ideal/superego points to only one stage of the development of the ego ideal and moral judgment.

As the center of morality, the ego ideal consists of values which posit an ideal relation or reconciliation of the desires of self and others. The function of a moral view is to provide a system of beliefs for adjudicating these conflicting claims. The central psychological conflicts confronting the individual, and at the heart of much of psychopathology, involve the tension between (the needs and the definition of) self and others. A number of psychologists, notably moral psychologists, have stressed the centrality of this conflict. Lawrence Kohlberg (Kohlberg and Mayer, 1972), for example, ties self-other conflict directly to the issue of morality, describing morality as "the reciprocity between the individual and others in his social environment" (p. 129). Carol Gilligan (1977) summarizes the perspective of Kohlberg and Piaget:

> Moral development, in the work of Piaget and Kohlberg, refers specifically to the expanding conception of the social world as it is reflected in the understanding and resolution of the inevitable conflicts that arise in the relations between self and others. The moral judgment is a statement of priority. . . . (P. 54)

Most moral philosophers would agree that morality is a person's or group's judgment of "the good," but they would add that morality also means altruism, or acting in the interests of others or the community. In so doing they are inserting a specific moral content into what should be a

105

formal definition. Nothing about the nature of "the good" requires that it must invariably mean "the good of others." As will be argued in Chapter 4, in early childhood "the good" means the good of oneself, and a similar view began to take root in Western philosophy with the theory of the social contract.

Part of the reason philosophers have mistakenly equated morality with altruism or with the good of the collectivity relates to a faulty view of reason, and a false antinomy of reason and desire, which have dominated Western ethical thought. Since Plato, moral philosophers (except for those who have actually taken Hume to heart) have almost uniformly believed that through proper use of reason, the individual will uncover and practice true morality, which generally means altruism or concern for the community. The enemy of reason is desire, which drives people toward particularistic earthly pleasures of no benefit to anyone else. In this view, reason is a guide for human action, not just a mode of cognition. This belief is intimately tied to the idea that desires represent short-term self-interest, whereas reason represents long-term self-interest, which in turn correlates with altruism. For Plato, proper understanding leads to a knowledge of the Form of the Good. For Hobbes, the law of nature, otherwise known as Reason, prescribes both self-preservation and the golden rule. For Rousseau, the individual who reasons correctly will pursue the general will. For Kant, proper use of reason leads one to impose upon oneself the categorical imperative to treat others as ends. For Rawls (1971), reason produces principles of justice which guarantee basic liberties and allow inequalities only to the extent that they foster the common good.

These views of the relation between reason, altruism, and long-run self-interest are nice sentiments, and frankly, I wish they were true. But they are not. Despite interminable attempts, no one has ever been able to prove that altruism and long-term self-interest coincide. In point of fact, the "golden mean" between partiality and impartiality is generally the best bet in terms of long-run "self-interest." David Gauthier asserts in *Morality and Rational Self-Interest*, "If all men are moral [altruistic], all will do better than if all are prudent [egoistic]. But any one will always do better if he is prudent than moral" (1970, p. 175). Gauthier uses the example of an arms race to illustrate his point. If neither side acts for the common good, both will be destroyed. If both act for the common good most of the time, but one of them gets caught cheating, both are again in trouble. The only way that self-interest and the common good coincide is if cheating is entirely detectable (p. 170). This, of course, is rarely the case in society, and certainly not in a large, industrialized society. The solution which represents the long-term self-interest of the country in an arms race is to act largely for the common good and present a firm illusion of detectability while cheating a little on the side.

106

One sees in Gauthier's terminology, however, the same confusion manifest in most moral philosophy. Gauthier equates morality with the common good or altruism, and prudence with self-interest or egoism. Yet if morality is a balance between the desires of self and other, or between individual and society, then one cannot a priori equate morality with the good of the other or the good of society. I may have wishes, and my society or someone else may have wishes, but nothing in the nature of "the good" in general requires that I consider the desires of others as "moral," and my own desires as immoral or amoral.[1]

Not only does morality not necessarily entail altruism, but reason cannot side with altruism, any more than it can choose "self-interest." The desires of self and the desires of others are simply competing desires; neither set of desires in itself is either moral or rational. The false antinomy of reason and desire that has pervaded moral philosophy since its inception stems from the incorrect assumption that reason can provide ends. The only ends of human actions are human desires, whether of self or others. Reason cannot choose between conflicting ends because reason can provide no criterion for choice. Philosophers generally agree that self-preservation is a rational desire. This is patently untrue, as Epicurus and Spinoza recognized centuries ago. Nothing could be less "rational" than spending one's life trying to stave off death when one knows that death is inevitable. Similarly, one can hardly call "rational," behavior which aims at preserving the lives of other mortal beings. Desires (i.e., motives) are neither rational nor irrational: they are a-rational. Reason can never prescribe ends because reason is a mode of cognition, not volition. Reason can help weigh the benefits of various potential actions in terms of desires, and it can help choose means to various ends, but it cannot choose between the ends themselves. That is the job of a moral value system, which may be informed by reason but cannot be determined by it.

To return to the ego ideal, a second, more speculative way of examining the ego ideal is to view it as an *immortality system*. From an ethological or sociobiological viewpoint, the ego ideal, like the self- and other-needs, is probably rooted in the structure of the organism. Sociobiologists (see, for example, Dawkins, 1976) contend that humans, like other animals, "desire" (to use the word in a metaphorical, if perhaps misleading way) the preservation of their genes. Each person shares genes proportionately with others in order of their relatedness to him. An individual's brothers, sisters, parents, and offspring are related to him by one-half; cousins, by one-eighth. Sociobiologists argue that natural selection favors individuals who

---

[1] In strictly logical terms one cannot maintain both a universalistic ethic and a belief that morality and altruism coincide: if the wishes of Fred are moral to Bill, Bill's wishes are moral to Fred, but Bill's wishes are not moral to himself, one runs into a contradiction. This kind of argument, of course, is sophistry.

care for their relations' lives as well as their own, and cross-cultural evidence corroborates this view. This theory was first proposed by Hamilton (1964), who produced empirical evidence to support his claim that natural selection selects animals that base decisions on something like calculations of their "inclusive fitness," which means an equation that considers reproductive costs and benefits to the animal as well as to related animals weighted by degree of relatedness. In other words, the "genes" of an animal that, for example, will sacrifice its own life for the safety of four siblings will be represented more highly in the gene pool of the next generation than those of a "selfish" animal because siblings share half of their genes; in terms of genetic transmission, four siblings are worth two selves.

Obviously, neither animals nor humans carry inclusive fitness calculators in their pockets, but a number of mechanisms could have evolved to maximize inclusive fitness (see Trivers and Hare, 1976, on the relation between inclusive fitness and the social organization of the social insects). For example, many animals (particularly primates) appear predisposed to protect members of their social group, and this is true of humans as well. In terms of inclusive fitness, this makes good sense since the probability is high that many members of the group will be biological relatives. (For a wonderfully balanced and appropriately cautious statement of sociobiological theory, see Maynard-Smith, 1978.) That people demonstrate concern for their relatives is, of course, no shocking statement, and that conflicts may arise is similarly no new insight, but the evolutionary argument is an important contribution of sociobiology. Clearly the individual requires some inner arbiter of competing claims.

The argument propounded here is that preservation and propagation of one's genetic material (maximization of "inclusive fitness") involves first, self-preservation, and secondly, preservation of related others (and other members of the group, given reciprocal altruism). The individual, one might say, is attempting to achieve immortality through these methods, preservation of self and preservation (and propagation) of others. A number of sociobiologists (see the volume on sociobiology and morality edited by Stent, 1978; Wilson, 1978) have noted the universality of moral beliefs cross-culturally and have speculated on the adaptive function and evolution of morals. Given that individuals frequently face conflicts between self-interest and the interests of significant others (who are not, of course, necessarily related others, though kinship was a far more prominent determinant of interaction in the hunter-gatherer societies in which people lived during the evolution of Homo sapiens), moral systems were likely to have evolved to adjudicate such conflicts, and a function of the ego ideal is, in the broadest sense, to reconcile self-preservation with the care for others. Again, the argument here is not that individuals make decisions by comparing the probability of their own death with a weighted probability of the death of kin. The implication, instead, is that the need for "immortality" is a motivating dynamism in humans that is elaborated through culture and experience, and that the ego ideal has as one function the striving for immortality.

Robert Jay Lifton makes a similar, though purely psychological, argument in *Boundaries: Psychological Man in Revolution* (1970; see also Lifton, 1979). He develops a theory of "symbolic immortality," claiming that "man requires a sense of immortality in the face of inevitable biological death" (p. 21, emphasis deleted). Lifton views "the sense of living on through" offspring as one "mode of immortality" (p. 22), and he writes, secondly, of a "theological mode" (p. 22). A third mode is "the sense one will live on in natural elements," and a fourth is the mode of "experiential transcendence," in which one experiences immortality through life itself (p. 23). From the perspective of the present theory, aside from self-preservation (and perhaps experiential transcendence), which must ultimately fail, humans share two avenues of immortality with animals: preservation of others and reproduction (Lifton's biological mode). Human beings have one additional path to immortality, however, peculiarly their own: symbolic immortality through objectification, i.e., through creativity broadly defined or "self-actualization." A person, unlike an animal, can create a lasting objectification of her own subjectivity. Lifton, in fact, points to human work as another path to immortality (p. 23). He concludes, in a passage which makes clear the bridge between his notion of symbolic immortality and the conception presented here of the ego ideal,

> [The symbolic modes of immortality] are constantly perceived inner standards, though often indirect and outside of awareness, by which we maintain feelings of connection, significance, and movement so necessary to everyday psychological existence. (P. 23)

These ethological and psychological arguments find a somewhat metaphysical parallel in *The Denial of Death* (1973), Ernest Becker's Pulitzer Prize-winning psycho-philosophical synthesis. Becker argues that culture, like character, is essentially a lie, a "hero-system" in which the individual's "heroics" serve to deny his own death. Becker contends that ". . . the idea of death, the fear of it, haunts the human animal like nothing else; it is a mainspring of human activity – activity designed largely to avoid the fatality of death, to overcome it by denying in some way that it is the final destiny for man." He continues:

> . . . the fear of death is indeed a universal in the human condition. To be sure, primitives often celebrate death . . . *because* they believe that death is the ultimate promotion. Most Westerners have trouble believing this anymore, which is what makes the fear of death so prominent a part of our psychological make-up. (P. ix)

109

Another explanation presents itself for the comparative absence of fear of death in some "primitives:" Western individuals are increasingly gaining meaning largely from their own personal existence, while "primitive" or "traditional" people – who saw death all around them, invested more energy in clan or community, and could not fancy themselves gods – synthesized self and other with an emphasis on other and community. The implication, which will be explored in Parts II and III, is that old age should be particularly a problem for modern individuals, who have invested more in their own lives. In the *Culture of Narcissism* (1978) Christopher Lasch documents precisely this state of affairs:

> In a society that dreads old age and death, aging holds a special terror . . .
> The usual defenses against the ravages of age – identification with ethical
> or artistic values beyond one's immediate interests, intellectual curiosity,
> the consoling emotional warmth derived from happy relationships in the
> past – can do nothing for the narcissist. (P. 41)

For the individual who is incapable of investing emotionally in others, death becomes especially terrifying and energy-absorbing, as the person is unable to "sublimate" self-love into a generative (Erikson, 1963) concern for her or his culture or future generations. Perhaps it is not accidental that existentialism, a profoundly individualistic philosophy, holds the fear of death as a central preoccupation.

The ego ideal, then, is the center of morality (responsible for the reconciliation of self and other) and an immortality system.[1] In actuality, the two functions are basically interrelated. The role of the ego ideal is to establish values and meaning, to help provide a sense of connectedness. It is the center of the individual's conception of a *summum bonum,* of an ultimate aim or set of aims which makes life worthwhile, and it provides the person with a basis from which to judge good and evil. Every healthy individual has such a meaning-system, whether it be a cultural legacy or an existential creation. It need not be largely conscious or entirely organized, though the extent to which it is both may be one aspect of ego ideal development.

The *integrating function* between ego ideal and ego real is responsible for feedback between the two structures.[2] This integrating function includes a *self-system,* i.e., a collection of self-representations or self-schemas. The term "self," as used in this book, refers to the whole person, "body and soul." The notion of "self" has a long history in psychology, stemming back

---

[1] As the skeptical reader may have noticed, one could accept the validity of the first function of the ego ideal without embracing the second, without significantly altering model.

[2] One could just as easily view this "integrating function" as a subcomponent of the ego real, since, for example, self-representations are aspects of cognition, which is a process ascribed to the ego real. I have presented this integrating function as a separate structure to underscore its significance in psychic life. One could similarly collapse the self-needs and other-needs into the ego real, though this would be less useful in highlighting motivational processes.

to William James and George Herbert Mead. (For a review, see Epstein, 1973). Interest in the self has ebbed and flowed since the early part of the century, and the concept of self is currently experiencing a renaissance independently in both mainstream psychology (e.g., Markus, 1980, 1982) and psychoanalysis (see Kohut, 1971, 1977). Both schools have tended to make two errors regarding the self. The first is to confuse the actual person with her image of herself. One sees this in both Epstein's thinking (1973), for example, and in Kohut's. As one philosopher has noted (Edgley, personal communication), one cannot logically consider the self a set of representations of the self because that would define the self as a representation of a representation of a representation, *ad infinitum*. Just as one would not define a chair as a cognitive representation of a chair, one should not define the self as a cognitive representation of the self. As noted above, "self" is used in this book to denote the whole person, and "self-system" refers to a constellation of representations of self. The second error is to confound "self" as a set of self-schemas (i.e., a theory of one's self) with self as an omnibus term that includes everything in personality, particularly a sense of "will" or agency. The same term cannot refer to both a collection of representations and a decision-making function or source of action. Curiously, one sees this in the work of psychologists with such diverse perspectives as Kohut, Epstein, Sullivan (1953), and Markus. Both errors are endemic to most social cognition research on self-schemas, which views self-schemas as somehow motivating.[1]

An aspect of the self-system is what may be called a *self-concept,* a generalized representation of the self that may be organized as a prototype or set of prototypes (Cantor and Mischel, 1979), or as a somewhat representative set of self-schemas (within the constraints of cognitive and defensive biasing). In the healthy individual the self-concept is a more or less accurate – though never by any means perfect – portrait of the self. It is imperfect both for cognitive reasons (we can never form a perfect schema of anything in the world, including ourselves) and defensive reasons (conscious recognition of various aspects of the self would be very painful, so we alter our cognitions). Though many aspects of the self-system are likely to be hierarchically arranged (see Epstein, 1973), particularly in adults, the self-system is not entirely organized, and its degree of organization differs by individual. A person has numerous self-representations, connected to various memories, wishes, feelings, and thoughts, and many of these may

---

[1] People do process information though self-schemas which guide their perception, but these schemas do not directly motivate action. A person does not act stingy because he sees himself as stingy; he may see himself as stingy because he acts stingy. Self-schemas only guide behavior to the extent that they are related to ideal self-schemas, in which case it is not the self-schema per se but the anticipated pleasure at fulfilling the ideal self-schema or the affect generated by the discrepancy between ideal and self-schema that is motivating.

111

be inaccessible and unintegrated into a general self-concept to avoid painful affect. The self-system includes both the conscious self-representations studied by empirical researchers (e.g., Markus, 1982) and the various unconscious – and often dynamically unconscious (Freud, 1912) – self-representations that influence much psychopathology and everyday behavior. Recent research supports the view, long held by clinicians, that many self-representations are stable aspects of personality that persist over time (Costa and McCrae, 1980; Block, 1981).

Kihlstrom and Cantor (1983) have applied cognitive theory to the concept of self and have considered different ways in which self-representations could be organized. They contrast, for example, a view of self-concept as a person-concept embedded within a system of other person-concepts, with a view of self-concept as a category of singular importance through which all or most information is processed. They also discuss whether the self-concept is organized as a prototype or "exemplar" (Medin and Smith, 1984) and articulately describe the way specific self-representations may be associatively linked to other aspects of experience. They do not, however, distinguish self from self-concept, which leads them mistakenly to believe that one can settle the debate about whether or not a stable core of self or "identity" exists by studying the organization of self-representations. A person could have a consistent core of central personality processes and see himself as fragmented, just as someone could behave in inconsistent ways yet perceive himself as having a stable identity. Kihlstrom and Cantor also do not, as they acknowledge, shed any light on the influence of affect on the organization of self-representations, and a crucial task for future theory and research about the self-system must be to incorporate an understanding of split-off and repressed self-schemas that computer models of cognition and social cognition lead one to ignore.

The ego ideal sets standards by which the ego real "should" act. The individual experiences the positive comparison of ego ideal and self-concept or specific self-representations (depending on the situation and defensive requirements) as positive self-esteem (compare Jacobson, 1954, p. 123). A negative comparison may result in low self-esteem, shame, or guilt, depending on context and ego development. Freud expressed basically the same thought about the relationship between self-image, ideals, and guilt, though in slightly different terminology (1921, p. 63). These comparison processes which may result in either low or high self-evaluation often proceed unconsciously, resulting in affects the cause of which is outside of awareness.

Decades ago William James (1890) proposed that self-esteem is the ratio of one's success to one's pretensions. Judgments of self-esteem arising in this way are one form of the cognitive-evaluative mismatches described in Chapter 2. Carl Rogers and his colleagues developed a

112

methodology for testing this aspect of self-esteem (Rogers and Dymond, 1954), and they argued that the measured discrepancy between ideal self and perceived self can be used as an index of maladjustment. Matters are not, however, so simple: psychopaths and pathological narcissists frequently fuse self-concept and ideal self (see Kernberg, 1975 for clinical evidence; Katz, Zigler, and Zelk, 1975, for empirical documentation that children who evidence antisocial behavior have lower discrepancies between ideal self and self-concept than normal children), and older children manifest more of a discrepancy between the two than do younger children (Katz and Zigler, 1967; Katz, Zigler, and Zelk, 1975).

The self-system also often becomes attached to various positive and negative affects through socially mediated processes. (For empirical evidence of the relation between parental warmth and affection and child's self-esteem, see Thomas et al., 1974.) In particular, many of our feelings about ourselves are determined by identification. One of the most difficult changes to make through psychotherapy is the alteration of ingrained negative valuations of the self which arose through internalization of parental valuations or through distorted construal of these valuations. A child who is abused, for example, faces the choice between seeing himself as evil, worthless, and therefore deserving of abuse, and seeing those perpetrating the violence upon him as evil. The former often results in chronically low self-esteem and characterological depression and masochism, whereas the latter places the child in the position of perceiving himself as at the mercy of a social world which is capricious and malevolent. One may conceptualize aspects of this latter option as "learned helplessness" (Seligman, 1975), though that does not capture by any means the phenomenology of finding oneself abandoned in a hateful world. That a child faced with these alternatives often chooses the former and consequently must bias information so as to maintain this self-image is not so counterintuitive if one examines the paradoxical felicific calculus – the affective cost-benefit analysis or "optimizing" principle – that results in this choice. Self-loathing for many people is affectively preferable to paranoia: to hate oneself in order to preserve an identification with someone powerful but objectively hateful at least permits the twin satisfactions of the hope of penance and the belief that the apparent tormenter who controls one's life is actually benevolent. For a child to construct, rightly or wrongly, the phenomenological reality that his supposed protector is actually his enemy is to doom himself to life in a world of tormentors, in which relationships with other people can result only in frustration, pain, and crushed hopes.[1]

---

[1] These very partial suggestions on the psychodynamics of child abuse, derived from working with patients who were abused, may help make sense of the paradoxical fact, explained in part by attachment theory, that abused children tend to cling to the very adults who abuse them, and that as adults they often suffer from chronic problems with self-esteem.

113

Judgments of self-esteem may occur at any level of generality (e.g., "I am a despicable person," "I am not very ethical," "I was not very honest in my dealings with him"). As these examples suggest, judgments of low moral self-esteem tend to evoke guilt, whereas that is not true of other aspects of self-esteem ("I am a poor soccer player") unless they are interrelated with moral or quasi-moral values ("my father expected me to be a professional athlete, and I let him down").

The level of generality of a judgment of self-esteem depends upon the level of generality of the component of ideal self that has been activated, and as a general rule, the higher the level of generality, the more powerful the affective response. I will suffer much less in terms of self-esteem if I determine that I will never be an adequate goalie, rather than that I am physically incompetent.

Though some researchers have tried to construct general measures of self-esteem (for reviews, see Wiley, 1979; Harter, 1983), the possibility of adequately doing so is doubtful since people differentially weigh different categories and levels of generality in making self-esteem determinations (see Rosenberg, 1979). For example, I am, in fact, a positively wretched soccer player,[1] though I thoroughly enjoy playing the game and subject myself to it regularly. I am, more generally, a rather mediocre athlete, and were I to rest my more global sense of self-esteem on my performance on the soccer field or the basketball court, mine would be a rather miserable lot. In contrast, a young man who frequently shows up at our weekly soccer games is appropriately named Jesús, and he would be depriving himself of a great deal of happiness were he not to emphasize his prowess at soccer in making judgments of self-esteem. Judgments of self-esteem are influenced, of course, by relatively short-term activation of self-schemas and ideal self-schemas, so that on the soccer field I am apt to feel less content with myself than when teaching.

People gain significant control over their self-evaluations by learning to limit snowball effects of minor failings, so that a momentary failure is not converted into a crisis of confidence. Harter (1981, 1983) has proposed, and provided data to show, that children have difficulty making discrete judgments in this regard and gradually learn (through, one may suspect, both cognitive maturation in ability to classify, and cognitively mediated conditioning through repeatedly experiencing severe distress caused by minor failures) to separate categories and level of generality. Psychoanalysts have similarly proposed that regulation of self-esteem is a basic ego function (see Reich, 1960), one that is often particularly deficient in people with certain character disorders. Such people will frequently report the devastating impact of a seemingly trivial remark that shattered their sense

---

[1] I will not list citations for this point, but I could amass quite a few references to attest to it.

of self-worth, and they appear to have minimal "reserves" of self-esteem to cushion even relatively minor threats to self-esteem.

A person can also gain some control over self-esteem valuations by altering and shaping set-goals to accord with reality constraints or avoiding situations that trigger low self-esteem. Had I maintained the unrealistic goal of being good at soccer, I would surely have given the game up years ago. Instead, I am pleased now when I score an occasional goal, make a decent pass, or avoid kicking the ball into my own goal. If I were unable to regulate my set-goals in this way, I would simply have to avoid elicitation of cognitive-evaluative mismatches. Years ago William James discussed the paradox of the "second oarsman or second pugilist in the world" who is "shamed to death" for losing a match, while "yonder puny fellow" who can beat no one suffers no chagrin about losing a match. James concludes, "With no attempt there can be no failure; with no failure, no humiliation" (1890, p. 310). The ability to regulate self-esteem is another developmental line that could in part be studied empirically.

Self-esteem, like ideal self, is likely to include a number of subcategories, though these will differ, as will their relative weightings, by person and culture. Studies in Western cultures have typically found major categories of self-esteem relating roughly to judgments about morality, competence, power, physical appearance, and interpersonal relations. Coopersmith (1967), for example, isolated four dimensions of self-esteem: competence, virtue, power, and significance (the acceptance, attention, and affection of others). Harter (1983) distinguishes self-esteem categories of competence, power or control, moral worth, and acceptance, and she argues, following Epstein (1973), that these categories are likely themselves to include subcategories (e.g., cognitive, physical, and social competence).

The ego real, the third subcomponent of ego processes, serves two functions: cognition and the regulation of emotion. The first function, cognition, will not be discussed extensively here. The ego real is the structure that responds to affective signals and sets control mechanisms in motion. As argued earlier, these mechanisms may be of three sorts: behaviors, coping mechanisms, and defense mechanisms.

Different situations and set-goals are likely to evoke different control mechanisms or type of mechanism. Some motives are fairly straightforward and require for their fulfillment in a given situation simple "scripted" behaviors to make use of readily available resources, e.g., peering into the refrigerator when one is hungry. Other situations may require more complex cognitive activity, as when the refrigerator is empty. In this case, the individual, cognizant of the feeling of hunger, will form a "plan" (Miller, Gallanter, and Pribram, 1960), such as going to the store, which will alleviate the mismatch between desire and actuality. These are the types of situations examined most frequently by cognitive-behavioral theorists, and if one intends personality theory as a broad schema through which to process information about people, then a theory of personality must be able to account for them. They may, in fact, comprise the majority of our thoughts and actions. Yet they are only part of the picture, the part that fits best with the rationalistic psychology inherited from the Enlightenment.

Many other situations and set-goals evoke far more complex processes because fulfillment is either not easily attained or conflicts with other valued ends. In these cases the sequence from feeling to behavioral response may be far more serpentine than activation of a script. A person will tend to choose the combination of behaviors, coping mechanisms, and defenses which she believes will "optimize"[1] affect. Such decision-making, as argued in Chapter 2, is generally only partially conscious and is a function of the ego real.

The utility or "optimizing value" of a coping or defense mechanism is appraised in terms of both its benefits (minimizing unpleasant affects or maximizing pleasant ones in the given situation) and its costs (distortion of cognitions or inattention to relevant stimuli which may lead to subsequent unpleasant emotions). The responses people use in various situations are likely to be arranged hierarchically in descending order of utility. In other words, they are ranked and evoked according to their perceived "adaptiveness," and in relatively normal development, these control mechanisms develop in efficiency as the person matures. This has been most clearly perceived regarding the defense mechanisms first examined by Freud and codified in Anna Freud's pathbreaking work on the *Ego and the Mechanisms of Defense* (1936; see also Vaillant's developmental-hierarchical model of defenses, 1977). Denial, uncontrolled fantasy confused with reality, and projection, for example, represent primitive mechanisms of defense adaptive only for a person with minimal tolerance for painful affect or confronted with massive affective threat. Defensive humor is an example of a far less reality-distorting, and therefore higher level or more mature mode of defense (Vaillant, 1977).[2] When a painful affect such as

---

[1] I use this term as a shorthand to mean maximization of pleasurable, and minimization of unpleasurable emotion. I use the term reluctantly, because it best conveys what I have in mind, but it is certain to come back to haunt me when some critic will contend that my use of a term from economics proves that this is one more bourgeois theory of human nature modeled after capitalist "acquisitive man."

[2] The term "defense mechanism" is retained here because it is a very useful concept, though its scope is considerably narrowed. The notion of defense in this context arose during a period in psychoanalytic thinking that viewed the ego as a weak, beleaguered structure, jostled about by its three masters (id, superego, and reality). Ego psychology, in contrast, ascribed more power and control to the formerly hapless ego. The notion of defense obscures the positive, adaptive aspects of the ego real's regulatory mechanisms, which I have instead referred to as coping and behavioral strategies. Psychoanalysis, as a psychology that emerged from the clinic, lacks a language to deal with adaptive functioning. A person who is disciplined is obsessive, one who does not let life get him or her down is

anxiety occurs, according to this model, ego processes ideally activate the most efficient – and often the most recently developed, i.e., developmentally most sophisticated – defense mechanism. If this mechanism fails or is anticipated to fail, the anxiety activates the next most efficient mechanism, and so on until the anxiety is eliminated or brought within a manageable level.[1] The model here resembles an economic analysis of a company owning multiple plants of varying marginal revenue products, with demand activating the most efficient plants first. I hasten to add that this is a simplified account, since defenses are flexibly created to meet momentary demands and are thus not all easily taxonimized. Any behavior or mental operation can be used defensively, but in general, the less a defense pays heed to reality, the less mature it can be said to be.

The developmental progression of control mechanisms, from the relatively inefficient to the relatively mature, can be seen in coping and behavioral responses as well, where the general maturational sequence is from behavior to intrapsychic transformations where the latter are appropriate. In other words, the child heightens her control over her impulses and emotions through various mental operations. The increasing ability to do so results from both cognitive maturation and affective selective retention of useful procedures (i.e., those that help regulate emotion are reinforced). In Mischel's delay of gratification experiments, for example, a child will be rewarded for having evolved mechanisms to control his momentary affects and impulses.[2]

Aside from ample clinical documentation, evidence from a variety of quarters demonstrates the developmental shift from behavioral to mental control operations.[3] The idea of progressive interiorization of action is

---

more on the hysterical side, a person who is intelligent is intellectualized, and so on. In many cases these are appropriate inferences, but to describe adaptiveness with the language of pathology can lead one astray. To speak, for example, of humor as a defense is often to miss the point, as anyone realizes who has had the unfortunate experience of joking with a psychologist or psychiatrist and receiving an analysis instead of a laugh. Humor, like much of behavior, can be used either defensively or to enrich life. The defense terminology often implies that personality is nothing but a precipitate of psychic battles or an accumulation of defenses. This is one way of analyzing character formation, but as an exclusive approach, it veils the extent to which people seek objects and experiences in ways that are not "defensive." I have therefore narrowed the use of the term to include only those emotion-regulating processes that are unconscious and must remain so for their efficacy.

[1] Mischel's (1984) recent observation of the breakdown of appropriate strategies and the resort to inappropriate aggression among a group of troubled children fits in well with this conception and documents individual differences in patterns of affect regulation.

[2] By "impulses" I mean actions set in motion by a wish, cognitive-evaluative mismatch, or other dynamic cognitive-affective schema.

[3] I am, of course, not suggesting that children use only the former, and adults, the latter. We all use both immature and mature modes of affect-regulation, though people differ on the extent to which they use different levels of control mechanisms chronically. Persistent overtaxing of capacities will lead to overutilization of immature control mechanisms, both because they become routinized and because the person has formed expectancies about environmental conditions.

central to Piaget's theory of cognitive development, though he does not stress its emotional consequences. Luria (1961) has argued for the importance of self-directed speech in gaining self-control, contending that children at first speak aloud to restrain themselves (as their parents do) and later "interiorize" this speech through intrapsychic self-direction. Kopp (cited in Harter, 1983) has studied children from 18 to 36 months of age in delay of gratification experiments and has found that by age three children make use of a number of behavioral strategies to control their impulses, such as sitting on their hands, singing, averting gaze, and talking to themselves. This is in marked contrast to the older children studied by Mischel and his colleagues, cited earlier, who could make use of more complex intrapsychic strategies.

Harris and Olthof (1982) asked children directly about their strategies for regulating emotion, questioning them about how they might make themselves stop feeling unhappy or angry. Children of all ages suggested behavioral strategies (e.g., go see a friend to become happy), but mental strategies were suggested almost exclusively by older children. Other studies (see Hoffman, 1979) have shown that older children are more likely to recognize that helping a person in distress will relieve their own empathic distress than two- and four-year-olds.

The ability to control one's impulses rests in part upon the development of strategies to modulate the intensity of momentary affects. Studies of the development of anger and aggression consistently show that younger children respond with more diffuse aggression (see Hartup, 1977), probably in response to a more diffuse, less modulated emotional signal. Izard (1978) has observed a similar trend regarding the experience of pain, noting a "change from diffuse distress that totally dominates the two-month-old during acute pain following inoculation to the more organized and centered distress experience of the six-month-old in the same situation" (pp. 404-5). Sullivan (1953) argued that "somnolent detachment" (falling asleep, exhausted, after prolonged crying) and apathy are primitive ways an infant copes with diffuse distress.

The ability to modulate emotion rests in part upon cognitive maturation and experience. An infant who perceives his environment to be inconsistent or malevolent will have more difficulty learning to modulate emotion because he lacks the expectation that his distress will be alleviated. Bruner (1981) postulates the importance of interpersonal expectancies in infants as young as three or four months, in modulating distress. He has observed that the infant's cry at four months often becomes less insistent and is punctuated with pauses in anticipation of adult response. The inability of a child to develop interpersonal expectancies of having his needs met during the first few years of life—whether through ineptness or malevolence of caretakers, a constitutional over-intensity of emotional experience that impedes development of modulatory techniques, a deficit in affect-modulation through some other cause, or an interaction of these – will frequently lead to an impulse disorder. From the child's point of view, this is quite reasonable: if he has no expectation that his wishes or needs will be fulfilled later, he has no reason to modulate current demands in anticipation of future rewards.

What should be clear from this analysis of ego real regulatory processes is that these are "adaptive" processes (see Hartmann, 1939) in the sense that the person is trying, within the context of her experience, to maximize pleasure and minimize pain. I use the phrase, "within the context of her experience," to underscore that we must always take a developmental approach in trying to understand the way a person chooses to manage affect through behavioral, coping, or defensive actions. Every effort to manage affect (for example every defense) has a history, and it is this history which interacts with current realities to produce a response. If a certain defense mechanism or coping strategy tends to work, a person is going to prefer that mechanism or strategy to others that have not been as useful in the past. This means that a person is not likely to try every control mechanism afresh in every situation and is instead likely to develop a defensive or coping "style." This is not by any means to imply that people have no response flexibility. A person is very likely to learn that certain behaviors, defenses, and coping strategies work in certain situations, and the extent to which a person generalizes particular strategies beyond these situations is an aspect of ego rigidity on which one would expect to find individual differences (and indeed, work by the Blocks on "ego rigidity" documents precisely that; see Block and Block, 1980).

Behavioral, coping, and defense mechanisms are thus likely to be significantly routinized, and the pattern of their routinization (including the degree of its flexibility) constitutes the personality's "deep structure" which one may call *character*. As can readily be seen, routinization itself can be used defensively: the person can essentially put himself on "automatic pilot" and avoid any affective turbulence. The line between habit, coping style, and ritual is also indistinct, as routinized procedures may become symbolically charged methods of warding off various perceived evils.

Living would be impossible without significant routinization. A person who thought about every stimulus impinging upon him and experienced affect with every conceivable move could not survive. Routinized standard operating procedures thus arise to reduce anxiety by reducing choice, and they may become dysfunctional if overused and rigidified. Once instituted, certain habits or rituals become valued in themselves, so that the breach of them becomes itself a source of anxiety.

Ego real processes respond in large measure to three sets of affects, those relating to self-needs and other-needs and those that arise because of "disequilibrium" or conflict within the ego itself. In terms of self-needs, the need for food provides a good example. When level of satiation declines, this need becomes motivating. What this means is that a mismatch arises between desire and actuality, such that needs exceed current fulfillment of the desire beyond a certain acceptable "equilibrium" level.[1] The result is a feeling, namely hunger. It is this feeling, not the physiological necessity for nutrition per se, that sets ego control processes in motion.

A wide variety of other-needs activate various ego control mechanisms. The analysis of mourning in Chapter 2 pointed to several other-need set-goals rendered unattainable by death of a loved one. These include desires for proximity to the person, desires for a certain level of social interaction, and concerns for the well-being of the deceased. Mourning involves an equilibration process through which various wished-for states (in this case, other-need set-goals) must be brought into line with the experienced actual state. Robert Kavanaugh has proposed a seven-stage model of the mourning process which views the individual as passing through periods of shock, disorganization, volatile emotions, guilt, loss and loneliness, relief, and reestablishment (1972, p. 107). Whether all of these stages always occur (and in an invariant sequence) is a question which need not concern us here. What is important is that Kavanaugh's model underscores not only an observation made earlier, that a number of negative affects seem to cluster together under acute distress, as in the grief experience, but also that the process of mourning is one of equilibration, in which the person must ultimately reconcile himself to a severe and permanent end to satisfaction of various set-goals.

Loneliness is another example of an affect evoked by frustration of other-needs. For simplicity, one may argue that a particular person desires a certain "amount" (including, to oversimplify, both quality and quantity) of human contact or social interaction. Different people require different types and amounts of interaction. Often the social isolate who claims to need no one is responding defensively to a conflict between a desperate need for intimacy and a history of frustration in human relationships. A patient who lived through his forties as a recluse insisted that he needed no one and would keep people away with barbed comments. Several years of psychotherapy uncovered the defensive nature of his isolation and revealed (or perhaps "uncovered") a warm and sensitive man who was so desperate to be loved that he would quickly and voraciously cling to women who showed interest in him, while pushing people away with his stinging remarks so they would stay away, thus preventing him from needing and

---

[1] Much of this process is obviously extra-conscious or nonexperiential, involving biologically programmed creation of feeling states through homeostatic mechanisms.

caring about them. It was both gratifying and fascinating to see his new-found (or perhaps newly rediscovered) gentleness toward others begin to spread to his relations with himself (as evidenced, for example, in his willingness for the first time to spend money on himself).

Hoffman (1980) has recently elaborated the notion of an empathic distress response, which from the perspective of the model developed here represents another affective response signaling the disturbance of an other-need set-goal. According to Hoffman, an individual may conceive a minimally acceptable standard of well-being for significant others, and if the person perceives the situation of the latter to fall below that minimum, the resulting affect will be an empathic distress response that may motivate the person to act. Hoffman views the generalization of this affective distress response to include people not personally known by the individual as an aspect of moral development.

A third set of needs to which ego processes respond includes those that arise because of "disequilibrium" or conflict within the ego itself, in particular those produced by a mismatch between ego ideal and perceived reality. As noted earlier, Freud pointed out that guilt often ensues from such a mismatch, and a number of psychologists from differing points of view, notably Carl Rogers (1954) and George Kelly (1955), have recognized the impact of discrepancies of this sort on self-esteem and the consequent effort to avoid ideal self/self-image disparities. From the perspective of the current approach, this can be understood in terms of the relationship between an ideal self-image (an aspect of the ego ideal) and a particular self-schema, the self-concept, or self-system referred to before as part of the integrating function "poised" between ego real and ego ideal.

To elaborate a previous example, suppose Joe College believes that he should not cheat on examinations but one day does so nonetheless. The negative affect that will probably arise is guilt, which will, in turn, set in motion ego real processes to eliminate the affect. One such process would be simply to suppress the emotion or repress the fact that he broke the rules. Another likely response would involve the defense mechanism of rationalization: he could tell himself that he would have done that well anyway had he had time to study, or that his instructor is such a jerk that he deserves to have students cheat, etc. Another response would be to do penance behaviorally or intrapsychically, by semideliberately doing poorly on the next exam to balance things out, by confessing to the professor, or by flagellating himself psychologically. Experimental research has demonstrated the use of both altruistic behavior and confession in the reduction of guilt (Regan, 1971). Other studies have documented the use of defensive processes in the maintenance of self-esteem (see Snyder and Smith, 1982), such as external attribution (i.e., attributing responsibility less to oneself)

121

for the harm done to another person during an experiment (Harvey, Harris, and Barnes, 1975).[1]

This is a rather everyday, "surface level" example of a process which is often unconscious and far less tied to daily adult existence. People often unconsciously hold themselves accountable for all kinds of actions and realities that were beyond their control, were egocentrically construed as resulting from their own behaviors or intentions, or occurred many years ago. A patient,[2] for example, lived with the guilt stemming from his belief (long forgotten) that he was responsible for driving his mother crazy, when in reality he was merely a child at the time and his mother's illness was probably in large measure biologically based. Many people with masochistic character structures spend their lives doing penance for alleged sins from early in their lives. Hurting themselves serves two functions. First, it allows them to identify with beloved parents who were often abusive or perceived as abusive. Secondly, if one conceives of oneself as bad, one can be, if not good, at least better, by recognizing and punishing oneself for one's badness. Nietzsche once said something to the effect that he who despises himself nevertheless esteems himself as a despiser. A patient once told me, quite similarly, that "the only way to be perfect is to admit how bad you are." In terms of the model presented here, in such a case guilt or low self-esteem activates self-punitive control mechanisms that, paradoxically, make the person feel good by atoning for his badness, and thus reduces the guilt or bad feelings about himself.

Another affect relating to ego processes is a form of anxiety stemming from a severe disturbance of the self-other balance of the ego ideal and/or a general concern about ego dysfunction (i.e., the feeling that one cannot cope or is falling apart). The defense mechanisms activated by such anxiety are likely to be much more generalized to the entire personality, and regressions to previous ego states are not uncommon. Such regressions by no means necessarily signal pathology. Adolescents, for example, fre-

---

[1] I do hope the reader will forgive my tireless (or tedious, depending on one's point of view) citation of studies documenting theoretical notions that she or he has probably recognized from personal experience since middle childhood. I am a half-breed (some might say mutt) who believes in a combination of empiricism and rationalism/symbolic interpretation. There are, however, pedigreed empiricists among us who do not believe in the existence of any phenomenon until it has been documented experimentally, and as I am trying to offer a theory of personality that will guide experimental research, I am bound by threat of excommunication to carry out the rituals of the discipline.

[2] I use the word "patient" here with reluctance since it can suggest a sometimes inappropriate medical model of the etiology and treatment of psychological problems. The frequently used term "client," however, strikes me as equally inappropriate, as if the person coming into therapy were a businessperson seeking a consultant, or a constituent seeking a favor from a corrupt official or "patron." My use of the word "patient" thus stems less from any conviction than from a situational factor, namely that I have recently been working in a medical setting. Chalk one up for situationism.

quently regress in the face of a surge of new feelings and impulses, altered cognitions, and in many cultures a widening of interpersonal relationships. Differentiation from early objects (Blos, 1967) is also significant in breaking down childhood response patterns, defenses, self-images, and ego ideal standards. As a consequence, adolescents often display extremely self-indulgent behavior, sometimes in alternation with severely ascetic behavior (Anna Freud, 1958).

Ego real processes thus respond to three "masters," to rephrase Freud: affects relating to self-needs, other-needs, and ego processes. They also respond to a fourth master, which includes those affects (often culturally transmitted) such as aesthetic values, that do not fall into any of these three categories. Behavior, as argued in Chapter 2, is thus primarily motivated by an affect, a set of affects, or a cognitive anticipation of affective consequences, not by "reason" alone.

A person who lacks developed anticipatory affect mechanisms may appear short-sighted and impulsive, but he or she is no less "rational" in the *aims* he or she is pursuing than the person who can anticipate the future effects of current action on later desires. Both people are trying to fulfill set-goals, and both are trying to maximize pleasurable affect and minimize painful affect, but only one of them is weighing future affective states into the balance. (The ability to anticipate emotion is another important developmental line.) The relative valuation of present and future affect, however, is a matter of individual judgment, a component of the decision calculus of the ego real.

This whole issue of what a person does with an affect when she gets one has a great deal of bearing on psychopathology and cognitive style. The style clinicians call "hysterical" is generally characterized by cognitive and behavioral impulsiveness, a tendency to find certain affects so pressing that something must be done immediately. As noted in Chapter 2, this often occurs in the cognitive realm: not only does the person with an "hysterical style" frequently repress or "forget" facts that cause anxiety, but he or she appears relatively unwilling to wrestle with cognitive ambiguity, instead dealing with more global images, changing beliefs to suit the occasion, and simply ignoring inconsistencies (Shapiro, 1965). The person whose style is "obsessive," in contrast, often tries to deal with affects by simply shutting them off. "Obsessives" may avoid intimacy because it can awaken affect, and they tend to weigh every conceivable detail in calculating every move.

Ego real processes, then, include a pattern of affect regulation usually called "character." The other function of the ego real is cognition, which is certainly related to processes of affect regulation. Cognitive development permits far more complex and effective ways of coping with emotions. Similarly, understanding something is one way of reducing anxiety relating to it, and cognitive ambiguity is highly anxiety-provoking. The question of

123

whether cognition is always "defensive" is the issue behind Hartmann's notion of a conflict-free ego sphere (1939) and behind the debates about whether cognition is independently motivated or is "drive-centered" in the literature attempting to reconcile Freud and Piaget (see Wolff, 1960; Greenspan, 1979). Much of this depends on whether one wants to perceive the glass as half empty or half full. Cognition is undoubtedly an effective mode of, or aid in, satisfying desires; cognitive activity also operates without any obvious incentives, as with Tolman's rats who formed cognitive maps in the absence of manifest reinforcement.

An example of ego real control mechanisms in response to multiple affective signals should help make all of this more concrete and relevant, as well as to show how the theory of personality proposed here can appropriate the most valuable aspect of psychoanalytic method and practice, namely the ability to explore the subtleties of unconscious processes and transformations. This example is from my own clinical work and is intended to illustrate, albeit very briefly and certainly not in much detail, the way the model of ego processes presented here can provide insight into clinical material of comparable depth to that of psychoanalytic psychology.

The patient is a tall black woman in her early forties who has a borderline personality disorder (see Kernberg, 1975; Stone, 1981). Descriptively, this means that, despite above-average intelligence, she has been unable to hold steady employment, has a history of unstable interpersonal relations, has a long history of self-destructive behaviors, and relatively often becomes overpowered by affects and motives over which she has minimal control. In terms of ego real functions, despite high level cognitive ability, her reality-testing becomes severely distorted in the presence of affects which she has difficulty modulating. Her internal representations or schemas of people in her life are highly variable, at times significantly distorted by intense emotions so that in the presence of such emotions she manifests what Kernberg has called "splitting," i.e., the separation of object-images into those which are all good and those which are all bad. Even in less stressful moments her object representations are biased by affective factors more significantly than those of people with more intact ego processes.

Her ego ideal structure is fragmented. She described on numerous occasions an existential emptiness and confusion about who she would like to be and what she should do with her life which one would not expect to see as a continuous aspect of normal postadolescent functioning. On various occasions she is tormented by primitive internalized and constructed images of herself as loathsome and destructive, which are often accompanied by self-punitive acts set in motion by ego ideal mismatches. As she has put it herself, the people whom she hoped to emulate as a child and who defined for her what is right and wrong turned out, in her estimation, to be vile and untrustworthy themselves. This left her, in her words, with "missing parts" of herself, or "gaps" in her personality (cf. Kohut's notion of missing segments of psychic structure, 1971). Dynamically, a central issue relates simultaneously to her being-in-the-world and being-with-others: how can she remain in a social world with people who, when she comes to be attached to them, either "die, abandon me, go crazy, or abuse me?" Her developmental history, exacerbated by her construal of it, rendered this an appropriate question, and it is a question that permeates borderline, schizoid, and psychopathic dynamics. It is also a question that cannot be adequately understood either in terms of "modeling," "social skills," "tasks," or "coping" on the one hand; or in terms of psychosexual stages or primitive drives and their derivatives on the other.

Those acquainted with principles of psychodynamic psychotherapy and with the treatment of patients with this level of pathology in particular will recognize that beyond supportive work aimed at helping her manage life crises, an important way to try to alter her character structure (and ultimately her behavior) is to deal extensively in the transference with her. By this I do not mean interpreting her actions in therapy as displacements from her father or mother, though this certainly occurred at times. Rather, I mean working with her relationship with the therapist as someone significant in her life in whom she is desperate to have hope, yet repeatedly interprets situations (such as the therapist's vacations) as evidence that she has placed her hope in vain and will only be fooled again. She had been treated with other therapeutic modes in the past, including both drug treatment and cognitive-behavioral therapy for her depression, but the end result was that she came to me following hospitalization because of another suicide attempt. One of the primary aims of psychotherapy with her was to have her participate in a relationship with someone who could be continuous for her, who could survive her love, her fury, her dependence, and her withdrawal without either dying, abandoning her, going crazy, or retaliating.

In the particular event that I would like briefly to explore, certain events which will not be described here had precipitated a crisis in the transference centered around two opposing feelings: she was both furious with me and found herself growing more and more attached. Her fury caused her to want to run from therapy for three reasons. First, she cared about me and was terribly frightened about what might happen to me if her rage were unleashed. In more formal terms, she experienced a cognitive-evaluative mismatch between a set-goal of my welfare and an expectancy of the consequences of her rage, which produced an affective state including fear and anxiety akin to Hoffman's empathic distress response. Secondly, ego ideal prohibitions against anger and violence (which for her were synonymous) and her own fear that she could not rein in her rage produced another

125

anticipatory affect that could best be handled by avoiding me entirely. Thirdly, for reasons stemming from her own history, she was scared that she would be overwhelmed by her anger and would lose her control over herself and become crazy. This is the form of ego-anxiety described earlier which involves fears of ego dissolution.

Her growing attachment to me also induced her to want to bolt therapy. As noted above, because she feared her own anger, her desire to protect me contributed, paradoxically, to her need to stay away. At the same time, she needed to defend against her attachment to, and dependence on me and her hope that I would be (again to use her words) her "protector" because of an anticipation or "expectancy" that I, like everyone else, would not continue to be there for her. This is somewhat akin to premature mourning for a loved object whom one shuts out of one's life for fear of losing him (see Lindemann, 1944).

More concretely, the events of a two week period suggested the working of a curiously syllogistic "psycho-logic" with two premises: "You are not abandoning me," and "I am a terrible and dangerous person," both of which she expressed fairly directly. The latter stemmed from primitive self-images relating to early experiences and identifications. The inconsistency between the two premises necessitated a cognitive or behavioral transformation to provide resolution. Five such transformations arose. The structure of the syllogism is as follows: if you are really not abandoning me and seem to care for me, and if I am awful and dangerous, then (1) you must be crazy; (2) you must be getting something, at my expense, which motivates you to stay in this relationship; (3) I had better run in order to protect you; (4) I had better drive you away for your own good by being hostile; or (5) you must be a wonderful person to put up with me. Indeed, in the space of four or five sessions, every one of these five transformations emerged. She expressed both fears, that I must be crazy and that I must have an ulterior motive, in fairly direct terms. She also skipped sessions and seriously contemplated stopping treatment, though her only consciousness of her motivation to do so was a diffuse feeling of fear. When she started coming again to her sessions, she displayed an enormous amount of hostility which only subsided when we explored the meanings and functions of this response. Alternating with many of these responses, she idealized me, seeing me as someone who must be superhuman to tolerate her despite her unworthiness.

The analysis of this example provided here is, of course, only the tip of a psychic iceberg. The patient's feelings and behaviors in this instance were clearly overdetermined, and I have selectively called attention only to certain aspects of some very complex compromise-formations. Yet this example has, I hope, suggested that the model proposed here may shed light not only on the higher level processes involved in everyday existence but also on the less "rational," often less conscious and more complex phenomena that constitute much of our psychic life.

To summarize, the model of the structure and dynamics of personality distinguishes five structures: the self-needs, a hierarchically arranged set of individual needs; the other-needs, which include social needs; the ego real, comprised of various cognitive and affect-regulation processes; the ego ideal, the psychic center of morality (and immortality) which establishes an ideal balance between the needs and desires of self and other; and an integrating function responsible for comparing ego ideal and self-system schemas.

Any adequate theory of personality must be not only structural and dynamic but developmental. The following chapter will now examine the development of personality, focusing on the relation between the development of narcissism and object relations, moral judgment and values, and ego processes.

4 The Development of Personality, Narcissism, and Moral Judgment

THROUGHOUT PSYCHOLOGY'S BRIEF history the notion of "stages," invariant sequences of unfolding needs or competences, has been an integral part of theorizing about psychological development. The field's two most imposing intellectual figures, Freud and Piaget, both proposed stage theories, one of psychosexual, and the other of cognitive development.

In recent years psychologists have begun to wonder whether in fact the invariance and orderliness of stages is a property of the object of study or an artifact of the schema-building of the observer (see Flavell, 1971, 1982; Keil, 1981). Of course, it is both: science, like all human cognition, entails the imposition of categories of thought upon sensory experience to make it meaningful and manageable. It was Piaget's genius that allowed him to discern an orderly sequence in cognitive development, but he was surely constrained by the "facts" to put something like formal operations at the end and not at the beginning of that sequence.

When a theorist introduces a term such as stage, just as when he introduces a concept like "structure," he must be careful to delineate precisely what he means, so that the concept does not, like a malevolent spirit, live on beyond its usefulness, wreak havoc on those who make its acquaintance, and elude the grasp of even those who invoke it frequently. In this chapter I will, indeed, invoke this charmed metaphor in a way perhaps best described through another metaphor. The conception is of sequential sets of processes that shape current functioning much as a series of waves shapes a shoreline. As one wave recedes, the next submerges it, laps up against the shore, and remolds the landscape upon which the first left its mark. In other words, a set of processes will be seen on the horizon, will reach a crest, and will gradually recede, to be replaced by another.

Like all metaphors, this one has its limitations, which should be made explicit from the start to avoid misinterpretations. First, it cannot illustrate fixations or developmental arrests, in which a wave fails to recede in its proper time. Secondly, it does not accommodate regressions, in which

128

previous waves return to the beach. Finally, the metaphor lacks an image of maturity, though it nicely illustrates the constant flow of experience that constitutes human life and perennially molds and remolds personality.

More formally, stages are sequentially organized ways of feeling, thinking, and behaving in the evolution of structures. In other words, they are waxing and waning methods of carrying out particular functions. To argue, as I did in Chapter 3, that certain control mechanisms develop from overt behaviors to intrapsychic transformations, is to say that the *method* for fulfilling the *function* of affect-regulation changes from action (e.g., sitting on one's hands) to thought (e.g., thinking about something else). At younger ages the child will rely primarily on the former, while at older ages he will use a combination of the two; and if mental strategies fail, he will resort once again to behaviors.

The aim of this chapter is to enunciate a theory of personality development, one that draws on the rich clinical and theoretical understanding developed over several decades by psychoanalytic clinicians as well as the growing empirical literature on child development that has enriched our knowledge of the way children think, feel, and behave. The chapter will begin with a discussion of current approaches to the development of narcissism and object relations, moral judgment, and ego processes, and will then show how a synthesis of these perspectives and recent research can paint a fuller picture of personality development.

The Development of Narcissism, Moral Judgment, and Ego Processes: Current Perspectives

A brief discussion of a persistent and growing problem in psychoanalytic theory provides a useful introduction to current perspectives on personality development. Classical psychoanalysis is a theory of drives and their vicissitudes, which argues that personality development is synonymous with psychosexual development. Since the 1940s, psychoanalytic theoreticians have been steadily recognizing the importance of understanding ego development and the development of object relations, and it has become increasingly clear that the latter aspects of maturation cannot be understood in psychosexual terms, however interlocked they may be. (For a masterful presentation of the history of this state of affairs and the inconsistent assumptions held by drive theorists and object relations theorists, see Greenberg and Mitchell, 1983.)

Classical psychoanalytic technique was intended to be applied only to patients with a certain level of "ego strength," who could tolerate delving into their fantasies and forming a highly emotion-laden relationship with the analyst. The classical model suggested that one could understand the pathology of these neurotic patients by looking for points of psychosexual fixation. A problem arose when psychoanalysts and psychodynamic psychotherapists began treating and charting the theoretical waters of pathology at a lower, more insidious "preoedipal" level. Cartographers with different tools and vantage points created an atlas of often conflicting maps of this region, which constitutes ego psychology and object relations theory.

Neurotic disorders presuppose, according to psychoanalytic theory, a conflict between desires and prohibitions, between impulses and the collection of identifications and ideals Freud called the superego. The problem with extending this line of thinking to "preoedipal" pathology (i.e., more severe than neurotic, and assumed to reflect psychic defects prior to the Oedipal years) is that many people with this kind of more severe pathology lack the solid core of identifications hypothesized to create the ego and superego and seem to face a much more malignant source of psychic pain than the neurotic: the question of whether they can survive, as a whole person with a complete identity, in a world of people who at times seem to them bent on their destruction, and whether they can experience their feelings – whether of hate, love, desperate need, or lust – without impulsively acting upon them, destroying, engulfing, or being engulfed.

Clinicians who worked with these people thus came to believe that what they were observing in their patients was a defect that began in the first years of life, before the establishment of morals embodied in the superego, when the child has to negotiate a place in the world as someone who is separate yet attached, and dependent yet able to trust that he will be cared for. Many theorists came to the belief that this defect ran much deeper than a neurotic solution to unrealistic wishes.

A model of psychosexual stages cannot alone account for pathology at this level, and the problem for psychoanalytic theory is the recognition that the hypothesized fixations of neurotics can occur at the same time as the developmental arrests of people with more severe pathology. If the era of the fixation does not, then, account for level of pathology, as psychoanalysis assumed, something else must account for the difference between someone who is neurotic and someone with a borderline disorder. A neurotic, according to the theory, can be orally fixated, which means a pathology arising in the first year of life. One sometimes encounters borderline patients with "anal" level pathology which is psychosexually more advanced, who are comulpusive, tightly defended to the point of brittleness, and prone to sadistic behavior and outbursts. In what way, then, does the neurotic differ from the borderline, the narcissistic character, the schizoid personality, or the psychopath? I would contend that the difference lies in the level of narcissism and object relations, moral functioning, and ego development. The present chapter will begin by examining current approaches to the understanding of each of those domains, and will then offer a developmental model that encompasses them.

130

THE DEVELOPMENT OF NARCISSISM AND OBJECT RELATIONS

In his *Analysis of the Self* Heinz Kohut relates the case of a patient described as suffering from a narcissistic disorder:

> Patient C., for example, had the following dream during a period when he was looking forward to being publicly honored and celebrated: "The question was raised of finding a successor for me. I thought: How about God?" (1971, p. 149)

Jean-Paul Sartre writes in all earnestness, "The best way to conceive of the fundamental project of human reality is to say that man is the being whose project it is to be God" (1957, p. 63). Patient C. has been diagnosed a narcissist; Sartre, a philosopher. One may question the validity of their diagnoses or suggest, as several psychoanalysts do, that the genus "narcissism" has both its normal and pathological species.

A number of theorists have defined narcissism a variety of ways; in the psychoanalytic literature since Hartmann (1950), the "libidinal cathexis of the self" has become the accepted definition. Freud defined narcissism as the libidinal cathexis of the ego. Hartmann amended this because one can make little sense of the cathexis of a structure responsible for cognition, perception, motility, defense, and the like. Freud had not systematically distinguished between ego, self, and self-concept, leaving his notions of narcissism and object love problematic.

The development of Freud's thought on narcissism has been traced a number of times (see Bing, McLaughlin, and Marburg, 1959; van der Waals, 1965; and Pulver, 1970) and will thus be treated only briefly here. Freud's earliest and most definitive statement on the subject is his rich and provocative paper, "On Narcissism" (1914), a dense and often confusing essay that has frequently been misunderstood. Freud developed his theory of narcissism prior to his later and final dual instinct theory (sex and aggression), and he never made a concerted effort to reconcile the two. The result has been a confusion in psychoanalytic theorizing about the relation between psychosexual theory and object relations theory.

Freud was not satisfied with his theory of narcissism (see Pulver, 1970), and with good reason: as Balint (1960) points out, Freud really presented three theories, not one. Balint refers to these as the theories of primary narcissism, primary object love, and primary autoerotism. Perhaps the most coherent extrapolation of Freud's argument is the following. Originally the psyche is unstructured, and libido is stored in an undifferentiated ego-id. This is the state of autoerotism, in which the neonate does not cathect—i.e., does not relate to—the world around him. With the differentiation of an ego and emergence of psychic structure, all the baby's libido cathects the ego (or, as Hartmann would say, the self). Freud calls this stage primary narcissism, and it is characterized by overvaluation of the self (cf. Piagetian egocentrism). With increased maturity some of the libido may remain attached to the ego, while a significant portion of it will be sent out in two directions. The first path is object love: the libido formerly cathecting the ego becomes attached to an object. Especially in psychosis, according to Freud, libido which was attached to objects is withdrawn again into the ego, which accounts for megalomania. The second path involves the creation of the ego ideal: libido from the ego becomes invested in an ego ideal, which is a sane way of preserving infantile narcissism.

Clinically, this developmental model has great explanatory power, although its theoretical and empirical difficulties are significant, and one can preserve most of its virtues while eliminating the unnecessary libido terminology. A variety of psychoanalytic writers have criticized or elaborated upon this framework and its numerous permutations. Balint, for example, attacks the whole notion of primary narcissism, arguing that the infant's first state is one of intense relatedness to her environment which Balint calls "primary love" (1960). Balint is certainly right in pointing out that the theory that the infant does not originally "cathect" the world is empirically incorrect. Sucking and grasping behaviors, for example, are present from birth, and if the baby did not relate to the world around her (and simply hallucinated all her needs, as Freud contends), every infant would die of malnutrition well before the end of the first month.

The relation between narcissism and object love is a lively topic of debate in psychoanalytic literature. Pulver soundly defeats the hypothesis, derived from libido theory, of an inverse correlation between object love and self-love, noting, on the contrary, that those who love themselves are most capable of loving others (1970, p. 335). Van der Waals sees an element of narcissism in every object relationship. He describes a mutually satisfying sexual relationship in terms of "giving satisfaction to one another by actually pursuing egoistic wishes" (1965, p. 298), which sounds something like a sexualized *Wealth of Nations* in which each individual pursuing his own self-interest leads – as if by an "invisible genital" – to a mutual orgasm.

The increasing prevalence (or perhaps, some would say, recognition) of narcissistic disorders has generated a significant amount of psychoanalytic theorizing about narcissism, and two analysts in particular, Otto Kernberg (1975, 1976) and Heinz Kohut (1971, 1977), have developed competing and hotly debated models. Like other psychoanalytic approaches to narcissism, their theories of narcissism are simultaneously theories of object relations since one's attitude toward oneself in relation to others is an integral part of one's relation to others. As Kegan has put it, object relations are really subject-object relations (1982, p. 77). The models of Kernberg and Kohut are the principal views of object relations and narcissism in currency today and will thus be briefly explored here.

Kernberg's work (1975, 1976) is an attempt to integrate insights from object relations theory (especially that of Klein, 1946, 1948; Fairbairn, 1952; and Jacobson, 1954, 1964) and ego psychology (especially Erikson, 1963) into psychoanalytic thinking without abandoning drive theory or the structural model (id, ego, superego). The basic logic of development, in broadest terms, is from a lack of awareness of self-other differentiation, to a differentiation of object- and self-representations based on affect (i.e., good versus bad), to an eventual construction of mature object representations (including self-representations) that integrate ambivalent feelings.

Central to Kernberg's developmental model is a movement from "splitting" to repression (and related defenses) as the ego's primary method of defense. Splitting, for Kernberg, means the separation of good and bad object representations. This mechanism originally stems from cognitive immaturity but later is used defensively against the perception of objects as both frustrating and gratifying. According to Kernberg, repression should attain primacy in the third year of life (1976, p. 69).

Kernberg delineates five stages in the development of object relations. The first he describes as a "Primary Undifferentiated" period (1976, p. 60), which corresponds to the first month of life. The psyche at this point, as in most psychoanalytic views of infancy, is basically unstructured, though forerunners to the ego start to emerge by the end of this phase.

The second stage is that of "Primary, Undifferentiated Self-Object Representations" (p. 60). During this period, which lasts roughly from the second to the sixth or eighth month, the infant develops a "good" self-object representation, which later develops into the core of the ego. This "good" representation does not distinguish self and other. "Good" at this stage means "me," and "bad" means "not-me" (p. 36). The good representation is invested with libido, and the bad representation, with aggression (p. 64).

The third stage, which ends between the eighteenth and thirty-sixth months, is that of the "Differentiation of Self- from Object-Representations" (p. 64). In this stage, self- and object-representations begin to separate within the "good" and "bad" camps, so that the child has images of good me, bad me, good mother, and bad mother. The child, however, still lacks integrated images of self and others since good and bad images remain separate. Splitting begins to be maintained actively in an effort to ward off anxiety (pp. 37, 67).

The fourth stage is that of the "Integration of Self-Representations and Object-Representations and the Development of Higher Intrapsychic Object Relations-Derived Structures," which begins in the latter part of the third year and lasts through the Oedipal period (p. 67). At this stage positive and negative self- and object-representations coalesce (p. 40), resulting in the formation of "total objects." In other words, the child develops integrated, ambivalent representations of self and others, and repression comes to replace splitting as a primary way of defending. Id, ego, and superego coalesce, as do images of self, object, ideal self, and ideal object.

The final stage is the "Consolidation of Superego and Ego Integration," in which ego identity solidifies and the superego matures (p. 72). The superego becomes depersonalized and abstract (p. 42), and the ego (which includes self- and object-representations) matures in its function of reality-testing.

Kohut's theory has stirred quite a controversy in psychoanalytic circles because he superimposes a "psychology of the self" upon classical psychoanalysis, arguing that a comprehensive psychology requires both a self psychology and a conflict psychology (1977, p. 78). His approach is predicated upon his notion of the "self," a term he uses in two different ways. In the *Analysis of the Self* he considers the self a collection of self-representations, analogous to an object-representation (1971, p. xv). In *The Restoration of the Self* his definition broadens considerably; here he refers to the self as a "psychological sector" comprised of ambitions, skills, and ideals (1977, p. 63). The former view of the self is consistent with previous psychoanalytic usage, whereas the latter poses the self as a structure on an equal footing with, if not superordinate to, id, ego, and superego.

In his later works (Kohut, 1977; Kohut and Wolf, 1978) Kohut views the self as a bipolar structure, consisting of ambitions on one side, ideals on the other, and "executive functions" poised between the two (1977, pp. 49, 54). The pole of ambitions emerges from the "grandiose self," an archaic structure that the infant erects to compensate for loss of primary narcissism. The pole of idealization arises from the "idealized parent imago," a similar vision of omnipotence, this time ascribed to the parent (1971).

Kohut's developmental theory begins, like Kernberg's (and almost every psychoanalytic writer), with an undifferentiated stage which Kohut calls "the stage of the fragmented self" (1971, p. 118). From this seething cauldron of drives, perceptions, affects, and whatever other condiments the infant desires in his ontogenetic primeval soup emerge the grandiose self and the idealized parent imago. Through these structures the baby attempts to preserve his original state of (imagined) perfection (1968, p. 86), ascribing omnipotence and omniscience to himself and to an idealized "selfobject" (1971, p. 3; cf. Winnicott's "transitional object," 1971) which he perceives as part of himself (Kohut, 1971, p. 25). What Kohut calls the nuclear self arises during the second year of life (Kohut and Wolf, 1978, p. 417) from the grandiose self, the idealized parent imago, and the rudimentary executive functions "arched" between them. This ushers in the "stage of the cohesive self" (1971, p. 32).

With the consolidation of the self, the child proceeds to the tasks of the

Oedipal years, as elucidated by classical psychoanalysis. During the Oedipal period the ego matures, and the idealized parent imago is introjected into the nascent superego (1971, p. 28) as well as the ego (where it performs functions largely related to drive-regulation, pp. 298-9). The ego also integrates facets of the grandiose self, providing goals, ambitions, and self-esteem (pp. 107, 299). Throughout life the narcissism of the grandiose self may be transformed into empathy, creativity, humor, and wisdom (1971, p. 299). Central to Kohut's theory is his contention that narcissism has both healthy and pathological transformations.

The theories of Kernberg and Kohut are complex, and the reader may have as much flavor for them after reading these very concise summaries as one has for Devon cream after eating a teaspoon of evaporated milk. Their theories converge and diverge on a number of issues (for an excellent discussion of their similarities and differences, see the panel discussion reported by Schwartz, 1973.) They differ, in particular, in their views on therapeutic technique and on specific beliefs about borderline and narcissistic pathology. At the theoretical level, perhaps the main difference lies in their energy concepts: Kernberg maintains a more Freudian stance, while Kohut moves somewhat away from the classical paradigm (which is a general difference between their approaches), practically positing a narcissistic drive (see Kohut's discussion of the "ego's capacity to tame narcissistic cathexes and to employ them for its highest aims," 1966; see also 1971, pp. 219-20) or at least viewing libido as a collection of several drives (1977, p. 23).

Their views have been debated in psychoanalytic circles as largely incompatible approaches, though one can detect a number of points of agreement between them. For example, parallel to Kohut's call for two complementary psychologies, one which examines the self and its defects, and the other which analyzes conflicts of a cohesive self, Kernberg distinguishes "two levels of internalized object relations," one of fragmented self- and object-representations, and the other of cohesive representations (1976, p. 245). Kernberg seems to agree with Kohut (1977, p. 227) that a firm self (and, he adds, cohesive object-representations) is an essential precondition for the experience of the Oedipus complex (1976, p. 200).

Further, Kohut's description of the "developmental stage" of the grandiose self, in which the child views himself as perfect and omnipotent and assigns "all imperfections to the outside" (1968, p. 96) sounds remarkably similar to Kernberg's stage in which "good" equals "me," and "bad" equals "not-me." Finally, Kohut's contrast of "vertical" and "horizontal" splits (1971, p. 193) is almost identical to Kernberg's contrast of splitting and repression. Both see splitting (Kohut's vertical splits) as characteristic of more severe pathology, and repression (Kohut's horizontal splits) as a later, less pathological phenomenon.

135

In general, object relations theorists of various theoretical stripes would agree on three broad suppositions. First, psychic development entails a gradual shift from a lack of realistic and cohesive self- and object-representations to the ability to form mature, multi-dimensional, ambivalently "cathected" representations. The person, in other words, gradually comes to experience herself and others as both good and bad, and is able to maintain positive feelings toward herself and others in the face of strong negative feelings and vice versa. Secondly, by the time this capacity has been achieved, significant ego development has occurred, as has the moral internalization which establishes the superego. Thirdly, with the establishment of the superego, the need-satisfying psychology of the preoedipal years begins to give way to a psychology in which one's own needs and impulses are tempered by internalized prohibitions and a recognition of the impact of one's actions on others.

MORAL DEVELOPMENT: CURRENT APPROACHES

Psychoanalytic thought on narcissism has had little relation to psychoanalytic theorizing about moral development. The latter is viewed in terms of the development of the superego, whereas theories of narcissism typically emphasize the preoedipal period. According to psychoanalytic theory, the superego arises as a precipitate of the Oedipus complex through the process of identification. As maturity approaches, the superego becomes less rigid and personalized, with internalized ideals and values substituting for internalized objects (introjects). In addition, the ego comes to assume many of the moral functions of the developmentally more primitive and punitive superego, though the mechanisms by which the ego comes to usurp moral authority are obscure.

The Freudian view of moral development suffers from four defects. The first is the connection between the development of the superego and the Oedipus-castration complex. (Elsewhere I have more thoroughly examined Freud's theory of internalization and the Oedipus complex and discussed the very problematic links to the superego and moral development; Westen, 1984b.) According to Freud the superego is the "heir to the Oedipus complex" (1933); by this he means that, in the male case, the child suffers an object loss when he gives up his mother as a sexual object, and he replaces the object with massive identifications with his father. He does this defensively, as a result of fear of castration. Thus, by introjecting his father, the boy develops a superego.

As even some writers within the Freudian tradition have recognized (see Flugel, 1945; Loevinger, 1976), the idea that the superego forms in "one fell swoop" (or a few fell swoops around age five) with the resolution of the Oedipus-castration complex is both implausible and contradicted by

136

empirical data. Psychoanalytic writers often speak of "archaic superego precursors" (Reich, 1954), early superegolike introjections of parental objects and/or demands. If such introjections occur before the Oedipal age, why should one suspect that a different mechanism is required to explain the formation of the rest of the superego? That preoedipal children have many isolated "pockets" of superego can be confirmed by any three-year-old's parents and suggests that superego formation need have little to do with Oedipal issues.

Freud's inability to conceptualize adequately the psychological development of females stems in large measure from this faulty view of the causes of superego development. In the male case, according to Freud, the child's fear of castration causes him to internalize the father and accept the father's morality. This poses a significant theoretical problem: since females cannot be castrated, why do they develop superegos? On several occasions Freud concluded that women must not have well-developed superegos, yet this is quite obviously incorrect. Empirical research, not to mention casual observation, suggests quite the opposite, that females in Western society (and in fact in almost all known societies) are socialized to focus on the needs of others and tend to hold more "humanistic" values (Hoffman, 1975). In point of fact, the majority of hysterics whom Freud analyzed were female, and he developed the notion that a conflict between internalized prohibitions and infantile sexual wishes is the root of neurosis in large part from his experience with hysterics. Freud's largely unsuccessful attempts (1925, 1931, 1933) at female psychology all fail precisely because he is trying to account for superego formation in terms of the Oedipus-castration complex. He should instead have recognized that if boys and girls both develop superegos, and only boys can fear impending castration, then the castration complex cannot explain superego development.

If Freud's hypothesized connection of superego and Oedipus-castration complex were true, one would expect that, in the male case, the father would vastly predominate over the mother in the boy's superego, i.e., that conscience should be largely derived from the father (see, for example, Freud, 1913, p. 157; 1923, p. 44). Again, reality runs counter to this prediction. Particularly in modern Western society, in which the father is often absent from the household for most of the day, moral training falls largely upon the shoulders of the mother. An empirical study by Hoffman and Saltzstein (1967) found that for both boys and girls, mother's child-rearing practices were more influential for child's moral development than father's. To try to answer this falsification of his theory, Freud might turn to the theory of the "negative Oedipus complex," which asserts that the child really wants both parents, so he identifies with each. In the male case, if the child is not to become homosexual, he must still internalize his father *more;* yet again, many if not most moral internalizations in most cultures are maternal or at least feminine.

A central problem here is the failure to distinguish between gender identification and moral internalization. The child's gender identification may in part stem from Oedipal issues; however, his moral internalization, except where it overlaps with his ideal image of his own sex, is not largely dependent upon the Oedipus complex. Indeed, one wonders, in the Freudian model, why the superego includes nonsexual injunctions: why does the child internalize the value of sharing, for example, which relates neither to sex nor aggression? The psychoanalytic model fails to separate ideal self-images formed through identification, some of which are gender-specific, from moral beliefs, which are largely independent of gender and Oedipal issues.

This is not to suggest that the Oedipus complex is not of tremendous psychological significance, at least in cultures with nuclear families, or that children do not develop prohibitions against incest.[1] The reader need only try for a moment to imagine himself or herself engaged in sexual intercourse with a parent to recognize the strength of these prohibitions. Rather, the point is that all moral development is not contingent, by and large, upon psychosexual development or the vicissitudes of the Oedipus complex.

A clinical example clearly differentiates Oedipal dynamics from moral development. The patient, a stocky middle aged man, was an only child from a midwestern Italian family. He had considerable conflicts around sexuality which inhibited enjoyment of a normal sex life, and had developed the fantasy as a child that his father's sexual activity with his mother had left her unable to bear more than one child. He also had difficulty establishing an identity as a competent male and had considerable conflicts around homosexual impulses. He had tried as a child to minimize identification with his father, who had a long history of trouble with the law, and had become something of a "confessor" to his mother, resulting in exacerbation of Oedipal issues.

The patient very early developed a hyper-moral stance and had been, through his twenties, a priest. From an Oedipal perspective, his choice of the priesthood was a compromise-formation: by being his mother's confessor he could be her closest confidante, while at the same time renouncing his Oedipal wish by renouncing masculine sexuality. This explanation, while true, ignores two other aspects of the compromise that cannot be

---

[1] It is not entirely clear, however, that these prohibitions stem either from childhood fantasies or from socialization. Evidence from Israeli kibbutzim (Shepher, 1971) suggests that the incest taboo may well have biological roots. It would certainly be an odd twist of fate if the castration complex were in part a rationalization of a biological aversion, a misattribution of a biologically based feeling of disgust.

explained psychosexually: first, in his culture the priesthood represents the pinnacle of power and worth, so that becoming a priest was a way to gain self-esteem and the esteem of others; and secondly, priests were the most available male figures of identification other than his father, so that in trying to reject identification with his father he could nonetheless develop an ideal of nondefective (though neuter) manhood.

What the psychoanalytic theory of superego formation least accounts for in this case is the patient's devout Catholicism and high moral standards. The Oedipal theory leads one to expect a linear correlation between identification with the father and strength of the superego. In this example, in contrast, moral development through internalization of religious values and identification with the Church occurred *at the expense of* identification with the father, who was seen as sinful and earthly. Because the patient could not, so to speak, find a father at home, he found a holy father in the Church. The questions the psychoanalytic theory cannot answer are why he, like most children, *wanted* to find someone with whom to identify, how moral development could occur in a man (who as an adult is very ethical and sensitive to the effects of his actions on others) despite problematic identification with his father, and how religion can offer a sense of meaning that has very little to do with infantile sexual issues.

A second problem with the psychoanalytic theory of moral development is that Freud left ambiguous the relationship between superego, ego, and the institution he called the ego ideal. While a literature has arisen on the concept of the ego ideal (which Freud developed in 1914 but never reconciled with his later structural model) and its relation to the superego (see, for example, Reich, 1954; Novey, 1955; Hartmann and Loewenstein, 1962), psychoanalysts have arrived at no consensus on this issue. Whether the ego takes on moral functions of the superego as maturity approaches is unclear (which is a necessary hypothesis since Freud views the superego as fairly primitive and not subject to historical change, whereas values do, in fact, change throughout the lifespan as well as historically), and whether the ego or superego ultimately determines action or is responsible for self-punishment is ambiguous. Issues about the functional relations between the three structures abound. Whether the rider or the saddle – let alone the horse – ultimately prevails is unclear in the Freudian paradigm.

A third difficulty, intimated above, is that Freud provides no mechanism for generational change in the superego. The child's superego "is in fact constructed on the model not of its parents but of its parents' superego" (1933, p. 67). In other words, cultural and historical conditions leave little or no imprint on the superego: once it is established, it is preserved forever. If the superego really is the psychic center of morality

139

(which is its function), then this is untenable. Moral values do, in fact, change over time, and one has little reason to believe that twentieth century "superegos" are exact or nearly exact replicas of the earliest Homo sapiens.

Finally, the Freudian notion of morality as represented by the superego is unable to account for true moral autonomy. Superego morality entails the following of parental or social rules. Existential philosopher Ortega comments, "Whether he be original or a plagiarist, man is the novelist of himself" (1961, p. 156). History and anthropology suggest that most people prefer to retype an aging manuscript – perhaps with an occasional change in punctuation – rather than to create an original piece of literature. In the moral realm, Freudian theory can accommodate only the plagiarist: the superego is passed from generation to generation like a family heirloom, and the mature individual is one whose depersonalized superego (i.e., a superego with generalized rules as opposed to internalized parental objects and their particular commands) acts in harmony with his selectively identifying ego (i.e., an ego which identifies with various objects selectively instead of wholesale). The problem with this model is that it confuses internalization with autonomy. That an individual no longer requires the vigilance of his parents in matters of morality may well be a sign of a more entrenched heteronomy, rather than a true autonomy. Such an individual does not act upon his own standards; he simply no longer requires active participation by his parents or society to ensure that he will perform in the manner *they* perceive as morally correct.

Put one more way, the psychoanalytic model of moral development fails in that it cannot explain an individual like Nietzsche. Nietzsche came to overturn the very core of his superego, questioning the notions of good and evil themselves, concluding that the dominant equation of "good" with "altruistic" is a perversion of true conscience (1887). Did Nietzsche possess a strong ego with an extraordinary capacity for "selective identification," or was he simply a psychopath or pathological narcissist? The Freudian framework can offer few other possibilities, and its inability to provide insight into such an individual is especially significant, given Freud's assessment of Nietzsche as possessing "a more penetrating knowledge of himself than any man who ever lived or was ever likely to live" (Kaufman, citing Jones, 1975, p. 20).

Outside of psychoanalysis, the leading models of the psychology of moral development are the cognitive-developmental models of Piaget and his disciple, Lawrence Kohlberg, and the social learning approach. For Piaget (1932), morality involves a respect for rules, and moral development proceeds in two stages. In the first stage the child's respect for rules is derivative of her respect for the authorities who teach the rules. In this

140

stage, which Piaget calls "conformity" or "constraint," the child views rules as immutable and eternal. Authority is absolute, and actions, not intentions, determine culpability. In the second stage of "cooperation" or "autonomy," the child perceives rules as the product of social interaction and group choice, not as divine mandates. With the second stage, which emerges roughly between ages eight and twelve, a mutual respect replaces the unilateral respect for adult authorities.

Kohlberg argues that moral development can be viewed in terms of six stages, organized into three levels of moral reasoning, each comprised of two stages (Kohlberg and Kramer, 1968; Kohlberg and Mayer, 1972). The first level of moral development Kohlberg calls "preconventional," in which the child accepts labels of good and bad but interprets them in terms of the power of those who create rules or the hedonistic implications of action (i.e., whether one will be punished or rewarded). In the first stage, the child is oriented toward punishment and obedience, and in the second, which Kohlberg calls "instrumental relativism," reciprocity emerges but "is a matter of 'you scratch my back and I'll scratch yours' not of loyalty, gratitude or justice" (Kohlberg and Kramer, 1969, p. 100).

At the second, or "conventional" level, the person comes to value the moral code of her family or society in itself, regardless of hedonistic implications. In both the third and fourth stages, the child maintains rules and commands to which she tries to conform. The third stage involves a "good boy"/"good girl" orientation, and the fourth is characterized by a "law and order" emphasis.

The third level, "post-conventional" morality, entails the belief in universal moral principles not tied to a particular authority or social group. In the fifth stage, a social contract prevails, and actions viewed as just are those with the greatest social utility; principles of democracy, legality, and contract predominate. In the final stage, morality involves universal principles: the individual chooses principles such as the greatest good for the greatest number, and she refuses to treat herself as an exception to those rules even when expediency contradicts them. In this stage the person believes in equality and the value of individual liberty.[1]

The cognitive approaches of Piaget and Kohlberg have proven valuable in two ways. First, they have attempted to operationalize, and, in the case

---

[1] Though he is never explicit about it, Kohlberg appears to believe that ontogeny recapitulates history in the development of morals. The idea of a social contract has its roots in Sophist philosophy but was not prevalent in the West until the eighteenth century. Similarly, Kohlberg appears to see twentieth century America as a prototype of moral development at the societal level, with its principles of democracy and formal equality, although he could and may equally argue that a future socialist society might better approximate the Stage 6 ideal. In a footnote to an article (Kohlberg and Kramer, 1969), he endorses the notion of societal evolution of morals (p. 106n).

141

of Kohlberg, measure the development of moral judgment, as opposed to theorizing about it using only case examples as data. Secondly, they have emphasized that children do not simply internalize parental prohibitions but actively construct their understanding of these principles. This is, of course, an extension of Piaget's constructivist epistemology to the moral realm. Piaget and Kohlberg both point out that a child's knowledge of moral rules, like all other knowledge, is constrained by the limitations of the child's cognitive apparatus. Though Freudians did not previously emphasize the cognitive side of superego development, they recognized from the start that the superego is the child's construction or representation of parental norms, not a direct reflection of parental rules. Kohlberg's perspective in particular has the added advantage of suggesting a stage of moral development beyond the collection of injunctions and prohibitions which comprises the superego.

Despite these merits, Kohlberg's theory, in particular, has been vigorously criticized (Kurtines and Greif, 1974; Hoffman, 1977), though often on methodological grounds, which will not be repeated here. Rather, I will focus on six more general problems with his approach to moral development. (For an excellent review of critical commentary on Kohlberg, see Lickona, 1976.) First, Kohlberg and Piaget are both guilty of smuggling a number of value judgments under their lab coats. This becomes particularly clear when one examines the philosophical underpinnings of their psychological theories. One could argue that the relation between Piaget and Kohlberg is similar to that of Rousseau and Kant: Piaget recapitulates Rousseau's error which influenced Kant, and Kohlberg recapitulates Kant's error by following Piaget. Rousseau asserts that deep within the human heart lies a divinely implanted morality. The primitive individual in a presocial state of nature could apprehend this moral law directly. Rousseau conceives of the "natural man" as a being motivated by self-interest and a natural compassion or "pity" that gives him pain to perceive the misfortune of another sentient being. Society has now corrupted and eliminated this natural man, but through reason one can rediscover the moral truth within one's breast. The truly free person is one who perceives and follows the dictates of his divinely-inspired conscience. Since all people reason alike, and the moral law is the same for all, if everyone were to withdraw to his corner of the world and discover and follow his conscience in the silence of the passions, the result would be a harmonious "general will." The general will, for Rousseau, is the collective will of the community, and its aim is the good of the group. In essence, conscience is identical to the general will, and to act autonomously is to follow this divine law.

The problem for Rousseau is that people do not always reason correctly, are often swayed by selfishness, and thus misperceive the Good. On

142

the societal level, the "will of all" does not always reflect the general will.[1] In the case of a disagreement between individual conscience and the will of all as to the morally correct action, the will of all must prevail because it is the closest approximation to the general will. If the individual disagrees with the collective belief, he must, to use Rousseau's curious phrase, be "forced to be free," since freedom consists in obedience to reason, which is embodied in the general will. The individual thus must be compelled to act "autonomously," i.e., freely. The same difficulty is endemic to Piaget's moral psychology: autonomy is defined in terms of conformity to group decisions.

Kant, like Rousseau, believes that reason can prescribe ends, and that freedom consists in subordinating individual desire to a "categorical imperative" to treat other people as ends in themselves as opposed to means to one's own ends. Reason, according to Kant, does not bow to particular interests; a rational morality is one that can be universalized (i.e., a person cannot make himself an exception to his own moral rules). For Kant, then, moral autonomy entails imposing upon oneself or "self-choosing" a set of preordained, ready-made principles (which are essentially rationalizations of Judeo-Christian morality). If a rational individual imposes upon himself a *different* set of principles, he must, according to Kant, be reasoning incorrectly, and not acting "autonomously." Similarly, for Kohlberg, post-conventional, self-chosen principles are by definition either social contractarian or universalizable Kantian moral commands. The problem is that one could conceivably develop and freely accept other types of moral values that, for example, cannot be universalized. Kohlberg, like Kant, would contend that a person of this sort is not acting "autonomously" (i.e., in line with Kohlberg and Kant's moral views), and he would add that the person's thinking is regressive (as in the often observed phenomenon among college students of Stage 2 morality following Stage 4).

This whole line of thinking rests upon the mistaken view, pervasive in moral philosophy, that reason can provide ends, and that the ends it chooses are altruistic ones. The fundamental difficulty with the moral philosophy of both Kant and Rousseau and the moral psychology of Piaget and Kohlberg is the assumption that all people who reason "correctly" will come to the same moral truth. This leads to a misbegotten view of autonomy that tries, unsuccessfully, to unite free thought with a preor-

---

[1] Plato recognized this problem and concluded that the philosopher who can understand the Good must also be a king who can implement and enforce it. Hobbes came to terms with the same issue, investing the sovereign with the power to decide moral questions. Similarly, Rousseau invents a divinely inspired "legislator" (and a tutor, on the individual level), modeled after Plato's philosopher-king, to direct society so that the will of all coincides with the general will. For Rousseau, as for Plato, the difficulty lies in determining who, in fact, is qualified to be the lawgiver. Hobbes provided the only consistent answer to this question yet devised: might makes right.

dained end. One cannot have both autonomy and moral absolutism: either one allows people to think autonomously, in which case one cannot be sure of the conclusions they will reach, or one demands that everyone accept the same moral view, in which case one must stifle all free thought. Rousseau, Kant, Piaget, and Kohlberg fail in their moral theorizing because they try to maintain the contradictory values of individual autonomy and moral absolutism. This is, indeed, one of the central conflicts of liberal moral and political philosophy.

The second problem with Kohlberg's theory is the confounding of two distinct phenomena: post-conventional morality as ability to form abstract conceptualizations and as self-chosen morality. One can see this confusion quite clearly by examining the evolution of his ideas. In 1963 he saw the highest level of moral development as involving the ability to generalize the norms of one's society (Kohlberg, 1963). This is a very Piagetian view, which essentially views moral maturity as the application of formal operational thinking to moral reasoning. By 1969, the definition of post-conventional morality had shifted to denote the "effort to define moral values which have validity and application apart from the authority of the groups or persons holding these principles and apart from the individual's own identification with these groups" (Kohlberg and Kramer, 1969, p. 101). In this latter view, the essence of post-conventional morality is that it is self-chosen, logical, and not derivable from one's specific culture. Note the difference between this approach and the earlier claim that moral maturity entails the ability to abstract a "formal system" from "a set of agreed-upon assumptions" (1963, pp. 29-30). These agreed-upon assumptions are rooted in the culture, not spontaneously generated or culture-free.

An example will make this criticism more clear. Thomas Aquinas was a very bright fellow, surely capable of formal operational thinking. Had he attempted a systemized Christian ethics, the project would likely have entailed an attempt to bring together the various moral laws of Christianity into a consistent set of values, perhaps derived from a few assumptions (e.g., about the nature of God). This would have been post-conventional in the cognitive sense, in that it would have applied abstract thinking to moral phenomena. Yet Aquinas's ethics would surely have been conventional in the sense that he would not have questioned the pillars of Christian faith as to what constitute morally correct and incorrect courses of action. Similarly, if a member of the Gestapo had taken Hitler's premises about purifying the human race and developed a consistent moral system from these principles, can one say that he displayed the same level of moral judgment as the member of the underground who rejected entirely the current "agreed-upon assumptions"?

This leads to the third problem, the confounding of cognitive *processes* with *content,* resulting in a view of moral development with a significant value bias. Kohlberg finds hedonism morally repulsive and consequently relegates it to Stage 2 morality, even though it frequently appears in late adolescence or early adulthood (see, e.g., Kohlberg and Kramer, 1969). As noted above, Kohlberg sides with the type of morality developed by Kant, with its rationalistic and individualistic bent. Stage 6 morality proclaims the rights of human beings as *"individual persons"* (p. 101), and Stage 5 involves a legalistic, social-contract orientation predicated on notions of individual rights. To say that one aspect of moral development involves the ability to develop coherent principles instead of ad hoc rules is entirely different than to argue for the psychological superiority of a particular moral view. One can think abstractly as a libertarian or reactionary just as one can as a liberal individualist.

Fourthly, this importation of content into the domain of process renders Kohlberg's theory culture-bound. That preindustrial, non-Western people tend not to reach Stages 5 and 6 is not surprising given that they are not indoctrinated from birth with social contract notions and proclamations of individual liberty, as are Americans. Kohlberg, like Piaget, tends to underestimate the extent to which both cognitive and moral schemas are culturally constituted.

A fifth problem is that the theory is sex-biased in favor of males (see Gilligan, 1982). Not only did Kohlberg generalize stages he discovered in studying a sample of males, but the type of morality he views as the pinnacle of moral development is one historically practiced primarily by male philosophers. More concretely, he explains the fact that women, in contrast to men, are more likely to remain at Stage 3 than at Stage 4 by noting that "personal concordance morality is a functional morality for housewives and mothers; it is not for businessmen and professionals" (1969, p. 108). I have difficulty seeing how a woman who cares for her family is less morally mature than a businessman who replaces workers with machines. Coles (1981) and others have criticized this model of moral autonomy for emphasizing the cognitive side of moral reasoning, which establishes men like Kant as moral giants, without regard to their actions.

This suggests a final objection, which many have raised, and which applies to both Kohlberg and Piaget, that cognitive-developmental approaches to moral development do not account for moral behavior. A person may have lofty ideals while nevertheless treating people like dirt; the ideals may serve as a magical amulet that protects the person from recognizing his actual baseness.

Aside from psychoanalytic and cognitive-developmental theories, the other major approach to moral development is social learning theory. (For a more complete account of competing views of moral development, see Lickona, 1976; Hoffman, 1980.) Social learning theorists argue that morality, defined as prosocial or altruistic behaviors (Mischel and Mis-

145

chel, 1976), is learned like any other kind of behavior, through cognitively mediated conditioning and socially mediated learning, particularly modeling. The production of moral or prosocial behavior depends both upon the (cognitive) competence and the inducement to do so (Mischel and Mischel, 1976; Bandura, 1977a). The competence involved in prosocial acts is primarily developed through watching other people perform them, and the incentive to perform them oneself comes from an assessment of response contingencies (i.e., one learns from both trial and error and vicarious conditioning that one will be punished or rewarded for certain acts). In addition, people learn to regulate their own behavior through self-reinforcement, by punishing failures to achieve standards and rewarding ability to delay gratification.

Social learning theorists, notably Mischel (Mischel and Mischel, 1976), have taken issue with both psychoanalytic and cognitive accounts of moral development. Against psychoanalysis, Mischel argues that the superego is not a unified structure, and that studies have demonstrated only modest correlations (around .3) between indexes of moral judgment, prosocial behavior, and guilt. Against Kohlberg, Mischel emphasizes the importance of social learning in the development of specific moral beliefs.

The social learning approach has considerable merit in explaining the roots of some prosocial actions in terms of cognitively and socially mediated learning. One can readily see how a child who is punished for fighting may come to see fighting as a maladaptive response. Further, Mischel's criticisms of psychoanalytic and cognitive-developmental theories are in some respects well taken. Psychodynamic psychologists too frequently speak of "the superego" as if it were a single, coherent agency, ignoring the impact of specific situations in evoking particular standards. Kohlberg is indeed guilty of failing to examine the extent to which his higher levels of moral development simply represent the modeling of culturally constructed moral systems.

Mischel's critique, however, also rests in part upon misunderstanding. That studies have demonstrated cross-situational inconsistencies in prosocial behavior is not problematic for psychoanalysis, which sees most behaviors as compromises between wishes and internal standards. One would expect, therefore, that situations that permit greater rewards for impulsive behavior will show a lower incidence of behavior in accord with superego standards. Psychoanalysis is predicated on the notion of psychic conflict, and nothing in the theory implies that people will always obey internalized standards.

Mischel equally misunderstands Kohlberg by equating moral development with the strengthening of "prosocial behaviors" and then showing that such behaviors are not linearly related to Kohlberg's stages. Kohlberg's moral situations are precisely those in which the person must choose

146

between *two* "prosocial behaviors," such as obeying the law versus saving one's wife's life. Kohlberg is thus interested in moral dilemmas and their resolution, not in the rate of altruistic responding. One might, in fact, expect the highest production of prosocial behaviors in many cultures and situations among people with conventional moral reasoning, who are interested in others' opinions of them and in the welfare of members of their particular group.

In situations of conflict the problems with the shallow focus on moral behaviors inherited from behaviorism become most apparent because at such points the whole question is which behavior is moral. Is a helpful Nazi, who "pitches in" and volunteers his time to the cause of the Final Solution behaving prosocially? Is the person who refuses to drop napalm on Southeast Asian peasants despite draft laws behaving antisocially? These kinds of questions are the stuff of moral angst, and they are entirely outside the scope of social learning theory.[1]

The social learning approach to moral development is problematic in other respects as well. While one can easily see how a child comes to the conclusion that untamed aggression will ultimately have unpleasant consequences for him, what this approach fails to explain is why such judgments are deemed *moral,* as opposed to *practical.* Why, for example, does the child come to see stealing as morally wrong, even when he can get away with it? Bandura would certainly be correct in arguing that the child may actually cheat despite the moral belief, but this does not explain why the child would feel guilty in doing so. If people respond to moral dilemmas in the situation-specific way social learning theory suggests, they should be able to discriminate situations in which they would do well to behave altruistically and experience guilt (understood by Mischel and Bandura as anticipation of bad consequences) as those in which they are likely

---

[1] They are also entirely ignored in psychological constructs such as "social skills," "social adjustment," and "social competence." Mischel, for example, contends that intelligence is highly correlated with honesty and social and interpersonal adjustment (Mischel and Mischel, 1976, pp. 86-7). It is difficult to see how anyone who has been affiliated with a university as long as he has could hold such a belief; academia is riddled with brilliant people who withdrew into their intellects because they could not deal with people, were scapegoats as children, are social isolates, are tremendously competitive, are misanthropes, or some delightful combination of these. In sum, one can be intellectually competent, as many people with borderline disorders are, yet be unable to maintain warm, lasting, and satisfying relationships with people. Further, to posit an abstract notion of "social skills" or "social competence" without considering the ends to which these alleged skills or competencies are used makes little sense. Hitler was tremendously adept at convincing people to follow him, and many "socially competent" people joined him. Millions of well-adjusted, milk-drinking American men are, at any given moment, ready to go to a foreign country (preferably an underdeveloped one) and kill "enemies" about whom they have not bothered to learn anything. Is this social competence? Erich Fromm perceptively raised these issues from a psychological perspective decades ago (Fromm, 1955), questioning the relation between social adjustment and sanity in an "insane" society.

to be caught. This is not, of course, how real people act or feel, though certainly the threat of punishment increases prosocial behavior. This is because it activates a second cognitive-evaluative mismatch, aside from that relating to moral standards or ideals, which involves fear for one's well-being.

The question the social learning account cannot address is why the child comes to view internalized moral standards as his own, as opposed to impositions to be avoided when possible. The function of modeling is to facilitate learning in the absence of direct reinforcement. In the case of moral learning, however, modeling often runs directly counter to one's conditioning, as when a child models the virtues of sharing and finds himself with one tenth of a piece of cake. According to Bandura, modeling occurs most in situations in which the consequences of various actions are ambiguous (1977a, p. 90). This is rarely the case in moral learning, since moral values are frequently self-abnegatory. The question, then, is why the child accepts as not only a prudent maxim, but as a moral truth various standards modeled from adults, many of which run counter to experience. If moral beliefs are expectations about response contingencies, then the same human beings Mischel characterizes as infinitely flexible in discriminating situationally appropriate responses are remarkably poor assessors of probable outcomes.

Another problem with the social learning approach to moral development relates to the notion of self-reinforcement. One can readily see how a person could learn to reinforce herself so as to maximize long-term self-interest. What cannot be explained from a social learning perspective is how a person could learn to resist temptation for the benefit of someone else. Delay of gratification and impulse control are not inherently moral. They may be used to further altruistic or egoistic ends (through maximization of long-term self-interest). As argued in Chapter 3, despite centuries of philosophical denial, nothing guarantees that altruistic morality and long-term self-interest coincide.

EGO DEVELOPMENT: CURRENT APPROACHES

A third approach relevant to an examination of personality development is one with its roots in psychoanalytic ego psychology, namely the study of ego development. Rapaport (1959) distinguished several historical periods in the development of Freud's thinking regarding the ego, from his earliest view of the ego as consciousness or "self" to his final statement in the *Outline of Psychoanalysis* (1939), in which he conceives of the ego as a structure responsible for perception, action, judgment, reality-testing, defense, and related functions. Freud's lifelong emphasis on the id and instinctual life led him to focus on the ego's defensive function. Heinz Hartmann inaugurated a new way of thinking about the ego in 1937 with his lectures on the ego, later published as *Ego Psychology and the Problem of Adaptation* (1939), in which he explored the function of the ego as an organ of adaptation to reality. (For a history of the evolution of the concepts of ego and ego development, see Blanck and Blanck, 1974; Loevinger, 1976a.)

Perhaps the clearest and most definitive statement of the psychoanalytic perspective on ego development is Hartmann, Kris, and Loewenstein's classic paper, "Comments on the Formation of Psychic Structure" (1946). Hartmann and his colleagues argue, in contrast to Freud's most frequent position that the ego develops out of the id, that ego and id develop out of undifferentiated matrix. The importance of this theoretical shift is that it establishes the presence from birth of strictly cognitive, reality-oriented ego functions. Freud, in contrast, viewed the ego (including its cognitive functions) as a precipitate of the frustration of drives. According to Hartmann, Kris, and Loewenstein, the psyche is originally undifferentiated in another sense: the infant lacks coherent representations of self and objects, so that self and other are not yet distinguished. This is an aspect of psychoanalytic ego psychology with which infancy researchers of most theoretical perspectives would agree (see Ainsworth, 1969).

According to Hartmann and his colleagues, psychic differentiation and development occurs for both cognitive-maturational and dynamic reasons. For example, before a child can tolerate absence of his primary caretaker, he must learn to modulate his need for immediate indulgence. Once he has matured cognitively to the point at which he can form a psychic representation of his mother and her love, he becomes even more vulnerable to anxiety because he can now fear loss of her or of her affection.

Like most currently practicing psychodynamic clinicians, Hartmann and his colleagues believe that the development of the ego "proceeds along with that of the child's object relations" (p. 23). With ego development comes an ability to form a constant representation of a love object despite the child's need-state. The development of object relations proceeds from an undifferentiated primary narcissism, to the use of others to satisfy drives and impulses, to the ability to love others in themselves and the internalization of the superego.

Erikson (1963, 1968) has proposed a theory of ego development (actually, psychosocial development) that tries to bridge Freud's more biological or organismic approach with an understanding of the role of culture and historical forces. He argues that people go through a series of "crises," by which he means turning points in psychological development in which the evolving psyche faces both danger and opportunity for growth. The first stage is "basic trust vs. mistrust," in which the task for the infant is to develop a sense of himself and his social world as safe and consistent

149

through time. In "autonomy vs. shame and doubt," the child needs to accept himself as a separate source of will and action. Problematic passage through this stage results in chronic shame, inability to tolerate separateness, or a faulty sense of self and will. The third stage, "initiative versus guilt," establishes the superego through identification. In "industry versus inferiority," the child comes to learn the ways of her culture and to develop competence in culturally prescribed areas, but the danger is a pervasive sense of incompetence and inferiority.

Adolescence (or thereabouts) is the age of "identity versus identity confusion," in which the person must develop or accept an identity which is objectively recognized (by his social group) and subjectively experienced as authentic and worthwhile. One of the many virtues of Erikson's theory is that it provides insight into psychic functioning and development after puberty. The task of the next stage, "intimacy vs. isolation," is to learn to love and become intimate with a person who is experienced as separate and worthy of commitment. In "generativity versus stagnation" the task is to feel productive and concerned for the next generation. The final stage is "integrity versus despair," in which the person either accepts that he has lived his one life and lived it well or feels a profound sense of despair and wasted opportunity. Of course, Erikson does not view these stages as "all-or-nothing;" rather, in each stage the person experiences a ratio of the opportunity to the danger (e.g., trust to mistrust), which influences passage through the next stage.

Outside of clinical practice, the main approach to ego development is that of Jane Loevinger and her colleagues (1966, 1976a). For two decades Loevinger has been developing a method, based on analysis of answers to a sentence-completion task, for empirically examining ego development. Her work is a pleasure to read because it is informed by a critical and theoretically sophisticated mind as well as by a body of verifiable data. (For reviews of her theory and research, see Hauser, 1976; Noam, Kohlberg, and Snarey, 1983).

Loevinger poses ego development as a "master trait," second only to intelligence in accounting for human variability on a variety of tasks (1966, p. 205). Ego development, for Loevinger, includes impulse control, character development, interpersonal relations, and conscious preoccupations (as well as, she claims at one point, "cognitive mode," 1976). Her theory is related to Kohlberg's theory of moral development both conceptually and empirically: like Kohlberg, she posits development from preconformist to conformist to postconformist stages, and her measure of ego development correlates highly with Kohlberg's measure of moral development (see Noam, Kohlberg, and Snarey, 1983).

Loevinger (1976a) views the ego as a process, not a thing, and she conceives of her stages as representing both a developmental sequence and

150

a character typology. The first stage she calls "presocial," during which the main task is to separate self from nonself. During the second, or "impulsive" stage, the child is preoccupied with his own wishes and impulses, and others are "seen and valued in terms of what they can give him" (1976, p. 16). The third stage is the "self-protective" stage, in which the child or the adult whose development has been arrested at this level has developed some capacity to control his or her impulses through anticipation of short-term rewards and punishments. The person remains essentially hedonistic, though Loevinger adds a sense of guardedness and vulnerability and a tendency to externalize blame.

In the "conformist" stage, the child identifies with powerful parental figures, and moral values are partially internalized. The conformist is cooperative, seeks approval, and identifies with a group; she or he is not attuned to internal psychological states or motivations. The next stage Loevinger calls "conscientious," in which internalization of rules has proceeded "to include self-administration of sanctions, self-evaluations, and self-selection of the rules to be followed" (1976b, p. 290). Introspection increases, and the person becomes aware of discrepancies between perceived self and moral standards. This stage received its name for two reasons. First, the person at this stage has developed an adult conscience. Secondly, though Loevinger is not entirely explicit about it, her prototype for this stage is the conscientious objector (see 1976a, p. 21). According to Loevinger, the modal or typical personality in Western societies is somewhere between the conformist and conscientious stages, at a transitional level she calls "self-aware" (p. 19).

The next stage is the "autonomous" stage, although it is preceded by another transitional period, the "individualistic level." At this level the person cherishes individuality and comes to appreciate internal conflicts, though the recognition and partial transcendence of conflicts is not more developed until the autonomous stage. In that stage the person recognizes and values the autonomy of both self and others. Unlike the individualistic person, the autonomous individual recognizes the limits of personal autonomy. The final stage, about which Loevinger says relatively little, is called "integrated," which she compares to Maslow's self-actualized person. Unlike the autonomous person, according to Loevinger, the integrated person has consolidated a sense of identity (p. 26).

While Loevinger's model offers, in broadest strokes, a useful way of conceptualizing ego development, in its particulars it is problematic in a number of respects. First, like Kohlberg's theory, while the model purports to be structural, in actuality it confuses content and structure. By and large a person who is liberal-to-leftist in an individualistic society will score higher than someone who is not, and given that liberal political values or individualistic attitudes are as much a product of socialization as ego

151

development, this poses a serious problem. For example, a person who completes a sentence completion item, "Education . . ." with "should be available to all" will be scored as conscientious, whereas one who answers, "is good for getting a job" will be classified as self-protective (Loevinger, Wessler, and Redmore, 1970). While this may indeed represent an ego-psychological difference, it may also simply reflect differential class, cultural, or historical circumstances. In hard economic times people are more likely to focus upon education's utilitarian value, and surely not everyone in a preliterate society or a working class neighborhood is developmentally stunted at a stage before conscience.

This confusion of content and structure leads to a second problem, the inference of ego-psychological differences from cultural differences. People at the conformist stage value niceness, helpfulness, and cooperation, whereas those at the self-protective stage are competitive and self-interested (1976, p. 18). New Yorkers are therefore by and large less developed than Georgians or rural Mexicans. In reality, people can internalize individualism just as they can internalize communalism. In both cases the psychological processes are similar, though the content is different.

Thirdly, because the measure focuses so heavily on conscious verbal responses, it does not discriminate intelligent, liberal people with severe ego defects from those who actually are quite integrated and ego-psychologically mature. Many, if not most, people with borderline personality disorders are very intelligent and many hold left-wing political beliefs; yet from an ego-psychological perspective, they are unable to modulate their emotions, have tremendous difficulty in regulating self-esteem, frequently blur self and other, and are often unable to maintain a coherent sense of self or identity. Such people are frequently attracted to extremist ideology because it splits the world into unambiguous categories of good and bad, maintains a sense of coherent goals and values, and permits expression of rage. It also fits in with their understanding of the world as cruel and malevolent while simultaneously fulfilling longings for a merger with others and for the end of real societal struggles that become projective screens for tremendous psychic battles. This is not, of course, to imply that all or most radicals are motivated by ego defects, or that armed or unarmed struggle is not frequently a reasonable response to state terrorism of the right or the left. Nevertheless, many severely disturbed people hold seemingly humanistic, egalitarian, or otherwise "enlightened" values that compensate for murderous rage or reflect the desperate need for unambiguous ideology upon which to rest identity, and these people would often score high on Loevinger's scale.

In general, Loevinger's model suffers from a lack of clinical grounding. I am not simply saying this as a snotty clinician who would like to claim that no one without clinical experience can understand personality. Unfortunately, I do not have enough clinical experience myself to make such a self-serving, condescending claim personally useful. Rather, I am simply arguing that Loevinger's model relies upon a number of stereotypes that clinical observation simply will not permit. For example, to view consolidation of a sense of identity as an accomplishment of the final "integrated" stage reached by only a few belies the experience of many of us who may not have reached such a stage but nonetheless clearly experience and are recognized by others to have a stable identity. Similarly, to argue that people at low levels of ego development do not experience profound depression (p. 20) is clearly wrong. Loevinger's prototype of psychic maturity appears to be the well analyzed adult, yet many such people, who are well aware of many of their more primitive conflicts, are much less able to rein in sadistic impulses and commit themselves to other people than some people without much introspective awareness who are nevertheless steady as an ox.

Finally, Loevinger's model and measure is too highly correlated with intellectual competence to be useful as a measure of ego development. Loevinger's model is highly correlated with IQ and verbal fluency (see Hauser, 1976). This is not simply a problem of discriminant validity (i.e., discriminating one construct from another; Campbell and Fiske, 1959). The problem, as suggested earlier, is that many brilliant people are ego-psychologically very primitive. One thus cannot justify the view that, for example, a person with "low ego level will not differentiate his notion of self from his ego ideal" because "persons of low level simply do not have that degree of conceptual complexity" (Loevinger, 1976, p. 100).

Recently Kegan (1982) has proposed another model of ego development that relies heavily on Piaget, though his model will not be elaborated here. Kegan has proposed a stage sequence in the evolution of "meaning-making" with considerable depth, though like other models that rely on Kohlberg's theory, he confuses content with process, as when he presumes that people whose morality centers on the good of a larger group are inherently higher level than those with a more particularistic focus (pp. 104-5).[1] Nevertheless, his theory offers a number of interesting insights and is part of an exciting new school of thought (see Selman, 1980; and the volume edited by Lee and Noam, 1983) that is attempting to bring together cognitive-developmental and clinical understanding.

From this brief review of approaches to various aspects of personality development, it should be apparent that the concerns of theoreticians interested in the development of narcissism and object relations, morality, and ego processes are clearly related. Theories of ego development and

---

[1] At other points he implies that the majority of people in the world cannot be intimate (p. 105), or that they lack a sense of self (p. 106).

theories of the development of narcissism and object relations underscore the same movement from an undifferentiated condition to pursuance of need-satisfaction to internalization and true concern for others that is examined by ego psychologists and moral psychologists who posit a shift from preconformist to conformist stages.

My aim in the remaining sections of this chapter is to offer an integrated theory of personality development that synthesizes the important insights of these approaches while avoiding their pitfalls. In particular, the theory will attempt to sketch a portrait of ego and moral development that avoids male-centered or ethnocentric ascription of content to stages and makes liberal use of contemporary research on child development to keep the theory closer to observable data than object relations theories which tend to posit unverifiable stages. In barest outline the theory proposes a movement from a stage in which self and other are not phenomenologically distinct; to a period in which a rudimentary self-concept is evolving but others are important primarily insofar as they fulfill one's needs; to a stage in which morals are increasingly internalized from significant others and the child comes to accept as legitimate the moral beliefs she is learning instead of following them for expedience; to a stage beyond internalization in which the person creates from her own experience values and moral beliefs that seem meaningful and valid. The presentation here will focus on the development of the ego ideal from a morality of self-interest in which the needs of others are secondary, to an internalized morality premised on the subordination of oneself to the higher authority of significant others, to a synthetic or integrative morality based on the recognition of the value and power of both self and others.

Internal Narcissism

For years psychologists have assumed, along with William James, that the infant's world is a bloomin', buzzin' confusion. Research on cognitive processes in infants has come to modify that view (for a review, see Cohen, 1979), suggesting that infants are capable of learning quite early in life, and that in the second half of the first year they are able to form nonlinguistic, though relatively abstract concepts (e.g., Cohen and Strauss, 1979).

Nevertheless, the evidence is clear that during the first months of life, reality is dimly perceived and relatively unorganized from the perspective of the infant. In part this reflects limitations in the perceptual apparatus of the baby: infants would likely be unable to discriminate different faces, and certainly facial expressions, in the first month or two solely for perceptual reasons (Souther and Banks, 1979, cited in Sherrod, 1981). Equally significant is the lack of experience and maturation of cognitive

154

capacities necessary to develop schemas through which to process information. Psychologists since Piaget and Bartlett have recognized the importance of schemas in both constructing and retrieving knowledge, and one need only imagine a condition in which one must construct all knowledge from scratch (with a little help from innate perceptual mechanisms) to grasp the extent to which infancy conforms to James's view. Further, in the earliest months a high percentage of the infant's time is spent in sleep, which limits the capacity to process and organize information.

Somewhere between the third and sixth months, gradual changes become perceptible. At around four months one begins to see differential social smiling, in which the infant smiles more at familiar than unfamiliar faces, suggesting some capacity to store and retrieve information about social stimuli. While the data are not entirely clear because of methodological problems, the weight of evidence suggests that infants cannot discriminate their mothers from strangers until the second quarter of the first year (Olson, 1981). As early as the fourth or fifth month, infants appear to possess rudimentary social expectations, showing signs of distress if their mothers violate expected patterns of social behavior by suddenly becoming silent, expressionless, or seemingly disinterested (Trevarthen, 1977; Oster, 1981).

The first six months[1] comprise a period in psychic development I will call *primary internal narcissism*. This period shares certain features with Freud's stages of autoeroticism and primary narcissism, though it assumes an infant actively engaged with, and within the limits of its cognitive and perceptual capacities, responsive to its environment (cf. Fast, 1981). Freud, in contrast, assumed that the infant begins life totally withdrawn from its environment and is as satisfied with hallucinatory wish-fulfillment as with satisfaction in reality. In this phase[2] of what will later be described as the stage of internal narcissism, the infant is pleasure-seeking, interested in quelling negative affects that are by and large produced through biological homeostatic mechanisms, and maintaining momentary pleasure, such as the presence of a familiar face or smell. Though in reality the infant is object-related from the start, its phenomenal world is initially, to use the psychoanalytic term, "objectless," which means devoid of stable and retrievable object representations.[3]

A significant feature of primary internal narcissism is the lack of differ-

---

[1] When I give chronological ages I am, of course, speaking only of approximations. The exact age in which a stage occurs is obviously influenced by constitutional and environmental factors.

[2] I use the term "phase" to refer to substages.

[3] A perennial problem in psychoanalytic theorizing is the confusion of objective and subjective perspectives in dealing with object relations. The infant interacts with people from its first days and is thus objectively object-related, though subjectively it cannot yet distinguish self from other or one object from another.

155

entiation of self and other. On this aspect of infantile experience, researchers and theorists of many different persuasions agree (see Ainsworth, 1969). The primary internally narcissistic infant has no concept of self, only a realm of experience, or what Rogers (1959) would call a "phenomenal field." Infants appear to develop differentiated object-representations or person-schemas[1] before they develop coherent self-schemas (Harter, 1983). The reason is fairly obvious: infants interact with different people, and they find the interaction with some more pleasurable or unpleasurable than others. They thus have both cognitive and dynamic reasons to learn to distinguish between people. "Interaction" with self, in contrast, is constant, allowing the illusion that reality and one's experience are identical.

To say that the infant lacks differentiated concepts of self and other is not to imply, as many theorists have, that the infant *confuses* self and other. It is very unlikely that when a three-month-old sees its mother walk away it thinks to itself, "There goes a piece of me." That a five-month-old can recognize specific people certainly suggests the presence of primitive object concepts, however difficult to retrieve. Rather than confusing self and others, the infant appears to lack stable and readily retrievable concepts of a self and of others separate from self. He simply does not process information using these categories because he lacks the ability to step back from himself cognitively in order to see that he and other people are independent animate objects located in space and time, not just here-again-gone-again images in his flow of experience. (For a fascinating application of differentiation notions to the development of gender identity, see Fast, 1978, 1979.)

Beginning somewhere between six and ten months is the phase of *secondary internal narcissism,* which predominates in normal development through twenty-four to forty-eight months. The defining characteristics of secondary internal narcissism are the emergence of primitive self-schemas and the use of others as extensions, mirrors, or tools of the self. Whereas in the primary phase the infant lacks a conception of self, in the secondary phase of internal narcissism self-images have emerged and developed content and boundaries, though frequently unrealistic. In other words, subjective and objective self have begun to converge, albeit only tentatively. As Piaget and Inhelder astutely note, "Freud talked about narcissism but did not sufficiently stress the fact that this was narcissism with a Narcissus"

---

[1] It would probably make sense to refer to these as "person-schemas" instead of "object representations" to avoid confusion. Both psychoanalytic and Piagetian psychologists refer to "objects," but with different meanings. By "object" Piaget intends any stimulus, animate or inanimate, which is an object of *thought*. The psychoanalytic notion originally meant an object of an instinct, and has gradually come to mean a representation of a stimulus endowed with human characteristics or one that is affectively "cathected."

(1969, p. 22). With secondary internal narcissism, narcissism has found its Narcissus.

Lewis and Brooks-Gunn (1979) argue that the infant's first sense of self is what they call an "existential self," a recognition that she is a causal agent distinct from others with separate actions and thoughts. During the second and third years the child develops a "categorical self," through which she learns to take herself as object and to categorize herself as possessing certain attributes.

The emergence of rudimentary self-schemas is obviously difficult to study empirically because it occurs in preverbal infants, though a sense of agency appears to emerge somewhere in the second half of the first year. The phenomenon of "social referencing," in which a person gauges the safety of a possible action by observing someone else's emotional reaction, arises in the last quarter of the first year, suggesting some degree of self-other differentiation (Klinnert et al., 1983).

The use of self-referent nouns and pronouns provides one index of the development of a sense of self during the second and third years. Self-referent nouns are common in the speech of verbal two-year-olds (Brown, 1973). Use of one's own name exclusively to refer to one's own picture as opposed to those of others is not normative until the end of the second year (Lewis and Brooks, 1978). Interestingly, Bossert (1982) observed that the use of the pronoun "mine" far outstrips use of other self-referent words in the speech of two-year-olds.

Because the ontogenesis of self-schemas is difficult to study empirically, researchers have focused on visual self-recognition as an indicator of the existence of a self-concept. In reality, these researchers only speak to the development of a body-self-concept, if not a visual-body-self-concept (as opposed, for example, to a tactile-body-self-concept, which may emerge somewhat earlier). Lewis and Brooks-Gunn (1979) argue that visual self-recognition occurs in 15- to 18-month-olds and is solidified by 21 to 24 months, though as Bossert (1982) observes, and a perusal of their data suggest, the data support no such conclusions. In a methodologically impeccable study, Bossert (1982) found that visual self-recognition is actually not solidified until sometime in the third year.

The second phase of internal narcissism is the first point at which tension arises between self and other because the infant had previously been unaware of the presence of the other. The infant now accepts the existence, but denies the legitimacy of the other and, particularly toward the beginning of secondary internal narcissism, is unable to understand the complicated goals, motives, and perspectives of significant others (see Bowlby, 1969; Selman, 1980). The child during this period is certainly object-seeking; however, she is still unable to view people as legitimate entities with their own, autonomous existences. The defining characteristic

157

of internal narcissism, both primary and secondary, is that the individual perceives only her own needs as legitimate. In terms of the ego ideal and moral development, internally narcissistic morality is a function of the child's own desires. Morality, a content of the ego ideal, at this stage is synonymous with the pursuit of pleasure. The infant perceives "the good" as that which is in accordance with her own desires.

The second phase of internal narcissism is the age of Winnicott's (1971) "transitional object." The transitional object, the archetype of which is the teddy bear, is an external object upon which the infant projects her own subjectivity; it is the "intermediate area between the subjective and that which is objectively perceived" (p. 3). Winnicott explains in *Playing and Reality:*

> It is not the object, of course, that is transitional. The object represents the infant's transition from a state of being merged with the mother to a state of being in relation to the mother as something outside and separate. (Pp. 14-15)

The realm of the transitional object is that of the secondary internally narcissistic ego, with its incipient subjective awareness of separation from caretakers. It is an early attempt at synthesizing subjectivity and objectivity after the two have become disjoint.

For the child (or the adult for whom aspects of ego development have been arrested) at this stage, people take on many of the characteristics of transitional objects: they function for the child as extensions of self, projections of self, mirrors of self, or tools for gratification. As early as six months the infant will begin to engage its caretakers in communication centered around its activities. Escalona (1968) notes a shift at this point toward more vigorous attempts to elicit and maintain social responses, which indicates, as well, an incipient differentiation of self and other.

Piaget's discussion of the development of symbolic play in early childhood in many ways parallels Winnicott's discussion of transitional phenomena. According to Piaget (Piaget, 1951; Piaget and Inhelder, 1969, pp. 57-63), the first form of play, "exercise play," occurs during the sensorimotor stage and involves repetition or preservation of actions that are in other contexts functional. The second form of play, "symbolic play," occurs especially between the ages of two and six, and it precedes a type of play characterized by objective, socially transmitted rules. "Symbolic play" lies somewhere between Piagetian assimilation and accommodation: it represents a transitional form of activity which in some sense acknowledges the reality of the external world but tailors this reality to the needs of the child. Symbolic play, like the transitional object, lies, to use Winnicott's (1971) phrase, in the "interstitial space" between subjectivity and objectivity.

158

Piaget contends that around eighteen months, with the move from sensorimotor to preoperational thought (Piaget, 1970), a fundamental change occurs in the relation between self and others:

> ... there occurs a kind of Copernican revolution, or more simply, a kind of general decentering process whereby the child eventually comes to regard himself as an object among others in a universe that is made up of permanent objects. ... (Piaget and Inhelder, 1969, p.13)

As can readily be seen from the description here of secondary internal narcissism, this phase is as thoroughly cognitive as affective or object relational. Indeed, the processes that lead to and comprise psychic development are so intertwined that to separate the various aspects of development is as implausible and artificial as it is necessary for understanding the various functions and capacities of the mind. As Robert Holt remarks:

> ... we should not proceed to develop one model for motivation, one to explain memory, and another for each of the traditional divisions of the old elementary texts, in the vain expectation that the unity of observed human functioning will somehow emerge from the joint, even "interactive," operation of these several models. Nature may be orderly, but it is not the creation of an obsessive-compulsive God who created thought one day, motivation another, and saw to it that there were proper boundaries between all such categories. (1976, p. 188)

In a somewhat different language, Piaget expresses the same thought:

> There is no behavior pattern, however intellectual, which does not involve affective factors and motives; but, reciprocally, there can be no affective states without the interventions of perceptions or comprehensions which constitute their cognitive structure. Behavior is therefore of a piece, even if the structures do not explain the energetics and if, vice versa, its energetics do not account for its structures. The two aspects, affective and cognitive, are at the same time inseparable and irreducible. (Piaget and Inhelder, p. 158)

The phase of secondary internal narcissism corresponds to Mahler's stage of "separation-individuation" (see Mahler, Pine, and Bergman, 1975), in which the child who is hatching from symbiosis with its mother tries to walk a tightrope between the development of autonomy on the one hand and the fear of aloneness, abandonment, and the regressive pull of merger on the other. In the "practicing" phase of separation-individuation, which Mahler correlates roughly with the period from ten to eighteen months, "the world is the junior toddler's oyster:"

> ... the child seems intoxicated with his own faculties and with the greatness of his own world. Narcissism is at its peak ... The chief characteristic of this practicing period is the child's great narcissistic investment in his own functions, his own body, as well as in the objects and objec-

tives of his expanding "reality." Along with this, we see a relatively great imperviousness to knocks and falls and other frustrations, such as a toy being grabbed by another child. (P. 71)

Psychoanalytic writers frequently attribute to the infant a fantasied sense of "omnipotence" (Freud, 1914; Winnicott, 1971). While the phenomenon to which they are pointing is certainly real, perhaps one would do better to speak of the infant's magical sense of "potency." One has little reason to suppose that infants routinely ignore the myriad cases in which their potency fails, or that all infants reason precisely the same in this regard. One need only observe a healthy two-year-old, however, to understand what psychoanalysts have in mind. The confidence with which the two-year-old will march into a neighbor's house with abandon, literally run circles around its parents, or willfully make its position clear on a wide range of matters can be truly astounding. The experience of a fortunate infant certainly promotes a magical sense of potency.[1] When she closes her eyes, the world gets dark. When she cries, her caretakers come to relieve her distress. The internally narcissistic infant does not recognize that between her actions and parental ministrations is a parent with a will and desires of her own. Empirical evidence documents this magical potency in late infancy. Marvin (cited in Shantz, 1975) found that two- and three-year-olds, unlike children even a year older, tend to insist that through their own power they can make their mothers return. By age four, children might instead respond that they cannot bring their mothers back "but herself can." Developmentally, children tend to attribute agency to themselves before attributing it to others (Watson and Fischer, 1977; Harter, 1983).

Self-other differentiation is incomplete in the secondary internally narcissistic child. During the apogee of this phase children are only beginning to sense that others have their own subjectivities or that the child himself has a private world of experience. Maccoby (1980) gives the example of the two-year-old who complains that her milk is not cold enough. When her mother protests that she just took the milk from the refrigerator, the little girl takes another sip and says, "See, it *is* warm!" (p. 262). This is similar to the three-year-old who covers her eyes and says, "You can't see

---

[1] The infant who is fortunate enough to experience this illusory potency or "omnipotence" develops what Erikson (1963) has called a sense of "basic trust" or Laing (1959) has termed "primary ontological security," a sense that his needs will be met through his own actions and those of others. For the infant who is not so fortunate, matters are quite different. To preserve a sense of safety in an untrustworthy environment, the infant or young child may defensively distort his sense of impotence to a view of total omnipotent control, withdraw into apathy and depression, develop an expectation that to survive he must take everything he can and avoid contact with people, or internalize primitively construed abusive "introjects" while simultaneously idealizing them and pretending they are benevolent.

me." As these examples suggest, ego development is intertwined with cognitive development, though neither is reducible to the other.

Similarly, as Vygotsky (1934) observes, it is not until three-and-a-half or four that the child begins speaking for others instead of producing egocentric monologues, and Piaget notes that egocentric language persists through age six (Piaget and Inhelder, 1969). This gradual change to truly social communication is both cognitive and object relational, representing both the ability to understand the listener's point of view and the *concern* for the listener's point of view.

As early as fourteen to twenty months the child, in what Sander (1975) refers to as the "self-assertion" stage of infant-mother interaction, comes to develop goals independent of, and often in opposition to his mother's wishes. This is the origin of moral conflict (i.e., the conflict between competing interests), and the internally narcissistic moral view resolves this conflict in favor of impulse. In other words, gratification is the *summum bonum*, so that the child responds primarily to conditioning or restraint.

The child does not come to recognize the existence of the private thoughts and desires of self and others until the third or fourth year. Research by Flavell and his colleagues (cited in Harter, 1983) documents that children begin to realize around age three that they have a private realm of thoughts that others cannot observe. Harter and Barnes (cited in Harter, 1983) found that three- and four-year-old children have difficulty differentiating their own emotions from those of their parents and that they cannot separate the causes of their emotions from the causes of their parents' emotions (e.g., "Daddy would be sad if he couldn't stay up and watch 'Hulk' on television"). By age three, children attribute intentions and motives to other people (Keasey, 1978), though whether they also attribute these to inanimate objects is unclear (Gelman and Spelke, 1981).

The child's gradual development of a sense of self, potency, and separateness from others is probably best chronicled by Mahler, particularly in her description of the period of "rapprochement" which she claims generally occurs between fifteen and twenty-four months (Mahler, Pine, and Bergman, 1975). During this period the child manifests an incipient fear of loss of love but retains much of his or her "anal" negativism (1975, pp. 76-7). According to Mahler and her colleagues, children during this period display two contradictory behavioral patterns: ". . . the 'shadowing' [incessant watching and following] of mother and the darting away from her, with the expectation of being chased and swept into her arms," which Mahler takes to indicate "both his wish for reunion with the love object and his fear of reengulfment by it" (p. 77).

The toddler is coming to differentiate self from others (p. 78), and that

161

every child Mahler observed experienced stranger anxiety during this period (p. 77) attests to the powerful psychic impact of the realization that,
not only can others exist independently of the child, but that they can
exert power over him as well. "The junior toddler gradually realizes that
his love objects (his parents) are separate individuals with their own personal interests" (p. 79). The child for the first time recognizes that his
wishes are not identical with those of his mother (p. 90). Whereas previously the child used the mother as a haven or "home base" for emotional
"refueling," his incipient awareness of her separate desires and existence
finds behavioral expression in his "continual bringing of things to mother,
filling her lap with objects that he had found in his expanding world" (p.
90). The mother at this stage is gradually changing for the child, from
transitional object to idealized love object. The toddler often expects the
mother magically to read his thoughts and fulfill his wishes (p. 95).

Characteristic of this period are indecisiveness, ambivalence, and rapid
mood swings (pp. 95-6). Mahler describes the central conflict of this age,
which Erikson (1963) has so aptly designated "autonomy versus shame
and doubt:"

> Around 18 months our toddlers seemed quite eager to exercise their
> rapidly growing autonomy to the hilt. Increasingly, they chose not to be
> reminded that at times they could not manage on their own. Conflicts
> ensued that seemed to hinge upon the desire to be separate, grand, and
> omnipotent, on the one hand, and to have mother magically fulfill their
> wishes, without their having to recognize that help was actually coming
> from the outside, on the other. (Mahler, Pine, and Bergman, p. 95)

Mahler nicely elucidates the affective side of the cognitive capacity to
separate self from other, observing that children in the period of rapprochement seek independence and autonomy as well as fear separateness,
as evidenced in rapidly alternating efforts to push the mother away and to
cling to her. This suggests, as well, the conflict the child is experiencing
between the desire for separateness and potency and the continued set of
feelings and behaviors generally described as "attachment." Another side
of this is a swing between undervaluation and devaluation of the self,
between omnipotence and impotence, and a similar oscillation regarding
others. This is the age Kernberg views as involving the splitting of all-good
and all-bad self- and object-representations.

External Narcissism

The shift from parents as transitional objects (or in Kohut's evocative
terminology, "selfobjects," 1977) to objects with an independent existence
is gradual and subtle and is evidence of the emergence of the second stage
of processes in the development of personality and moral judgment which

162

will here be called *external narcissism.*[1] Two interrelated events mark the emergence of external narcissism, which begins some time between three and five years, and is generally consolidated during preadolescence or adolescence.[2] The first involves object relations and social cognition, and the second involves the form of moral judgment, though the two are intertwined. First, the person not only becomes capable of more fully understanding the wishes and feelings of other people, but she or he comes to *value* the interests of significant others. Secondly, the meaning of "the good" changes from need-satisfaction to values and standards of behavior internalized from significant others. Whereas in internal narcissism the child's wishes and desires serve as the basis of his morality, in external narcissism the morals and ideals of significant others begin to function as ego ideal set-goals, an ideal self starts to emerge, and the individual must base her self-esteem on the capacity to achieve *externally* derived ideal standards.

The first aspect of the emergence of external narcissism has been described by psychoanalytic theorists variously as the development of whole objects or total objects, object constancy (Kernberg, 1976), libidinal object constancy (Mahler, Pine, and Bergman, 1975), and true object love. One must be cautious in using terms such as these which have acquired over the

---

[1] By "narcissism" I mean the belief in the value and power of the self, regardless of whether that narcissism occurs or is sustained through lack of differentiation, primitive defenses, identification with powerful others, or other normal and pathological mechanisms. I could just as easily have named the stages without reference to narcissism, though I chose to do so to emphasize continuity with models of narcissism and object relations.

[2] My unwillingness to pinpoint ages precisely stems less from the desire to evade falsification than from two issues, one empirical and the other conceptual. First, developmental variability across individuals and cultures is so great that one simply cannot propose absolute ages. Secondly, the conceptualization of "stages" proposed here, which views them as waxing and waning processes used to fulfill certain functions, suggests a different model of change than in either a continuity or a discontinuity model of personality development. Rather than development being easily represented graphically by a straight line from the origin with a slope of one, as in a model of continuous linear development; or as a series of linear progressions with steep slopes punctuated by long plateaus, as in a discontinuity model (with stage transitions conceived as sudden spurts of growth); this conceptualization views stages as sets of processes best illustrated by overlapping curves, with the slope of an early stage largely being negative as a new stage emerges. Transitions are represented as areas of overlap, where one set of processes recedes and another develops, so that one cannot unambiguously point to an age and correlate it with a particular stage. These different models of growth may be illustrated as follows:

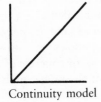   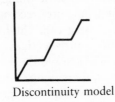

Continuity model Discontinuity model Alternative model

years many, and often inconsistent meanings. "Whole objects" is a good example. Whole objects are usually juxtaposed with part-objects, which are representations of isolated aspects of a person. The problem is that some have meant by this distinction something very concrete, namely the representation of mother *qua* mother instead of breast, while others have intended something more general and metaphorical, namely the ability to love an object in itself instead of loving it solely for its need-gratifying aspects. The former occurs quite early, certainly by eighteen months if not much sooner, while the latter tends not to be solidified until five or six. A third meaning of "whole objects" is the ability to store and retrieve a single representation of an object that is both frustrating and gratifying.

The emergence of externally narcissistic processes occurs in the period described by Kernberg as the consolidation of self- and object-representations and psychic structure and by Kohut as the stage in which a cohesive self has emerged. The first aspect of this development involves a gradual shift from use of others as transitional objects or tools of gratification to the recognition and valuing of autonomous others. While this shift is not primarily cognitive, in that it entails a change in valuation of others and not just understanding of them, it is certainly connected with, and dependent upon cognitive development. It relies, for example, upon the development of empathy, which Hoffman (1979, 1980) has masterfully traced from primitive conditioning and contagion in infancy to more complex affectively and cognitively mediated distress and understanding of others' internal states in older children and adults.

It also rests upon the development of "role taking" (for a review, see Higgins, 1981) or "perspective taking" (Selman, 1980) capabilities through which a person comes to understand others' psychological experience. In a methodologically diverse and exquisite programme of research, Selman (1980) has attempted to chart the development of perspective taking through five periods. The first is undifferentiated and egocentric perspective taking which roughly corresponds to ages three to six. (Selman does not examine perspective taking in children younger than three years of age.) At this level the child distinguishes self from other physically but not psychologically and is unable to separate subjective feelings from objective reality. The second stage is one of "subjective perspective taking," in which the child forms relatively simple conceptualizations of others, and attributes an illusory observability and unity to their thoughts and feelings. The child cannot, at this developmental juncture, recognize ambivalence in others.

In the third, "self-reflective" stage, the child is able to take the perspective of another person. At the fourth level, the young adolescent can step back from both her own perspective and the perspective of concrete others to take a more objective, third-person approach that integrates multiple perspectives. Finally, in the fifth stage, the person is fully aware of the distinction between self-presentational appearance and psychic reality, is able to form complex object representations, and has some awareness of the depths of psychological functioning, including the existence of unconscious motivational processes. (For an excellent summary of related research on the development of social cognition, see Shantz, 1975.)

The second aspect of the emergence of externally narcissistic processes is that alongside a differentiation of self-schemas from ideal self-schemas is a change in the form of morality or sense of "the good." The criterion of need-satisfaction recedes as the standard of good and evil and is replaced by "internalized" standards. "Internalization" is another one of those constructs that should not be used without explicitly stating what one means. It is an omnibus term in psychoanalysis that does not draw certain very important distinctions. One such distinction, which has often been ignored because of the ambiguous place of object relations concepts in the Freudian structural model, is between object representation and identification. If one conceives of cognition as an ego function, then any mental representation or schema is "internalized into the ego." Yet this is an altogether different phenomenon from the internalization process Freud described in "Mourning and Melancholia" (1917) through which a person makes a lost object part of himself (e.g., takes on many of its characteristics) and thus incorporates the object "into the ego." Freud himself failed to distinguish the cognitions people form of significant others from the internalizations that in part constitute the ego and superego.

One can distinguish several distinct phenomena through which aspects of an object or ideal are "internalized." The first is object representation, or the formation of a person-schema, in which the individual forms a cognitive representation of the object. The second is modeling (Bandura, 1977), in which the person develops the competence to imitate some aspect of the object's behavior. The third is internalization of function, in which behaviors or attitudes of the object or aspects of the relationship with the object are replaced by self-regulatory ego functions, such as the ability to restrain oneself from tempting but dangerous acts or the regulation of self-esteem (see Reich, 1960). In other words, the person develops the capacity to carry out intrapsychically a function previously fulfilled by the object. Anna Freud (cited in Maccoby, 1980) provides an excellent example of this phenomenon:

> A little girl, just two years old, had always been put to bed by her mother, and there was a familiar bed-time routine. For the first time, the mother was away over night, and the child was being put to bed by a baby-sitter. The child had great difficulty going to sleep, and even though she was very tired, kept her eyes open after she was tucked in and the sitter had tip-toed out of the room. Through the open door, the sitter hears the child say, imitating her mother's voice: "Goodnight my dearest." (Pp. 14-15)

One could consider internalization of function a subcategory of modeling, in which the "behavior" being modeled is intrapsychic, i.e., a mental operation.

A fourth process is moral internalization, in which injunctions are established as moral standards and values are learned and accepted. Fifth, and often related, is the formation of ideal self-schemas, both moral and nonmoral. At the most primitive levels these may be idealized and distorted self-schemas or object representations (or what psychoanalysts call "introjects"). Finally, the person may alter self-schemas or self-concept to accommodate representations of idealized objects or ideal self.

The relationship between these processes is complex and has never been adequately elucidated. For example, partly in the service of affect and partly for strictly cognitive reasons, people form schemas of significant others. The nature of social schemas and the cognitive distortions involved in social information processing have been studied at length by social cognition researchers (see, e.g., Nisbett and Ross, 1980). The nature of representations of other people has also been a focus of object relations theory in psychoanalysis. In psychoanalytic metapsychology the place of such representations is ambiguous. As noted earlier, object representations have frequently been viewed as "internalizations" in the ego or superego. A child can, however, form a schema of her father without internalizing her father or his attributes as an ideal. Inadequacies in social information processing (e.g., in the formation of object representations) invariably affect moral internalizations: a child with a schema of a parent which is distorted for cognitive or motivational reasons will necessarily form problematic ego ideal internalizations when introjecting distorted images of the parent as moral internalizations. This is an area in which one must bear in mind the warning of cognitive-developmental theorists from Piaget onward that moral "internalizations" always involve active cognitive processing by the child and are never perfect representations of parental demands or attributes.

The phenomenon one may properly call identification is actually a composite of several of these processes. First, the child must form a cognitive representation of the object or the aspect of the object with which he is identifying. A second process involves the setting up of this object or attribute as an ego ideal set-goal that establishes a standard to be attained. Thirdly, the child imitates the desired attribute or behavior, trying to make himself more like the object. Finally, he adjusts his self-concept or specific self-schemas to reflect the altered ideal and behavior. This will often, additionally, involve a defensive distortion of self-schemas to allow the child the sense that she or he actually is like the parent or object of identification.

Disentangling these various processes also allows one to distinguish between modeling and identification. Bandura (1977) has argued that we should jettison the concept of identification and replace it with the more observable notion of modeling or imitation. In contrast, psychoanalytic psychologists usually use the term "identification" to refer to any occasion in which a person appropriates the thoughts, feelings, or behavior of someone else, usually an authority figure. As opposed to either of these two views, the present approach suggests a useful distinction between modeling and identification: modeling means cognitively mediated imitation, whereas identification refers to a process in which modeling of behaviors or attributes is motivated by the establishment of the object or attributes as an ideal, and in which the person expects to gain pleasure or reduce displeasure by adjusting self-schemas accordingly. In other words, whereas modeling usually occurs in many situations as a way to produce appropriate responses in the absence of direct reinforcement, identification involves the alteration of ideal self-images as well as self-images relevant to those ideals.

All identification thus has a component of modeling, but all modeling does not entail identification. The distinction between the two is clearest regarding the internalization of moral beliefs. Modeling of self-abnegatory rules would not occur without identification because direct conditioning would override it. Such rules are, however, internalized through identificatory processes because acting or believing like the parent is itself rewarding since it allows one to fulfill an ideal of becoming like the idealized object. With identification, unlike nonidentificatory modeling, the reward or "reinforcement" is in the process itself, not in the potential to produce more suitable behavior in the modeled domain. When the little boy imitates his father shaving, he does not do so because he knows that ten years later he will benefit from having practiced shaving as a child; he does so because being like his father is pleasurable.

This all raises the question of why the externally narcissistic child identifies with parents at all and comes to accept their moral views as legitimate. I will propose three mechanisms through which this can occur. In so doing I will not hypothesize that every child identifies for precisely the same combination of reasons to the same degree. It is time that the psychodynamic understanding of development move away from nomothetic accounts of allegedly universal phenomenology to a greater recognition that one must be extremely cautious in ascribing particular thoughts to "the Oedipal age boy," "the child," or the like. For example, before doing clinical work I suspected that the psychoanalytic notion of "penis envy" was a flight of Freudian fancy, an ideological projection of culturally constructed and learned beliefs about male superiority. In reading clinical accounts of penis envy, in which anger at men or jealousy of various privileges granted to males in Western society were interpreted as manifestations of penis envy, I was convinced that clinical data were being too readily assimilated into theoretical constructs, which indeed, they often are. I was therefore rather surprised when a female patient, in the context of discussing her revulsion for women and her sense of their profound inferiority, described her early sense of her body as missing something. In psychotherapy one does, in fact, come across penis envy of this sort, and when one thinks about the concreteness of childhood cognition, it is not surprising that a little girl who sees her brother getting advantages because of his sex may view the source of her misfortune as a missing penis. Yet we have no reason to suppose that "the generic girl" – i.e., every girl – undergoes precisely the same experiences and thought processes to develop a view that women are inferior, that their inferiority stems from a physical defect, that mother was responsible for the child's defectiveness, and therefore that father is to be loved. Many little girls have not seen male genitals yet nevertheless develop conscience, and it is certainly to be expected that of those girls who unconsciously view the vagina as a defect or a wound (which many do), an equal number are likely to blame the father for it as the mother, since the father, unlike the mother, appears to be intact. The point of this is not that we should abandon nomothetic accounts and focus exclusively on individual differences. Rather, we should be careful in causally attributing phenomena such as conscience, which are nearly universal and appear in people with vastly differing capacities for complex symbolization, to complicated and individually highly variable mental processes.

The first reason for identification, and probably the most important, relates to the maintenance of self-esteem. When the child has matured cognitively to the point at which he must begin to relinquish the magical sense of potency of infancy and to recognize his inferiority with respect to his parents, he can regain or maintain a sense of his own power and value by becoming like someone who appears all-powerful and all-valuable. He thus begins to establish moral demands and ideal self-images that become set-goals to which he must aspire. Adler emphasized the child's sense of inferiority with respect to his parents, and Freud offered a hypothesis very similar to that proposed here several years before he came to believe in the origin of the superego through resolution of the Oedipus complex. In his essay on narcissism (1914) he argued that with the move away from narcissism and the formation of an ego ideal, the child trades his illusory infantile omnipotence for the worship of a new ideal. One need not suppose that the infant has a sense of omnipotence for this mechanism to operate. Rather, the infant does appear to have a magical sense of potency, and with cognitive development, he forms goals or wished-for self-images that he now realizes are beyond his capacities.

Ausubel (1952) has described the process through which the infant relinquishes an hypothesized infantile omnipotence for what he nicely calls "satellization," in which the child is "relieved of the burden of justifying his adequacy on the basis of actual performance ability" by identifying with seemingly omnipotent parents. In so doing he shares in their magnificence much as "the retainers of a powerful potentate would revel in the glory of their liege" (pp. 57-8). Ausubel argues that satellization proceeds from a "devaluation crisis," in which the child begins to realize that his parents are fulfilling his needs because they, as autonomous beings, *want to* and that getting what one wants depends upon the executive abilities possessed by adults (Ausubel, 1958). Satellization will not occur appropriately if the child is rejected by the parents or valued only for achievements in which the parents can bask (cf. Freud's essay on "those wrecked by success" and the "exceptions," 1916, and Jacobson's elaboration of it, 1959).

One of the implications of Ausubel's view is that the child gains enhanced self-esteem simply by feeling like part of his parent or his parent's entourage, without even having to adjust his behavior. In other words, by redefining his self-schemas to include a likeness or relationship to a parent or parents, the child attains set-goals of being like these omnipotent, omniscient beings. This has implications for cross-cultural study of the self-system and self-esteem as well, because in cultures in which the individual is not considered a separate unit apart from significant others, self-esteem is less likely to depend as much upon factors such as individual competence, morality, etc., and more upon the status of relevant groups or fulfillment of group ideals. This phenomenon is not limited to non-Western societies and can be seen both in the behavior of children, who revel in their parents' successes because they identify with parents, and in the experience of people whose identity prominently includes significant others, so that, for example, a housewife may feel bad about herself when her husband must accept a low-status job or proves incompetent at work.

Kohut (1971, 1977) has elegantly described the shift from internal to external narcissism examined by Ausubel in terms of devaluation and satellization in a way informed by clinical observation of adults with borderline and narcissistic pathology rooted in this developmental era. This is the period of transition from a fragmented self to a cohesive self and the emergence of a grandiose self and an idealized parent imago.[1] One could argue that a grandiose self has roots in an infantile sense of potency but is then defensively elaborated with the growing recognition of lack of power and control. The child thus develops an image of himself as able to do anything, to stand alone, to surmount all odds. The idealized parent imago gradually emerges from parental selfobjects (i.e., transitional objects that serve as extensions of self) and later becomes incorporated into what I am

---

[1] The orthodox Kohutian will, I hope, forgive me if I extend Kohut's ideas somewhat, using them as transitional objects with which to play and mingle my own thoughts.

169

calling here the ego ideal. Grandiose self and idealized parent imago[es] both become established as aspects of ideal self, and with development the child both tones down these omnipotent fantasies and learns to tolerate greater discrepancies between ideals and self-image.[1]

A second source of identification and idealization of parental figures is the need for security. Both Ausubel and Maslow (1954) have pointed to the need for security in the formation of idealized "omnipotent parent" schemas. If the child is to maintain basic trust after recognizing his relative powerlessness, he must be able to put his faith in what one might call a *benevolent other* in whose hands he must put his very existence. The inability to maintain this trust in a benevolent other – whether because the child's affective life is constitutionally so intense that others seem incapable of keeping one safe and satisfied, because those upon whom he relies are so defective in some respect that identification is problematic, or because of experiential or environmental factors such as chronic infantile and childhood illness – can be psychologically devastating. This is observable in the most extreme form in the experience of infants who grew up without nurturance or attachment in sterile foundling homes as first described by Spitz as "hospitalism" (1946).[2] It is also central to the experience of people with profound character pathology and is manifest in a transference frequently filled with fears of rejection or abandonment, intense longing for a benevolent other (or, as a patient once called me, "my protector") juxtaposed with a tremendous fear of attachment, themes of poorly differentiated victims and victimizers, and an alternating sense of one's own dangerousness and unworthiness and the dangerousness and unworthiness of significant others. The child in such a position will generally both reject identification and withdraw into fantasies of secure aloneness on the one

[1] Kohut argues that one of these two "poles" of the "self" can often compensate for defects in the other. One can readily see how serious difficulty with either grandiose self or idealized parent imago(es) could lead to serious pathology. If the child cannot develop a sense of himself as competent, powerful, and valuable in the face of recognition of limitations, he is likely chronically to devalue himself or defensively to create a self-image of total grandeur, which is the psychic complement to extreme devaluation. The result is likely to be an over-dependence on others or an intense need for "narcissistic supplies" from devalued others. Difficulty forming an image of idealized parent figures will result in an inability to identify and consequently in what Kohut calls "missing segments" of psychic structure, the continuation of a morality of need-satisfaction, and a falling back upon a grandiose self-concept that is fragile in the face of cognitive development. In people with borderline pathology one frequently sees defects in both "poles," so that the person oscillates between intense need for an unambivalently positive, idealized object of identification and a fiercely independent stance as a person who needs no one, who can satisfy his own needs and will do so because no one else is to be trusted.

[2] While there has been some controversy about whether psychological deficits in such children stem largely from affective factors relating to attachment or simply from lack of stimulation, recent evidence quite clearly demonstrates the profound impact on character of lack of adequate figures of attachment even in children who received adequate stimulation (Tizard and Hodges, 1978).

hand, and identify with primitive hostile "introjects" who must be abusing him because he deserves the abuse on the other. The result of an inability to believe in and identify with a benevolent other is what one might call (to appropriate Sullivan's term, 1953) a "malevolent transformation" of the object world. Later experience of intense and disorganizing affect will often cause a regressive activation of these primitive schemas.

The identification process that establishes an externally narcissistic ego ideal and forces the child to relinquish need-satisfaction as his highest good is the most important form of a more general mechanism that underlies much of modeling, moral internalization, and identification, which entails the internalization of objects and behaviors that one desires for oneself but does not possess. This mechanism encompasses both the learning of adaptive modeled behaviors (including "internal behaviors") and identification with those whose status one envies (cf. Whiting, Kluckhohn, and Anthony's "status envy" hypothesis of identification, 1958). It underlies both the massive internalizations that result in the formation of conscience and later identifications with significant others, cultural heroes, and the like. The logic of this process is quite simple: if someone has something you want or knows something you want to know, watch that person and copy the behavior; and if someone is tremendously powerful and valuable, make yourself like him or her, and you are likely to become more powerful and valuable (or at least to have the pleasure of thinking you are).

The third factor promoting identification and the internalization of moral rules is cognitively mediated conditioning and social learning. The child learns to expect punishment for particular actions and rewards for others, and she discovers that she can optimize emotion by following certain maxims. This explanation, incidentally, encompasses Freud's castration hypothesis, which asserts that the boy actively represses Oedipal wishes to avoid castration or allay fears of it. Gender identifications and gender-appropriate Oedipal object choice also stems from social learning: the child learns that certain behaviors are appropriate for members of her or his sex, and also that one can gain pleasure from being, for example, coy in relationships with members of the opposite sex, particularly the opposite sex parent.

The wish to avoid painful affects and attain pleasurable ones is an important source of moral development which can explain why the child learns certain prudential rules and performs certain actions in order to gain approval. What it cannot explain is why she or he considers these rules morally correct as opposed to practically useful, often obeys them in the absence of a watchful parental eye, and identifies with the parents as idealized authorities whose notions of good and bad are as objective as the rising and setting of the sun. If moral internalization were strictly a function of conditioning or social learning, people would come to believe in a totally situation-specific morality, in which one need never experience guilt

171

and only need be upset if one breaks rules and gets caught. In reality, however, most people beyond the age of seven or eight do not simply regard moral injunctions as convenient rules of thumb to maximize self-interest (Kant, in fact, specifically defined such maxims as outside the bounds of morality): they view them as standards of behavior that give meaning to their lives and transcend self-interest. The trauma – and the achievement – which the child experiences during this period is that he must trade his own potency or "omnipotence" for that of his parents. In so doing he must submit to their morality, but in return he receives a new form of power and value, an external narcissism. The internalization of moral values thus involves a shift in the perceived locus of power and value. The internally narcissistic person tries to incorporate others into his orbit; the externally narcissistic person has become a satellite in the orbit of significant others.

Whereas the internally narcissistic person attempts to externalize the internal, to make the subjective objective, the externally narcissistic person attempts to internalize the external, to make the objective subjective. To put the matter differently, the internally narcissistic individual views external reality and external objects as extensions or mirrors of himself. The externally narcissistic individual, in contrast, perceives himself as an extension or mirror of external reality (of an external object, e.g., parent, family, or society). External narcissism has, to date, been the norm in all human cultures and is illustrated in its most extreme form by the soldier who gives his life for his country, perceiving his own body as an agent of the group or state.

From an ego-psychological point of view, the shift to external narcissism is the central dynamic operating during the "Oedipal" years. Certainly Oedipal issues are significant in most, if not all cultures, and particularly those with nuclear families. The Oedipus complex is not, however, solely an aspect of psychosexual development; it is also one facet of the gradual relinquishment of infantile power, value, and centrality – affectively complementary to Piagetian cognitive "decentering" – which occurs sometime between late infancy and late childhood.

I should make absolutely clear that I am not therefore arguing for the nonexistence or unimportance of the Oedipus complex, which no one who does clinical work with his eyes open could possibly do. Rather, I am making two more specific arguments. First, the Oedipus complex is not responsible for the bulk of moral internalizations. Aside from the strictly sexual aspects of the Oedipus complex, the recognition that one cannot possess the desired parent is an aspect of a broader recognition in early childhood that one cannot have everything one wants, and that if one wishes to have the love or privileges of significant others one must accommodate oneself to a world that is not under one's magical control.

Secondly, I am arguing that the time has come for psychodynamic psychologists to recognize what has gradually become apparent since the development of ego psychology but which no one has been willing to say: that the development of personality involves the maturation of various ego processes (including cognition, social cognition, self-representation, ego ideal formation, and understanding and modulation of affects), and that what Freud called psychosexual development is only a developmental line, albeit an important one. The schemas a person forms about sexuality originate in childhood, and later information is processed through those schemas unless the schemas accommodate to new information. Such accommodation may not obliterate early affective responses that remain attached to cognitive representations or symbols, even when the representations themselves undergo various transformations. These schemas interact with, but are not isomorphic with the various schemas and scripts (Abelson, 1981) a person forms in interaction with early parental objects. All problems with authority are not, after all, problems with Oedipal authority; all anxiety is not castration anxiety; all envy is not penis envy; all conflicts do not surround sexual gratification or the need to discharge pent-up aggressive energy; and all psychological development is not born of conflict.

External narcissism develops in two phases. First, at the inception of external narcissism, the child has formed schemas of "bad me," "good me," and the like, and he has constructed primitive schemas of parental rules that are used in the service of avoiding punishment and gaining rewards. This phase roughly corresponds to Kohlberg's preconventional level. The child at this point obeys parental commandments, but they are not, in large measure, the "child's own." They are expedient but not morally obligatory. Characteristic of this phase is what Piaget calls "moral realism" (1965), the belief that punishment "naturally" follows a "bad" action. For the young child, Loevinger observes, "physical principles, psychological principles, and moral necessity" are largely indistinguishable (1976b, p. 287). This is the period Loevinger describes as the beginning of the "conformist" stage, and the epoch Kegan (1982) labels the "imperial" stage, in which the child has learned to take her own impulses as an object of thought and therefore to be able to control them. Being "bad" at this stage is experienced primarily in terms of fear of punishment and shame, though one begins to see the rudiments of guilt.

During the second phase, which usually begins in middle to late childhood, conscience becomes fully developed as the child comes to believe in the morals she is internalizing, irrespective of their hedonic value. Research by Harter (1983) suggests that children do not often experience shame in the absence of another person until middle childhood (around age eight). While rudimentary guilt experiences have been observed in children as

173

young as two (Zann-Waxler, Radke-Yarrow, and King, 1979) and appear to be important in early object relations (if one can cautiously use reconstructions from adulthood as data), full guilt responses generally do not emerge until around six years (Hoffman, 1979).

The ability to experience guilt and internalize moral values to which one is committed relies upon a number of cognitive-affective developments, such as the greater organization and coherence of self-schemas, the development of ideal self-schemas, the ability to tolerate discrepancies between ideal self and self-concept so that one can develop what psychoanalysts call an "observing ego" which allows one to observe oneself even in the face of painful affect, the ability to regulate affect more successfully so that guilt is not disorganizing and an observing ego is capable of operating, and the continued evolution of perspective-taking skills.

Ample evidence suggests that children's self-schemas begin concrete and gradually become more abstract as they grow older (Livesley and Bromley, 1973; Bannister and Agnew, 1977; Montemayor and Eisen, 1977; Harter, 1983), which fits well with the kind of developmental sequence posited by Piaget for nonsocial cognition. Harter (1983) has nicely applied Piagetian theory to the development of self-schemas. The preoperational child, she contends, would not be troubled by logical contradictions between perceived attributes of self and would not show hierarchical ordering of self-images. With the transition to concrete operations (roughly between ages five and eight), self-images would become hierarchically classified and logically related, though they would continue to focus primarily on concrete, observable details. Formal operations brings the ability to think abstractly about oneself and one's attributes and mental processes.

A coherently structured set of ideal self-images also emerges during the second phase of external narcissism, superseding the unsystematically organized and activated ideal self set-goals of earlier years. Older children are also more capable of preventing wished-for self-images from distorting self-images beyond recognition. Studies by Ruble and her colleagues (summarized in Ruble and Rholes, 1981) demonstrate that young children's self-attributions are significantly positively biased and are relatively independent of actual success or failure. This is a good illustration of the interaction of cognitive, affective, and defensive processes: the child's inability to reality-test about her own abilities is certainly a cognitive deficit, but it is motivated or maintained beyond its strictly cognitive-developmental basis to avoid unpleasant affect. One can thus see how the development of more mature ways of regulating emotion (in this case, defenses) is intimately related to social-cognitive development, moral development, development of self-system and ideal self, and personality development more generally.

In terms of moral development, in the second phase of external narcis-

174

sism the person's morality is aptly characterized by Kohlberg's appellation of "conventional." This is the period of the entrenchment of the agency Freud described as the superego. The person in this phase holds many specific and unsystematic moral beliefs internalized from parents and others, but he also has learned more general principles and categories of moral judgment that he can apply to given situations. In addition, Sullivan describes the emergence of "supervisory patterns" at this time that remain for life (1953, pp. 239-40). These are internal "personifications" (e.g., "the hearer," "the spectator") who perform the functions of self-observation and editing of behavior and self-presentation in order to preserve self-esteem and the respect of others. Thus, alongside the development of ideal self-images, conscience, and recognition of what others are thinking comes a concern with self-presentation. Several studies summarized by Hauser (1976, p. 931) suggest that most American adults function at the level of secondary external narcissism. Depending on culture and circumstance, the orientation of the person in either phase of external narcissism, but particularly in the second, may be primarily toward pleasing authorities, conforming to peers, or supporting the larger community and upholding its rules. Garbarino and Bronfenbrenner (1976) have articulately described the way environmental factors can influence these orientations.

In the latter part of the second phase of external narcissism the person frequently selectively identifies with the values, ideals, beliefs, and attributes of nonparental significant others. Particularly in pluralistic Western cultures, during the latter part of this phase the person may experience conflicting internalizations, such as the conflict between earlier moral beliefs and ideal self-images and those of peer groups counter to parental or societal values. Part III will more thoroughly examine the relationship between culture, social change, and the phenomenon one might call ego ideal splits, in which the person is torn between conflicting value systems.

The most ontogenetically primitive externally narcissistic ego ideal often corresponds to the severe, punitive, self-abnegatory superego described in many clinical accounts. Adolescent personality development in some cultures may require in part the distantiation from, and working-through of these earliest introjects and prohibitions. One way this process may be carried out is through replacement of early objects of identification by nonparental, often peer identifications. Peter Blos describes the use of peer internalizations in the process of differentiation in adolescence:

> ... the group shares and thus alleviates individual guilt feelings that accompany the emancipation from childhood dependencies, prohibitions, and loyalties ... Contemporaries ease the way to membership in the new generation within which the adolescent has to establish his social, personal, and sexual identity. Whenever peer relationships simply replace childhood dependencies, then the group has miscarried its function. In

175

such cases, the adolescent process has been short-circuited with the result
that unresolved emotional dependencies are made permanent personality
attributes. (1967, pp. 177-8)

As Blos's analysis makes clear, adherence to ideals internalized from others
is still external narcissism, whether the new objects of identification are
parental or otherwise. Kohlberg and Gilligan (1971) contend in "The Adolescent as a Philosopher" that identity crises and relativistic notions can
occur in individuals who are still conventionally moral. The "countercul-
ture" of the 1960s, they argue, required an old form (submission) with a
new content (rebellion); the adolescent merely obeyed a different external
object.

Synthetic Narcissism

Internal narcissism as a stage of personality development is characterized
by an equivalence of "the good" with "good for me." The internally
narcissistic standard of right and wrong is gratification. With external
narcissism, the source of morality is an externally imposed set of standards. The externally narcissistic conception of "the good" is "the good as
I understand significant others to define it." Externally narcissistic morality is a standard against which one judges one's actions, a standard that
frequently conflicts with the standard of gratification. The final stage in
personality and moral development is *synthetic narcissism,* which may
provide the final form, though not necessarily the final content of the ego
ideal. The *form* of the ego ideal is its developmental level, e.g., external
narcissism; the *content* is the particular set of values, moral beliefs, and
ideal self-images at a given time. The synthetically narcissistic ego ideal
contains a personal philosophy or ethic, an original, synthetic reconciliation of self and other. It represents neither a grandiose return to infantile
narcissism nor an overvaluation of others, as in external narcissism. Synthetic narcissistic processes rest upon a mutual potency self and other.[1]
The synthetically narcissistic ego ideal insures that the Kantian categorical
imperative is extended to oneself. Neither self nor others may consistently
be treated only as means to an end, though the particular balancing act
(i.e., the content of the moral system) is idiosyncratic and not prescribable
by any theory of personality growth or "maturity."

[1] One should note, in addition, that synthetic narcissism involves the recognition of realistic
limits on the potency of both self and other. Whereas the internally narcissistic person
overvalues his own wishes, value, and/or power, the externally narcissistic individual attributes too much power and value to parents or society. Synthetic narcissism represents a
more realistic view of human power and its limits. I should point out, as well, that by
"synthetic" I am referring to the synthesis of values and ideals that occurs with this stage
and to the dialectical process of transcending internal and external narcissism. I do not
intend by "synthetic" any connotation of artificiality.

176

The phase of the emergence of synthetic narcissistic processes may sometimes correspond to Kenneth Keniston's (1968, 1970) concept of "youth," in which the individual is psychologically, but not sociologically adult. The youth has worked through many of his childhood conflicts; however, he is unable or unwilling to come to terms with his society and its institutions. For Keniston this is not a pathological development but often a healthy source of social change (1968). One could argue that in youth the individual differentiates from her society in a manner parallel to the differentiation of the adolescent from domestic (parental) society. According to Keniston, the youth is not immature. On the contrary, the synthesis which the individual may achieve upon the resolution of this stage represents a healthy, realistic reconciliation of self and society, in which the "relatedness yet separateness of both is affirmed" (1970, p. 642). He adds,

> Thus the "resolution" of the self-society tension in no way necessarily entails "adjusting" to the society, much less "selling out" – although many youths see it this way. On the contrary, individuation refers partly to a psychological process whereby self and society are differentiated internally. But the actual conflicts between men and women and their societies remain, and indeed may even become more intense. (P. 642)

In a Sullivanian tone, Keniston traces interpersonal development from parity to complementarity to the mutuality of youth (p. 643). In an Eriksonian moment, he claims that in youth the individual faces the danger of estrangement from herself or her society, stating that "we can define the central developmental possibilities of youth as individuation vs. alienation" (p. 643).

While Kohlberg's ascription of a particular content to post-conventional morality is not in keeping with the notion of a self-chosen, autonomous system of values, the idea embodied in the concept of a stage beyond the acceptance of the dominant ideology of family or society is central to the notion of synthetic narcissism. Periods in which synthetically narcissistic processes emerge are existential, in the sense that the person lacks a set of assumptions upon which to base values, ideals, and a sense of meaning. The person who has established some degree of synthetic narcissism is, of course, never entirely free of unconscious and more primitive injunctions and ideal self-images, though she has gained some degree of autonomy over many of these early internalizations and no longer accepts internalized and societal moral beliefs and decrees as her own simply because they were issued by seemingly omnipotent authorities.

Synthetic narcissism represents a pinnacle of psychic differentiation. Theorists of moral development have failed to note that the inability to separate the moral values of parents and society from one's own is a problem in differentiation, an inadequate distinction between self and other. Synthetic narcissism involves a differentiation between the moral views of self and significant others, an ability to separate "mine" from "thine" in the realm of values. It does not, however, represent a pseudo-independence, a defense against primitive fears of intimacy or merger. It rests upon the recognition that values do not inhere in the universe but are created, and that one needs some vantage point from which to adjudicate legitimate competing desires of oneself and others.

The content of the synthetically narcissistic ego ideal may range from *predominant* self-orientation to *predominant* other-orientation, but it is bounded on the one side by devaluation of the self, and on the other, by the devaluation of others. The content is also not likely to be stagnant, and as the individual ages, assumes new roles, undergoes new experiences, and is faced with old and often unknown conflicts from the past evoked in new situations, the content is likely to change.

Synthetic narcissism represents an alternative view of moral autonomy to that derived from Kant and Rousseau, and embodied in current approaches to moral psychology. Kant proposed that the categorical imperative is an a priori morality mandated by reason. Curiously, this a priori morality is a philosophized version of the morality Kant's parents and society instilled in him. Indeed, the morality that Kant's "autonomous" individual must obey is not a priori at all: it is *a dependenciori*. The child internalizes his parents' morality not, as Kant argues, because he is rational, but because his rationality is only poorly developed, because he mistakenly takes his parents or society for gods. Would a "rational" human being really accept the doctrine that to himself he should be just one more person among many, that he should treat himself just as he treats everyone else because he, like they, are rational beings? Such a view, one might argue, demonstrates a *lack* of adequate "reality-testing" or reason: to ourselves we are not *e pluribus unum*, we are not just another face an objective observer would miss in a crowd.

Kohlberg, like Kant, speaks of moral autonomy as the choosing and willing upon oneself of a moral code. While the notion of a truly post-conventional morality makes sense, Kohlberg errs, just as Kant does, in trying to prescribe what the content of that moral code must be. For Rousseau, Kant, Piaget, and Kohlberg, an individual who produces a moral system contrary to theirs is reasoning incorrectly and acting heteronomously. Psychoanalysis, too, shares some of these assumptions about moral autonomy. The child becomes morally autonomous when he has internalized parental prohibitions, at which point "the ego submits to the categorical imperative of its super-ego" (1933, p. 38). Freud recognized throughout his career that the superego is often primitive and a source of misery to the individual, yet he could never quite formulate a path beyond superego morality. Social learning theory describes mechanisms to account for conformity to social standards, but it lacks an explanation for either rebellion or creativity, moral or otherwise.

Synthetic narcissism offers an alternative conception of moral autonomy that avoids allegedly "scientific" or "rational" prescription of a universal ethics. I would suggest that moral philosophy abandon the attempt to uncover a priori moral principles through supposedly rational inquiry, and instead examine the *method* of formation of moral beliefs in order to understand the possibilities and limits of moral autonomy.

The reader may wonder, if one does not prescribe a set of allegedly mature moral beliefs, what is to prevent the "synthetic narcissist" from being a mass-murderer. I have argued that the content of the synthetically narcissistic ego ideal cannot be determined a priori. Content, however, is constrained by form. The first form of the ego ideal involves the inability to perceive others as legitimate, and the second form denies independent legitimacy to the self. The content of the third form, synthetic narcissism, is bounded by these two extremes. Synthetically narcissistic processes entail, by definition, a valuing of both self and others as ends in themselves. The particular balance between these two valuations, however, is indeterminate and varies by individual, culture, and historical era. Synthetically narcissistic value systems may be largely self-oriented or predominantly other-oriented, but pure self- or other-orientation is a point they cannot reach without regression to a previous ego ideal synthesis. Maturity of object relations entails the recognition and valuation of others' existence as well as one's own. Murderous and indiscriminate rage based on infantile experience and fantasy empirically does not correlate with maturity of object relations and ego development.

Before concluding, it is important to bear in mind the conception of "stage" underlying the developmental model offered here. Stages are waves of processes, methods of fulfilling certain functions which crest and recede. "Pure" examples of the ideal types of internal, external, and synthetic narcissism obviously never exist. An unalloyed synthetic narcissism, for example, would involve the working through of every facet of one's conception of good and bad developed throughout early life and beyond. The pure case thus represents something of an upper bound which one may asymptotically approach. While some core of an integrated ego ideal may be unitary, remnants of past syntheses obviously persist, as archaic schemas and their corresponding affects are evoked by various thoughts and experiences.

One should also bear in mind that the stages described here are comprised of complex sets of processes, not single processes or functions, involving cognition, social cognition, self-representation, affective arousal and management, and the holding of values and ideals. I have described the development of this congeries of processes as personality development, subsuming within that term the development of narcissism and object relations, moral judgment, and ego processes. From another vantage point, one may do well to try to disentangle the various processes to get a clearer picture of their interrelated yet distinguishable developmental trajectories. I have painted in thin, broad strokes, but am asserting that one may find in this canvas the potential for a more colorful portrait.

Conclusion

To justify adoption of a new theory, one must be able to show, first and foremost, that the proposed view is more congruent with observable data, is more internally consistent, and/or is more economical than previous theories. These chapters have been in part comparative, pointing to deficiencies in other views, but they have not been systemically so. I hope to provide a more thorough summary and critique of the major approaches to personality at a later date. The assumption behind the eclecticism underlying the present work is that previous approaches have a great deal to offer, but none is adequate for the task of integrating current research and clinical understanding.

Apart from the question of the relative merits of this approach versus other views of personality in dealing with various research and clinical findings, the present perspective has four advantages. First, this approach allows an integration of theoretical understandings derived from clinical experience as well as more verifiable empirical work from the laboratory. The approach presented here not only synthesizes a number of theoretical perspectives, but it relies upon both clinical and experimental data. My own view is that the two are complementary and equally valid sources of information. Verification is obviously less problematic with replicable laboratory experiments, and when an important phenomenon can be tested experimentally it is imperative to do so instead of relying on one's beliefs or unsystematic observations. One should not, however, underestimate the extent to which the use of ideas by a community of clinicians is a selection process that weeds out concepts without much utility or those that do not explain the data of clinical observation.

While psychoanalytic psychologists tend to ignore important sources of empirical data, academic psychologists largely hold an outdated nineteenth century view of science which posits that accumulating "facts" and sticking them all in a textbook constitutes knowledge, and that one can test entire theories experimentally and therefore choose between them on strictly empirical grounds. Unfortunately, philosophers of science have abandoned this naive brand of positivism that does not even accord with the experience of the natural sciences which these psychologists are trying to emulate. A paradigm of personality that can be corroborated or disconfirmed with a few well-designed experiments cannot have broad application to significant phenomena. One can test various aspects of a paradigm and either refine them, conclude that they explain the data well enough, or decide that one must search for a more accurate or useful general approach, but as Kuhn (1970) has made so clear, the fate of a broad theoretical approach does not rest upon isolated anomalies, which face every paradigm.

A useful distinction made by philosophers of science is between the context of discovery, in which new approaches are developed, and the context of justification, in which they are put to empirical test. Experimental techniques are far more convincing in the context of justification, but they are of limited utility in trying to formulate a broad theory of human mental processes and behavior. Relying solely upon networks of studies that sample thirty-minute slices of behavior of usually homogeneous populations through questionnaires or experimental procedures to guide one in formulating a gestalt of personality is comparable to examining with a microscope fifty one-millimeter sections of the ceiling of the Sistine Chapel and attempting to piece together what Michelangelo was trying to portray.

What generally happens is that the psychologist scaffolded six inches from the ceiling with his microscope will inform his understanding of the whole by sneaking an occasional glance from his idiosyncratic perspective. In other words, he will draw from his microscopic studies, but he will primarily fall back upon his own life experience as a source of more general assumptions or hypotheses. Researchers who study self-concepts come upon the idea of the existence and importance of them through introspection. Because such concepts are not observable, they would probably not have been discovered experimentally. When Fiske (1981) draws upon the "old flame phenomenon," she is drawing from personal experience; when Little (1983) models human behavior after the process of publishing an article, he is clearly gaining his understanding of motivation and action from his own life; when academic psychologists construct theories about the centrality of feelings of competence or control they do so first by looking inward and only secondarily by peering outward.

In other words, while in the context of justification experimentalists gain fuller understanding by examining large samples, in the context of discovery they rely primarily upon a sample of one, bolstered, of course, by their knowledge of various research traditions. Thus, while the research psychologist has the edge in the context of justification, the clinician who observes the most intimate personal experiences, longitudinally and in depth, of many people other than himself, has the broader data base in the context of discovery. I suspect that the farther psychology moves from a stimulus-response approach, the more professionals of the field will come to recognize that we cannot limit ourselves to quantifiable accounts of relatively simple phenomena built upon implicit assumptions derived from idiosyncratic experience, and that the findings of clinicians who daily encounter the deep structures of meaning and dynamic processes of concrete individuals are, though less verifiable than experimental evidence, not only admissible but essential as sources of data and theory-building.

Secondly, the present theory provides a more sophisticated account of the relation between thoughts and feelings than previous approaches and can accommodate both cognitive and dynamic explanations. A simple example is in the oft-noted tendency of people to ignore information discrepant from their schemas. Clearly this stems in part from the nature of human information-processing: new data are assimilated into existing schemas, so that information less expected is less easily perceived. Yet one should also note that the presence of information that conflicts with one's ways of thinking can also be very threatening and anxiety-provoking, so that ignoring discrepant data can be reinforced, i.e., defensively motivated. My own understanding of personality was initially primarily psychodynamic, and when I began reading Bandura's work, I had to fight my impulse at every step of the way to toss it aside as rubbish. My life would have been much easier at the time if it had, in fact, been rubbish. Unfortunately, sinister fellow that he is, Bandura had to disappoint me by being articulate. The result was that I was faced with conflicting schemas, and the reader must judge for herself or himself whether the schema I have constructed to gain a better understanding (cognitive explanation) and to allay my anxiety (dynamic explanation) has some utility or is grossly distorted by either cognitive error or dynamic pressure.

Motley's research on the experimental production of slips of the tongue demonstrates beyond doubt that such errors can result from either cognitive or dynamic interference. One can similarly reinterpret a whole host of phenomenon observed by cognitive social psychologists, such as self-serving biases in attributions (Greenwald, 1980), or contradictory evidence on the impact of negative mood states on behavior (Clarke and Isen, 1982), by considering motivational and cognitive factors in combination.

Sadly, the discipline has for years been largely polarized between those who feel compelled to deny any impact of dynamic processes and those who ascribe motivational significance to every act. For example, in their interesting book on social inference and its shortcomings, Nisbett and Ross (1980) downplay the possibility that people could deliberately keep thoughts or wishes from awareness, arguing that "what is unconscious is normally unconscious for the simplest of reasons: People lack the machinery for bringing the relevant facts into conscious purview" (p. 245). The model of human nature informing their work is that people are like "intuitive scientists" or "intuitive psychologists" (Ross, 1977) who form hypotheses, test them through their experience, and frequently come to incorrect conclusions because of faulty experimental design or inference.

Yet if one really wishes to pursue the intuitive science metaphor, one should correct the idealized and distorted image of science that underlies it. Scientists and psychologists do indeed form and test hypotheses and make cognitive errors, yet they also falsify data, pour out meaningless studies in the quest for tenure, divide decent articles into several papers to increase their stack of publications, list themselves as first author on publications in collaboration with struggling younger colleagues who may have done most of the work, write scathing critiques of colleagues' work out of personal enmity, collapse variables in "legal" but dubious ways to attain significance, favorably cite the work of probable reviewers in articles they would like published, jockey for power in academic committees, make passes at attractive students currently in their classes or under their control, imagine themselves the greatest researcher in their profession, wear lab coats to make themselves feel like scientists, give students unconscionably low grades to satisfy sadistic impulses – the list goes on, and I will stop before revealing my own favorite vices.

Human beings are creatures who both think and feel, and any theory that begins with the assumption of the primacy of either cognition or dynamics can only be a partial theory. It is a pity that we, like Oedipus, seem compelled to blind ourselves in the face of information we do not wish to believe. Unlike Oedipus, however, we tend to gouge out only one eye while being unaware of our monocular vision, convinced that we are seeing things in proper perspective. I am arguing that we must keep one eye on cognition, one on affect and dynamics, and integrate the two impressions to form a coherent single image. We will always be blind to data on the periphery of our understanding, but we can at least be certain that we are seeing in depth.

Thirdly, a good theory must be able to guide research, and the avenues of exploration generated or accommodated by the theory proposed here are many. For example, while I have argued for a general process of ego development, one can delineate a nearly infinite number of developmental lines, such as the development of affect and specific affects, cognition and specific cognitive processes, social cognition (including social causality, person perception, social reasoning, understanding of social rules, and understanding of affect and motivation), object relations, control mechanisms and specific coping or defensive processes, self-schemas, ideal self-images, moral beliefs, psychosexual phenomena, and generalized and specific set-goals. Many of these have, of course, been studied at considerable length through the years. The advantage of the current approach is that they may now be housed under one theoretical roof.

The theory also suggests directions for empirical studies of interactions

183

between many of these processes, such as affect, cognition, and affect regulation. For example, efficient mechanisms of emotional regulation are unlikely to develop while affect remains global and overwhelming. This relies both upon strictly affective development as well as on the emergence of the cognitive capacity to form expectancies about the probable outcome of various control mechanisms and to attribute and isolate causes of distress. Any faulty link in a complex chain – from perception and cognition of stimulus, to affect, to attribution of causes and quality of affect, to efficiency of control mechanisms – may lead to psychic dysfunction. Not only can poor cognitive processing lead, for example, to inappropriate affect, which can cause primitive defensive functioning, but low level defenses generally distort cognition, leading to a circle of pathology. Similarly, Damon (1977) has found that the maturity of children's responses to questions about fairness decreases when the candy to share is in sight, and psychoanalytic experience leads one to believe that affect can often disrupt mature cognitive functioning.

A fourth advantage, and from a practical perspective probably the most important, is that the theory holds out the promise of aiding in some limited way in our understanding of psychopathology and processes of therapeutic change. One of the main advantages in this regard is that it may provide a theoretical underpinning for psychodynamic psychotherapists who find Freud's clinical theory valuable but reject psychoanalytic metapsychology (for the distinction between clinical theory and metapsychology in psychoanalysis, see the volume edited by Gill and Holzman, 1976). It may also help in effecting a rapprochement between psychodynamic psychotherapists, counselors (the majority of whom are primarily influenced by Rogers), and cognitive-behavioral clinicians. Psychodynamically oriented clinicians often view the work of the latter two groups as dealing with surface phenomena instead of with the roots of psychic problems, whereas counselors and cognitive and behaviorally oriented clinicians often criticize psychodynamic psychotherapists for reducing every problem to an infantile sexual conflict.

Both are sometimes right, and those mental health professionals who come into contact with serious pathology as well as momentary problems of living often find themselves, especially when working with children and their families, flipping from one paradigm to another in the course of a day or even a therapy session. The approach proposed here may ultimately provide a more integrated perspective. With the exception of a few random examples, I have avoided in this work any systematic application of the theory to psychopathology since I lack either the extensive clinical experience required for such a task or the hubris to embark upon it without enough experience. I will therefore leave this to more experienced and

184

knowledgeable clinicians and perhaps to myself years hence when I have accumulated more experience, more hubris, or both.

A final advantage of the theory presented here is that it can, as the remainder of the book will attempt to show, be integrated into a general social scientific model that allows one to transcend artificial and often limiting disciplinary boundaries. One cannot understand the structure, dynamics, and development of personality entirely in isolation from sociocultural structure, dynamics, and change. The examination of these sociocultural phenomena is the task to which Part II now turns.

II A Theory of Culture

5 Social Theory in Sociology and Anthropology

IN HIS INTELLECTUAL history of social thought from 1890 to 1930, H. Stuart Hughes argues that the two issues which permeated the thought of the theorists who paved the transition from philosophy to social science were the questions of what human nature is, and how an observer endowed with it can study it objectively (1958, p. 24). The first issue, the nature of human nature, is of course an old one, and efforts to answer it in the last hundred years have formed the content of the social sciences. In sociology and anthropology, as in psychology, the last few decades have witnessed a wariness and weariness of grand theories; hope has faded that an overarching perspective in any of the social disciplines can capture reality without domesticating it into vapid overgeneralization. The result has been greater attention to lower order generalizations which hover much closer to observation. This has clearly had a salutary effect, promoting a more thorough understanding of specific aspects of social life and behavior, and discouraging metaphysical abstractions with only minimal grounding in reality.

Yet in turning to theories of the middle range, one encounters the disconcerting fact that, over time, such theories often prove equally falsifiable and worse still, uninteresting. The paradox of microtheories is that they tend either to prove false, and are therefore discarded; or true, and therefore exhausted. The theorist who spins a larger theoretical yarn must always remember that he is, like the writer of a historical novel, doing an enormous amount of background research for a project that in some respects resembles fiction, though he has the gratification of writing a novel instead of a short story.

The second question, relating to the objectivity of social science, is in some ways even more vexing. We owe in large measure to Marx an awareness that our understanding of the social world is always historically conditioned. Freud added insult to this intellectual injury, cautioning that our thought is distorted, as well, by our own personal dynamics. This basically philosophical issue could largely be ignored by empirical re-

189

searchers if not for a more concrete, derivative issue. Any human science that attempts to be historical or developmental faces the difficulty of separating development of the subject from development of the object. This is no more true in any field than in anthropology. When one reads the accounts of small scale preliterate societies provided by fieldworkers in the first half of this century, one gets the pervasive sense of highly solidary, tradition-bound groups with relatively homogeneous values and beliefs. In contrast, the pages of the *American Anthropologist* today are filled with actor-based models and accounts of individual decision making among non-Western peoples. The question one must immediately ask is whether the nature of the cultures being studied has changed that dramatically, which it has; whether anthropology as a discipline has become far more sophisticated, which it has; or whether the broad culture responsible for producing anthropologists has become more individualistic, which it also has. The answer is thus a rather resounding and unhelpful "yes." We are in somewhat of the position of passengers on a train moving rapidly in one direction, trying to write a complete account of life on a passing train. The problem is magnified when one is immersed in both the life of another culture and in the changing life-world of one's own discipline.

To pursue for a moment the analogy of the observer on the train, the best research strategy is to watch carefully as the train passes, take numerous photographs of particular moments, and if possible, jump aboard the passing train for as long as one can without jeopardizing one's chance to jump back aboard one's own. That is to say, an optimal approach would look at changes in the culture across time, analyze its structure and dynamics at any given point, and try to understand reality from the standpoint of the culture being studied (in order to deepen one's own understanding). In more jargonistic terms, the examination of sociocultural phenomena should be diachronic, synchronic, emic, and etic.

A theory of culture or society[1] that is both illuminating and useful must explicitly accommodate these four perspectives. It must, further, forge a network of links between the four, so that one is not left with empty classification. The aim of Part II is to propose such a theory. Chapter 5 will begin with reviews of sociocultural theories in sociology and anthropology. Chapter 6 will then provide a model of the structure and dynamics of society. Finally, Chapter 7 will offer a diachronic theory of the evolution of moral values in human groups.

[1] I use the terms "society" and "culture" here as omnibus terms to include the ensemble of sociocultural phenomena of a given social group, similar to the use of "psyche" or "personality" in Chapter 1. Anthropologists sometimes contrast "society," referring to concrete social relations and institutions, with "culture," referring to the realm of ideas (cf. Ortner, 1984). I will retain that usage in this chapter while reviewing other theories but will thenceforth generally use the terms "society" and "culture" interchangeably in the comprehensive sense defined above.

Classical Social Theory and the Sociological Tradition

The ideas of sociology's three most important classical theorists, Karl Marx, Max Weber, and Emile Durkheim, were all inspired by the massive changes that occurred with the Industrial Revolution. Similar changes inspired the modernization literature of the postwar era as well as subsequent approaches, such as world-systems theory, that have tried to explain socioeconomic development and underdevelopment. The questions and answers posed by the classical social theorists were of such significance and brilliance that they have continued to set the agenda for generations of sociologists.

For Marx, the dynamic in history lies in the material infrastructure of society, in the contradictions between the forces of production (tools, technology, etc.) and the relations of production (class relationships of ownership and distribution). In speaking of a "material" infrastructure, Marx does not, of course, mean "material" in the philosophical sense of mind versus matter. Rather, the material realm that lies behind sociocultural reality is the realm of material interest. Politics and culture, according to Marx, reflect contradictions in the mode of production; the mode of production includes the forces and the relations of production. In other words, if one wishes to understand values, literature, politics, or religion, one must explore the dynamics of class from which these "superstructural" phenomena emerge.

Economic infrastructure is thus the key to sociocultural superstructure, and every mode of production except communism contains within itself the seeds of its own destruction when relations of ownership serve as a fetter on economic development. Feudal social relations, for example, could not accommodate manufacture; the latter requires wage laborers who are not tied to particular estates or occupations. Capitalist social relations will similarly serve as an integument that must, and will, ultimately be destroyed, as monopolization of capital proceeds alongside the progressive pauperization of the masses.

For each mode of production one can identify a ruling class whose interests dominate social and legal relations. In Marx's evolutionary scheme human society moves from a classless primitive communism to slavery, feudalism, capitalism, and ultimately socialism and communism, though many have argued about whether or not a society could skip a stage or two. The Marxist revolutions of this century have all been predicated on the belief that such leapfrogging is possible since communist revolutions have not yet arisen in any capitalist societies, where Marx expected them to occur. Just as the bourgeoisie displaced the aristocracy as the dominant class with the rise of capitalism, the proletariat will, in Marx's scheme, supersede the bourgeoisie and will put an end to class conflict and exploitation. Presenting Marx's thought in three paragraphs is as enlightening as referring to Einstein as the man who said, "Everything is relative," but this capsule summary must here suffice. Marx's social theory will be examined in greater detail throughout Part II.

For Weber, history's "motor" lies in progressive rationalization, which entails increased bureaucratization and the "disenchantment" of the world, by which he means secularization and the diminishing attribution of intention to natural events. Weber is particularly concerned with political sociology, and he isolates three forms of authority: traditional, charismatic, and rational. Traditional authority is historically primitive, though it still exists to some degree in all twentieth century societies and is predominant in many. Traditional authority is legitimized with reference to the past and emphasizes custom and tradition. Charismatic authority flows from the "charisma" or awesome character of a "quasi-magical" (Aron, 1970, p. 247) leader. Rational (or "rational-legal") authority rests upon laws and entails ever-growing bureaucracy. In a society dominated by traditional or rational authority, a charismatic leader sometimes emerges who creates a new authority that later becomes "routinized." Traditional authority is rapidly disappearing as the mystical qualities attached to traditional states (and perhaps, Durkheim would argue, societies) gradually disappear. The fate of humankind is thus rational-legal authority, perhaps punctuated by the periodic emergence of charismatic figures.

Unlike Marx, who argues that since the state is a reflection of class conflict it will wither away in a classless society, Weber contends that the requirements of advanced technology necessitate an ineluctable bureaucracy. Weber also criticizes Marx's one-sided emphasis on economic variables as the determinants of sociocultural structure. While Weber concurs that economics are often decisive, he views causality as multidirectional, stressing the critical role of ideals. Ideals and values are both the creations and creators of society, according to Weber, and he argues as a significant example that capitalism owes its origin in part to certain religious developments in Protestantism (Weber, 1958). Weber certainly did not denigrate the importance of material conditions as determinants of sociocultural phenomena. Rather, socioeconomic causes are one of a number of causal influences on sociocultural reality, if not the major one. Yet ideas, he noted in a famous metaphor, can also be causally significant as the "switchmen" that shift a society from one "track" or trajectory to another.

Whereas Marx's view of historical evolution is optimistic, Weber is ambivalent, noting that the rational means associated with rational authority and capitalism may lead to irrational ends, that history may place humanity in an "iron cage." Unlike Marx and Durkheim, Weber firmly separates fact and value, arguing that science can never legislate ends, but it can assist in the selection of means. Again, a few paragraphs hardly do justice to as thorough and encyclopedic a mind as Weber's; his views will be utilized further in Part III.

Durkheim, unlike Marx and Weber, demonstrated a keen interest in preagricultural, "primitive" societies. In such societies, he argues, the *conscience collective* (translated as either "collective consciousness" or "collective conscience"), the supraindividual set of sentiments that unites the group, dominates individual consciousness. For Durkheim, the progress of civilization involves the shift from "mechanical solidarity," a cohesiveness based upon the collective consciousness and mutual attraction of similar individuals, to "organic solidarity," a cohesiveness based upon interdependence and the division of labor.

The problem, he contends, is that organic solidarity does not develop fast enough to replace the mechanical solidarity of the past. The result is that individuals experience a sense of normlessness, a societal condition he calls "anomie." Durkheim believes that social science can rescue humankind from anomie in essentially two ways. First, by exposing the source of the current malaise, it can suggest alternative institutions to replace obsolete mechanisms of social integration such as religion and ritual. Secondly, Durkheimian sociology asserts that the gods of primitive society are symbolic representations of society itself. By exposing this idolatry, social science can lead humanity to venerate the true, unalienated object of human devotion, society. (This is a very Comtean reading of Durkheim, suggested by Aron, 1970.)

Like Marx, Durkheim points to the atomism of contemporary society and hopes for a more mature society that would unite the advantages of technology with the solidarity of primitive community. Like Weber, he stresses the breakdown of tradition, and Durkheim's conceptualization of the decreasing role of the collective consciousness in many ways parallels Weber's view of the disenchantment of the world. Once more, such a short presentation is necessarily a crude presentation of the work of a great thinker, though Durkheim's theory will receive further exploration throughout the following chapters.[1]

Twentieth-century sociologists have operated from a number of implicit and explicit perspectives, but the main theoretical position that emerged was structural-functionalism, particularly associated with Talcott Parsons (1951; Parsons and Shils, 1951). Parsonian structural-functionalism (or functionalism for short) drew inspiration from the classical social theorists (particularly Weber and Durkheim). Parsons' functionalism examines the

---

[1] For a very lucid presentation of the ideas of the classical social theorists, see Raymond Aron's two short volumes on the *Main Currents of Sociological Thought*, 1968 and 1970; see also Giddens, 1971.

193

interaction between three systems: society, culture, and personality. It looks at sociocultural reality as a complex whole, in which various traits or structures exist because they fulfill particular functions. The primary units of analysis (for the functionalists) are the roles and statuses into which individuals become socialized; these must always be examined in context of an interdependent system. Functionalism has been increasingly rejected over the last three decades, for reasons to be discussed at greater length later, including its difficulties in elucidating intrasocietal conflict and the teleological character of the notion of function.

No method and model of comparable scope and impact has surfaced in sociology since functionalism, though a number of schools of thought have emerged. Social exchange theory, for example, attempts to analyze society in terms of the costs and benefits of various social interactions for individual actors (see Homans, 1961). Phenomenology has had an important impact on sociology, especially through the work of Alfred Schutz (1967a, 1967b) and the ethnomethodologists (see, e.g., Garfinkel, 1967; Psathas, 1973), who examine the perceived reality or "life-world" of a given social group or set of individuals. The world-systems theory of Wallerstein (1974, 1978) and his disciples has expanded the level of sociological analysis outward from the traditional focus on a single society to what he calls the world-system. Wallerstein argues that to understand problems of underdevelopment in the Third World from other than a world-systems perspective is to miss the extent to which the fate of the developing or "peripheral" areas is dependent upon their interactions with the "core" and "semiperipheral" powers whose interests dominate the world capitalist system. The legacy of functionalism persists alongside these other approaches, as no single paradigm has come to dominate the field.

Affinity and Consanguinity in Anthropological Theories

Throughout this century anthropologists have shown an enormous interest in structures of kinship and marriage. To aid them in their studies they have erected elaborate terminology, unflinchingly analyzing systems of "patrilateral cross-cousin marriage" and the like. Anthropology itself has an extraordinarily complicated kinship structure that seems to defy interpretation. The relationship, for example, between social and cultural anthropology is obscure (see Singer, 1968); some would argue that they are identical twins, others would see them as half-sisters, and still others would deny any kinship between them at all. Anthropology has wed many theories and theorists in this century, and only the most skilled ethnologist could determine whether this marriage structure involves polygyny, polyandry, or serial monogamy. As anthropologist Clifford Geertz laments,

... so far as anthropology is concerned, it is almost more of a problem to get exhausted ideas out of the literature than it is to get productive ones in, and so a great deal more of theoretical discussion than one would prefer is critical rather than constructive, and whole careers have been devoted to hastening the demise of moribund notions. As the field advances one would hope that this sort of intellectual weed control would become a less prominent part of our activities. But, for the moment, it remains true that old theories tend less to die than to go into second editions. (1973, p. 27n)

One can, nevertheless, delineate the major lines of development of the sociocultural side of anthropology. Nineteenth century anthropology, like much of nineteenth-century thought, was enamored with the concept of evolution. L.H. Morgan in the United States and Sir Henry Maine, Sir James Frazer, and Edward Tylor in England all proposed evolutionary views of the development of culture. With a few notable exceptions from Ancient Greece to eighteenth century France, anthropology began with these thinkers, who were struck basically by the strangeness of "primitive"[1] societies. European colonization and missionary activity were at their peak, and reports of strange and mysterious practices from all over the world began to attract attention. While the evolutionist anthropologists disagreed in their particular developmental schemes, their formulations largely suggested a general movement in human history from a state of savagery, in which people were animistic and premoral, to civilization, with its science, humanism, and Victorian morality.

Anthropology divorced itself from evolutionism when the Boasian revolution of the early twentieth century demonstrated that the evolutionist paradigm was unfaithful to the facts. Franz Boas, the dominant figure in American anthropology for roughly forty years, questioned the evolutionist assumption that one can neatly place all cultures on a single continuum (see Boas, 1940). Boas was avowedly antitheoretical, and he insisted that his students record every aspect of a culture, from its kinship terms to its recipes. Instead of proposing broad unilinear or universal theories of cultural evolution, Boas's historical particularist school examined specific instances of culture change and attempted to look at the way a given trait had been diffused, independently invented, or reworked by a particular culture. Boas also played an instrumental role in making prolonged fieldwork a central part of anthropological training.

Boas and his students advocated cultural relativism, both as a descrip-

---

[1] The term "primitive" will be used here temporarily since it occurs in the work of so many of the writers to be discussed, and will refer to preliterate societies with minimal social differentiation and relatively simple technology.

tive and a prescriptive rule. Cultures, they argued, vary in almost every respect, and other cultures cannot and should not be judged by Western standards. While the prescriptive ethical argument that one society's morality is as good as another's is no longer axiomatic for all anthropologists, the emphasis on the uniqueness (as opposed to universal aspects) of all cultures and the methodological mandate that a culture should be studied in its own terms are still prevalent in anthropology. Ernest Gellner remarks:

> Like members of other tribes, anthropologists are socialized by means of legends. . . . The legend by means of which anthropologists are molded runs something like this: Once upon a time, the anthropological world was inhabited by a proto-population who were *ethnocentric*. They collected information about primitives mainly in order to poke fun at them, to illustrate the primitive's inferiority to themselves . . .
>
> One day the Age of Darkness came to an end. Modern anthropology begins with good, genuine, real modern fieldwork. The essence of such fieldwork is that it does see institutions, practices, beliefs, etc. *in context*. At the same time , ethnocentrism is overcome. (1974, pp. 28-9)

Boas's students, while imbued with their teacher's relativism, were generally more theoretically inclined. Anthropologists such as Alfred Kroeber (1948), Ruth Benedict (1934), and Margaret Mead (1963) were associated with a school of thought that looked for *culture patterns* and was not averse to comparative work. Like Boas, those associated with the culture pattern approach emphasized the importance of viewing a cultural trait in context as a part of a systematic configuration. They attempted to isolate the unconscious value commitments held by those in a given culture, similar to the way cognitive anthropologists have attempted to build models of native understanding. However, a significant difference is that the culture pattern approach, like contemporary symbolic anthropology (see, e.g., Geertz, 1973, 1983), examined cognitive-affective value structures rather than simply cognitive classificatory schemas. Reflecting their Boasian heritage, writers of this school tried to understand the way a culture would refashion a trait diffused from another culture in order to assimilate the trait to its overall pattern.

Anthropology and the Boasian tradition effected a trial separation that was never formalized in a divorce, but anthropology remarried in the meantime. Around the time of the development of the culture pattern approach, functionalism emerged as a dominant paradigm, particularly in Great Britain. The functionalist approach has its roots in the work of Durkheim, who took an organismic view of society and was primarily concerned with the nature and preservation of social solidarity. For Durkheim, laws, moral values, religious ideas, and other cultural traits serve the purpose of maintaining societal integration. Like Durkheim, twentieth-century functionalists examine sociocultural institutions by exploring their functions for the group. Functional analysis began in anthropology with the work of Radcliffe-Brown and Malinowski in the 1920s. Just as England and America have been viewed as two nations divided by one language, in many ways Radcliffe-Brown and Malinowski are two theorists separated by one theory, though Malinowski placed greater emphasis on the needs of individuals within the group. As in sociology, functionalism as a coherent body of theory has lost its predominance in anthropology. Its influence, however, is manifest in much current ethnography as well as in the work of anthropologists such as Victor Turner (1969) who are not themselves associated with functionalism as a school. Indeed, much of sociological and anthropological analysis continues to be functionalist in the broader sense of explaining social facts in terms of their functions for groups or individuals, as will be discussed in more depth below. (For a historical review of the evolution of British functionalist anthropology, see Goody, 1973.)

CONTEMPORARY APPROACHES: STRUCTURALISM AND THE OPPOSITION

Anthropology's two most recent suitors are structural and ecological anthropology. While anthropology has been engaged in the structuralist enterprise for quite some time, the two have never exchanged vows because of structuralism's reluctance to be tied down. What I mean by this is that structuralism has provided a *method* for studying various aspects of culture, which involves finding oppositions or contradictions in a given domain and showing how certain aspects of culture mediate those oppositions. It has also advanced several specific *theories* of, for example, kinship structure (Lévi-Strauss, 1969a). What it has not done is to provide a general *model* or unified theory of culture and society comparable to functionalism, or to psychoanalysis or behaviorism in psychology. Its reluctance to be tied down can be seen even in the difficulty its adherents have in trying to define so basic a concept as "structure."

Rather than attempting to summarize the history of structuralist thought, a task for which I lack both space and competence, I will instead briefly explicate the ideas of the architect and master of structuralism, Claude Lévi-Strauss.[1] Lévi-Straussian structuralism bears the imprint of a number of perspectives and disciplines, of which linguistics and Durkheimian functionalism are among the most important. He accepted from both

---

[1] The most intelligible presentation of Lévi-Strauss's ideas I have come across is, surprisingly, that of a psychologist, Howard Gardner (1981). (See also Leach, 1970; Scholte, 1973; and Werner, 1973.)

the assumption that one must look at culture as a system, and consequently that the elements of that system must always be analyzed in context. He went further in arguing that culture is essentially a system of communication, much akin to a language, and that therefore cultural phenomena can be treated as arbitrary signs that are only intelligible in the context of the system of signs comprising the particular cultural domain.

An example should make this a bit more concrete. Since the nineteenth century, anthropologists have proposed numerous theories of the phenomenon of "totemism," in which different clans in a given territory are associated with certain species of animals or plants. In his book on totemism, Lévi-Strauss (1962) argues that the Australian clansman who claims to be a kinsman of the turtle is not a precocious Darwinian. To take the relation between one clan and one species out of context would, according to Lévi-Strauss, be a mistake. Rather, the relations among cultural groups (clans) are being expressed metaphorically in totemic beliefs by the relations among natural groups (species). A series of clans (A,B,C, and D) is logically analogous, for example, to a series of animals (raccoon, turtle, eagle, and bear), and thus the latter represent the former. That one particular clan happens to be called bear as opposed to eagle is a historical fact of minimal importance; the particular species chosen is an arbitrary sign, of significance only within the context of the totemic "language" or system of signs.

Central to Lévi-Strauss's version of structuralism is the claim that the human brain is essentially like a digital computer, so that we inherently think in terms of binary oppositions. In the final analysis, anthropology is really a neurophysiologically based cognitive psychology, as all of culture is reducible to the innate structure of human cognition. Behind the surface structure of any aspect of sociocultural reality—whether it be totemism, mythology, or kinship systems—lies a deep structure involving certain binary oppositions and a middle term mediating between them. For example, Lévi-Strauss's analysis of kinship (1969a) reveals that reciprocity and exchange are innate characteristics of mind that allow mediation between groups. The binary opposition "us/them" is mediated by the exchange of women, which facilitates solidarity among otherwise separate groups.

Lévi-Strauss applies the same method to mythology. For example, in his analysis of the Oedipus myth, Lévi-Strauss claims that the binary opposition of overvaluation/undervaluation of kin is symbolically related to the opposition of autochthonous origin/denial of the autochthonous origin of humankind (1963, p. 215). As the "purpose of myth is to provide a logical model capable of overcoming a contradiction" (p. 229), one set of oppositions which is problematic becomes equated with another which can be mediated by a third element and thus resolved. As Lévi-Strauss writes, "mythical thought always progresses from the awareness of opposites to their resolution" (p. 224). The same method can be applied to the culinary realm, where, Lévi-Strauss argues in *The Raw and the Cooked* (1969b), people often structure their meals in the ways they do, not because the foods are good to eat, but because they are "good to think."

This is obviously not the place to provide a detailed discussion of the problems with Lévi-Strauss's position or with structuralism more generally, though brief mention of some of the more salient difficulties is in order. Personally, I find much that is intriguing in Lévi-Strauss's work, though I cannot but admit sympathy with a critique like Marvin Harris's (1978), replete with headings such as, "The Raw, the Cooked, and the Half Baked," and "Will the Real Oppositions Please Stand Up." I have already suggested that structuralism lacks a model of how society is structured, why people perform rituals when they do, how groups adapt to their environments, how human societies have changed evolutionarily, and various similar questions which must at least in principle be answerable by a general model of culture. Thus, structuralism cannot purport to be such a model, though specific structuralist theories have addressed aspects of culture and society in an often enlightening fashion.

As a method and a set of theories, Lévi-Straussian structuralism is problematic. Numerous critics have pointed out that a scientific method must allow replicable analysis, or at the very least must provide specific analytical procedures. Lévi-Strauss's approach instead calls for the anthropologist to play with a myth, for example, until she or he finds something intellectually satisfying. Determining those elements of a myth on which one wishes to focus is largely a matter of taste or whim. In his analysis of the Oedipus myth, for example, Lévi-Strauss chooses to find significance in the names of some of the characters. Labdacos has some connection with lameness, and Oedipus, with a swollen foot. Why he did not choose to explore associations to Eteocles's or to Europa's name is unclear. In general, determining which cultural elements one will choose to consider as the constituents or units of analysis is arbitrary. Lévi-Strauss is not particularly concerned with this problem, nor is he concerned with the argument that his analyses may simply reflect his own associations, rather than the thought of the natives. His response to this question is worth quoting in some detail:

> ... [W]hat does this matter? ... [I]t is in the last resort immaterial whether ... the thought processes of the South American Indians take shape through the medium of my thoughts, or whether mine take place through the medium of theirs. What matters is that the human mind, regardless of the identity of those who happen to be giving it expression, should display an increasingly intelligible structure as a result of the doubly reflexive thought processes acting one upon the other. ... (1969b, p. 13)

199

Frankly, in clinical practice I would be startled by such severe boundary confusion in a neurotic patient. In any case, this kind of argument can hardly be taken seriously without making extraordinary theological assumptions about the cosmic unity of human minds.

A further problem appears in a part of the quotation that I omitted, in which Lévi-Strauss states that "the final aim of anthropology is to contribute to a better knowledge of objectified thought and its mechanisms . . ." That is a very peculiar view of anthropology, and one which betrays Lévi-Strauss's failure to grasp the dynamic, noncognitive aspects of culture. If culture merely reflects brain physiology, the brain Lévi-Strauss has in mind is one without a limbic system. To say that one aspect after another of culture is reducible to unconscious binary brain processes can only leave one wondering about those unconscious brain processes Freud uncovered, which are affective, and which motivate much of social life. Are wishes and fantasies binary?

When one begins to reflect on this notion of binary oppositions without cloaking it in metaphorical and often obscure prose, one wonders what Lévi-Strauss could possibly mean in saying that people inherently think this way. The fact that I can count to five certainly appears to be a falsifying instance. That some of our thought is binary is obvious; that our psychic deep structure is binary is at best devoid of meaning and at worst nonsensical. How does one make sense of schemas or gestalts that guide perception, and that certainly form an unconscious cognitive deep structure involved in processing information? These schemas are themselves alogical and certainly not binary; the same is true of imagistic thinking.

Much of the problem stems from the assumption that culture is itself a form of communication. No one would doubt that many, if not most cultural phenomena have communicational value. Yet to suppose that everything from kinship to cooking is merely, or even primarily communicational is again to take a naively cognitive, nondynamic view of culture from the cortex. People do not act because they think. They think because they want to act. The metaphor of culture as communication – and it is just a metaphor – is fraught with all kinds of ambiguities. Who is communicating to whom? If it is ourselves communicating to ourselves, why do we not simply shut up and think our thoughts instead of trading women, tabooing the flesh of bears, and making up stories of fellows like Oedipus?

The "signs" and "symbols" of cultural "discourse" are not, after all, arbitrary. It is not a matter of indifference whether I symbolize my distaste for someone by slitting his throat versus avoiding him in the subway. In some cases the medium is indeed the message, but in others, the medium is simply the medium, and Lévi-Strauss leaves us without a clue as to what the message would be or, more importantly, why anyone would want to send it. I should point out again that my complaint is not with structuralist explanations per se. Rather, I am simply arguing that as a general theory of sociocultural reality, structuralism is inadequate.

ECOLOGICAL ANTHROPOLOGY: OF CALORIES AND CULTURE

Structuralism's main rival for the hand and heart of sociocultural anthropology in the last two decades has been ecological anthropology. Orlove defines the latter as "the study of the relations among the population dynamics, social organization, and culture of human populations and the environment in which they live" (1980, p. 235). Ecological approaches examine the way various sociocultural phenomena foster adaptation of a population to its environment. This approach to anthropology tends to focus on material conditions and thus overlaps with economic anthropology in both its content and its assumption of rational actors pursuing "survival," "material interest," or "adaptation."

Ecological anthropology has its roots in the work of Leslie White (1949) and Julian Steward (1955, 1968), two men who were instrumental in restoring respectability to evolutionism in anthropology. White, who was profoundly influenced by Marx, was (unlike many later ecological anthropologists) interested in the broad sweep of history, in the evolution of human society as a whole. He was convinced that in reacting against nineteenth-century evolutionary schemes, the historical particularists had pushed the pendulum too far in the other direction. White proposed a unidirectional, universal[1] model of evolution based, not on the development of religion, ideals, or culture, but on the progressive harnessing of energy. He thus emphasized the role of technological development as the prime mover in cultural evolution.

Steward (1955), who had originally been trained in the Boasian tradition, also, like White, came to believe that approaches that center on cultures as systems of ideals and beliefs are deficient in their failure to examine the material conditions of a society, and especially the relations between a culture and its environmental resources. Rather than proposing a universal scheme aimed at explaining society as a whole, Steward preferred to examine particular societies and their adaptations to their specific environments. He was interested in showing that, in different geographical regions, similar cultural complexes would emerge under similar environmental conditions. He was not, strictly speaking, an environmental determinist. He argued that the environment influences a "culture core," but that other elements of culture are relatively autonomous.

It should be evident that ecological anthropology is essentially function-

---

[1] I have profited here from Carneiro's (1973) discussion of universal, unilinear, and multilinear evolution.

alist in the broader sense of the term, if by that one means that it explains the presence of traits in terms of their functions. An approach that centers on adaptation must necessarily attempt to show how various cultural processes either serve or hinder adaptation, and how the latter tend to be selected against.[1] Whereas the functionalism of Radcliffe-Brown focused on the function of cultural practices for the maintenance of societal integration, ecological "functionalism" focuses on processes that serve survival. As Alland (1975) has pointed out, ecological explanations are subject to the same problems as functionalist explanations. One could perhaps press the point even further, to argue that analysis in terms of evolutionary selective retention of various traits is basically functionalist, since those traits that serve a purpose are likely to be retained, and those that do not will be randomly selected and hence subject to extinction.

What should also be made clear is that when one speaks of the influence of "environment," one is always actually talking about the relationship between the environment and the "needs" operative in a given system. At the most obvious level, shortages of available proteins would not provoke responses by a population if proteins were not needed by humans as biological organisms. At a less obvious level, the psychological need for a stable and coherent way of understanding the world necessitates culturally constructed categories of meaning just as surely as the need for food necessitates the collection or cultivation of foodstuffs. As I shall argue below, functional analysis is not itself problematic; what becomes problematic is a single-minded functionalism that focuses only on certain sets of needs, whether they be social or material, and ignores other needs which are equally determinative of sociocultural processes.

Two problems have consistently confronted ecological approaches, from White and Steward to the present. The first is that to the extent that a human population comes to regulate an ecosystem itself, then one can no longer explain social facts in terms of ecological necessities. To put the matter differently, what makes an ecological account less appropriate for humans than for other animals is that human beings produce their own means of subsistence.[2] This problem forces the ecological anthropologist to expand her notion of environment to include the "internal" environment of a culture, such as class structure and technological capacity, if she does not wish to limit her discussion to small scale hunter-gatherer societies. That this problem has led anthropologists back to Marx is not surprising.

The second problem involves determining the appropriate unit of analy-

---

[1] For a cogent discussion of the relationship between adaptation and evolution, see Alland and McCay, 1973.

[2] I am quite certain that someone has said this in precisely the same way, though I cannot find the reference, and offer my apologies to whomever I am unwittingly plagiarizing.

sis. White focused on universal evolution of "society" as a whole. Steward examined multilinear evolution by studying specific cultures. Current anthropologists tend instead to hold one of two perspectives. Some, such as Roy Rappaport (1968, 1979), take populations as the unit of analysis. A population is defined in terms of an ecosystem, and a single society may contain more than one population (and perhaps vice versa). The advantage to focusing on populations is that one can make use of general principles of ecology valid for all other animal species, though ecological approaches influenced by systems theory tend to suffer from the same difficulties in explaining intrasystemic conflict endemic to all systems approaches to social life.[1]

The alternative approach to the unit of analysis problem in ecological anthropology is to focus on decisions of individual actors (see, for example, Barth, 1959; Goldschmidt, 1971; Britan and Denich, 1976; and Laughlin and Brady, 1978). Actor-based or decision-making theories tend to focus on economic/technological decision making, as opposed to the wider aspects of culture, such as ritual and religious belief, examined by those who do not take the individual as the relevant unit (e.g., Rappaport, 1979). Such approaches often argue that rational cost-benefit analysis, not traditionalism, accounts for stasis in preliterate societies, and that change can be similarly explained as a reiterative process whereby many people in roughly identical circumstances reach similar conclusions (e.g., Barth, 1967; Britan and Denich, 1976).

This, of course, raises that thorny issue, hotly debated among economic anthropologists (see Cook, 1973), as to whether this rational economic actor model really applies to anyone, let alone to preindustrial peoples. Even setting that aside, the actor-based approach can often verge on a paradoxically antianthropological, psychological reductionism based on a naively rationalistic model of personality. In some ways this approach merely avoids answering the unit of analysis problem because it fails to consider the extent to which both the aims and cognitive understandings of individual actors are culturally conditioned. In a peculiarly pre-Durkheimian way, the individual actor model often neglects the culturally constructed cognitive representations and affective preferences that mediate between individual and environment.

---

[1] Some who focus on populations also consider ecosystems as units of analysis, though this does not eliminate the problem of intrasystemic conflict. Not only do the "interests" of populations and ecosystems often diverge, but even in a group with as minimal social differentiation as the Maring of New Guinea, whose ecology and culture Rappaport has described, interests of various "subsystems" do not coincide with the interests of the population as a whole. Nevertheless, in my judgment Rappaport's 1979 collection of essays is among the most provocative and insightful works of theoretical anthropology in the last decade, as he attempts to bring together an analysis of ecological relations and systems of meaning.

The advantage to this individualistic approach is that it avoids the hypostasization of culture and the concomitant failure to explain the actions of concrete social actors characteristic of a previous era in anthropology. Further, as exemplified by Britan and Denich's excellent article on decision making in times of rapid social change (1976), this approach avoids the often static nature of functional analysis by using the same principles to explain relative stasis and relative change. Even the latter article, however, runs into trouble in accounting for the "needs" that motivate individual actors. For example, in their examination of a fishing population on St. Brendan's Island in Newfoundland, the authors claim that "decision-making processes" and "dimensions of choice" were not dramatically altered despite massive social change: "People continued to evaluate profits and risks in the light of their own social obligations and their access to resources and alternatives" (p. 68). The question an ecological approach, and especially one oriented toward individual actors, cannot address here is why people made their decisions "in light of their own social obligations" and what these obligations were. A broader theory of society requires one to consider social needs alongside material needs in the understanding of social forms and processes.

Coombs's (1980) fascinating application of decision theory to subsistence strategies illustrates both the tremendous promise and the limitation of decision models. Coombs argues that one can construct a payoff matrix that models the choices facing a population in allocating resources for various subsistence strategies. He compares different decision rules, particularly the "minimax" strategy and the "Bayes" strategy. The minimax strategy means the maximization of minimum payoffs. Using this rule, an allocation of time, effort, and other resources that is likely to provide the highest nutritional rewards in the worst circumstances will be selected even above a strategy that is generally much more advantageous but occasionally produces a low yield. The Bayes strategy, unlike the minimax, maximizes *average* yield over time and is unconcerned with temporary failures.

Coombs very impressively distinguishes conditions under which these two strategies (or points on the continuum between them) are more likely to be adopted. For example, he argues that the minimax rule is more likely to be observed in populations with minimal storage capacities and greater environmental inconsistency. Such populations are more responsive to periods of low yield because they cannot draw on reserves during hard times. Coombs argues that one need not assume rational planning to make this model work: if, for example, a subsistence strategy chosen by a population without storage capacities yields a payoff during one season below subsistence level, the population will begin to starve or migrate from the area, so that populations remaining in an area will "tend to exhibit strategies within the 'viable range' set by the minimum-payoff function" (p. 197).

Decisions models of this sort are tremendously useful, especially as a corrective to "culturological" accounts that minimize the impact of subsistence decisions on culture and social structure, though they are limited in a number of respects (with which many of their adherents would, I suspect, agree). For example, Coombs's model takes populations as units of analysis (p. 196). It is not clear how populations collectively make decisions, nor is it clear what happens when members of a population have conflicting interests. This becomes problematic the further one moves from egalitarian societies, where segments of the population may co-opt group decisions for their own benefit. Decision models generally fail to incorporate a very important variable: the distribution of power and resources.

A second problem is that one cannot always escape the problematic assumption of rational, well-informed decision-makers by turning to selection pressure as the mechanism for subsistence strategy selection. Under severe environmental contingencies selection pressures will, indeed, select particular strategies, though even in those situations cognitive and affective processes mediate decisions to migrate, to maintain dysfunctional practices, and the like, as will be explored in Chapter 9. Under other circumstances, one cannot factor out the psychological and cultural factors that influence choice of strategies because a much wider range of strategies will provide a minimum above subsistence level. Again, I doubt Coombs would disagree, though this certainly limits a purely "rational" decision model.

A third problem is that decision models of this sort assume nutritional needs as the sole determinant of production strategies, which is never the case, though again is more applicable where natural selection operates on the margins of subsistence. What is considered adequate nutrition is itself in some measure culturally determined: most Europeans would not be likely to make use of a nutritionally acceptable reliance on rats and insects unless threatened with starvation (though impoverished Frenchmen have been known to eat escargot; I have fallen on such hard times myself on occasion). Further, people generally produce far more goods of various sorts than is nutritionally required.

A final problem is that military action or coercion is another way of procuring "payoffs," either as a response to production below subsistence level or (as the history of this century amply illustrates) even when a group is economically well situated. Decisions to take military action rely upon other sociocultural (and psychological) factors and are also subject to selection pressures. As I will argue in Chapter 9, societies are likely to manifest hierarchically organized responses (control mechanisms) to various contingencies which can be activated in different ways.

While ecological anthropology has proven extremely fruitful in the generation of hypotheses and in the understanding of human adaptation, like structuralism it has been short on general models of the structure, dynamics, and development of human groups. As Rappaport notes, ecological anthropology "does not constitute a general theory of culture," and he argues that all of culture cannot and should not be explained in ecological terms (1979, p. 62). To continue with an already ailing marital metaphor, one might say that ecology has provided anthropology with numerous propositions, but not enough proposals. One conspicuous exception is Marvin Harris's (1979) attempt to develop a general theory of culture, which deserves attention here since it is perhaps the most explicit and comprehensive paradigm that has emerged since functionalism.[1]

Unlike other observers (Friedman, 1974; Godelier, 1977), I do not consider Harris's materialism particularly "vulgar" (though his critiques of other theorists and theories do occasionally border on it; I am, unfortunately, prone to this excess myself). In fact, Harris's advocacy of his brand of anthropology in *Cultural Materialism* (1979) is a model of how one should ideally (or should I say materially) present a paradigm in any discipline: unambiguously state one's epistemological position, spell out in detail one's method and theoretical assumptions, present specific theories utilizing the method, and systematically critique competing paradigms. In so doing one makes conscious one's scientific unconscious, and thus allows others to understand and challenge one's ideas.

Harris argues from the outset that one must separate emic from etic, and mental from behavioral events. The terms "emic" and "etic" were originally derived from "phonemic" and "phonetic," and they have come to signify the perspective of the natives and that of an outside observer, respectively. A significant difference between the linguistic roots (phonemic and phonetic) and their anthropological analogs that is often overlooked is that whereas the phonemic is always a subset of the phonetic, the same relation does not hold between emic and etic. In other words, of all the sounds that are phonetically discrete, only a subset will be phonemically meaningful in a given linguistic community; "d" and "th," for example, are not phonemically differentiated in many languages. In contrast, the emic is not simply a subset of the etic. Native understanding of a food prohibition or ritual may be quite disparate from the anthropologist's understanding; the Zande belief in witchcraft is not a subset of Evans-Pritchard's understanding of the origins of misfortunes.

Harris also calls for a strict separation of mental and behavioral events. He justifies this move on operationalist grounds that one can use different operations to make scientifically acceptable statements about each realm. It is somewhat ironic that he wrote *Cultural Materialism* in 1979, after a decade in which psychologists had moved away from behaviorism because

---

[1] Portions of this and a later section are adapted from Westen, "Cultural Materialism: Food for Thought or Bum Steer?" *Current Anthropology, 25,* December 1984.

they found that this separation is precisely what one cannot do, that one cannot explain behavior without examining the cognitions that mediate between stimulus and response.

In any case, Harris makes these distinctions because he wants to show that the emic and mental can be explained in terms of the etic and behavioral. Harris shares with Marx the belief that consciousness is derivative of material conditions. Ideas, according to Harris, are causally of marginal significance in comparison to techno-econo-ecological reality. Marx had, for analytical purposes, separated society into material infrastructure and cultural-political superstructure. Harris expands and reworks this scheme, distinguishing what he calls infrastructure, structure, and superstructure.

Rejecting Marx's categorization of relations of production as part of the infrastructure, Harris includes subsistence technology, "techno-environmental relationships," ecosystems, and work patterns as comprising the mode of production. Harris also contends that Marx failed to consider the importance of the "mode of reproduction" in determining culture and social structure, and he includes in this category such factors as demography, mating patterns, infant care (evidently child care is derivative, whereas infant care is not), and population control mechanisms. Together the modes of production and reproduction so defined constitute the infrastructure. Cultural materialism rests upon the assumption that most of sociocultural reality is determined by, and thus predictable from, a knowledge of the material infrastructure. What Harris calls the "structure" includes domestic and political economies (including household patterns, roles, political organization, social hierarchies, war, etc.). The "superstructure" includes the arts, ritual, advertising, recreational activities, and science, which comprise the behavioral superstructure; and the knowledge, thoughts, and ideology that constitute the emic and mental superstructure (1979, pp. 52-4).

Infrastructure is basic, according to Harris, because it provides the main interface between nature and culture (p. 55). The central postulate of cultural materialism is the "principle of infrastructural determinism":

> The etic behavioral modes of production and reproduction probabilistically determine the etic behavioral domestic and political economy, which in turn probabilistically determine the behavioral and mental emic superstructures. (Pp. 55-6)

What Harris means by this, in terms of method, is that one should assume that any aspect of culture is determined by infrastructural variables and construct explanations accordingly. Any residual "error variance" should then be explained in terms of structure, or, if need be, superstructure. The model is thus primarily unidirectional, with causality running from infrastructure to structure to superstructure. Harris does, however, postulate a "feedback" process from emic or mental superstructure to the rest of the system, though he has never described the process in any detail in his theoretical work nor ever explicitly resorted to such explanation in his analyses of specific phenomena.

Elsewhere (Westen, 1984a) I have criticized Harris's model in considerable detail. I will not reproduce those arguments here, though I will sketch a few of the more salient problems. First, despite his belief in infrastructural determinism, Harris admits the existence of "system-transforming values," conceived as "feedback between infrastructure and superstructure" (p. 303). The problem with this is that in times of social change and disintegration of older structures of meaning and authority, one cannot speak of systemic feedback because a functioning system *no longer exists*. The use of the word "feedback" here masks a significant problem with the principle of infrastructural determinism. The analysis of "system-transforming values" brings one inevitably to the Weberian notion of ideas as "switchmen." Weber intended this notion as an antidote to Marxian determinism, and it is a view fundamentally incompatible with cultural materialism. If ideas can be the switchmen of modern events, they no doubt could have played a similarly influential role in the revitalization movements that have appeared throughout human history (Wallace, 1980). The idealistic blueprints of a group of German-influenced Russian intellectuals in 1917 have surely altered the infrastructures as well as ideologies of hundreds of millions of people.

Secondly, like all ecologically oriented approaches, cultural materialism runs into the problem of determining the appropriate unit of analysis. When one argues that essentially rational cost/benefit analysis determines cultural traits, one must be careful to specify which costs and which benefits accrue to which individuals or groups. This is particularly problematic in stratified societies, in which various individuals and subgroups have conflicting material interests. This issue dovetails with the problem, endemic as well to Marxian materialism, of how ideology comes to reflect the interests of dominant classes. This is central to Harris's claims, but in direct opposition to his theoretical assumptions. For example, Harris writes of the "deepening misery of the lower castes and classes" brought on by "politico-economic exploitation and Malthusian penalties" (p. 108). His demystification of the world religions asserts that Confucianism, Taoism, Buddhism, Hinduism, Christianity, and Islam were all invented or co-opted by self-interested elites: "By spiritualizing the plight of the poor, these world religions unburdened the ruling class of the obligation of providing material remedies for poverty" (p. 110). In sum, peasants tend to act on their rational interests, "provided, of course, that their perceptions are not subject to continued manipulation by classes or factions that benefit from the status quo" (p. 300). It should be apparent that this is an emic superstructural explanation: the structure of society depends upon the "perceptions" of the peasants. Not only is this an emic line of argument, but it is one that places the problem of unit of analysis in stark relief. What would happen if the peasants stopped believing these self-serving mystifications of the ruling classes? Would this destroy "adaptiveness" to the ecosystem?

The problem here with the cultural materialist position is the same one encountered by all ecological approaches, particularly those which take populations or cultures as the unit of analysis: as soon as intrasocietal conflict becomes as, or more significant than convergent interests, one can no longer make simple arguments about adaptiveness producing cultural traits. The difficulty lies in showing why one group or class sacrifices its "adaptiveness" for the "adaptiveness" of another group or class. Harris claims that "[i]t is always cheaper to produce obedience through mystification than through police-military coercion" (p. 102). This, however, negates the whole point he has so forcefully argued throughout his work, that behind apparent mystification (whether in pollution rites, food prohibitions, or incest taboos) lies good common sense from an adaptive point of view. In analyzing stratified societies, he thus abandons this assumption and starts talking about the force of irrational beliefs. He would therefore have us believe that until 10,000 B.C. people were not mystified and tended to operate as rational actors, but with the rise of agriculture, literacy, increased knowledge, and the like, suddenly people lost their rationality. To put it differently, Harris assumes a rational psychology of self-interest which applies to everyone except peasants and proletarians. With the rise of stratification comes the development of two kinds of people with radically different psychologies: those who think well (and can thus trick their fellows) and those who do not.

This leads to a final problem with cultural materialism, its inadequate psychology. When he is at his most consistent, Harris locates cost-benefit analysis at the level of the individual, and he even speaks of "infrastructural cost-benefit analysis" (p. 193). The problem is that such analysis is emic and mental, not infrastructural and behavioral, so that the ultimate causes of behavior and culture must be superstructural. According to Harris, "the objective of cultural materialism is to predict both ideas and behavior from a knowledge of behavior" (p. 271). This is a far more ambitious goal than even that of Skinner, who was content to ignore ideas and predict behavior from behavior. As demonstrated by the move away from behaviorism in psychology, even Skinner's more modest goal proved unattainable, as psychologists came to recognize that people's thoughts and feelings have an immense impact upon their behavior.

I should once again point out that in criticizing Harris's overall model I am not advocating the abandonment of specific cultural materialist explanations. Harris and his colleagues have made many brilliant contributions to anthropology, and it would be a mistake to conclude that such contributions are misbegotten. Rather, the point is that Harris's materialism, like structuralism, is inadequate as a general theory, and indeed, that both materialist and structural analysis must be integrable into a more encompassing theory.

Social-Cultural Theory: Prospects and Retrospects

This review of social-cultural theory in sociology and anthropology is obviously an abbreviated one that hardly does justice to an exceedingly complex subject. I have not, for example, discussed two significant approaches, symbolic anthropology (see, e.g., Schneider, 1968; Turner, 1969; Geertz, 1973, 1983), which examines culture as a meaning-system or system of symbols and attempts to describe a culture's conceptual universe; and Marxist anthropology, notably structural Marxism (see Althusser, 1971; Friedman, 1974; Godelier, 1977), which applies Marxist categories (notably "mode of production") to precapitalist societies, emphasizes asymmetrical power relations, and considers symbolic culture as "ideology" that masks class conflict. As in the other social sciences, anthropology in the last decade has largely seen a move away from broader paradigms and systematic theorizing. Sherry Ortner summarizes the current state of affairs in an excellent review of anthropological theories of the last two decades:

> The field appears to be a thing of shreds and patches, of individuals and small coteries pursuing disjunctive investigations and talking mainly to themselves. We do not even hear stirring arguments any more. Although anthropology was never actually unified in the sense of adopting a single shared paradigm, there was at least a period when there were a few large categories of theoretical affiliation, a set of identifiable camps or schools, and a few simple epithets one could hurl at one's opponents. Now there appears to be an apathy of spirit even at this level. We no longer call each other names. We are no longer even sure of how the sides are to be drawn up, and of where we would place ourselves even if we could identify the sides. (1984, pp. 126-7)

In looking back upon the various approaches discussed, one notices that two issues stand out which must be addressed by any general theory of sociocultural phenomena. The first is the relation between ideas and material reality. Each of the major approaches in sociology and anthropology has taken an implicit or explicit stand on this question. Materialist theories from Marx to the present ascribe priority to the material realm. Weber recognized the causal significance of both. Durkheim, while most interested in "ideal" phenomena such as religion and solidarity, was well aware of the importance of material factors and in fact related the rise of organic, and demise of mechanical solidarity to increased population density. Anthropology until the 1950s tended to focus more on the ideal, looking for self-maintaining patterns of culture, social mechanisms for maintaining solidarity, and the like. Structuralism can largely be viewed as within the "idealist" tradition, though Lévi-Strauss adds the peculiar twist of neurophysiological reductionism. Ecological anthropologists conceive of culture and behavior as mechanisms of adaptation to the environment, though some, such as Rappaport, have over the years moved toward a position that grants importance and autonomy to the cultural realm.

This issue of the relation between "ideal" and "material" is as important today in the social sciences as it was historically in philosophy. In its essentials, the problem lies in showing how and why the two Cartesian clocks – of mind and mechanism – tick together. If ideas are not simply reflections of material infrastructures, and social relations are not merely actualizations of ideas, one must develop a more sophisticated theory of the processes by which the twin quests for nutrition and meaning interrelate. In particular, one must be clear to separate two aspects of the "ideal:" cognitions, which *mediate* between reality and human action; and "ideals" proper, which *motivate* human action. Another way to put this is to distinguish maps *of*, from blueprints *for* (Geertz, 1973).

Within the material realm, one must be careful to separate two meanings of "material." On the one hand, one could mean "things," as opposed to ideas. If one defines "material" this way, one can readily see how the world of concrete things (e.g., tools, local fauna and flora, climatic and demographic variables) influences human life, but one cannot argue that these things motivate human action. They may mediate between desire and fulfillment, but they do not determine the aims of human behavior. If, on the other hand, one means material as in "material interest," one is speaking at once of something psychological and economic. Material interests are, in this sense, motivating, though why one should isolate economic self-interest as the sole or primary dynamic in human culture is unclear. Other needs are also dynamically important, such as the needs of individuals for identity and human relationships, and the needs of collectivities for integration and shared structures of meaning. Beyond perhaps the need for food (which is itself culturally articulated), one cannot construct a notion of material self-interest that is not culture-bound; the equation of rationality, material interest, and self-interest is itself a product of Western culture, and every culture fashions for itself beliefs about what constitutes a person's material interest. In some cultures, for example, power is seen as an aspect of material interest, but this is by no means universal. I will argue in Chapter 7 that the belief in a connection between rationality and material self-interest that emerged in the West in the last few centuries represents a significant shift in human values from a previously nearly universal system of values that did not equate "what makes sense" with "what is good for *me*."

The relationship between emics and etics is an aspect of this issue of ideal and material. The question is whether one can develop an adequate theory of culture or society that is either strictly phenomenological or strictly causal-mechanical. At its most basic level, the question is essentially philosophical: what is the aim of social science? Whether one believes that the goal is interpretive understanding or causal explanation will obviously influence one's method and theory. Even if one is primarily interested in causal explanation, however, one cannot escape the question of whether people act because of environmental contingencies or because they have certain needs, desires, and perceptions of environmental contingencies. More concretely, in terms of research, can one study people *as if* subjective states and shared systems of meaning were inconsequential? It is gradually becoming clear that one cannot construct sophisticated etic models that do not take into account emic understandings, just as in psychology one cannot understand the way a person behaves, copes, or defends without examining the way he construes reality and the wishes and fears that motivate his actions.

Rappaport (1968, 1979) has discussed this issue in relation to his distinction between cognized and operational environments. The operational environment is the actual set of environmental forces that impinges upon a population. The cognized environment is the population's understanding of these forces. The two diverge, as in the beliefs of many peoples in the efficacy of witchcraft. In some cases, of course, mind does appear to lord over matter, as when fear induced by voodoo actually produces "voodoo death." Rappaport suggests that the way cognized and operational environments diverge is central in determining the survivability of a population.

The second problem relates to the unit of analysis and centers on the relationships between individuals and larger collectivities. Historically social and cultural theorists have predominantly focused on the level of the group. Marx focused on class as an analytical unit. Durkheim prescribed the explanation of social facts in terms only of other social facts. Functionalist and culture pattern theorists centered on groups or cultures. While the unit of analysis in structuralism is obscure, structural anthropologists have never focused on individuals.

Individualistic analysis became prominent in anthropology with ecological studies, though concerns about using the group as level of analysis surfaced at least as early as Leach's (1954) *Political Systems of Highland Burma,* in which the problem of delimiting group boundaries became clear. A further development in anthropology, the recognition of significant intragroup differences in the understanding of collective rules and concepts (Pelto and Pelto, 1975), has also rendered a focus on collectivities problematic.

As noted earlier, shifting to the individual as unit of analysis does not solve the problems it was intended to circumvent. Often this endeavor loses sight of what has historically been most distinctive about sociological and anthropological investigations, namely, the elucidation of supraindividual social and cultural processes that can only be explained holistically rather than atomistically. To reduce what Durkheim called "collective representations," which are passed from generation to generation, to individuals' schemas is to miss the point of their collective nature, and as pointed out earlier, one cannot understand the goals of individual actors without examining their cultural background. Focusing on individuals often leads to a psychological reductionism based on fuzzy and rationalistic images of human motivation, and it can offer little by itself in explaining why individuals pursue anything other than food and sex. A significant problem is the confounding of analysis which focuses on the individual with the assumption of self-oriented actors. As should be clear from Part I, human beings are social creatures who form attachments and pursue many social objectives; they are not solely economic policy-makers who make all judgments in terms of "rational" cost-benefit analysis.

The distinctive notion of "adaptation" contributed by evolutionist and ecological anthropologists is made problematic by a failure to deal effectively with the unit of analysis problem. As noted in the discussion of cultural materialism, especially in stratified societies in which individuals and subgroups have conflicting material interests, one person's adaptiveness is another's demise. As Williams (1966) noted in a seminal sociobiological tract, the question is whether adaptation occurs on the level of individuals pursuing reproductive success, or whether populations or species evolve adaptive mechanisms of their own. Williams (cited in Alland, 1973) asks the provocative question of whether an adapted population of bumblebees is the same thing as a population of adapted bumblebees. The issue of the relation between units of analysis, and of individuals and collectivities, is a central focus of this book, and I shall argue throughout that it must be a central and explicit focus of any general social scientific perspective at any level of analysis.

If one were, then, to enumerate the prerequisites of a general theory of sociocultural reality, one would perforce include the following. (1) It must specify the dynamic forces that energize the system and motivate individual actors. (2) It must show theoretically and empirically how various societal institutions respond to, and mediate these sometimes conflicting needs. (3) The theory must examine the interplay between these dynamic forces and the environment and history of the group being studied. (4) It must distinguish, and elucidate the relationship between cultural cogni-

213

tions of this interplay and the actual relationship between biological, psychological, and social needs and the human and nonhuman environment. (5) The model must distinguish, and elucidate the relationship between normative "social structure" and actual "social organization" (Firth, 1951). In other words, one must examine both the norms governing social behavior (the study of which dominated earlier anthropology) and the actual interactional patterns emphasized by writers such as Bott (1957) and other network analysts (e.g., Boissevain, 1974). Both conformity to, and deviation from normative patterns must be explicable in terms of dynamic factors and concrete opportunities. (6) It must distinguish, and explore the relationship among cultural ideals, cognitions of reality relevant to these ideals (i.e., whether the ideals are being met), the actual reality (aspects of the operational environment), and mechanisms responsible for correcting discrepancies between ideals and cognized and operational reality. (7) It must distinguish, and elucidate the relationship between the actual functioning of a society and its image of its functioning (similar to the difference between operational and cognized environments, though pertaining to the "internal environment"). (8) It must permit examination of prominent culturally constructed cognitive-affective schemas or collective representations, which both motivate action and mediate experience. (9) The model must distinguish various culturally cognized and noncognized subgroups with shared and unshared interests and elucidate the mechanisms by which conflicts of interest are mediated. (10) The theory must provide insight into the relationship between all of the factors described above over time and help establish the degree to which different processes can vary independently. (11) Finally, the theory must be integrable with an understanding of dynamics, cognition, and behavior at the individual level.

This is obviously a mighty list, and one against which the theories reviewed here do not, by and large, fare well. To take the example of Lévi-Straussian structuralism, how it provides insight into many of these processes and relationships is difficult to see. In a rather opaque review of Lévi-Strauss's perspective (as such reviews tend to be), Scholte writes of Lévi-Strauss's "ontological subordination of the individual and the subjective to the collective, and the systematic and methodological priority of logical and objective explanations to emotional and utilitarian ones" (1973, p. 654). It is precisely because he *chooses* between the individual and collective and the cognitive and emotional that Lévi-Strauss's structuralism cannot be anything more than a subset of a more general theory that recognizes that human beings are both individual organisms and members of collectivities (I have my doubts about seeing them as vessels of a cosmic consciousness), and that they feel and wish as well as think. As I argued in Part I, the idea that human beings act in the world for "cognitive" reasons

214

is largely mistaken, though certainly cognitive processes mediate both our perceptions and the alternative forms of action we consider.

I will not claim that my own perspective does stellarly against this list, though it at least attempts to differentiate and explicitly address all of these issues and is thus, I would contend, better than available alternatives. The model has not yet been tested in the field, however, so I must propose it tentatively as an approach with greater explanatory power but only potential utility in guiding research. While I will use many examples in the following chapters, I beg the reader's patience in waiting until Chapter 10 for a more thorough reinterpretation of anthropological data in terms of the proposed theory.

6 Societal Structure and Dynamics

THE FIRST REQUIREMENT of any social theory is that it elucidate the dynamic forces which energize a society and motivate its individual actors. For Marx, these forces are competing class interests, though why anyone desires anything other than food is unclear in his system because it lacks a systematic psychology. Marx himself astutely argued against the imputation of universality to historically specific valuations of various social goods; one is left with a theory that sees classes as aggregates pursuing what are ambiguously called their "interests." The dynamic behind social life for Durkheim and most of the functionalists is the quest for solidarity, which is actualized in such institutions and practices as religion and ritual. For Weber, people pursue power, status, wealth, and other unspecified values.

Early evolutionists were less concerned with dynamic forces than with descriptive evolutionary schemes, though one could, with ahistorical hindsight, view natural selection as the dynamic process responsible for societal evolution. The culture pattern theorists argued for a consistency principle in culture itself which rearticulates a diffused cultural element in order to assimilate it into the cultural gestalt. Structuralists tend to avoid dynamics and focus instead on cultural cognition, though this is an oversimplification, particularly for anthropologists, like Victor Turner, who wed structural, symbolic, and functional analysis. Turner, in analyzing the *Isoma* ritual of the Ndembu, points out that the symbols and their relations in this fertility ritual are not simply "a set of cognitive classifications for ordering the Ndembu universe. They are also, and perhaps more importantly, a set of evocative devices for rousing, channeling, and domesticating powerful emotions . . ." (1969, pp.42-3). Structuralism lacks a clear theory of the dynamic forces behind ritual, myth, food preparation, table manners, and the like. Ecological theories posit the striving for survival or adaptation among individuals, cultures, or populations as the source of social action, though they are deficient in providing a general theory of what people do when their bellies are full and their neighbors are peaceful.

216

Group-needs and Member-needs

I will attempt to systematize the various dynamic forces in a given society by distinguishing two separate sets of needs: collective needs and individual needs. While many theorists have assumed the convergence of these in their models, the two types of needs are analytically distinct and may often come into conflict.

The distinction to which I am calling attention is similar to that described by Marx, following Hegel, of civil and political society. For Hegel, civil society is the "complex of organised social ties which knot individuals together by the cords of self-interest" (Hook, 1962, p. 300). The state, for Hegel, is the "institutional sublimation of all social difference" (p. 22), similar in many ways to Rousseau's concept of the general will. In Marx's early, more Hegelian writings, he similarly distinguishes between civil and political society. While in the *German Ideology* his use of "civil society" embraces the entire material infrastructure (1963, p. 127), in his even earlier writings Marx describes civil society as the realm of individual self-interest: "Practical need, egoism, is the principal of civil society" (1975a, p. 239, emphasis deleted). Political society, in contrast, is the realm of the "general interest" (p. 239).[1]

Political society and civil society are terms that denote two clusters of needs operating in the societal "system" which will here be called *group-needs* and *member-needs*. The group-needs consist in part of the needs related to societal cohesion and sociality stressed by functionalists. Radcliffe-Brown, the cofounder of anthropological functionalism, describes sanctions as "reactions on the part of a community to events affecting its integration" (1965, p. 211). Similarly, he argues that the "performance of rites serves to cultivate in the individual sentiments on whose existence the social order depends" (p. 146). According to Ralph Linton (1945), societies have needs independent of the needs of their members; in response, social systems must develop techniques for indoctrinating individuals, provide rewards and punishments for socially acceptable and unacceptable behavior, and create relatively nonconflictual culture patterns (p. 24).

Even in the "simplest," least differentiated societies, people have multiple loyalties to different subgroups, though the degree to which this situation is disharmonious or conflictual varies considerably. At the simplest level, age-grading and gender distinctions often produce subgroups who share special bonds of interest and affection. Male solidarity, for example, is often prized in hunter-gatherer societies, where it may also be

---

[1] Marx's notion of political society, like that of Hegel, often confounds the general or group interest with the actual apparatus of the state; the two may be entirely different. In fact, for Marx, the state as repressive apparatus only comes into existence when the state or "political society" as nonconflictual general interest becomes a mere fantasy.

ecologically adaptive. Individuals in primitive societies tend to have ties to groups on different levels, such as clan and tribe or band and family. These group attachments are frequently hierarchically ordered. An old man among the Ojibwa would not sacrifice the tribe for solidarity among old men. A peasant may value both her village and her family, but she usually knows which comes first in a conflict of interest (although this varies by society). Similarly, an American may have attachments to his home state, but these attachments are generally secondary to his nationalistic sentiments. In discussing the problems of emerging nations in the Third World, Geertz points to the potential for conflict between private interests, various collective interests, and what he describes as a "civic sense," a "definite concept of the public as a separate and distinct body and an attendant notion of a genuine public interest, which though not necessarily superior to, is independent of and at times even in conflict with, both private and others sorts of collective interest" (1963, p. 156). (For excellent discussions of conflicting loyalties, see Gluckman, 1955; Sahlins, 1968.)

The problem that emerged in anthropological writings by the 1950s was that one could not always speak unambiguously about functions for "the group" because individuals were often found to have ties to more than one group. Simple functionalist arguments (and I will later argue that the same is true of Marxist-derived "class functionalist" approaches) tend to underestimate the extent of affectional ties to multiple collectivities. As Etzioni remarks, "Society may be viewed as a set of Chinese nesting boxes; smaller units exist and function within larger ones" (1974, p. 337). Durkheim (1915) recognized the possibility that an individual actually may relate to several collective consciousnesses, though he paid the problem little attention. Gellner, among others, has noted that many members of "primitive" and "peasant" societies have a sliding scale conception of morality, rather than a simple ingroup/outgroup image of social relations; social obligations are "graduated and enforceable according to context" (1968, p. 134). Attachments may thus be diverse and hierarchically related, and they frequently outweigh material considerations in determining concrete acts of individuals.

LeVine and Campbell (1972, p. 4) delineate two types of loyalty patterns discovered by anthropologists: the pyramidal-segmentary type and the cross-cutting type. These are ideal types, of course, which often coexist within a single society. The pyramidal-segmentary type involves the nesting pattern described by Etzioni in which individuals have loyalites to groups that are subgroups of larger collectivities. Especially in the event of conflict between levels, individuals may have to rank their loyalties, and they may do so parochially, favoring the local group, or less parochially, favoring a larger unit. Cross-cutting loyalty systems, the second type, involve multiple (and often military) loyalties to groups based on descent, residence, or age.

A "pacifying network of cross-cutting ties" (p. 48) often arises and may become relatively institutionalized, as individuals presented with competing claims must mediate these claims and often press for peaceful solutions. Gluckman (1955) has explored the way competing loyalties can bind a society together by forcing individuals to press for resolution of conflicts between competing groups to which they have ties. Guetzkow (1955) has focused on the problem of multiple and conflicting loyalties, especially in developing nations.

The member-needs, in contrast, relate to the hierarchy of individual needs discussed in Part I. Member-needs are the purely individual desires that exert pressure on the societal "system" as well as on the ecosystem. When ecological anthropologists speak of adaptation, they are usually referring to the processes by which individuals or populations fulfill member-need set-goals for food, shelter, and safety. Member-need/environment interactions have both emic and etic dimensions, as will be discussed further below. Different individuals in a given society establish different set-goals, and these are frequently culturally patterned, so that, for example, members of different classes or status groups may not demand similar things from society. This is especially true in more complex, stratified societies. Particularly in periods of rapid social change, different groups may demand satisfaction of set-goals not previously desired or provided. Society's failure to fulfill the new needs may cause this class to deny the legitimacy of the system, where previously legitimacy was not in question.

Culture Processes: Culture Real and Culture Ideal

Definitions of the term "culture" are as varied as the writers who use the word. Tylor established an early and inclusive view of culture as "that complex whole which includes knowledge, belief, art, morals, law, custom, and any other capabilities and habits acquired by man as a member of society" (1958, p. 1). In a review of the concept of culture, Kroeber and Kluckhohn (1952) analyze several hundred definitions proposed by various authors. I will now throw one more fish in the water in the hope of displacing a number of schools of thought.

Group-needs and member-needs represent two clusters of set-goals confronting society. To the extent that conflicts arise between set-goals, particularly between the "instrumental" needs of individuals and the requirements for preservation and solidarity of the group, society requires some arbiter of competing claims. That arbiter is culture. Two structures, *culture real* and *culture ideal,* form that which, along with an integrating function between the two, will here be considered *culture.* "Culture" as used here is analogous to "personality" at the individual level of analysis. Aspects of the culture real correspond to typical notions of the social system or social structure (compare Parsons and Shils, 1951, p.54). It includes the concrete culture "on the ground" as well as the body of shared and unshared cognitions. The culture real includes social organizations, economic institutions, kinship systems, and political systems. More systematically, the culture real is the set of cognitions, behaviors, and institutions which respond to social and individual set-goals operative in a given collectivity. Defining this structure in terms of its function, it is the aspect of society responsible for maintaining various set-goals or "homeostases" and for providing an (emic) image of reality. It includes the relatively concrete social norms that govern role behavior; the actual pattern of social interactions or "social organization" that Firth (1951) juxtaposed to "social structure;" the "cognized environment," including representations of the group and collective functioning; and the institutionalized and noninstitutionalized control mechanisms responsible for meeting individual and social set-goals and resolving conflicts.

The "equilibration"[1] function of culture real deserves attention because it has not been *systematically* treated before as a result of fuzzy systems concepts. Many anthropologists have profitably written of various cultural mechanisms that maintain "homeostasis," but their analysis has not proceeded much further because of a failure to specify a theory of societal dynamics (i.e., the needs that "energize" the system, and the way societal mechanisms mediate conflicting demands). As long as one treats society or culture as a system with monolithic ends that the various subsystems cooperate in pursuing, one will not be able to explore the numerous set-goals established and attained in a society. A society has numerous homeostases, not a single one, and these homeostases relate to specific needs.

Ecological anthropologists influenced by systems theory have examined various sociocultural processes as control mechanisms. Rappaport, for example, argues that members of a population "compare the states of the systems in which they participate, as these states are indicated by signs, with their culturally determined notions of what they think they should be (reference or ideal values)" (1979, p. 98, emphasis deleted). His analysis of Maring ritual cycles in *Pigs for the Ancestors* (1968) suggests that when cognized reality indicated by signs deviates from reference values, various control mechanisms (such as rituals) come into play to reduce the disparity. The reader should note the similarity between this view and the notion of cognitive-evaluative mismatches at the individual level in Part I. Rappaport astutely emphasizes the distinction between culturally encoded (emic) reference values and the actual (etic) "goal ranges" which reference values should ideally, but frequently do not, approximate. If, for example, certain

---

[1] I will use this term with reservations as in Part I, to refer to the regulation of individual and collective set-goals through various control mechanisms.

information sets off control mechanisms erroneously, or the (emic) reference value is outside the (etic) goal range and necessary control mechanisms are not activated when they should be or are activated when they should not, the results could be disastrous. Rappaport centers on reference values and goal ranges involving "biological well-being" (1979, p. 98), but the argument here is that the model of set-goals, feedback, and control mechanisms can be extended to encompass *all* the needs that energize the system.

Wynne-Edwards (1962) has tried to show how animal populations biologically develop control mechanisms to regulate population. Abernathy (1979) argues that human groups use mechanisms such as infanticide, gerontocide, suicide, marriage age delays, intercourse taboos, warfare, and similar mechanisms to regulate population. She claims that the feedback that triggers these control mechanisms is the perception of scarcity (at the individual level). Dickeman (1975) has shown how the Tikopia consciously and collectively control population size when it begins to become dangerously large by limiting sexual intercourse to once per week. Such mechanisms may be culturally patterned and thus constitute cultural control mechanisms, or they may simply be statistical artifacts of reiterative individual decisions. The former case (culturally constituted control mechanisms) does not require that all individuals who participate in carrying out the mechanism experience similar situations or that they all recognize the actual set-goal/reality disparity. In this case, feedback interpreted at the collective level or by key individuals can set off a mechanism the function of which members of the group do not understand. In the latter case, in contrast, individuals must consciously or unconsciously recognize the discrepancy between desire and reality and act in similar ways because of similar alternatives and similar cost-benefit analyses. Even in this latter case, however, the way individuals will construe a situation and the alternatives they will consider and choose are culturally conditioned. These matters will receive further attention in Chapter 9.

Groups frequently respond collectively to threats from neighboring groups, often even changing geographical location, social structure, or political organization. Evidence from West Africa documents the impact of pressure from neighboring states, producing responses such as migration and state formation in societies previously without complex political organization (Netting, 1972; Cohen, 1976). Societies also respond to dangers from within by projecting them upon other societies, as the history of twentieth-century international relations corroborates and as La Barre (1966) has shown for the Aymara. White (1972) has commented on a mechanism through which another nation's leaders are vilified while "the people" of that society are viewed sympathetically.

Scapegoating is a defense used by all societies, whether the scapegoat is internal or external to the group. The phenomenon of scapegoating on the family level has been analyzed impressively by Bermann (1973) from a systems perspective. Scapegoating or persecution of deviants on the collective level serves a number of functions. First, it draws attention away from the culture's own defects, as when a nation blames poverty on its poor or expresses moral indignation at welfare fraud while expanding licit and illicit opportunities for tax evasion by the rich. As this example shows, scapegoating can obviously be used by one class or segment of the population to avoid attention to its own wrongdoings. A second function of scapegoating is to isolate a danger and thus to contain it. If the scapegoat is internal to the group, not only can the danger be contained, but the deviant can be controlled, punished, and even induced to despise himself, which in turn bolsters the collective "defense" and allows the society to master the danger.

Similar control mechanisms arise in relation to social needs not directly related to subsistence or survival. Turner (1969, p. 10) found that periods of high social conflict in Ndembu villages correlated with a high frequency of rituals, suggesting that rituals can function as control mechanisms activated by social conflict to restore social order. Examples of ritual fulfilling social functions can be culled from any functionalist ethnography. Ritual not only serves as a control mechanism in relation to various needs of a single group, but it also can mediate conflict between different group levels in segmentary societies or between groups which command competing loyalties in nonsegmentary collectivities. In so doing, ritual preserves or enhances various attachments simultaneously.

Turner, for example, describes how the *Isoma* ritual mediates conflicting loyalties in Ndembu society (1969). Various aspects of *Isoma* symbolism mediate conflict between loyalties based on matrilineal descent and patrilocal residence. Rappaport's analysis of Maring rituals and beliefs documents the use of these cultural phenomena for the enhancement, and expression of the solidarity, of two groups simultaneously. A sacrifice of pigs occurs with the planting of the *rumbim*, which signifies the beginning of a period of repayment of the ancestors for their help in war. Although the dead supposedly devour the spirits of the pigs, the living consume the flesh. Even though the Red Spirits are the dead who provided aid in wartime, most of the meat is sacrificed to the spirits of the lower ground. The flesh of the pigs sacrificed to the latter spirits is presented to allies of the local group and thus both repays them for their aid in war and expresses intergroup solidarity. At the same time, the sacrifice also, by designating a portion of the meat to the Red Spirits (and that meat can only be eaten by agnates), expresses solidarity among the local group and particularly among the men who have fought together.

As these examples suggest, control mechanisms may be highly symbolic responses to many different set-goals. In her brilliant analysis of concepts of pollution and taboo, Mary Douglas (1966) argues that actions and objects become taboo, impure, and dangerous when they challenge collective classificatory beliefs or "fall between the cracks" of social relations. She argues, for example, that the food taboos in Leviticus can be explained better in terms of their threat to the established view of the world (e.g., certain animals do not fit into a sharp separation of animals of sea, land, and air, so they become taboo) than through materialist explanations that search for the "rational" roots of every belief. "Even if some of Moses' dietary rules were hygienically beneficial," she remarks, "it is a pity to treat him as an enlightened public health administrator, rather than as a spiritual leader" (p. 4l).

Objects of thought that fall between the cracks of collective cognitive schemas can provoke anxiety in much the same way as facts that cannot be assimilated into an individual's way of understanding the world can be extraordinarily threatening, especially if the person is one for whom control is a central issue. Douglas documents the way a culture may use pollution beliefs and rituals to circumscribe a threat to its collective cognitive constructs: the danger of the ambiguous cases may be focused on one particular case which becomes threatening and impure, leaving the rest of the structure intact. This effectively deflects attention from other aberrant phenomena:

> In a given culture it seems that some kind of behavior or natural phenomena are recognized as utterly wrong by all the principles which govern the universe. There are different kinds of impossibilities, anomalies, bad mixings and abominations. Most of the items receive varying degrees of condemnation and avoidance. Then suddenly we find one of the most abominable or impossible is singled out and put into a very special kind of ritual frame that marks it off from other experience. The frame ensures that the categories which the normal avoidances sustain are not threatened or affected in any way. Within the ritual frame the abomination is then handled as a source of tremendous power. (Pp. 194-5)[1]

Douglas also notes that pollution beliefs emerge "when moral rules are obscure or contradictory," or when norms defining standard operating procedures are not enforceable or reinforced by sanctions. She points out that where the threat of physical violence is uninhibited with respect to a

---

[1] To the reader acquainted with the philosophy of science, a particular word in this quotation signals a fascinating parallel. That word is "anomalies," and the parallel is with Kuhn's (1970) discussion of the anomalies that arise which threaten a given scientific paradigm and ultimately trigger a scientific revolution. As will be argued in Chapter 13, the phenomena Douglas has so astutely observed in "primitive" societies are collective mechanisms to control anomalies, very similar to mechanisms operative in scientific communities used to abort paradigm shifts.

223

given act, pollution beliefs do not arise (p. 168). This suggests, as will be elaborated in Chapter 9, that collective control mechanisms may be ordered hierarchically, with activation of the most efficient mechanisms generally occurring first. If more efficient mechanisms fail, less "adaptive" strategies may be necessary. Cultural control mechanisms may be relatively institutionalized or routinized, or they may arise spontaneously to meet a particular situation or crisis.

Numerous other cultural beliefs and institutions can be employed in ways similar to those described by Douglas. Witchcraft, for example, can be used to maintain social solidarity and control when lines of authority are ambiguous (see B. Whiting, 1950; Swanson, 1960; Douglas, 1966). Swanson (1960) notes that in Western history, witch crazes arose during periods of social upheaval or breakdown of authority, and similar epidemics of witchcraft have occurred throughout the Third World.

The culture ideal is the societal analog (and Part III will try to show that they are related by more than analogy) of the individual's ego ideal. Somewhat like the ego ideal, it represents the culture's center of morality and ideal reconciliation of society, its subgroups, and its individual members. The culture ideal as proposed here resembles a slightly delimited version of Kroeber's classic concept of culture, which he defines as a "set of ideas, attitudes, and habits – 'rules' if one will – evolved by men to help them in their conduct of life" (1963, p.10). In contrast to "real culture," which consists largely of behaviors, anthropologist Ralph Linton contends that a culture has "ideal patterns" which express a people's normative consensus about that which *should* be (1945, pp. 43-53); these ideal patterns correspond in many ways to the culture ideal. The culture ideal similarly resembles Shils's concept of the "central cultural system" (1975, p. 38) and has affinities to his "central value system" (p. 4).

As this discussion suggests, the concept of a "culture ideal" is hardly revolutionary; a number of other anthropologists and sociologists have developed similar ideas. In the *Rules of Sociological Method* Durkheim suggests that certain ideals of the *conscience collective* have an abstract, yet real existence:

> . . . collective habits find expression in definite forms: legal rules, moral regulations, popular proverbs, social conventions, etc. As these forms have a permanent existence and do not change with diverse applications made of them, they constitute a fixed object, a constant standard within the observer's reach, exclusive of subjective expressions and purely personal observations. (1938, p.45)

Elaborating upon the Durkheimian tradition, Radcliffe-Brown comments that "an orderly social life amongst human beings depends upon the presence in the minds of the members of a society of certain sentiments, which control the behaviour of the individual in his relation to others" (1952, p. 157).

224

Here Radcliffe-Brown, in speaking of self-other relations, provides a tie between the concept of culture ideal as enunciated here and ego ideal as previously presented; this connection will be discussed in depth in Part III. For Radcliffe-Brown, rites have as one function the maintenance and transmission of ideals from one generation to the next. Similarly, Parsons discusses collective "moral standards," which constitute "the main focus of the evaluative aspect of the common culture . . ." (1970b, p. 22).

A number of authors from the culture pattern school have developed concepts similar to that of culture ideal. Loosely following Bateson (1936), Kroeber distinguishes the *eidos* of a culture ("its appearance, its phenomena, all about it which can be described explicitly"), which corresponds to aspects of culture real, from the *ethos* of a culture ("the system of ideals and values that dominate the culture and so tend to control the type of behavior of its members") (1948, pp. 101-2), which corresponds to the culture ideal.

Perhaps the anthropologist whose thoughts come closest to the view proposed here is Clifford Geertz. Geertz recognizes that the image of a culture pattern is overly mechanistic and implies too much consistency and articulation. Nevertheless, culture does in some sense form a cohesive whole:

> The appropriate image, if one must have images, of cultural organization, is neither the spider web nor the pile of sand. It is rather more the octopus, whose tentacles are in large part separately integrated, neurally quite poorly connected with one another, and yet nonetheless manages both to get around and to preserve himself, for a while anyway, as a viable if somewhat ungainly entity. (1973, p. 408)

Geertz proposes that one view culture less as a set of customs and traditions than as a set of rules and instructions analogous to a computer program (p. 44), a program that is never entirely actualized (p. 250). Culture and social structure (culture ideal and real), he argues, interact, and the attempt to reduce one to the other is futile (pp. 143-4). Materialists are certainly justified in arguing against a pure idealism that views ideas as entirely independent of material reality. Yet to argue that ideals reflect social structure (or an aspect of social structure, such as class) misunderstands the function of ideals and the dynamic interaction of ideals and action. The culture ideal serves as a program for action, not just a legitimation of existing reality. When Gellner notes that Islamic religion is a "blueprint of a social order" (1968, p. 127), he is in no sense implying that such a social structure (culture real) exists; rather, what this suggests is that Islamic society would like the culture real to approach this ideal.

In his fieldwork in Bali, Geertz found that, as in many preindustrial societies, an ideal image of the past serves as a valued model for the present. The Balinese "search the past not so much for the causes of the present as for the standard by which to judge it, for the unchanging pattern upon which the present might properly be modeled but, which through accident, ignorance, indiscipline, or neglect, it so often fails to follow" (p. 334). In terms of the model proposed here, an ideal of the past guides activity in the present, and when too great a discrepancy occurs between ideals and cognized reality, control mechanisms are activated to try to bring the "system" back in line with culture ideal reference values or set-goals.

Another related viewpoint is Robert LeVine's notion of a "psychosocial adaptive compromise" between society and its members (1973, p. 157). Connecting micro- and macro-levels of analysis, LeVine points out that an institutionalized compromise between socioeconomic demands and individual needs may be transmitted intergenerationally through a normative structure (p. 57). He astutely notes that the normative synthesis created may deny the needs of either individual or society:

> Institutional forms of adaptation between personality and sociocultural systems can be seen as compromise-formations in which constraints and demands of both personality genotype [core personality] and its normative environment are represented. Although movement is toward a steady-state in which the more pressing demands of both sides are adequately satisfied, many particular institutionalized adaptations are "bad" compromises, in which one side or another is overrepresented. (P. 132)

The view of culture as compromise-formation is extremely important and will be developed further in Part III. Cultures serve two masters: individuals and groups. Culture ideal set-goals establish the ideal relation between these masters in the form of a moral system. Culture real institutions and processes attempt to actualize this relationship in the form of social structure and action. To the extent that certain collective and individual set-goals cannot be fulfilled, elements of culture ideal will represent a "projective system" (Kardiner, 1945), a set of social and individual fantasies which may take the form of art, literature, or ideas. One cannot dismiss Marx's view of religion as a fantasy—a cry of the oppressed, an "opiate" of the masses—out of hand. Certainly many aspects of religion serve precisely this psychocultural function. As a general view of religion, however, this is too cynical. When a peasant expresses in religious form the desire for a return to the egalitarianism of a past age, he is not simply "letting off steam." He is calling for a particular order, and if the contradiction between the ideal and reality becomes too great, he begins to face a choice. The stability of most historic agricultural societies suggests not only the realities of power in the particular societies but also that this critical point of choice has simply not been reached.

Culture ideal – the realm of values – sets the standards by which culture real – the "social system" – must act. The dialectic between the real and the ideal is mediated by cultural cognitions, including a picture of the way the society is actually operating. If the hiatus between culture ideal and the cognized model of culture real becomes chronic or acute, the society may distort its conception of its institutions (its "group-concept," one might say) or its ideals. It may deny that, in fact, culture real is failing to meet the mandates of culture ideal. In slightly different terms LeVine documents this phenomenon, observing that certain norms in a culture may be preserved only by maintaining the pretense that they are rigidly enforced (1973, p.143). He gives the example of incompetent leaders being quietly deposed contrary to cultural norms with little notice. Similarly, Kenneth Keniston describes as the "institutionalization of hypocrisy" the process by which a culture ignores many of its own inconsistencies and shortcomings (1968, p. 237).

Alternatively, a culture may maintain an adequate image of itself in such cases, leading to the possibility of apathy or instability. As Merton notes, these processes need not apply uniformly throughout a society. The conflict between cultural ideals and the actual situation of a particular class may become acute (1968, pp. 199-201), resulting in "deviant" behavior, for example, or a kind of withdrawal Merton calls retreatism (pp. 207-9).

The Cyrenaica Bedouin as described by Peters (1967) have, according to their own emic conceptions, a segmentary system with political ties based on unilineal agnatic descent. They believe that political alliances should be, and are, based strictly on degree of lineage ties. Yet when Peters actually mapped out the organization of real political ties in concrete situations, he discovered that alliances were influenced heavily by ecological and economic factors and were more often formed with distant lineages than with those specified by cultural ideals. The Bedouin explain away the various exceptions and thus maintain the pretense that the ideals are governing behavior, though "in doing so they are as truthful as anyone anywhere whose traditions do not fully apply to the exigencies of their existence" (Cohen, 1973, p. 868).

The analytical separation of a culture's ideals from its cognitions about reality, from reality itself, and from actual social structure and social organization is critical. Simply to separate emic from etic cannot suffice. The emic meaning-system of a culture includes both its culture ideal (the evaluative standards of what should be) and cognitive elements of culture real (beliefs about how things really are). It is the discrepancy between culture ideal set-goals and these cognitive aspects of culture real that activates cultural control mechanisms, not the discrepancy between ideals and actual social organization or social structure. Were a society not to recognize a mismatch between its ideals and its practices, mechanisms for adjusting the situation would not be motivated. In this respect, the observer must look to the emic or cognized model of social functioning in constructing an etic explanation of the processes that activate control mechanisms. Yet one must not equate emic or cognized with *conscious* understandings. The Bedouin in the above example may well not be conscious that their ideals are only one determinant of their actions, and one frequently overruled. This is not to say that they are not *cognizant* that their political alliances are influenced by pragmatic, as opposed to ideal considerations. One cannot, on an etic level, account for the sophistication of their rationalizations without assuming unconscious awareness (and defensive operations aimed at minimizing the disruptive consequences that would ensue from conscious acknowledgment of the causes of their behavior) of the discrepancy between their actions and ideals. Later in this chapter I will demonstrate the importance of disentangling the often confounded notions of emic and conscious beliefs.

The necessity of distinguishing the elements of a culture's meaning-system that are imperative (culture ideal) from those that are cognitive (culture real) does not imply that fact and value always remain separate and separable. In this regard, Geertz's discussion of the anthropological distinction of ethos and worldview is instructive. The ethos is comprised of the moral, aesthetic, and evaluative elements of culture; it is "the tone, character, and quality of their life, its moral and aesthetic style and mood; it is the underlying attitude toward themselves and their world that life reflects" (1973, p. 127). The worldview, in contrast, is "their picture of the way things in sheer actuality are, their concept of nature, of self, of society" (p. 127). The discussion thus far has emphasized the function of aspects of worldview (cognitive culture real) in providing information as to the state of actualization of ethos (culture ideal). Ethos and worldview, however, are not always so separate, particularly in certain types of society and in institutions such as religion. As Geertz observes,

> Religious belief and ritual confront and mutually confirm one another; the ethos is made intellectually reasonable by being shown to represent a way of life implied by the actual state of affairs which the world view describes, and the world view is made emotionally acceptable by being presented as an image of an actual state of affairs of which such a way of life is an authentic expression. (P. 127)

The model presented here thus proposes four societal structures (bearing in mind that "structure" means the same as in Part I, a constellation of functionally related processes): group-needs, which include social sentiments and requisites; member-needs, which are comprised of the individual needs of society's members; culture real, which includes cognitions, behaviors, and social institutions; and culture ideal, society's center of morality, which provides an ideal reconciliation between conflicting set-goals and expresses unfulfilled social and individual desires. The boundaries between these structures are obviously not entirely rigid; they are ideal-typical constructs, not absolute and entirely faithful representations of reality. Before concluding this section, I would like to apply this model to three thorny issues, and to show how the notions of "function," "class," and "emics and etics" may, with the same names but slightly different interpretations, smell somewhat sweeter.

Function and Functionalism: The Uses and Abuses of Teleology

As mentioned earlier, within the last twenty-five years functionalism has come under severe attack (see Lockwood, 1956; Dahrendorf, 1958; Hempel, 1958; Homans, 1964; Geertz, 1973), though a few have rallied to its cause (see Cancian, 1960; Merton, 1968). Four serious problems confront functional analysis. The first is its well-noted difficulty in explaining dysfunction. When one embarks upon an examination of the way certain sociocultural phenomena fulfill a function for a group, one can easily assume away the question of how traits may be dysfunctional or what happens when particular functions are not being adequately fulfilled.

This leads to the second charge often leveled against functionalism, that it has difficulty explaining change. The system-maintaining functionalist view of society does tend to emphasize systems that fight to preserve the status quo, and theories of the evolution of the set-goals that serve as regulatory ideals are generally missing. Specific rituals, institutions, or myths may change, but structural change which alters system goals and often the mechanisms used to maintain those goals has seldom been explained through functional analysis.

A third problem is the difficulty in elucidating intrasocietal conflict. Functionalist accounts tend to view anything from religion to deviance as necessary for maintaining societal "equilibrium." This perspective has difficulty accounting for struggles for power, status, and wealth within a group. The specific resolution of these struggles can often account for the phenomena functionalists frequently describe as functional for the group rather than as products of competing desires for limited resources.

A final problem is the teleological nature of functionalist analysis. Natural science banished Aristotelian teleology from the court of King Knowledge several centuries ago, no longer accounting for a phenomenon like the sun by pointing out that humans need the light. In contrast, functionalism explains a phenomenon in terms of the function or purpose it serves, which many view as a return to an outmoded form of explanation (see Rappaport, 1979, on formal versus final causes).

229

Much of the difficulty with functional analysis can be alleviated by replacing vague notions of homeostasis and good of the group with specific accounts of particular set-goals, their resolution, and the mechanisms through which these resolutions are selectively retained. In this way one can similarly avoid the difficulties encountered when one speaks of ecological "adaptation," which parallel the problems of functionalism described above. A cultural trait rarely serves one function; a trait that fulfills more than one goal is more likely to be retained over time, and individuals and groups are likely to use or distort existing institutions or traits to satisfy their current aims. As Merton contends in his enlightening essay on "Manifest and Latent Functions," a cultural item may have multiple functions (1968, p. 195) (in psychoanalytic parlance, it is "overdetermined"), and one must therefore examine the function of a sociocultural trait from the perspective of various subgroups and individuals as well as the larger collectivity one is studying (p. 134). To this extent, the crucial point is not that one must abandon functional analysis entirely, but that in its place one may usefully substitute a *multifunctionalism* that recognizes and distinguishes various set-goals operative in a given society.

This substitution of multifunction for function – i.e., of overdetermination for determination – has a bearing on all the criticisms leveled against functionalist approaches. As soon as one abandons the assumption of a monolithic system with interdependent parts in the service of nonconflictual ends, one opens up the possibility of explaining dysfunction, change, and conflict. The old functionalist image of a harmonious system is an ideal type that may be approximated more closely by certain societies or types of society than others, and I will argue in the next chapter that the anthropologists who studied small-scale preliterate societies earlier in this century may not have been so mistaken in using this model to guide their understanding. Yet in a general model one can assume no such thing, and if one pays attention to conflicting needs, one will be able to see and begin to explain the internal battles for scarce social and material resources that inevitably arise, as well as the relatively harmonious pursuit of collective ends.

The compromises erected to maximize competing and cooperative interests within the context of existing power relations are likely to be "dysfunctional" for one group or another, and they may even prove dysfunctional, if not fatal, to the group as a whole. Not only are various institutions and practices compromise-formations that may serve conflicting masters both simultaneously and inadequately, but such practices may prove faulty even in the absence of significant conflict as a result of simple shortsightedness, cognitive error, or runaway selection processes that maximize short-term

230

interests of individuals or collectivities but produce unforeseen and disastrous consequences in the long run.

In a sense, one can view Marx and Durkheim as presenting two different functionalisms, one of the group as a whole, and the other of classes. To explain the presence of ideology as a reflection of the needs of a class is logically no different from an explanation based upon the needs of a larger, more inclusive collectivity. Neither the group functionalist nor the "class functionalist" position generally provides much enlightenment as to the mechanisms by which group or class needs come to influence ideology or events; hence the problem of teleology. Steven Lukes, for example, nods approvingly at a study which claims that U.S. Steel Corporation's reputation as a powerful corporate entity in Gary, Indiana, somehow, mysteriously, prevented air pollution regulation in that town, despite the fact that the company neither took any action nor even took a stand on the issue. (I did not track down the original study and rely on Lukes's presentation of it, 1974, pp. 41-2.) This kind of analysis resembles animism more than social science. Similarly, when Godelier condemns "those ideological prejudices of which anthropologists and economists are the conscious or unconscious vectors" (1977, p. 43), he does not share with his readers the processes through which these unwitting social scientists acquire vectorhood, or, for that matter, the mechanisms that have allowed him to escape ideology and see reality as it is. These examples show how Marxist class analysis can run into the same pitfalls as functionalist and ecological analysis. I am not arguing that Marxist analyses are generally inaccurate. I am simply saying that we should not accept class interest as an explanation of a phenomenon without understanding the concrete mechanisms through which members of a class act in its behalf or trick others into doing so. I am further contending that Marxist analysis is a class functionalism and is therefore not immune to criticisms of functionalist and systems approaches. In arguing for his brand of Marxist anthropology, Friedman (1974) deplores "tautological" functionalist explanations of the form, "the function of X is to do Y for a culture." Yet when Marx contends that political ideology serves the interests of the dominant class, or religion appeases the exploited masses, could one not equally phrase this as, "the function of ideology is to maintain the interests of the dominant class?"

The first step one must take in making a functionalist argument is to show that the individuals or groups involved derive some (conscious or unconscious) emotional gratification or need-satisfaction from developing or perpetuating a given act. For example, if one wants to show that a ritual among the Navaho serves the function of maintaining tribal solidarity, one must first demonstrate that individuals in that society at some level value (have an attachment to) the tribe, expressed in set-goals relating to

231

its welfare. Were this not the case, the ritual would not prove "reinforcing" to members of the tribe and would thus be preserved only be accident.[1] Boehm (1982) makes a similar point, developing the notion of "hedonic selection" of cultural traits in a very insightful essay on cultural selection.

This problem of teleology must be squarely faced by any theory that examines traits or processes in terms of functional consequences. To argue that a cultural phenomenon exists because it must exist for a group or population to survive is an abuse of teleology unless one can at least suggest a plausible explanation for the development and selective retention of the phenomenon. This is not usually terribly difficult to do and is therefore not a particularly stringent requirement. Unlike the objects of natural scientific inquiry, human beings are purposive creatures who not only can recognize phenomena responsible for need-fulfillment but can also anticipate the consequences of various processes (cf. Bennett, 1976). One way, then, for a trait to be produced and/or maintained is through conscious or unconscious recognition of its value. The trait may, alternatively, produce secondary consequences (or latent functions), which are themselves consciously or unconsciously cognized and therefore hedonically selected.

A significant proportion of functional practices and traits are not, however, cognized in this sense, which raises questions about mechanisms for selective retention. One function of the valuing of tradition and the intergenerational transfer of beliefs, values, and practices is the maintenance of traits and practices which fulfill certain needs. These practices become routinized and are therefore neither open to regular scrutiny nor demanding of conscious or unconscious recognition of their specific value in order to be retained. High valuation of tradition makes more sense in relatively stable societies in which patterns of set-goals do not change greatly over the years and the compromises encoded in traditional practices remain fairly close to the balance of power and ideals that regulate the society. In periods of rapid social change, traditional sociocultural compromise-formations may not fulfill new set-goals and expectations of particular individuals, subgroups, or emerging wider collectivities (see Geertz, 1963), so that these newly psychologically disenfranchised factions may no longer find obedience to tradition rewarding. An individual or group is just as surely disenfranchised

---

[1] Similarly, on a more cognitive level, to make a structuralist argument that "primitives" view nature and culture as parallel systems that can be related to one another systematically, one must demonstrate that at some conscious or unconscious level, the people do think in these terms. After explaining that primitive peoples neither think in abstract ways nor even have words that mean "nature" or "culture," Leach adds, "yet primitive people must still be aware of the distinction . . ."(1966, p. 335). This, however, is nonsense: if the people who perpetuate a myth, ritual, or totemic system do not understand its meaning, one would hardly expect such a system or trait to be transmitted intact.

232

when a new desire emerges that existing institutions cannot satisfy as when old obligations are no longer being met (see Huntington, 1968, on conditions for social unrest).

Another type of selection, which one can strictly call cultural selection, occurs when a society fails to produce a trait without which it cannot survive (e.g., the development or acquisition of steel weapons when confronted with iron age adversaries) or produces and maintains a practice so dysfunctional to the group or population as a whole that the group or population perishes. Without being teleological in the illegitimate sense, the social scientist cannot frequently account for the preservation of traits through this form of natural selection. The reason is that a given sociocultural "system" includes so many discrete phenomena that individual traits and processes are unlikely to produce this sort of cultural selection unless they are massively dysfunctional. Most such traits will produce results dysphoric to members of the group and therefore be selected against through hedonic selection rather than selection of cultures as wholes. Clusters of traits may produce this sort of selection, but rarely will a single trait be so determinative of survival. In a broad sense, one can argue that had a culture developed or not developed a certain wide class of practices it may have been more or less likely to survive, but one cannot, by and large, account for specific rituals, for example, in terms of this form of group selection unless the ritual was clearly, yet unrecognizably disastrous.

What I am advocating is that social scientists need not abandon the mode of explanation that can broadly be construed as functionalist, a mode utilized by ecological anthropologists and Marxists as well as those influenced by Durkheim, Parsons, Malinowski, and Radcliffe-Brown. Instead, I am arguing that we shift the question from a rather misleading and unproductive one, namely, "What is the function of trait X for group Y?" to a number of interrelated questions. First, what goals is trait X fulfilling? To answer this question one would need to explore set-goals related to group-needs and member-needs, culture ideal, and valued norms in the population under study. Secondly, what compromises are encoded in trait X, and what do these compromises suggest about power relations in the society? Thirdly, what is the emic understanding of trait X and its functions, and how can one explain the persistence of X if emic understanding differs substantially from the etic model one has constructed of the relationship between set-goals and the trait? Fourthly, how well is trait X meeting the goals that it hypothetically should satisfy, and how closely does the culture's own appraisal of its functionality in this sense conform to an etic appraisal? Fifthly, in what ways does trait X as a functional phenomenon spill over into other sociocultural areas? In other words, does X itself have unintended consequences for other set-goals it creates or thwarts, and does its relation to these set-goals create tensions in other parts of society?

A multifunctional analysis of this sort is certainly not sufficient for understanding every aspect of a society. A more thorough understanding requires an examination of specific cultural and historical factors that shape specific solutions. Without distinguishing the needs and specific set-goals that propel social life, however, one cannot examine the interaction between these aims and the sociocultural and environmental realities responsible for creating the phenomenon one observes. A given trait may provide a partial response to a particular set-goal, but it is likely to serve several masters simultaneously, as it becomes embellished and altered through use by concrete individuals and groups. If this is what one means by "function," then the concept of function is likely to persist as a cornerstone of social scientific method.

Class as a Multifaceted Phenomenon

The concept of class is a central one in social science, especially in sociology. Marx first explored its emic and etic dimensions, though in different terms, in the *Eighteenth Brumaire of Louis Bonaparte*. In that work he distinguished a class in-itself from a class for-itself. A class in-itself is a group of people who, from the perspective of an observer, share a relation to a mode of production. The urban proletariat forms a class in-itself because various workers are in the same position vis-à-vis the economic infrastructure; i.e., they are wage laborers. A class for-itself is a class whose members recognize their common material interests and identify with, and seek the solidarity of their class. The situation in which a class in-itself is not a class for-itself establishes the possibility of what Marx calls "false consciousness." False consciousness occurs when members of a class fail to recognize their material self-interest.

This perspective clearly has significant merit, though it glosses over a number of crucial distinctions that can be made by using the model proposed here. Goldstone (1982) has suggested that revolutionary crises in early modern Europe had roots in dynamics of population growth and price escalation. He contends that in Europe in the sixteenth and seventeenth centuries, landed elites were divided in terms of material interest: landlords dependent on fixed rents faced a declining standard of living as prices rose, whereas others who controlled produce marketing reaped harvests of gold. The question one may wish to ask at this point is whether or not the landed elites constituted a class. They were in part similarly situated vis-à-vis the mode of production, and they may have associated with each other and identified with their "class" and its privileged status, but their material interests were quite divergent.

234

A similarly ambiguous case occurs in world systems theory. Factory workers in America and Africa may be similarly related to the world capitalist mode of production in that they are wage laborers who participate in manufacture. Yet the interests of the two groups are markedly different: American laborers, despite their class position in the United States, nevertheless reap some of the benefits of living in a core country which extracts resources from the periphery. In terms of material interests, then, industrial workers in the United States share some interests with American corporate executives and some with laborers from Zimbabwe. To fit these relationships into unified categories of class is thus very difficult. Further, American workers may know nothing about conditions in Zimbabwe and not conceive of themselves as sharing anything, let alone material interests, with their African counterparts. Does their emic understanding have implications for whether or not they form a class?

I would argue that in order to speak coherently, one must distinguish several ways of defining a class. First, one could argue that individuals form a class to the extent that they share member-need material interests. In other words, to the extent that they benefit similarly from economic practices, one could say that they share class interests. In this sense, as long as the American Medical Association lobbies to have payments for mental health care restricted to medical doctors, then psychologists and social workers who may be doing precisely the same things in their practices and receiving comparable payments from private patients are not part of the same class.

Secondly, to the extent that certain members of a society have similar set-goals, whether or not their interests conflict, one can consider them a class. This view of class focuses on values and patterns of consumption. From this perspective peasants and workers, or rural and urban workers, may form a class because they have a comparable standard of living and comparable economic desires. By this view, as well, many preagricultural societies tend to be classless, in that individuals have similar needs and values.

A third meaning of class bases distinctions on relation to a mode of production. In this view, all laborers form a class. This is, of course, problematic because one must decide whether modes of production are specific to nations or whether one can coherently speak of a world-capitalist system. Complicating matters further, to distinguish in a complex society which people are related in which ways to a mode of production is difficult. Is lower level management a different class from higher level management? If a foreman is seen as management and thus barred from union membership, are he and his working class compatriots members of the same class? Certainly in more complex societies, if not in most stratified societies, classes are continuous, not discrete phenomena. One may further complicate mat-

235

ters by including patterns of association as aspects of class. One could argue that people with similar interests, needs, or relation to a mode of production only form a class if they tend to associate more with one another than with other members of society.

These three ways of looking at class all involve etic definitions. One must, as well, consider two emic aspects of class. First, one could argue that a class exists if and only if individuals in that class perceive their commonality of material (member-need) interest. By this definition, an Irish worker in Boston and an Italian worker in Boston do not share a class if they despise each other because of ethnic stereotypes. A second emic definition of class would focus on whether or not a (group-need) attachment to the class exists. In other words, do the members of the alleged class value the class as an object of (noninstrumental) attachment? Do they see their class as something to which they are committed, as to their family or nation?

These five aspects of class may vary in part independently, and the extent to which they covary is an empirical question in each particular instance. Simply because several members of a society share a common set of self-need concerns or interests does not imply anything, for example, about their social relations with one another. They need not interact, nor must they view themselves as a class in order to act in similar ways, particularly if they are tied in similar ways to a mode or modes of production. To impute any solidarity to such a group, one must show an affectional group-need involvement, i.e., that they identify with the class as a discrete group and seek its solidarity. As Marxists have painfully discovered, "objective" (etic) class varies at times independent of attachments. Weber expresses the same idea in his distinction between communal and societal action, which in many ways resembles the distinction between group-needs and member-needs (1946, p.183). An individual may be attached to family or ethnic group and feel no special attachment to his class. More to the point, both bourgeoisie and proletariat may share common attachments, e.g., to the nation or the state, as should have been the lesson of World War I, when many Marxists supported their own countries when the war erupted. One cannot in any sense label these attachments to nation "false;" they do exist, and they are not merely the creations of greedy dominant classes. Such attachments to a group are as old as human history, and they cannot simply be dismissed as false consciousness.

People may certainly be deluded about their economic self-interest. That American workers can vote en masse for a right wing millionaire who pretends concern for the average worker certainly smacks of false consciousness in this sense, though the issue of whether or not an outside observer can know more about a person or group than that person or group knows (e.g., what their "real" interests are) is as difficult in this context as it is in psychotherapy. Yet material self-interest is only one of the factors that motivates social life. Equally important are affectional ties (as expressed, for example, in nationalism) which are neither derivative of, nor less real than economic interests. That Marxists have come to identify true interests with economic interests to the exclusion of the attachments that also make life meaningful is ironic, given Marx's emphasis on the atomism and fetishism of capitalist society. I argue in a work in progress that this problem stems from Marx's paradoxical acceptance of the im-plicit – and relatively rationalistic – theory of personality embedded in the same liberal philosophies he set out to criticize.

This is not, of course, to deny that, as Kelman (1969) has argued, "instrumental" loyalties can lead to "expressive" loyalties, and vice versa. Rather, it is to argue that people may act against their material interests without having a false consciousness. If history at certain junctures ap-pears to be the history of class conflict, this represents a limiting case in which the intensity of other group-need attachments approaches zero. If such a situation arises, as it perhaps may in periods of sociocultural disin-tegration, this primacy of class and breakdown of attachments must be explained, not assumed as a methodological principle.

Conscious and Unconscious Emics: The Case of the Starving Cow

The third issue to be discussed here in terms of the proposed model is the distinction between conscious and unconscious emics, which, to date, an-thropologists have neglected to examine.[1] The best way to explore this distinction is by analyzing an example, and I have chosen one that has already been discussed by Harris in terms of emics and etics. Harris is well known in anthropology for, among other things, his fascinating attempt (1966) to show that the Hindu belief in the sacred cow and prohibition of beef consumption can be explained in terms of ecological adaptiveness. This was a significant case for Harris's emergent materialist perspective because it was one often cited as a refutation of ecological and materialist principles.

In a later work Harris (1979) reported on his first-hand investigations of the ecology of the sacred cow in the state of Kerala in southern India. Harris observed that the mortality rate was twice as high among male as among female calves. All the farmers "ardently affirmed the legitimacy of the standard Hindu prohibition against the slaughter of domestic bovines" (pp. 32-3) and denied any deliberate shortening of the lives of domestic

---

[1] Bateson's (1936) concept of eidos, like many notions of culture patterns, does refer to unconscious value commitments and ways of looking at things; however, I am speaking here not only of those ideas and ideals that are not conscious but of beliefs, values, and expecta-tions that are dynamically unconscious, i.e., that are deliberately kept from awareness.

237

cattle, though they were aware of the differential mortality rates of males and females. Harris elicited from the farmers their explanations of this phenomenon:

> When I asked farmers to explain why male calves got sick more often, several suggested that the males ate less than the females. One or two suggested that the male calves ate less because they were not permitted to stay at the mother's teats for more than a few seconds. But no one would say that since there is little demand for traction animals in Kerala, males are culled and females reared. (P. 33)

In other parts of India, where traction animals are in demand, the mortality rate is higher for females than for males. Harris notes the discrepancy between emic and etic reality in Kerala. Emically, according to Harris, the farmers are caring for their cattle in accordance with Hindu law, and males are not being differentially mistreated. Etically, male cattle are being systematically starved to death. Harris does not point out that the alleged cognitive error of the farmers who do not see that they are starving the males for sound economic reasons is *motivated*, not accidental. For the farmers to admit to "bovicide" would produce fear and guilt at breaking Hindu law and would force them either to refrain from this practice or cast off their religious beliefs, neither of which is an appealing option.

Harris further analyzes this instance to show the utility of distinguishing the various combinations of etic, emic, behavioral, and mental events. He separates out the four combinations in this situation in terms of four propositions:

I   Emic/Behavioral: "No calves are starved to death."
II Etic/Behavioral: "Male calves are starved to death."
III Emic/Mental: "All calves have the right to life."
IV Etic/Mental: "Let the male calves starve to death when feed is scarce."
    (P. 38)

This way of looking at the situation does not, however, hold up under scrutiny. None of these statements is any more behavioral or mental than the others. The emic/behavioral proposition, for example, is a cognition, not a behavior; it is no more behavioral than proposition IV. Both statements I and IV are mental: statement I is a (mistaken) construal of reality, and IV is an (unconscious) rule for behavior. Further, while Harris distinguishes four propositions that are somewhat at odds with each other, he cannot *explain* their relationship. What, for example, accounts for the discrepancy between emic and etic understanding of the situation?

One can readily understand this from the perspective advocated in this chapter. The main question to be answered is how and why the actual (etic) situation (proposition II, that male calves are starved to death) is transformed into an inaccurate cognized (emic) model (proposition I, that no calves are starved to death). The key to understanding this is the

238

conflict between two set-goals. On the one hand, when feed is scarce, preservation of useless male cattle threatens member-need material welfare. On the other hand, a religious aspect of the culture ideal demands that all calves have the right to life (proposition III), and that therefore killing them is morally wrong. In Kerala nutritional set-goals were apparently more potent in determining behavior, as the culture real behavioral norm emerged to let male calves starve to death when feed is scarce (proposition IV).

This behavioral outcome is, however, only part of the story and is a response to only one of the conflicting set-goals (desire for material welfare). The failure to satisfy the cultural ideal not to murder cattle would, if recognized, produce fear and guilt. The discrepancy between the reality of male bovicide (proposition II) and the ideal of preservation of all cattle (proposition III) produced an altered cognition: no calves are being starved to death (proposition I). The culturally approved mechanism of denial accompanied by the systematic starvation of male calves is a compromise-formation hedonically selected to optimize emotion.

This suggests that the farmers had, in fact, *two* emic, cognized models that are contradictory: male calves are starved, and male calves are not starved. The latter is a transformation of the former, distorted by a hedonically selected control mechanism: denial. The belief that calves are being starved is thus an unconscious emic, replaced defensively by a conscious emic belief. We can know of the unconscious emic belief only by inference, though three pieces of information suggest its presence: (1) the farmers are neither stupid nor blind and therefore are likely to recognize, especially when probed by Harris, that they are differentially starving male calves; (2) the farmers protest too much, as in the quotation from Harris above, which suggests a resistance to the cognition that they are killing males, a resistance that is understandable in the context of the cultural ideal against doing so; and (3) one cannot account for the motivated transformation of etic reality into its cognized opposite without assuming awareness of the killing, which would prompt an affective response and consequent control mechanism.

One could, of course, analyze this case at the level of the individual farmer in terms of a conflict between self-need and ego ideal set-goals, producing an affect that motivates a behavior (starving males) and a defense (denial). This would, however, miss the fact that the ideal against killing cattle is endemic to the culture and thus may have wider significance. More importantly, it would ignore the extent to which this defense is culturally constituted. Not only do individual farmers deny the reality of what they are doing, but they turn a blind eye to the similar misdeeds of their compatriots, who are also breaking rules meaningful to them. Without cultural acceptance, this control mechanism at the individual level could not be maintained. Part III will explore in detail the notion of culturally constituted defenses (see Spiro, 1965) and will produce an extended example to show how one can bring together individual and cultural analysis to explain such phenomena as the cattle-killing in Kerala.[1]

The three previous discussions — of functionalism, class, and emics and etics — hardly constitute "proof" that the theory proposed here is superior to competing frameworks, though I hope these analyses have at least suggested the potential utility of this approach. So far the model has focused on sociocultural structure and dynamics. The following section will delve into the arena of sociocultural change and will present a theory of the evolution of morals in human groups, focusing on the structure described here as the culture ideal.

---

[1] This raises an important potential problem in extending ethnoscientific analysis into affectively charged domains. When one studies botanical categorization, one is likely to find discrepancies within a single informant's cognitive schemas simply because of cognitive error, or between informants because of the vagaries of socialization and the idiosyncratic processing of information at the individual level. With categories that are not so affectively neutral one is unlikely to be able to build a model of native understanding without examining defensive transformations of knowledge. In the above case, one could not map the cognitive domain centering around the death of male calves in a straightforward manner because the farmers hold two contradictory beliefs, that males are being starved and that they are not. The same problem is endemic to simplistic cognitive approaches in psychology that study such phenomena as the self-concept, which is not a logically sound, consistent structure that can be comprehended without examining defensive distortions in cognition. When a thirty-five-year-old patient tells her therapist in the course of the same hour that she is a great lover and that she is a virgin, the therapist has good reason to believe that her self-perception as a great lover is a defensive transformation of her image of herself as sexually inadequate. One will understand very little about the cognitive domain of the self-concept in this case if one does not examine the interplay of affect, cognition, and defensive distortion of cognition.

7 The Development of Collectivism and the Culture Ideal

THROUGHOUT THIS BOOK I have argued that the conflicting needs of self and other and of individual and society are the stuff of which moral conflict is made. The function of morality, in this view, is to provide an ideal resolution of conflicting demands, both at the psychological and sociocultural level. One would expect that historical change would bring with it an alteration of this delicate balance. A plethora of ideas and evidence from a number of sources suggests that the culture ideal of human societies has been, and is in the process of undergoing a fundamental revolution in the relative valuation of individual and group. To demonstrate this movement, and accompanying changes in cultural forms, is the central aim of this chapter.

In an essay on the psychological implications of collectivism, D.F.Y. Ho defines "collectivism" in a fairly standard fashion:

> In contrast to individualism, collectivism affirms that to preserve and enhance the well-being of the group is the supreme guiding principle for social action. It demands that the interests of the group must take precedence over those of the individual. (1979, p. 144)

This definition sounds remarkably like a societal analog to the popular conception of the term "narcissism"; collectivism, so defined, appears similar to a "group narcissism." As Part I showed, however, narcissism is not a simple phenomenon that remains stable through time; it passes through a series of developmental transformations. This chapter will attempt to show that something similar is true of collectivism. A brief comparative analysis of the thought of Durkheim and Marx is instructive here.

Durkheim defines morality in terms of the group. For Durkheim, as for most thinkers, morality has a social derivation:

> Everything which is a source of solidarity is moral, everything which forces man to take account of other men is moral, everything which forces him to regulate his conduct through something other than the striving of his ego is moral, and morality is as solid as these ties are numerous and strong. . . . (1933, p. 398)

241

He continues:

> ... [M]orality consists in a state of dependence. Far from serving to emancipate the individual ... it has, on the contrary, the function of making him an integral part of a whole, and consequently, of depriving him of some liberty of movement ... ... [M]an is a moral being only because he lives in society, since morality consists in being solidary with a group. ... (1933, p. 399)

For Durkheim, in the movement from mechanical to organic solidarity, the collective consciousness accounts for a steadily decreasing portion of individual consciousness. Just as Weber perceives a progressive disenchantment of the world, Durkheim recognizes that the realm of the sacred declines with progressive "civilization." Alternatively, perhaps sociologist Edward Shils is more to the point in noting a "dispersion of charisma" (1975, p. 99) or a "shift in the locus of charisma" (p. 106) (translate "sacred" for "charisma") from the group to the individual.

In any case, according to Durkheim, with the rise of organic solidarity, social cohesion is restored, and with it, morality. The problem with Durkheim's formulation is that while he is correct in seeing the morality of the person in a mechanically solidary society as a derivative of his relationship to society, he is incorrect in extending this observation to organically solidary society. In the latter case, in fact, the situation is reversed: organically solidary society derives its morality from its individual members, not vice versa, as this chapter will attempt to demonstrate. The difference is not just semantic; it is fundamental. While Durkheim's argument in the *Elementary Forms of Religious Life* (1915), that in a primitive society the real object of worship is society itself, is a stroke of brilliance, he errs in extending this view to organically solidary societies because in such societies the individual, not the collectivity, is the primary locus of moral valuation. Organic solidarity is thus incompatible with his notion of morality. Although Durkheim recognizes the necessity of social structural change concomitant with the progressive individuation of individuals, he fails to see that the shift from mechanical to organic solidarity necessitates a change in the nature of morality itself.

Marx's analysis of the relations between civil and political society is enlightening here as well. For Marx, bourgeois society (in essence, the epoch of Durkheim's organic solidarity) is marked by the separation or disjunction of civil and political society. The state (again, not referring to the actual apparatus), Marx argues, exists only in contradiction to its civil presuppositions: the democratic state asserts equality and universalism precisely because they do not exist in civil society (p. 219). He comments:

> [M]an leads a double life ... [H]e lives in the political community, where he regards himself as a communal being, and in civil society, where he is active as a private individual ... (1975a, p. 220).

> This secular conflict . . . reduces itself . . . to the conflict between the general interest and the private interest, the split between the political state and civil society. . . . (P. 221, emphasis deleted)

Marx's argument is that, historically, humanity moves from a union of political and civil society, to their separation, and ultimately again to their reunion, in which individual and general interest coincide. A problem with this formulation is the faulty nature of its dialectic: the true thesis of which the fiction of political society is the antithesis is the fiction of civil society. In other words, while Marx observes that "bourgeois" or "organically solidary" society (the correlation between the two is obviously not totally complete) involves the alienation of the individual from a true communal life (from actual "political society"), he does not recognize that prebourgeois society may represent an alienation of the person from a true individual life ("civil society"). In terms of the theory being developed here, the culture ideal is moving from a belief in the moral value of the group to a belief in the moral value of the individual, and a sense of separate selfhood is becoming progressively more pronounced. Whereas in the former case individuals find meaning in the value of the group, in the latter, the group derives its meaning from the value of individuals.

A number of theorists have posited dichotomies similar to Durkheim's distinction of mechanical from organic solidarity. Ferdinand Tönnies, whose work undoubtedly influenced Durkheim, similarly distinguished between *Gemeinschaft* (community) and *Gesellschaft* (society) (Tönnies, 1957). The former is based upon "the assumption of perfect unity of human wills as an original or natural condition" (p. 37), while the latter is "a mechanical aggregate and artifact" (p. 35) (note that his use of "mechanical" is precisely the opposite of Durkheim's). Tönnies contends that in the Gemeinschaft, people "remain essentially united in spite of separating factors, whereas in the Gesellschaft they are essentially separated in spite of all uniting factors" (pp. 64-5).

Robert Redfield, in a similar vein, distinguishes "folk" society from "urban" society (Redfield, 1947), just as Pitrim Sorokin contrasts "familistic" and "contractual" relations (Sorokin, 1947). Talcott Parsons' "pattern variable" approach provides a somewhat more complex variation on the same theme: the ideal type of action in a mechanically solidary society would be characterized by affectivity, particularism, ascription, diffuseness, and collectivity-orientation, as opposed to action in an organically solidary society, with its affective neutrality, universalism, achievement orientation, specificity, and self-orientation (Parsons and Shils, 1951).

Ten thousand years ago, before the development of agriculture, all human societies were comprised of hunters and gatherers, largely living in social units called "bands," if archaeological evidence and the hunter-gatherer societies extant in the nineteenth and twentieth centuries provide any indication. Such societies tend to be relatively egalitarian, with minimal social differentiation, division of labor, and political complexity. Division of labor that does exist tends to be based on age and sex. Bands are typically comprised of 25 to 50 people and are formed through kinship association. Membership is somewhat fluid, with disputes often settled by members switching to another band. Band societies, like most preliterate societies, tend to be highly cooperative. Individual ownership and notions of private property are unusual in the least complex societies. As hunter-gatherer societies evolve into more rigidly bounded and organized tribal societies, an incipient political organization may emerge, though kinship remains the primary basis of social relations, and discrete political, religious, and technological realms are not clearly differentiated. To the extent that a group maintains territorial ties, the territory is a property or possession of the entire community, not specific individuals. Natural abundance and increased techno-economic complexity tend to erode the egalitarianism of hunter-gatherer and tribal societies, as individualism, greater political organization (and especially the prevalence of chiefdoms), and social stratification begin to emerge. I am of course speaking in terms of ideal types. In reality the extent of political complexity, division of labor, or differentiation of clear group and territorial boundaries is continuous, from the relatively undifferentiated social relations of the least complex hunter-gatherer societies to the relatively stratified tribal societies with powerful chiefs that verge on being primitive states.

The morality of preliterate societies focuses on the needs and cohesion of significant groups, and the values of a clan or tribe become embodied in institutional arrangements. Carleton Coon provides an example of the handling of interclan murder among the Nootka, a tribe of Northwest Coast American Indians, which has parallels – albeit not always such drastic ones – among many preliterate societies:

> If a man of one clan was killed by a man of another, the aggrieved clan as a body demanded the death of a man of rank equal to that of the deceased. The man selected to be the victim accepted his sentence calmly and died bravely. (1971, p. 293)

In analyzing such a case, one cannot simply say that the action of the individual of the murderer's tribe who calmly faces execution for the crime of a comrade is somehow a "reflection" of social structure, or that the procedure that trades one death for another is functional for the group because it inhibits internecine strife. That such an act of bravery is functional for the group may well be true, but that does not explain why the condemned individual, or his kin, accepts his fate as legitimate. In general, to make a functionalist argument that an act or element of the culture real occurs despite a negative effect on particular individuals because it meets certain needs of the group is to make an extraordinary assumption about

244

the culture ideal: that it emphasizes the needs of the group as a unit. If, indeed, this is true for a particular society, this fact needs to be explained and underscored, not assumed. The argument here is that the culture ideal of "primitive" societies (and any exception requires a particular, causal explanation) – as well as, to one extent or another, preindustrial societies more generally – is characterized by an emphasis on the value and authority of the group. To the extent that this condition holds in a society, its culture ideal will be defined (as will the culture in general) as characterized by *communitarian collectivism,* which implies a collectivism or cohesion based upon a belief in the *legitimate primacy of the group.*

One can distinguish two variants of communitarian collectivism. The first, and historically more primitive form, will here be called *primary communitarian collectivism.* This variant is associated generally with pre-agricultural and less complex societies, though many such societies which are more developed technologically or more fortunate ecologically more closely approximate the second type of communitarian collectivism. In the primary version, cultural representations of nature, culture, and individuals are minimally differentiated. Religion is group religion, and various symbolic expressions of the group are endowed with a supernatural potency or "omnipotence."

The second variant is *secondary communitarian collectivism,* which emerges with increased abundance, social stratification, and/or agriculture as primary mode of subsistence. In secondary communally collectivistic societies, greater differentiation of nature, culture, and individuals has occurred. With this differentiation comes an assault on individual desire codified in the classical religions and in peasant ideology. The value and power of society is frequently projected upon an object, often a political leader, who symbolizes the collectivity and its values.

Primary Communitarian Collectivism

Three features of primary communally collectivistic cultures (from this point onward to be referred to simply as "primary societies") are particularly striking: the predominance of group-needs in the culture ideal, as evidenced in primitive religion, ritual, and myth; minimal differentiation of group, individual, and nature; and a belief in the magical potency or "omnipotence" of the group.

Religion in primary societies is group religion; religious membership coincides with membership in the group (Scharf, 1970, pp. 41-6). The classic statement on the nature of clan religion is provided by Durkheim. Putting in the most accurate terms an idea that permeated much of nineteenth century Western philosophy (notably that of Hegel and Comte), that society is really its own god, Durkheim writes that the god of the clan

245

is the clan itself, "personified and represented to the imagination under the visible form of the animal or vegetable which serves as totem" (1915, p. 236). Generalizing, he describes religion as "a system of ideas with which individuals represent to themselves the society of which they are members, and the obscure but intimate relations which they have with it" (p. 257). As will be noted below, this formulation of the essence of religion has considerable validity in the case of less differentiated societies; however, it gradually loses its veridicality the farther one moves from ideal-typical communitarian collectivism.

Historian of religion E.O. James reinforces Durkheim's view that religion in "primitive" societies serves an important function in maintaining social cohesion:

> In primitive society the deepest emotions and most heartfelt wants, hopes and fears are aroused . . . chiefly within the corporate life of the community . . . Under the precarious condition in which the human species lived when it first emerged from its mammalian ancestry, and in which it has remained in primitive society throughout the ages, corporate life has been essential . . . [R]eligion has exercised a powerful unifying influence. (1964, p. 12)

Fellow religious historian Joseph Kitagawa posits that religion in the primary society reinforces tradition and solidifies social control (1967, p. 49). Anthropologist Clyde Kluckhohn adds, referring to peasant societies as well, "The *ultima ratio* of nonliterates strongly tends to be 'that is what our fathers said it was' . . . The Eskimo saying 'we keep the old rules in order that we may live untroubled' is well known" (1942, p. 101).

A number of ethnographers have pointed to the relationship between religion and solidarity in various societies. According to Melford Spiro, the inhabitants of Ifaluk in Melanesia use the fear of the dead to inhibit hostility and maintain amicable ingroup relations (1952). Countless observers have remarked upon the functional uses of witchcraft beliefs in reducing internal strife within a group (for a general analysis of this phenomenon, see B. Whiting, 1950; Mair, 1969). Witchcraft accusations conveniently control deviance and provide scapegoats for pent-up hostilities. Among the Azande, witchcraft accusations are directed only at outsiders, which reinforces kinship solidarity and provides an outlet for hostility (Evans-Pritchard, 1937). According to psychological anthropologist John Whiting (1955), the Paiute deter crime with their sorcery beliefs; those who break rules or simply have nasty dispositions are often convicted of sorcery and punished severely. John Middleton (1960) contends that the Lugbara in Africa insure obedience to social rules through their beliefs in the malevolent powers of the souls of the deceased. In an article titled, "Sorcery, Sin, and the Superego" (1959), Whiting argues that beliefs in witchcraft and the efficacy of the spirits of ancestors serve the same role

246

and often complement internalization of social norms. In terms of the structural model proposed in the previous chapter, such beliefs, like other aspects of religion in communally collectivistic societies, constitute culturally institutionalized control mechanisms to maintain solidarity and intragroup cohesion. The question becomes how and why the goal of solidarity becomes so paramount in such societies as a moral aim that it easily overrides individual desires.

Turning to ritual and myth, as sociologist Robert Bellah attests, Durkheim's position in several respects "seems still to be largely acceptable" (1964, p. 272). Bellah adds, "The ritual life does reinforce the solidarity of the society and serves to induct the young into the norms of tribal behavior" (p. 272). Kluckhohn is more specific about the social functions of myths and rituals:

> ... myths and rituals are adaptive from the point of view of the society in that they promote social solidarity, enhance the integration of the society by providing a formalized statement of its ultimate value-attitudes, and afford a means for the transmission of the culture with little loss of content. (1942, p. 110)

A classic statement of the functionalist position is Radcliffe-Brown's assertion that the primary basis of ritual, as well as myth and magic, is "the attribution of ritual value to objects and occasions which are either themselves objects of common interests linking together the persons of a community or are symbolically representative of such objects" (1939, p. 82). Kitagawa notes that rituals are primarily "corporate acts of the whole tribe or the community" (1967, p. 47), and where they are not, they are socially established. As evidence for the functionalist view of ritual, Kluckhohn notes that with the growing encroachment of white civilization, Navaho ceremonials correspondingly increased in frequency, suggesting that increased ritual was one response to threats to group survival (1942, 102n).

Turner's superb exegesis of Ndembu "rituals of affliction" shows how various rites used to restore health or reproductive abilities among the Ndembu are used to heal the community as well. Ritual therapy, he writes, "becomes a matter of sealing up the breaches in social relationships simultaneously with ridding the patient ... of his pathological symptom" (1967, p. 360). Turner became a confidante of a ritual doctor and accompanied him to many rituals of affliction. Turner discovered that when the Ndembu doctor is trying to divine the cause of illness, he explores the tensions in community life. Death, illness, and misfortune among the Ndembu are "usually ascribed to exacerbated tensions in social relations ... Divination therefore becomes a form of social analysis, in the course of which hidden struggles among individuals and factions are brought to light, so that they may be dealt with by traditional ritual procedures" (p. 361).

The Ndembu ritual doctor thoroughly "researches" the social situation, listening to gossip and even to the patient's dreams. In the course of treatment he induces members of the community to confess any grudges or hostilities toward the patient. In one case Turner described at length, the patient was a disliked member of the community who nevertheless held a position of power because of his ascribed status, and in the course of the "cure," the patient was forced to shed a great deal of blood while members of the community were induced to confess their sins and hostilities. This cure was an effective compromise-formation: it made the patient pay for his character defects and undoubtedly gave those who were angry at him some cause for satisfaction, while simultaneously healing the disorder of social relations. At the end of the ritual, people were jubilant, and even enemies smiled at one another: "Men and women who had been on cool terms with one another until recently, shook hands warmly and beamed with happiness" (p. 391). Social bonds had thus been reinforced.

Sacrifices perform a role similar to that of many other rituals, with often even more concrete results. Sacrificed objects can either be destroyed or consumed, and as Firth (1963) points out, the latter possibility is by far the more common. Not only does sacrifice reinforce communal ties through its ritual aspects, but it ensures more equitable distribution of food as well. Especially in those communally collectivistic societies that rely upon individualized production to a relatively greater extent, one frequently finds redistributive rituals of one form or another. The Kaupauka Papuans, for example, are often viewed as an extraordinarily individualistic culture for a preindustrial society; private property and accumulation are stressed. Yet the highest value in their society is generosity, and the individual who succeeds as a producer but fails as a giver finds himself severely punished (Pospisil, 1958, 1963). This kind of situation occurs more often in agricultural communities, and Barrington Moore notes that in these societies, "a high degree of inequality may not only be acceptable but even regarded as very desirable, as long as in the end it somehow contributes to the social good as perceived and defined in that society" (1978, p. 41). Dumont (1965b, 1966) has commented similarly on the Indian caste system.

Myth, like ritual, has as one function the reinforcement of group sentiments. Kluckhohn contends that myths, like rituals, "facilitate the adjustment of the individual to his society" through sublimation of the individual's antisocial tendencies (1942, p. 104). He notes, "It is surely not without meaning that essentially all known chant myths take the family and some trouble within it as a point of departure" (p. 104). Lévi-Strauss maintains a similar viewpoint on the nature and content of myths. Edmund Leach, in summarizing the work of Lévi-Strauss, emphasizes the latter's belief that primitive myth uniformly has the moral implication – in contrast to the ideas of "modern" (European) society – that "Hell is ourselves" (Leach, 1970, p. 37). In explicating Lévi-Strauss's view of conflict in primitive mythology, Leach points out that the disaster that befalls mythic characters "always originates in the circumstances that a human being fails to fulfill his or her proper obligations toward a deity or clansman" (p. 88). What Lévi-Strauss means in claiming that the basic message behind myth is "Hell is ourselves," according to Leach, is that "self-interest is the source of all evil" (p. 88).

The social function of myth is not simply to emphasize the moral legitimacy of the group, though this is undoubtedly extremely important. In an excellent review article on "Theories of Myth" (1969), Percy Cohen contends, unlike Lévi-Strauss, that "the fact that myth has a narrative form is not accidental: for a narrative has a beginning, a moment of time in which a series of events is anchored." A function of myth, he claims, is to reinforce tradition; myth "anchors the present in the past" (p. 349, emphasis deleted). Similarly, Eliade submits that myth is always "an account of a 'creation' " (1963, pp. 5-6). Kitagawa adds that, for "primitive and archaic man," the ultimate meaning in life involves "participation in the divine act of creating and maintaining cosmos (order)" (p. 48). Malinowski unites these various insights on the nature of myth in a masterful passage:

> ... [M]yth is the statement of an extraordinary event, the occurrence of which once and for all established the social order of a tribe or some of its economic pursuits, its arts and crafts or its magical beliefs and ceremonies ... It justifies by precedent the existing order ... The function of myth is to strengthen tradition and to endow it with a greater value and prestige by tracing it back to a higher, better, more supernatural and more effective reality of initial events. (1931, pp. 70-1)

As this quotation suggests, one need not view various theories of myth as necessarily incompatible. Lévi-Strauss, for example, claims that myths mediate cultural contradictions (1966). The reader should note the similarity between this view and Freud's notion of a compromise-formation. In mediating contradictions, myth could allow the expression of repressed individual (or social) desires (compare Kardiner's "projective system," 1945), while cloaking them in a form acceptable to the "collective consciousness" (culture ideal). Thus, myth can be viewed not only as an agent of social control and purveyor of group-centered morality but also as a mediator or compromise-formation. Further, in some cases myth may also represent a form of primitive science, much anthropological thought to the contrary. (The debate between evolutionists and creationists in the United States, for example, still rages.) The point of all this is that a given social institution may serve multiple functions. Cohen aptly calls this the "principle of functional economy" (p. 351), and the similarity of this characteristic of culture to Freud's contention that on the individual level an action or trait

249

may be "overdetermined" is unmistakable (see Waelder [1936] for a discussion of the "principle of multiple function" in psychoanalysis).

A second aspect of primary communitarian collectivism is the relative lack of symbolic differentiation, or fluidity of boundaries between culture, nature, and individual. A salient aspect of this is an oft-noted fusion or confusion of the natural and social worlds. Tribal societies, according to anthropologist John Bennett, "perceive the self (humans) as largely in synthesis with the environment whereas industrial societies appear to develop the most pronounced sense of self detached from the environment" (1976, p. 750). For "primitives," Kitagawa claims, everything is a Thou in Buber's sense: any natural object may be endowed with purpose and intention (pp. 50-1). Arguing that "early man would seem to have drawn but little distinction between himself and his animal, bird, and reptile cousins," Bouquet gives the example of a Papuan who "included the crested dove, the black cockatoo and even a particular iguana as members of his tribe" (1962, pp. 42-3). Similarly, early observers of the Iroquois in the eighteenth century repeatedly noted their tendency to address entreaties to inanimate objects. In 1745 one European (cited in Druke, 1980) reported an incident in which an Indian attempted to drive stakes into the ground to make a hut but was having difficulty doing so. He then implored the stones not to give him trouble, explaining, " 'We poor Indians cannot use iron instruments like you Europeans; but we have other means which we have learned from our Grandfathers, and we have it much easier if we talk to spirits and call them friends, and mingle threats therein, then we succeed.' " For years anthropologists have wrestled with this confusion of culture and nature under the rubric of "totemism," but they have not reached a consensus as to its meaning or meanings. (This may, of course, be another case of multiple causality.)

When anthropologists first noticed this peculiar fusion of humanity and nature (e.g., when an Australian aborigine claimed to be a "turtle"), their reaction was one of surprise and perplexity. Contemporary anthropologists, socialized via Gellner's myth quoted in Chapter 6, no longer react with such awe, though they are still quite unsure as to why people take on these beliefs that seem to conflict with sensory experience. In their untroubled acceptance of such phenomena, anthropologists are acting much the same way as many neurotics act when confronted by the inexplicable and uncontrollable: they pretend, through denial or obsessive rituals, to be in control. (Clearly Malinowski's theory, 1954, that magic arises in those anxiety-provoking situations in which normal behavior and science fail, has some validity.)

Something is going on that is clearly in need of explanation when one is confronted with an Australian who is convinced that he is, in every ontological sense, a turtle. Such a person is not simply speaking metaphorically, nor is the Nuer who believes that twins are birds (Evans-Pritchard, 1956). Both the Australian and the Nuer are accepting, in spite of their senses, a socially transmitted classificatory schema. This itself is not a phenomenon peculiar to members of less complex societies: individuals in every culture internalize schemas about the nature of reality, though a more stringent empiricism appears to be a historical development unparalleled in any preliterate society. What *is* distinct about this representation of reality, this culturally shared and transmitted schema, is its relative indifference to a distinction that appears to "us" obvious, and which in fact is obvious to children in all cultures by two or three years of age.

Parallel to this fusion of the social and natural worlds is a comparatively diffuse boundary between the collective and the individual. Identity in communally collectivistic cultures tends to center around group affiliations to a greater extent than in more complex societies. The clear and rigid distinction of a concept of self that has come to be accepted as "natural" in Western culture over the last four centuries is foreign to many primary cultures, which frequently entirely lack a comparable concept. As Geertz has noted,

> the Western conception of the person as a bounded, unique, more or less integrated motivational and cognitive universe, a dynamic center of awareness, emotion, and judgment, and action organized into a distinctive whole and set contrastively both against other such wholes and against its social and natural background, is, however incorrigible it may seem to us, a rather peculiar idea within the context of the world's cultures. (1974, p. 31)

In a recent study Lambe and I (1983) explored conceptions of the soul in a sample of sixty preliterate societies and found that the overwhelming majority failed to posit a one-to-one correspondence between souls and individuals. Almost all cultures studied on which data were available believed that the soul frequently slips out of the body on occasions such as illness or dreaming. More to the point, most cultures either posited multiple souls that do not together form some composite "self," or they saw the soul as a diffuse quality frequently not coextensive with the empirical individual. I am not, of course, advancing the absurd thesis that in some dark, mysterious, primordial era whole groups of people existed who were so lacking in boundaries of self that they could not distinguish between their own bodies and someone else's. As Boas (cited in Fogelson, 1982, p. 97) pointed out, no known language lacks personal pronouns to indicate "I, thou, and he." Rather, I am arguing that primary cultures do not assume the individual to be the basic unit of social relations, and that they do not conceptualize a unified self with a bounded subjectivity, an individuated identity, and a core of experience always residing within the body and separate from social existence.

251

Data from cultures across the world documents the lack of a conception of a separate and unified self in primary cultures (see Fogelson [1982] for an excellent review; see also Geertz, 1974; Shweder and Bourne, 1982). The study of "enthnopsychology" or "enthnopersonality," which examines cultural conceptions of personhood, has provided voluminous evidence in this regard (e.g., Druke, 1980; Straus,1982). The Mehinaku of Brazil posit multiple souls, including a "shadow soul," a "sweat soul," and an "eye soul" (Gregor, 1981). The shadow soul, when stolen by a spirit or another person, can produce illness. The sweat soul is one of many souls that becomes an animal of the forest when the person dies. The eye soul, the most important, wanders while the person is dreaming and lives in the "village in the sky" after death.

The Tshidi of Southern Africa, as described by Comaroff (1980), do not confine the "self" to the "visible limits of the body." The self "extends to encompass the more general sphere of personal influence upon the environment, inhering in words, footprints, and personal possessions. In fact, mortuary practice among the Tshidi suggests that something of the self is lodged in all those persons who, in a very literal sense, share its substance – those who give it life, those to whom it has given life, and those with whom it has regular sexual contact" (pp. 643-4). Comaroff notes that the Tshidi do not posit an "interior entity" that "sets apart the experiencing self and the exterior impingements on it," adding that mental events such as memories and dreams are viewed as "the products of external forces acting upon the person" (p. 644). The Tshidi self is relational, "enmeshed in a web of influences, a field of relations with other people, spirits, and natural phenomena . . . ." (p. 644).

In a pioneering ethnopsychological study, Lee (1950) examined the conception of self among the Wintu Indians. She found that the Wintu, like other communally collectivistic cultures, do not possess a differentiated conception of self, and indeed, Wintu language lacks a corresponding term. The Wintu, according to Lee, "conceive of the self not as strictly delimited or defined, but as a concentration, at most, which gradually fades and gives place to the other. Most of what is other for us, is for the Wintu completely or partially or upon occasion, identified with the self" (p. 134). The Wintu, for example, do not use "and" to refer to people who are socially closely related: "Instead of analyzing the *we* into: *John and I,* they say *John we,* using John as a specification. Only when two individuals who are not already in relatedness are brought together, is the *and* used" (p. 134). Similarly, Lee observes, in Wintu myths people are described spatially and behaviorally, not in terms of internal mental processes, and rarely do introspective statements occur. Further, the Wintu rarely use the terms "left" and "right," in which spatial orientation is rendered egocentrically:

> When the Wintu goes up the river, the hills are to the west, the river to the east; and a mosquito bites him on the west arm. When he returns, the hills are still to the west, but, when he scratches his mosquito bite, he scratches his east arm. The geography has remained unchanged, and the self has had to be reoriented in relation to it. (P. 139)

This relative undifferentiation of self was nicely expressed in Lee's experience of trying to elicit autobiographical statements from one of her informants. The person began with a story of her husband, and when Lee insisted on the informant's *own* life history, the first three-quarters of the narrative that followed (which the person called "my story") described the lives of relatives. Finally, the woman began to discuss " 'that which was in my mother's womb' " and proceeded to speak of her own life (p. 140).

Questions of subjective motivation are often irrelevant or less pronounced than objective actions in conceptions of justice in many less complex societies. As Anthony Wallace points out, the deadly and criminal nature of violating a taboo (e.g., touching a tabooed object) does not depend on volition: when Oedipus unwittingly slept with Jocasta, he still had to pay the price (1966, p. 62). Piaget calls this emphasis on the external act moral realism. In his *Moral Judgment of the Child* (1932) he argues that this moral realism is characteristic of "primitives," and that the transformation of moral realism to a more subjective sense of responsibility "goes of a piece with the psycho-sociological transformation that characterizes the passage from the theocratic conformity of so-called 'primitive' societies" to the consciousness of modern times (p. 337).

While primary societies (both band and tribal) nearly universally lack conceptions of bounded selfhood, tribal societies tend to have more clearly articulated group boundaries. Band societies often have rather diffuse boundaries; with greater socioeconomic and political development one uniformly finds rigidification in this respect. LeVine and Campbell (1972) provide a useful analysis of the issue of group boundaries in their excellent book on ethnocentrism. As they point out, rigid group boundaries rarely emerge in acephalous (stateless) societies; firmer boundaries appear to be associated more generally with societies at a higher level of technological and political complexity. Administrative centralization and a more institutionalized political apparatus tend to demarcate more clearly the lines of who will follow and who will not. Permanent settlement, as opposed to shifting locations and bands, occurs with the move to agriculture as mode of subsistence, and the solidification of territorial boundaries and the need to develop rules for intergenerational transfer of land promote solidification of group boundaries.

To summarize this second feature of primary societies, their collectively transmitted schemas manifest a relative indifference to distinctions between nature, culture, and individual. Collective units, to the extent that

253

they are well-defined (which they are in more complex tribal societies), are not well distinguished from their members, nor is culture clearly separated cognitively from nature.

A third aspect of such societies is an attribution of power to the collectivity, which one may call a magical "potency" or "omnipotence," and which is not unrelated to the moral primacy of the group and the fusion of nature and culture. In the primary society, nature and morality are interdependent. George Homans makes a similar point, arguing that the primitive, like the peasant, "feels that unless all the moralities of his society are observed, nature will not yield her fruits" (1941, p. 87). Incest, intragroup violence, or breaches in ritual will lead, with the inexorability of a law of nature, to such natural disasters as crop failures. de Laguna's (1954) Tlingit informants used the words de Laguna translated as "laws of nature" in referring to the expected consequences of the failure to observe certain taboos: "Failure to observe them means death to oneself and to one's relatives" (p. 174).

Numerous examples demonstrate the belief in the "omnipotence" or supernatural potency of the group. This potency is related to a belief in the efficacy of social actions such as ritual to control nature; it is also related to the dangerous power of breaches of the socio-moral order to set in motion catastrophic environmental contingencies. The Saulteaux Indians of North America search for a culprit if food becomes scarce. Like many communally collectivistic societies, they attribute illness to human causes, notably witchcraft (Hallowell, 1955, pp. 144-5, 268-9). The !Kung Bushmen believe that the relationship between various hunters and corresponding animals is responsible for the weather; if a man kills the wrong kind of animal, a force called *N!ow* is released, which affects the climate (Marshall, 1957). According to Anthony Wallace, through various tactics, such as putting fresh water in the mouths of recently killed animals, some Eskimo groups try to avert natural disasters (1966, p. 90). Wallace explains how these beliefs maintain social control and inhibit deviance: infractions threatening to the community are believed to threaten the natural order and require public confession; the group may impose such a severe punishment as banishment upon an individual who continually violates shared rules.

As Lévi-Strauss documents, clans often believe themselves to have magical control over their corresponding totemic species (1959, p. 188). W. Lloyd Warner ties this belief to a functionalist argument in relation to the Murngin:

> The Murngin in their logic of controlling nature assume that there is a direct correlation between social units and different aspects of nature, and that control of nature lies in the proper control and treatment of social organization . . . The society is disciplined by the threat of what will

254

happen to nature, the provider, if the members of the group misbehave. (1937, p. 87)

The Ndembu believe that various forms of affliction such as illness result from the action of shades (spirits) of ancestors who have been offended by the actions of the living. Notable among these actions, as noted before, are attitudes and behaviors that threaten intragroup solidarity, and especially those that prevent kin from "living well together" (Turner, 1967, p. 360). One can see here how even the uncontrollable – illness and misfortune – is believed to stem from the group, through bad actions of the living and consequent responses of the dead. By attributing even evil to the group, the Ndembu can more easily believe in their ability to master it. If evil is externally generated, it cannot be controlled, whereas if it stems from human behavior, it can be managed through greater adherence to group-centered moral rules and through compensatory ritual action. The ritual evoked by affliction or social crisis performs a triple function: it is believed to control the affliction and thus reinforces the sense of potency of the community, it reminds members of the culture that they must behave morally and fulfill social expectations if they are to avoid misfortune, and it brings the group together and thus in a very real sense strengthens the bonds of the community and makes more likely harmonious social relations.

The primary culture, then, is characterized by a moral primacy of the group, evidenced in religion, ritual, and myth; relatively ambiguous boundaries between nature, culture, and individuals; and a belief in the special potency of the group, which combines the sense of the sanctity of society and its rules with the lack of differentiation between social and natural laws to produce an understanding of morality and the cosmos that overestimates the role of human agency. These features are consistent with the threefold definition of the "primitive worldview" proposed by Robert Redfield. Redfield (1952) argues that this worldview includes, first, a failure to differentiate humanity from nature; secondly, a view of people as participating in nature; and thirdly, a belief that the universe is morally significant, that a person's relationship with the universe, like her relationship with other people (and other animate beings), must be moral. Redfield's description, like that summarized above, is obviously an ideal type that exists only in social scientists' heaven. On earth the student of the natural or human world suffers eternal damnation: for every apple that neatly falls in Newtonian fashion, a snake lurks in the background, ready to stalk its theoretical prey.

Secondary Communitarian Collectivism

With growing specialization and social differentiation, the primary type of communitarian collectivism begins to give way to a secondary version.

255

This frequently occurs with the development of agriculture or any massive ecological windfall that permits the growth of private property and some significant rigidification of class structure. Again, the correspondence is not complete, as many of the characteristics that will be described as facets of secondary communitarian collectivism begin to emerge in more complex hunter-gatherer societies.

In the secondary type of communitarian collectivism, the needs of the group still prevail in the culture ideal; however, group predominance is no longer so easy to maintain. The nature of this type of collectivism can be explored through an analysis, first, of cultural differentiation of self, society, and nature; secondly, of the classical religions; and thirdly, of peasant ideology (using the term "ideology" in the nonpejorative, more generic sense of systems of ideas).

Mauss has traced the evolution of the concept of distinct selfhood, differentiated from nature and culture, in his brilliant essay on the history of the *personne morale*. Mauss argues that the concept of a self-conscious *personne morale* or moral actor began to solidify in the centuries immediately preceding and following the Common Era. Mauss's inferences are acute, as he suggests, for example, that the end of the right of the father to kill his sons in Roman society implies that the sons have achieved full personhood even in the father's lifetime.

Mauss writes of the "transition from the notion of persona – man invested with a status – to the notion of man as such, of the human person" (p. 85, emphasis deleted). He argues that the meaning of *persona* evolved from "mask" or "role" to the present notion of "person." The notion of an individual who is conscious, autonomous, and free emerged with Greek philosophy and Roman law. Mauss contends that not until the eighteenth or nineteenth century did the concept of the person become the "category of the self," which is "still being slowly erected, clarified, specified, and identified with self-knowledge, with the psychological consciousness, almost into our own times" (p. 87).

Jaynes (1976) has tried to argue that consciousness did not emerge until the first millenium B.C., a few thousand years after the development of agriculture. As it stands, his argument poses too rigid an "us-them" stereotype, one which seems unlikely in the face of ample anthropological data which suggest that preagricultural people do not all hallucinate regularly like schizophrenics. One can, however, make sense of the argument if one translates for "consciousness" the consciousness of self, distinct from others. Jaynes carefully examined the language of the *Iliad* and found that the characters in the *Iliad* do not ponder their actions, nor do they introspect (p. 72). Rather, "The Iliad is about *action* and it is full of action – constant action. It is really *about* Achilles' acts and their consequences, not about his mind" (p. 79).

According to anthropologist Anthony Wallace, not until a clergy emerges that has communal interests in mind does a society become aware of itself as an entity, one which requires rites and rituals (such as calendrical rituals) for the maintenance of faith (1966, p. 131). Robert Bellah argues that in the "primitive" society, myth and religion hover so close to reality that a "sense of gap" between the real and the ideal rarely occurs (1964, p. 271; see also Stanner, 1958). In "archaic," as opposed to primitive religions, Bellah argues, the distinction becomes much sharper between the human and the divine (p. 274), but the function of religion in maintaining social solidarity remains the same:

> The social implications of archaic religion are to some extent similar to those of primitive religion. The individual and his society are seen as merged in a natural divine cosmos. Traditional structures and social practices are considered to be grounded in the divinely instituted cosmic order and there is little tension between religious demand and social conformity. Indeed, social conformity is at every point reinforced with religious sanction. (P. 275)

When the "historic" religions develop, he claims, the separation between the group, nature, and the individual becomes more pronounced. "The identity diffusion characteristic of both primitive and archaic religion," he contends, "is radically challenged by the historic religious symbolization, which leads for the first time to a clearly structured conception of the self" (p. 277).

Similarly, Kitagawa claims that, unlike earlier religions, the classical religions of the Near East, Far East, India, Greece, and Rome which began to develop around the middle of the fourth millenium B.C. "recognize the distinction between 'man, society, and nature' as well as among 'past, present, and future' . . ." (1967, p. 50). Unlike their predecessors, the classical religions demonstrate "a high degree of sophistication and systemization of theoretical, practical, and sociological aspects of religion" (p. 50). Kitagawa observes that the classical religions uniformly derogate the phenomenal world (p. 50). Bellah concurs, adding that the de-emphasis of empirical reality parallels the denigration of the empirical self: religious thought begins to posit a core self with a "consistency belied by the fluctuations of mere sensory impressions" (pp. 278-9).

These facets of the classical religions, which developed only a few thousand years ago, suggest two features of secondary communitarian collectivism. First, that the differentiation of society from nature and individuals is accompanied by a relative devaluation of empirical nature and self is no accident: the one element in the trinity of nature, society, and self that escapes denigration is society. Secondly, the main threat to a society whose cohesion was formerly guaranteed by relative lack of social and cultural differentiation is suddenly viewed as the greatest of sins: individual desire.

These implications point to a single conclusion, that the secondary culture is one in which social-structural and symbolic differentiation threaten the belief in the value and power of the sacred collectivity. A symbolic differentiation of nature and culture challenges the magical potency of culture, and a symbolic differentiation of culture and self alongside a social-structural differentiation of classes and interest groups challenges communalistic systems of values. The reader should not be surprised to find that, as Kitagawa (following Eliade) notes, the classical religions all express a "nostalgia for a lost paradise" (p. 60).

The historic religions, in contrast to their "primitive" predecessors, are relatively universalistic; a person is no longer defined "chiefly in terms of what tribe or clan he comes from," and "it is for the first time possible to conceive of man as such" (Bellah, p. 277). Simultaneously, one finds everywhere a religious assault upon individual desire. "Religion," remarks Edward Sapir, "has always been the enemy of self-satisfaction" (1949, p. 139), and nowhere is this more true than in the classical religions. Bellah documents the point:

> But historic religion convicts man of a flaw more serious than those conceived by earlier religions. According to Buddhism, man's very nature is greed and anger from which he must seek a total escape. For the Hebrew prophets, man's sin is not particular wicked deeds but his profound heedlessness of God, and only a turn to complete obedience will be acceptable to the Lord. For Muhammad, the *kafir* is . . . the ungrateful man who is careless of the divine compassion. For him, only Islam, willing submission to the will of God, can bring salvation. (P. 277)

According to the Buddha, the root of misery is desire (*tanha*), which stands in the way of Nirvana; the individual must strive to escape the "conceit of individuality" (James, 1964, pp. 81-5). Jainism called for the containment of individual passion (p. 79). Christianity thrusts upon the individual an original sin, and pride is elevated to the status of a deadly passion. All the classical ethical religions, Scharf observes, "emphasize the importance of brotherly or parental-filial relations among members . . ." (p. 148).

An analysis of the ideology and values of peasant society provides further insight into the nature of secondary communitarian collectivism. Academics, unlike normal users of language, become uncomfortable when confronted with simple definitions; if a definition is meaningful, we suppose, something must be amiss. This is certainly the case regarding the terms "peasant" and "peasant society." Every peasant knows precisely what a peasant is, but sociologists have found difficulty agreeing upon a definition. According to Eric Wolf, who has devoted a career to studying and awakening sociological interest in peasantry, peasant societies "stand midway between the primitive tribe and industrial society" and constitute "a phase in the evolution of human society" (1966, p. vii). Other authors stress that peasants, unlike hunter-gatherers, have contact with "towns, markets and high cultures" (Bailey, 1966, p. 317). This is the view of Redfield, who, following Kroeber, views peasant cultures as part-cultures always related to a Great Tradition (see Redfield, 1953; Redfield and Singer, 1954). Foster (1973) emphasizes that, unlike "primitives," peasants do not have an autochthonous (self-generated) culture; i.e., they borrow their culture from the Great Tradition of the city. Shanin attempts a more definitive description:

> The peasantry consists of small agricultural producers who, with the help of simple equipment and the labour of their families, produce mainly for their own consumption and for the fulfillment of obligations to the holders of political and economic power. (1966, p. 240)

Perhaps the best characterization comes from Geertz, who defines peasant societies as "societies with too many resemblances to our own for us to stigmatize them as primitive and too few for us to celebrate them as modern" (1966, p. 329).

A comparable controversy exists as to the nature, if any, of peasant culture. The three main traditions of thought about peasant culture are those of Redfield, Banfield, and Foster. Redfield paints a rosier picture of peasant life than the others (1947, 1953), though he is hardly naive, as some of his detractors suggest. He views peasant culture as a "folk society" characterized by homogeneity and cooperation, similar in many ways to Durkheim's mechanical solidarity. Banfield, like Foster, takes issue with this more romantic view, describing as "amoral familism" the principles by which Italian peasants interact, competing for scarce resources (1958; for a rather negative review of Banfield, see Davis, 1970). Whereas Rousseau is the theoretical ancestor of Redfield, political scientist Banfield seems to have been influenced by Hobbes. This situation seems a bit like that which inspired Bertrand Russell's remark that the animals studied by American behaviorists act like Americans, "running about in random fashion," whereas those described by German behaviorists resemble Germans, "sitting and thinking" (cited in Skinner, 1974, p. 20). Foster's view, while closer to that of Banfield, is something of a rapprochement between them. Foster argues that the peasant worldview is shaped by the "image of Limited Good" (1965). According to Foster, peasants quite realistically see the competition for resources as a zero-sum affair, and they consequently discourage any of their fellows from accumulating resources or standing out in any way.

The disparity between these three perspectives can only in part be reduced to the preconceptions of their authors. Part of of the problem results from the lack of a coherent definition of culture (and in particular, culture ideal). Foster himself would not deny that, while peasant social structure may create suspicion and antagonism, the *ideal* of clan or village unity is

259

everpresent (1973, p. 39). The time periods and cultures studied by various observers of peasant societies without doubt influence the results of their investigations. If one looks at the debate about the definition of peasant society itself, one realizes that part of the reason some contemporary rural sociologists do not believe that a peasantry exists in anything near ideal-typical purity is that such a peasantry scarcely does exist anymore. Forty years ago, one could not say the same thing. Similarly, if one is seeking a picture of the peasant culture ideal prior to the effects of modernization, one would certainly not examine the peasantry in many areas of Italy, birthplace of the Renaissance. Again, one is confronted with the problem of making observations about life on a passing train.

One can, despite differences of opinion on various matters, make certain generalizations about culture ideal in preindustrial, agrarian societies. Peasant morality centers upon the group, whether the group emphasized is extended family, village, or larger society (Wolf, 1966, p.17). Generally the village community is a moral unit with strong sentimental bonds (Dobrowolski, 1958, p. 293). Ayrout (1963) claims that in the Egyptian village (in the first half of this century, at least) the village community is more important (i.e., a more important group-need attachment) than family or clan. In other peasant societies, the extended family or clan commands more loyalty. In either case, the authority of tradition and the good of the group define peasant morality. Summarizing the general consensus as to the nature of peasant culture (ideal), Shanin writes of the "preeminence of traditional and conformist attitudes, i.e. the justification of individual action in terms of past experience and the will of the community . . ." (1971, p. 15). Elsewhere Shanin expands upon this view, taking off from the perspective of Pitt-Rivers:

> Pitt-Rivers notes the main features of a closed community to be habitual personal contact, widespread endogamy, homogeneity of values, emphasis on strict conformity, intense group solidarity and marked egalitarianism; this may serve as a generalization of much recent anthropological research into specific peasant cultures. (1966, p. 247)

Family life, according to Shanin, exerts powerful social pressure and discourages individualism; individual desire "is markedly subordinated to the formalized restraints of accepted family role behavior" (p. 243).

Foster's analysis leads him to the same conclusion, namely, the importance of tradition and the denigration of individualistic striving. Peasants are conservative, he claims, "because individual progress is seen as – and in the context of the traditional society in fact is – the supreme threat to community stability . . ." (1965, p. 310). This description of peasant ideology is remarkably similar to the view presented earlier of religion in the secondary society.

Peasant ceremonials and rituals, as well as various mechanisms for the redistribution of wealth, reinforce group solidarity. Not only do many rituals take place on the familial level, but rituals always exist at the level of the village or local group as well (Wolf, 1966, p. 97). Wolf argues, in a functionalist moment,

> in a peasant community men must often depend on each other if only for that sense of continuity which renders life predictable, and hence meaningful. Thus, we shall find in peasant communities ceremonial which involves men as members of a community, and which acts to uphold their common social order, to purge it of disorder, to restore its integrity . . . In many kinds of festivals, peasants in different parts of the world celebrate their sense of interdependence and affirm the rules governing it. (P. 98)

Arguing that "social order," not "the examined life," is the aim of peasant religion, Wolf concludes in a Durkheimian passage:

> Moreover, its rules are enjoined upon the interacting parties from above. Representing the interests of the wider community, such rules appear to stand above and beyond it, to have a reality of their own independent of the rival claims of the contestants. They are said to be supernatural. (P. 99)

Foster contends that peasant societies use various sanctions (supernatural and otherwise) to enforce social control and prevent divergence from norms of moderation and equality. The punishments meted out to deviants are often informal and spontaneous, including "gossip, slander, backbiting, character assassination, witchcraft or the threat of witchcraft, and sometimes actual physical aggression" (1965, p. 305). He adds, "Concern with public opinion is one of the most striking characteristics of peasant communities" (p. 305).

Peasant societies also maintain solidarity through various redistribution or "leveling" mechanisms. Foster provides a common Latin American example, in which an individual who has become too successful is induced to sponsor an extravagant fiesta. He explains why peasant fiestas are enormously expensive and why so many life transitions (e.g., baptism, marriage, and death) are marked by extravagant rites: "These practices are a redistributive mechanism which permits a person or family that potentially threatens community stability to restore the status quo . . ." (p. 305). Similar practices occur with some frequency in "primitive" societies as well (the potlatch certainly comes to mind), and one senses a continuity between primary and secondary cultures in this emphasis on egalitarianism for the sake of solidarity, though this is by no means universal. As Wolf observes, egalitarianism often permeates the goals of peasant social movements, which frequently "center upon a myth of a social order more just and egalitarian than the hierarchical present" (1966, p. 106). Such myths, he remarks, "may look backwards, to the re-creation of a golden age of justice and equality in the past," or they may look forward, "to the establishment of a new order on earth . . ." (p. 106).

The nature of peasant movements (see Wolf, 1969) provides important insight into the values of peasant communities. In his classic work on the *Social Origins of Dictatorship and Democracy,* comparative historian Barrington Moore argues that, unlike the case in Japan, Germany, England, and France, the peasantry in Russia and China "provided the main destructive revolutionary force that overthrew the old order . . . ." (1966, p. xvi). That these same two countries in which the peasantry prevailed (until the government became entrenched and autonomous) adopted a communalistic creed suggests that the culture ideal of the *ancien régime* may be of some importance in explaining revolutionary outcome. This is not to suggest that a cultural explanation can be substituted for a sociopolitical and socioeconomic one; class structure, the nature of the old regime state, and the role of the international system have obviously played important causal roles in the outcome of every social revolution since 1789, if not before (see Skocpol, 1979). Rather, the argument here is that one cannot fully understand the nature of either "revolutionary situations" or "revolutionary outcomes" (Tilly, 1978) without examining cultural – and psychocultural – variables. Specific case studies by Scott (1976) and Sewell (1980) suggest the importance of peasant ideologies for revolutionary outcomes.

Even Theda Skocpol, who claims to present a "nonvoluntarist" approach that avoids the unnecessary pitfalls of "purposive" explanation (1979, p. 32-3) in her tremendous book, *States and Social Revolutions,* fails to follow her nonpurposive principles. "Just as the socioeconomic basis of the French peasant community explained the accomplishments and limits of the peasant revolution in France," she contends, "so did the qualitatively different basis of the *obschina* provide the key to the content of the peasant victory in Russia." Awaiting a socioeconomic explanation, the reader is told that the crucial factor is that the Russia *obschina* "did not *legitimate* private landed property as such. Rather 'all land belonged to God,' and the peasant community as a whole strove to gain access to as much as possible and then distribute it roughly equally to households . . ." (p. 139, emphasis added). This is hardly an explanation that avoids purposive cultural variables. Similarly, if one cannot understand the course of the Chinese Revolution without explaining why many Chinese businessmen became "converts to various Western ideals and turned into vociferous advocates of Chinese national autonomy and assertion against the humiliating privileges of the imperialist powers" (p. 242), then one cannot avoid psychocultural explanation. The point being made here is essentially the same as that made by Weber in *The Protestant Ethic and the Spirit of Capitalism* (1958): ideas constitute one important variable among many in explaining an event. The disconcerting fact about social science is that causal explanation is necessarily multidirectional. Ideas cause both events and other ideas; similarly, events cause ideas and other events. Social explanation does not fit neatly into a Cartesian separation of a realm of purpose and a realm of mechanism, and neither "realm" unilaterally determines the other. (Quite paradoxically, the most important falsification of a pure Marxian materialism or any other method that reduces ideals to activities is the Bolshevik Revolution, in which a small cadre of intellectuals, supported by the ideals and ideas of a nineteenth-century German thinker, molded an entire society to fit an entirely ideal – and idealistic – mental blueprint.)

One can conclude from this discussion of classical religion and peasant ideology that the culture ideal of the secondary culture, like that of the primary variant, is characterized by emphasis on the primacy of group needs as moral aims. The difference between the two reflects the greater sociocultural differentiation and individuation of the secondary type. In the primary form of communitarian collectivism, the group is phenomenologically not fully distinct from its members or from nature, and it is believed to possess an extraordinary potency. In the secondary form, the culture recognizes the existence, but not the legitimacy of individuals. In other words, concomitant with the growth of individualism and the recognition of the emerging chasm between individual and collectivity is a global assault on individual desire and a reassertion of group-centered morality.

In both variants, but particularly in the secondary type, one finds a tendency for societies to project their alleged value and power upon real or imagined objects. An analogy here is to Winnicott's (1971) transitional object, the "intermediate area" between subjectivity and objectivity. As elaborated in Part I, the transitional object for the individual arises in a stage of ego development in which the individual first recognizes the existence – but not yet the legitimacy and intrinsic value – of others. The child projects his own subjectivity upon an external object that is valued, but not phenomenologically fully distinct from self. Similarly, the societal "transitional object" may be a god, an icon, a flag or emblem, a leader, a group, an ideology, or even a societal institution (e.g., a polity). The common characteristic of all these objects is that they are objects of projection of societal force. Durkheim describes this phenomenon in an insightful passage from *The Elementary Forms:*

> Also, in the present day just as much as in the past, we see society constantly creating sacred things out of ordinary ones. If it happens to fall in love with a man and if it thinks it has found in him the principal aspirations that may move it, as well as the means of satisfying them, this man will be raised above the others and, as it were, deified. Opinion will invest him with a majesty exactly analogous to that protecting the gods. This is what has happened to so many sovereigns in whom their age had faith: if they were not made gods, they were at least regarded as direct

263

representatives of the deity . . . [I]t is society alone which is the author of these varieties of apotheosis. . . . (1915, pp. 243-4)

The early Egyptians saw their rulers as gods incarnate. Shinto religion claims that the emperor is descended from a sun-goddess (James, 1964, p.110). More recently, Geertz has observed that the Balinese see the political order as a reflection of the cosmos, equating the king with the supreme god (1973, 1981). The traditional Chinese viewed the emperor as the "son of Heaven," and the doctrine of the divine right of kings in the age of absolutism in the West argued for legitimacy on supernatural grounds.

One can find similar parallels in the history of many cultures. Cora DuBois, for example, has described a relationship between society, state, and rulers once prevalent throughout Southeast Asia. Remarking on the presence of a "magico-religious god-king symbolizing a world order," she claims that the "wealth and sexual potency of the ruler, the splendor of the court and temples were projected and sublimated expressions of cultural well-being" (1964, p. 31). Part III will explore the relationship between this process at the societal level, in which a culture projects its own value and power upon a leader who both controls and is controlled by it, and the concomitant process at the psychological level whereby individuals share in this splendor and magnificence by identifying with such a leader. What is crucial to note is that state and god-king represent the collectivity and its moral order itself. The state, writes DuBois, is "the symbol of a world order, and the expression of a system of proprieties in human and superhuman relationships" (p. 31). Contrasting the phenomenon in Southeast Asia with feudal Europe, DuBois observes that the "lords seem to have been less the masters of the surfs and more an expression of the peasantry's greatness" (p. 31). While this latter assertion no doubt underestimates the extent to which such sentiments could be manipulated by the dominant classes for their own purposes, her point is clear that the peasantry were not simply being duped: by establishing a symbol of their greatness and solidarity, they could make this greatness and solidarity concrete and real and could so participate in it.

Turner describes a similar relationship between ruler and people among the Ndembu of northwestern Zambia. The paramount chief of the Ndembu serves not only as a political leader but as a symbol of the community: "He is, symbolically, also the tribal territory itself and all its resources. Its fertility and freedom from drought, famine, disease, and insect plagues are bound up with his office, with both his physical and moral condition" (1969, p. 98). The projection of the power and value of the group upon an individual leaves the community open to the everpresent danger that this individual will act on his own desires and subvert social institutions for his personal gain. Not surprisingly, much of the initiation rite that installs a new Ndembu chief is devoted to reviling him for his previous selfishness and demanding that he relinquish personal motives for the benefit of the community. A homily delivered during this initiation rebukes and exhorts the chief-elect as follows:

> "You are a mean and selfish fool . . . Put away meanness, put aside anger, give up adulterous intercourse . . . You must eat with your fellow men, you must live well with them . . . You must give up your selfish ways, you must welcome everyone, you are the chief!" (P. 101)

Turner observes that in the course of the homiletic, the chief-elect is chided for "his selfishness, meanness, theft, anger, witchcraft, and greed. All these vices represent the desire to possess for oneself what ought to be shared for the common good" (p. 104).

In both historical and anthropological discourse one frequently finds confrontations between those who argue that the state emerges as a result of conflict between emerging classes and those who contend that the state arises for the common defense or for the pursuit of collective goals (for an excellent review, see Cohen, 1978). Both are in part right, since in early states one finds an uneasy amalgam of communally collectivistic attachment to a collectivity and the emergence of groups and individuals who co-opt social and governmental institutions for their own benefit. Godelier (1978) has articulately discussed this issue, arguing that dominant individuals and groups in early states were likely in many cases historically to have gained legitimacy for their status by exchanging religious service for subsistence. As Godelier puts it, "the monopoly of the means (to us imaginary) of reproduction of the universe and of life must have preceded the monopoly of the visible means of production, i.e., of those means which everyone could and had to produce in order to reproduce . . ." (p. 767). Godelier rightly notes that force can nevertheless substitute for legitimacy when the latter has broken down and the peasantry begins to feel exploited. In other words, secondary societies are societies with separate individuals and subgroups as well as a communal culture, and while that culture remains communally collectivistic, one will find in such societies institutions and practices that clearly benefit one class. Most of social life and culture is overdetermined, so that institutions or cultural traits that began as collectivistic may gradually become exploitative and vice versa. Often legitimacy and exploitation coexist in a way that is uneasy both for the members of the culture and for those who wish to understand it.

In both forms of communitarian collectivism, the person is perceived, if distinctly, as an extension or microcosm of the group. The member of the communally collectivistic society is willing to die for the group because its existence is seen as transcending his own, of being more legitimate, of being moral. With increasing individuation, however, this balance between individual and collectivity is bound to dissolve. The use of an individual as a symbol of the group is an intermediate step between the primary com-

265

munitarian collectivist lack of differentiation between group and self and a more thorough separation of the two.[1] The deification of an individual may also occur in times of social breakdown, when society is looking for an ideal, as will be discussed in Chapter 13.

The culture that symbolizes itself through the medium of an individual as a societal transitional object is thus, in some sense, using the individual as its totem. A remark by Lévi-Strauss is of significance here. Arguing in *The Savage Mind* that totemism of one sort or another exists in every society, he comments in passing that in contemporary Western society totemism "has merely been humanized. Everything takes place as if in our civilization every individual's personality were his totem . . ." (1966, p. 214). If one takes "totem" to mean either a societal transitional object or a primitive undifferentiation of the group and an object, then Lévi-Strauss is undoubtedly correct in asserting that every culture to date has had its totems. Yet his comment suggests more than this: it suggests that in contemporary society, the totem is rapidly becoming the individual. More to the point, the locus of value and power appears to be shifting from group to individual. The following section will attempt to show that this is the case, as well as to explore the corresponding culture ideal and the transformed nature of collectivism in a society no longer premised on the belief in the legitimate primacy of the group.

Individuated Collectivism

In an essay on the relation between Indian and Western conceptions of the individual, Louis Dumont (1965b) argues that the individual in the West is seen as a source of value, comparable to the Hindu notion of *dharma*, signifying the moral order (see also Dumont, 1965a). Dumont argues that in the modern West the individual is "valorized," whereas the "self" or "individual ego" is negatively valued in the India of the Upanishads. Dumont writes,

> With us, modern Westerners, the ontological unit is the human indivisible being. In traditional India it is always a whole, whether big or small, an entirety embodying relations, a multiplicity ordered by its inner, mostly hierarchical, oppositions, into a single whole. (1965b, p. 99)

He adds that the distinction between nature and culture parallels historically that between individual and collectivity.

The "valorization" of the individual in contemporary Western society

---

[1] The use of a different class of object to represent the group, as occurs in totemism, frequently occurs in relatively simple societies, but this reflects the level of symbolic differentiation of culture from these natural symbols. With the symbolic use of an individual as a group's "totem," an incipient differentiation of group and self has emerged, though the boundaries are not firm, as one can stand for the other.

266

represents a fundamental shift in the relative valuation of self and society. Again, a brief discussion of the theories of Durkheim and Marx is instructive. Durkheim suggests the importance of the differentiation of individuals in his concept of organic solidarity. Organic solidarity represents group cohesion based upon specialization and interdependence. Utilizing the organic metaphor borrowed from Comte and so pervasive in (especially nineteenth century) social science, Durkheim contends that individuals in an organically solidary society function like organs in the "body politic." Organically solidary society, he claims in a passage that seems to echo Adam Smith, "is characterized by a co-operation which is automatically produced through the pursuit of each individual of his own interests" (p. 200).

Marx points to the same phenomenon, though he evaluates it in much more negative terms. Marx astutely observes that in bourgeois society, the group (political society) is a means to the ends of individuals (civil society):

> ... citizenship, the political community, is reduced by the political eman-
> cipators to a mere means for the conservation of these so-called rights of
> man and ... the citizen is therefore proclaimed the servant of egoistic
> man ... [I]t is man as bourgeois, i.e., as a member of civil society, and
> not man as citizen who is taken as the real and authentic man. (1975a, p.
> 231, emphasis deleted)

What Marx does not point out is that the movement from "prebourgeois" to "bourgeois" society involves a reversal of means and ends. No longer does the individual exist for society; rather, society exists for the individual. Durkheim errs in conceiving of morality as inherently self-abnegatory and group-centered. To the contrary, a selfless morality is only the morality of communitarian collectivism. In a culture characterized by *individuated collectivism*, in contrast, morality is the morality of self-interest. In the former case, societal cohesion is prior to self-interest. In the latter, cohesion, if it exists, is only a by-product of self-interest.

A number of writers document the shift from communitarian to individuated collectivism. Social-political theorist Roberto Unger speaks in similar terms of the movement from social relations based on kinship to relations based on role. He argues that kinship, estate, class, and role form a historical continuum "in which individual identity is increasingly distinguished from group existence, or the self is ever more separated from others" (1975, p. 165). Christopher Lasch, taking off from the work of Riesman and his colleagues (1961), suggests that personality structure is changing from inner-direction to narcissism (1978, p. 42). The narcissist, for Lasch, is the individual "who sees the world as a mirror of himself and has no interest in external events except as they throw back a reflection of his own image" (p. 47). In contrast, the individual in the communally collectivistic culture may perceive himself as a mirror of his society. The difference could not be more fundamental.

At a more concrete level, Redfield's work on Yucatan (1941) provides an example with parallels throughout the Third World. Redfield found that as Yucatan became less isolated and homogeneous, three cultural changes occurred: disorganization of the culture, secularization, and individuation (p. 339). Part III will attempt to show that while cultural disorganization may appear in any rapidly changing society and is likely to abate, the individualization that comes with "modernization" is not an artifact of rapid social change and is not likely to recede.

General evolutionary trends in the development of culture real have received treatment in numerous places and will receive only brief mention here. Models of universal and unilinear evolution have begun to emerge as evolutionism continues to regain respectability in anthropology (e.g., Carneiro, 1970, 1973). In terms of technological development, a sequence from hunting, fishing, and foraging societies, through herding and agricultural, to industrial societies appears rather clear, though numerous questions about details of this general sequence are by no means approaching resolution. Division of labor and social stratification progressively increase, at least through some point in economic development. The minimal distinctions of hunter-gatherer societies based primarily on age and sex burgeon into distinctions based on class and, additionally, on roles and statuses that are achieved rather than ascribed. One can discern a rough sequence of political evolution, from acephalous societies, to chiefdoms, to states and empires, though again the degree to which every society conforms to such a pattern is a significant question.

In summarizing general evolutionary trends of the culture real, I should make absolutely clear that I am proposing neither that all change is of this macroevolutionary sort (and that cultural differences and microevolutionary adaptations are not equally significant), nor that development of the culture ideal is independent of these processes. As in the study of personality, an adequate understanding of sociocultural phenomena requires an approach that is both nomothetic and idiographic, which can elucidate broad developmental or evolutionary trajectories as well as individual cases. In terms of the culture ideal, Chapter 11 will attempt more systematically to show the relationship between developments in the culture real and the emergence of individuated collectivism (and its psychological concomitants).

To examine the movement from communitarian to individuated collectivism, one could probably equally study literature, philosophy, or religion. I will illustrate this revolutionary shift through two brief excursions, one into the sociology of religion, and the other into the history of Western moral philosophy.

A key issue in the sociology of religion is the nature of secularization and the relationship between religion and modernization. (For analyses of the role of religion in contemporary society, see Herberg, 1955; B.R. Wilson, 1966; and Luckmann, 1967). Berger and Luckmann emphasize the privatization of belief in modernized societies (1963, p. 70), in which religion becomes a more personal matter. Joachim Wach comments:

> Modern Western man is all too prone to think of the solitary individual first and last, yet the study of primitive religions shows that, individual experiences notwithstanding, religion is generally a group affair . . . There is no denying that on a higher [technologically more advanced] level of civilization a more strongly individualized attitude developed. (1958, pp. 121-2)

The idea that the average individual needs no social mediation between himself and the Absolute has appeared rarely in human history, and the withering away of the Absolute itself (and a socially constructed cosmology) is a relatively recent phenomenon.

Robert Bellah proposes a broad and bold scheme for the history of religions in his classic article on "Religious Evolution" (1964). Bellah delineates five stages of religious development: primitive, archaic, historic, early modern, and modern. Unlike the first three types, he claims, early modern religion begins to place positive emphasis on the individual. Bellah describes the evolution of religion as a progressive understanding and acceptance of individuality:

> The historic religions discovered the self; the early modern religion found a doctrinal basis on which to accept the self in all its empirical ambiguity; modern religion is beginning to understand the laws of the self's own existence and so to help man take responsibility for his own fate. (P. 288)

Religious trends suggest "the increasing acceptance of the notion that each individual must work out his own solutions" and that the church can "provide him a favorable environment for doing so, without imposing on him a prefabricated set of answers" (p. 289). That with the individualism of early modern religion came an emphasis on faith is not surprising. Unlike outward, public rituals, faith is subjective and not amenable to group verification. Central here is the decline of the group. Unlike the case in earlier societies, "modern" religion is no longer fused with the interests of society as a whole (Scharf, 1970, p. 86).

The development of Western moral philosophy provides another index of the rise of individuated collectivism in the West. For all intents and purposes Western moral philosophy began in the first millenium B.C. with the ancient Greeks, though it is certainly unlikely that any society has existed (for long) that lacked a moral code. The earliest records of Greek moral views, found in the Homeric epics, suggest the kind of morality here called communitarian collectivist, in which morality is synonymous with the good of the group. *Agathos*, "the good," is defined in terms of fulfillment of one's role in society. Alasdair MacIntyre writes in his *Short His-*

tory of Ethics, "The society reflected in the Homeric poems is one in which the most important judgments that can be passed upon a man concern the way in which he discharges his allotted social function" (1966, p. 5). The goodness of a person was a factual, "objective" question: if he fulfilled his function, he was good; if not, he was bad; and if he was a member of a different society, he was not a moral actor at all. Determinations of goodness could be considered objective because the end – the good of the society – was assumed, so the only question was whether or not one fulfilled one's duties toward promoting that end.

The belief that the moral views of one's culture are absolute and natural is conceivable only when the culture is inadequately differentiated from nature, and when the moral views of other cultures are not seriously considered. By the fifth and sixth centuries B.C., Athenian society in particular was too cosmopolitan to maintain this undifferentiated moral absolutism. One could probably argue that moral philosophy began with the Sophists, who developed the distinction between *phusis* (nature) and *nomos* (social convention). The Sophists concluded that when in Crete, do as the Cretans, i.e., that one should follow the conventions of one's society. The Sophists were the first to distinguish, as the liberals later would, between natural man[1] (a volatile, premoral, egoistic creature) and social man (a civilized being who follows social rules), and they sided with the latter. One should note that the recognition of the threat of individual desire appeared simultaneously with the recognition that society and nature are not identical, that society's rules are not the same as natural laws.

"Much of the political philosophy of Plato and Aristotle," writes J.W. Gough, "was concerned to combat these subversive opinions" of the Sophists (1936, p. 12). Unlike the Sophists, who viewed goodness as essentially arbitrary and relative, Plato argued that the Good is real and objective, but that only the true philosopher can apprehend it. The Good is a Platonic Form, if not the supreme Form. According to Plato, if one thinks correctly, one will uncover one true morality, the Form of the Good. Plato does not believe that proper understanding can produce two contradictory moral views: only one view can approximate the Good, and the other must be wrong.

Plato was the founder of the dichotomy of reason and desire, which he derived largely from Orphic and Pythagorean beliefs about conflict between the soul and the body, and which has persisted in moral philosophy ever since. This view sees humans as impulsive creatures who must use reason to keep the passions in check. Reason (or understanding) is thus intimately connected with morality; it is also related to social function. For

---

[1] I use the word "man" throughout this section as a generic term when I am trying to preserve the original language of various philosophical positions.

270

Plato, the person, like everything else in nature, has a function or *telos*. A knife performs the function of cutting, and a soldier performs the function of protecting the *polis*. Just as one can objectively determine if a knife is a good knife (i.e., if it performs its function well), so one can objectively decide if a person is fulfilling his role; to do the Good is to fulfill one's social function well.

While Aristotle's ethics differ in many respects from Plato's, his moral philosophy responds to the Sophists' position with an even more vigorous reestablishment of the fundamentals of the moral *status quo ante*. Like Homer, Aristotle concerns himself with the hero or the "magnanimous" man, but also as in the Homeric myths, the noble, heroic, or magnanimous man is only examined within the context of the moral community. For Aristotle even more than for Plato, a person's function is her or his social function, so that a person without a state cannot be moral. In his *Politics* Aristotle thus argues that life without law is devoid of goodness. If one were to impose upon Aristotle the language of modern political philosophy, one might say that moral freedom consists in obedience to the law (at least to the law of a good *polis*). The state, for Aristotle, is both morally and logically prior to the individual; his concept of the *polis* is organismic, and to speak of an individual outside of a *polis* is like speaking of an eye without a person to use it. The phrase "use it" is important here: the state is the highest aim, and the individual exists as a servant of the community. One should note that this reflects a communally collectivistic value system: the individual is perceived as an agent or extension of the state, and the Good is synonymous with the good of the community.[1] Aristotle also proposed the doctrine of the "golden mean," which makes some considerable sense as a loose maxim to keep "everything in moderation," but which is nonsensical as a formal rule. Russell amusingly illustrates the difficulties with the golden mean:

> There was once a mayor who had adopted Aristotle's doctrine; at the end of his term of office he made a speech saying that he had endeavored to steer the narrow line between partiality on the one hand and impartiality on the other. (1945, p. 174)

With the fall of the Greek *polis* and the rise of empires of unprecedented power and territorial scope, the kind of public morality suitable for life in a small city-state began to give way to a more private morality among many philosophers. Of course, the moral views of the vast majority at that time hardly rested upon the ruminations of a relatively small number of philosophers. Moral rules for most people were, and still are, part and parcel of their religious orientations.

---

[1] Also important to note is that Aristotle's term for "society" (*polis*) is the same as his word for "state," so that when he asserts that "man is a political animal," he means, as well, that man is a social animal.

After Aristotle and the disintegration of the *polis,* philosophy became a "philosophy of retreat" (Russell, p. 232). Life was precarious, and one could count only on one's subjectivity. Philosophers withdrew in resignation from social life, and one sees in both Stoic and Epicurean philosophy the attempt to explain how a person devoid of a community within which to interact and to which to devote her or his efforts can still find meaning and live a virtuous life. Similar questions would arise over a thousand years later when the affluence and societal disintegration of life after the city-state would be in some ways duplicated with the Renaissance, the birth of the modern nation-state, and the Industrial Revolution. The precariousness of existence was, however, far greater in the age of the Stoics and Epicureans, and one finds in their philosophy a retreat to private life that appears to be an unhappy substitute for public morality, whereas the philosophers of a later era would rejoice in their individualism. In Stoic and Epicurean philosophy one still finds the disdain for physical pleasure characteristic of a secondary communally collectivistic culture; the human being's raison d'être was to live a good life with a minimum of pain, not a maximum of earthly pleasure.

At the same time, two other developments occurred that would vastly change the way people conceived of morality. The first was the rise of a generic conception of "man," as opposed to man in a particular society. The second was the predominance of monotheism, with the image of a God whose domain was the entire world and all humankind, not just a limited geographic area or a particular people. Many of the moral duties previously circumscribed to a particular people became universalized (while others became isolated to smaller social units, such as the agricultural village or extended family). Whereas moral philosophers through Aristotle saw the individual as an actor who must fulfill his role in society's play, now God often replaced society as the Supreme Director, and the good thespian would receive his Academy Award in another life. This was true not only in Christian theology; Epictetus, a Stoic, viewed people as actors in God's play, whose virtue consists in playing their parts well.

From the fifth century A.D. to the fifteenth, Western moral philosophy was essentially Christian philosophy. Augustine dominated philosophy during most of the Middle ages, uniting Platonism with Christianity to form a synthesis that would predominate until Aquinas wedded Christian theology with Aristotelian teaching in the thirteenth century. Augustine's understanding of God and Scripture is thoroughly Platonic: even his account of the steps toward coming to an understanding of God in *The City of God* is almost identical to Plato's account of the philosopher's ascent from the cave. Plato's Forms are Augustine's God, and just as earthly affairs for Plato are "unreal," transitory, and inferior to the Forms, so, for Augustine, is worldly existence a poor imitation of God and his true City.

For Plato, sensory existence is the apprehension of an inferior universe, whereas true understanding is knowledge of the Forms. To follow one's bodily desires above one's reason and understanding is to pursue life in an inferior world. Similarly, after years of profligacy, Augustine came to the belief that the spirit is higher than the flesh, and that one must, as far as possible, leave the demands of earthly existence behind and commune with God.

Aquinas was concerned about potential conflicts between reason and faith. According to Aquinas, reason never contradicts Scripture; the learned can use their reason to supplement their faith, but the two cannot come into conflict. Further, for Aquinas, God is the goal of human desire, perhaps the ultimate desire, so reason and faith cannot contradict desire. Drawing upon the concept of a "natural law" first invoked by the Sophists, Aquinas sees the natural laws that govern human life as compatible with divine law. The desires for self-preservation, procreation, life in a community, and knowledge of God are all, for Aquinas, part of natural law or human nature. The individual is still not the focus of attention. While Aquinas asserts that natural law limits the latitude of kings in making their decisions, the notion of autonomous individuals with preordained rights is absent from Aquinas' thought. As d'Entreves comments,

> The emphasis is on natural law, not on natural rights. What is stressed is the duty of the state rather than the rights of the individual . . . In fact, it is not from the individual that we are asked to start, but from the Cosmos, from the notion of a world well ordered and graded, of which natural law is the expression. (1970, p. 49)

Within a few centuries, the individual would loom far larger on the philosophical horizon. Rather than deriving the function of the individual from the nature of the cosmos or community, philosophers would begin to search for the function of the natural and social worlds in the nature of the individual. The dogma of Aquinas had gradually replaced the dogma of Augustine, but by the fifteenth century, neither dogma could withstand the competition of an emerging worldview. Philosophers often refer to Machiavelli as the founder of modern political philosophy for a variety of reasons. From the perspective of the social theory presented here, the decisive characteristic of the philosophy of Machiavelli that distinguishes it from its predecessors is its individualism: with Machiavelli, Luther, and Hobbes one finds that the locus of philosophical attention is no longer society, and the object of moral concern is moving from community to individual. MacIntyre makes the point in relation to Machiavelli and Luther:

> Machiavelli and Luther mark in different ways the break with the hierarchical, synthesizing society of the Middle Ages, and the distinctive moves into the modern world. In both writers there appears a figure who is

273

absent from moral theories in periods when Plato and Aristotle dominate it, the figure of "the individual." In both Machiavelli and Luther, from very different points of view, the community and its life are no longer the arena in which the moral life is lived out. (P. 121)

The Machiavellian individual seeks power and security. Morals are simply means to these ends. Machiavelli is not without his communalistic sentiments: many of his ultimate aims are nationalistic, and one can sense throughout his works the pain he feels at the disunity of Italy. Machiavelli's was a first step toward individuated collectivism, though as any parent knows, first steps are always hesitant, and apprehensively undertaken.

Luther, too, was an ambivalent individualist. The morality he preached was the same altruistic value system the Bible had mandated for centuries, and the self-abnegatory tendencies of Protestantism were almost as severe as, if not more severe than ascetic elements of Catholicism. Yet Luther's religious vision added an element that was revolutionary: the belief that each individual is free to interpret the Scripture on his own. A second, and equally individualistic aspect of his teaching is the doctrine of justification by faith. Luther argued that one's place in heaven is secured, not by outward acts of altruism, but by inner devotion. This marks a turn toward individuated collectivism in two ways. First, the demotion of good works (i.e., altruistic actions) to an epiphenomenon of faith ipso facto rendered one's duties to others less important. Secondly, works are publicly verifiable, whereas faith is subjective and accessible only to the individual. Goodness is thus an inner characteristic that only the individual can judge; the community has lost its power to ascribe good and evil.

The most decisive move toward individuated collectivism was the philosophy of the social contract, especially that of Hobbes. Even this was an ambivalent move, and the early liberals seemed hardly aware that they were enunciating a new moral vision. But they were.

Commentators on Hobbes have often argued that he does not propose a theory of ethics, that he is a hedonist, not a moral philosopher.[1] Yet a careful reading of Hobbes suggests that, in fact, his hedonism *is* a moral philosophy. In the *Leviathan* he asserts:

> For Morall Philosophy is nothing else but the Science of what is *Good,* and *Evill* . . . *Good,* and *Evill,* are names that signifie our Appetites, and Aversions; which in different tempers, customes, and doctrines of men, are different. (1968, p. 216)

---

[1] The doctrine of ethical egoism has always been the black sheep of moral philosophy, and many philosophers have even thrown it out of the litter. (For reviews of philosophical conceptions of ethical egoism, see Machan, 1979; Regis, 1980.) As I argued in Chapter 3, this is the result of muddled thinking. Morality means an ultimate judgment of the good, of a person's *summum bonum,* and nothing in the nature of the thing requires that this be equivalent to the good of others or the good of the group.

For Hobbes, natural law is divine law, and it commands the individual to secure his own preservation. To guarantee one's life and "commodious living," the individual must contract into a state. Thus, Hobbes derives all social life and government from the needs and rights of the individual. Humans are not, as Aristotle contends, social by nature: they are solitary creatures who only have truck with one another for egoistic purposes.

A pure egoism of this sort, however, was too radical for a person of the seventeenth century, and Hobbes argued that reason and natural law also prescribe the golden rule, "that no one should do unto another that which he would consider inequitable for the other to do unto him" (Hobbes, 1972, p. 73). When passions are relatively silent and reason is intact, a person will come to recognize his natural duty or law. Seldom, however, is she or he not stirred by desire, and no one always reasons correctly. For this reason the individual in civil society needs an absolute sovereign to delineate good and evil. Whereas the individual in the state of nature interprets natural law for himself, the member of civil society must obey the sovereign, who is the ultimate authority on moral matters. Thus, from the premise of the sovereign individual, Hobbes deduces the sovereign state. Hobbes's thought, like all liberal political philosophy, marks a transition from one moral view to another, from a belief in the value and power of the collectivity or its representative to a belief in the value and power of the individual. That Hobbes lived in a society whose "social structure" or culture real was in the early phases of revolutionary change should not be surprising in view of his ethical ambivalence. Culture real and ideal are distinct only in theory.

In the seventeenth and eighteenth centuries the notion of a social contract flourished. Many of the major moral and political philosophies at the time were concerned to paper over the conflict between individual and society that was becoming so salient as feudalism gave way to capitalism and the seeds of industrialization began to take root. Locke and the Cambridge Platonists, like Hobbes (and Plato), likened morality to mathematics: through proper reasoning, everyone would arrive at the same moral truth, and this truth or law of nature, as in Locke, equates altruism and long-run self-interest. In all facets of eighteenth-century Western culture, in the midst of communally collectivistic systems of belief as old as human life, "the individual" began to make his appearance in a morality play with a changing script. The rise of the novel, with its portrayal of "the problems of individuals in society" (Harris, 1968, p. 17), can hardly be divorced from this new individualism. In the novels as well as the philosophical works of Rousseau, for example, one finds in as poignant a fashion as conceivable the conflict between the needs of individual and community. Rousseau was torn between the desires for autonomy and submergence which Pye so ably describes in his study of political modernization in

Burma (1962), and which Weinstein and Platt (1969) characterize as prominent in Rousseau, the French Revolution, and the Enlightenment in general. At one moment Rousseau may sound like Emerson, whereas in the next he can be mistaken for Fichte or Comte. Judith Shklar, a recent interpreter of Rousseau, argues that Rousseau proposed two incompatible and alternative utopias, one of the private man and the other of the totally public man, the Spartan who devotes his life to the public weal (Shklar, 1969).

The link between these two models, for Rousseau as for Plato, is the lawgiver whose genius expresses and directs the public will. For both Plato and Rousseau, the prototype of this great man is Lycurgus, the mythical founder of Sparta, upon whose brilliance rested a *polis* in which mothers would shed no tears for sons who died in defense of the motherland. In Rousseau one perceives the fine line between narcissism and collectivism, between idealization of the all-powerful, all-valuable individual and the omnipotent, all-important collectivity, which has led some commentators to view Rousseau as the grandfather of Hitler.

Deep within the human heart, asserts Rousseau, lies a divinely implanted morality. Primitives in a presocial state of nature could apprehend this moral law directly. Rousseau conceives of natural man as a being motivated by self-interest and a natural compassion or "pity" that gives him pain to perceive the misfortune of another sentient being. Society has now corrupted and eliminated this man, but through reason one can rediscover the moral truth within one's breast. One notices in this account a changing conception of the nature of human desire. Alongside the desires vilified since Plato and Christian philosophy are natural passions that promote altruism. One finds similar ideas in the work of several of Rousseau's contemporaries, such as Hume and Adam Smith. As Rorty (1982) has observed, in previous times "the passions" were considered "the poor relations of the mind . . . ." (p. 160), to be kept in check by reason and will. With developing individualism, even such a private, frequently disruptive force started to lose some of its more malevolent connotations.

In England in the nineteenth century the liberalism that began with the social contract was transformed into utilitarianism. Bentham, like Hobbes, argued that pleasure and pain are the only possible criteria of good and evil. For Bentham and the early utilitarians, pleasures were seen as quantitative and commensurable, so that one could conceive of comparing the utility of various proposals by comparing units of utility or "utils." The best social policy is thus one that maximizes utility, providing the greatest good for the greatest number. While certainly a liberal himself, Bentham argued that the notion of "natural rights" propounded by liberal philosophers – the idea that human beings possess inalienable, unabridgeable rights – is philosophical nonsense.

J.S. Mill altered Benthamite utilitarianism in essentially two ways. First, he moved somewhat in the direction of believing that not all pleasures are commensurable, asserting that some pleasures are "higher" than others.[1] Secondly, he placed more positive value upon the development of the individual, which meant that he had to reconcile two potentially conflicting aims: the development of the individual and the good of other individuals (the greatest good for the greatest number). As in all liberal philosophy one finds in the utilitarians an inability to come to grips with potential conflicts between individual and communal aims. To move from the statement that everyone desires his own happiness to the statement that everyone should desire the happiness of the greatest number – even above his own – is problematic, and to reconcile a concept of individual growth with a communalistic ethic requires a far more adequate recognition of the problem than the utilitarians demonstrated.

A final school of thought in the last two centuries relevant to the present argument is existentialism. With Kierkegaard one encounters the view that the individual, in good Protestant fashion, must commune with God by himself. In this sense Kierkegaard's philosophy is individualistic, although the value system he embraces is that propounded in the Bible. Nietzsche makes a further, and more violent, step toward an unabashed individualism. For Nietzsche, Christian morality is a slave morality that sacrifices men of greatness to the resentful, swinish multitude. The truly noble man, the "superman," is a proud, volatile, aristocratic fellow whose grandfather is Aristotle's magnanimous man. The difference between Nietzsche's and Aristotle's visions of the great man is that for Aristotle, the great-souled man is moral within the context of the social whole. Nietzsche's superman, in contrast, is not a social creature; he uses other people as he would use a washcloth. The reader should recognize in this philosophy the essence of pure individuated collectivism, in which others are extensions, or tools for the use of the self. In Nietzsche the concept of

[1] This idea is, in a sense, a precursor to the notion developed here of a hierarchy of needs. Yet if one were to consider the impact of a view of hierarchically arranged desires upon a Millian utilitarian ethic, the results would be quite interesting. For example, if one assumes that different people in a society may have different levels of set-goals, then utilitarianism would argue against equality. To equalize material welfare of a rich person and a poor person would generally provide the latter with a far higher level of happiness than the former. A utilitarianism informed by the psychological theory proposed here would thus probably view justice as two-tiered: one "tier" would pay cognizance to the differential distribution of various sorts of goods required to produce an egalitarian distribution of "happiness," and the other would attempt to raise the level of need and set-goals of those less fortunate to approach those of greater fortune.

"society" or "community" as a positive value has dropped out entirely. Even Nietzsche, however, cannot tolerate the thought of the individual whose sole moral aim is pleasure: the superman is a creature who must continually "overcome" himself, stifle his animal nature, and perennially put himself through painful trials. The end result of his philosophy is thus not altogether far from ascetic Protestantism.

The early Sartre provides perhaps the best example to date of unalloyed individually collectivistic morality. For Sartre, "Hell is the other." To participate in social life is to sacrifice oneself, to become engulfed in a "viscous," slimy realm from which one may never return. Playing a role in society is being-for-others instead of being-for-oneself and constitutes an act of "bad faith" or self-deception. The contrast between this philosophy and the view with which moral philosophy began is dramatic: for the earliest philosophers, to fulfill one's role in society is to behave morally, whereas for Sartre, to play a part in society's farce is the ultimate act of *immorality*, the quintessential sin against oneself.

This brief history of the Western tradition of moral philosophy has obviously been schematic and incomplete. The purpose was not to review the entire history of Western moral philosophy but to illustrate the vast difference between the starting point of ancient moral philosophy and the presuppositions and conclusions of moral philosophers since the rise of individuated collectivism. If one were to pinpoint a particular philosophical tradition that ushers in the new moral view, one would undoubtedly point to liberalism, and to the philosophy of the social contract in particular. The early liberal contractarian thinkers were the reluctant heralds of a new age, marked by a radically different notion of morality and legitimacy. Hobbes, Locke, Rousseau, and their cohorts all grasped that the individual must now be the starting point of a philosophical investigation into the nature of human existence because the type of existence that began to emerge in the seventeenth and eighteenth centuries was of a markedly different nature.

To say that the early liberals "mirrored" the socioeconomic reality of their times is to place an undue priority on a single, though critical variable in a web of synergic causalities. The individual's relationship to culture – real and ideal, including social and economic institutions as well as ideas and ideals – is that of the artist, not the photographer. Many people mirror their culture as precisely as possible, though their artistic technique is often only poorly developed. If the term "culture" appears to be an ideal type bereft of meaning, because no member of any society is entirely "typical," one can in part blame the tools and artistry. Not all art, however, is representational, and some individuals, if not all in some limited way, will portray reality in a manner seemingly "untrue" to the "objective" object but more faithful to the interaction of their playful subjectivity

278

and the universe outside them. Finally, another kind of woman or man – Weber's charismatic leader, Erikson's Gandhi or Luther, perhaps Hegel's world-historical individual or Nietzsche's superman – transcends the object, painting over objective reality itself and creating a new image that others will, faithfully and unfaithfully, transcribe and mingle with their own subjectivity.[1]

In this sense one must view the early liberals as both the observers and the architects of a new epoch and a new consciousness, ushering in the era of individuated collectivism. All started with the premise of individual man, shorn of attachments to family and nation, seeking his own good. This man, however, was nowhere developed in the age of the social contractarians, either in fiction or in fact, and to allow such an individual to survive was intolerable for them. Hobbes, Locke, Rousseau, and even Kant, all accepted, in the beginning, the sovereignty of the individual, but each could only justify this radical presupposition by the morality of the *ancien régime:* none of them could ever have endorsed individualism as a premise if he had not believed the public welfare or the General Will to be the logical conclusion. As Roberto Unger puts it,

> These philosophers whom we usually regard as the deepest exponents of the liberal doctrine – Hobbes, Rousseau, and Kant – may have begun with the program of making the world safe for individuality, but they invariably concluded in one way or another with the defense of the state against the individual, of the species against its members, of universal or abstract against particular or concrete humanity. (1975, p. 163)

The contractarians were caught between two ages with two moralities, and their philosophy betrays their profound ambivalence. Indeed, the liberal notion of reason, by including both self-interest and altruism, masks the fundamental moral contradictions of human existence: self versus other, society versus individual. Hobbes asserts that the law of nature proclaims in one breath both self-preservation and the golden rule; Adam Smith sees the pursuit of self-interest as naturally conducive to the common good; Kant views the individual's reason as the path to his duty to others; Mill justifies individualism on the basis of the greatest good to the greatest number. Only the existentialists accept the individual as both aim and object, but even Sartre retreats into Marxism, warding off pathological narcissism and the transition from philosophy to insanity.

In individuated collectivism, then, culture real is more complex and differentiated, and individual desires become legitimate and moral. Society becomes an extension or agglomeration of individuals, not a morally charged totality, though it may still command some feelings of attachment. Such a society does not yet exist in pure form, and one may wonder

---

[1] I am speaking, of course, of a continuum, not of a typology.

whether or not it could exist at all. For the past few centuries, however, humankind has been moving in this direction, and the trend has accelerated in the present century.[1]

Synthetic Collectivism

Nothing guarantees that individuated collectivism will be carried through to its logical extreme. As Karl Popper (1957) maintains, the social scientist must be careful to avoid mistaking trends for laws. At this point, to suggest a form of cultural organization beyond individuated collectivism is merely to present a logical possibility. The "stage" of *synthetic collectivism* by no means necessarily implies an abolition of private property, nor a withering away of the state, nor a Marcusean genital utopia. Nor, for that matter, is a society approaching the ideal type ever likely to exist. The synthetically collectivistic culture is one that recognizes the legitimacy of both collectivity and individual, of sociality and self-interest. Neither society nor the individual is consistently conceived as a means to an end; the Kantian categorical imperative is extended to both. In such a society the foundation of social cohesion is dual: self-interest and group feeling both

---

[1] One could make an interesting, though highly speculative evolutionary argument compatible with the hypothesized movement from communitarian to individuated collectivism. Biological evolutionists now reject the view that natural selection occurs between species, looking instead at competition between individuals or genes (with some even suggesting sperm-to-sperm combat in the quest for the golden egg). The reason for this rejection of "group selection" is that group selection could only occur in species that are geographically and ecologically isolated, in which case the group or species could battle as a unit to maintain its niche. This condition, however, is unusual since most species are larger and more territorially dispersed. Even if reciprocal altruism develops (Trivers, 1971), in most species "cheating" can lead an individual to greater reproductive success. For example, the argument for a standard biological approach to human evolution would suggest that an individual who pretended to do his share for his mates but really stole food and raped clandestinely would reproduce more than his honest fellows. The problem with this standard individualist approach is that at a certain point in hominid evolution, selection begins to operate on the cultural level, and group selection does start to occur. (For discussions of cultural selection, see Lumsden and Wilson, 1981; Boehm, 1982, and Durham, 1982.) A society without "cheaters" could easily supplant a group with members who lived by the laws of the jungle. Human groups are relatively stable, and warfare occurs between groups. In a hunter-gatherer society, group-centered values are generally "adaptive" for protecting against the vagaries of food collection and hunting, and for making war. If a neighboring tribe attacks, a group with strong solidarity may survive, while one with an "every person for himself" mentality would quickly perish. At a certain historical point, however, greater individuation may come to benefit the group. The correlation between technological development and individuation in the last few centuries may not be accidental. Interestingly, Charles Darwin comments in *The Descent of Man*, his work on human evolution, that the "so-called self-regarding virtues . . . have never really been esteemed by savages, though now highly appreciated by civilised nations." He adds that "actions were regarded by savages and were probably so regarded by primeval man, as good or bad, solely as they obviously affect the welfare of the tribe, – not that of the species, nor that of the individual member of the tribe" (1905, pp. 488-9).

contribute to cultural integration,[1] though obviously conflict between them will never be eliminated.

So much for sweet reveries. Humanity will be lucky enough to survive the current century, let alone muse of a culture that could simultaneously affirm individual liberty and collective sentiment. The diachronic model proposed here suggests that the culture ideal of human societies is rapidly shifting from communitarian to individuated collectivism. With communitarian collectivism, morality is defined in terms of the group. In the primary variety this group is not clearly differentiated from nature and self. In the secondary form such differentiation has proceeded, but with it comes a universal denigration of individual desire. With individuated collectivism the locus of value and power shifts from the collectivity to the individual. Rather than individuals being conceived as means to societal ends, society begins to be viewed as a necessary vehicle for the satisfaction of individual desire.

If the relationship between the model of personality of Part I and that of culture presented in Part II appears simply to be one of analogy, the reader has been deliberately misled for the sake of theoretical clarity. The attempt has been made to create two plausible, logically consistent, largely independent models, one of personality and moral development at the individual level and the other of the evolution of several aspects of cultural differentiation and morality at the collective level. In truth, the two models must be integrable, just as the models of the structure and dynamics of personality and of culture must be as intertwined theoretically as the reality they depict. Part III will now attempt such a synthesis.

---

[1] One could "read Durkheim" to make him consistent with the analysis here, viewing synthetic narcissism and organic solidarity, for example, as isomorphic, and "finding" a similarity between individuated collectivism and anomie. This practice of reading one's own ideas into a thinker is common in social science and philosophy (and has undoubtedly been done in this book as well) and often passes for humility. Quite the contrary, it generally represents displaced narcissism. When author X extols the brilliance of author Y for having discovered in an earlier age that which only now author X is making explicit, X is really saying in a socially acceptable form, "My ideas sure are brilliant!" Kohut's concept of the "idealizing transference" (1968) is clearly relevant here. For a mild amusement, the reader should see Lévi-Strauss's attempt (1962, pp. 99-104) to "read" Rousseau as the first structuralist. As Jane Loevinger (1976b) has put it, scientists are like lovers: they find signs of their beloved everywhere.

III Personality and Culture: A Synthesis

8 Culture and Personality: Dying Species or Vigorous Hybrid?

IN ONE OF the most impressive essays ever written on the common ground between psyche and society, Malinowski comments,

> The problem of the relation between group and individual is so pervading and ubiquitous that it cannot be treated detached from any question of culture and of social or psychological process. A theory which does not present and include at every step the definitions of individual contributions and of their integration into collective action stands condemned. (1939, p. 962)

The aim of Part III is to integrate the theory of personality of Part I and the theory of culture of Part II to move a step closer, albeit a small step, to the fulfillment of Malinowski's prescription. The present chapter will begin by reviewing past and present approaches to the study of personality and culture. Chapter 9 will examine the relationship between psychic and sociocultural structure and dynamics, placing the model of set-goals, affects, and control mechanisms in cultural context. Chapter 10 will discuss the psychology of communitarian collectivism. Chapter 11 will explore the psychodynamics of modernization, and Chapter 12 will examine some aspects of personality and social change, reinterpreting data relating to a crisis surrounding a ritual in changing times in Java. Chapter 13 explores the relation between personal identity and cultural integration, and the final chapter examines the psychology of individuated collectivism, concluding with some comments on morality and individuation.

The Totem-Pole-Is-a-Symbolic-Penis Approach

One can find historical antecedents to any school of thought; all contemporary ideas are, no doubt, a detailed footnote to Plato, and Plato's thought is probably itself a footnote to some magnificent anonymous australopithecine. Similarly, one could cite Rousseau's *Discourses,* Darwin's *Expression of Emotions in Man and Animals,* or Wundt's volumes on *Folk Psychology* as early works on culture and personality, but the field began in earnest with

285

the publication of Freud's *Totem and Taboo* in 1913. The tradition Freud originated in culture and personality can be conveniently called the "totem-pole-is-a-symbolic-penis" approach. This is perhaps too snide since Freud made some tremendously incisive observations, but it calls attention to the fact that Freud and his early anthropological disciples began thumbing through Frazer's *Golden Bough* (1922) and traveling to Australia only with the intent of finding sexual imagery and the Oedipus complex behind all social institutions and primitive beliefs. This was necessarily so because Freud's psychological theory posited that the actions and beliefs of the normal adult are best understood as sublimations of sexual and aggressive drives; if this is true, then the collection of the actions and beliefs of an aggregate of people – i.e., culture – must ipso facto be one vast sublimation.

Assuming that ontogeny recapitulates phylogeny, Freud began *Totem and Taboo* with the assumption that "savages" must be like children; children, in turn, are like neurotics because neurotics are fixated at childish levels of functioning. Freud's equation of savages, neurotics, and children was not simply based upon deductive reasoning; it rested upon some uncanny similarities that haunt anthropologists to this day. In particular, Freud observed the similarity between the omnipotence of thought and the animism of children (which Piaget would later develop; see also Jahoda, 1958), and two characteristics of many preliterate societies: the ascription of intention to inanimate aspects of the environment and the practice of magical rites believed to control natural phenomena. Freud argued that just as the individual passes through narcissism to a stage of object finding to maturity, society similarly passes through animistic, religious, and scientific stages. Freud's evolutionary thinking was hampered by his reliance upon English evolutionist anthropology which had already been thoroughly debunked by Boas and the American anthropologists with whose work Freud was not familiar.

Freud sought to explain in *Totem and Taboo* the relationship between totemism and exogamy, arguing that the two bases of totemism are the prohibition against killing the totem animal and the proscription of incest. These two prohibitions, he noted, are symbolically identical to the main features of the Oedipus complex, the thwarted desire to kill and replace the father and the frustrated desire to sleep with the mother. In the course of arguing for this symmetry, Freud made some profound observations about the ambivalence that lies behind taboos (and behind "joking relationships," which would later be elaborated by Radcliffe-Brown). In trying to connect the two levels of analysis, however, he resorted to mythmaking that could rival anything in *The Golden Bough*. In summarizing Freud's theory of the origin of culture, Evans-Pritchard begins, "Once upon a time – the tale deserves a fairy-story opening – when men were more or less apelike creatures, the dominant father-male of the horde kept all of the females for himself" (1965, p. 42). The "sons" in this Darwinian horde one day rebelled against the dominion of the father, proceeded to kill him, and, "cannibal savages as they were" (Freud, 1913, p. 142), to make a meal of him. Afterwards they felt remorse, and the event made such a strong impression on humankind (actually, mankind) that the memory of this event found its way, in good Lamarckian fashion, into our genetic makeup. The brothers then forbade incest, declaring it taboo.

Taboos, Freud continues, are like neurotic touching phobias, so culture, in the last analysis, becomes a collective neurosis which preempts the need for personal neuroses (p. 73). As civilization progresses, so does repression (p. 97), which implies, as Freud later developed in *Civilization and its Discontents* (1930), that civilization entails a progressively greater burden of repression on the individual. Freud assumed that "uncivilized" peoples, in contrast, are totally uninhibited (see 1913, p. 161).

As noted before, if one does not mind panning for gold in murky waters, Freud's anthropological thought contains numerous brilliant nuggets. The similarity between phobias and taboos, for example, is striking and leads one to wonder about possible similarity of function. Somewhat less can be said for the theoretical creations of Freud's orthodox anthropological disciples, notably Geza Roheim. Roheim was determined to look for genitals behind every loincloth, and needless to say, he was never disappointed. According to Roheim (1943), culture is caused by delayed infancy: it arises as a defense mechanism against infantile traumas and represents "the colossal efforts made by a baby who is afraid of being left alone in the dark" (p. 131). Finding self-evident Freud's assumption of the "structural and fundamental identity of neurosis and civilization" (p. 29), Roheim argues, foreshadowing later approaches to culture and personality, that every culture has its own "ontogenetic trauma," and that each culture type is determined by that particular conflict area created by its infant-rearing practices. From this he proceeds to reduce every aspect of culture, from myth to money, to primitive sexual issues. For example, he informs the reader that "a mutual mother-child situation underlies trade," and thus "trade partners are united by the umbilical cord" (pp. 67-8), and that "the reverence paid to cattle is due to Father Bull and Mother Cow" (p. 86). His explanation of the origins of agriculture is worth quoting, if for no other reason than as a warning against our tendency to become bewitched by our own metaphors and paradigms:

> Evidently "defloration" refers to the breaking of the ground and the big vulva means deep planting. We may now suggest that the unconscious meaning of taking roots out of the ground was originally the body destruction phantasy of pulling "good body contents" out of the mother's body and that the restitution phase of this phantasy led, by chance, to the origin of the cultivation of these plants. (pp. 73-4)

287

The Cultural Configuration Approach

The orthodox Freudian approach to culture and personality, then, proved untenable, though later offshoots of the psychoanalytic position have proven far more useful. The second major theoretical tradition in the culture and personality field is the "configurational" or "culture pattern" approach, which later grew into the "national character" literature that flourished during the Second World War. This tradition is associated with the students of Boas, especially Margaret Mead and Ruth Benedict. Boas had emphasized, in his studies of cultural diffusion among the North American Indians (1940), that cultures *selectively* borrow from each other, and that the selection mechanism must be viewed in psychological terms.

This was the starting point for the configurational approach, the most representative example of which is probably Benedict's *Patterns of Culture* (1934). For Benedict, as for all the configurational theorists, "The life history of the individual is first and foremost an accommodation to the patterns and standards traditionally handed down in the community" (p. 2). The cultural configuration perspective emphasizes the extent to which culture molds the individual and his personality, and it thus pays special attention to socialization as the key to transmission of culture. Culture, in this view, determines not only motivation but cognition: "No man ever looks at the world with pristine eyes. He sees it edited by a definite set of customs and institutions and ways of thinking" (p. 2).

As LeVine (1973) emphasizes in referring to the configurational approach as the "culture-is-personality" view, the theorists of this persuasion saw personality as largely a reflection of culture. According to Benedict, ". . . the great mass of individuals take quite readily the form that is presented to them" (1934, p. 235). Benedict argues that individual and group are neither separable nor mutually antagonistic. She recognizes, however, that some individuals become "deviants" because they cannot adjust to the particular culture pattern. A metaphor one could use to describe the view of individual and society in the configurational approach is that culture is a sculptor which chisels away at the individual until he or she conforms to its ideal pattern. Some rocks, however, are recalcitrant to sculpture, and they ultimately remain unfinished slabs or become broken and deformed by the hammer of the frustrated artist.

Benedict's theory is configurational in the sense that she sees every culture as characterized by some internal ordering principle, pattern, or configuration. A given culture selects traits from the "great arc" of possibilities (p. 21). Culture, like personality, is ordered and cohesive: "A culture, like an individual, is a more or less consistent pattern of thought and action" (p. 42). Like other configurational theorists, Benedict argues that what "really binds men together is their culture, – the ideas and the stan-

288

dards they have in common" (p. 14). In *Patterns of Culture* she provides examples of three kinds of culture, Dionysian (characterized by excess), Apollonian (emphasizing self-control), and paranoid, though she does not believe this to be an exhaustive list of cultural types. During the Second World War, a number of anthropologists conducted, sans fieldwork, studies of large-scale urban societies, largely America's enemies, searching for patterns referred to as "national character." (For a thorough review of this literature, see Inkeles and Levinson, 1969.)

Four main problems confront the configurational approach. First, it tends to assume that the only needs operative in culture are those of the group, so that the needs of the individual are given little theoretical attention. This is related to the second problem, the assumption of the child as passive recipient of culture. As Edward Sapir (another student of Boas who placed more emphasis on the individual's reactions to socialization) argues, culture is "gradually and gropingly discovered" (1934) by the individual, not just imposed from above. Thirdly, as LeVine (1973) points out, the configurationist view exaggerates the extent to which cultures are consistent and integrated. Finally, it assumes an "ideal congruence" (Inkeles and Levinson, 1969) between personality and culture that may not exist in a given culture. In other words, the configurationist position assumes a perfect "fit" between personality and culture.

The Personality Mediation Approach

The third approach to culture and personality LeVine (1973) calls the "personality mediation" approach because personality is seen as mediating between social institutions (notably child-rearing practices) and cultural expressions of personality. This view was first enunciated by Abram Kardiner (1945), a psychoanalyst who collaborated with anthropologist Ralph Linton. Kardiner distinguishes between "primary institutions," which are the child-rearing practices of a society, and "secondary institutions," which include religion, folklore, and related institutions (p. 29). Primary institutions create a "basic personality structure" in individuals, and part of this personality structure, common to the members of the society, is a "projective system" which creates the secondary institutions (p. 25). Projective systems are "excrescences developed from nuclear traumatic experiences . . ." (p. 39); in other words, conflictual issues or traumatic early experiences create pockets of emotionally charged beliefs, fantasies, and wishes, which in turn become translated into cultural myths, legends, and beliefs. One should note the similarity between Kardiner's model and the models of two other theorists: Roheim and Marx. Like Roheim, he sees cultural traits as products of early traumas. Like Marx, he sees personality and culture as products or reflections of social structure (which at times he seems to include with child rearing under the rubric of primary institutions). "The social order, and its institutions," he writes, "is the source of all projective systems . . ." (p. 44). He continues:

> The fantasy or projective screen hides social realities, and one cannot come to grips with them because the fantasy screen itself becomes the chief object of preoccupation and is mistaken for the reality to be dealt with. (P. 45)

The above passage is fully consonant with Marx's analysis of the way conflicts in the "infrastructure" produce a "superstructure" which is only an imaginary, reified realm that serves to make social life "opaque." Kardiner's formulation also has a Durkeimian ring (as well it should, because his collaborator, Linton, was heavily influenced by functionalism), claiming that religious conceptions mirror social realities. In some ways, Kardiner's theory is an attempted reconciliation (though not necessarily an intentional one) of Durkheim, Marx and Freud: like Durkheim, it sees cultural phenomena as manifestations of social life; like Marx, it stresses tensions in the social structure; and like Freud, it emphasizes tensions in child rearing that create fixations.

In a classic work, John Whiting and Irvin Child (1953) elaborated Kardiner's model in order to test a number of hypotheses about the relationship between child rearing and personality. Whiting and Child were originally part of the interdisciplinary group at the Yale Institute of Human Relations whose aim, manifest in Whiting and Child's *Child Training and Personality* (1953), was to combine psychoanalysis and Hullian learning theory, and to integrate the psychological theory with anthropological data. Whiting and Child performed statistical analyses of data from seventy-five cultures using the Human Relation Area Files to test correlations between initial indulgence and severity of socialization and certain cultural beliefs about disease. For example, they found statistically significant correlations between severity of socialization for aggression and the belief that illness results from aggressive acts, such as aggression against spirits or the use of magical weapons (p. 153).

The model they employed to explain their data is similar to Kardiner's. They argued that "maintenance systems" (economic, political, and social institutions) produce child training practices, which in turn create "personality variables" (they do not ever speak of personality per se; personality remains a black box in this analysis), which ultimately produce projective systems (beliefs about supernaturals, myths, art, etc.).

Over the last twenty-five years Whiting and his associates have altered the model slightly. In its most recent form, the model begins with an interaction of a culture's environment and history, which produces maintenance systems. Ecological variables have thus gained in importance. The maintenance system, in turn, produces the child's learning environment, which interacts with innate propensities to produce an adult, who then creates "projective-expressive systems" (Whiting & Whiting, 1975). This model is titled, significantly, "A Model for Psycho-Cultural Research," as opposed to "A General Model of Culture and Personality." This underscores two issues. First, Whiting and his colleagues are interested in operationalizing their concepts, and of all the researchers in the social sciences, they are among the most successful in combining articulate constructs with meaningful empirical investigations. The work of John and Beatrice Whiting and their colleagues has contributed substantially to our understanding of cross-cultural child development.

Secondly, Whiting and his colleagues have moved farther away from speaking of "personality" at all; in this sense they have drifted closer to cognitive-behavioral psychology and farther from psychoanalysis. This move seems to reflect as much a lack of a sophisticated alternative to Freudian personality theory as it does a commitment to social learning theory. Whiting remains psychodynamic in the sense that he continues to view projective systems as culturally-determined "neurotic" defenses to avoid idiosyncratic personal neuroses. Over the years, however, he has come to view Freudian psychosexual theory, with its emphasis on toilet training, for example, as far less useful than Freudian notions like defense mechanisms. As opposed to the psychosexual theory, he believes that "the real game is learning to behave socially . . ." (Whiting, personal communication). This is an especially significant shift since it is born of both field experience and correlational studies by a researcher originally committed to both learning theory and psychoanalysis.

The contributions of the Whitings and their colleagues cannot be overestimated. In particular, their Six Culture Study (see Whiting and Whiting, 1975) provides an extraordinary comparison of different approaches to socialization and the effects of these on personality. The Whitings have used a multitude of methods, including field observation, interviewing, quantitative and qualitative coding of directly observed practices, and correlational research to document the impact of ecological variables and child-rearing practices on personality and culture. Nevertheless, at the theoretical level, the Whiting model, like that of Kardiner, suffers from a number of defects. Perhaps most significantly, it is only a partial model, in two senses. It is partial, first, in that it must rely upon other theories for hypotheses; it cannot, for example, furnish hypotheses about the relationship between child rearing and religious symbolism because it lacks a theory of personality development. While the model can assert that maintenance systems affect child-rearing practices, or that these practices influence personality processes, it cannot explain how or why this occurs. Specific hypotheses (e.g., severe infant rearing contributes to the production and maintenance of polarized religious cosmologies; see Lambe and

Westen, 1983) must be derived from other theories that explain the mechanisms by which environmental stimuli affect personality. Whiting has recognized this all along, and in *Child Training and Personality* he and Child explicitly stated that they were plugging into the model hypotheses from learning theory and psychoanalysis.

The model is incomplete in another, more important way. While Whiting acknowledges that causal arrows may occasionally run in the opposite direction from those proposed in the model, the model fails to account for the reciprocally causal relationship between values and social structure. Whether value changes always precede or follow social structural (culture real) changes is an open matter, but what is clear is that ideals about the way society should operate affect its modus operandi. Once values are produced, they act as a guide for action; if the group deviates too far from its ideals, control mechanisms are likely to be activated to bring ideals and actuality back into "equilibrium." An example that would prove difficult to explain from the Whiting's model would be the Russian Revolution: surely changes in early socialization cannot account for the Marxist ideals of the Bolshevik leaders, who then shaped society in accordance with their ideals. In the Whitings' system, ideals are products of child rearing, which, once produced, seem to influence only the projective system. The Whitings' projective system, like Kardiner's secondary institutions, confounds two aspects of personality and culture. The first includes those "expressions" or "projections" of personality that are functionally inert, like Rorschach responses; once produced, they accumulate, but they do not motivate action. The second includes values and ideals that are not simply "expressions" which fulfill their cathartic function and then drop out of the system. Values, unlike expressive "excrescences" or "projections," are dynamic. Aside from its incompleteness, as the example of the Russian Revolution suggests, the model also has difficulty explaining change. Cultural change may be much more rapid than changes in socialization practices, which suggests other mechanisms operative in the creation of culture.

An additional problem, as LeVine (1973) notes, is that the division of culture into aspects that are utilitarian ("instrumental") and thus causal and those that are expressive and thus noncausal does not withstand close scrutiny. Many child-rearing practices have expressive (e.g., magical) components, and many "projective" beliefs have utilitarian or social structural components (e.g., rituals associated with supernatural beliefs). If, for example, a parent places a heavy cross on the neck of her child because she believes the cross will frighten away demons, one cannot maintain that the practice of placing the cross on the child's neck, as in the model, was determined by the ecology and social structure, while the belief is a projection of individual conflicts. Beliefs and actions are intertwined. This is a similar objection to that raised earlier against Marvin Harris's model.

The Kardiner/Whiting model is, further, too psychologically reductionistic. It suggests that symbolic culture is like the Rorschach protocol of the average member of a society. (One is reminded here of the family therapy assessment practice of administering a set of TAT cards to a family and making them agree on a response; see Handel, 1967.) Myth, art, and religion do not, however, only express the tensions and conflicts of the individual: they reflect and mediate, as well, tensions within the structure of social relations. Swanson (1960) found statistically significant correlations between certain forms of social structure/group composition and religious beliefs, irrespective of child-rearing practices, which he interpreted, following Durkheim, as demonstrating that supernatural beliefs are symbolic representations of group structure. Between Whiting and Swanson lies a multifunctionalist approach that allows for the presence of both individually (and frequently reiterative) and socially derived representations.

Finally, as noted by LeVine (1973), the Whiting model postulates an unmediated ecological effect, which ignores the extent to which ecological issues become relevant only by being cognized (cf. Rappaport, 1979). In fact, the place of cognition is highly ambiguous in this model. In the Whitings' latest model, cognition must be an individual process, which is caused by child rearing, but which (like projective aspects of personality) is largely inert. This model provides no mechanism through which cognition affects the maintenance system. It also fails to account for collective cognitions or shared "paradigms."

Darwin Meets Oedipus

The fourth major approach to culture and personality research is Robert LeVine's (1973) synthesis of Freudian psychology and neo-Darwinian evolutionism. Culture, for LeVine, is an organization of ideas and rules, and personality mediates between environment and behavior. LeVine distinguishes three hierarchically related personality processes: behavior, personality dispositions (the potential for given behaviors), and personality organization (the overall structure in which dispositions are embedded). He further contrasts personality "genotype," the enduring and idiosyncratic "deep structure" of the individual, which includes ego processes and "motivational residues of early experience" (p. 116); with personality "phenotype," the socially conditioned behavioral patterns of the individual, which also includes a self-concept. Whereas genotype is formed by innate tendencies and early socialization experiences and is fixed by the Oedipal age, phenotype is variable and "reflects the normative consensus of society" (p. 123). Genotype places constraints on later phenotypic development, and while deliberate parental behavior may affect personality phenotype, parental suppression of genotypic traits leads to sublimation, not extinction. Another constraint upon phenotype is social norms. The individual may adapt to these norms through willing conformity or "co-erced conformity," or he may be allowed latitude in choosing norms be-cause of his society's "normative pluralism" (p. 142). Roles (which seem to bridge personality phenotype and social institutions) represent a com-promise-formation of individual genotype and social norms (p. 137).

LeVine's neo-Darwinian argument is that individual behavior is an adaptive response to the social and physical environment, and socialization practices represent a "preadaptation" to future environments (p. 101). An evolutionist argument requires variations in a population and mechanisms of selective retention/duplication of "mutations" (Campbell, 1965). Ac-cording to LeVine, the source of unplanned variation is personality, and the mechanism for selection of personality traits is "provided by the socio-cultural environment in its normative aspect . . ." (p. 105). The mechanism for retaining and duplicating positively selected variations is the cognitive activity and "deliberate socialization acts" of parents. Socialization thus mediates between adult and child, and here the differences between LeVine and Whiting are at their apogee. Whereas for Whiting child training causes personality, which causes cultural manifestations such as values, for Le-Vine, cultural norms also impinge upon adult experience and are trans-lated into socialization practices and ultimately into the personality of the next generation. Thus, whereas Whiting's model is largely linear and uni-directional, LeVine's is recursive.

In general, LeVine points to four loci in the nexus of individual, culture, and ecology at which Darwinian mechanisms of variation and selective retention are operative (pp. 132-4). The first involves the adaptation of early child-care customs to ecological pressures. For example, as Munroe and Munroe (1975) note, cross-cultural evidence suggests that all cultures provide more than the physical minimum of care necessary for infants, and one can suppose that, given high infant mortality rates (at least in techno-logically less advanced societies), cultures that provide inadequate early care perish or change their practices to avoid extinction.

The second area of evolutionary adaptation is that discussed earlier, through which deliberate socialization in response to normative pressures selects personality dispositions from the unplanned variations of personal-ity. This selection process is similar to the process described by Benedict in which culture selects personality traits from the "great arc" of variations.

The third locus of variation and selection occurs in secondary adapta-tions of individual personality to normative environments. What LeVine has in mind here is that the adult is continually conditioned by his social environment to express or suppress aspects of his personality genotype.

This mechanism is similar to social exchange theory, which relates rewards and sanctions on the societal level to positive reinforcement and punishment on the individual level (see Homans, 1961; for a cross-cultural statement of exchange theory, see Gergen et al., 1980).

The final locus of evolution relates to the adaptation of aggregate personality characteristics of populations to normative environments through the selective pressure of social sanctions. LeVine argues that societies reward certain phenotypic traits, so that gradually those traits become more frequent in the culture, and parental norms and socialization practices may even become so routinized that little feedback between socialization methods and social sanctions and rewards is necessary. This latter possibility, he argues, is more typical of societies with low status mobility.

LeVine's model is by far the most sophisticated theory of personality and culture to date, and it is one that anthropologists in the field who are not even particularly interested in personality could profitably use. It addresses a central issue, namely the relationship between ecological conditions and norms, and perhaps its most impressive feature is its applicability to societies that are relatively stable as well as to those that are rapidly changing. The discussion of the relation between socialization practices at the level of concrete individuals and broad social norms is superb, examining parental incentives to socialize children in specific ways. The advantage to this way of thinking is that it allows one to go beyond simple descriptions about how people in more stable societies inculcate cultural values in their children, and to show how people can be induced to alter their beliefs and values in times of rapid social change.

LeVine's approach is deficient in two respects. First, like Whiting's model, LeVine's is incomplete. It relies for its understanding of the dynamics and development of personality upon psychoanalytic theory. This type of reliance on other theories is a problem endemic to the whole field of "culture and personality" and stems from the field's self-conceptualization. Researchers in this area have seen the purpose of their work as to serve as a bridge between conceptualizations of personality and of culture. The problem is that adequate theories of either personality or culture have proven difficult to develop and have therefore not been forthcoming, so that one is left with a bridge without concrete pillars. In other words, a sophisticated theory of culture and personality must be just that: a sophisticated theory of personality, of culture, and of the relation between the two. The probability is not high of developing an adequate bridge theory into which one can plug a variety of models.

A second problem stems from LeVine's acceptance of Freudian personality theory. Psychoanalytic theory asserts that personality is largely formed by the Oedipal age, and in some measure this is certainly true.

295

LeVine depends upon this Freudian hypothesis in his distinction between personality phenotype and genotype. This leads him incorrectly to assume that the conflict between *individual* needs and social requisites is isomorphic with the conflict between *infantile* needs and social requisites. His discussion of the way cultural practices, such as roles, mediate between personal desires and social norms is very insightful, but he underemphasizes the extent to which the group may interfere with *adult* needs that are not reducible to childish desires and precipitates of infantile conflicts. In Western culture earlier in this century, for example, a woman's desire for professional competence would conflict (and still often does) with social norms, and the result could be some form of compromise-formation (e.g., volunteer activity). The woman's desire for competence, however, may not be primarily an infantile wish. Erikson (1963) and others have convincingly shown that human motivations and concerns develop throughout adult life, and one would expect that wishes and desires at any point in the lifespan could conflict with the wishes and desires of others or the needs of collectivities with which the person is connected.

Approaches Past and Present

This review of theories of culture and personality is in no sense exhaustive, though it has attempted to cover the major paradigms. (For a fuller account, see Spiro, 1965; Spindler, 1978; Bourgignon, 1979; Jahoda, 1980; and Klineberg, 1980.) Though no other broad perspective has arisen in culture and personality, a few other approaches and trends deserve brief mention. First, a number of theorists deny any need for culture and personality theory or research. LeVine labels this the "anti-culture-personality" approach, and it includes evolutionists such as Leslie White (1949), who believed in the legitimacy of treating culture "as if it were independent of human beings . . . ." (p. 144), and Durkheim in his more militantly sociological moods. Secondly, the work of McClelland (1962) and his associates on achievement and affiliation motives has fostered much cross-cultural work, although McClelland does not offer a general model of culture and personality. Thirdly, a number of writers have attempted to synthesize the work of Marx and Freud, and although they are rarely considered in accounts of the field of culture and personality, their work has nonetheless been significant (the most important examples of which include Fromm, 1947, 1955; Marcuse, 1955; Weinstein and Platt, 1969, 1973; and Habermas, 1972).

Interest in culture and personality reached its peak in the 1940s and 1950s, and in recent years this interdisciplinary specialty has largely been absorbed into psychological anthropology (Hsu, 1972; Bourgignon, 1978) and cross-cultural psychology (Triandis, 1980). Psychological anthropology attempts to understand personality variables within the context of anthropological data and theory. Cross-cultural pscyhology is a brand new subdiscipline primarily engaged in testing hypotheses developed in Western cultures and adapting experimental procedures to different cultural contexts. A recent six-volume *Handbook of Cross-Cultural Psychology* (Triandis, 1980) has been published, with an emphasis on reviews of empirical studies and descriptive models. This endeavor is likely to prove a welcome corrective to ethnocentric psychological pronouncements on "human nature," and one can expect cross-cultural psychology to find its way into introductory textbooks within the next decade. Many of the general models currently guiding research in cross-cultural psychology are descriptive rather than explanatory, in which the authors draw in as many arrows as possible between ecology, child rearing, cognition, norms, values, social structure, and the like.

An approach receiving significant attention in the *Handbook* is Harry Triandis's theory of "subjective culture" (see Triandis, 1972). Triandis defines subjective culture as "a cultural group's characteristic way of perceiving its social environment" (p. 3), and he goes about trying to find group differences on this dimension. This approach nicely highlights the cultural influence on social cognition frequently unacknowledged by American researchers, though it is problematic in several respects. Triandis's definition of "subjective culture" is inconsistent from one passage to the next. Only one page after the first definition cited above, he defines subjective culture as a cultural group's "characteristic way of perceiving the *man-made* part of its environment" (p. 4, emphasis added). This is totally different from the perception of the social environment because now the definition includes perceptions of tools, art, automobiles, and the like, not just people. A second issue is the failure to distinguish between cognitions and values, so that the latter are viewed as part of the former. This is a typical problem of social cognitive models, which frequently conflate cognition and conation. Triandis views subjective culture as motivational because he defines it as including people's perceptions of social norms and values. He fails to note that, as a general rule, people are motivated by their values, not their perceptions of other people's values. To the extent that they act on their perceptions of other people's values, they manifest a system of moral beliefs or other-need-related set-goals which exhort, "I should act as others tell me to act." This is a particular value system, not a general psychological principle, and individuals and cultures differ on the extent to which people value this kind of conformity.

Thirdly, as Gustav Jahoda notes (1980, pp. 95-6), Triandis fails to distinguish subjective culture as an attribute of individuals and as an attribute of groups. This leaves unclear the issue of the relation of individual to collective cognitive constructs.[1]

Many have argued that culture and personality as a field is heading for a well-deserved obsolescence, to be superseded by its more vigorous offspring, psychological anthropology and cross-cultural psychology. This would be unfortunate for two reasons. First, given the extent to which anthropologists have come to recognize intracultural variation and have found imperative the study of individual decision makers, the need intensifies, not diminishes, for a theory without disciplinary bounds, one that can examine simultaneously individual choices and the cultural context. Secondly, cross-cultural psychology could easily develop in the direction of proliferation of disparate strands of unsystematic research. The empirical study of microprocesses is a fundamental aspect of the accumulation of knowledge, but the significance of such investigations is multiplied a thousandfold when the topics investigated are part of a systematic effort at elucidating, expanding, and/or disconfirming aspects of a larger paradigm. Theoretical elaboration of the relationship between personality and culture thus remains indispensable. As Draguns has commented, "Culture and personality as a research area is by no means moribund and, to paraphrase Mark Twain, the news of its death is highly exaggerated" (1979, p. 138). The remainder of this book is devoted to a theoretical synthesis of the structure, dynamics, and development of personality and culture.

---

[1] Triandis's aims of research and implicit philosophy of social science also lead to a trivializing of his efforts. He expresses his basic aim: "We must develop general or culture-free laws, such as, 'the greater the rewards experienced in an interpersonal relationship, the more positive the affect experienced in the presence of the other person' " (p. 5). If laws such as this are the pot of gold at the end of the social scientific rainbow, then a torrent of research will only produce fool's gold.

9 Psychic and Sociocultural Structure and Dynamics

PERSONALITY DEVELOPS IN the context of culture, just as culture only exists through the thoughts, feelings, and behaviors of concrete people. One would thus expect that the dynamics of individual mental life and action dovetail with the dynamics of cultural life and action. The motives of individual actors press for solutions within the sociocultural context, and the dynamics of culture reciprocally condition both cognitive-evaluative mismatches and methods for their resolution. The present chapter will examine the relationship between the structure and dynamics of personality and of culture. It will first discuss the relation between psychological motives and cultural processes. It will focus in particular on the way culture helps fulfill psychological motives through the patterning of individual and collective responses. Secondly, it will try to show how a single model can account for both stasis and change and will explore evolutionary processes in culture and personality.

Psychological Motives and Cultural Processes

Chapter 2 argued that motivation at the psychological level can be understood in terms of cognitive-affective schemas, and that people form affect-laden set-goals of desired states. A mismatch between the goal or ideal and cognized reality produces an aversive feeling that motivates action. Much of this process can occur without actual affective mediation through cognitive anticipation of affective consequences of actions or through cognitive processes serving a feedback function, as when a person recognizes and corrects minor divergences from a plan, script, or goal.

At the societal level, Chapter 6 proposed that collectivities form set-goals as well, and that divergences from these set-goals similarly evoke control mechanisms to eliminate the mismatch. These set-goals may be moral rules or ideals, desired levels of solidarity, standards for behavior, desired levels of material welfare, or other goals. Collective set-goals need not be represented in the minds of individuals: they may instead be en-

299

coded in rules surrounding ritual performance, so that, for example, intragroup tension sets in motion rituals that heighten solidarity. More often than not, however, these collective set-goals will simultaneously be individual set-goals acquired through socialization and experience. Members of a culture may value the welfare and solidarity of various collective units as ends in themselves, so that collective valuations of social "objects" are converted into personal set-goals. This may occur because the group is an object of attachment, an object of identification, a source of meaning, or a source of satisfaction of self/member-needs. As writers on nationalism have noted, for example (see Guetzkow, 1955; Kelman, 1969), individuals may develop nationalistic sentiments and loyalties and ascribe legitimacy to the nation-state on the basis of either "instrumental" or "expressive" needs. Kelman (1969) argues that the individual may develop loyalty toward the nation-state as a unit because it fulfills his own egoistic needs (e.g., for protection), because it fulfills his needs for participation in a larger collectivity, or both. People can form attachments to groups just as they can to other people, animals, and fantasy objects (such as imaginary playmates, or culturally constructed religious objects). Lee (1957) notes that among the Hopi, "parents have been known deliberately to try to shift a child's affection from concentration upon one family member, to diffusion among the group" (p. 20). This nicely illustrates the continuity of attachment to parents and the larger society of which they are a part, particularly in communally collectivistic societies.

Individuals' set-goals are greatly influenced by cultural valuations, and an important task for cross-cultural empirical research would be to try to document the acquisition of culturally constructed cognitive-affective schemas. A person learns to attach evaluations to cognitive representations of other people, herself, and aspects of reality in ways congruent with collective schemas through processes described in Part I, such as observational learning, modeling, identification, and cognitively mediated conditioning. Evidence reviewed earlier on "social referencing" (Klinnert et al., 1983) suggests that the use of other people's affective responses begins in the first year. Developmental studies have documented the ability of young children to understand the affective significance of other people's facial expressions (Oster, 1981), which is likely to serve a very useful function in helping the child to choose behaviors in the face (so to speak) of minimal experience.

Moral standards and ideals at the individual level are in most cultures largely reconstructed from the supraindividual "collective representations" that have been described here as culture ideal. The internalization of values, moral rules, and ideals is not a mechanical process through which a child gradually reproduces linguistically encoded rules as one might copy a computer file to a tape. Ego ideal set-goals, values, and beliefs are, as Piaget would say, constructed – or, perhaps, one might say, reconstructed – through ritual and interaction as much as through verbal instruction.

Prevailing "value paradigms" may become transformed into psychological values and set-goals in a number of ways. The most direct approach is through the simple teaching of values by authorities whom the person considers legitimate. A second approach is through imitation: the individual follows the example of others and thus gains an often unconscious knowledge of culturally constructed systems of meaning. A third method is the use of positive and negative sanctions for various actions, often coupled with direct exhortations. A fourth is through symbolic forms such as myths and fairy tales. The stories told to children, as McClelland (1962) and others have demonstrated convincingly, express certain value themes a culture imparts to its members. Similarly, Lévi-Strauss, as noted earlier, views myths as mediating between oppositions, and he sees the meaning behind all myths (in the societies described here as communally collectivistic) as "Hell is ourselves," by which he means that failure to do one's duty to kin or group is the root of all evil. The reader familiar with Kuhn's philosophy of science should recognize the similarity between the heuristic use of folklore and mythology and Kuhn's notion of the shared "exemplars" (1970) with which a scientific community socializes its new members. Exemplars, for Kuhn, are shared or collective examples or problem sets which have been solved in a particular way by a scientific community, and which suggest to the members of that community the appropriate way to understand and solve problems. With both scientific paradigms and cultural ideals, conformity to the dominant paradigm occurs through a number of "socialization" techniques such as those outlined above, and seldom will a culture use only one technique to inculcate its creed since multiple techniques provide a greater probability that the paradigm will be followed and learned correctly.

One is reminded here of Lévi-Strauss's discussion of why myths, and oral literature in general, are "so much addicted to duplication, triplication, or quadruplication of the same sequence." He contends that the "function of repetition is to render the structure of myth apparent" (1963, p. 229), that the more the repetition, the greater the probability of communicating the message. Mythic meanings are often themselves a repetition of cultural messages, which may be values or more strictly cognitive schemas or ways of seeing things. Where Lévi-Strauss errs is in concluding that cross-cultural universals in myth suggest inherent properties of mind or brain physiology. The myths he has studied are all products of communitarian collectivist societies, and the universal properties he believes he has discovered are thus properties of that type of society. While some oppositions are inherent in social life, such as the conflict on the individual level between the aims of self and others, or on the societal level, between

301

individual and group, the particular resolution which myth or other aspects of culture generates to mediate that opposition is not an innate property of mind. Lévi-Strauss's fascinating conclusion that the meaning of myth in "primitive" cultures seems to be that "Hell is ourselves" tells us something extraordinarily significant about that kind of culture. It does not, however, tell us anything about the particular resolution of self-other and individual-group conflicts in industrial societies, and if the analysis of individuated collectivism in Chapter 7 has any validity, an entirely different synthesis has begun to emerge in the "modern" world. This suggests, as well, the futility of searching for common denominators among the world's religions for common or "universal" human moral codes. These moral paradigms are uniformly the product of a particular kind of society, and humankind appears to be in the midst of the most fundamental moral revolution in its history, a revolution that is setting on its head the traditional way of "mediating" between person and person which has prevailed since the rise of human groups. Whether this great shift is for better or for worse is another matter altogether.

Culture not only shapes wishes and ideals of individuals, but it is shaped by them as well. As argued in Chapter 6, cultural phenomena are compromise-formations that reflect individual as well as collective needs. Individual action is oriented toward satisfaction of both egoistic and social motives, just as collective action is oriented toward fulfilling needs of social units as well as individuals. One cannot understand the goals people pursue without understanding their social relations, just as one cannot understand cultural institutions, practices, and values divorced from individual motivation. Nor can one simply consider culture an instrument for adaptation (as in Bennett, 1976) because cultural values also *define* adaptation, by prescribing whose interests are to be promoted.

Cultures, like individuals, respond to discrepancies between ideal states and actualities. Since cultures are comprised of individuals, one would expect some congruence of individual and collective set-goals. One would also expect culture to provide patterned responses to mismatches, potential mismatches, and goals that recur across time and person, and indeed this is the case.

At the most obvious level, social institutions such as economic and political organizations, practices, and technology provide institutionalized responses to recurrent problems, such as production, reproduction, and defense. One can see the relation between set-goals and institutions of this sort most clearly when these institutions are changing. Earle (1980) has applied economic theory to production decisions in preindustrial societies, and has argued convincingly that as marginal costs of pursuing particular subsistence strategies change (e.g., through environmental or technological change, resource depletion, etc.), mix of subsistence strategies will shift toward those with lower marginal costs. Earle points out that since the cost of exploiting a resource and its maximum potential yield are both influenced by social organization, changes in group organization may be (consciously or unconsciously) motivated by the desire to make better use of available resources for survival. Smith (1983) has similarly made some interesting arguments about the impact of foraging strategies on social organization. Barth (1956) has shown the impact of both political and economic pressure on the social organization of ethnic groups coexisting in Swat, North Pakistan. He found that in high-altitude areas which were ecologically marginal for one group because of their subsistence mode, political organization was altered and "economized" to compensate (p. 1081).

Culture thus provides institutionalized political and economic arrangements to fulfill various set-goals. It also shapes individuals' responses to affective signals as well as their definition of situations as problematic. Psychological literature on stress, coping, and problem-solving tends to underemphasize the extent to which available options are culturally constructed. John Bennett, in contrast, defines culture as "the precedents that people use to construct patterns of coping" (1976, p. 851). Like Bennett, Christopher Boehm (1983) argues for the importance of what he calls "adaptive problem-solving," through which members of a culture anticipate possible developments and outcomes and select behavior accordingly. This problem-solving is both shaped and constrained by culturally constructed alternatives and definitions of situations.

This can be seen most clearly in the literature on decision making in preindustrial societies. As was argued earlier, much of this literature is limited by a failure adequately to consider the role of culturally mediated constructions of reality and alternatives in individual decision making. The same is true of "optimal foraging" theories, which typically ignore cultural influences on cost-benefit analysis (see Bishop's comment in Smith, 1983). Others who advocate decision models recognize the role of cultural cognitions and values but tend to ignore them because they cannot readily fit into models of rational decision making (see, for example, Earle's switch from speaking of "biological and cultural needs" to "calories needed to maintain the population," 1980, p. 16).

Culture provides decision rules (see Quinn, 1975) for numerous aspects of life, which represent collectively patterned "plans" and "scripts." In other words, both the cognitive-affective motivational schemas and the control mechanisms activated in relation to them are in part culturally patterned. On the whole, European social psychologists have been far more cognizant of the social origin of many behavioral schemas than their American counterparts. For example, Forgas (1981) has discussed the relation between "social episodes" (basically the same as what others call

303

"scripts") and the larger culture. These interaction schemas "are not only intra-individual cognitive objects, but also the building blocks of particular cultural milieux which can be objectively established and consensually validated" (p. 166).

Much of human behavior is routinized, and goals, scripts, and other plans for action encoded in schemas become activated often unconsciously or habitually, just as wishes do. A significant portion of this routinized behavior is socially created. Routinized thoughts, feelings, and behaviors at the individual level can also be connected to routinized cultural schemas through roles. Spiro theorizes that roles provide a link between the needs of individuals and groups:

> ... if ... social roles are capable of satisfying personality needs ... these needs may serve to motivate the performance of roles. But if social systems can function only if their constituent roles are performed, then, in motivating the performance of roles, personality not only serves its own functions but it becomes a crucial variable in the functioning of social systems as well. (1961, p. 100)

A person need not create all or most of her own roles, any more than she must construct from scratch all her own wishes, problem-solving techniques, plans, and scripts. Performance of role behavior can be doubly satisfying: not only do societies generally reward appropriate, and sanction inappropriate role behavior, but performance of role requirements makes life predictable and thus less anxiety-ridden for oneself and others.

Berger and Luckmann present a similar argument in *The Social Construction of Reality* (1967) in their discussion of "habitualization." Habitualization, they argue, occurs on both the individual and societal levels because it "makes it unnecessary for each situation to be defined anew, step by step" (p. 54). According to Berger and Luckmann, habitualization is a method of relieving tension (p. 57), and it crystallizes in role behavior. On the societal level, roles are aspects of social institutions. By taking on a role, the person is therefore integrating herself into those institutions, while making them part of herself. As Berger and Luckmann put it, "By playing roles, the individual participates in a social world. By internalizing these roles, the same world becomes subjectively real to him" (p. 74).

Roles become subjectively real, as well, through their impact upon the self-system. Subjectively experienced and valued roles are frequently aspects of a sense of identity, which are simultaneously consensually validated. Roles may come to be valued in the same way other phenomena come to hold affective significance. One important way is through identification, as one can observe by watching the enjoyment young children get from playing at being their parents, superman, or other objects of identification.

While roles arise and become institutionalized in response to individual and collective set-goals, they may become dysfunctional in a number of ways. They may be particularly unpleasant for some people, especially those forced into deviant or low status roles. Roles also become, like habits and scripts of individuals, valued in their own right because their breakdown produces uncertainty and anxiety. Social norms and roles may thus persist beyond their utility not only because of a social inertia but because they have taken on autonomous value, independent of their original functions. "Tradition," writes Ruth Benedict, "is as neurotic as any patient" in its "overgrown fear of deviation . . ." (1934, p. 252).

Defense mechanisms may also be culturally patterned. Freud pointed to the defensive function served by many cultural institutions and Spiro (1965) has described in detail how Burmese monasticism serves as a "culturally constituted defense mechanism." Based on data from interviews, observation, and projective testing, Spiro argues that the option of a monastic life in Burma performs multiple functions. It allows individuals who would otherwise likely manifest fairly severe pathology to express their conflicts in an adaptive and socially approved way. Simultaneously, it provides for the culture not only religious personnel, but a way to integrate potential deviants into society in a socially acceptable manner. In other words, Burmese monasticism is overdetermined, a product of both individual and collective needs.[1]

Not only may cultures provide mechanisms through which individuals may resolve conflicts or express unconscious wishes, but they may pattern intrapsychic defenses and coping strategies more directly. One can readily observe this in families, which often have institutionalized mechanisms for conflict resolution which then become internalized by family members. Similarly, a child may learn to deny unpleasant aspects of reality through observations of his parents, and he may also be conditioned to rely on denial or repression himself by experiencing the unpleasant consequences of threatening the denial of those around him. The case of the starving cows in Kerala presented in Chapter 6 is illustrative of culturally constituted defenses. Cultures tend to pattern modes of regulating emotion as well as modes of emotional expression, as anyone who has travelled from Germany to Italy can attest.

Cultural control mechanisms tend to be hierarchically organized, with the least costly ones activated first, even though cultures differ in the degree to which they utilize less "adaptive" measures, and in times of extreme threat, responses are likely to be less effective and more dangerous. This is largely because dangers to the group or survival produce more intense, less modulated affects in individuals, who in turn react in more

---

[1] I hope Spiro will forgive me for simplifying his very subtle arguments almost beyond recognition.

305

reality-distorting ways. In times of cultural disintegration, institutionalized procedures for regulating conflict break down, making more likely the use of violent action.

Stasis and Change

In the previous section, it was argued that not only are cultural processes compromise-formations that reflect multiple and competing set-goals, but that culture in turn shapes individuals' aims, their assessment of situations, and the control mechanisms they use to regulate emotion. Social institutions at times preempt the need for idiosyncratic responses to affects and set-goals, while at other times they shape the intrapsychic life of individuals.

The remainder of the chapter will briefly try to show the mechanisms through which cultural traits are preserved and discarded. I will contend that a single model can account for relative stasis and relative change, avoiding the pitfalls of functionalist models which assume an unchanging equilibrium or steady-state. The basis of the theory is the notion, developed in Part I, of affect as a mechanism of selective retention of responses.

In an excellent unpublished paper on cultural selection, Boehm (1983) distinguishes between intentional and automatic selection processes. Automatic selection relies upon the random variation and selective retention of cultural traits through natural selection described by Campbell (1965), which operates on all biological organisms. With human beings, in contrast, as others have noted (e.g., Pelto and Pelto, 1975), an additional mechanism for selection of traits[1] is intentional, purposive behavior. What Boehm adds is a mechanism for selection of traits, which is affect. He argues that behaviors and strategies are chosen through "hedonic selection," i.e., that behaviors which threaten survival are selected against, while those that enhance it are preserved.

This mechanism is thoroughly in accord with the view proposed here, that, on the individual level, affect is a selective retention mechanism for the selection of behavior, coping mechanisms, and defenses, though the present view is not limited to behaviors used for survival. Boehm adds a second mechanism, which he calls "rational preselection," through which people choose courses of action on the basis of their expectations. This is also consonant with the theory proposed here which posits, like social learning theory, that people need not learn solely through trial and error.

I would add two additional distinctions. The first is between reiterative and collectively patterned decision making. In the former, a trait appears

---

[1] I am using the word "trait" here to be concise, as an omnibus term for ideas, beliefs, behavior patterns, implements for production, etc.

in a culture because many decision-making units (whether individuals, households, etc.) are faced with similar situations and therefore choose similarly. In the latter, they choose similarly because of a collective decision. The two, of course, are not entirely distinct, since reiterative decisions occur within a common culture which leads individuals to define problems and solutions similarly.

A second distinction is between conscious and unconscious selection. As in the case of the Keralan farmers starving their male cows, decisions affecting the reality observed by an ethnographer can be not only unconscious, but dynamically unconscious (i.e., deliberately unconscious). Much of cultural selection is neither "rational" nor conscious. Similarly, cultural traits may have latent functions of which individuals are unaware, but which nevertheless are in part responsible for their hedonic selection. A person in a culture that accuses those who threaten solidarity of practicing witchcraft and punishes them accordingly may have no idea that his fury at the alleged witch maintains solidarity.

If one examines various approaches to decision making in anthropology, one generally finds an unacknowledged affective component. For example, when Barth (1967) shows how household structure changes among the Fur of the Sudan depending on the "relative advantage of joint production over separate production" (p. 667), he does not explicitly mention a mechanism that explains why people would, for example, shift to cooperative farming. They do so because it makes them less hungry, because it decreases their toil, or because they believe it will do so. Similarly, Earle (1980) elegantly shows how a group could shift its subsistence mode as marginal cost of the present strategy increases. The mechanism that accounts for the shift, however, is again affective: a leaner hunt produces hunger or displeasure, as does increased time searching for prey. Our own economic behavior is similarly affectively motivated, though mediated through money.

Affective or hedonic selection may account for the preservation of momentary behaviors, more extended and patterned plans or scripts, or broad behavioral dispositions. It may also, as LeVine (1973) would argue, account for the selective retention of norms, child-rearing practices, and personality traits. One can bring together aspects of symbolic and structural anthropology with ecological anthropology by recognizing that affect motivates and selects control mechanisms related to a host of set-goals, many of which are unrelated to survival. A myth that mediates a cultural contradiction (or a personal conflict) in a way that provides members of the culture with a symbolic resolution will be selected just as will a trait that solves a dietary dilemma.

One should bear in mind that causality here is not unidirectional. While affect has an important role in selecting cultural traits, culture plays an important role in shaping individuals' set-goals so that they find certain situations and solutions to problems pleasurable and others unpleasurable.

Three other mechanisms account for selection of aspects of culture. First, whole cultures can be selected on the basis of collective characteristics, such as solidarity in fighting and preying upon enemies, ability to deal with potential disasters such as famines, and mechanisms of handling intragroup conflict (see Alexander and Borgia, 1978).

Secondly, particularly in less rapidly changing societies, culturally encoded solutions to problems may be relatively impervious to change because tradition itself is valued. In other words, adherence to past strategies may itself be a broad strategy that is hedonically selected as a guide for behavior.

Finally, a trait may be preserved for strictly cognitive reasons, or because it accords with psychological experience. For example, the Ndembu believe that the dead are most restless, and visit the living most frequently, shortly after death (Turner, 1967, p. 9). This may well be in part dynamically motivated by the desire for the dead to remain with the living, at least while the cognitive-evaluative mismatch is the most intense. Yet it also stems from a simple observation, that people "see" the dead more often when they need to, i.e., before they have had time to work through their grief.

More enduring aspects of personality may also affect selection of traits. Members of a fierce or unfriendly culture like the Aymara (La Barre, 1966) are likely to find myths about loss and oral incorporation more memorable than myths about fairies and flowers, so that the former themes will more likely be transmitted intact across generations than the latter. In other words, personality is also a selective retention mechanism, and given the vagaries of intergenerational transmission of culture and the tendency of people to remember and pass on themes most salient to them, cultural traits such as myths and rituals with psychodynamic or "sociodynamic" meaning are likely to be preserved over time. Collective representations are generally overdetermined, reflecting both individual motivations and the requisites and conflicts of social relations. Thus, when Douglas (1966) argues that body boundaries are used to symbolize social relations and not the conflictual issues of individuals, she is no doubt overstating one causal factor. The margins of bodies may well symbolize the dangers of social relations at the margins, but they also are likely to have special meanings in terms of psychological development. The more levels on which a cultural belief or trait is meaningful, the more likely it is to be preserved.

In this chapter I have described cultural change as if it were a piecemeal process, with a bit of drift here, a pinch of cultural evolution there, and a "culture" somehow remaining in the process. In reality, different cultures

308

have differing abilities to change and to assimilate new content without a crisis of integration, and beyond a critical threshold, members of a culture may begin to feel that the social order is being subverted. This, in turn, activates control mechanisms that may or may not avert a crisis. The following chapters will explore the relationship between personality and rapid social change, cultural breakdown, and modernization.

10 Personality and Communitarian Collectivism

CHAPTER 4 PROPOSED that personality and moral development proceeds from internal to external to synthetic narcissism. The internally narcissistic child is a seeker of gratification, and to the extent that others are differentiated from self, they are seen as instruments for the child's fulfillment. With external narcissism, ideal self-images, values, and conceptions of right and wrong are internalized from significant others and from the larger society. Conflicts between ego ideal set-goals and competing wishes lead to anxiety, shame, and guilt. Synthetically narcissistic processes rest upon greater differentiation of one's own ideals and values from those of the group or early introjects, and represent a synthesis of self and other in which neither is consistently used as a tool for the other.

When placed back to back, the resemblance between this model and the model of the development of culture and morality is striking, and the reader is likely to think to himself, "Aha! This is one more 'individual writ large' theory of society." A political scientist with expertise in political and socioeconomic development read an early draft of these ideas several years ago and responded that the developmental models made a great deal of sense, but that they were *too neat*. I did not appreciate that comment until some time later, but when I began to shed my desire for metaphysical ordering principles by which to make sense of the world, I started to search for data that would throw the theory a bit off, so that the symmetry would not be so perfect.

Unfortunately, more research produced even greater symmetry. At first, for example, I had not distinguished two phases of communitarian collectivism, but the literature on peasant societies and the classical religions, and some cross-cultural evidence on hunter-gatherer versus agricultural societies to be reviewed shortly, literally imposed such a distinction upon the theory. Why this symmetry should appear I cannot entirely explain. In part it stems from similar processes occurring on both the societal and individual levels (e.g., differentiation and "equilibration").[1] No doubt, it is also in part an artifact of an idiosyncratic attempt to make sense out of a sea of data. As we have known since Kant, our understanding of the "noumenal" world is always mediated by the categories we use, and philosophers, psychologists, and anthropologists since his time have recognized that not all of those categories are innate a prioris. Somewhere in that noumenal realm, "the facts" are having a good laugh at our expense, but in the realm of human thought, "reality" is a defenseless, voiceless creature which can only long to demand of us, "Hold! Enough! I am not that way at all!" Or as William James has written,

> Probably a crab would be filled with a sense of personal outrage if it could hear us class it without ado or apology as a crustacean, and thus dispose of it. "I am no such thing," it would say; "I am MYSELF, MYSELF alone." (1902, p. 26)

Since crabs comprise only a small percentage of theoreticians, their views are undoubtedly not well represented. Every theory must thus be advanced with the caveat that it is partial theory, the product of a selective mind influenced by other selective minds, but this does not mean that it cannot be valuable, or that it may not be less inadequate than previous perspectives. Anyone who says he has a "good" theory about the way human beings operate individually or collectively is probably grandiose, a bit foolish, or some subtle combination of the two. A person who claims that he has a *better* model than those of his predecessors may well be those things, but he may also be right.

Chapter 7 proposed the following theory of sociocultural evolution, focusing especially on the culture ideal. In the initial state, primary communitarian collectivism, the group is not clearly differentiated from its environment or its members. Society and nature are perceived as indivisible, and the group ascribes to itself magical power to control natural events. The *summum bonum* of such a society is the good of significant groups, and individuation is less pronounced than in later forms of society. In secondary communitarian collectivism, the needs of the group are still paramount, but with progressive differentiation and an emerging chasm between individual interest and communal interest, individualism becomes an explicit and cardinal sin. Secondary communitarian collectivism probably begins with cultivating modes of subsistence or ecological abundance, which allows individual accumulation, private property, and increased security. In both primary and secondary communitarian collectivism, the

---

[1] Unlike many theorists who emphasize differentiation or systems theory, however, I do not see these as broad metaphysical principles that inhere in the universe; rather, I view them as heuristics or metaphors that in many cases "seem to work."

311

defining feature is that for society the individual exists, if at all, as an extension of itself, as a means to societal ends. Morality is defined by the communally collectivistic culture ideal in terms of group needs.

The next "stage" is individuated collectivism. Western society has been moving towards the ideal type of individuated collectivism for centuries, and the modernizing nations of the Third World are shifting in that direction. The defining characteristic of individuated collectivism is its reversal of means and ends: society becomes the means for achieving individuals' ends, as opposed to communitarian collectivism, in which the individual is a means to societal ends. In individuated collectivism, in contrast to communitarian collectivism, morality is defined by individual needs, not less clearly differentiated social needs; it is the morality of self-interest.

A possible third "stage," synthetic collectivism, would involve a dialectical synthesis of the earlier stages. The synthetically collectivistic culture recognizes the legitimacy of the social needs of the group as well as the personal needs of the individual. Morality extends both to society as a whole and to its members. Whether such a collectivity could ever exist and what it would look like if it did is beyond the possibilities of social forecasting.

The problem with which one must deal straight away in trying to relate personality variables to the sociocultural model of development is the issue of whether or not "primitives" really think differently than "we" do. The issue comes down to a paradox. On the one hand, communally collectivistic cultures have a number of pervasive and clearly fallacious ways of looking at reality which have been variously dubbed "animistic," "prelogical," and the like, which center on mistaken views of cause and effect that tie cosmic events to human actions. On the other hand, a group comprised of individuals who could not link cause to effect would quickly perish, and ethnographic observation of decision making in preliterate societies hardly supports the image of the confused savage.

Cross-cultural psychologists have tried to approach this question through empirical studies of individuals in different cultures (see, for example, Volumes 3 and 4 of the *Handbook of Cross-Cultural Psychology,* which are devoted to perception, cognition, and psychological development). The results of these studies have been conflicting and often ambiguous, largely because of the methodological problems of designing culture-free tests. While cross-cultural Piagetian research seems largely to suggest that individuals in preindustrial societies are less likely to achieve formal operations (the ability to think abstractly)(Ashton, 1978), researchers such as Michael Cole (see Cole, 1975) argue that this is an artifact of the tests, although Cole's approach is to *assume* that everyone reasons alike and to keep changing the tests until preliterate people do well. One can hardly doubt that education, to name one important factor, is a catalyst to the development of abstract thinking. Yet it is nonetheless true that, given ecological pressures, to assert that the majority of people in any society function at the concrete or preoperational level is, as Gustov Jahoda puts it, "nonsense almost by definition" (1980, p. 116).

This is, then, a thorny issue, and it is not the aim of this book to take up issues of cross-cultural cognition. To get a grasp on the issue as it bears on the present work, however, requires that one go back to the first articulated position on "primitive" mental life, in the work of Lucien Lévy-Bruhl. Lévy-Bruhl's book on the primitive mind (1923) has been thoroughly vilified by anthropologists because he argued for a contrast between the mystical thought of primitives and the rational thought of moderns, and he overstated his case in both directions. I will argue, however, that he was right in arguing that the differences may not be psychological in the sense that individuals in primitive societies do not know how to think correctly. Rather, he maintained, the differences can be found at the *cultural* level in the collective representations of the two types of society, representations which, I will argue, are essentially analogous to Kuhnian paradigms. Once one recognizes the differences in shared cognitive schemas, one can still speak of psychological differences in two senses. First, to the extent that these collective representations are made a part of the individual's own conceptual universe, then one can say that, in some sense, the individual operating from a schema that sees human actions as capable of offending the forest is cognitively inferior (though I know this statement will make some relativistic hearts murmur). Secondly, ecological requirements in industrialized and nonindustrialized societies lead to the development of different cognitive and perceptual skills, though one has no reason to suppose that the tribesman cannot out-compete the urbanite in a number of skills for which he has been trained which would not have been developed in his industrial counterpart.

The issue then resolves itself into the nature of collective representations in communally collectivistic societies. The argument here is that certain important features of some of the most important of these representations can be reduced to a lack of cultural differentiation and a belief in the magical potency of the group. By cultural "differentiation" I am not referring here to institutional differentiation (increased division of labor, political complexity, technological complexity, etc.), though that would be a legitimate use of the term. I am focusing instead on differentiation in the symbolic realm, in the conception of self, society, and nature. The two are obviously highly correlated, though the extent to which they are is an empirical matter beyond the scope of the present work.

Two questions immediately arise. First, how does this lack of differentiation at the cultural level relate to the psychological functioning of con-

313

crete individuals. Secondly, how is it that people can actually fail to discriminate animate from inanimate, so that they speak to inanimate objects as if they were human, and how is it that people believe they can affect or coerce cosmic affairs through their deeds and misdeeds? If one tries to reduce this question to individual cognition, one will get nowhere, especially since the distinction between animate and inanimate is one of the earliest ontogenetic discoveries at which the child arrives (see Gelman and Spelke, 1981). The individual tribesperson is certainly capable of discriminating between a relative and a raccoon. If she fails to do so, however, she fails because her individual "reason" has been overridden by a force greater than herself, namely culture.

Chapter 7 argued that primary cultures do not conceive of the self as a distinct and unique entity apart from social relations. To examine the relation between these cultural conceptions of self and the psychology of concrete individuals, it will be useful to explore some particular cases.

Frederica de Laguna wrote a pioneering article thirty years ago on the concept of the individual among the Tlingit of Northern Coastal Canada (1954). The Tlingit self, according to de Laguna, has a social aspect defined by lineage, sib, moiety, ancestral status, and actions of both the person and her or his living relatives; a corporeal aspect or body; a spiritual aspect or soul, which is not temporally connected with the body; a set of names; and a supernatural aspect. De Laguna points out that these various aspects do not have any systematic relation to each other, and that they "are not clearly integrated to constitute a unique or single entity" (p. 172).

The body is seen[1] as a "garment" worn by the soul. The person is alleged to have multiple souls, associated with each of the person's multiple names. The Tlingit give many names to the same person, and they frequently treat a person as they would treat someone with the same name, particularly her namesake. For example, a widow will address a child who was named after her husband as "husband." The Tlingit take quite seriously this identity conferred by name: two individuals with the same name are often equated, and they treat one another with a special warmth. Names are socially imposed aspects of identity, and one sees in Tlingit practices regarding names a lack of clear differentiation between discrete individuals and a tremendous social control over identity.

These naming practices relate to Tlingit notions of reincarnation. The person with multiple names is believed to take on traits of each of her or his namesakes. The Tlingit is assured of immortality in this way; he will live on in spirit as well as in name. The dead are believed to choose the mothers who will give birth to them in their next incarnation, and people

---

[1] For simplicity, I will write in the ethnographic present.

314

frequently inform the potential mothers of their choice while still alive. These ideas of reincarnation and aspects of self associated with namesakes are not cultural categories devoid of meaning to the concrete individual: not only are people expected, quite early in life, to remember past lives, but the force of social expectations and the strength of identifications with others closely related to the deceased are likely to exert a powerful influence in shaping the person's identity.

"Identity" is probably not an appropriate word in referring to the Tlingit conception of personhood, since "identity" implies wholeness, or a oneness of cognized self. According to de Laguna, "The distinction between being oneself irresistible, skillful, or lucky and of making others, animal or human, respond in desired ways is not always clearly drawn" (p. 174). Identity, as in other communally collectivistic societies, is socially defined, not personal. The fatherless orphan, the illegitimate child, and the child of incestuous or slave descent is "socially incomplete." Such a child, writes de Laguna, is "incomplete as a person because he lacks the proper ancestral lines" (p. 175).

Social status, self-esteem, and moral responsibility are not rendered on the basis of personal actions or accomplishments. One's status and worth depend upon one's ancestry and the actions of living relatives, as well as one's own attributes and behaviors. Again, these cultural beliefs and values have a direct impact on the person, whose own valuations of self are determined as much by his social relations and social identity as by his own characteristics. This is an aspect of self-esteem that Western psychologists have missed, focusing strictly on valuations of aspects of self as the self is defined in the contemporary West. Where self-concept is not limited to attributes of what appears to *us* a discrete individual, judgments of self-esteem (i.e., comparison of ideal self with self-concept or self-images) will not be isolated to judgments of the empirical individual because neither self-schemas nor ideal self-schemas are rigidly bounded.

The Tlingit conception of self is, then, not of an individuated self. Nor, one might add, is it clearly differentiated from supernatural objects or aspects of nature. De Laguna nicely summarizes:

> The individual for the Tlingit is thus not a unitary self, distinct from all others, but is both compounded of and linked to other selves: his ancestors, his descendents, and even his contemporaries. His self not only "participates" to some extent in theirselves . . . but also, to varying degrees, "participates" in animal spirits and in other supernatural beings, and even in portions of the inanimate world. (P. 191)

The Tlingit were a considerably more complex society than many of the aboriginal societies of Australia and Africa, yet one discovers even at this level of complexity an absence of a concept of differentiated and unitary selfhood. The same is true of the Northern Cheyenne, whose notions of self Straus (1977, 1982) has described in detail. Straus (1977) points out, as did Mauss (1938), that every culture appears to have a concept of a "person," of who or what is considered a moral being, and that this concept need not be the same as the category of "human." The category of moral actor or person may include nonhuman creatures or supernaturals, and it may exclude many humans. This is the case among the Cheyenne, for whom personhood is conferred only upon those who "know the Way," who are properly socialized. Non-Cheyenne are not persons, nor are those who have sinned and been exiled. Children are "persons-in-becoming" who, if "improperly socialized," may "never make the transition from animal to human, from natural to cultural . . ."(p. 343).

Like the Tlingit and most other preliterate cultures, the Cheyenne conceive of the self as having multiple parts. One is a life principle, translated as "having physical life" (1982, p. 113). A second is sometimes translated as "soul," which Straus translates as "breath," "air," "word," and "consciousness." This aspect of self is associated with power. A third aspect of self is often glossed as "spirit," and it means the consciousness of moral order, of the Cheyenne Way (p. 119). The final, and most important aspect is the heart, which is considered "the personal core of the individual: it is his ethnic identity and the seat of his 'deep' motivations" (p. 122). It is of interest that this core of the self is located at once in the moral community and in the empirical person.

The Cheyenne conception of the person is that she or he is part of an interdependent whole. The Cheyenne explain behaviors not in terms of personality traits or personal motivations but in terms of relationships (1977, p. 355). Further, like other nonindustrial societies (see Miller, 1984), they tend to describe people behaviorally instead of making dispositional attributions. For example, instead of calling a person aggressive, they would generally say, "he fights a lot" (1982, p.121).

Like the Wintu described by Lee (1950), when asked for autobiographical statements, the Cheyenne Straus interviewed did not provide personal histories. Instead, they frequently began, "My grandfather . . ." (p. 122). According to Straus, "Intrapsychic and interpsychic processes are not distinguished in Cheyenne perspective. The Cheyenne self participates in, and cannot be defined by contrast with, other Cheyenne selves. Motivation is understood to be seated in the heart, symbol of social relationship, and is presumed to be inherently social" (p. 125). Straus argues that individuality certainly exists among the Cheyenne, but it is not valued the same as in the West. Rather, as one of her informants put it, " 'the individuals are like the poles of a tipi—each has his own attitude and appearance but all look to the same center (heart) and support the same cover' " (p. 125).

For the Cheyenne as for the Tlingit, participation in the moral community is a path to immortality. The Cheyenne believe that in the afterlife they will be reunited with their ancestors. The dead are literally kept alive in the community of the living: they are seen as participating members, more powerful than mortals, who both continue to interact with the living and extend the tribal community "in time and space" (p. 117). Cheyennes fear loneliness and isolation, which they see as resulting from individuation and consciousness of self. Cheyenne culture, like Tlingit culture, is relatively differentiated for a communally collectivistic society, and Cheyenne, like other North American Indian tribes, is frequently described as "individualistic" (though this is clearly relative to other hunter-gatherer societies). Straus summarizes the Cheyenne conception of personhood:

> The Western concept of person . . . is clearly foreign to Cheyenne culture, where the individual is "whole" only insofar as he has a unique position in a greater whole, where the environment ("background") is part of him and he is part of the environment such that he cannot be "set contrastively against it." (1977, p. 355)

She concludes that "development and motivation are understood as relational and systematization of personality is thus of little concern – indeed there is no concept comparable to 'personality' . . ." (p. 355).

A third example is provided by the Tallensi, whose concepts of self and personhood have been explicated in a masterful essay by Fortes (1971) on the Tallensi concept of the *personne morale*. Fortes notes, following Mauss (1938), that personhood is socially defined. Among the Tallensi, specific crocodiles are granted personhood because they are believed to be, or to contain, the spirits of the ancestors. These crocodiles are "the vehicles of ancestral spiritual immortality, the living shrines, as it were, of the ancestors" (p. 292). This notion of immortality through ancestorhood emerges again and again in the ethnography of communally collectivistic societies, and as will be suggested shortly, it suggests a psychological function of the belief in the value and magical potency – in a word, the sacredness – of the collectivity.

The Tallensi concept of *nit*, or person, implies both biological existence and moral and ritual status, whether that status is conferred upon real or fantasied social "objects." As in all primary societies, to be a *personne morale* is to be a participant in the social order. To become a person requires, for the Tallensi, "normal and legitimate birth into a family, lineage and clan which automatically stamps upon the individual his patrilineal status and binds him in the advance to the observances and prescriptions that go with this" (p. 296). The Tallensi "soul" is less an inextricable aspect of selfhood than a "double of the individual, accompanying him rather than being integral with him" (p. 300). The soul wanders during sleep and may appear in someone else's dream.

Fortes summarizes the relation between Tallensi personhood and the social order in a passage worth quoting at length:

317

The centre of gravity of all the constraints, mystical and material, that shape a person's life are felt to lie outside him – in the mystical powers of Earth and ancestors and Fate, in the determinance of descent and kinship and so forth. Personhood comes thus to be in its essence externally oriented. Self-awareness means, in the first place, awareness of oneself as a *personne morale* rather than as an idiosyncratic individual. The moral conscience is externally validated, being vested, ultimately, in the ancestors, on the other side of the ritual curtain.

The soul is not limited to personal existence and will outlast the living person by being "projected on to material objects." Fortes concludes:

Person is perceived as a microcosm of the social order, incorporating its distinctive ... norms of value and implementing a pattern of life that finds satisfaction in its consonance with the constraints and realities (as defined by Tallensi culture) of the social and material world. (P. 317)

In this quotation Fortes connects the Tallensi concepts of person and self with broader aspects of Tallensi culture: the valuation of the larger community, the view of the individual as extension or microcosm of the group, the sense of primacy of social rules over individual desires, and the belief that this primacy is in the nature of things, not a social construction or a matter of convention. The same constellation of values and beliefs appears in communally collectivistic societies in disparate parts of the globe. The Hopi, for example, use rituals of intensification to guarantee that Nature will yield its agricultural bounty. The aim of these rituals, according to Dorothy Lee (1957), is to ensure the well-being of the universe, and only incidentally of the individual. Lee adds:

Eventually, through the maintenance of this harmony, the human group thrives, the sun moves along its established course from solstice to solstice, the thunderclouds gather and release their rain, the corn sprouts and roots and fills and ripens. (P. 22)

The examples presented here were obviously not randomly selected; they were chosen because the Tlingit, the Cheyenne, and the Tallensi are among a small group of cultures whose concepts of self have been systematically explored, and because they exemplify the understanding of personhood and its relation to the moral community endemic to primary cultures. In all of these cases one finds, at the level of cognition, no concepts of unique individuality separate from the group, and at the level of ideals, a valuation of collective ends.

As all of these examples suggest, undifferentiated selfhood cannot be entirely separated from other aspects of communitarian collectivist culture, notably the moral primacy of the group, the magical potency of collective action, and the relative undifferentiation of the human and the natural. Primary societies do not distinguish between collective schemes and the reality they depict: beliefs about the consequences of breaking taboos are not hypotheses; they are laws of nature. To put this another way, the primary society is relatively less likely to take its own ideas and ideals as object, as something upon which to reflect. I am not suggesting that "primitives" never philosophize; rather, that the distinction between collective categories and natural phenomena in these cultures is relatively indistinct. It is not a difficult move from the culture's constructing a "paradigm" of its universe which describes the sun as rising and setting to the culture's belief that the sun rises and falls *because* the group knows this to be true or performs certain actions. One sees this among the Hopi, who have converted the natural – and uncontrollable – cycle of seasons into a product of human agency. It is no wonder that themes of world destruction emerge in times of cultural breakdown in communally collectivistic societies: when nature and culture are indistinct, the destruction of cultural categories and norms appears to spell the demise of the world order.[1]

Sir James Frazer, a nineteenth century evolutionist anthropologist, argued (1922) that one can perceive a movement historically from a magical, to a religious, to a scientific stage. Lévi-Strauss points out that one cannot draw a distinction between magic and religion in the least complex societies because both are manifestations of an undifferentiation of the natural and the human: ". . . religion consists in a humanization of natural laws and magic in a naturalization of human actions – the treatment of certain human actions as if they were an integral part of physical determinism." He concludes that the "notion of supernature exists only for a humanity which attributes supernatural powers to itself and in return ascribes the powers of its superhumanity to nature" (1966, p. 221).

The primary society's undifferentiation from nature is thus directly related to its sense of magical potency: to the extent that nature and culture are inseparable, then the power of nature is the power of culture. Hence, a threat to the social order is a threat to the cosmic order, and one should therefore not be surprised to find that dangers to the collectivity are the source of many rituals, and that moral beliefs center around preservation of the social order. The "primitive worldview" is thus, to use Douglas' words, "personal, anthropocentric, and undifferentiated" (1966, p. 112), or as Lewis has put it,

> The cosmos, events in nature, and particularly their impingement on human affairs through fortune and mishap, all unfold inexorably in response to man's behavior towards his fellows. Nature, and the mystical forces which animate it, respond dutifully to whatever dramas occur in social relations. (1976, p. 148)

---

[1] The world-destruction fantasies of schizophrenics stem from a similar undifferentiation of self and other at the individual level, as the person symbolizes annihilation of the self as destruction of reality.

If a lack of differentiation of nature and culture renders culture magically potent, then an absence of clear distinctions between self and society results in the potency of undifferentiated selfhood. In other words, through the value and power of the group, the person in the primary society attains a sense of significance and participation in a magical potency. Many rituals perform precisely this function: the person simultaneously experiences the reality of solidarity and the awe or "collective effervescence" (Durkheim, 1915) it evokes, while participating in ritualized action believed to have considerable efficacy. The worldview of the primary culture is thus psychologically functional: it provides a sense of value, potency, and security to the persons who live it. To put this another way, by internalizing collective cognitive and value paradigms,[1] the externally narcissistic person shares in communitarian collectivism. Where the individual in an individually collectivistic society may strive to be a god, the person in a communally collectivistic society is an undifferentiated part of God.

When one examines a number of practices common in primary communitarian collectivist societies, one finds that they perform the function of guaranteeing social potency or "omnipotence." The greatest threats to this magical potency are natural events that seem beyond social control, but precisely those events become viewed as products of social action. When one looks, for example, at "rites of intensification" or transitional rites marking the movement from one season to another, one finds that these are not simple "celebrations" of the change of seasons: they are *explanations* of the change. In other words, through these rituals, the group guarantees that the change will occur as it is supposed to occur. One notes here a collective defensive maneuver by which necessity is converted into choice, so that the culture ordains that which is going to happen anyway. At the risk of becoming tedious in drawing parallels to individual psychology, one cannot but notice the resemblance to what psychoanalysts call the "ego's attempt to master," which is often tied to Freud's notion of "repetition compulsion." The idea behind the ego's attempt to master is that when a traumatic event occurs which the individual cannot avoid, one way to deal with the event is to bring it symbolically under one's control. Freud's formulation of the repetition compulsion stemmed from his observation of the tendency of traumatic events to be continually remembered and re-experienced, for example, in dreams. This phenomenon at first

---

[1] I use the term "paradigms" here advisedly. Chapter 13 will explore the relation between Kuhn's notion of paradigms and a number of phenomena at the individual and collective levels of analysis, such as cultural revitalization movements and rites of passage. Unlike Kuhnian paradigms, these phenomena are as thoroughly affective or evaluative as they are cognitive. Wolin (1968) and Ryan (1972) have drawn from Kuhn's work to speak of "moral paradigms" or "value paradigms." In appropriating a concept like Kuhn's, one must, of course, be careful to avoid transposing its ambiguities (see the volume edited by Lakatos and Musgrave, 1970) onto another realm.

seemed to Freud to contradict his principles of psychic economy because it appeared to provide a clear case in which the person was pursuing gratuitous pain. With characteristic brilliance, Freud then recognized that the repetition compulsion was a way in which traumatic material could be worked through: by deliberately presenting itself with the trauma, "the ego" was not only *controlling* the traumatic event but also making the experience of the trauma a matter of choice, not imposition. Thus, through repeatedly subjecting itself to the trauma, the ego could master it by controlling it and confining it to particular times of the ego's own choosing.

Aside from rites of intensification, one could provide a host of examples of a similar "if you can't beat 'em, join 'em" mechanism operating at the cultural level. Communally collectivistic societies characteristically explain social disasters in terms of failure to perform rituals correctly, in-group antagonisms, and the like. Perhaps the one event most threatening to societies, because it continually and inexorably mutilates them, is death, and one finds a collective mechanism similar to the ego's attempt to master as one cultural response to death. Lienhardt's (1961) description of Dinka religion provides a classic example. The highest clans among the Dinka are the spear-masters, a hereditary priesthood. When a spear-master is old and weak,[1] he calls his people and tells them to gather together to bury him alive. The Dinka harbor no illusion that the man will not die; rather, as Lienhardt makes clear, through this ritual they affirm the group's control over death. According to Lienhardt, the fundamental principle of the ritual is twofold: that for certain masters of the fishing spear death must be deliberate, and that it must be the occasion for a public celebration (p. 313). These two facets are, in actuality, intertwined because the former asserts societal potency and control (the "culture's attempt to master") and the latter reflects and intensifies social solidarity.

This latter aspect becomes more apparent in examining particular accounts of the ceremony. One informant cited by Lienhardt described the attitude of the spear-master and the participants in the ritual:

> And he [the spear-master] will not be afraid of death; he will be put in the earth while singing his songs. Nobody among his people will wail or cry because their man has died. They will be joyful because their master of the fishing-spear will give them life (*wei*) so that they shall live untroubled by any spirit. (P. 500)

The burial ritual not only brings the group together, but it supposedly purges malevolent spirits threatening the group. These malevolent forces may be natural forces such as death itself, which threaten the group's integrity and control, or they may be social forces which threaten to

---

[1] Again, I am writing in the ethnographic present. The colonial authorities put a stop to such practices.

splinter the group or dissolve social bonds. Lienhardt cites a fairly clear case, that of the spear-master Deng Deng, in which the burial brought together, and reinforced ties between, clans that could potentially be at odds (p. 302).

Among the Western Dinka, people believe that the spear-master may carry an affliction of the community with him to the grave. In one case, for example, a spear-master was buried clutching a tsetse fly (p. 309). As Lienhardt demonstrates, the Dinka ritual is not just a form of catharsis or an "expressive" act:

> In his death, then, the Dinka master of the fishing-spear is made to represent to his people the survival with which masters of the fishing-spear are associated in myth and present day ritual. Nor, in one sense, are the Dinka deceiving themselves in maintaining that the death of an old master of the fishing-spear produces a renewal of life in his people. (pp. 318-9)

He concludes:

> Notions of individual personal immortality mean little to non-Christian Dinka, but the assertion of collective immortality means much, and it is this which they make in the funeral ceremonies of their religious leaders. (P. 319)

Thus, social solidarity and reaffirmation of community are produced simultaneously with a social triumph over death. Why the mechanism of triumph – social mastery of the inevitable – is so similar to the individual mechanism known as the ego's attempt to master becomes readily apparent when one recognizes that both mechanisms may be used to answer, on two different levels, the same fundamental issue: the problem of theodicy. The internally narcissistic child has established his sense of basic trust on the premise that life is consistent and need-satisfying, and he is likely to imagine for himself a larger role in producing this state of affairs than reality suggests. He knows, for example, that if he sucks at the nipple, the tension he experiences, hunger, diminishes. If the nipple is not present, he lets out a cry, which causes the nipple to appear. I once watched a baby carry on for several minutes in the cold Michigan winter by repeatedly dropping a snowball out of its stroller and crying for its return. Each time the baby cried, he was rewarded with the snowball, which he promptly tossed down again. What a sense of omnipotence this baby must have developed! In the course of experience, however, every infant experiences frustration, and ultimately this frustration must call into question his basic assumptions about his magical potency. I call this a question of theodicy because the infant must come to grips with the presence of evil (defined at this point in terms of his or her own desires) in a system with a powerful deity. That is also why Chapter 4 used the term "potency" in place of "omnipotence," because one suspects that the child learns quite quickly that his dominion is not absolute.

322

The mechanism of the ego's attempt to master may thus arise as one answer to this theological crisis. Eventually the child resolves this crisis by converting, one might say, to another religion. By endowing his parents or, later, society with extraordinary value and power, he maintains his "faith" or "basic trust." Shortly thereafter he may learn that this does not necessarily resolve the problem of theodicy. He must still come to terms with evil in the world (which, however, he may define quite differently than before), but he now has a new ally in his quest for religious understanding: culture.

The communally collectivistic culture is equally vulnerable to the problem of theodicy because it sets itself up as its own deity. If evil cannot be eliminated – e.g., if death cannot literally be conquered – then at least it can be controlled. The society may thus symbolically, as in Dinkaland, turn death into its opposite, collective immortality. As will be discussed in later chapters, this resolution of the problem of theodicy will be disrupted if it loses its personal meaning, either because societal power or legitimacy come into question or because the individual no longer accepts collective immortality as his *summum bonum*. In communally collectivistic societies, however, the potency and value of the group are maintained through mechanisms such as the "culture's attempt to master," magic, and ritual.

Malinowski recognizes the relationship between such practices and the needs of individuals and groups for "positive affirmations of stability, success, and continuity" in a world always fraught with uncertainty and ambiguity (1939, p. 959). He argues that beliefs in sorcery and black magic constitute a way of accounting for evil, a way that leaves open the possibility of controlling this malevolence. When one examines the primitive pollution beliefs so elegantly analyzed by Douglas, one finds that these beliefs about the impure always relate directly to the issue of the potency versus the powerlessness of society, and that the connection she makes in her title, *Purity and Danger*, is between the pure (the sacred, the group) and the dangerous (the areas, cognitive or behavioral, in which the group has lost its control). One major function of purity beliefs is to mediate and thus resolve this polarity.

Lienhardt's account of the Dinka burial of the spear-master also makes clear the function of communally collectivistic values, often expressed through ritual, in assuring immortality. The same phenomenon appeared in the cultures described earlier. The Tlingit attain immortality through the transmission of names. The Cheyenne preserve the lives of the deceased by allowing them to interact with the living, and believe that through death a person becomes united with the ancestors. For the Tallensi, symbolic immortality is concretized: ancestors can be seen directly in their transformed state as sacred crocodiles. Immortality for the Tallensi can only be achieved through the community, in this case the lineage; a person who leaves no successor to "perpetuate his status by descent and kinship" cannot become an ancestor (Fortes, 1971, p. 308). To become an ancestor one must also live by the rules of the community. The Tallensi who commits sacrilege or mortal sins (e.g., homicide within the group) loses his status as a person and consequently his ability to become an ancestor and thus achieve immortality.

Notions of collective immortality are expressed in many, if not all communally collectivistic societies. For example, the Atuot are Nilotic pastoralists of the Southern Sudan. Nilotic cultures like the Atuot and the Nuer are frequently described as individualistic for "primitive" cultures. Yet even for the Atuot, immortality can be achieved only through the agnatic group. According to Burton, "collective immortality is represented in physical form by the herd of cattle in which agnates share rights of use and ownership. Individual immortality is possible only through the memory of a name, derived from one of these cattle" (1978, p. 614). Burton relates a conversation with one Atuot who was asking about the purpose of Burton's writing, to which Burton replied that he was relaying information that would live on after his own death. To this the Atuot responded, "This is the same with our ropes. Every cow has its own rope and each rope is our writing. The writing of our ancestors are these cows in the camp" (p. 614).

Among the Maring of New Guinea, a man may join an agnatic group by participating in the ritual planting of *rumbim*. In so doing he mingles his soul, "life stuff," or "shadow" (called *min*) with those of others and the wider community. According to Rappaport,

> By clasping *rumbim*, a man participates in, as it were, a corporate life whose span is greater than his own. Such a view of clan *min* is suggested by a standard phrase in the speech of heroes in accounts of how brave men have faced death. "It does not matter if I die. There are more Merkai (or Kamungagai, or Kwibigai, etc.) to hold the land and father the children." (1979, p. 109)

Rappaport adds that the clan may not be immortal, but its life is longer than that of the individual, and this immortality (or extended mortality) is symbolized in the *rumbim*.

Geertz (1974) extracts a similar meaning from the symbolic actions and expressions of the Balinese. In elaborating a dramaturgical metaphor of Balinese culture, Geertz emphasizes that roles, not individual selfhood, are central in Balinese experience and interaction:

> Physically men come and go, mere accidents in a happenstance history, of no genuine importance even to themselves. But the masks they wear, the stage they occupy, the parts they play, and, most important, the spectacle they mount remain, and comprise not the facade but the substance of things, not least the self. (P. 62)

The donning of masks in Bali not only minimizes individuality, but it also guarantees immortality through participation in a play that never goes out of production:

> there is in Bali a persistent and systematic attempt to stylize all aspects of personal expression to the point where anything idiosyncratic, anything characteristic of the individual merely because he is who he is physically, psychologically, or biologically, is muted in favor of his assigned place in the continuing and, so it is thought, never-changing pageant that is Balinese life. It is dramatis personae, not actors, that endure; indeed, it is dramatis personae, not actors, that in the proper sense really exist. (P. 62)

The communally collectivistic system of values and beliefs thus serves another important psychological function: it provides the person with a sense of immortality. To value the group and to seek its solidarity and longevity is to provide oneself an avenue for continued life, either as a shade or name that lives on in the memories of the living or as a participant in a world of sacred, even if not individuated, ancestors. In a culture without crystallized boundaries of individual selfhood, collective immortality is simultaneously individual immortality. Where the ethnographer could immortalize himself through personal achievement and publication of thoughts and information known only to himself, the Atuot could extend his life indefinitely through cultural symbolism regarding cattle, the Maring could preserve his *min* through ritual relation with others, and the Balinese could participate in a sacred and perpetual drama.

This sense of immortality may well not be illusory. As Craig (1979) has argued, "kinship gives life meaning by providing people with a mechanism by which both their substance and their personal values . . . survive them" (p. 95). Not only may kin and community preserve one's blood or beliefs, but through ritual the community may literally preserve the ideas and values of many generations through the actions of the living. Lévi-Strauss is well-known for his contention that through ritual a culture transmits a message to itself; the culture is both sender and receiver. Rappaport (1979) extends this notion to suggest that through ritual a message encoded by *previous* generations is decoded or received by current members of the community. In their enactment of the ritual, the living themselves become transmitters and recipients of immortal messages from the past, and in conforming to the structure of the ritual, the members of a community express their acceptance of the message, if not merge themselves with it (pp. 192-3).

Whereas in both primary and secondary communitarian collectivism the ultimate moral value is the welfare of the group, in secondary communally collectivistic cultures one finds this ethical maxim explicit, and typically explicitly opposed to individual desire. I will argue that it must be made explicit because individuation has proceeded (and with it the heightened

325

separation of private from public ends) to a level that threatens the dominant culture ideal which views community as raison d'être.[1]

The most interesting study along these lines is Guy Swanson's *The Birth of the Gods* (1960), a tremendously creative correlational study based on well reasoned theoretical underpinnings. Swanson wanted to test and expand Durkheim's contention (1915) that supernatural beings are symbolic representations of social relations, and he proceeded to examine a number of hypotheses using a sample of fifty preindustrial cultures drawn from the Human Relations Area Files (for a description of the files and their uses, see Naroll and Cohen, 1970). Swanson argues that every group has a moral basis, but that unstable or ambiguous moral relationships between individuals or subgroups will evoke supernatural sanctions to buttress these relationships (1960, p. 159). He contends that supernatural controls are used in all (preindustrial) societies, whether hunter-gatherers, nomads, or cultivators, but that these beliefs become explicit only when unstable or ambiguous relationships arise.

Swanson wanted to discover what kinds of social conditions are associated with the use of supernaturals to bolster the society's moral code, which he hoped would allow him to learn about the relationship between magic and ethical religion. He found that four factors are significantly correlated with supernatural sanctions: presence of social classes ($p<.005$), debt relations ($p<.01$), individually owned property ($p<.05$), and primogeniture ($p<.05$). He interpreted these results as demonstrating that interpersonal differences in wealth correlate with supernatural sanctions. When any two of these variables were simultaneously present, correlations ranged from 92 to 100 percent (p. 168). He also found that grain crops as primary form of subsistence and population density correlate at a statistically significant level with presence of supernatural sanctions (pp. 168-9). Finally, he discovered that the presence of a large number of noncommunal groups (i.e., specialized groups with interests that diverge from those of the community) correlates with high gods who actively participate in human affairs.

One could interpret Swanson's findings a number of ways, and one explanation that has been advanced regarding similar results in another area will be discussed shortly. The interpretation advanced here is that the use of more active supernaturals to enforce communally collectivistic values emerges only when the previous moral order is threatened by the

---

[1] On the family level, David Reiss (1982) has noted that explicit rules begin to arise only when implicit norms have begun to break down, and a number of writers (e.g., Gellner, 1964; Berger and Luckmann, 1967) have noted a similar process on the cultural level. One may wonder, in terms of individual psychology, if this may not be a component of adolescent philosophizing: as Gellner (1964) notes in relation to culture change, philosophy emerges only when the old order has begun to disintegrate.

awareness of individuals and classes with interests divergent from those of the wider community. Greater individuation, a heightened separation of private from public ends, private property, and economic surplus are generally associated with the rise of agriculture.

This hypothesis is consistent not only with the analysis of peasant societies and the classical religions presented in Part II, but it is also supported by a number of cross-cultural empirical studies which have unambiguously shown that, as opposed to hunter-gatherer societies, agricultural societies produce – and "deliberately," through socialization practices – individuals who emphasize obedience to authority and conformity to the needs of the group. The classic study along these lines is Barry, Child, and Bacon's investigation of the "Relation of Child Training to Subsistence Economy" (1959). The study has some methodological weaknesses (for example, cultural diffusion may explain much of the variance, since most of the hunter-gatherer societies stressing achievement are American Indian groups), but their basic findings have since been replicated (see Berry, 1967). They used as their independent variable accumulation of food resources (which correlates with agriculture and husbandry, as opposed to hunting and fishing) and found a statistically significant correlation (on a sample of 104 cultures) with socialization for "responsibility" and "obedience" as opposed to "achievement," "self-reliance," and "independence." Combining variables to form a dichotomy of compliance versus assertion, they found a .94 correlation between these traits and subsistence category (p. 59), with agricultural societies high on compliance.

The explanation they offer for their findings has remained unquestioned in their literature, though one may wonder whether it actually accounts for the magnitude of the correlations. Barry et al. contend that the nature of adult economic roles determines socialization practices and ultimately character: in agricultural and husbandry societies innovation is feared, whereas in hunting and fishing societies, "individual initiative and development of high individual skill seem to be at a premium" (p. 52). This formulation is problematic in three regards. First, hunting large game requires intricate coordination of activities, so that one would expect cooperation to be highly valued in many hunter-gatherer societies. Secondly, in hunter-gatherer societies, women's gathering activities provide a large percentage of the group's subsistence, which should suggest that if economic roles determine personality characteristics, gathering should also have its psychological consequences. Gatherers who innovate, however, will frequently bring home poisonous berries. The more adaptive path for gatherers in many situations would probably be for the community to collect a list of acceptable plants, fruits, and berries and suggest conformity to that list. Finally, given the vast difference between hunting (a predominantly male occupation) and gathering (a predominantly female occupation), one

327

would expect significant sex differences in hunter-gatherer societies in terms of independence, self-reliance, and related variables. Available data, however, suggest quite the opposite. In tests of field-dependence versus field-independence in migratory hunting and gathering groups, for example, Witkin (1975) reports that sex differences are relatively uncommon, especially compared to sedentary cultivating societies. These data bear directly on Barry et al.'s hypothesis in that Witkin correlates field-dependence with conformity to social cues.

This is not to say that ecological and economic factors do not play an immense role in determining psychological characteristics, or that seeming differences in values between hunting and agricultural societies do not in part reflect differential environmental pressures. Rather, the argument is that Barry et al.'s ecological explanation cannot alone account for the correlations observed, which suggests the need for an additional hypothesis. The hypothesis proposed here is a psychosociological one, namely that the differences in part reflect greater social and symbolic differentiation in agricultural societies, which has the byproduct of creating heightened conflict between individual and group. The result of this conflict is a cultural attack on individual desire (especially when opposed to group needs) which uniformly appears with the development of agriculture as primary mode of subsistence.

I will not attempt here to explain why a greater differentiation of self from community, or of culture from nature, appears with the rise of agriculture (or with greater technological and political complexity in hunting societies). I lack the comprehensive knowledge of the classical religions and the anthropology of chiefdoms and early states one would need to speculate with any confidence about such matters. One would suspect, however, that the causes of this change in cultural conceptions of self, society, and nature are, like most important cultural shifts, at once economic, sociological, psychological, political, and cultural. From an economic standpoint, critical changes include the ability to store produce; the technological capacity to use large numbers of people in the building of irrigation systems, public monuments, and the like; and the origin of markets. From the sociological side, geographical mobility, rigidified stratification, and contact with other cultures seem important. Psychologically, a number of experiences may converge to produce a sense of independent selfhood, particularly those associated with mobility. Politically, the rise of empires and complex state organizations fosters separation of private and public spheres, and particularly a separation of the social from the political. Finally, at the cultural level, changes in ideas and ideals set in motion by technological advances develop a semiautonomous existence, creating new ways of looking at self and society that in turn produce changes in other spheres. Just as the emergence of markets may foster a sense of individuality when trade partners are individuals rather than groups, cultural conceptions of individuality may foster the sense that innovation is desirable or that one can leave one's place of origin in the pursuit of profits, with economic, sociological, psychological, and political ramifications.

If one must have prime movers, no doubt the "demo-econo-technological" realm is the most important in setting in motion the wheels of social change. Yet ecological and economic forces do not change and leave psychological and cultural forces intact. Nor do culture and personality passively shift with the winds of technology: the way people understand and evaluate changes has an immense impact upon the fate of those changes and the form future developments will take. This is nowhere more clear than in the second great technological revolution (the first was agricultural), the industrial revolution, which has shaped the history of the present era. Chapter 11, on the psychodynamics of modernization, will now explore the relation between psychological processes and this massive change.

11 The Psychodynamics of Modernization

S INCE THE END of the Second World War, many Western eyes have cast ambivalent glances toward the Third World, and a multitude of non-Western eyes have reciprocated. Cognizant of the upheavals and transformations to ensue, social scientists in the early postwar era tried to develop the conceptual tools through which to understand the great transformation in the South. Many of the early theories accepted evolutionist principles stemming from nineteenth century anthropologists such as Morgan and Maine; societies bereft of modern technology represented images of a lost and simple world, and an analysis of change in underdeveloped countries could provide insight into the Western past.

Throughout the 1950s and 1960s, the impact of functionalism on theories of modernization was profound. The functionalist approach of Talcott Parsons found expression in works such as Marion Levy's two-volume opus, *Modernization and the Structure of Societies* (1966). The term "modernization" became popular in the 1960s, as did the comparative historical approach (see, for example, Black, 1966).

By the 1960s the audience for the literature on modernization had spread to the Third World, and in 1968 Samuel Huntington expanded the focus of analysis from societal evolution to political stability with the publication of *Political Order in Changing Societies*. At the same time, writers such as Gusfield (1967) and Whitaker (1967) began to question the whole notion of modernization, with its assumption of a movement from a condition called "tradition" to another referred to as "modernity." Other authors continued those attacks through the following decade (Tipps, 1973; Shiner, 1975; Migdal, 1979), arguing from examples in the contemporary Third World that modernity may not, in fact, constitute a single syndrome.

During the 1970s *dependencia* theory arose in Latin America as an alternative to views that looked for the obstacles to modernization in the internal dynamics of premodern societies. The dependency theorists, of Marxist extraction, looked for the causes of "underdevelopment" in the structure of international capitalism. Simultaneously, the term "modern-

330

ization" fell into disrepute (and disuse) because of its seeming value bias. Instead of speaking of "relatively modernized" versus "relatively non-modernized" countries (Levy, 1966), social scientists began to contrast "developed" with "underdeveloped" or "developing" nations. This new terminology generally stresses *economic* development, as opposed to the earlier concepts, which emphasized the sociological concomitants of technological change. Berger, Berger, and Kellner note the "terminological gyrations used to refer to those not yet fully blessed with 'modernization' or 'development' ":

> One used to speak of "backward" societies. These then came to be called "underdeveloped," and later (as an expression of optimism) "developing." Clearly, to be less than "modern" or "developed" has a stigma attached to it. (1974, p. 13)

The term "modernization" will be summoned from the dead in the present chapter for essentially two reasons. First, on a practical level, both psychology and sociology (as well as political science) attach special meaning to the word "development," and the use of that term in a book which crosses the social sciences would lead to incessant ambiguities. Secondly, whereas the sociological concept of development implies a prior social theory (i.e., development from and toward *what?*) which often remains only implicit, the notion of modernization need not imply either a value judgment or a fixed starting or ending point (though in past writings it may have implied both).

Some have argued that modernization implies the categories of "tradition" and "modernity," and that these categories are deficient as analytical tools. The notion of modernization, however, does not inherently suggest that all "premodernized" societies are the same, or that all "modernized" nations are similarly homogeneous. Though many modernization theorists do, in fact, lump all premodernized societies together in the residual category of "tradition," to suggest that a process called modernization occurs does not necessarily prevent one from seeing that modernization can "happen" to primarily hunter-gatherer, nomadic, or peasant societies (whether or not one accepts *those* ideal types). To argue, for example, that a process exists called "cooking" does not imply that all uncooked foods are alike or that cooking necessarily leads to a given end; cooked steak is different from cooked eggs.

As to the assertion that modernization implies a value judgement, this need not be the case. To claim that cooking is a process does not suggest that it is good. Similarly, simply because one finds nuclear weapons repugnant does not suggest that one eliminate the term "bomb" because of its possible implications. If one can prove that, empirically and logically, certain traits covary, one is justified in referring to the complex as a conceptual unit. This does not imply that no other way of grouping the

331

data would prove useful; it simply suggests that one can gain an intellectual hold on that subject by pointing to, or even exaggerating, particular common traits (see Weber, 1949).

Viewing modernization as a process rather than an end-state avoids many of the difficulties associated with the term. Huntington (1971) makes a similar point regarding political development, arguing that one can focus on social processes – including industrialization, urbanization, commercialization, literacy expansion, and occupational mobility – which empirically covary. Elsewhere, Huntington (1968) systematizes a number of processes associated with modernization. "At the intellectual level," he writes, "modernization involves the tremendous expansion of man's knowledge about his environment," the spread of literacy and education, and the heightened significance of mass communications (pp. 32-3). Demographic processes of modernization include "a marked increase in health and life expectancy, increased occupational, vertical, and geographical mobility, and in particular, the rapid growth of urban population as contrasted with rural" (p. 33). He further describes the social and economic processes associated with modernization:

> Socially, modernization tends to supplement the family and other primary groups having diffuse roles with consciously organized secondary associations having much more specific functions ... Economically, there is a diversificaiton of activity as a few simple occupations give way to many complex ones; the level of occupational skill rises significantly ... subsistence agriculture itself declines in significance compared to commercial, industrial, and other nonagricultural activities. (P. 33)

Daniel Lerner similarly observes in an essay on modernization in the *International Encyclopedia of the Social Sciences* that "the urban explosion is systemic with the population explosion and the literacy explosion..." (1968, p. 390). He contends that these processes form a unitary syndrome, "suggesting that perhaps they went together [empirically] so regularly because, in some sense, they *had to* go together" (1958, p. 438).

Thus, while its circumstances necessarily differ across time and space, modernization inexorably affects a variety of aspects of life. The burgeoning of science and technology revolutionizes methods of production and alters perspectives on the world. Modern mass media begin to exert daily impact on the lives of the multitudes. Education and the spread of literacy transform ways of thinking that may have remained relatively stable for generations. Urbanization and increased mobility caused by more sophisticated forms of transportation dramatically alter the conditions of existence; whether by enclosure movements, decrees, threat of starvation, or various other positive and (more frequently) negative incentives, folkways are disrupted, and rural peasants and tribespeople find themselves metamorphosed into urban laborers. Modernization involves not only the addition of new institutions but the destruction of old ones. Peter Marris (1974) has nicely emphasized the role of psychological loss in the process of social change. Political scientist Karl Deutsch has given the name "social mobilization" to the process by which "major clusters of old social, economic, and psychological commitments are eroded or broken and people become available for new patterns of socialization and behavior" (1961, p. 494).

The psychological factor in modernization is often overlooked or dismissed as unimportant. Those who assume that collective behavior is minimally influenced by the psychology of those who are carrying it out, like those who suppose that as technology changes consciousness will follow, will no doubt find little to recommend an approach that suggests that revitalization movements, resurgence of fundamentalist religion, and various ambivalent or unambivalent reactions to modernizing trends and institutions have a psychological component. One would be thoroughly justified in rejecting as absurd an approach to modernization that did not accept as axiomatic the centrality of issues of class, power, and technological change. Yet the members of societies exposed to the processes of modernization are not abstractions; they are living, breathing people who respond—and respond affectively—to migration from ancestral homelands, breakdown of culturally constructed systems of meaning, or the terror of being trapped in the line of fire in interminable civil wars.

Since the 1950s, a small but significant literature has arisen attempting to explicate the psychodynamics of modernization. The conclusions of the various theorists have included the inference of causal relationships between social change and personality, the isolation of particular character traits conducive to economic development, and attempted answers to the question of whether the "modern" personality is qualitatively different from the "traditional" personality.

The aims of this chapter are twofold. First, it will provide a critical review of the literature on the psychodynamics of modernization. Secondly, extracting the common conclusions of previous studies and drawing upon the model of personality developed in Part I, it will analyze the effects of the modernization process upon the individual in terms of two significant changes in the ego ideal: a breakdown of internalized structures of meaning and a heightened emphasis of self.

Psychology and Modernization: Empirical, Psychodynamic, and Sociological Approaches

One can conveniently separate the literature on the psychology of modernization into three groups: empirical, psychodynamic, and sociological approaches. This section will summarize and assess the major works in the field, turning first to four empirical studies, then to two psychodynamic perspectives, and finally to one more sociological approach.

LERNER'S PASSING OF TRADITIONAL SOCIETY

The first major work to appear on the psychology of modernization was Daniel Lerner's (1958) *The Passing of Traditional Society,* a study of modernization in six Middle Eastern countries. In Lerner's formulation, the media play the central role in psychological modernization. Modern mass media expose the individual to new and different viewpoints and cultures, provide him with increased information, and allow him vicariously to experience situations other than his own. For Lerner, the predominance of mass media results in the "mobile personality" characterized by the individual's heightened empathy for ways of life other than his own. He argues that empathy is "the basic communication skill required of modern man" (p. 412). Not only is Lerner's modern individual empathic and mobile, he is participant (p. 50). The participant individual formulates opinions and seeks information upon which to base his views. Central to his psychological structure is his new feeling of potency, his sense of his ability to affect his environment.

Modernization for Lerner is a syndrome which is unidirectional and worldwide; it is not, he contends, a Western phenomenon. The shift from a predominance of oral to mass communication breaks down old authority structures, freeing the nonempathic, constricted traditional person from his prepositivist fetters. Lerner isolates three stages – urbanization to literacy to mass media – through which a society passes on its way to modernity. Unlike many subsequent writers, Lerner is careful to point out that the causal relationship between psychological and social modernization is not unidirectional: ". . . a communication system is both index and agent of change in a total social system . . . [O]nce the modernization process is started, chicken and egg in fact 'cause' each other to develop" (p. 56).

Lerner, exemplifying the Western optimism (or imperialism, from a different standpoint) characteristic of the 1950s, professes to demonstrate empirically that the mobile person, even in a "transitional" society, is happier than his traditional counterpart (p. 101), although his data prove that this is only true if the society is already in a state of upheaval. Finally, he points to the possibility and consequences of unbalanced growth in psychological and socioeconomic modernity, arguing that if the ratio of nontraditional people to traditional institutions is too high, revolution may occur (cf. Huntington's formula for political instability, 1968).

Lerner's attempt was pathbreaking and in many ways insightful, and his formulation has influenced every major writer in the field. It fails, however, in a number of respects. First and foremost, his model conflates the

334

modernizing with the modernized. He describes empathy as the "inner mechanism which enables *newly mobile* persons to operate in a *changing world*" (pp. 49-50, emphasis added). He further describes it as "a high capacity for arranging the self-system on short notice" (p. 51). These are characteristics adaptive for individuals in changing times, but this conception tells little about the psychology of the individual in a more stable, highly modernized country.

Secondly, Lerner over-emphasizes the role of the media, which causes him, for example, to ignore the impact of socialization in early childhood, which psychoanalysts, in contrast, consider crucial in personality formation. Lerner's emphasis on mass media implies that a starving child placed in front of a television will become as "modern" as a more comfortable, secure individual in the same situation. Further, communications structure and the breakdown of traditional authority are not, as Lerner seems to posit, inextricably bound. One wonders what happens, for example, when traditional authorities gain absolute control over the mass media, eliminating the exposure to conflicting views and multiple alternatives Lerner stresses. This suggests that the crucial explanatory variable may be the breakdown of an internalized or external absolute authority, rather than the media, which may simply be one key institution that helps effect this change.

DOOB'S BECOMING MORE CIVILIZED

Defining "civilization" as "the culture, or way of life, possessed by modern literate and industrial nations in Europe and America" (1960, p. 2), Leonard Doob sets out in *Becoming More Civilized* to explain why people modernize and what happens to them when they do. In attempting to differentiate between civilized and uncivilized peoples, he lists a number of features characteristic of the latter, including smaller social units, greater concern with social rules, largely autarchic economies, slow rate of change, greater dependence on the vagaries of nature, less tendency to question belief, and simplicity (pp. 26-36). Civilized people are basically characterized by the opposite features, and modernized people in general value "traits which indicate initiative, independence, and self-confidence" (p. 141).

Doob formulates twenty-seven hypotheses and tries to test each one empirically. His method is quite broad and varied, utilizing questionnaires and projective techniques in his own research on three African tribes and a Jamaican sample, as well as relying upon the data of similar studies conducted by researchers such as A.I. Hallowell (1955), George Spindler (1955), and Lerner. He attempts to compare acculturated with nonacculturated groups in each society, using Western education as an index of acculturation.

335

Among his most significant hypotheses (which all seem to have proven correct, at least to some extent), Doob argues that acculturation leads to increased aggressiveness (p. 80) and discontent (p. 74), an hypothesis contrary to Lerner's view. He claims that modernizing individuals are more sensitive to others than are modern or premodern people, though his evidence here is clearly ambiguous (pp. 135-6). He proposes that after people change "from old to new ways, they are a little less likely to be dogmatic concerning the validity of their own beliefs and the goodness of their own values" (p. 169). He adds, in addition, that people who are modernized or modernizing are more adept at dealing with novel situations than their traditional counterparts (p. 125) and concludes, "Basic changes in personality are likely to occur as people become adequately civilized" (p. 256). He does point out that it is by no means clear that civilization is a blessing, adding, "It is certain only that we are destined or doomed to be civilized" (p. 267).

Doob's work has the advantages of conceptual clarity and readability, but it is a "period piece" that certainly did not rise above the times. Value biases aside, the most significant problem with his hypotheses and distinctions is that they are generally trivial. He argues that modernized people are more tolerant of delayed gratification of their goals, but he fails to note that the "goals" which "uncivilized" people often refuse to postpone include aims such as eating. He hypothesizes that people who have elected to change their ways "are likely to feel antagonistic toward traditional leaders who did not reveal similar changes" (p. 117). In another flash of insight, he hypothesizes that a central change in behavior is likely to have "more repercussions" than a peripheral change (p. 236).

Not only are the questions and answers he poses largely uninteresting and commonsensical, but his method is fundamentally flawed. He uses amount of Western education as an index of modernization, which renders his study an analysis of the effects of Western education, not modernization. An individual educated in a traditional school may still develop "modern" ideas, and a person educated in a Western school may reject modern notions entirely. Exposure to Western ideas does not necessarily make one "Western" or "modern," any more than exposure to the Bible makes one religious.

MCCLELLAND'S ACHIEVING SOCIETY

In a controversial and ambitious psychological examination of history and historical change, David McClelland (1961) attempts, through the analysis of children's stories, to demonstrate the causal relationship between the need for achievement (*n* Ach) and economic development. In *The Achieving Society* McClelland contends that a rise in *n* Ach *precedes* economic development, and that the achievement motive is highest in the fastest growing countries while declining in wealthy nations past their take-off (to use Rostow's term, 1960). The link between *n* Ach and economic development, McClelland claims, is the entrepreneur.

McClelland examines other motives or needs as well, arguing that achievement and affiliation needs are inversely correlated. Further, he modifies Riesman and colleagues' (1961) theory of the development of "other-directedness," arguing that preceding a period of rapid technological development is an era in which the "force which holds society together has shifted from tradition, particularly impersonal institutional tradition, to public opinion which helps define changing and functionally specific interpersonal relationships" (p. 192, emphasis deleted).

Drawing upon the work of Lerner and Fromm, he argues that this change to a morality based upon the generalized or "anonymous other" (pp. 195-6) is conducive to economic development in that it allows increased flexibility and reduces parochialism detrimental to development. He concludes that the achievement motive and other-directedness are two independent variables that lead to economic growth. Making explicit his attack on materialism, he emphasizes the primacy of ideology, asserting, "There is no real substitute for ideological fervor" (p. 430).

The Achieving Society is a provocative work that inspired further research, particularly through its creative methodology. Nevertheless, it does not demonstrate what it purports to show. The main problem with McClelland's argument is his attempt to establish the temporal and explanatory priority of ideological factors and motivations, a priority which – whether true or not – is not supported by his data. McClelland emphasizes the role of child rearing in creating orientations toward achievement and other-directedness. At one point, however, he states, "Social and economic conditions influence the extent to which one generation provides early self-reliance training for its children" (p. 129). If this is, indeed, true, then one must ultimately look to social and economic conditions for the cause of changes in child rearing which lead to heightened achievement motivation, which defeats his argument. He cannot escape Lerner's chicken-egg question because he is unable without recourse to extra-psychological or extra-familial conditions to explain the origin of changes in child-rearing practices. By demonstrating that achievement motivation rises with development *rate* and declines with development *level* he is, at best, proving an important psychosocial *correlation;* at worst, he is simply showing that people will strive to better their condition if opportunities to do so exist.

Further, characteristic of a number of psychological studies of modernization and particularly of McClelland's, is the subtle change from "is" to "ought," from social science to social policy (to use Weber's distinction, 1949). Musing over the rise and fall of various civilizations, McClelland laments that the Florentines "lost their interest in achievement. Their dreams changed. They became more concerned with love and friendship, with art, with power struggles" (p. 437). McClelland concludes the book suggesting a variety of ways to increase achievement motivation and other-directedness and thus, one may suppose, avoid a Florentine-style decline into preoccupation with art and love.

INKELES AND SMITH'S *BECOMING MODERN*

The most comprehensive of a number of attitude studies attempting to isolate a modern personality is Alex Inkeles and David H. Smith's (1974) *Becoming Modern,* a massive study of the psychology of modernization in six developing countries. Asserting that modern nations require modern people, Inkeles and Smith construct an instrument for measuring "Overall Modernity," the *OM Scale* (p. 35). They posit that psychological modernity is a syndrome, not a congeries of unrelated attitudes and orientations. Describing the modern individual, they write:

> He is an informed participant citizen; he has a marked sense of personal efficacy; he is highly independent and autonomous in his relations to traditional sources of influence, especially when he is making basic decisions about how to conduct his personal affairs; and he is ready for new experiences and ideas, that is, he is relatively open-minded and cognitively flexible. (P. 290)

Like Lerner, Inkeles and Smith maintain that psychological modernity is worldwide, not simply Western. The modern person is the "instrumental activist" (p. 112) who believes in his own ability to have an impact. He is open to change and experience, yet informedly opinionated; he is a seeker of knowledge and a believer in the dignity of others; and, while less past-oriented than his traditional counterpart, he does not forsake kith and kin.

Inkeles and Smith's modern person is an industrial worker, but he hardly fits Marx's image of the proletarian. Asserting that Marx's real contribution is in his social psychology (p. 10), they contend that a person's occupation does, indeed, in many ways determine his consciousness. Claiming that the factory is "an effective school in modernity" (p. 174, emphasis deleted), they use largely correlational data to demonstrate that occupation, education, and influence of mass media account for 90 percent of variation in OM scores, with education the most important independent variable. They conclude, finally, that the Freudian view that personality is largely a fait accompli by age six is false, pointing to changes in OM scores caused by differential experiences well beyond the Oedipal age.

Inkeles and Smith's work is painstaking in its attempts at empirical study of a phenomenon prone to receiving anecdotal and impressionistic examina-

338

tion, but is flawed in a number of ways. First and foremost, they presume that modernity resides in the industrial working class. One wonders, reading *Becoming Modern*, about the place of entrepreneurs, lawyers, doctors, and professionals: can one really understand "modern" psychology without examining the middle class, which, at least in the West, created "modern" culture and in almost all countries is a chief purveyor of modern life and ideology? If the factory worker is participant, efficacious, autonomous, and open, can one surmise that his white collar compatriot must possess the same qualities to an even greater degree since he is more educated and has an occupation more conducive to self-development? In other words, if the move from rural to urban labor results in a qualitatively different psychology, one wonders if the transition from blue to white collar occupation will result in another new psychology.

Secondly, characteristic of the vast majority of empirical studies, Inkeles and Smith conflate modernizing or "transitional" individuals with people in more stable developed nations. They assert that the "essential feature of our modernization study . . . is its emphasis on the *change* in the social and physical environment which men experience as they shift from the more traditional settings of village, farm, and tribe to city residence, industrial employment, and national citizenship" (p. 156). If this is, indeed, the essential feature of their study, the OM Scale may actually measure ease of adaptation to a changing environment, rather than modernity per se.

Thirdly, and critically, their choice of factors representing modernity significantly biases their results. Discussing their methods, they write:

> We proposed, then, to classify as modern those personal qualities which are likely to be inculcated by participation in large-scale modern productive enterprises such as the factory, and, perhaps more critical, which may be required of the workers and the staff if the factory is to operate efficiently and effectively. (P. 19, emphasis deleted)

Given their choice of modern traits for the OM Scale as those caused by factory experience, to proceed, as they do, to measure the correlation between working in a factory and OM score, and to conclude that working in a factory does, indeed, cause modernity, is fallacious. They essentially prove that working in a factory produces attitudes consonant with working in a factory; they claim, instead, to prove that working in a factory causes psychological modernity. Inkeles and Smith's OM Scale not only fails to measure the factory-modernity correlation, but as the median partial correlation between factory work and OM score is only .18 (p. 174), they effectively prove, if anything, that their instrument is not even a terribly good indicator of factory attitudes produced by factory work. They also factor out potentially important variables, such as class, by holding socioeconomic level constant.

Finally, their instrument is ethnocentric and geared to American middle class values. For example, one element of "modernity" which they test is the "valuing of technical skills, and the acceptance of it as a valid basis for distributing rewards . . ." (p. 23, emphasis deleted). At one point equating "tradition" with "deprivation" (p. 277), they, like McClelland, eventually make the crucial shift from "is" to "ought," gradually transforming the book into something of a "how to" manual for the modern capitalist.

PYE'S POLITICS, PERSONALITY, AND NATION BUILDING

Of the literature on the psychodynamics of modernization, Lucian Pye's (1962) *Politics, Personality, and Nation Building* is among the most successful in discussing and elucidating the topic it claims to explain. Pye, dissatisfied with the simple traditional-modern dichotomy, attempts to explicate the dynamics of "transitional" society and politics. Influenced by the work of Erik Erikson, Pye is interested in the confluence of personal and societal identity crises. He suggests that the central contradiction facing transitional individuals is the choice between self-development and submergence, between autonomy and security. Correspondingly, society must reconcile the prerequisites of efficient state building with those of national identity.

Transitional politics, he argues, may be a route for creativity or comradeship. The transitional individual is insecure, having lost trust in his peers, authority, and himself. The result is aggression and anxiety, and the individual may seek escape from these feelings either by developing personal skills and a sense of mastery or by following a charismatic leader and submerging himself in the group.

Pye enunciates three stages of socialization relating to political affairs: cultural socialization, political socialization, and political recruitment. In a transitional society, unlike a stable, "traditional" one, these three phases are disjoint. The result is a polity characterized by, among other factors, a political sphere not differentiated from society, totalistic party ideologies, freedom of leaders in policy formulation caused by the predominant quality of loyalty, interchangeable political roles, and prevalance of charismatic leaders. Pye's analysis is compelling and often extremely insightful, in large measure because he combines a thorough interdisciplinary understanding with sensitive observation through fieldwork in Burma.

HAGEN'S THEORY OF SOCIAL CHANGE

Hagen, an economist who argues that "economic theory has rather little to offer toward an explanation of economic growth" (1962, p. 8), posits, like McClelland, that the roots of economic development are psychological. Hagen contends that the traditional or "authoritarian" personality and the

340

modern or "innovational" personality are situated on opposite ends of a continuum (p. 72). The traditional person's identity, unlike that of the modern individual, is, as psychoanalytic theory asserts, largely determined by the age of six. The authoritarian personality is the result of indulgence in early life followed by extreme constraint, culminating in an Oedipus complex marked by severe repression (and fears of homosexuality) and a consequent dearth of creativity. The authoritarian, traditional individual has passive-aggressive and dominant-submissive tendencies as a result of intense rage and repression. He feels impotent, taking his society and environment as given.

The modern, innovational personality, in contrast, has access to his unconscious and is thus capable of creativity. He depersonalizes a smaller field of individuals than his traditional counterpart and emphasizes succorant-nurturant and manipulative needs. The crucial link between personal and social change which explains the emergence of innovational individuals is "withdrawal of status respect" (p. 185). Initially, one can suppose, everyone is authoritarian. As a result of physical displacement by force, denigration of valued symbols, inconsistency of status symbols, or nonacceptance in a new society, a group and its members experience withdrawal of status respect, a depreciation of the group and its members in the eyes of society. The eventual result is retreatism, a somewhat schizoid withdrawal from the world. Ultimately, groups experiencing this state of affairs may turn to technological innovation to prove their worth. Rich or landed "deviants" are similarly liable to innovational personalities since their status protects them from societal repression and frees them to create new technology.

Hagen's work is inconsistent, interspersing novel and fascinating passages and chapters with cumbersome, and often illogical analyses. His concept of the innovational personality, and particularly the "anxious innovator" (p. 141), is highly suggestive, and his analysis of responses to social stress, derived from Robert Merton (1968), contains many valuable ideas. He postulates that an individual at a time of societal upheaval may respond by retreatism; rititualism, the continued acceptance of obsolete values and institutions; innovation; or reformism, which, unlike innovation, seeks to change the existing society.

The faulty link in his theory is the concept of withdrawal of status respect and the subsequent sequence to retreatism and innovation. His explication of the dynamics of the sequence entails an extremely detailed, tortuous, and generally unlikely Freudian examination of changing father-son relationships. Further, the causes of withdrawal of status respect all in some way stem from the emergence of a bourgeoisie (whether from internal or external developments), which undercuts the argument for the primacy of psychological factors. If withdrawal of status respect results from altered class relations, withdrawal of status respect is the sine qua non of the innovational personality (which is both stated and contradicted in the course of the book), and the innovational personality is the root of economic development, then to find the ultimate cause of technological advance one must look for an explanation of changes in class structure, which may or may not lie in the psychological realm.

BERGER ET AL.'S HOMELESS MIND

In *The Homeless Mind* (1974), Peter Berger, Brigitte Berger, and Hansfried Kellner present a thoughtful account of the relationship between individual consciousness and modernization, taking into consideration the critique of the modernization paradigm which had arisen in the literature. Arguing that one cannot assume modernization or "development" to be either inexorable or beneficial (pp. 12-13), they posit, as does Max Weber (their chief intellectual ancestor), that the social scientist should examine reciprocal relations of causality between various spheres of society (e.g., economic and religious). Berger et al. examine their subject from an approach to the sociology of knowledge developed by Berger and Luckmann (1967), and they painstakingly attempt to separate those processes that must inherently form a "package" (p. 91) from those that may only incidentally covary. They assert that some of the factors associated with modernization and modernity may be manipulable, while others are resistant to human tampering; the more interesting question, they claim, is that of the "parameters of choice" (p. 25).

Like Inkeles and Smith, Berger et al. focus on the "everyday consciousness of ordinary people engaged in technological production" (p. 29). They hope to show that the "life-world" (p. 62) of the member of modern society is essentially dissimilar to that of the premodern person. They ascribe to the modern individual a sense of "homelessness" (p. 77), a lack of grounding in a socially created identity. The "essential ordeal of modernization" involves the "collective and individual loss of integrative meanings" (pp. 141-2). They note that premodern societies typically achieve symbolic integration through religion, but that this "integration is in most cases critically challenged by the onset of modernization" (p. 140). Fundamental to the consciousness of the modern individual is the *pluralization of life-worlds* to which he is exposed (p. 62); he finds himself confronting a problem of choice unknown to his traditional counterpart, largely as a result of urban and media influences (p. 64).

Berger et al. enumerate four distinctive characteristics of modern identity. First, modern identity is "peculiarly open" (p. 73). Like Robert Lifton's description of "Protean man" (1970), Berger et al.'s analysis emphasizes the fluidity and transitory character of modern identity. Secondly, modern con-

342

sciousness is subjectivistic and relativistic. Because reality and value appear constantly in flux, only internal states seem real: a "subjective realm of identity is the individual's main foothold in reality" (p. 74). Thirdly, modern identity is "peculiarly reflective" (p. 74); the incoherence of modern life renders continual analysis and re-analysis imperative. This reflectiveness extends not only to the external world, but to the self, which "becomes an object of deliberate attention and sometimes anguished scrutiny" (p. 75). Finally, modern identity is "peculiarly individuated," and modern ideologies legitimate this individuation (p. 75). The private sphere tends to compensate for the disruption of the public domain (pp. 166-7), as individual dignity replaces "honor" as a prime value in society (p. 80).

Berger et al. differentiate between primary carriers of modernization and secondary carriers. They attach central importance to technological production and bureaucracy (paying implicit tribute to Marx and Weber, respectively), denoting these as primary carriers. They isolate cities and pluralism as important secondary agents of modernization (p. 16).

Like Inkeles and Smith, Berger et al. view modern technological production – factory work – as requiring particular forms of consciousness and cognition, including an awareness of a hierarchy of experts, a mechanistic style of work, the segregation of work from private life, an anonymity of social relations, and a "tinkering attitude" (pp. 30-6). The "symbolic universe of modernity" (p. 101) thus includes such features as rationality, a problem-solving approach, and a maximization or progressivity ethic (the belief that everything can be improved) (pp. 102-3). Bureaucratic influence promotes conceptions such as competence, "proper procedure," orderliness, organizability, and anonymity (pp. 46-56). The secondary carriers of modernization, which include urbanization and pluralism as well as other factors such as education and mass media, all tend toward a diversification and relativization of beliefs.

Each of these carriers also brings with it a specific set of discontents. Technology requires rationalization, which results in the need to control impulses, and hence repression. In addition, the anonymity of social relations fostered by technology leads to anomie and a sense of the meaninglessness of existence (p. 163). Bureaucracy, and political bureaucracy especially, leads to alienation "from the polity and its symbols, as political life becomes more abstract and anonymous" (p. 165). Pluralization of lifeworlds, which seems to represent the summation of the secondary carriers and their effects, generates the sense of homelessness (p. 165).

Thus, modernization is a mixed blessing, and the reactions to it may vary. Berger and his colleagues believe in the influence of ideology on action, and they distinguish three types of idealogical reaction to modernization: ideologies endorsing modernization, ideologies opposed to it (which they call counter-modernization ideologies), and ideologies "that seek to control or

343

contain modernization in the name of values that are conceived to be independent of that process" (p. 143). Berger et al. note, regarding the third alternative, that the notion of manipulating reality and its processes is a "modern" approach. They comment, "Nothing could be more modern than the idea that man has a choice between different paths of social development" (p. 158). In addition to these three options, in later stages of modernization a "de-modernizing" impulse arises, which often converges with counter-modernizing tendencies (p. 169). The authors recommend a democratically oriented socialism as perhaps the most promising social organization for modernizing nations of the Third World since it combines community with progress (p. 153). They warn, however, that socialism is not a panacea for the "intrinsic discontents of modernity," suggesting that the Marxist conception of "alienation" is incomplete (p. 206).

Like Pye's *Politics, Personality, and Nation Building*, *The Homeless Mind* is excellent in its substitution of critical analyses for critical assumptions. The attempt to separate the essential from the extraneous aspects of modernization, for example, is both extremely useful and necessary for an adequate study of modernization and its psychological concomitants. Similarly, the discussion of the movement from an ethic of honor to an ethic of duty, and the suggestion that the two need not be conceived as totally antithetical (pp. 87-8), is original and enlightening. What is perhaps most impressive about this book is that the authors beautifully mix observation with theory without letting the theory determine their observations.

The Homeless Mind is problematic in two respects. First, like most of the works explicated above, Berger et al. fail to question the critical assumption that psychological modernity corresponds to factory consciousness. Neither Adam Smith nor Karl Marx would view the dominant ideology of the modern age as emanating from the working classes. If modern ideology is, in fact, the ideology of the lower classes, the observation of this "trickle up" effect is new to social science. One wonders, as well, how factory life and relations with an impersonal, all-powerful bureaucracy produce the individuation and pluralization of life-worlds ascribed to modern society. Perhaps one might more accurately suppose that several aspects of modernization have different psychological concomitants, and that these aspects may in part differentially affect different classes.

This leads to a second problem, the issue of causality. Though they are careful to stress mutually reinforcing factors, Berger et al. give priority to the consciousness-producing effects of technology and bureaucracy. The problem, intimated above, is that working on an assembly line and dealing with a large bureaucratic "machine" may well produce a "mechanistic" style of work but will hardly be conducive to the individuated, reflective, differentiated, and open identity described as "modern." Something else must be the prime causal factor in creating modern consciousness.

CONCLUSION: APPROACHES PAST AND PRESENT

The literature on psychodynamics of modernization,[1] the most significant and representative of which has been reviewed here, is varied in both content and quality. Yet the various studies almost uniformly underline two central psychological changes heralded by modernization: the belief in the efficacy (and value) of the self and the erosion of traditional (external and internalized) structures of authority and meaning. In terms of the content and form of the ego ideal as described in Part I, psychological "modernity" appears to represent a greater orientation toward self and a shift away from relatively unproblematic internalization and maintenance of nonconflicting authority. In more technical terms, the central argument of this chapter is that modernization brings with it a change in the composition of the ego ideal in two ways: by unbalancing the traditional equilibrium between self and other through heightened emphasis on self, and by sabotaging traditional structures of authority and value, presenting the individual with significantly conflicting internalizations. The following two sections will explore some aspects of modernization that contribute to these changes.

The reader should be forewarned that the proposal that modernization produces a more self-oriented individual for whom internalization of authorities, culturally constructed values, and structures of meaning is problematic is in no sense intended to suggest that all people in industrialized societies fit this pattern or that no people in preindustrial societies do. Indeed, this type of personality is only beginning to emerge as a predominant personality configuration in the industrialized West, though the propagation of more self-oriented value systems is increasing its frequency. While most groups and classes in contemporary industrialized societies have, at least to some extent, been exposed to the factors that result in the breakdown of unproblematic authority, the number of individuals who have experienced the conditions necessary for a greater emphasis on self is considerably smaller. That the configuration marked by a breakdown of authority and a stress on self is claimed to be moving toward primacy is based on a long historical trend, and the following two sections of this chapter attempt to isolate those factors which are, and have been, moving personality in this direction. Some of these variables are operative for certain groups or classes in preindustrial societies, and to the extent that they are, one will find elements of psychological "modernity" in affected individuals. The total configuration, however, has never been more than an isolated phenomenon in the preindustrial world.

---

[1] The focus here on the psychodynamics of modernization is not meant to imply the absence of other psychological concomitants of modernization. Cognitive changes, for example, occur with the spread of literacy (Goody, 1977; Scribner and Cole, 1981).

Modernization and the Content of the Ego Ideal: Self versus Other

Modernization alters the content of culture ideal and ego ideal through greater individuation and heightened emphasis on the value and power of the individual self. It does so in several ways. First and most importantly, when modernization brings about a change in material conditions, it alters the individual's sense of personal security and predominant level of functioning on the hierarchy of self-needs. While obviously no individual operates strictly on one level, economic factors greatly influence, and often determine the most significant needs confronting an individual. Pre-industrial societies are uniformly more vulnerable to the vicissitudes of nature than are modernized societies. The person in a society for which accumulation of foodstuffs is difficult or population density taxes available resources is ever cognizant of the food he requires, aware that a bad harvest, draught, or flood could spell the end of his existence, despite elaborate village or communal mechanisms for emergency relief. (The landed rural elite or rich peasant, on the other hand, may find himself much more immune to nature's whims, which suggests one arena in which one would expect psychological differences.)

Along with greater perceived security of the self, the tremendous lengthening of lifespan which accompanies technological advance through better medical care, nutrition, and information allows the individual to live under the illusion of his own immortality. In nonindustrial societies, death is much more a fact of life. The individual most affected by the processes of modernization, in contrast, never lives as close to death as his preindustrial counterpart (though see Lifton on "nuclearism," 1970, 1979) and is exposed less to the death of peers until later life.

Secondly and related, a number of "modern" experiences foster a sense of individual competence, of efficacy of the self apart from any larger community. Literacy and education provide the individual with a better basis for attacking problems and understanding the world. With technological and scientific advances, nature loses some of its mystical power, as do the communal rituals previously used to placate or control it. The "modern individual"[1] is consequently less likely to accept her environment as given. Instead of constantly changing herself to suit her environment, a trait Lerner and Inkeles and Smith postulate as modern, the modern individual may conceive of her natural and social environments as more malleable.

Unlike much of the nonmodern person's sense of efficacy, the modern individual's feelings of competence and efficacy are largely individual. In-

---

[1] I will temporarily use this abominable term to refer to the self-oriented individual maximally exposed to the processes being described here, though I promise to discard it shortly.

creased division of labor provides the individual described as modern in this sense (who is often not, as in Inkeles and Smith's description, the unskilled laborer forced to turn a bolt on an assembly line, who has as little control over his life and labor as his rural compatriot) with an area of special competence, a vocational niche which allows him to feel (whether correctly or otherwise) that, in at least some way, his special ability distinguishes him from others. Unlike nonmodern individuals, whose skill is more likely to be exercised in groups, an individual whose labor is performed to a greater extent in isolation will develop a more individualized sense of competence and productivity. Generalizations of this sort usually (to generalize again) perform less service for their original authors than for critics who perennially cite them out of context. The point is that as individuals come to segregate work from family life, to perform more specialized roles, and to develop areas of competence that are not part of the culture's general store of knowledge (see Berger and Luckman, 1967), they will develop a more differentiated and valued sense of self.[1] One cannot read a text on physics in groups, and few of the most significant and innovative discoveries in history have arisen in large groups. Einstein's theory of relativity was hardly developed around a table, and Marx shared authorship of only a few of his works with even Engels.

Greenfield and Bruner (1968) have proposed a fascinating hypothesis about the relation between literacy and individualism. They cite evidence to suggest that formal education fosters a separation of thought and its referents that ultimately leads to heightened self-consciousness. Reviewing a large number of cross-cultural empirical studies of cognition and cognitive development, Greenfield and Bruner found that people without schooling tended not to distinguish their thoughts from reality. Greenfield and Bruner argued that school promotes this distinction by de-contextualizing knowledge and clearly separating word and thing. Knowledge distinguished more clearly from reality implies the presence of a knower, distinct from other knowers with different points of view: "When names, or symbols in general, no longer inhere in their referents, they must go somewhere; and the logical place is the psyche of the language user" (p. 389).

Thirdly, to the extent that a person has the mode of immortality available to her which has been described as "objectification" or "creativity broadly defined," the creation in the world of a more or less lasting

---

[1] The Marxist is sure to object at this point that, like most bourgeois modernization theorists, I am mistaking industrialization for capitalism. It is difficult to imagine, however, how one could maintain an industrial society of any sort without, for example, segregating work from family or neighborhood life. The household as unit of production is hardly a viable option for *any* industrial society, however communalistic. Similarly, technological advances over preindustrial societies require specialization of expertise, which, I would argue, inherently promotes a more individualized sense of competence or efficacy.

representation of her own subjectivity, she will be likely to invest corre-spondingly more in herself. Again, the argument here is not that every person in an individually collectivistic society, or that no one in a commu-nally collectivistic society is capable of objectifying his existence. The nomad or peasant, however, can leave no lasting proof of his appearance on the earth other than his offspring. The industrial worker in contempo-rary modernized societies (capitalist and otherwise), similarly, while ca-pable of creating more than his own subsistence, rarely sees, and has little control over the fruits of his toil; in Marxian terms, he is alienated from the products of his own labor (1974, p.327). Perhaps it would not be too psychologistic to suggest that part of what Marx presciently described as fetishization of commodities in capitalist societies is the result of fulfill-ment of the physiological and security needs of large numbers of people without corresponding opportunities to develop a sense of mastery or competence, resulting in a "fixation" on the level of security and comfort.

A fourth factor resulting in heightened psychological individualism is the shaping of character according to the requisites of industrial society (see Fromm, 1947). This shaping process accords well with LeVine's (1973) description of personality characteristics as selectively retained ac-cording to norms and adaptive pressures. In conditions of scarcity, such as those encountered by many agricultural societies, self-interested individu-als are anathema to the group. With heightened productivity, this zero-sum ethos which Foster (1965) describes as the "image of limited good" begins to break down, and with increased division of labor, society re-quires individuals capable of more complex and flexible problem solving, innovation, and specialized expertise. As the Whitings and their colleagues have demonstrated through their analysis of child-rearing practices, soci-eties are remarkably adept at developing ideals consonant with social and productive requirements. The individualism resulting from this factor (which is obviously intertwined with the others) is intensified by industrial capitalism, which shapes people to focus on their desires for personal consumption (see Galbraith, 1971) and fosters what Fromm has described as a "marketing orientation" (1947, 1955).

Fifthly, and also exacerbated by capitalism, is the effect of commercial-ization and wage labor on sense of separateness and deservingness of personal reward. Concepts of individual ownership no doubt contribute to individualism, as does the experience of receiving personal monetary com-pensation for one's labor separate from family instead of partaking of the distribution of collective products. Though capitalism was originally re-sponsible for this system of distribution, as noted earlier, it is difficult to see how one could return to the household as primary unit of production or run an industrial economy without significant commercialization and monetization.

Finally, several processes of modernization shift the balance in ego ideal and culture ideal between self and other, and individual and collectivity, by altering interpersonal relations. Increased geographic mobility allows people to stray farther from kith and kin, so that familistic or communitarian values seem no longer appropriate. The breakdown of extended family living arrangements allows for greater intergenerational differentiation of self and less emphasis on duty to kin. While decreasing family size is in no sense a necessary concomitant of modernization, historically (with the rise of more effective contraception and changing values about the merits and demerits of large families), one wonders about the effects of smaller sibships on individuation and emphasis of self. Children of large families often experience less individualized attention and gratification from parents, and they tend to have more difficulty carving out a niche or identity strictly their own. If this is true in achievement-oriented societies such as our own, where personal competence can be a source of separate identity, it is likely to be even more the case where status is in large measure ascribed rather than achieved, specialization of function is less developed, and individualism is discouraged. Though I am unaware of any clear data on this, large families also seem to foster a greater sense of group identity, a more cooperative attitude, and a willingness to subordinate one's own desires to those of others.

These various aspects of modernization thus lead to a heightened emphasis of self. This destabilization and reworking of communitarian collectivist values in favor of individualism may begin to occur over a single lifetime, or, as is more often the case, changes in culture ideal gradually becoming internalized by individuals and intensified over successive generations.

Modernization and the Form of the Ego Ideal: The Apostasy of Early Internalizations

Modernization not only disrupts the content of the ego ideal (the self/other balance), but it alters the form as well. As conceptualized in Part I, in the second phase of external narcissism the person selectively identifies with nonparental significant others, groups and values. A number of aspects of modernization, particularly in its earlier phases, lead to a disruption of the smooth intergenerational transmission of ideals and systems of meaning, and a consequent experience of conflicting internalizations.

First and foremost is the breakdown of shared structures of meaning which occurs as old social forms give way, and frequently, as Durkheim observed, new ones only slowly develop and gain legitimacy. This state of affairs may arise because of technological advance, migration, colonialization, or similar forces. Those who migrate to urban areas, for example, encounter many new individuals and groups and may break old ties of attachment and commitment. Historically, modernization has entailed the breakdown of tribal and village societies and the formation of nation-states. Whether this process resembles "social mobilization" (Deutsch, 1961), with its virtual elimination of old affiliations, or allows many "primordial sentiments" (Geertz, 1963) to coexist in "joint sovereignty" (Migdal, 1979) with new and larger groupings, the process entails massive changes in patterns of investment and consequent disruption of traditional values.

The breakdown of communally collectivistic systems of values does not simply confront the individual with a sense of anomie. It has a much more concrete, personal component as well. In the first few years of life a child introjects the parent as an idealized figure of power and value. If, however, the child comes to see the parent as impotent, if not backward, the internalization proves dysfunctional: the parent can offer neither guidance nor perfection. In our culture, one sees this phenomenon in, for example, children of alcoholics, who often experience tremendous conflict in trying to reject identification with a seemingly defective parent.

In a rapidly changing society, the parent may appear to his or her children singularly incompetent in dealing with reality. Indeed, the perception may not be altogether incorrect: the parent may be maintaining atavistic behaviors and attitudes which the child recognizes as poorly adapted to the changing environment (see Mead, 1949, p.518). Further, the skills required by a rapidly modernizing society often render the young more qualified than the old (Lasch, 1979, p. 213). Relations between the generations may thus be stood on their heads: whereas in communally collectivistic cultures the old do tend to appear the wisest by virtue of their experience, in a changing society, younger individuals may have the upper hand because of their flexibility and exposure at an early age to technological society. This dominance of the young and the new makes maintenance of early internalizations problematic and fosters "other-directedness" (Riesman, 1961) in individuals who remain externally narcissistic. The crowd may thus come to replace, or at least confront, the elders.

Further, education, science, and the media converge to threaten old values, ideology, and myths. The relative inefficiency of traditional methods of production or medicine can suggest to the individual that tradition in other areas, too, may be less than optimal for determining action. In the contemporary Third World in particular, the existence of more advanced technology can threaten the traditional authority by virtue of its seeming advantages. Traditional systems of meaning may thus become subjectively connected with a sense of inferiority, to which individuals may react, for example, by wholesale accommodation to the new or by the desperate attempt to revitalize and prove the superiority of the old.

350

Especially in agricultural societies in which leaders function as symbols of collective power and significance, the erosion of meaning, value, and authority extends to the political sphere, as society's leaders and the collectivity itself lose their appearance of potency. Before significant specialization, the emperor or chief may be able to claim superior knowledge in all matters, sacred and secular. With increased division of labor, however, the doctrine of the leader's omnipotence and omniscience becomes both questionable and dangerous. This was clearly the case in China under Mao in the late 1950s and 1960s. Mao repeatedly tried to maintain the primacy of politics over economics, and in so doing caused disaster during both the Cultural Revolution and the Great Leap Forward. By asserting the power of will over economic forces (a peculiarly idealist doctrine for a Marxist), he attempted, in the style of a traditional chief (or Chinese emperor), to exert his "omnipotent" force against material forces.

Two other factors that influence the transmission and maintenance of communally collectivistic ideals are urbanization and increased mobility. A common theme of philosophers and sociologists since the beginning of the Industrial Revolution is the anonymity of city life and its impact on social control. Durkheim contends that urban anonymity attenuates traditional ties and the *conscience collective* because "the attention of each is distracted in too many directions, and because, moreover, one is known less" (1933, p. 298). Geographical (and, as Lerner would stress, psychological) mobility also allows the person to escape notice and to experience separateness from his community of origin and its values. As Fromm has noted, the escape from embeddedness may lead to a sense of psychological separateness and freedom, but it may also lead to anomie and turning outward toward replacement objects of authority and significance (1947).

The kind of conflict between systems of values that generally occurs rather early in the modernization process does not appear as prevalant in stable industrialized societies, though a significant number of individuals in "developed" countries continue to experience conflicting internalizations, which is related to what Berger and his colleagues call the pluralization of life-worlds (see also Garbarino and Bronfenbrenner, 1976). Whereas Lerner would emphasize the role of the media in alerting people to multiple ways of being and thinking, Margaret Mead (1949) suggests that a crucial factor is the separation into nuclear families, which can result in a dual and contradictory socialization process, with one set of values and beliefs learned at home and other views propounded elsewhere. Anthropologist Clyde Kluckhohn (1944) points to the role of the school in producing a more contradictory socialization process, with children being exposed to the views of teachers, peers, and older children.

Further, the later entry of "modern individuals" into adult society inhibits uncritical acceptance of societal norms, gives individuals who are

351

not yet totally "socialized" time and latitude for developing and perceiving alternate ideologies, and prevents premature closure of identity by delaying psychic investment in the social system. Remarking that in many preindustrial societies adolescence and even childhood are aborted (1968, p. 242), Kenneth Keniston asserts that "puberty rites more often serve to hasten the child toward adulthood than to permit him anything like the possibility of adolescent turmoil, emotional growth, and independence" (p. 243). As will be argued in Chapter 13, one function of initiation rites is to assure intergenerational and cultural continuity by imposing a culturally constructed identity on the initiate. In so doing, the culture preempts the initiate's ability to create an idiosyncratic or unconventional identity, and in the process promotes the initiate's integration and investment in the social order. (For other hypotheses as to possible functions of initiation ceremonies, see Whiting, Kluckhohn, and Anthony, 1958; Burton and Whiting, 1961; and Young, 1962, 1965.)

Conclusion

Various processes connected with modernization thus produce two prominent effects on personality: a heightened emphasis of self and a breakdown or conflict of external and internalized structures of meaning and authority. The first appears to be associated more with the later stages of technological development, while the latter occurs with the greatest intensity in the early periods of transition from preindustrial to industrial society. Lest the focus here on the psychodynamics of modernization be mistaken for psychological determinism, I must reiterate that psychological factors are but one link in the complex network of multiple and reciprocal causal relations that links psyche and society. Understanding of psychological aspects is not a replacement for, but a complement to, analysis of the socioeconomic and sociopolitical forces involved in the process of modernization.

This chapter began by discussing the concept of modernization and suggesting that it can be useful as an analytical tool. In social research, to group together several attributes or processes under a single rubric, one must demonstrate that these attributes are necessarily related both empirically and logically. Whatever one's beliefs about whether non-European societies have ever developed a social form precisely like European feudalism, one does not include the use of a European language in the definition of feudalism because it is not logically related to the concept. In the case of modernization, not only have its various processes such as urbanization, literacy expansion, and technological development consistently appeared together empirically, but one can readily see that they are logically related as well (e.g., technological growth requires literate workers, engineers, and managers).

352

By relating psychological phenomena to these processes, this chapter has shown that modernization ultimately affects the content of the ego ideal through greater emphasis of the separateness, efficacy, and desires of self, and disrupts the form of the ego ideal by challenging traditional authority. To the extent that an individual in a modernized or modernizing society does not encounter the factors responsible for these changes, he is less likely to experience the psychological effects, though he may internalize cultural values not entirely relevant to his life situation.

What should be underscored here is that these psychological changes result from modernization in particular and not simply from colonialism, capitalism, or social change in general. Writers on the psychology of colonization such as Mannoni (1964) and Fanon (1963) have stressed factors such as feelings of inferiority, racism, and oppression, which may or may not produce psychological changes in similar directions. Perhaps the best commentaries on the psychological effects of capitalism are Karl Marx's early writings on alienation (see, in particular, the "Economic and Philosophical Manuscripts," 1975) and Erich Fromm's various books (for a good summary of his work, see *The Sane Society,* 1955).

The greatest methodological problem in studying and theorizing about as massive and historically specific a phenomenon as modernization is that one cannot grow it in one's laboratory in a petri dish or have sixty college freshmen undergo it under controlled conditions. The best one can do is to watch it while it happens in as many places as one can, read about its previous occurrences, and try to experiment mentally in testing hypotheses about particular variables by comparing reasonably similar cases, if any exist, in which the independent variable of interest was not present. Additionally, one must make greater use of logical inference to fill in missing knowledge, hypothesizing causal links and, where the empirical data do not help distinguish between two causal explanations, trying to decide which, if either, makes better sense.

Because modernization and capitalism arose together and have co-occurred in most of the societies on which we have much data, one must obviously be cautious in making causal distinctions between the two. Marxists have traditionally accepted as axiomatic that individualism, the loss of communal ties, and alienation are the handiwork of capitalism. Marx argues that money, private property, wage labor, and fetishism of commodities are the roots of "bourgeois" individualism.

The evidence and arguments provided in this chapter should give one pause before making that assumption. While I have been careful to note those cases in which capitalism and modernization produce similar psychological effects, a number of processes have been examined which, independent of capitalism, can be expected to result in greater self-orientation. For example, not only are lengthened lifespan and greater physical security conducive to individualism, but the requirements of a technological society point in the same direction. The implications for Marxist theory of this psychological tendency toward self-orientation *intrinsic* to the processes of modernization must be developed elsewhere, but one should note that they lend doubt to the belief that simply by eliminating private property and rearranging social institutions one will eradicate "bourgeois" subjectivity and the conflict between private and public interest.

12 Personality and Sociocultural Change

A N EXPLORATION OF the psychological effects of modernization or any form of social change must examine the impact of the various processes on the *individuals* involved. Living in a nation-state (as opposed to a village community) or tilling the fields with mechanized implements does not necessarily "modernize" the structure of one's personality. A significant problem with many of the studies reviewed in the previous chapter is the implicit assumption that everyone in a "modern" society must be psychologically "modern," and everyone in a premodern society must have a "premodern" personality. Many of these works ignore important similarities between individuals and groups in modernized and non-modernized societies. They seem to assume that the small-town minister and urban philosopher in a modernized society must be psychologically equivalent, that the wealthy landlord and marginal peasant must have the same needs and concerns, and that the tribal warrior is somehow different from the modern soldier in motivation or rationality.

The present chapter will explore the relation between personality processes and a central aspect of modernization (and social change in general), the experience of the breakdown of shared structures of meaning. It will then examine a specific case, of a disrupted funeral ritual in Java in changing times, in order to demonstrate the utility of the approach being offered here.

The reader will forgive, I hope, an inattention in the present work to the impact on personality of exploitation, civil war, torture, and other experiences confronting people in the Third World, for whom class conflict, power struggles among elites, and unwitting enmeshment in a global struggle between imperialistic superpowers are at least as important influences on their lives as modernization. Other researchers with greater experience and first-hand knowledge are far more competent to treat those subjects than I, and they are not elaborated here only because of limitations of space and expertise. We are desperately in need of psychocultural studies of the plight of refugees, as well as of the ever-growing numbers of people who have been emotionally and physically mutilated by terrorist governments of the right or left.

Personality and the Breakdown of Meaning

In the society in which cultural integration has broken down, the individual is unable simply to internalize the culture ideal as her ego ideal. Again, I must make clear that I do not intend "internalization" to mean a passive process through which culture leaves its brand on the individual's hide or heart. Internalization is an active process through which a person gradually and gropingly reconstructs, on the basis of her current understanding and ways of thinking, beliefs and values external to herself. In a changing society, the external meaning-system is itself disrupted, rendering internalization problematic. Durkheim has described this state of affairs as anomie. "Our faith has been troubled," he writes, "tradition has lost its sway; individual judgment has been freed from collective judgment" (1933, p.408). Individuals in such a society are ripe for mass movements which provide collective affirmation of identity and an omnipotent ideal, whether it be a group or its transitional object, a charismatic leader.

A number of empirical investigations have explored this state of affairs, many of them drawing upon the concept of "acculturative stress" first enunciated by Hallowell (1955). Such studies have generally found that, whereas in some cases acculturation produces little psychological disruption, in general the individual undergoing acculturation experiences a transitional period of "crisis and fragmentation" (Berry, 1980, p. 261). Those who conform to new cultural influences in such situations usually experience far less "stress" than those who try to reaffirm their traditional identity or those who remain fence-sitters (pp. 264-5).

Faced with the process of modernization, a person in a changing society will frequently respond in different ways in different situations to maximize attainment of various wishes and set-goals. At the global level, however, one can delineate a few broad patterns the person may choose in coping with conflicting internalizations and a breakdown of culturally constructed meanings.

The first is a holding onto previous values and authority, which frequently involves a regression to early and relatively primitive internalizations and often a radical denial of any positive aspects of new ideologies. Internalizations which have been rejected are generally perceived as threats, and these internalizations, or thoughts and actions consonant with them, are often vilified and projected outward. This outcome of the conflict of internalizations or life-worlds is related to Berger et al.'s notion of counter-modernizing impulses, and to Adorno et al.'s conceptualization of the "authoritarian personality" (1950).

A second alternative is the rejection of previously predominant internalizations in favor of new or transient ideals. Largely because of the influences of Western culture and modernization, this may be the predominant personality "type" of the twentieth century. Erich Fromm refers to a variant of this alternative as an "escape from freedom," an automaton conformity which "is the solution that the majority of normal individuals find in modern society" (1947, p. 185). The person may be other-directed, sensitive to the vicissitudes of popular opinion and ideology, similar to the shame-oriented individual Riesman and his colleagues (1961) describe as obeying a noninternalized external ideal. This response to conflicting internalization frequently occurs in Western adolescence, and it may continue through life or be replaced by another identity synthesis. It often occurs among people who migrate from rural to urban areas, who may abandon attitudes, loyalties, and beliefs as well as mode of subsistence. Even many generations after the migration to the city or conscious acceptance of new ways, the basic values the individual transmits to his young children may remain the traditional values consciously rejected or superseded. Like the person who rejects new values and internalizations, the person who accepts them frequently must spend enormous energy repressing conflicting systems of belief and value, often learned in early childhood. This phenomenon is not confined to Third World countries, as any Western woman knows who formed her image of ideal womanhood from her housewife-mother and later rejected stereotyped sex-roles. Many women whose early socialization took place before significant cultural changes in sex-role expectations feel very conflicted between their adult values and more primitive identifications and wishes from early childhood. They frequently try to repress early internalizations, though repressed wishes are frequently expressed through fantasies or selection of fantasy material to read or watch, such as romance novels or soap operas that purvey sexual stereotypes. Correspondingly, men who as adults have shed cultural sex-role stereotypes routinely find unconsciously incorporated patterns and repressed wishes expressed in the role relationships they establish with their wives or lovers.

A third option, not always distinct from the second, is to leave the conflict unresolved.[1] This may take one of two forms. The first resembles what Hagen (1972) and Merton (1968) call "retreatism" (see also Fromm, 1947, p. 185): the individual fails entirely to choose, holding identity formation in abeyance. As this approach continues in time (particularly past adolescence), the line between it and more serious ego pathology becomes decreasingly distinct.

---

[1] A fourth way of resolving conflicting internalizations is to move toward synthetic narcissism, though this is particularly difficult in times of upheaval, in which polarization is much more likely.

357

The second form has been nicely described by Lifton in his concept of "Protean man" (1968, 1970). The "Protean style of self-process" is comparable to Eriksonian identity confusion, yet it is not, Lifton maintains, pathological (1970, p. 44). Protean man, according to Lifton, suffers from a diffuse anxiety or existential guilt, "the guilt of social breakdown," which stems from inner disharmony, from "a sense of having no outlet for his loyalties and no symbolic structure for his attachments" (p. 59). The Protean person cannot readily form a cohesive ego ideal and instead erects a transient synthesis that can never assuage his feelings of "formlessness" (Lifton, p. 60). According to Lifton, Protean man arises in all periods of rapid social change, not just in the present day (1970, p. 63).

Lifton's Protean man is endlessly shifting his identity. One is reminded in this context of Helene Deutsch's classic article on the "As-if Personality" (1942), a theoretical precursor to writings on borderline and narcissistic conditions. The similarity is not accidental because Protean man lies somewhere between Eriksonian identity confusion and borderline psychopathology. The Protean individual, like his borderline counterpart, suffers from a problem of identity, a difficulty in piecing together a coherent value system and sense of continuity or self-sameness through time.

Lifton describes the tendency of men and women in such unstable times to see the world in black and white, to form "all-or-nothing alignments" (1963, p. 129). Again, one cannot miss the parallel with borderline psychopathology: Kernberg (1975) has described a mechanism used by some (he claims all) borderline personalities called "splitting," i.e., viewing certain people as all-good and others as all-bad. One reason a similar mechanism appears in both Protean and borderline individuals is that they are wrestling with some of the same issues, such as how to find meaning in life, how to form commitments to goals and people, and how to maintain separate selfhood without being submerged. Lifton observes that imagery of death and rebirth pervades the phenomenology of Protean man, and one cannot but note that the same is true of borderline pathology: themes of annihilation, for example, are common in borderline Rorschach responses (Kwawer et al., 1980).

The fear of annihilation and the hope for rebirth of the Protean individual represent the pervasive concerns of a person without identity, who fears the loss of psychological selfhood and longs to be reborn as whole. The fear of death that preoccupies both Protean existence and much existential philosophy is also the natural concomitant of a world without stable values and attachments, because without these, the person has no sense that things he values will live beyond him. To put it another way, a life without commitments – to ideals and to people – forecloses the possibility of immortality.

Other writers have spoken to this same issue. Viktor Frankl writes of the "feeling of the total and ultimate meaninglessness" of life that many of his patients express:

> They lack the awareness of a meaning worth living for. They are haunted by the experience of their inner emptiness, a void within themselves; they are caught in that situation which I have called the "existential vacuum." (1959, p. 167)

Before turning to the analysis of a specific case, another approach to the relationship between personality and rapid social change, that of Weinstein and Platt (1969, 1973), deserves mention. Weinstein and Platt are limited by their strict adherence to psychoanalytic theory (replete with ids and libidinal regressions), but one can probably say that a better integration of psychoanalysis and sociology could not be made. They astutely recognize that people become attached to society (in a psychological, object-relational sense) as well as internalize society's moral mandates. Internalization of values, they contend, "occurs most intensively and extensively in relatively undifferentiated groups and communities" (1969, p. 32).

Weinstein and Platt argue that modernization brings with it a greater demand for autonomy and political inclusion, but that in the transition to modernized life individuals face a conflict between the "contradictory evaluative structures" of passivity and autonomy (p. 37). They provide a compelling analysis of the French Revolution to demonstrate that the Revolution, like the Enlightenment as a whole, was characterized by an ambivalence between autonomy and the traditional "passivity" (p. 108). They argue that the philosophers of the Revolution attempted to shed only parts of the *ancien régime* because they failed to recognize that they were advocating a value change that would require the demise of both church and monarchy (pp. 51-7). As was argued in Chapter 7, liberal social contract philosophers – and among them, the French Revolution's greatest thinker, Rousseau – found themselves caught between two ages with competing moralities, and their ambivalence betrayed their failure to recognize themselves as the products and producers of a fundamental moral revolution.

According to Weinstein and Platt, the major period of psychological conflict has shifted from the Oedipal period to adolescence (1973, p. 70). Though the situation is clearly not either/or, one could perhaps interpret this to mean that whereas for the individual in communally collectivistic society the fundamental psychic Rubicon involves the acceptance and internalization of external authority, for the person in a changing or individually collectivistic society an additional and fundamental issue is the formation of identity in a culture with multiple and conflicting worldviews. Weinstein and Platt extend their analysis more generally to social change, arguing that "social-structural events can interrupt an 'average expectable environment' at any time and force an identity crisis and a redefinition of the world" (p. 71). They contend that the breakdown or failure of idealized social objects – introjects gone sour, one might say – can lead to revolutionary activity and identity change:

> The failure of cultural and social symbols and mandates, a failure which violates, contradicts, or renders ineffective or disappointing internalizations at all levels of personality, constitutes the primary source of radical demands against the environment and leads to the reformation of identity. (P. 84)

Communitarian collectivism is not a "social fact" divorced from psychological functioning. The group as idealized social object allows the person to maintain esteem, trust, a system of morals and meaning, and a sense of immortality. As the child shifts his object of devotion from self to society, he trades an internal narcissism for a communitarian collectivism. Collectivism is thus, one might say, a pseudonym of narcissism, though neither is reducible to the other. The externally narcissistic projection of value and power upon the communally collectivistic group fulfills a dual function, providing a sense of meaning and security or "basic trust" to both. When this function begins to break down, however, as it does with modernization, the result is a crisis of individual and cultural integration.[1]

A Javanese Example

I would like now to explore an instance in which just such a crisis of meaning occurred, and in the process to demonstrate how the theory of personality and culture proposed here can elucidate a specific case. The measure of a model, after all, is its ability to distinguish and explain that which was previously less thoroughly understood. The case is of a funeral of a preadolescent boy described by Geertz in his well-known essay on ritual and social change in Java (1973). Geertz's aim in that essay was to show that neither social structure (culture real) nor culture (culture ideal) is reducible to the other, and that disharmony between the two can serve

---

[1] This transferring of a sense of value and power from self to society occurs in stratified communally collectivistic societies, just as it does in more egalitarian groups, and the breakdown of legitimate authority can occur in the same ways. In a stratified society, however, it can also occur if subordinate groups develop a sense of their own exploitation. Marxist anthropologist Godelier has split with more orthodox Marxists in proposing that coercion does not, in fact, account for the willingness of all seemingly exploited groups to accept the status quo, and he hypothesizes that originally stratification and unequal distribution were indeed conceived as legitimate (1974). Similarly, Weinstein and Platt contend that in societies with social classes, individuals internalize "any object that stands in a superordinate relationship to ego," but that if the object fails to meet its obligations, it loses its "license to authority" (1969, p. 149). In a sensitive work on the sense of injustice, Barrington Moore has similarly observed that, historically, ". . . failures of authority to meet its expressed or implied obligations to provide security and advance collective purposes" threaten the legitimacy of the system of authority (1978, p. 46).

as a catalyst to social change. I am largely in agreement with his analysis, though my intent is to show how one can more fully flesh out the relationship between social structure, cultural values, individuals' structures of meaning, and ritual.

Geertz wrote the essay following fieldwork in Modjokuto, a small Javanese town, in the early 1950s. Population growth, urbanization, monetization, and occupational differentiation – in a word, incipient modernization – had begun to "weaken traditional ties of peasant social structure" (p. 148), as well as to alter the syncretic peasant religion amalgamated from Hindu, Buddhist, Islamic, and indigenous animistic traditions. Part of this transformation involved a shift from social ties primarily between individuals and families based on geographical proximity (which Geertz connects to the ecological advantages of agricultural cooperation), to ties based on ideology (as well as class, ethnicity, etc.). Superimposed upon the still extant religious valuation of communal ties was a growing schism, spreading outward from the cities, between Moslem reformists (*santri*) calling for a return to the ways of the Koran, and Marxist-leaning, Hindu-animist *abangan*. The primary ritual reinforcing traditional solidarity was the *slametan*, a communal feast that served as both a rite of passage and a rite of intensification on various occasions, aimed at honoring the ancestors and bolstering solidarity. The conflict between the values embodied in the slametan and the emerging chasm between santri and abangan was nowhere more evident than in the *kampongs*, transitional towns in which peasants were gradually exposed to, and metamorphosed by, the values and tensions of urban society.

In the kampongs, santri and abangan lived in close proximity, and the traditional cultural values stressing solidarity with one's neighbors uneasily coexisted with growing consciousness of intracultural conflict on religious/political lines. Geertz stresses that religion spilled into politics and vice versa, as two parties, the Masjumi and Permai, represented the Moslems and the anti-Moslem Marxist abangans, respectively. In Modjokuto, as in other areas of Java, Permai was a political-religious cult that combined the slametan ritual with religious and political concepts.

For a number of social and political reasons, tensions were mounting between the Masjumi and Permai. During Geertz's stay, a young boy living in the kampong with his aunt and uncle died suddenly, which brought on the event that Geertz masterfully detailed. A funeral in Java is normally a calm, tearless affair, in which unrestrained display of affect is discouraged. The aim of the ceremony, which is a variation of slametan in which people immediately flock in from neighboring areas, is to produce in the mourner a feeling of *iklas*, "a kind of willed affectlessness, a detached and static state of 'not caring,' " and for the neighborhood group a state of *rukun*, or " 'communal harmony' " (p. 153).

361

Commemorative slametans are held at fixed intervals for the next three years. One can readily see how this series of rituals is "overdetermined" by individual and collective needs. At the collective level, it makes solidarity between relatively independent households experientially real through sharing of food and communal assembling, and in so doing fosters a group-need attachment that also makes ecological sense. At the individual level, the funeral rituals channel the grieving process in such a way as to maintain a sense of meaning and gradually to reduce other-need set-goals requiring the loved one's presence. This function is made clear in the notion of *iklas*, which aptly expresses the ultimate aim of the mourning process: to reduce the need for the deceased person to the point of "not caring" or "affectlessness." In this respect, that the funeral rituals appear over a span of time and not simply once, reflects the psychological requisites of the grieving process. Western students of grief have observed the potential for pathological grief reactions in those who try, once and for all and from the start, to deny the pain of mourning. Repeated slametans are thus psychologically adaptive. Emphasis on communal solidarity also makes psychological sense since it helps quell the pain of loss of one attachment by augmenting attachment to another object, the group.

In the event witnessed by Geertz, however, sociocultural change prevented the funeral ceremony from fulfilling its psychocultural functions. The funeral ritual was traditionally directed by the local religious official, or Modin. The Modin for the kampong was a Masjumi leader, whereas the dead boy's uncle, who had to arrange for the funeral since the boy's parents had to come from a distance, was an active Permai. At the direction of a higher official, the Modin refused to officiate at the ceremony, which left the boy's uncle and the converging crowd of santri and abangan neighbors paralyzed.

No one but the Modin knew the correct procedure for carrying out a funeral, and as time passed, people became more frightened of what the dead boy's soul might do if not properly attended to. The santris, who were largely members of the Masjumi, were crowded together, "chatting quietly to one another about everything but the problem at hand" (p. 156). In this one can recognize a collective mechanism of defense aimed at denying the magnitude of the crisis which was already causing "nervousness" among a nearby group of women. This provides a good illustration of how one cannot simply separate emics from etics. The description in terms of defense is clearly etic, and the people involved would no doubt have explained the content of their conversation differently. Yet the situation is far less clear regarding their emic view of the magnitude of the crisis. At a conscious emic level, they may well have denied the significance of the problem. At an unconscious emic level, however, they obviously perceived the collective paralysis and normative disorder; otherwise the defense would not have been set in motion. The anthropologist must thus separate conscious emics from unconscious emics, just as the psychodynamic psychologist distinguishes between the patient's conscious and unconscious beliefs and feelings.

Normally the boy's relatives would prepare for the funeral by taking the boy on their laps and washing his body. "But the relatives," observed Geertz, ". . . were by now so deeply shaken and confused that they were unable to bring themselves to hold the boy on their laps in the customary fashion" (p. 157). When eventually three reluctant volunteers had been recruited to do the job, confusion persisted around the technicalities of preparing the body. The boy's aunt finally broke down and wept unrestrainedly, which made the situation even more tense and prompted a frantic attempt to comfort her. From a theoretical perspective, what one sees here is the breakdown in the web of meanings that makes life understandable, predictable, and secure. Conflicting cultural ideologies had created a situation in which a ritual necessary for channelling grief, promoting solidarity, and, like all rituals, maintaining a sense of continuity and coherence to life and social life in particular, could not be performed. The lapse in the culture real norm of carrying out the funeral in the prescribed manner was itself unsettling since it negated the routine and expectable as well as demonstrated concretely that the social order and communality were falling apart. This breach in prescribed behavior also had the psychologically devastating effect of leaving unchanneled a grieving process which everyone expected to be controlled through the ritual.

The aunt's tears thus reflected both her grief, which would have manifested itself differently had the collective mechanism for channelling the emotion been functioning as usual, and a doubly painful assault on structures of meaning that made the world stable and comprehensible; not only had her nephew died, but her social world was crumbling. The response of those around her who frantically tried to console her can be viewed as a collective control mechanism or defense activated by the breakdown of a norm (that one does not weep). At an individual level, one can view the responses of the women who tried to comfort her as control mechanisms instigated by anxiety caused by the perception of a broken norm and consequent threat to their own structures of meaning. A friend of the uncle then suggested that the boy simply be buried and the ritual ignored; at the collective level, just as at the individual level, routinized action which no longer fulfills its function – the management of feelings – becomes discardable or, in Skinnerian terms, "extinguished."

At this point the boy's parents arrived, and the father, a rather apolitical man, resolved the issue by calling for the traditional Islamic ceremony. The Modin then directed the ceremony, the santris had their day and sang their chants, and the slametan was finally served. Three days later the first commemorative slametan occurred, but no santris appeared, and "it was as much a Permai political and religious cult meeting as a mourning ritual" (p. 160). The funeral had thus, as ritual, done precisely what rituals tend to do: to manifest concretely the state of the "body politic." Yet this informational aspect of ritual, which Rappaport (1979) calls its "indexical" function (i.e., providing an index of the state of some variable), conflicted with another function of ritual, which aims at reinforcing solidarity. In more stable times, despite petty squabbles and infighting, when people assemble for ritual they submerge their individual differences in a spirit of solidarity. The very act of assembling and of performing in unison or in complement to one another, concretely demonstrates the reality of a sacred solidarity which itself masks the disharmonies of the profane world. In theoretical terms, ritual can be a routinized control mechanism that responds to the gap between culture ideal (solidarity) and culture real (ingroup antagonism) by making solidarity real in the here and now. In so doing, it reinforces both the ideal and the perception that reality conforms to the ideal. In this Javanese example of a ritual in the context of monumental social change, the ritual properly performed its function of making concrete aspects of culture real (particularly the state of social relations) and culture ideal, yet in so doing it backfired by revealing in the starkest form that the ideal of territorial solidarity was no longer *real,* that the culture ideal was now itself divided and conflictual, and that solidarity could not be achieved. In other words, it adequately performed its informational or indexical function of reflecting the state of solidarity, but whereas this indexical function had previously reinforced a more dynamic function of *promoting* solidarity, now the informational and dynamic functions were disharmonious.

That the santris did not appear for the commemorative ritual is testimony to the power of the ritual in expressing the state of the culture. The experience of three days earlier had taught the santris that they were no longer part of a homogeneous culture in which neighbors were compatriots. What better indication of this state of affairs than a failed ritual, destroyed by ideological factionalism? For the abangans, the ritual made clear not only the end of territorial communality but also their own reliance upon the santris. This no doubt fed into feelings about domination from, or inferiority to the santris, who tended to be of a higher class than the abangans. The control mechanism utilized by this subpopulation on the occasion of the commemorative slametan was to turn the ritual into a political-religious meeting, affirming the solidarity of the Permai, in contraposition to the santris.

This affirmation of solidarity, however, could not overcome the reality of conflict in the culture ideal. On the one hand, the old ideals preached the solidarity of a communally collectivistic culture, while on the other hand, the new ideals for the Permai preached solidarity of their own group, pitted against the Masjumi or santris. For the Permai leader who led the political-religious ritual, this conflict was resolved by transferring his loyalty primarily to the Permai and thus siding with the new morality. For the dead boy's father, however, the situation was not so clear, as revealed in a speech he delivered at the commemorative slametan:

> He kept telling himself it was just the will of God, but it was so hard, for nowadays people didn't agree on things any more; one person tells you one thing and others tell you another. It's hard to know what is right, to know what to believe . . . He said he was trying to be *iklas*, to tell himself it was just the will of God, but it was hard, for things were so confused these days. It was hard to see why the boy should have died. (P. 161)

This speech reveals three interrelated aspects of the father's life-world. First, his ego ideal had become conflicted; he no longer knew what was right because he was faced with competing ideologies. Secondly, the norms upon which he had come to depend, which served the social and psychological function of maintaining order and predictability, had been shattered. Thirdly, with traditional norms, values, and rituals destroyed, he could no longer channel his grief in accordance with cultural prescriptions, nor could he ascribe any meaning to his son's death. The failure to find meaning in his suffering further exacerbated his grief, producing a speech his audience found disquieting and inappropriate.

In a lucid analysis, Geertz assimilates this event to a conflict between a cultural system inherited from rural society and a social structure based on *Gesellschaft* principles. The kampong is a transitional society, and its residents found meaning in the old values of territorial communality, while being functionally integrated into the social system through urban ties of wages, bureaucracy, and secondary associations.

This perspective has much merit, though it underestimates the extent to which the conflict exists not only between culture (ideal) and social structure (culture real) but within the ideal itself. Geertz argues that much of the problem involved the interpenetration of religious meanings and political meanings, but he views political meanings as an aspect of social structure. What his analysis misses is that the political meanings themselves are aspects of an emergent meaning-system with its own ideals which evolves from, but is not identical with, social organization. In other words, while the kampong residents demonstrated their adherence to the old ideals by gathering for the slametan, the end result of the affair evidenced a conflicting adherence to a new morality that militated against neighborhood solidarity. Put differently, not only did culture ideal and culture real conflict, but the culture ideal itself was conflictual and ambiguous, as reflected in the demise of the communal ritual of a more homogeneous, solidary age.

One can now begin to diagram some of the causal factors that produced, and were set in motion by this event. Culture real changes in the techno-ecological sphere, which included the influence of foreign capital, urbanization, modernization, and altered social structure, led to a nascent ideology in conflict with the traditional peasant communitarian ethos. Solidarity began to be defined in terms of common ideology and instrumental interests, as opposed to territorial contiguity. This conflict in the culture ideal in turn influenced a culture real element, the funeral ritual. The misfiring of this ritual shattered the web of meanings that held together the emic reality of individuals in the kampong and prevented them from handling their grief in the prescribed manner. In so doing it initiated individuals' defenses and coping strategies aimed at dealing with the anxiety of cultural breakdown, either through various forms of withdrawal or through the attempt to put together a more satisfying culture. The breakdown of a ritual, the function of which was to reinforce solidarity, also, by its very dysfunction, not only failed to reinforce communal sentiment, but further suggested and thus abetted its demise. The attempt to construct a new and more satisfying culture ideal (e.g., through nationalism, Marxism, or an Islamic state) may itself lead to alterations in technological, ecological, and economic structure.

Thus, an alteration in the culture real produced changes in both culture real and culture ideal which themselves produced further changes. The recursive processes involved cannot be understood exclusively in terms of cybernetic feedback mechanisms, and as this example shows, one can be far more precise in detailing the forces that lead from ecological and social structural variables to ideals and back again as well as the relation between individual and collectivity in times of cultural breakdown.

13 Breakdown and Recovery: Paradigmatic Processes in Personal Identity and Cultural Integration

CHAPTER 9 EXAMINED a number of issues related to cultural stasis and change, arguing for the presence of self-regulating control mechanisms and processes that can account for minor as well as extraordinary sociocultural changes. Cultural institutions – including the beliefs, political organizations, and economic institutions of culture real and the ideas, ideals, and moral mandates of culture ideal – synthesize multiple and often competing demands. To the extent that the solutions encoded in culture can no longer meet these demands, the culture is likely to experience a crisis of integration, i.e., a psychocultural crisis in which cultural beliefs and values no longer seem satisfying to members of the culture and patterns of behavior and social interaction are substantially disrupted (cf. Wallace, 1956).

A crisis of cultural integration may occur for a number of reasons. Altered set-goals relating to member-needs (e.g., a threat to life or security) or group-needs (such as shifting units of attachment, which often accompanies modernization) may impose new requirements on the culture and disrupt various aspects of the culture real or force a resynthesis of the culture ideal. In terms of culture real and ideal, cultural diffusion may produce altered norms; institutional changes in the culture real may have unintended consequences for cultural integration; political dynamics may alter the culture ideal; innovations may have intended and unintended consequences for culture real and ideal; societal control mechanisms may have unintended effects when reverberating though the psychocultural "system" (cf. Smelser, 1963, p.11); and demographic factors may have cultural consequences that ultimately prove disruptive. In most cases, minor disruptons produce mechanisms to restore "equilibrium"; however, in some instances, cultural integration breaks down, and a new worldview, including both culture ideal and real, must emerge if the group is to survive. As noted before, when a cultural synthesis breaks down, individual identity becomes problematic. The crucial question here is how one can conceive of the processes by which individual identity and cultural

367

integration disintegrate and resynthesize, and how these processes interrelate. To explore this question, this chapter will examine six seemingly unrelated processes – scientific revolution, cultural revitalization, personal religious experience, identity crisis and formation, brainwashing, and rites of passage – and demonstrate that they share a common pattern that allows one to gain a clearer understanding of one aspect of the relationship between personality and culture.

Kuhnian Scientific Revolutions

Thomas Kuhn (1970) argues that science does not involve, as previously supposed, the orderly accumulation of facts or the verification or disconfirmation of hypotheses. Rather, he contends, science "progresses" through the development, breakdown, and reformation of scientific paradigms. These paradigms, in the broadest sense, are "universally recognized scientific achievements that for a time provide model problems and solutions to a community of practitioners" (p. viii). In periods of "normal science," researchers are puzzle-solvers who try to resolve minor anomalies that have arisen. Such scientists tackle these anomalies with the assumption or faith – one is tempted to say "basic trust" – that through proper experimentation and perhaps minor adjustments of the theory, the anomaly will be resolved within the context of the paradigm. Normal science thus involves the assimilation (in the Piagetian sense) of new data to an existing paradigm (p. 53). The paradigm provides rules that tell scientific practitioners what both the world and the science are like, though these rules become explicit only when a paradigm is beginning to break down (p. 47). One cannot avoid the parallel, remarked upon earlier, that in both personality and culture, the "grammar" of belief and action becomes explicit only when a preexisting identity synthesis or cultural integration begins to totter. Normal science, according to Kuhn, "often suppresses novelties because they are necessarily subversive of its basic commitments" (p. 5). Built into normal science is a resistance (perhaps in the psychodynamic sense?) to change and to anomalies that threaten the paradigm.

The reader cannot but notice here the similarity to Mary Douglas's account of taboo and pollution beliefs in communally collectivistic societies. Pollution beliefs, she argues, relate to anomalies that fall between the cracks of collective classificatory schemas. As she remarks at one point, "Ideas about contagion can certainly be traced to reaction to anomaly ... The initial recognition of anomaly leads to anxiety and from there to suppression or avoidance ..." (1966, p. 15). Her account of the sequence of recognition of anomaly to anxiety to defense against anxiety is a subclass of the systems model used throughout this book, in which feedback sets in motion control mechanisms to restore "equilibrium."

We can turn this analysis against our own science and see that scientific anomalies, like the objects of cultural taboos, are dangerous and powerful: they are dangerous because they threaten the very edifice upon which we rest our understanding of the world, and they are powerful precisely because they are outside our control. We, like our "primitive" brethren, guard against these evil forces through elaborate purification rituals, and perhaps one would not be too far afield in suggesting that the elaborate statistical analyses to which social scientists submit their data may in part serve this function. Indeed, to take this example a step further, perhaps it is no accident that statistical techniques confer what has been inappropriately labeled "significance" upon data which themselves may be useless or irrelevant. Douglas argues that cultures often single one anomaly out of many onto which they project the danger of all anomaly, and by ritually controlling that particular danger, they symbolically restore order and deny the problems with their conceptual "paradigms." The runaway processes involved in overspecialization and attention to microdetails characteristic of so much of contemporary social science may represent, in part, the same mechanism. By narrowing his interests to the reaction time of three-year-olds in sandbox experiments, the individual researcher symbolically masters his lack of a larger context or paradigm and focuses his attention on resolvable questions that provide quantifiable, if irrelevant results. At the collective level, this frenetic search for the understanding of the insignificant displaces the scientific community's attention from its cognitive vacuum to masterable details.

Different scientific communities, like different cultures, utilize different control mechanisms to deal with anomaly. If the reader will excuse a personal anecdote, I once attended a case presentation at a prestigious psychoanalytic institute in which a well-known analyst beautifully presented material on a boy who had been in analysis for many years. The boy's mother was seriously disturbed and had wished to abort him, and the material quite clearly suggested that this was a young man who had never experienced the consistency and "unconditional regard" that permit the development of a sense of basic trust and ulimately foster the formation of a coherent identity. No one familiar with the work of the heretical psychoanalyst Heinz Kohut, whom many in the psychoanalytic community have recognized to be at the extreme outer margins of the Freudian paradigm, could have failed to perceive that the presenting analyst was speaking Kohutese without acknowledging it. As a prophylactic measure against this implicit infusion of a foreign and dangerous construct, one of the senior psychoanalysts at the institute stood up promptly after the presentation and began raising questions about when the boy had been circumcised, his homosexual strivings, and the like (no doubt reflecting the cognitive castration anxiety of the analyst . . .), all of which issues were extraordinarily irrelevant to the central problems of a young man who was unwanted by his mother, had been tossed from relative to relative in his childhood, and had never been able to find the love and consistency in another person so basic to human happiness and health. After the discussion, I proceeded (perhaps with unconscious maliciousness of which at the time I was unaware) to ask the analyst who had presented the case if he thought Kohut's theory could provide any insight into the boy's dynamics. To this he replied, with the manner of a bishop gently reminding an errant priest of his duty to the church, "You know, we don't *believe* in Kohut here."

To return to Kuhn, when the anomalies produced through normal scientific puzzle-solving cannot be handled through routine procedures, they begin to generate a feeling within the scientific community that the paradigm is inadequate. A period of "extraordinary science" appears in which researchers, motivated by cognitive disharmony, search for new ways to make sense of reality. These periods are marked by a competition between segments of the scientific community (1970, p. 8), comparable, one might note, to the conflicting internalizations and identity fragments that compete for primacy in periods of individual identity confusion. During the period of extraordinary science, Kuhn observes, a researcher or small group of researchers motivated by the "essential tension" of the inadequacy of a collective cognitive schema develops a new paradigm which leads to something similar to a "gestalt switch." Others in the scientific community come to recognize the usefulness of the new approach (though many older scientists must simply die off before the paradigm shift is completed) and become converted to it (p. 19), so that eventually this new paradigm provides a basis for a new tradition of normal science. A paradigm, Kuhn argues, is never discarded before a new one appears to take its place (p. 77). Once the new paradigm has taken hold, textbooks are literally rewritten in line with the new paradigm, so that old paradigms are viewed as having tried to answer questions in which the new paradigm is interested (whereas the older paradigms may really have been concerned with a different set of issues).

New paradigms, then, change the questions asked, not just the answers posed, and the convert to a paradigm is often unable to switch gestalts, to see things from the previous perspective. On the psychological level, one wonders if a similar phenomenon to the rewriting of textbooks and the failure to understand the issues of paradigms lost provides a complementary explanation to Freud's repression theory of infantile amnesia.[1] Information stored under different cognitive ordering principles (e.g., Piagetian sensorimotor or preoperational thought) may be inaccessible to conscious-

---

[1] Schachtel (1947) and Neisser (1962) have proposed similar cognitive explanations; see also Kihlstrom (1981).

ness based upon a different set of cognitive "paradigms." "Secondary revision" of latent dream content may, similarly, have as much to do with the problems of transition from one way of thinking to another as with ego censorship of repressed material.

Kuhn suggests that paradigm changes are comparable to changes of worldview, and it is at this point that his ideas begin to converge with phenomena on a cultural level, in Wallace's description of revitalization movements.

Revitalization Movements

The similarity between Kuhn's model of scientific revolutions and A.F.C. Wallace's (1956) model of cultural revitalization movements represents one of those striking examples of simultaneous discovery of the same phenomenon, often by researchers (as in this case) in entirely different fields. Six years before Kuhn published the first edition of *The Structure of Scientific Revolutions,* Wallace (1956) studied nativistic movements, religious revivals, messianic movements, millenarian movements, utopian communities, cargo cults, and similar phenomena and found that in each case, a new cultural "gestalt" emerged that was embodied in what he calls a revitalization movement. Wallace defines a revitalization movement as a "deliberate, organized, conscious effort by members of a society to construct a more satisfying culture" (p. 265). While he does not make clear the relative extent to which values and cognitions are involved, he argues that revitalization movements alter, at the individual level, what he calls the person's "mazeway," a mental image of herself, her culture, and her general "behavioral environment" (Hallowell, 1955). The precipitating factor that leads to the need for mazeway resynthesis is a repeated and irresolvable anxiety or stress that cannot be eliminated within the current mazeway (though Wallace does not distinguish whether this stress is the result of cognitive disharmony or noncognitive need-frustration). A collective effort to reduce this anxiety through mazeway resynthesis constitutes a revitalization movement. According to Wallace, and one cannot miss the parallel with Kuhn, the individual will not abandon one mazeway, no matter how dysfunctional or obviously inaccurate, until he has a new one to replace it (1961, p. 161).

Wallace isolates five stages of revitalization which constitute a "structure of the revitalization process" (compare Kuhn's "structure of scientific revolutions"):

> The structure of the revitalization process, in cases where the full course is run, consists of five somewhat overlapping stages: 1. Steady State; 2. Period of Individual Stress; 3. Period of Cultural Distortion; 4. Period of Revitalization (in which occur the functions of mazeway reformulation,

371

communication, organization, adaptation, cultural transformation, and routinization); and finally, 5. New Steady State. (1956, p. 208)

In the steady state, "For the vast majority of the population, culturally recognized techniques for satisfying needs operate with such efficiency that chronic stress within the system varies within tolerable limits" (p. 268). During the period of increased individual stress, cultural mechanisms for stress-control begin to break down as a result of such factors as ecological changes, economic distress, acculturation, etc. The third stage is the period of cultural distortion, in which individuals are forced to choose various maladaptive and idiosyncratic forms of stress-reduction (such as regressive clinging to the old mazeway, alcoholism, intragroup violence, and psychosomatic disorders), and ultimately the old mazeway fails to provide individuals with a sense of meaning.

If the culture is to survive, a revitalization movement must arise that can provide a "new synthesis of values and meanings" (p. 270), often religious in character. This period is comparable to Kuhn's "extraordinary science," in which an individual or small number of individuals produces a new synthesis which promises to relieve the stress produced by the demise of the old paradigm. A prophet undergoes a personality transformation during the period of revitalization, which often occurs in a dream or hallucination and involves a new mazeway gestalt. The prophet is frequently an unstable person such as a shaman, who believes that he is in touch with the supernatural. He begins to preach his novel vision and attract converts, and the new synthesis eventually revitalizes the community and becomes institutionalized. The stage of revitalization Wallace compares to Weber's (1947) concept of the routinization of charisma.

Sixteen years after publication of his classic article on revitalization movements, Wallace linked his approach with that of Kuhn in another tremendous essay, "Paradigmatic Processes in Culture Change" (1972), in which he subsumed revitalization movements under the rubric of "paradigmatic" processes in culture. He argues in this later article that after the original innovation (whether scientific, technological, or religious) comes a period of paradigmatic core activity roughly similar to Kuhn's normal science. Alongside core development he notes a number of processes that generally follow from a paradigmatic cultural innovation. The first are processes of "exploitation," by which an economic, military, religious, or political organization exploits the paradigm for its own interests (p. 470). A second set of processes Wallace calls "functional consequences," in which effects of the paradigm ripple through various aspects of society. The paradigm has something of a multiplier effect, in that original consequences provoke responses which in turn set off a chain of action and reaction. A final process is "rationalization," which includes ethical, political, and other justifications offered by the paradigmatic community to its members and to affected members of the larger society. Wallace concludes the article with an interesting speculation about the way a trait or practice may pass from one society to another through acculturation or diffusion without transferring with it the relevant paradigmatic context or deep structure.

While psychological variables are almost absent from Wallace's later article, his model of revitalization provides a link between individual psychology and cultural dynamics in times of culture change. As will become clear through an analysis of religious experience, identity formation, brainwashing, and rites of passage, paradigmatic processes analogous to those discussed by Kuhn and Wallace occur on the level of personality as well as that of culture.

The Structure of Religious Experience

The classic work on personal religious experiences is William James's *Varieties of Religious Experience*, which would be worth reading for its esthetic beauty even if James had nothing to say. (James, like Freud, Erikson, and Geertz, is a member of that underpopulated species which provides the archaeological missing link between those who can think and those who can write.) Religious experience, James contends, and conversion experience in particular, involves the process by which a formerly divided self becomes unified:

> To be converted, to be regenerated, to receive grace, to experience religion, to gain an assurance, are so many phrases which denote the process, gradual or sudden, by which a self hitherto divided, and consciously wrong, inferior and unhappy, becomes unified and consciously right, superior and happy, in consequence of its firmer hold upon religious realities. (1902, p. 157)

James argues that religious experience in may ways resembles the "conversions" of adolescence (p. 164). The various impulses of the child "begin by being a comparable chaos within us" and "must end by forming a stable system of functions . . ." (p. 143). The period of "order-making and struggle" is likely to be one of unhappiness (p. 143). The root of the need for rebirth, James argues, is "an incompletely unified moral and intellectual constitution" (p. 141). This lack of complete unification represents an inadequate synthesis of the ego, and in particular of the self-concept and the morality system or meaning-system described in this book as the ego ideal.

James maintains that religion is only one way to unify a troubled soul. Remedying "inner incompleteness and inner discord," he contends, "is a general psychological process" (pp. 146-7). James observes a pattern to this process of unification: "In all these instances we have precisely the same psychological form of event, — a firmness, stability, and equilibrium succeeding a period of storm and stress and inconsistency" (p. 147). This process of establishing equilibrium or unification may occur suddenly or gradually. In either case it involves a feeling of wholeness and moral certainty, a reconciliation of subjectivity and objectivity. James quotes the manuscript of a clergyman:

> I remember the night, amd almost the very spot on the hilltop where my soul opened out, as it were, into the Infinite, and there was a rushing together of the two worlds, the inner and the outer . . . The ordinary sense of things around me faded . . . It was like the effect of some great orchestra when all the separate notes have melted into one swelling harmony. . . . (P. 67)

Considering accounts of experiences such as these, James delineates three characteristics of the faith-state or "state of assurance" that occurs during the religious experience (pp. 198-9). First, it is characterized by a sense of peace and harmony. Secondly, it entails "the sense of perceiving truths not known before" (p. 199). Finally, in the faith-state the world appears to have undergone an objective change.

The connection between this state of assurance (the stage in the religious experience in which equilibrium is restored) and the new paradigm that emerges with a Kuhnian scientific revolution or the new steady state that appears in the process of cultural revitalization is not difficult to apprehend. In all three, a sense of peace and harmony is restored where previously tension, disorder, and inconsistency prevailed. In all three the individual feels that he has come upon a new truth, a new bedrock to his understanding. Finally, in all three, a new *Weltanschauung* has arisen, so that the world appears suddenly to have changed.

In the course of religious experience as described by James, the individual synthesizes a new self-concept and a new ego ideal. In so doing he brings coherence to his life; he develops an altered sense of truth and of his relation to the external world. Prior to this new synthesis, the individual experiences the dread of nothingness; he lacks identity, he lacks an essential relation to his fellows, and he lacks a sense of meaning and coherence. John Lame Deer, a Sioux medicine man, recounts his experience of the vision quest, a form of collectively patterned religious experience common to several North American Indian tribes:

> I was still lightheaded and dizzy from my first sweatbath in which I had purified myself before going up the hill . . . Even now, an hour later, my skin still tingled. But it seemed to have made my brain empty . . . Blackness was wrapped around me like a velvet cloth. It seemed to cut me off from the outside world, even from my own body. It made me listen to voices within me. I thought of my forefathers, who had crouched on this hill before me . . . I thought I could sense their presence . . . I trembled and my bones turned to ice. (Lame Deer and Erdoes, 1972, pp. 14-15)

374

In this passage one finds all of the characteristics of what can be described as a void in ego identity: a lack of coherent self-concept, a fragmentation of ego ideal processes, and a consequent inability to know what plans to pursue. One also sees in this passage an attempt to ascend from this existential vacuum. Lame Deer begins by purifying himself, by shutting himself off from the impure past. At this point he feels like his *brain is empty,* like nothing is inside of him. Psychotherapists hear similar statements daily in their practices, and one could hardly express with more precision the feeling of emptiness of an existence without identity, without a raison d'être and a "self" to pursue it. Lame Deer felt cut off from both the world and himself: divorced from his prior self-concept and ego ideal, from a prior relationship between self and other, he was left without a relation to either. He could hear voices within him, old introjects and identity fragments competing for his attention. Finally, he felt an overwhelming presence, and his identity resynthesis had begun.

The discussion of religious experience thus leads to an analysis of identity, and one should not be surprised to find another example of a pattern of breakdown and resynthesis.

Identity Crisis and Identity Formation

The "father" of identity is Erik Erikson, who has devoted a number of books and papers to the subject (see Erikson, 1968). Like many fathers, Erikson has begotten several children, most of whom have inherited similar qualities: his definitions of identity are various, though related. In *Childhood and Society* he claims that the "sense of identity provides the ability to experience one's self as something that has continuity and sameness, and to act accordingly" (1963, p. 42). In *Identity: Youth and Crisis,* a collection of articles, he speaks of identity as a "process 'located' in the core of the individual and yet also in the core of his communal culture, a process which establishes, in fact, the identity of these two identities" (1968, p. 22, emphasis deleted). Later in the same book he unites these two versions:

> Ego identity is the awareness of the fact that there is a self-sameness and continuity to the ego's synthesizing methods, the style of one's individuality, and that this style coincides with the sameness and continuity of one's meaning for significant others. (P. 50, emphasis deleted)

One can offer a slightly more precise definition by using the theory of personality proposed in Part I. Identity is a function of the ego and entails integration between ego ideal, a coherent self-concept which permits the experience of a subjective sense of continuity and sameness, and ego real processes realistically attempting to fulfill relatively stable and consistent ideals. By "integration" between these structures I mean that not only do

375

the functions of the ego ideal make demands upon those of the ego real, but the ego real mediates between reality and ego ideal, tempering ego ideal processes in accordance with concrete possibilities. The choice of an occupation, for example, both conditions and is conditioned by ego ideal set-goals, which must adapt to this choice as well as provide guidelines for its selection. This definition of identity could alternatively be stated as the creation or acceptance of a conception of morality and the attempt to actualize it, the formation of an ideal balance between self and other and the pursuit of it, or the establishment of a coherent immortality system and the realistic attempt to fulfill its demands. This definition involves all three subcomponents of the ego, and one can readily see how a disturbance in one can lead to difficulty in the others. For example, inability to form a coherent set of ideals and commitments renders one less able to carry out stable plans and long-term goals, which in turn produces a subjective sense of incoherence.

Erikson has described the existential void experienced in identity crisis as a "play with nothingness," an "adventure in reaching inner rock bottom to find something firm to stand on" (1958, p. 104). One finds the same idea expressed in Descartes' *Meditations* or in Kierkegaard's discussion of the infinite resignation, after which one can make a leap into faith. Erikson writes of this "rock bottom attitude" as "an attempt to find that immutable bedrock on which the struggle for a new existence can safely begin and be assured of a future" (p. 103).

One can construct from Erikson's work an implicit model of the pattern of identity development which runs roughly as follows. A childhood pre-identity synthesis gives way to a period of identity confusion. Overlapping with, and following this stage may be, in some cultures and classes, a period Erikson calls "psychosocial moratorium," in which the individual is free to dramatize and experiment with various values, roles, and patterns of behavior (1975, pp. 199-200). Identity confusion and moratorium are followed by identity formation, which marks the transition to adulthood.

Identity formation, for Erikson, entails the integration of old identifications into a cohesive whole. Asserting that identity formation "begins where the usefulness of identification ends," he argues that "identity arises from the selective repudiation and mutual assimilation of childhood identifications and their absorption in a new configuration . . ." (1968, p. 159). This quotation is somewhat reminiscent of Ruth Benedict's notion of culture as a configuration (she and Erikson use the same word) which selects from the great arc of cultural traits. Wallace (1956) speaks of cultural revitalization in similar terms as the formation of a new gestalt out of existing cultural materials.

Erikson places issues of identity in social perspective, arguing that identity is a process at the core of personality as well as at the core of culture. It is a process, he asserts, that establishes "the identity of these two identities" (1968, p. 22). Erikson points out that different cultures deal with the problem of identity in different ways, whether through ritualized ceremonies or the teaching of social and technological methods of "mastering dangerous forces which take the form of enemies, animals, and machines." In each case, he concludes, "the young person finds himself part of a universal framework which reaches back into an established tradition, and promises a definable future" (1958, p. 114). Societies thus fashion identities for their young people to accept, yet in times of rapid technological change, institutionalization breaks down, and the child can no longer step into culturally constituted identity syntheses (1968, p. 38). At such times, charismatic leaders arise whose identity serves as a model for a troubled era. Erikson's studies of Luther (1958) and Gandhi (1969) attempt to show how a "great man's" confrontation with a Jamesian divided soul leads to a cultural resolution of a crisis of identity and integration. Again, one cannot miss the parallels with Kuhn and Wallace, though Kuhn speaks only of cognitive revolutions.

Erikson thus emphasizes that identity is socially conditioned, with societies narrowing and guiding individual choice, particularly through puberty rites that "replace a horror of undefinedness, dramatized by rituals, with a defined sacrifice and a sacred badge" (1968, p. 87). One would thus expect to find some relation between the process of identity-formation and initiation rites in communally collectivistic societies. This is, in fact, the case, as will be discussed shortly. First, however, it will be useful to examine another form of socially patterned identity reformation, brainwashing.

Brainwashing as Forced Identity Resynthesis

In a penetrating study of the psychology of "brainwashing," Robert Lifton (1963) examined the processes of thought reform in postrevolutionary China through extensive psychiatric interviews with a number of individuals who had been subjected to it. Lifton contends that thought reform has two major elements: confession and reeducation (p. 5). Brainwashing involves an imposed identity change (p. 380) in individuals whose identities may previously have been secure, and it is accomplished through the "penetration by the psychological forces of the environment into the inner emotions of the individual . . ."(p. 66).

Imagery of death and rebirth pervades the thought reform experience. The aim of brainwashing is to destroy one identity and replace it with another, and the individual is thus symbolically killed and reborn:

The physical and emotional assaults bring about the symbolic death; leniency and the developing confession are the bridge between death and rebirth; the reeducation process, along with the final confession, create the rebirth experience. (p. 66)

Two features of the above quotation deserve attention. First, the symbolism of death and rebirth has been encountered before in these pages, in the discussion of Protean and borderline personalities and in William James's account of rebirth in religious experience. This suggests that some shared factor underlies identity processes, religious experience, and brainwashing. Secondly, a peculiar pattern has once more begun to emerge—breakdown, transition, and resynthesis—which seems endemic to processes of identity formation and cultural integration.

Lifton proposes a four-stage model of the processes through which thought reform destroys and resynthesizes identity. The first stage is the "great togetherness," in which the individual is surrounded by an omnipotent group which informs him of his disease and promises a cure (pp. 380-1). Characteristic of the entire ordeal is a surrender of autonomy and identity to the group (pp. 67-8). The group demands that the individual relinquish his independent thought and identity and accept the will of the group on trust, which Lifton relates to the issue of Eriksonian basic trust (p. 422). The group appears omniscient, and for all intents and purposes it is, because the individual is never out of its sight; Lifton also speaks of the "shared omnipotence" of the group (p. 427).

The second stage Lifton calls the "closing in of the milieu" (p. 381). This is undoubtedly the most painful period, in which the aim is to dissolve every attachment, self-image, or previous internalization that could interfere with the imposed identity. The individual is forced symbolically to kill everyone and everything that ever meant anything to him. In this stage and the last, the individual is subjected to merciless interrogation and is denied sleep for long periods of time (sometimes more than a week). One is reminded here of the vision quest which, like many other forms of collectively induced identity crisis, is precipitated by mind-altering stimuli such as sleep-deprivation, drugs, or torture. One of Lifton's interviewees told Lifton of this experience, "You are annihilated . . . exhausted . . . You feel that all is lost . . ." (p. 23).

The fear of annihilation—of both life and identity—is central to the thought reform experience. The prisoner is presented with an alternation of threats of annihilation and leniency (p. 73). This serves the psychological function, one might argue, of forcing a trade of dependence and submission for security.

The third and fourth stages entail a steady indoctrination of the individual with the imposed ideology (or, one might say, paradigm). The third stage marks the beginning of personality resynthesis and "ends on a note of togetherness . . ." (p. 385). The stage is the stage of rebirth, which centers around the signing of a confession, which purges the individual of his impurity and signals to the community that he has been reborn.

Lifton speaks of the brainwashing environment as a "purging milieu" which combines a "demand for absolute purity" with an "obsession with personal confession" (p. 425). The confession is, no doubt, a purification ritual (analogous to baptism) which serves both individual and societal functions. Yet a significant question remains as to why the purity must be absolute, why the individual is forced to believe in a strict dichotomy of good and evil, and why any intrusion of impure thoughts leads to the violent need for purification. One can again make use of Douglas' analysis of purity and danger, and one realizes that the society which creates the brainwashing milieu—and the individual who becomes "reformed"—may have few intermediate control mechanisms that would allow some tolerance of ambiguity. Any impure thought must immediately be purged.

Here Lifton provides another link between psychological and sociocultural processes in his notion of "totalism." He refers to the convergence of "immoderate ideology with equally immoderate individual character traits" as "ideological totalism" (p. 419). Lifton argues that ideological totalism is "most likely to occur with those ideologies which are most sweeping in their content and most ambitious—or messianic—in their claims, whether religious, political, or scientific" (p. 419).

It is at this point that some connecting links become clear between Lifton, Kuhn, Wallace, and Douglas. The ideologies that are likely to be most sweeping are those that arise in periods of massive social upheaval. Lifton himself points out that totalism seems to be a property of movements characterized by "revitalizing enthusiasm" (p. 455), though he appears unfamiliar with Wallace's work. In times of breakdown of a cultural paradigm, anxiety is at its peak, and the mechanisms previously used to control fear and anxiety have proven ineffectual. These are the mechanisms Douglas describes, high-level control mechanisms that presuppose a culture which, while experiencing normal mismatches between goals and achievements, is essentially in little danger of disintegration. In periods of massive change, however, anxiety and terror are nearing their upper limit, and high level defenses and coping strategies are a luxury the culture cannot afford. The result is a polarization of good and evil at the collective level parallel to a similar tendency toward splitting at the individual level.

Revitalization movements occur in periods of cultural breakdown, and in less turbulent times communally collectivistic societies provide culturally determined identity syntheses that perform the dual function of maintaining societal integration and personal identity. These syntheses are often transmitted through rites of passage, especially those that occur shortly before or during adolescence, and an examination of these rites provides a final example of paradigmatic processes which create an identity that is personally meaningful and socially integrative.

Rites of Passage as Forced Identity Resynthesis

The definitive work on rites of passage and initiation ceremonies is the brilliant French sociologist Arnold van Gennep's (1908) *The Rites of Passage*. (For more recent work on initiation ceremonies, see Young, 1965.) van Gennep observed that many rites of passage follow a sequence of three stages: separation, transition, and incorporation. In the separation phase, the individual is removed from his previous existence and secluded with the other initiates. The purpose of the separation period is to eliminate past beliefs and attachments, to separate the individual from his past life and leave him in a state of existential emptiness. That the novice in the midst of initiation is frequently considered *dead* is therefore not surprising (p. 75). He is often physically and mentally weakened through drugs, sleep deprivation, or torture, the purpose of which is to make him forget his childhood.

In the transition phase, the initiate is indoctrinated with the ways of the group and provided with the makings of a new identity. In the stage of incorporation, he is "reborn" with a new identity and reincorporated into the community with a new status. van Gennep describes a typical course of initiation:

> In some tribes the novice is considered dead, and he remains dead for the duration of the novitiate. It lasts for a fairly long time and consists of a physical and mental weakening which is undoubtedly intended to make him lose all recollection of his childhood existence. Then follows the positive part: instruction in tribal law and a gradual education as the novice witnesses totem ceremonies, recitations of myths, etc. The final act is a religious ceremony . . . and, above all, a special mutilation which varies with the tribe (a tooth is removed, the penis is incised, etc.) and which makes the novice forever identical with the adult members. (P. 75)

The striking feature of this account is that it is identical in almost all respects to Lifton's description of the process of thought reform. The individual undergoing brainwashing is made to feel dead, annihilated, self-less, and totally dependent. He is physically and mentally weakened in order to exorcise his past, to "empty his brain" of prior beliefs, attachments, and values. He is then indoctrinated with the "correct" ideology, so that the myths presented to him throughout his experience become his own, and he must join in recitations of the new values and beliefs until his controllers are satisfied that he is sincere. Finally, his new identity is solidified and collectively acknowledged through a stage of rebirth, which culminates in his signing a confession and excising and exorcising his evil past. The group extracts a confession from him, just as the initiation group extracts a tooth.

Initiation, like brainwashing, takes place in an enveloping milieu, a "total institution" (Goffman, 1961). It does so in part because a purpose of both is to establish in the individual an identity based on an ego ideal that accepts the collectivity as a powerful, all-knowing, all-valuable end to human action. A "total institution," as occurs in initiation or brainwashing (and sometimes in the monastery or the military), is especially effective in this regard because it approximates this godlike collectivity: it is magically potent because it wields total control over the individual, it is omniscient because the person can never escape its view, and it is all-valuable because it offers the only source of meaning and security in a world that threatens annihilation.

During the initiation ceremony, van Gennep notes, the initiates are outside the boundaries of the larger collectivity, of the profane world. While under the control of the initiating group, they have severed their relationship to their previous society:

> During the entire novitiate, the usual economic and legal ties are modified, sometimes broken altogether. The novices are outside society, and society has no power over them, especially since they are actually sacred and holy, and therefore untouchable and dangerous, just as gods would be. Thus, although taboos, as negative rites, erect a barrier between the novices and society, the society is defenseless against the novices' undertakings. (P. 114)

This connection of the sacred, the dangerous, and the powerful provides a link between van Gennep's analysis and that of Douglas. Douglas argues that ritual harnesses the power and danger at societal boundaries. The initiate, Douglas points out, "has no place in the social system and is therefore a marginal being . . ." (1966, p. 117). He is not only marginal because he is removed from the purview and control of the larger collectivity, but he is marginal in two other senses as well: during the initiation he is outside of the social order because he lacks a socially constructed identity, and he is also cognitively marginal because he fits into neither the category of child nor that of adult.

Just as communally collectivistic cultures may attempt to create the identities of their members through initiation rites and thus maintain societal potency, van Gennep includes under the rubric of rites of passage those rites of intensification which celebrate and guarantee natural phenomena such as the passing of the seasons. In each case, rites of passage and rites of intensification maintain societal potency. In the former, including puberty as well as marriage rites and other ceremonies that commemorate and sanction a change of status, this control is real because the group is actually determining the identity and status of the individual. In the

381

latter, this "omnipotence" is illusory, but it is fundamental to maintaining that sense of individual and collective basic trust without which individual identity and cultural integration are inconceivable.

Conclusion: Paradigmatic Processes and the Identity of Two Identities

When one compares the pattern of the various phenomena described here – scientific revolutions, revitalization movements, religious experiences, identity crises and resolutions, brainwashing, and rites of passage – one finds a strikingly similar form which is called here (following Wallace, 1972) a *paradigmatic process*. Whether described in terms of two, three, four, or five stages, this pattern always involves the breakdown of a prevailing synthesis, a period of emptiness and transition, an overlapping stage in which the seeds of a new synthesis take root, and a period of resynthesis or paradigmatic neogensis.[1] Kuhn's model of scientific revolution differs from the others only in the sense that it involves paradigms that are primarily cognitive (although, of course, every scientific paradigm contains norms of scientific practice).[2]

In each of these paradigmatic processes, one sees a movement from form to formlessness and back again to form. The formless period is a "liminal" period (van Gennep, 1908; Turner, 1969), betwixt and between, in the interstices of individual and collective existence, and it appears remarkably similar across these very dissimilar processes. In the formless or liminal stage – of revitalization, of religious experience, of identity formation, of brainwashing, of initiation – the culture or individual experiences a disquieting state of emptiness, of anomie, of marginality. The same is true of the Protean or borderline personality, who in some ways is perpetually liminal, forever on the outskirts of consistency, identity, and integration with others. Perhaps it is no accident that those for whom this liminality is central – the borderline personalities described by psychoanalysts like Kohut as lacking a cohesive "self" – are labeled by the psychiatric community as *borderline*, falling between the cracks of psychiatric diagnosis just as they frequently fall between the cracks of selfhood and society.

A striking feature of these paradigmatic processes is that they are essen-

---

[1] A similar phenomenon has been observed on the family level by David Reiss (1982), who has developed a concept of the "family paradigm." Psychologists for some time have recognized equilibration processes in groups (e.g., Bales, 1953; Katz and Kahn, 1978), and one might expect that the structural model of society presented here could be adaptable to groups, such as families, at different levels of complexity and size. The term "equilibration," however, does not entirely convey the idea of paradigmatic development.

[2] Though his model will not be discussed further here, it suggests that certain cognitive processes in individuals and groups seem to follow a pattern similar to the breakdown and creation of ego and cultural syntheses.

382

tially the same for individuals and groups. In *Loss and Change,* Peter Marris (1974) notes that scientific revolutions "are not unlike the personal and social crises, where our sense of the meaning of life seems fundamentally threatened by contradictions and inconsistencies we can no longer ignore" (p. 131). In the phenomena described in this chapter (with the partial exception of Kuhn), these crises occur with the dissolution of an entire worldview, an identity synthesis or cultural integration that rests upon the interrelation of a series of ideals and a set of beliefs and practices. It is in this area that one encounters, in Lifton's words, "the very tenuous psychic boundaries between identity crisis, psychosis, theological innovation, and individual and historical revitalization" (1974, p. 29).

In communally collectivistic cultures, rituals such as rites of passage are employed at those junctures in the life cycle that present changes in status and alterations in the culture's conception of the individuals involved. At the societal level, as Douglas would point out, rites of passage are like other rituals that restore order to formlessness, that provide collective control over forces at the margins of social structure and cognition. Yet at the psychological level, rites of passage also confer order on chaos, by imposing a renewed, socially constructed identity on those who are themselves seeping into the margins, into formlessness, fragmentation, and nothingness.

In conditions of social breakdown and in the current age which lacks rites of passage comparable in power to those of communally collectivistic societies, identity can no longer rest upon unquestioned internalization of a collective paradigm. Communal identifications and social roles suffice less as personal identity, and the *issue* of identity becomes the *problem* of identity.

In the contemporary world and in times of social stress in the world we have lost, a period of Protean existence appears to be the fate of a significant number of individuals. Protean individuals, particularly in changing times, are seekers of wholeness and truth, and periodically, as Weber recognized, a charismatic authority may appear as a model for identity resynthesis. Charisma is to Weber what the sacred is to Durkheim: a special, uncanny power, the polar opposite of the profane (see Weber, 1947, p. 361). The charismatic leader is, for the follower, an externally narcissistic object who can give to the person what earlier objects can no longer provide: security, meaning, direction, and immortality.

Freud recognized this when he spoke of transference phenomena in crowds and mass movements, and he tied the issue to the ego ideal (1921). Indeed, the sacred lies in the realm of the ego ideal: the sacred object is the magically potent object—whether self, other, or collectivity—which restores order, meaning, and value to our lives. The charismatic leader is an individual who has known the depths of despair and the agony of fragmentation, and who creates an identity for others in the process of creating an identity for himself. "Now and again," Erikson writes, "an individual is called upon (called upon by *whom,* only the theologians claim to know, and by *what* only bad psychologists) to lift his individual patienthood to the level of a universal one and to try to solve for all what he could not solve for himself alone" (1958, p. 67).

The charismatic leader often serves, as well, as a societal transitional object, a displaced symbol of the sacredness of social relations. One thus finds a curiously fine line between narcissism and collectivism, especially with the breakdown of communitarian collectivism, in which the individual identifies with a divine hero as well as a sacred collectivity. In the West, one could ask for no better examples of this than among the Romantics, such as Byron and Rousseau, who longed to be both the great man and the faceless participant in a harmonious social divinity.

Historically, nationalism has served as a repository for communal "primordial sentiments" (Geertz, 1963) in the wake of attachments to village, tribe, and clan. In the social and psychological short run, it performs a useful function, translating the group-centered morality of a rapidly passing era into a contemporary form, providing an orientation toward the world and the person's place in it, in an environment characterized by continuous revolution.

In the long run, however, the historian must ask what is to be learned from the experiences of the earlier modernizers in their more nationalistic periods. If the reader will forgive one last analogy with individual development, the similarity is all too clear between the clinical phenomenon of pathological narcissism (see Kohut, 1971; Kernberg, 1975) and the pathological nationalism that has led to so much death and destruction in the current age. In the former, the individual views the world as centering on him, and gratification is his *summum bonum.* The pathological narcissist experiences others only as they relate to his needs, and he projects upon them characteristics which, because of his own dynamics, he needs to project. Any radical psychological position – whether it be egocentric or ascetic, loving or aggressive, impulsive or rigid – always presupposes its opposite, and the pathological narcissist must protest his greatness all the more because of his unconscious (and more painful, conscious) feelings of worthlessness and impotence.

I need not spell out the analogous dynamics of a collectivity with a tenuous hold on cultural integration which similarly doth protest too much. This is not to say that leaders of the Third World must capitulate to an inevitable cult of the individual, shunning nationalism as the last gasp of tribalism that it is. To the contrary, the possibilities in the "underdeveloped" world for erecting social institutions that simultaneously promote and direct the individualism inherent in the modernization process while recreating a sense of community may be greater than in the West. Precisely in "underdevelopment" lies the flexibility to engage in new experiments in social forms, and the information and theorizing that the Third World has at its disposal are incomparably superior to those that were available to the West in its periods of institutional solidification. The rapidity and intensity of social change thrust upon the peoples of the underdeveloped world, however, leads to that tendency Lifton has described as totalism, and in transitional periods this totalism may combine with the breakdown of normal rules regulating the relationship of human beings to one another to legitimize incomparable acts of inhumanity.

Nationalism thus has its psychological and social uses, and it will not begin to fade until the psychological effects of modernization are universal. If nations of the Third World are not, however, simply to reenact the imperialism and militarism of their predecessors in modernization, nationalism must be seen for what it is: a regressive solution. It was useful and necessary for emancipation from the colonial powers, and no doubt it will prove useful in erecting new institutions, but it is – if I may relinquish my role as "social scientist" – a pathological and displaced invocation of tribal solidarity. Fate has decreed that nationalism will be a major dynamic of this century and the next, but we can in no way predict or control whether the charismatic leaders who channel it will follow in the footsteps of Gandhi, or the bootmarks of Hitler.

14 Personality and Individuation

THE AIM OF Part III has been to integrate the theory of personality proposed in this book with the theory of culture. The last four chapters have examined the relationship been personality processes, communitarian collectivist culture, and social change. This final chapter will explore the psychology of individuated collectivism and will conclude with a brief discussion of moral individuation in psychological and sociocultural perspective.

The literature on the psychodynamics of modernization discussed in Chapter 11 provides one set of indicators of a shift toward self-orientation that occurs with modernization. A second line of evidence, especially convincing because of its methodological rigor and the broad scope of its authors' knowledge, comes from the Six-Culture study by John and Beatrice Whiting and their colleagues. This research involved intensive fieldwork over a number of years by a team of researchers interested in the relationship between child rearing, personality, and culture. The investigators coded interpersonal interactions on a number of dimensions for children and their parents in six cultures with varying subsistence patterns. Particularly relevant from the standpoint of the thesis developed here is the variable of altruistic versus egoistic children's social behavior. Whiting and Whiting (1973, 1975) found a strong correlation between this dimension and sociocultural complexity (institutional differentiation and technological development), such that egoistic social behaviors correlated highly with complexity. The Whitings suggest that a key variable in explaining that difference is the mother's workload. In simpler societies, the mother has less time for the child, and the child must take on more household responsibilities, such as caring for younger children. While this may explain some of the variance, it is only a partial explanation. It would suggest, for example, that as the number of working mothers increases, the trend toward egoism will reverse, which is unlikely. Chapter 11 tried to dissect and separate the necessary from the contingent features of modernization, and specific child-rearing variables, such as maternal availability, need not always occur with modernization. That socialization practices *have*, in fact, changed in line with this heightened emphasis of self tells us something extremely important about socialization, values, and socioeconomic processes, and supports LeVine's analysis of selective retention of socialization practices.

The Six-Culture study does not provide the only evidence of heightened self-emphasis at the individual level associated with the processes of modernization. Madsen (1971) and his colleagues have developed a number of experimental game situations to test the relative cooperativeness and competitiveness of children, and they have consistently found that competitiveness as opposed to cooperativeness varies directly with factors associated with modernization, such as urbanization, education, social mobility, and industrialization. Marin, Mejia, and deOberle (1975), for example, found significant differences in the cooperative and competitive behavior of rural and urban children in Colombia. Madsen and his colleagues have carried out similar experiments comparing urban and rural children in Mexico (Madsen, 1967) and urban Israeli versus kibbutz children (Shapiro and Madsen, 1969), and Miller and Thomas (1972) compared urban and rural groups in Canada. In each case significant differences in the expected direction were found.

These results appear in studies of class differences as well, supporting the argument that differential effects of the processes of modernization on different groups within a culture will produce differences in self-orientation. Emmy Werner summarizes the trend:

> Generally speaking, children from traditional cultures on all continents, in Latin America, in Africa, in the Middle and Far East, and in Australia, tend to be more cooperative than children from transitional and Western cultures. Within a given culture, children from rural areas tend to be more cooperative than children from urban areas, and children from lower socio-economic-status homes tend to cooperate more than children from middle-class homes. (1979, p. 519)

Kagan and Carlson (1975) studied assertiveness in Mexican and American children and found that urban, middle class, Anglo-American children were more assertive than semirural, poor, Anglo-American or Mexican-American children. No differences were found between the latter two groups, but both were significantly more assertive than poor, rural Mexican children. In a longitudinal study of urban Mexican and American children, Holtzman, Diaz-Guerrero, and Swartz (1975) found that fourteen-year-old boys from working-class families in both cultures were significantly higher on a dimension called "affiliative obedience" and lower on "active self-assertion" than boys from upper middle class families, and that the lower class Mexican group was highest on affiliative obedience of any of the groups studied. Werner (1979) concludes from the available evidence that "the urban working class in a society developing toward modern industrialism still tends to be the primary carrier of traditional sociocultural premises . . ." (p. 295). In general, as Werner points out (p. 319), poverty generally correlates with greater group-orientation.

Further evidence of heightened self-orientation of adults in modernized versus relativity nonmodernized areas is provided through analysis of cross-cultural patterns in the personality dimension called "Machiavellianism" (see Christie and Geis, 1970; Geis, 1978). The various measures of Machiavellianism developed by these researchers attempt to measure the extent to which an individual believes that people are manipulable, is willing to manipulate them, and is successful in doing so. Again, the evidence is clear: Machiavellianism correlates with modernization. A Spanish study by de Miguel (cited in Christie, 1970) found a correlation of .89 between Mach score and industrialization of the province in which an individual lived and had been reared. A Chinese study similarly discovered a "relationship between traditionalism and low Mach scores" significant at the p<.005 level (cited in Christie, 1970). Geis (1979) reports the results of a Nigerian study in which Mach scores of 80 percent of urban children fell above the median, while those of 80 percent of rural children fell below.

In considering all of this evidence from various quarters, one need not accept the conceptual and methodological positions of all the various researchers. Cross-cultural research is extremely difficult to carry out with any degree of validity (for the methodological issues involved, see Vol.II of the *Handbook of Cross-Cultural Psychology*, 1980), but researchers agree that the best way to try to deal with issues of validity is using multiple measures. The data reviewed so far come from a variety of largely independent empirical traditions, and while the conceptualizations used and the traits tested vary somewhat from one approach to the next, all of these studies relate to the issue at hand – the relationship between modernization and self-orientation – and provide striking confirmation of the thesis of Chapter 11, that the processes of modernization produce a greater emphasis of self.

Evidence of this shift toward greater self-orientation with modernization comes from studies of socialization practices as well. Munroe and Munroe (1975), after reviewing some of this evidence, somewhat hesitantly admit,

> A popular stereotype holds that modern Western individuals have lost certain qualities characteristic of those who live in a simpler way. Supposedly Westerners are self-oriented, highly competitive, and constantly pushing for achievement, while non-Westerners are more group-oriented, cooperative, and accepting of things as they are . . . Recent work surprisingly supports the stereotype. . . . (P.314)

Available data suggest that the difference is not between Westerners and non-Westerners: it is between those affected in certain ways by the processes of modernization and those not so affected.

Cross-cultural studies of socialization practices demonstrate this shift and suggest that ego ideal values of parents become translated into socialization practices that foster similar values and corresponding behavioral patterns in their children. In one study, Mussen and Beytagh (1969) examined socialization practices of parents and personality traits of children in Puerto Rico. They compared families in which the husband worked in an industrial setting with those in which the husband remained in agricultural work (though both sets of parents came from a rural area). They found that parents in the agricultural families stressed traditional values, were more restrictive, and were more punitive in their child rearing, emphasizing obedience and conformity. The industrial parents had moved toward socialization practices emphasizing achievement, self-reliance, and decreased authoritarianism. Werner provides a summary of research on socialization in contemporary preindustrial groups:

> If we look at the socialization values prevalent around the world today, we see that most traditional societies of sub-Saharan Africa, Asia, and Latin America stress authoritarianism, a sense of mutual interdependence, and an external locus of control. Children are reared with deference to elders, with respect for order, and with stress on obedience and cooperation. Family solidarity, or service to the collective group – in short, mutual obligations to the common good – are greatly valued, and there is an acceptance of the ephemeral nature of life and the cycle of birth, death, and renewal. (P. 337)

She contrasts this picture with socialization practices of "modernized" or "modernizing" groups and subgroups, observing that the latter "stress socialization values that emphasize egalitarianism across generations and sexes, individualism, self-reliance, and personal aspirations" (p. 337).

Cross-cultural psychological studies thus suggest that the processes of modernization produce an individual who comes to view himself as the source of power and value once attributed to the group. As sociologist Richard Sennett writes in *The Fall of Public Man,* "In modern social life adults must act narcissistically to act in accordance with society's norms" (1974, p. 326). "Masses of people," he argues, "are concerned with their single life-histories and particular emotions as never before . . ." (p. 5), and he attributes this to capitalism and to "secularism" (the force that explains everything capitalism does not).

The analysis of Chapter 11 suggested that, while capitalism quite likely reinforces the trend toward individualism, it is not capitalism but modernization that is primarily responsible for this trend. Many of the factors hypothesized to result in a breakdown of internalized and external struc-

389

tures of authority can occur in any period of rapid social change. Social processes associated with the growth of modernization add an attribute unique to industrial and industrializing societies: an emphasis of self.

In Part I it was proposed that an individual's view of morality is synonymous with the balance between self and other forming the content of a significant component of the ego ideal. This suggests that the heightened awareness and emphasis of self associated with modernization is tantamount to a new morality, and one can see in the early liberals a distinctive shift in moral theorizing in that direction. Sennett writes of the obsessive "desire to reveal one's personality in social dealings" of contemporary Western society (p. 11), and one is reminded here of Lévi-Strauss's comment, quoted earlier, that our personalities have become our totems. Swanson argues that in preindustrial societies sacred objects symbolically represent what he calls "sovereign" groups. A group has sovereignty "to the extent that it has original and independent jurisdiction over some sphere of life . . ."(1960, p. 20). One recognizes, in examining Swanson's definition, that the individual is rapidly becoming sovereign in a variety of areas, and indeed, one finds precisely that sentiment in liberal political philosophy. More explicitly, if the sense of the sacred reflects experience with the sovereign, then individuated collectivism implies the sacredness of the individual. One should thus not be surprised to find that in the movement toward individuated collectivism over the last few centuries, philosophers (and politicians) have spoken of the sanctity of the individual and God-given, inalienable individual rights.

To make clear the relationship between personality and historical change in the understanding of "the good," one can say, then, that greater psychological individuation and emphasis of self are the psychological flip-side of individuated collectivism, just as lesser individuation and a higher valuation of collective aims is the psychological concomitant of communitarian collectivism. Between these two ideal types, of course, individuals of any kind may appear. It cannot be stressed enough that this is only the view from theoretical Olympus, and that mere mortals do not always concern themselves with, or conform to, the desires of competing theoretical supernaturals.

We need not concern ourselves greatly in a social scientific tract with synthetic collectivism. "Pure" synthetic collectivism would represent, to connect individual and collective levels of analysis, a collectivity that recognized the independent value of both sociality and individuality, in which a significant part of the population developed some synthetically narcissistic ideals. Synthetic collectivism is obviously as much an ideal as an ideal type: the synthetically narcissistic individual in the synthetically collectivistic culture would be a creator and a lover, or perhaps, one might say, a Nietzschean individual in a Marxian community. Erich Fromm describes this type of individual in his definition of mental health:

> Mental health is characterized by the ability to love and to create, by the emergence from incestuous ties to clan and soil, and by a sense of identity based on one's experience of self as the subject and agent of one's powers, by the grasp of reality inside and outside ourselves. . . . (1955, p. 68, emphasis deleted)

Indeed, this is the message of Freud and Marx. For Freud, the key to health is *lieben und arbeiten*, love and work (and one might wish to add "play"). For Marx, the individual who is truly free is a productive member of a real community:

> Only in community with others has each individual the means of cultivating his gifts in all directions; only in the community therefore, is personal freedom possible . . . In the real community the individuals obtain their freedom in and through their association. (1973, p. 161, brackets deleted)

In this sense, one can view the last two centuries as a fortification of two half-truths. In the nineteenth century, one set of thinkers, including Hegel, Fichte, Saint-Simon, and Comte, viewed the needs of society as the legitimate ends of human endeavor. Opposing them, a variety of philosophers, including Humboldt, Stirner, Kierkegaard, Spencer, and Nietzsche, refused to sacrifice the individual to this collective deity. In our own century, people have spoken of an iron curtain between the "communist" and the "capitalist" worlds, with half of humanity proclaiming the sanctity of the isolated individual and the other half brandishing the sanctity of the group. In reality, each great camp demands the denial of half of humanity, the alienation of the person from half of what makes life worthwhile.

In proposing a "stage" of synthetic collectivism, I am in one sense switching hats, from the feathered cap of the so. scientist to the straw hat of the philosopher. Even the maddest of hatters knows, however, that the two hats fit one head, and indeed, much of the same fabric went into the construction of both. On logical grounds, I was compelled to propose the construct of synthetic collectivism because of the rather unlikely, but conceivable possibility of a society in which synthetic narcissism is more prevalent than in our own.

It was suggested in Part I, somewhat off-handedly, that synthetic narcissism may offer a relatively content-free model of moral autonomy (again, within the constraints of mature object relations). One would be naive to suppose that this or any view is culture-free, somehow transcending the times. The concept of synthetic narcissism would not have arisen in a communally collectivistic culture because the moral presuppositions of that type of culture make such a viewpoint incomprehensible. It is a conception of moral autonomy that presupposes considerable differentiation of self and other, and is thus a product of the twentieth century. It may nevertheless be a useful conception for an epoch in which institutions and ideals are changing at a speed unprecedented in human history, in which tradition may be an inadequate guide to action.[1]

In ethical thought from Plato to Rawls, philosophers have demanded that however one approaches moral philosophy, one must conclude with a preordained set of principles. The situation is highly reminiscent of philosophical preoccupation in a bygone era with "rational" proofs of the existence of God. In communally collectivistic cultures moral laws are as immutable as natural laws because they are seen as an aspect of nature. Since Plato, and especially since Hobbes, moral philosophy has reflected the ambivalent valuation of both individual reason and a particular (communitarian) end, but the belief in the verity of the end has largely prevailed. John Rawls, to use a more recent example, attempts to rest his principles of justice upon the thought of any rational individual, yet he admits that he is interested in elaborating the moral perspective "widely thought reasonable" (1971, p. 121) in Western culture, and that his assumptions and arguments have been specially chosen "so that we get the desired solution" (p. 141).

No scientist or philosopher of science would respect the conclusions of a researcher who rigged his experiments so that they produced the "desired solution." No moral philosopher – or individual attempting to decide how to guide her life – should, either. As in science, we can never prove the veracity of our current theories, but we can guarantee that the method – the use of reason, emotion, and experience – is more likely than contending methods – such as conformity to dogma – to help us understand the object of our investigation. In ethics as in science, true autonomy requires an independence of thought that transcends blind acceptance of the wisdom of the ages, or, for that matter, blind rejection of prevailing opinion.

Moral inquiry differs from scientific inquiry in that the object is also the aim, that our objective is an imperative, and this imperative differs by individual, society, and epoch. Morality is the product of human beings in social interaction. It represents a reconciliation of the needs of self and other, individual and society, and it is bound to do an injustice to one or the other. Such is the nature of human existence. The tragic achievement of autonomous, individuated man[2] is that he is aware of moral conflict but is left without a priori moral principles with which to make a choice.

---

[1] Not only are the psychocultural preconditions for synthetic narcissism largely absent in communally collectivistic cultures, but synthetic narcissism would probably be "maladaptive" for both individuals and groups at that level of sociocultural complexity.

[2] I hope the reader will forgive this untimely intrusion of sexist language. I am looking for a word that means simultaneously individual and collective humankind, and the English language lacks any word but "man" that conveys this dual meaning.

392

Ethical principles, to our dismay, are not engraved upon our hearts, and moral philosophy must finally come to grips with the fact modern surgery should have demonstrated once and for all: deep within the human breast lies only blood and tissue.

Human beings do not enter the world – individually or collectively – in order to discover and put into operation a preexisting, a priori morality mandated by God, Nature, or Reason. The origin of human society marks the genesis of morality, and the birth and development of every individual heralds the rebirth or conception of a particular moral view. Man must develop a morality by himself, and if he cannot do so satisfactorily, he and morality will leave the world as simultaneously as they entered.

References

Abelson, R.P. (1981). Psychological status of the script concept. *American Psychologist, 36,* 715-29.

Abernathy, V. (1979). *Population pressure and cultural adjustment.* New York: Human Sciences Press.

Abramson, L.Y., Seligman, M.E.P., and Teasdale, J.D. (1978). Learned helplessness in humans: critique and reformulation. *Journal of Abnormal Psychology, 87,* 49-74.

Adams, R.N. (1981). Natural selection, energetics, and "cultural materialism." *Current Anthropology, 22,* 603-24.

Aderman, D., Brehm, S.S., and Katz, L.B. (1974). Empathic observation of an innocent victim: the just world revisited. *Journal of Personality and Social Psychology, 29,* 342-7.

Adler, A. (1929). *The science of living.* New York: Anchor/Doubleday, 1969.

Adler, A. (1939). *Social interest.* New York: G.P. Putnam.

Adorno, T.W., Frenkel-Brunswick, E., Levinson, D.J., and Sanford, R.N. (1950). *The authoritarian personality,* New York: W.W. Norton.

Ainsworth, M.D.S. (1969). Object relations, dependency, and attachment: a theoretical review of the infant-mother relationship. *Child Development, 40,* 969-1025.

Ainsworth, M.D.S. (1979). Infant-mother attachment. *American Psychologist, 34,* 932-7.

Alexander, R.D. and Borgia, G. (1978). Group selection, altruism, and levels of organization of life. *Annual Review of Ecology and Systematics, 9,* 449-74.

Alland, A. and McCay, B. (1973). The concept of adaptation in biological and cultural evolution. In J.J. Honigmann (Ed.), *Handbook of social and cultural anthropology.* Chicago: Rand-McNally.

Alland, A. (1975). Adaptation. *Annual Review of Anthropology, 4,* 59-73.

Allport, G.W. (1937). *Personality: a psychological interpretation.* New York: Henry Holt and Company.

Allport, G., Bruner, J.S., and Jandorf, E.M. (1949). Personality under social catastrophe: ninety-nine life-histories of the Nazi revolution. In C. Kluckhohn and H.A. Murray (Eds.), *Personality in nature, society and culture.* New York: Alfred Knopf.

394

References

Althusser, L. (1971). *Lenin and philosophy*, B. Brewster (Trans.). New York: Monthly Review Press.

American Psychiatric Association. (1980). *Diagnostic and statistical manual of mental disorders* (3rd ed.). Washington, D.C.: American Psychiatric Association.

Anderson, J.R. (1976). *Language, memory, and thought*. Hillsdale, New Jersey: Lawrence Erlbaum.

Anderson, J.R., and Bower, G.H. (1973). *Human associative memory*. Washington: Winston.

Apter, D. (1965). *The politics of modernization*. Chicago: University of Chicago Press.

Aquinas, St. Thomas (1945). *Introduction to Saint Thomas Aquinas*, A.C. Pegis (Ed.). New York: Modern Library.

Aristotle (1947). *Introduction to Aristotle*, R. McKeon (Ed.). New York: Modern Library.

Arlow, J. and Brenner, C. (1964). *Psychoanalytic concepts and the structural theory*. New York: International Universities Press, Journal of the American Psycho-analytic Association Monographs No.3.

Aron, R. (1968). *Main currents in sociological thought*, Vol.1. New York: Doubleday.

Aron, R. (1970). *Main currents in sociological thought*, Vol.2. New York: Doubleday.

Asendorph, J.B. and Scherer, K.R. (1983). The discrepant repressor: differentiation between low anxiety, high anxiety, and repression of anxiety by autonomic-facial-verbal patterns of behavior. *Journal of Personality and Social Psychology, 45*, 1334-46.

Ashton. P.T. (1978). Cross-cultural Piagetian research: an experimental perspective. In *Stage theories of cognitive and moral development: criticisms and applications*, Reprint No.13, Harvard Educational Review.

Augustine (1961). *Confessions*. Middlesex: Penguin Books.

Ausubel, D.P. (1952). *Ego development and the personality disorders*. New York: Grune and Stratton.

Ausubel, D.P. (1958). *Theory and problems of child development*. New York: Grune and Stratton.

Averill, J.R. (1979). The functions of grief. In C.E. Izard (Ed.), *Emotions in personality and psychopathology*. New York: Plenum Press.

Ayrout, H.A. (1963). *The Egyptian peasant*. Boston: Beacon Press.

Bailey, F.G. (1966). The peasant view of the bad life. In T. Shanin (Ed.), *Peasants and peasant societies*. Middlesex: Penguin Books, 1971.

Baldessarini, R.J. (1977). *Chemotherapy in psychiatry*. Cambridge: Harvard University Press.

Bales, R.F. (1953). The equilibrium problem in small groups. In T. Parsons, R.F. Bales, and E.A. Shils (Eds.), *Working papers in the theory of action*. Glencoe, Illinois: Free Press.

Balint, M. (1960). Primary narcissism and primary love. *Psychoanalytic Quarterly, 29*, 34-40.

Balint, M. (1968). *The basic fault*. London: Tavistock.

References

Ball, J.F. (1977). Widow's grief: the impact of age and mode of death. *Omega, 7,* 307-33.

Bandura, A. (1967). The role of modeling in personality development. In C.S. Lavatelli and F. Stendler (Eds.), *Readings in child development and behavior* (3rd ed.). New York: Harcourt, Brace, Jovanovich, 1972.

Bandura, A. (1969). *Principles of behavior modification.* New York: Holt, Rinehart and Winston.

Bandura, A. (1977a). *Social learning theory.* Englewood Cliffs, New Jersey: Prentice-Hall.

Bandura, A. (1977b). Self-efficacy: toward a unifying theory of behavioral change. *Psychological Review, 84,* 191-215.

Bandura, A. (1982). Self-efficacy mechanism in human agency. *American Psychologist, 37,* 122-47.

Bandura, A. and Rosenthal, L. (1966). Vicarious classical conditioning as a function of arousal level. *Journal of Personality and Social Psychology, 3,* 54-62.

Banfield, E. (1958). *The moral basis of a backward society.* New York: Free Press.

Barry, H., Child, I.L., and Bacon, M.K. (1959). Relation of child training to subsistence economy. *American Anthropologist, 61,* 51-63.

Barth, F. (1956). Ecologic relationships of ethnic groups in Swat, North Pakistan. *American Anthropologist, 58,* 1079-89.

Barth, F. (1967). On the study of social change. *American Anthropologist, 69,* 661-9.

Bartlett, F. (1932). *Remembering.* New York: Columbia University Press.

Bateson, G. (1936). *Naven.* Cambridge: Cambridge University Press.

Beck, A.T. (1967). *Depression: clinical, experimental, and theoretical aspects.* New York: Harper and Row.

Beck, A.T. (1967). *Cognitive therapy and the emotional disorders.* New York: International Universities Press.

Becker, E. (1973.) *The denial of death.* New York: Free Press.

Bellah, R.N. (1964). Religious evolution. In R. Robertson (Ed.), *Sociology of religion.* Middlesex: Penguin Books, 1969.

Bem, D.J. (1972). Self-perception theory. In L. Berkowitz (Ed.), *Advances in experimental social psychology,* Vol.6. New York: Academic Press.

Benedict, R. (1934). *Patterns of culture.* New York: Mentor/New American Library.

Bennett, J.W. (1976). Anticipation, adaptation, and the concept of culture in anthropology. *Science, 192,* 847-53.

Berger, P., Berger, B. and Kellner, H. (1974). *The homeless mind.* Middlesex: Penguin Books.

Berger, P. and Luckmann, T. (1963). Sociology of religion and sociology of knowledge. In R. Robertson (Ed.), *Sociology of religion.* Middlesex: Penguin Books, 1969.

Berger, P. and Luckmann, T. (1967). *The social construction of reality: a treatise in the sociology of knowledge.* New York: Anchor Books.

Berkowitz, L. (1972). Social norms, feelings, and other factors altering helping and altruism. In L. Berkowitz (Ed.), *Advances in experimental social psychology*, Vol. 6. New York: Academic Press.

Berkowitz, L. (1978). Do we have to believe we are angry with someone in order to display "angry" aggression toward that person? In L. Berkowitz (Ed.), *Cognitive theories in social psychology*. New York: Academic Press.

Bermann, E. (1973). *Scapegoat*. Ann Arbor, Michigan: University of Michigan Press.

Berry, J.W. (1967). Independence and conformity in subsistence-level societies. *Journal of Personality and Social Psychology, 7*, 415-18.

Berry, J.W. (1980). Social and cultural change. In H.C. Triandis and R.W. Brislin (Eds.), *Handbook of cross-cultural psychology*, Vol.5. Boston: Allyn and Bacon.

Bertalanffy, L. von. (1973). An outline of general systems theory. *British Journal of the Philosophy of Science, 1*, 134-63.

Bibring, E. (1941). The development and problems of the theory of the instincts. *International Journal of Psycho-Analysis, 22*, 102-31.

Bibring, E. (1953). The mechanism of depression. In P. Greenacre (Ed.), *Affective disorders*. New York: International Universities Press.

Bing, J. and Marburg, R., reporting (1962). Narcissism. *Journal of the American Psychoanalytic Association, 10*, 593-605.

Bing, J., McLaughlin, F., and Marburg, R. (1959). The metapsychology of narcissism. *The Psychoanalytic Study of the Child, 14*, 9-28.

Binswanger, L. (1958). The existential analysis school of thought. In R. May, E. Angel, and H.F. Ellenberger (Eds.), *Existence*. New York: Basic Books.

Binswanger, L. (1963). *Being-in-the-world: selected papers of Ludwig Binswanger*. New York: Basic Books.

Black, C.E. (1966). *The dynamics of modernization: a study in comparative history*. New York: Harper and Row.

Blanck, G. and Blanck, R. (1974). *Ego psychology: theory and practice*. New York: Columbia University Press.

Block, J. (1981). Some enduring and consequential structures of personality. In A.I. Rubin et al. (Eds.), *Further explorations in personality*. New York: Wiley.

Block, J.H. and Block, J. (1980). The role of ego-control and ego-resiliency in the organization of behavior. In W.A. Collins (Ed.), *Development of cognition, affect, and social relations, Minnesota symposium on child development*, Vol. 13. Hillsdale, New Jersey: Lawrence Erlbaum.

Blos, P. (1967). The second individuation process of adolescence. *Psychoanalytic Study of the Child, 22*, 162-86.

Boas, F. (1940). *Race, language and culture*. New York: Free Press.

Boehm, C. (1982). A fresh outlook on cultural selection. *American Anthropologist, 82*, 105-25.

Boehm, C. (1983). Adaptive problem solving and the study of cultural selection. Unpublished manuscript.

Boissevain, J. (1974). *Friends of friends: networks, manipulators, and coalitions*. Oxford: Basil Blackwell.

References

Bolles, R.C. (1970). Species-specific defense reactions and avoidance learning. *Psychological Review, 71*, 32-48.

Bolles, R.C. (1972). Reinforcement, expectancy, and learning. *Psychological Review, 79*, 394-409.

Bolles, R.C. (1975). *Learning theory*. New York: Holt, Rinehart and Winston.

Boss, M. (1977). *Existential foundations of medicine and psychology*. New York: Aronson.

Bossert, L.D. (1982). *The ability to differentiate the self and other in two-year-olds: the role of contingency and feature cues*. Unpublished doctoral dissertation, University of Michigan.

Bott, E. (1957). *Family and social network*. London: Tavistock.

Bouquet, A.C. (1962). *Comparative religion* (6th ed.). Middlesex: Penguin Books.

Bourgignon, E. (1979). *Psychological anthropology: an introduction to human nature and cultural differences*. New York: Holt, Rinehart, and Winston.

Bower, G.H. (1981). Mood and memory. *American Psychologist, 36*, 129-48.

Bowlby, J. (1961). Process of mourning. *International Journal of Psychoanalysis, 42*, 317-40.

Bowlby, J. (1969). *Attachment and loss*, Vol.1, *Attachment*. New York: Basic Books.

Bowlby, J. (1973). *Attachment and loss*, Vol.2, *Separation*. New York: Basic Books.

Brenner, C. (1974). On the nature and development of affect: a unified theory. *Psychoanalytic Quarterly, 43*, 532-56.

Brenner, C. (1976). *Psychoanalytic technique and psychic conflict*. New York: International Universities Press.

Britan, G. and Denich, B. (1976). Environment and choice in rapid social change. *American Ethnologist, 3*, 55-72.

Broadbent, D.E. (1977). The hidden preattentive processes. *American Psychologist, 32*, 109-18.

Brown, A.S. (1979). Primary effects in semantic memory retrieval process. *Journal of Experimental Psychology: Human Learning and Memory, 5*, 65-77.

Brown, N.O. (1959). *Life against death: the psychoanalytic meaning of history*. Middleton, Connecticut: Wesleyan University Press.

Brown, R. (1973). *A first language*. Cambridge: Harvard University Press.

Bruch, H. (1973). *Eating disorders*. New York: Basic Books.

Bruner, J.S. (1971). The growth and structure of skill. In K.J. Connolly (Ed.), *Motor skills in infancy*. New York: Academic Press.

Bruner, J.S. and Goodman, C.C. (1947). Value and need as organizing factors in perception. In J.S. Bruner, *Beyond the information given: studies in the psychology of knowing*. New York: W.W. Norton, 1973.

Bruner, J.S. and Klein, G.S. (1960). The functions of perceiving: New Look retrospect. In J.S. Bruner, *Beyond the information given: studies in the psychology of knowing. New York: W.W. Norton, 1973*.

Bull, N. (1951). The attitude theory of emotion. In *Nervous and Mental Disease Monographs*. New York: Coolidge Foundation.

Burton, J.W. (1978). Ghosts, ancestors and individuals among the Atuot of the Southern Sudan. *Man, 13*, 600-17.

References

Burton, R.V. and Whiting, J.W.M. (1961). The absent father and cross-cultural identity. *Merrill-Palmer Quarterly, 7,* 85-95.

Campbell, D.T. (1965). Variation and selective retention in socio-cultural evolution. In H.R. Barringer, G.I. Blanksten, and R.W. Mack (Eds.), *Social change in developing areas.* Cambridge: Schenckman.

Campbell, D. and Fiske, D. (1959). Convergent and discriminant validation by the multitrait-multimethod matrix. *Psychological Bulletin, 56,* 81-105.

Campbell, D. (1975). On the conflicts between biological and social evolution and between psychology and moral tradition. *American Psychologist, 30,* 1103-26.

Cancian, F. (1960). Functional analysis of change. *American Sociological Review, 25,* 818-26.

Cantor, N. and Kihlstrom, J.F. (1982). Cognitive and social processes in personality. In G.T. Wilson and C. Franks (Eds.), *Contemporary behavior therapy.* New York: Guilford.

Cantor, N. and Mischel, W. (1979). Prototypes in person perception. In L. Berkowitz (Ed.), *Advances in experimental social psychology,* Vol.12. New York: Academic Press.

Cantor, N., Mischel, W., and Schwartz, J. (1982). A prototype analysis of psychological situations. *Cognitive Psychology, 14,* 45-77.

Carneiro, R. (1970). A theory of the origin of the state. *Science, 169,* 733-8.

Carneiro, R. (1973). The four faces of evolution. In J.J. Honigmann (Ed.), *Handbook of social and cultural anthropology.* Chicago: Rand-McNally.

Carr, S., Debbs, J., and Carr, T. (1975). Mother-infant attachment: the importance of the mother's visual field. *Child Development, 46,* 331-8.

Christie, R. (1970). Social correlates of Machiavellianism. In R. Christie and F.L. Geis, (Eds.), *Studies in Machiavellianism.* New York: Academic Press.

Christie, R. and F.L. Geis, Eds. (1970), *Studies in Machiavellianism.* New York: Academic Press.

Clark, M. and Isen, A. (1982). Toward understanding the relationship between feeling states and social behavior. In A. Hastorf and A. Isen (Eds.), *Cognitive social psychology.* New York: Elsevier.

Cohen, L.B. (1979). Our developing knowledge of infant perception and cognition. *American Psychologist, 34,* 894-9.

Cohen, L.B. and Strauss, M.S. (1979). Concept acquisition in the human infant. *Child Development, 50,* 419-24.

Cohen, P.S. (1969). Theories of myth. *Man, 4,* 337-53.

Cohen, R. (1973). Political anthropology. In J.J. Honigmann (Ed.), *Handbook of social and cultural anthropology.* Chicago: Rand-McNally.

Cohen, R. (1976). The natural history of hierarchy: a case study. In T.R. Burns and W. Buckley (Eds.), *Power and control: social structures and their transformation.* London: Sage.

Cohen, R. (1978). Introduction. In R. Cohen and E.R. Service (Eds.), *Origins of the state: the anthropology of political evolution.* Philadelphia: Institute for the Study of Human Issues.

Cole, M. (1975). An ethnographic psychology of cognition. In R. Brislin et al. (Eds.), *Cross-cultural perspectives on learning.* New York: Sage Publications.

References

Coles, R. (1981). Psychoanalysis and moral development. *American Journal of Psychoanalysis, 41,* 101-13.

Collins, A.M. and Loftus, E.S. (1975). A spreading-activation theory of semantic processing. *Psychological Review, 82,* 407-28.

Comaroff, J. (1980). Healing and the cultural order: the case of the Barolong boo Ratshidi of southern Africa. *American Ethologist, 7,* 637-57.

Cook. S. (1973). Economic anthropology: problems in theory, method, and analysis. In J.J. Honigmann (Ed.), *Handbook of social and cultural anthropology.* Chicago: Rand-McNally.

Coombs, G. (1980). Decision theory and subsistence strategies: some theoretical considerations. In T.K. Earle and A.L. Christenson (Eds.), *Modeling change in prehistoric subsistence economies.* New York: Academic Press.

Coon, C.S. (1971). *The hunting peoples.* Middlesex: Penguin Books.

Cooper, J.F., Bloom, F.E., and Roth, R.H. (1978). *The biochemical basis of neuropharmacology.* New York: Oxford University Press.

Coopersmith, S. (1967). *The antecedents of self-esteem.* San Francisco: Freeman.

Costa, B.T., Jr. and McCrae, R.R. (1980). Still stable after all these years: personality as a key to some issues in adulthood and old age. In P.B. Baltes and O.G. Brim (Eds.), *Life span development and behavior,* Vol. 3. New York: Academic Press.

Craig, D. (1979). Immortality through kinship: the vertical transmission of substance and symbolic estate. *American Anthropologist, 81,* 94-6.

Crowell, D.H., Blurton, L.B., Kobayashi, L.R., McFarland, J.L., and Young, R.K. (1976). Studies in early infant learning: classical conditioning of the neonatal heart rate. *Developmental Psychology, 12,* 373-97.

Dahrendorf, R. (1958a). Toward a theory of social conflict. In A. and E. Etzioni (Eds.), *Social change.* New York: Basic Books, 1964.

Dahrendorf, R. (1958b). Out of utopia. *American Journal of Sociology, 64,* 115-27.

Damon, W. (1977). *The social world of the child.* San Francisco: Jossey-Bass.

Darley, J.M. and Latane, B. (1968). Bystander intervention in emergencies: diffusion of responsibility. *Journal of Personality and Social Psychology, 8,* 377-83.

Darwin, C. (1872). *The expression of the emotions in man and animals* (2nd ed.). Chicago: University of Chicago Press, 1965.

Darwin, C. (1895). *The descent of man.* New York: Appleton and Co.

Davis, J. (1970). Morals and backwardness. *Comparative studies in society and history, 12,* 340-53.

Dawkins, R. (1976). *The selfish gene.* Oxford: Oxford University Press.

deCharms, R. and Muir, M.S. (1978). Motivation: social approaches. *Annual Review of Psychology, 29,* 91-113.

de Laguna, F. (1954). Tlingit ideas about the individual. *Southwestern Journal of Anthropology, 10,* 172-91.

Demos, J. and Demos, V. (1969). Adolescence in historical perspective. *Journal of Marriage and Family, 31,* 632-8.

400

d'Entreves, A.P. (1970). *Natural law: an introduction to legal philosophy*. London: Hutchinson University Library.

Des Pres, T. (1976). *The survivor: an anatomy of life in the death camps*. New York: Pocket Books.

Deutsch, H. (1942). Some forms of emotional disturbance and their relationship to schizophrenia. *Psychoanalytic Quarterly, 11*, 307-21.

Deutsch, K. (1961). Social mobilization and political development. *American Political Science Review, 55*, 492-506.

Dickeman, M. (1975). Demographic consequences of infanticide in man. *Annual Review of Ecology and Systematics, 6*, 107-37.

Dobrowolski, K. (1958). Peasant traditional culture. In T. Shanin (Ed.), *Peasants and peasant societies*. Middlesex: Penguin Books, 1971.

Dollard, J. and Miller, N. (1950). *Personality and psychotherapy: an analysis in terms of learning, thinking, and culture*. New York: McGraw-Hill.

Doob, L.W. (1960). *Becoming more civilized: a psychological exploration*. New Haven: Yale University Press.

Douglas, M. (1966). *Purity and danger: an analysis of concepts of pollution and taboo*. Middlesex: Penguin.

Draguns, J.G. (1979). Culture and personality: old friend, new directions. In L.H. Eckensberger, W.J. Lonner, and Y.H. Poortinga (Eds.), *Cross-cultural contributions to psychology*. Holland: Swets and Zeitlinger.

Dienstbier, R.A., Hillman, D., Lehnkoff, J., Hillman, J., and Valkenaar, M.F. (1975). The emotion-attribution approach to moral behavior: interfacing cognitive and avoidance theories of moral development. *Psychological Review, 82*, 299-315.

Druke, M.A. (1980). The concept of personhood in seventeenth and eighteenth century Iroquois ethnopersonality. In N. Bonvillain (Ed.), *Studies in Iroquoian culture*. Occasional Papers in Northeastern Anthropology, No. 6.

DuBois, C. (1964). *Social forces in Southeast Asia*. Cambridge: Harvard University Press.

Dumont, L. (1965a). The modern conception of the individual: notes on its genesis. *Contributions to Indian Sociology, 8*, 85-99.

Dumont, L. (1965b). The functional equivalents of the individual in caste society. *Contributions to Indian Sociology, 8*, 13-61.

Dumont, L. (1966). *Homo hierarchicus: the caste system and its implications*. Chicago: University of Chicago Press.

Durham, W.H. (1982). Interactions of genetic and cultural evolution. *Human Ecology, 10*, 289-323.

Durkheim, E. (1915). *The elementary forms of the religious life*. New York: Free Press.

Durkheim, E. (1933). *The division of labor in society*. New York: Free Press.

Durkheim, E. (1938). *The rules of sociological method*. New York: Free Press.

Duval, S. and Wicklund, R.A. (1972). *A theory of objective self-awareness*. New York: Academic Press.

Dweck, C.S. and Gilliard, D. (1975). Expectancy statements as determinants of reactions to failure: sex differences in persistence and expectancy change. *Journal of Personality and Social Psychology, 32*, 1077-84.

Earle, T.K. (1980). A model of subsistence change. In T.K. Earle and A.L. Christenson (Eds.), *Modeling change in prehistoric subsistence economies*. New York: Academic Press.

Eisenstadt, S.M. (1968). Empires. In D. Sills (Ed.), *International Encyclopedia of the Social Sciences*, Vol.5. New York: Macmillan.

Eisenstadt, S.M. (1969). *The Political Systems of Empires*. New York: Free Press.

Endler, N.S. (1980). Person-situation interaction and anxiety. In I.L. Kutash and L.B. Schlesinger (Eds.), *Handbook of stress and anxiety: contemporary knowledge, theory, and treatment*. San Francisco: Jossey-Bass.

Epstein, S. (1973). The self-concept revisited, or a theory of a theory. *American Psychologist, 28*, 404-16.

Erdelyi, M.H. and Goldberg, B. (1979). Let's not sweep repression under the rug: toward a cognitive psychology of repression. In J.F. Kihlstrom and F.J. Evans (Eds.), *Functional disorders of memory*. Hillsdale, New Jersey: Lawrence Erlbaum.

Erikson, E. (1958). *Young man Luther: a study in psychoanalysis and history*. New York: W.W. Norton.

Erikson, E. (1963). *Childhood and society*. New York: Basic Books.

Erikson, E. (1968). *Identity: youth and crisis*. New York: Basic Books.

Erikson, E. (1969). *Gandhi's truth: on the origin of militant nonviolence*. New York: W.W. Norton.

Erikson, E. (1975). *Life history and the historical moment*. New York: W.W. Norton.

Escalona, S.K. (1968). *The role of individuality: normal patterns of development in infancy*. Chicago: Aldine.

Etzioni, A. and Etzioni, E., Eds. (1964). *Social change*. New York: Basic Books.

Evans, M.B. and Paul, G.L. (1970). Effects of hypnotically suggested analgesia on physiological and subjective responses to cold stress. *Journal of Consulting and Clinical Psychology, 35*, 362-71.

Evans-Pritchard, E.E. (1937). *Witchcraft, oracles and magic among the Azande*. Oxford: Clarendon Press.

Evans-Pritchard, E.E. (1956). *Nuer religion*. Oxford: Clarendon Press.

Evans-Pritchard, E.E. (1965). *Theories of primitive religion*. Oxford: Oxford University Press.

Fairbairn, W. (1954). *An object-relations theory of the personality*. New York: Basic Books.

Fanon, F. (1963). *The wretched of the earth*. New York: Grove Press.

Fast, I. (1978). Developments in gender identity: the original matrix. *International Review of Psycho-Analysis, 59*, 265-73.

Fast, I. (1979). Developments in gender identity: gender differentiation in girls. *International Journal of Psycho-Analysis, 60*, 443-53.

Fast, I. (1981). Infantile narcissism and the active infant. Unpublished manuscript.

Fenz, W.D. (1967). Gradients of psychological arousal of experienced and novice parachutists, as a function of an approaching jump. *Psychosomatic Medicine, 29,* 33-51.

Festinger, L. (1957). *A theory of cognitive dissonance.* Evanston, Illinois: Row, Peterson.

Feyerabend, P. (1975). *Against method.* London: Verso Editions.

Firth, R. (1951). *Elements of social organization.* London: Watts.

Firth, R. (1963). Offering and sacrifice: problems of organisation. *Journal of the Royal Anthropological Institute, 93,* 12-24.

Fiske, S. (1982). Schema-triggered affect: applications to social perception. In M.S. Clarke and S.T. Fiske (Eds.), *Affect and cognition: the 17th annual Carnegie symposium on cognition.* Hillsdale, New Jersey: Lawrence Erlbaum.

Flavell, J.H. (1971). Stage-related properties of cognitive development. *Cognitive Psychology, 2,* 421-53.

Flavell, J.H. (1982). On cognitive development. *Child Development, 53,* 1-10.

Fleming, R., Baum, A., and Singer, J.E. (1984). Toward an integrative approach to the study of stress. *Journal of Personality and Social Psychology, 46,* 939-49.

Flugel, J.C. (1945). *Man, morals, and society: a psycho-analytical study.* London: Duckworth.

Fogelson, R.D. (1982). Person, self, and identity: some anthropological retrospects, circumspects, and prospects. In B. Lee (Ed.), *Psychosocial theories of the self.* New York: Plenum Press.

Fortes, M. (1971). On the concept of the person among the Tallensi. In *La notion de personne en Afrique noire.* Paris: Colloques International.

Foster, G. (1965). Peasant society and the image of limited good. *American Anthropologist, 67,* 293-315.

Foster, G. (1973). *Traditional societies and technological change* (2nd ed.). New York: Harper and Row.

Frankl, V. (1959). *Man's search for meaning: an introduction to logotherapy.* New York: Pocket Books.

Franklin, J.S., Schiele, B.C., Brozek, J., and Keys, A. (1948). Observations on human behavior in experimental semistarvation and rehabilitation. *Journal of Clinical Psychology, 4,* 28-45.

Frazer, J.G. (1922), *The golden bough.* New York: Macmillan.

Freedman, J.L., Wallington, S.A., and Bless, E. (1967). Compliance without pressure: the effect of guilt. *Journal of Personality and Social Psychology, 7,* 117-24.

Freud, A. (1936). *The ego and the mechanisms of defense.* New York: International Universities Press.

Freud, A. (1958). Adolescence. *Psychoanalytic Study of the Child, 13,* 255-78.

Freud, A. (1973). The concept of developmental lines. In S. Sapir and A. Nitzburg (Eds.), *Children with learning problems: readings in a developmental-interaction approach.* New York: Brunner/Mazel.

Freud, S. (1900). *The interpretation of dreams.* New York: Avon Books, 1965.

Freud, S. (1901). *The psychopathology of everyday life.* New York: W.W. Norton, 1965.

References

Freud, S. (1905). *Three contributions to the theory of sex.* New York: E.P. Dutton, 1962.

Freud, S. (1912). A note on the unconscious in psychoanalysis. In P. Rieff (Ed.), *Freud: general psychological theory.* New York: Collier, 1963.

Freud, S. (1913). *Totem and taboo.* New York: W.W. Norton, 1950.

Freud, S. (1914). On narcissism: an introduction. In P. Rieff (Ed.), *Freud: general psychological theory.* New York: Collier, 1963.

Freud, S. (1915). The unconscious. In P. Rieff (Ed.), *Freud: general psychological theory.* New York: Collier, 1963.

Freud, S. (1916). Some character-types met with in psycho-analytic work. In P. Rieff (Ed.), *Freud: character and culture.* New York: Collier, 1963.

Freud, S. (1917), Mourning and melancholia. In P. Rieff (Ed.), *Freud: general psychological theory.* New York: Collier, 1963.

Freud, S. (1920). *Beyond the pleasure principle.* New York: W.W. Norton, 1961.

Freud, S. (1921). *Group psychology and the analysis of the ego.* New York: W.W. Norton, 1959.

Freud, S. (1923). *The ego and the id.* New York: W.W. Norton, 1960.

Freud, S. (1925). Some psychical consequences of the anatomical distinctions between the sexes. *Standard edition,* Vol.19, 243-60.

Freud, S. (1926). *Inhibitions, symptoms, and anxiety.* New York: Basic Books, 1959.

Freud, S. (1930). *Civilization and its discontents.* New York: W.W. Norton, 1961.

Freud, S. (1931). Female sexuality. *Standard edition,* Vol.21, 223-46.

Freud, S. (1933). *New introductory lectures on psychoanalysis.* New York: W.W. Norton, 1965.

Freud, S. (1939). *An outline of psycho-analysis.* New York: W.W. Norton, 1949.

Freund, K.W. (1977). Should homosexuality arouse therapeutic concern? *Journal of Homosexuality, 2,* 235-40.

Friedman, J. (1974). Marxism, structuralism, and vulgar materialism. *Man, 9,* 444-69.

Fromm, E. (1947) *Man for himself: an enquiry into the psychology of ethics.* New York: Holt, Rinehart and Winston.

Fromm, E. (1955). *The sane society.* Greenwich, Ct.: Fawcett Books.

Fromm, E. (1962). *Beyond the chains of illusion: my encounter with Marx and Freud.* New York: Simon and Schuster.

Galbraith, J.K. (1971). *The new industrial state.* New York: Mentor/ New American Library.

Garbarino, J. and Bronfenbrenner, U. (1976). The socialization of moral judgment and behavior in cross-cultural perspective. In T. Lickona (Ed.), *Moral development and behavior: theory, research, and social issues.* New York: Holt, Rinehart and Winston.

Garcia, J., Hawkins, W.G., and Rusiniak, R.W. (1974). Behavioral regulation of the milieu interne in man and rat. *Science, 185,* 824-31.

Garcia, J. and Koelling, R.A. (1966). Relation of cue to consequence in avoidance learning. *Psychonomic Science, 4,* 123-4.

Garcia, J. and Rusiniak, K.W. (1980). What the nose learns from the mouth. In D.

References

Muller-Schwarze and R.M. Silverstein (Eds.), *Chemical signals*. New York: Plenum Press.

Gardner, H. (1981). *The quest for mind: Piaget, Lévi-Strauss, and the structuralist movement* (2nd ed.). Chicago: University of Chicago Press.

Garfinkel, H. (1967). *Studies in ethnomethodology*. Englewood Cliffs, New Jersey: Prentice-Hall.

Gauthier, D.P., Ed. (1970). *Morality and rational self-interest*. Englewood Cliffs, New Jersey: Prentice-Hall.

Geertz, C. (1963). The integrative revolution: primordial sentiments and civil politics in the new states. In C. Geertz (Ed.), *Old societies and new states*. New York: Free Press.

Geertz, C. (1973). *The interpretation of cultures*. New York: Basic Books,

Geertz, C. (1974). From the natives' point of view. *American Academy of Arts and Sciences Bulletin, 28*, 26-43.

Geertz, C. (1981). *Negara: the theater state in nineteenth-century Bali*. Princeton: Princeton University Press.

Geertz, C. (1983). *Local knowledge: further essays in interpretive anthropology*. New York: Basic Books.

Geis, F. (1978). Machiavellianism. In H. London and J.E. Exner (Eds.), *Dimensions of personality*. New York: Wiley.

Geis, F. (1979). Machiavellianism: a cross-cultural perspective of manipulative social behavior. In L.H. Eckensberger, W.J. Lonner, and Y.H. Poortinga (Eds.), *Cross-cultural contributions to psychology*. Holland: Swets and Zeitlinger.

Gellner, E. (1964). *Thought and change*. London: Weidenfeld and Nicolson.

Gellner, E. (1968). A pendulum swing theory of Islam. In R. Robertson (Ed.), *Sociology of religion*. Middlesex: Penguin Books, 1969.

Gellner, E. (1974). Concepts and society. In B.R. Wilson (Ed.), *Rationality*. Oxford: Basil Blackwell.

Gelman, R. and Spelke, E. (1981). The development of thought about animate and inanimate objects: implications for research on social cognition. In J.H. Flavell and L. Ross (Eds.), *Social cognitive development: frontiers and possible futures*. Cambridge: Cambridge University Press.

Gergen, K.J., Morse, S.J., and Gergen, M.M. (1980). Behavior exchange in cross-cultural perspective. In H.C. Triandis and R.W. Brislin (Eds.), *Handbook of cross-cultural psychology*, Vol.5. Boston: Allyn and Bacon.

Gibbs, J. (1977). Kohlberg's stages of moral judgment: a constructive critique. In *Stage theories of cognitive and moral development*, Reprint No.13, Harvard Educational Review, 1978.

Giddens, A. (1971). *Capitalism and modern social theory: an analysis of Marx, Durkheim, and Max Weber*. Cambridge: Cambridge University Press.

Gill, M. and Holzman, P., Eds. (1976). *Psychology versus metapsychology: psychoanalytic essays in memory of George S. Klein. Psychological Issues*, Monograph 36, Vol.9, No.4.

Gilligan, C. (1977). In a different voice: women's descriptions of self and morality. In *Stage theories of cognitive and moral development*, Reprint No.13, Harvard Educational Review, 1978.

References

Gilligan, C. (1982). *In a different voice*. Cambridge: Harvard University Press.

Gluckman, M. (1955). *Custom and conflict in Africa*. Glencoe, Illinois: Free Press.

Godelier, M. (1974). Infrastructures, societies, and history. *Current Anthropology, 19*, 763-71.

Godelier, M. (1977). *Perspectives in Marxist anthropology*, R. Brain (Trans.). Cambridge: Cambridge University Press.

Goffman, E. (1961). *Asylums*. New York: Doubleday.

Goldberger, L. and Breznits, S., Eds. (1982). *Handbook of stress: theoretical and clinical aspects*. New York: Free Press.

Goldfried, R. and Robins, C. (1979). Self-schema, cognitive bias, and the processing of therapeutic experiences. *Advances in Cognitive-Behavioral Research and Therapy, 2*, 33-80.

Goldschmidt, W. (1971). Introduction and Epilogue. In R.B. Edgerton (Ed.), *The individual in cultural adaptation: a study of four East African peoples*. Berkeley: University of California Press.

Goldstone, J. (1982). World-systems theory. *Annual Review of Sociology, 8*, 187-207.

Goody, J. (1973). British functionalism. In R. Naroll and F. Naroll (Eds.), *Main currents in cultural anthropology*. Englewood Cliffs, New Jersey: Prentice-Hall.

Goody, J. (1977). *The domestication of the savage mind*. Cambridge: Cambridge University Press.

Gordon, P.C. and Holyoak, K.J. (1983). Implicit learning and generalizability of the "mere exposure" effect. *Journal of Personality and Social Psychology, 45*, 492-500.

Gough, J.W. (1936). *The social contract: a critical study of its development*. Oxford: Clarendon Press.

Gould, R. (1978). *Transformations: growth and change in adult life*. New York: Simon and Schuster.

Granberg, D. and Brent, E. (1983). When prophecy bends: the preference-expectancy link in United States presidential elections, 1952-1980. *Journal of Personality and Social Psychology, 45*, 477-91.

Gray, J.A. (1979). A neuropsychological theory of anxiety. In C.E. Izard (Ed.), *Emotions in personality and psychopathology*. New York: Plenum Press.

Greenberg, J. (1980). Attentional focus and locus of performance causality as determinants of equity behavior. *Journal of Personality and Social Psychology, 38*, 579-585.

Greenberg, J.R. and Mitchell, S.A. (1983). *Object relations in psychoanalytic theory*. Cambridge: Harvard University Press.

Greenfield, P.M. and Bruner, J.S. (1968). Culture and cognitive growth. In J.S. Bruner, *Beyond the information given: studies in the psychology of knowing*. New York: W.W. Norton, 1973.

Greenspan, S. (1979). *Intelligence and adaptation*. New York: International Universities Press.

Greenwald, A.G. (1980). The totalitarian ego: fabrication and revision of personal history. *American Psychologist, 35*, 603-18.

References

Gregor, T. (1981). "Far, far away my shadow wandered . . ."; the dream symbolism and dream theories of the Mehinaku Indians of Brazil. *American Ethnologist, 8*, 709-20.

Guetzkow, H. (1955). *Multiple loyalties.* Princeton: Princeton University Press.

Guntrip, H. (1971). *Psychoanalytic theory, therapy, and the self.* New York: Basic Books.

Gusfield, J.R. (1967). Tradition and modernity: misplaced polarities in the study of social change. *American Journal of Sociology, 72*, 351-62.

Gutmann, D. (1974). The country of old men: cross cultural studies in the psychology of later life. In R. LeVine (Ed.), *Culture and personality: contemporary readings.* Chicago: Aldine.

Haan, N. (1977). *Coping and defending: processes of self-environment organization.* New York: Academic Press.

Haan, N. (1982). The assessment of coping, defense, and stress. In L. Goldberger and S. Breznits (Eds.), *Handbook of stress: theoretical and clinical aspects.* New York: Free Press.

Habermas, J. (1972). *Knowledge and human interests,* J.J. Shapiro (Trans.). London: Heinemann.

Hagen, E. (1962). *On the theory of social change: how economic growth begins.* Homewood, Illinois: Dorsey Press.

Hall, C. and Lindzey, G. (1978). *Theories of personality* (3rd ed.). New York: Wiley.

Hallowell, A.I. (1955). *Culture and experience.* Philadelphia: University of Pennsylvania Press.

Hamilton, W.D. (1964). The genetical theory of social behavior. *Journal of Theoretical Biology, 6*, 1-52.

Handel, G. (1967). Analysis of correlative meaning: the TAT in the study of whole families. In G. Handel (Ed.), *The psychological interior of the family.* Chicago: Aldine.

Harris, M. (1966). The cultural ecology of India's sacred cattle. *Current Anthropology, 7*, 51-9.

Harris, M. (1979). *Cultural materialism: the struggle for a science of culture.* New York: Random House.

Harris, P. and Olthof, T. (1982). The child's concept of emotion. In G. Butterworth and P. Light (Eds.), *Social cognition: studies of the development of understanding.* Chicago: University of Chicago Press.

Harris, R.W. (1968). *Reason and nature in the eighteenth century.* London: Blandford Press.

Harter, S. (1981). A model of intrinsic mastery motivation in children: individual differences and developmental change. In W.A. Collins (Ed.), *Minnesota symposium on child development,* Vol. 14. Hillsdale, New Jersey: Lawrence Erlbaum.

Harter, S. (1983). Developmental perspectives on the self-system. In M. Hetherington (Ed.), *Handbook of child psychology,* Vol.3. New York: Wiley.

Hartmann, H. (1939). *Ego psychology and the problem of adaptation.* New York: International Universities Press.

407

References

Hartmann, H. (1950). Comments on the psychoanalytic theory of the ego. *Psychoanalytic Study of the Child*, 5, 74-96.

Hartmann, H., Kris, E., and Loewenstein, R. (1946). Comments on the formation of psychic structure. *Psychoanalytic Study of the Child*, 2, 11-38.

Hartmann, H. and Loewenstein, R. (1962). Notes on the superego. *Psychoanalytic Study of the Child*, 17, 42-81.

Hartup, W.W. (1977). Aggression in childhood: developmental perspectives. In M. Hetherington and D. Ross (Eds.), *Contemporary readings in child psychology*. New York: McGraw-Hill.

Harvey, J.H., Harris, B., and Barnes, R.D. (1975). Actor-observer differences in the perception of responsibilities and freedom. *Journal of Personality and Social Psychology*, 32, 22-8.

Harvey, J.H. and Weary, G. (1981). *Perspectives on attributional processes*. Dubuque, Iowa: W.C. Brown.

Hauri, P. (1976). Dreams in patients remitted from reactive depression. *Journal of Abnormal Psychology*, 85, 1-10.

Hauser, S.T. (1976). Loevinger's model and measure of ego development: a critical review. *Psychological Bulletin*, 83, 928-55.

Heinemann, L. and Emrich, H. (1971). Alpha activity during inhibitory brain processes. *Psychophysiology*, 7, 442-50.

Hempel, C. (1958). The logic of functional analysis. In L. Gross (Ed.), *Symposium on sociological theory*. Evanston: Row, Peterson.

Helson, R. and Mitchell, V. (1978). Personality. *Annual Review of Psychology*, 29, 555-85.

Higgins, E.T. (1981). Role taking and social judgment: alternative developmental perspectives and processes. In J.H. Flavell and L. Ross (Eds.), *Social cognitive development: frontiers and possible futures*. Cambridge: Cambridge University Press.

Hilgard, E. (1979). Divided consciousness in hypnosis: the implications of the hidden observer. In E. Fromm and R.E. Shor (Eds.), *Hypnosis: developments in research and new perspectives* (2nd ed.). New York: Aldine.

Hinde, R.A. (1970). *Animal behavior: a synthesis of ethology and comparative psychology* (2nd ed.). New York: McGraw-Hill.

Hobbes, T. (1968). *Leviathan*. Middlesex: Penguin Books.

Hoffman, M. (1975). Sex differences in moral internalization. *Journal of Personality and Social Psychology*, 32, 720-9.

Hoffman, M. (1977). Moral internalization: current theory and research. In L. Berkowitz (ed.), *Advances in experimental social psychology*, Vol.10. New York: Academic Press.

Hoffman, M. (1978). Toward a theory of empathic arousal and development. In M. Lewis and L. Rosenblum (Eds.), *The development of affect*. New York: Plenum Press.

Hoffman, M. (1980). Moral development in adolescence. In J. Adelson (Ed.), *Handbook of adolescent psychiatry*. New York: Wiley.

Hoffman, M.L. and Saltzstein, H.D. (1967). Parent discipline and the child's moral development. *Journal of Personality and Social Psychology*, 5, 45-7.

References

Holroyd, K.A. and Lazarus, R. (1982). Stress, coping, and somatic adaptation. In L. Goldberger and S. Breznitz (Eds.), *Handbook of stress: theoretical and clinical aspects*. New York: Free Press.

Holt, R. (1976). Drive or wish? A reconsideration of the psychoanalytic theory of motivation. In M. Gill and P. Holzman (Eds.), *Psychology versus metapsychology: psychoanalytic essays in memory of George Klein. Psychological Issues*, Monograph 36, Vol.9, No.4.

Holtzman, W.H., Diaz-Guerrero, R., and Swartz, J.D. (1975). *Personality development in two cultures: a cross-cultural study of children in Mexico and the United States*. Austin: University of Texas Press.

Homans, G. (1972). Anxiety and ritual: the theories of Malinowski and Radcliffe-Brown. In W.A. Lessa and E.Z. Vogt (Eds.), *Reader in comparative religion: an anthropological approach* (3rd ed.). New York: Harper and Row.

Homans, G. (1961). *Social behavior: its elementary forms*. London: Routledge and Kegan Paul.

Homans, G. (1964). Bringing men back in. In A. Ryan (Ed.). *The philosophy of social explanation*. Oxford: Oxford University Press, 1973.

Hook, S. (1962). *From Hegel to Marx: studies in the intellectual development of Karl Marx*. Ann Arbor: University of Michigan Press.

Horney, K. (1950). *Neurosis and human growth: the struggle toward self-realization*. New York: W.W. Norton.

Hsu, F.L.K., Ed. (1972). *Psychological Anthropology* (2nd ed.). Cambridge: Schenkman.

Hughes, H.S. (1961). *Consciousness and society: the reconstruction of European social thought, 1890-1930*. New York: Vintage Books.

Hunt, J. McV. (1965). Intrinsic motivation and its role in psychological development. *Nebraska symposium on motivation*, D. Levine (Ed.). Lincoln: University of Nebraska Press, *13*, 189-282.

Huntington, S.P. (1968). *Political order in changing societies*. New Haven: Yale University Press.

Huntington, S.P. (1971). The change to change. *Comparative Politics, 3*, 283-322.

Inkeles, A. and Levinson, D.J. (1969). National character: the study of modal personality and sociocultural systems. In G. Lindzey and E. Aronson (Eds.), *Handbook of Social Psychology* (2nd ed.), Vol.4. Boston: Addison-Wesley.

Inkeles, A. and Smith, D.H. (1974). *Becoming modern: individual change in six developing countries*. Cambridge: Harvard University Press.

Izard, C.E. (1977). *Human emotions*. New York: Plenum Press.

Izard, C.E. (1978). On the ontogenesis of emotions and emotion-cognition relationships in infancy. In M. Lewis and L.A. Rosenblum (Eds.), *The development of affect*. New York: Plenum Press.

Jacobson, E. (1954). The self and the object world. *Psychoanalytic Study of the Child, 9*, 75-127.

Jacobson, E. (1959). The "exceptions": an elaboration of Freud's character study. *Psychoanalytic Study of the Child, 14*, 135-54.

Jacobson, E. (1964). *The self and the object world*. New York: International Universities Press.

References

Jahoda, G. (1958). Child animism: I. A critical survey of cross-cultural research. *Journal of Social Psychology, 47:* 197-212.

Jahoda, G. (1980). Theoretical and systematic approaches in cross-cultural psychology. In H.C. Triandis and W. Lambert (Eds.), *Handbook of cross-cultural psychology*, Vol I. Boston: Allyn and Bacon.

Jahoda, M. (1977). *Freud and the dilemmas of psychology*. London: Hogarth.

James, E.O. (1964). *History of Religions*. London: Hodder and Stoughton.

James, W. (1890). *Principles of psychology*, Vol. 1. New York: Wiley.

James, W. (1902). *The varieties of religious experience*. New York: American Library, 1958.

Jaynes, J. (1976). *The origin of consciousness in the breakdown of the bicameral mind*. Boston: Houghton Mifflin.

Joffe, W. and Sandler, J. (1967). Some conceptual problems involved in the consideration of disorders of narcissism. *Journal of Child Psychotherapy, 2,* 56-66.

Johnson, J., McCauley, C., and Copley, J.B. (1982). The quality of life of hemodialysis and transplant patients. *Kidney International, 22,* 286-91.

Jung, C.G. (1928). The relations between the ego and the unconscious. In *The portable Jung*, J. Campbell (Ed.). New York: Penguin Books, 1971.

Jung, C.G. (1971). *The portable Jung*, J. Campbell (Ed.). New York: Penguin Books.

Kagan, J. (1976). Emergent themes in human development. In P.H. Mussen, J.J. Conger, and J. Kagan (Eds.), *Readings in child and adolescent psychology*. New York: Harper, 1980.

Kagan, S., and Carlson, H. (1975). Development of adaptive assertiveness in Mexican and United States children. *Developmental Psychology, 11:* 71-8.

Kahneman, D. (1973). *Attention and effort*. Englewood Cliffs, New Jersey: Prentice-Hall.

Kanfer, F. (1980). Self-management methods. In F. Kanfer and A.P. Goldstein (Eds.), *Helping people change: a textbook of methods* (2nd ed.). New York: Permagon Press.

Kanfer, F.H. and Hagerman, S. (1980). The role of self-regulation. In L.P. Rehm (Ed.), *Behavior therapy and depression: present status and future directions*. New York: Academic Press.

Kant, I. (1948). *Groundwork of the Metaphysic of Morals*, H.J. Paton (Trans.). New York: Harper Torchbooks.

Kardiner, A. (1945). *The Psychological frontiers of society*. New York: Columbia University Press.

Katz, D. and Kahn, R. (1978). *The social psychology of organizations* (2nd ed.). New York: Wiley.

Katz, P. and Zigler, E. (1967). Self-image disparity: a developmental approach. *Journal of Personality and Social Psychology, 5,* 186-95.

Katz, P.A., Zigler, E., and Zelk, S.R. (1975). Children's self-image disparity: the effects of age, maladjustment, and action-thought orientation. *Developmental Psychology, 11,* 546-50.

Kaufman, C. (1974). Biological considerations of parenthood. In R. LeVine (Ed.), *Culture and personality: contemporary readings*. Chicago: Aldine.

References

Kaufman, W., Ed. (1975). *Existentialism from Dostoevsky to Sartre.* New York: New American Library.

Kavanaugh, R. (1972). *Facing death.* Middlesex: Penguin Books.

Kazdin, A.E. (1978). Conceptual and assessment issues raised by self-efficacy. *Advances in Behavior Research and Therapy, 1,* 177-85.

Keasey, C.B. (1978). Children's developing awareness and usage of intentionality and motives. In C.B. Keasey (Ed.), *Nebraska symposium on motivation,* Vol. 25. Lincoln, Nebraska: University of Nebraska Press.

Kegan, R. (1982). *The evolving self: problem and process in human development.* Cambridge: Harvard University Press.

Keil, F.C. (1981). Constraints on knowledge and cognitive development. *Psychological Review, 88,* 197-227.

Kelly, G. (1955). *The psychology of personal constructs.* New York: W.W. Norton.

Kelman, H.C. (1969). Patterns of personal involvement in the national system: a social-psychological analysis of political legitimacy. In J.M. Rosenau (Ed.), *International Politics and Foreign Policy.* New York: Free Press.

Kelman, H.C. and Lawrence, L. (1972). American response to the trial of Lt. William L. Calley. *Psychology Today,* June.

Keniston, K. (1968). *Young radicals.* New York: Harcourt Brace Jovanovich.

Keniston, K. (1970). Youth: a "new" stage of life. *American Scholar, 39,* 631-54.

Kernberg, O. (1975). *Borderline conditions and pathological narcissism.* New York: Aronson.

Kernberg, O. (1976). *Object-relations theory and clinical psychoanalysis.* New York: Aronson.

Kierkegaard, S. (1843). *Fear and trembling.* In *Fear and trembling and the sickness unto death.* Princeton, New Jersey: Princeton University Press, 1954.

Kihlstrom, J.F. (1981). On personality and memory. In N. Cantor and J. Kihlstrom (Eds.), *Personality, cognition, and social interaction.* Hillsdale, New Jersey: Lawrence Erlbaum.

Kihlstrom, J.F. and Cantor, N. (1983). Mental representations of the self. In L. Berkowitz (Ed.), *Advances in experimental social psychology,* Vol.15. New York: Academic Press.

Kitagawa, J.M. (1967). Primitive, classical and modern religions. In J.M. Kitagawa (Ed.), *The history of religions: essays on the problem of understanding.* Chicago: University of Chicago Press.

Klein, G.S. (1967). Motives and thought: structure and force in motivated ideas. In R. Holt (Ed.), *Motives and thought: psychoanalytic essays in honor of David Rapaport. Psychological Issues,* Monograph 18/19, Vol.5, No.2-3.

Klein, M. (1946). Notes on some schizoid mechanisms. *International Journal of Psychoanalysis, 27,* 99-110.

Klein, M. (1948). *Contributions to psycho-analysis, 1921-1945.* London: Hogarth.

Klineberg, O. (1980). Historical perspectives: cross-cultural psychology before 1960. In H.C. Triandis and W.W. Lambert (Eds.), *Handbook of cross-cultural psychology,* Vol.1. Boston: Allyn and Bacon.

Klinnert, M.D., Campos, J.J., Sorce, J.F., Emde, R.N., and Svejda, M. (1983).

411

References

Emotions as behavior regulators: social referencing in infancy. In R. Plutchik and H. Kellerman (Eds.), *Emotion: theory, research, and experience*, Vol. 2, *Emotions in early development*. New York: Academic Press.

Kluckhohn, C. (1942). Myths and rituals: a general theory. In W.A. Lessa and E.Z. Vogt (Eds.), *Reader in comparative religions: an anthropological approach* (3rd ed.). New York: Harper and Row, 1972.

Kluckhohn, C. (1944). *Mirror for man: a survey of human behavior and social attitudes*. Greenwich, Connecticut: Fawcett Books.

Kohlberg, L. (1963). The development of children's orientations toward a moral order. I. Sequence in the development of moral thought. *Vita Humana, 6,* 11-33.

Kohlberg, L. and Gilligan, C. (1971). The adolescent as a philosopher. *Daedalus, 100,* 14-70.

Kohlberg, L., and Kramer, R. (1969). Continuities and discontinuities in childhood and adult moral development. *Human Development, 12,* 93-120.

Kohlberg, L., and Mayer, R. (1972). Development as the aim of education. In *Stage theories of cognitive and moral development*, Reprint No.13, Harvard Educational Review, 1978.

Kohut, H. (1966). Forms and transformations of narcissism. *Journal of the American Psychoanalytic Association, 14,* 243-72.

Kohut, H. (1968). The psychoanalytic treatment of narcissistic personality disorders. *Psychoanalytic Study of the Child, 23,* 86-113.

Kohut, H. (1971). *The analysis of the self: a systematic approach to the treatment of narcissistic personality disorders*. New York: International Universities Press.

Kohut, H. (1977). *The restoration of the self*. New York: International Universities Press.

Kohut, H. and Wolf, E. (1978). The disorders of the self and their treatment. *International Journal of Psychoanalysis, 59,* 413-25.

Kovacs, M. and Beck, A.T. (1979). Cognitive-affective processes in depression. In C.E. Izard (Ed.), *Emotion in personality and psychopathology*. New York: Plenum Press.

Kroeber, A.L. (1948). *Anthropology: culture patterns and processes*. New York: Harvest.

Kroeber, A.L. and Kluckhohn, C. (1952). *Culture: a critical review of concepts and definitions*. Cambridge: Papers of the Peabody Museum of American Archaeology and Ethnology, Harvard University, No.47.

Krohn, A. (1974). Borderline "empathy" and differentiation of object representations: a contribution to the psychology of object relations. *International Journal of Psychoanalytic Psychotherapy, 3,* 142-65.

Kubler-Ross, E. (1969). *On death and dying*. New York: Macmillan.

Kuhn, T. (1970). *The structure of scientific revolutions*. Chicago: University of Chicago Press.

Kurtines, W. and Greif, E. (1974). The development of moral thought: review and evaluation of Kohlberg's approach. *Psychological Bulletin, 81,* 453-70.

Kwawer, J.S., Lerner, H.D., and Lerner, P.M., and Sugarman, A. (1980). *Border-*

line phenomena and the Rorschach test. New York: International Universities Press.

LaBarre, W. (1966). The Aymara: history and world view. *Journal of American Folklore, 79*, 130-44.

Laing, R.D. (1959). *The divided self*. New York: Penguin Books.

Laird, J.D. (1974). Self-attribution of emotion: the effects of expressive behavior on the quality of emotional experience. *Journal of Personality and Social Psychology, 29*, 475-86.

Lakatos, I. and Musgrave, A., Eds. (1970). *Criticism and the growth of knowledge*. Cambridge: Cambridge University Press.

Lambe, R. and Westen, D. (1983). The etiology of borderline disorders: a cross-cultural study of the relationship between infant care and borderline phenomena. Unpublished manuscript.

Lame Deer, J. and Erdoes, R. (1972). *Lame Deer, seeker of visions*. New York: Simon and Schuster.

Landau, R.J., and Goldfried, M.R. (1981). The assessment of schemata: a unifying framework for cognitive, behavioral, and traditional assessment. In P.C. Kendall and S.D. Hollon (Eds.), *Assessment strategies for cognitive-behavioral interventions*. New York: Academic Press.

Lasch, C. (1978). *The culture of narcissism: American life in an age of diminishing expectations*. New York: W.W. Norton.

Laszlo, E. (1972). *The systems view of the world*. New York: George Braziller.

Laughlin, C.P. Jr. and Brady, I.A., Eds. (1978). *Extinction and survival in human populations*. New York: Columbia University Press.

Lazarus, A. (1968). Learning theory and the treatment of depression. *Behavior Research and Therapy, 6*, 83-9.

Lazarus, R. (1981). The stress and coping paradigm. In C. Eisdorfer, D. Cohen, A. Kleinman, and P. Maxim (Eds.), *Models for clinical psychopathology*. New York: Spectrum.

Lazarus, R. (1982). Thoughts on the relations between emotion and cognition. *American Psychologist, 37*, 1019-24.

Lazarus, R., and DeLongis, A. (1983). Psychological stress and coping in aging. *American Psychologist, 38*, 245-54.

Leach, E. (1966). Ritualization in man in relation to conceptual and social development. In W.A. Lessa and E.Z.Vogt (Eds.), *Reader in comparative religion: an anthropological approach*. New York: Harper and Row, 1972.

Leach, E. (1970). *Claude Lévi-Strauss*. New York: Penguin Books.

Le Bon, G. (1895). *The crowd*. New York: Balantine, 1969.

Lee, D. (1950). The conception of the self among the Wintu Indians. In D. Lee, *Freedom and Culture*. Englewood Cliffs, New Jersey: Prentice-Hall, 1959.

Lee, D. (1957). Personal significance and group structure. In D. Lee, *Freedom and Culture*. Englewood Cliffs, New Jersey: Prentice-Hall, 1959.

Lerner, D. (1958). *The passing of traditional society: modernizing the middle east*. New York: Free Press.

Lerner, D. (1968). Modernization: social aspects. In D. Sills (Ed.), *International Encyclopedia of the Social Sciences*, Vol. 10. New York: Free Press.

413

References

Leventhal, H. and Everhart, D. (1979). Emotion, pain, and physical illness. In C.E. Izard (Ed.), *Emotion in personality and psychopathology*. New York: Plenum Press.

LeVine, R. (1973). *Culture, behavior, and personality*. Chicago: Aldine.

LeVine, R.A. and Campbell, D.T. (1972). *Ethnocentrism: theories of conflict, ethnic attitudes, and group behavior*. New York: Wiley.

Levinson, D. (1978). *The seasons of a man's life*. New York: Ballantine Books.

Lévi-Strauss, C. (1959). The bear and the barber. In W.A. Lessa and E.Z. Vogt (Eds.), *Reader in comparative religion: an anthropological approach*. New York: Harper and Row, 1972.

Lévi-Strauss, C. (1962). *Totemism*. Boston: Beacon Press.

Lévi-Strauss, C. (1963). *Structural anthropology*. New York: Basic Books.

Lévi-Strauss, C. (1966). *The savage mind*. Chicago: University of Chicago Press.

Lévi-Strauss, C. (1969a). *The elementary structures of kinship*. Boston: Beacon Press.

Lévi-Strauss, C. (1969b). *The raw and the cooked*. New York: Harper and Row.

Levitt, E.E. (1980). *The psychology of anxiety* (2nd ed.). Hillsdale, New Jersey: Lawrence Erlbaum.

Levy-Bruhl, L. (1923). *Primitive mentality*. L.A. Clare (Trans.). London: Allen and Unwin.

Levy, M.J. (1966). *Modernization and the structure of societies: a setting for international affairs*, Vols. 1 and 2. Princeton: Princeton University Press.

Lewinsohn, P., Weinstein, M., and Shaw, D. (1969). Depression: a clinical-research approach. In R.D. Rubin and C.M. Franks (Eds.), *Advances in behavior therapy*. New York: Academic Press.

Lewis, I.M. (1976). *Social anthropology in perspective*. Middlesex: Penguin Books.

Lewis, M. and Brooks, J. (1978). Self-knowledge and emotional development. In M. Lewis and A. Rosenblum (Eds.), *The development of affect*. New York: Plenum Press.

Lewis, M. and Brooks-Gunn, J. (1979). *Social cognition and the acquisition of self*. New York: Plenum Press.

Lewis, M. and Rosenblum, L., Eds. (1978). *The development of affect*. New York: Plenum Press.

Lickona, T. (1976). Critical issues in the study of moral development and behavior. In T. Lickona (Ed.), *Moral development and behavior: theory, research, and social issues*. New York: Holt, Rinehart and Winston.

Lienhardt, G. (1961). *Divinity and experience: the religion of the Dinka*. Oxford: Oxford University Press.

Lifton, R.J. (1963). *Thought reform and the psychology of totalism: a study of "brainwashing" in China*. New York: W.W. Norton.

Lifton, R.J. (1968). Protean man. *Partisan Review*.

Lifton, R. (1970). *Boundaries: psychological man in revolution*. New York: Vintage Books.

Lifton, R.J., Ed. (1974). *Explorations in psychohistory: the Wellfleet papers*. New York: Vintage Books.

Lifton, R. (1979). *The broken connection*. New York: Touchstone Books.

414

References

Lindemann, E. (1944). Symptomatology and the management of acute grief. *American Journal of Psychiatry, 101,* 141-8.

Linton, R. (1943). Natavistic movements. In W.A. Lessa and E.Z. Vogt (Eds.), *Reader in comparative religion: an anthropological approach.* New York: Harper and Row, 1972.

Linton, R. (1945). *The cultural background of personality.* New York: Appleton-Century.

Little, B.R. (1983). Personal projects: a rationale and method for investigation. *Environment and Behavior, 15,* 273-309.

Lively, W.J. and Bromley, D.B. (1973). *Person perception in childhood and adolescence.* London: Wiley.

Locke, J. (1960). *Two treatises of government.* New York: Mentor Books.

Lockwood, D. (1956). Some notes on "The Social System." *British Journal of Sociology, 1,* 134-46.

Loevinger, J. (1966). The meaning and measurement of ego development. *American Psychologist, 21,* 195-206.

Loevinger, J. (1976a). *Ego development.* San Francisco: Jossey-Bass.

Loevinger, J. (1976b). Origins of conscience. In M. Gill and P. Holzman (Eds.), *Psychology versus metapsychology: psychoanalytic essays in memory of George S. Klein, Psychological Issues,* Monograph 36, Vol.9, No.4.

Loevinger, J., Wessler, R., and Redmore, C. (1970). *Measuring ego development II: scoring manual for women and girls.* San Francisco: Jossey-Bass.

Luckmann, T. (1967). *The invisible religion.* New York: Macmillan.

Lukes, S. (1974). *Power: a radical view.* London: Macmillan.

Lumsden, C. and Wilson, E.O. (1981). *Genes, mind, and culture: the coevolutionary process.* Cambridge: Harvard University Press.

Luria, A. (1961). *The role of speech in the regulation of normal and abnormal behaviors.* New York: Liveright Books.

Luther, M. (1961). *Martin Luther: selections from his writings,* J. Dillenberger (Ed.). New York: Anchor Books.

Maccoby, E.E. (1980). *Social development: psychological growth and the parent-child relationship.* New York: Harcourt Brace Jovanovich.

Machan, T.R. (1979). Recent work in ethical egoism. *American Philosophical Quarterly, 16,* 1-15.

Machiavelli, N. (1961). *The prince.* Middlesex: Penguin Books.

MacIntyre, A. (1966). *A short history of ethics.* London: Routledge and Kegan Paul.

Madsen, M.C. (1967). Cooperative and competitive motivation of children in three Mexican subcultures. *Psychological Reports, 20,* 1307-20.

Madsen, M.C. (1971). Developmental and cross-cultural differences in the cooperative and competitive behavior of young children. *Journal of Cross-Cultural Psychology, 2,* 365-71.

Mahler, M., Pine, F., and Bergman, A. (1975). *The psychological birth of the human infant: symbiosis and individuation.* New York: Basic Books.

Mair, L. (1969). *Witchcraft.* New York: McGraw-Hill.

Malinowski, B. (1931). The role of magic and religion. In W.A. Lessa and E.Z.

References

Vogt (Eds.), *Reader in comparative religion: an anthropological approach.* New York: Harper and Row, 1972.

Malinowski, B. (1939). The group and the individual in functional analysis. *American Journal of Sociology, 44,* 938-64.

Malinowski, B. (1954). *Magic, science and religion, and other essays.* New York: Doubleday.

Mannoni, O. (1964). *Prospero and Caliban: the psychology of colonization.* New York: F.A. Praeger.

Marcuse, H. (1955). *Eros and civilization: a philosophical inquiry into Freud.* Boston: Beacon Press.

Marin, G., Mejia, B. and deOberle, C. (1975). Cooperation as a function of place of residence in Columbian children. *Journal of Social Psychology, 95,* 127-8.

Markus, H. (1980). The self in thought and memory. In D.M. Wegner and R.R. Vallacher (Eds.), *The self in social psychology.* New York: Oxford University Press.

Markus, H. (1983). Self-knowledge: an expanded view. *Journal of Personality, 51,* 543-65.

Marris, P. (1974). *Loss and change.* London: Routledge and Kegan Paul.

Marx, K. (1844). Economic and philosophical manuscripts. In *Karl Marx: early writings,* Q. Hoare (Ed.). New York: Vintage Books, 1975.

Marx, K. (1852). The eighteenth brumaire of Louis Bonaparte. In R.C. Tucker (Ed.), *The Marx-Engels reader.* New York: W.W. Norton, 1972.

Marx, K. (1859). *Capital,* Vol.1. New York: International Publishers, 1967.

Marx, K. (1972). *The Marx-Engels reader,* R. Tucker (Ed.). New York: W.W. Norton.

Marx, K. (1975). On the Jewish question. In *Karl Marx: early writings,* Q. Hoare (Ed.). New York: Vintage Books.

Maslach, C. (1979). The emotional consequences of arousal without reason. In C.E. Izard (Ed.), *Emotion in personality and psychopathology.* New York: Plenum Press.

Maslow, A. (1954). *Motivation and personality.* New York: Harper.

Maslow, A. (1962). *Toward a psychology of being.* Princeton, New Jersey: D. Van Nostrand.

Masters, J.C. and Santrock, J.W. (1976). Studies in the self-regulation of behavior: effects on contingent cognitive and affective events. *Developmental Psychology, 12,* 334-48.

Mauss, M. (1938). A category of the human mind: the notion of person, the notion of "self." In M. Mauss, *Sociology and psychology: essays,* B. Brewster (Trans.). Boston: Routledge and Kegan Paul.

May, R. (1953). *Man's search for himself.* New York: Signet Books.

Maynard-Smith, J. (1978). The concepts of sociobiology. In G. Stent (Ed.), *Morality as a biological phenomenon: the presuppositions of sociobiological research.* Berkeley: University of California Press.

McClelland, D. (1961). *The achieving society.* Princeton: D. Van Nostrand.

McConaghy, N. (1976). Is a homosexual orientation irreversible? *British Journal of Psychiatry, 129,* 556-63.

416

References

McFall, R.M. (1982). A review and reformulation of the concept of social skills. *Behavioral Assessment, 4,* 1-33.

Mead, M. (1949). Social change and cultural surrogates. In C. Kluckhohn and H.A. Murray (Eds.), *Personality in nature, society, and culture.* New York: Alfred Knopf.

Mead, M. (1963). Socialization and enculturation. *Current Anthropology, 4,* 184-8.

Medin, D.L. and Smith, E.E. (1984). Concepts and concept formation. *Annual Review of Psychology, 35,* 113-38.

Meichenbaum, D. (1977). *Cognitive-behavior modification: an integrative approach.* New York: Plenum Press.

Meichenbaum, D., Butler, L., and Joseph, L.G. (in press). Toward a conceptual model of social competence. In J. Wine and M. Smythe (Eds.), *The identification and enhancement of social competence.* Washington, D.C.: Hemisphere.

Mendelson, M. (1974). *Psychoanalytic concepts of depression.* New York: Spectrum.

Menninger, K., Mayman, M., and Pruyser, P. (1963). *The vital balance.* New York: Viking.

Merton, R. (1968). *Social theory and social structure.* New York: Free Press.

Meyer, D.E. (1973). Correlated operations in searching stored semantic categories. *Journal of Experimental Psychology, 99,* 124-33.

Meyer, D.E. and Schvaneveldt, R.W. (1971). Facilitation in recogniizing pairs of words: evidence of a dependence between retrieval operations. *Journal of Experimental Psychology, 90,* 227-34.

Middleton, J. (1960). *Lugbara religion: ritual and authority among an East African people.* London: Oxford University Press.

Migdal, J. (1979). Social control and social change. Unpublished manuscript.

Mill, J.S. (1962). *Utilitarianism, on liberty, essays on Benthem,* M. Warnock (Ed.). New York: Meridian/New American Library.

Miller, A.G. and Thomas, R. (1972). Cooperation and competition among Blackfoot Indian and urban Canadian children. *Child Development, 43,* 1104-10.

Miller, G.A., Gallanter, E., and Pribram, K.H. (1960). *Plans and the structure of behavior.* New York: Holt, Rinehart, and Winston.

Miller, I.W. and Norman, W.H. (1979). Learned helplessness in humans: a review and attribution-theory model. *Psychological Bulletin, 86,* 93-118.

Miller, J. (1984). Culture and the development of everyday social exploration. *Journal of Personality and Social Psychology, 46,* 961-78.

Miller, N. and Dollard, J. (1941). *Social learning and imitation.* New Haven: Yale University Press.

Mischel, W. (1968). *Personality and assessment.* New York: Wiley.

Mischel, W. (1973a). Toward a cognitive social learning reconceptualization of personality. *Psychological Review, 80,* 252-83.

Mischel, W. (1973b). On the empirical dilemmas of psychodynamic approaches: issues and alternatives. *Journal of Abnormal Psychology, 82,* 335-44.

Mischel, W. (1976). *Introduction to personality* (2nd ed.). New York: Holt, Rinehart and Winston.

417

References

Mischel, W. (1979). On the interface of cognition and personality: beyond the person-situation debate. *American Psychologist, 34,* 740-54.

Mischel, W. (1984). Convergences and challenges in the search for consistency. *American Psychologist, 39,* 351-64.

Mischel, W. and Mischel, H.N. (1976). A cognitive social-learning approach to morality and self-regulation. In T. Lickona (Ed.), *Moral development and behavior: theory, research, and social issues.* New York: Holt, Rinehart and Winston.

Mischel, W. and Moore, B. (1980). The role of ideation in voluntary delay for symbolically-presented rewards. *Cognitive Therapy and Research, 4,* 211-21.

Moltz, H., Lubin, M., Leon, M., and Numon, M. (1970). Hormonal induction of maternal behavior in the overiectomized rat. *Physiology and Behavior, 5,* 1373-7.

Monahan, L. (1975). Mother-infant and stranger-infant interaction: an ethological analysis. Unpublished doctoral dissertation, University of Indiana.

Montemayor, R. and Eisen, M. (1977). A developmental sequence of self-conceptions from childhood to adolescence. *Developmental Psychology, 13,* 314-19.

Moore, B. (1966). *Social origins of dictatorship and democracy.* Boston: Beacon Press.

Moore, B. (1978). *Injustice: the social bases of obedience and revolt.* London: Macmillan.

Moore, B., Clyburn, A., and Underwood, B. (1976). The role of affect in delay of gratification. *Child Development, 47,* 273-6.

Motley, M. (1980). Verification of "Freudian slips" and semantic prearticulatory editing via laboratory-induced spoonerisms. In V.L. Fromkin (Ed.), *Errors in linguistic performance: slips of the tongue, ear, pen, and hand.* New York: Academic Press.

Motley, M. and Baars, B.J. (1976). Laboratory induction of verbal slips: a new method for psycholinguistic research. *Communication Quarterly, 24,* 28-34.

Mowrer, O.H. (1947). On the dual nature of learning: a reinterpretation of "conditioning" and "problem-solving." *Harvard Educational Review, 17,* 102-48.

Munroe, R.L. and Munroe, R.H. (1975). *Cross-cultural human development.* Monterey, California: Brooks/Cole.

Mussen, P. and Beytagh, L.M. (1969). Industrialization, child-rearing practices, and children's personality. *Journal of Genetic Psychology, 115,* 195-216.

Naroll, R. and Cohen, R. (1970). *Handbook of methods in cultural anthropology.* New York: Natural History Press.

Neisser, U. (1962). Cultural and cognitive discontinuity. In T.E. Gladwin and W. Sturtevant (Eds.), *Anthropology and human behavior.* Washington, D.C.: Anthropological Society of Washington.

Neisser, U. (1976). *Cognition and reality.* San Francisco: W.H. Freeman.

Netting, R.M. (1972). Sacred power and centralization: aspects of political adaptation in Africa. In B. Spooner (Ed.), *Population growth: anthropological implications.* Cambridge: M.I.T. Press.

418

References

Nietzsche, F. (1956). *The birth of tragedy and the genealogy of morals.* New York: Doubleday.

Nietzsche, F. (1954). *The portable Nietzsche,* W. Kaufman (Trans. and Ed.). Middlesex: Penguin Books.

Nisbett, R.E. and Ross, C. (1980). *Human inference: strategies and shortcomings of social judgment.* Englewood Cliffs, New Jersey: Prentice-Hall.

Nisbett, R.E. and Wilson, T.D. (1977). Telling more than we can know: verbal reports on mental processes. *Psychological Review, 84,* 231-59.

Noam, G.G., Kohlberg, L. and Snarey, J. (1983). Steps toward a model of the self. In B. Lee and G.G. Noam (Eds.), *Developmental approaches to the self.* New York: Plenum Press.

Novey, S. (1955). The role of the superego and ego-ideal in character formation. *International Journal of Psycho-Analysis, 36,* 254-9.

Nunberg, H. (1955). *Principles of psychoanalysis.* New York: International Universities Press.

O'Dea, T.F. (1970). *Sociology and the study of religion: theory, research, and interpretation.* New York: Basic Books.

Olson, G.M. (1981). The recognition of specific persons. In M.E. Lamb and L.R. Sherrod (Eds.), *Infant social cognition: empirical and theoretical considerations.* Hillsdale, New Jersey: Lawrence Erlbaum.

Orlove, B.S. (1980). Ecological anthropology. *Annual Review of Anthropology, 9,* 235-73.

Ortega, J. (1961). Man has no nature. In W. Kaufman (Ed.), *Existentialism from Dostoevsky to Sartre.* New York: New American Library, 1975.

Ortner, S.B. (1984). Theory in anthropology since the sixties. *Comparative Studies in Society and History, 26,* 126-66.

Oster, H. (1981). "Recognition" of emotional expression in infancy? In M.E. Lamb and L.R. Sherrod (Eds.), *Infant social cognition: empirical and theoretical considerations.* Hillsdale, New Jersey: Lawrence Erlbaum.

Parkes, C.M. (1970). "Seeking" and "finding" a lost object: evidence from recent studies of the reaction to bereavement. *Social Science and Medicine, 4,* 187-201.

Parsons, T. (1951). *The social system.* New York: Macmillan.

Parsons, T. (1970a). The father symbol: an appraisal in the light of psychoanalytic and sociological theory. In *Social structure and personality.* New York: Free Press.

Parsons, T. (1970b). The superego and the theory of social systems. In *Social structure and personality.* New York: Free Press.

Parsons, T. and Shils, E. (1951). Categories of the orientation and organization of action. In T. Parsons and E. Shils (Eds.), *Toward a general theory of action.* Cambridge: Harvard University Press.

Pavlov, I. (1927). *Conditioned reflexes.* London: Oxford University Press.

Pearlin, L.I. and Schooler, C. (1978). The structure of coping. *Journal of Health and Social Behavior, 19,* 2-21.

Pelto, P. and Pelto, G. (1975). Intra-cultural diversity: some theoretical issues. *American Ethnologist, 2,* 1-18.

Pennebaker, J.W. (1980). Self-perception of emotion and internal sensation. In

References

D.M. Wegner and R.R. Vallacher (Eds.), *The self in social psychology*. New York: Oxford University Press.

Pervin, L. (1977). *Current controversies and issues in personality*. New York: Wiley.

Peters, E. (1967). Some structural aspects of the feud among the camel-herding Bedouin of Cyrenaica. *Africa, 37,* 260-82.

Pettijohn, T., Wong, T., Ebert, P., and Scott, J. (1977). Alleviation of separation distress in three breeds of young dogs. *Developmental Psychobiology, 10,* 373-81.

Piaget, J. (1926). *The language and thought of the child*. New York: Humanities Press, 1951.

Piaget, J. (1932). *The moral judgment of the child*. New York: Free Press, 1965.

Piaget, J. (1951). *Play, dreams and imitation in childhood*. New York: W.W. Norton.

Piaget, J. (1970). Piaget's theory. In P. Mussen (Ed.), *Carmichael's manual of child psychology* (3rd ed.). New York: Wiley.

Piaget, J. and Inhelder, B. (1969). *The psychology of the child*. New York: Basic Books.

Plato (1974). *The republic*. Indianapolis: Hatchett Publishing Co.

Plutchik, R. (1980a). A general psychoevolutionary theory of emotion. In R. Plutchik and H. Kellerman (Eds.), *Emotion*, Vol.1. *Theories of emotion*. New York: Academic Press.

Plutchik, R. (1980b). *Emotion: a psychoevolutionary synthesis*. New York: Harper and Row.

Poole, F.J.P. (1982). The ritual forging of identity: aspects of person and self in Bimin-Kuskusmin male initiation. In G.H. Herdt (Ed.), *Rituals of manhood*. Berkeley: University of California Press.

Popper, K. (1957). *The poverty of historicism*. London: Routledge and Kegan Paul.

Pospisil, L. (1958). *Kaupauka Papuans and their law*. New Haven: Yale University Press.

Pospisil, L. (1963). *Kaupauka Papuan political economy*. New Haven: Yale University Publications in Anthropology, No. 67.

Powers, W.T. (1973). *Behavior: the control of perception*. Chicago: Aldine.

Pribram, K. (1980). The biology of emotions and other feelings. In R. Plutchik and H. Kellerman (Eds.), *Emotion: theory, research, and experience* , Vol. 1, *Theories of emotion*. New York: Academic Press.

Psathas, G. (1973). *Phenomenological sociology*. New York: Wiley.

Pulver, S. (1970). Narcissism: the term and the concept. *Journal of the American Psychoanalytic Association, 18,* 319-41.

Pye, L. (1962). *Politics, personality, and nation building: Burma's search for identity*. New Haven: Yale University Press.

Quinn, N. (1975). Decision models of social structure. *American Ethnologist, 2,* 19-45.

Rachman, S.J. (1978). *Fear and courage*. San Francisco: Freeman.

Radcliffe-Brown, A.R. (1972). Taboo. In W.A. Lessa and E.Z. Vogt (Eds.), *Reader*

420

in comparative religion: an anthropological approach. New York: Harper and Row.

Radcliffe-Brown, A.R. (1965). *Structure and function in primitive society*. New York: Free Press.

Rapaport, D. (1953). On the psychoanalytic theory of affects. *International Journal of Psychoanalysis, 34*, 177-98.

Rapaport, D. (1957). Cognitive structures. In *The collected papers of David Rapaport*, M. Gill (Ed.). New York: Basic Books, 1967.

Rapaport, D. (1959). An historical survey of psychoanalytic ego psychology. In *The collected papers of David Rapaport*, M. Gill (Ed.). New York: Basic Books, 1967.

Rappaport, R.A. (1968). *Pigs for the ancestors*. New Haven: Yale University Press.

Rappaport, R.A. (1979). *Ecology, meaning, and religion*. Richmond, California: North Atlantic Books.

Rawls, J. (1971). *A theory of justice*. Cambridge: Harvard University Press.

Redfield, R. (1941). *The folk culture of Yucatan*. Chicago: University of Chicago Press.

Redfield, R. (1947). The folk society. *American Journal of Sociology, 52*, 293-308.

Redfield, R. (1953a). *The primitive world and its transformations*. Ithaca: Cornell University Press.

Redfield, R. (1953b). The natural history of the folk society. *Social Forces, 31*, 224-8.

Redfield, R. and Singer, M. (1954). City and countryside: the cultural interdependence. In T. Shanin (Ed.), *Peasants and peasant societies*. Middlesex: Penguin Books, 1971.

Rees, W.D. (1975). The bereaved and their hallucinations. In B. Schoenberg et al. (Eds.), *Bereavement: its psychosocial aspects*. New York: Columbia University Press.

Regan, J.W. (1971). Guilt, perceived injustice, and altruistic behavior. *Journal of Personality and Social Psychology, 33*, 124-32.

Regan, D., Williams, M., and Sparling, S. (1972). Voluntary expiation of guilt: a field experiment. *Journal of Personality and Social Psychology, 34*, 42-5.

Regis, E., Jr. (1980). What is ethical egoism? *Ethics, 91*, 50-62.

Rehm, L.P. (1977). A self-control model of depression. *Behavior Therapy, 8*, 787-804.

Reich, A. (1954). Early identifications as archaic elements in the superego. *Journal of the American Psychoanalytic Association, 2*, 218-38.

Reich, A. (1960). Pathologic forms of self-esteem regulation. *Psychoanalytic Study of the Child, 15*, 215-32.

Reiss, D. (1982). *The family's construction of reality*. Cambridge: Harvard University Press.

Rescorla, R.A. and Solomon, R.L. (1967). Two-process learning theory: relationships between Pavlovian conditioning and instrumental learning. *Psychological Review, 74*, 151-82.

Riesman, D., Denny, R., and Glazer, N. (1961). *The lonely crowd*. New Haven: Yale University Press.

References

Robertson, R., Ed. (1969). *Sociology of Religion*. Middlesex: Penguin Books.

Rodin, M, Michaelson, K., and Britan, G.M. (1978). Systems theory in anthropology. *Current Anthropology, 19*, 747-62.

Rogers, C. (1959). A theory of therapy, personality, and interpersonal relationships, as developed in the client-centered framework. In S. Koch (Ed.), *Psychology: a study of a science*, Vol.3. New York: McGraw-Hill.

Rogers, C. (1961). *On becoming a person*. Boston: Houghton Mifflin.

Roheim, G. (1943). *The origin and function of culture*. New York: Anchor Books.

Rorty, A.O. (1982). From passions to emotions and sentiments. *Philosophy, 57*, 159-172.

Rosch, E. (1978). Principles of categorization. In E. Rosch and B.B. Lloyd (Eds.), *Cognition and categorization*. Hillsdale, New Jersey: Lawrence Erlbaum.

Rosenberg, M. (1979). *Conceiving the self*. New York: Basic Books.

Rosenblatt, J.S. (1969). The development of maternal responsiveness in the rat. *American Journal of Orthopsychiatry, 39*, 36-56.

Ross, L. (1977). The intuitive psychologist and his shortcomings. In L. Berkowitz (Ed.), *Advances in experimental social psychology*, Vol.10. New York: Academic Press.

Rostow, W.W. (1963). *The stages of economic growth: a noncommunist manifesto*. Cambridge: Cambridge University Press.

Rotter, J.B. (1954). *Social learning and clinical psychology*. Englewood Cliffs, New Jersey: Prentice-Hall.

Rotter, J.B. (1966). Generalized expectancies for internal versus external control of reinforcement. *Psychological Monographs, 80*, Whole No.609.

Rousseau, J.J. (1964). *The first and second discourses*. New York: St. Martin's Press.

Rousseau, J.J. (1974). *Emile*. London: J.M. Dent and Sons.

Rousseau, J.J. (1978). *On the social contract: with Geneva manuscript and political economy*. New York: St. Martin's Press.

Roxborough, I. (1979). *Theories of underdevelopment*. Atlantic Highlands, New Jersey: Humanities Press.

Rubenstein, C., Shaver, P., and Peplau, L.A. (1982). Loneliness. In Krebs, D. (Ed.), *Readings in social psychology: contemporary perspectives* (2nd ed.). New York: Harper and Row.

Ruble, D.N. and Rholes, W.S. (1981). The development of children's perceptions and attributions about their social world. In J.H. Harvey, W. Ickes, and R.F. Kidd (Eds.), *New directions in attribution research*, Vol. 3. Hillsdale, New Jersey: Lawrence Erlbaum.

Russell, B. (1945). *A history of western philosophy*. New York: Touchstone Books.

Ryan, A. (1972). "Normal" science or political ideology. In P. Laslett, W.G. Runciman, and Q. Skinner (Eds.), *Philosophy, Politics, and Society*, 4th series. Oxford: Basil Blackwell.

Sahlins, M.D. (1965). On the sociology of primitive exchange. In Association of Social Anthropologists of the Commonwealth Monograph No. 1, *The relevance of models for social anthropology*. New York: Praeger.

References

Sahlins, M.D. (1968). *Tribesmen*. Englewood Cliffs, New Jersey: Prentice-Hall.

Sander, L.W. (1975). Infant and caretaking environment: investigation and conceptualization of adaptive behavior in a system of increasing complexity. In J. Anthony (Ed.), *Explorations in child psychiatry*. New York: Plenum Press.

Sandler, J. and Rosenblatt, B. (1962). The concept of the representational world. *Psychoanalytic Study of the Child*, 17, 128-45.

Sapir, E. (1934). Emergence of a concept of personality in a study of cultures. In *Selected writings of Edward Sapir in language, culture and personality*, D. Mandelbaum (Ed.). Berkeley: University of California Press.

Sapir, E. (1949). *Culture, language and personality*. Berkeley: University of California Press.

Sartre, J. (1957). *Existentialism and human emotions*. New York: Wisdom Library.

Sartre, J.P. (1971). *Being and nothingness*. New York: Citadel Press.

Sartre, J.P. (1976). *Critique of dialectical reason*. New York: New Left Books.

Schachtel, E.G. (1947). On memory and childhood amnesia. *Psychiatry*, 10, 1-26.

Schachter, S. and Singer, J.E. (1962). Cognitive, social, and physiological determinants of emotional state. *Psychological Review*, 69, 397-9.

Schank, R.C. and Abelson, R.P. (1977). *Scripts, plans, goals, and understanding*. Hillsdale, New Jersey: Lawrence Erlbaum.

Scharf, B.R. (1970). *The sociological study of religion*. London: University Library.

Scheier, M.F., Fenigstein, A. and Ross, A.H. (1974). Self-awareness and physical aggression. *Journal of Experimental and Social Psychology*, 10, 264-73.

Scheier, M.F. and Carver, C.S. (1982). Cognition, affect, and self-regulation. In M.S. Clark and S.T. Fiske (Eds.), *Affect and cognition: the 17th annual Carnegie symposium on cognition*. Hillsdale, New Jersey: Lawrence Erlbaum.

Schneider, D.M. (1968). *American kinship: a cultural account*. Englewood Cliffs, New Jersey: Prentice-Hall.

Scholte, B. (1973). The structural anthropology of Claude Lévi-Strauss. In J.J. Honigmann (Ed.), *Handbook of social and cultural anthropology*. Chicago: Rand-McNally.

Schutz, A. (1967a). *Collected papers*, Vol.1, M. Natanson (Ed.). The Hague: Martinus Nijhoff.

Schutz, A. (1967b). *The phenomenology of the social world*. Evanston: Northwestern University Press.

Schwartz, L., reporting. (1973). Technique and prognosis in the treatment of narcissistic personality disorders. *Journal of the American Psychoanalytic Association*, 21, 617-32.

Schwartz, N. and Clore, G.L. (1983). Mood, misattribution, and judgments of well-being: informative and directive functions of affective states. *Journal of Personality and Social Psychology*, 45, 513-23.

Scott, J.P. (1980). The function of emotions in behavioral systems: a systems theory analysis. In R. Plutchik and H. Kellerman (Eds.), *Emotion*, Vol.1, *Theories of emotion*. New York: Academic Press.

Scribner, S. and Cole, M. (1981). *The psychology of literacy*. Cambridge: Harvard University Press.

References

Seligman, M. (1972). Phobias and preparedness. In M.E.P. Seligman and J.L. Hager (Eds.), *Biological boundaries of learning*. New York: Appleton.

Seligman, M. (1975). *Helplessness: on depression, development, and death*. San Francisco: W.H. Freeman.

Seligman, M., Abramson, L., Semmel, A., and Von Baeyer, C. (1979). Depressive attributional style. *Journal of Abnormal Psychology, 88*, 242-7.

Seligman, M. and Johnston, J.C. (1973). A cognitive theory of avoidance learning. In F.J. McGuigan and D.B. Lumsden (Eds.), *Contemporary approaches to conditioning and learning*. Washington, D.C.: Winston.

Selman, R.L. (1980). *The growth of interpersonal understanding: developmental and clinical analyses*. New York: Academic Press.

Selman, R.L. and Byrne, D.F. (1974). A structural-developmental analysis of role-taking in middle childhood. *Child Development, 45*, 803-6.

Selye, H. (1936). A syndrome produced by diverse nocuous agents. *Nature, 138*, 32.

Sennett, R. (1974). *The fall of public man: on the social psychology of capitalism*. New York: Vintage Books.

Sewell, W.H. Jr. (1980). *Work and revolution in France: the language of labor from the old regime to 1848*. Cambridge: Cambridge University Press.

Shanin, T. (1971). *Peasants and peasant society*. Middlesex: Penguin Books.

Shantz, C.U. (1975). The development of social cognition. In E.M. Hetherington (Ed.), *Review of child development research*, Vol. 5. Chicago: University of Chicago Press.

Shapira, A. and Madsen, M.C. (1969). Cooperative and competitive behavior of kibbutz and urban children in Israel. *Child Development, 40*, 609-17.

Shapiro, D. (1965). *Neurotic styles*. New York: Basic Books.

Sheehy, G. (1976). *Passages: predictable crises of adult life*. New York: E.P. Dutton.

Sherrod, L.R. (1981). Issues in cognitive-perceptual development: the special case of social stimuli. In M.E. Lamb and L.R. Sherrod (Eds.), *Infant social cognition: empirical and theoretical considerations*. Hillsdale, New Jersey: Lawrence Erlbaum.

Shevrin, H. (1978). Evoked potential evidence for unconscious mental processes: a review of the literature. In A.S. Pragishvili, A.E. Sherozia, and F.V. Bassin (Eds.), *The unconscious: nature, functions, and methods of study*. Tbilisi, USSR: Metsiereba Publishing House.

Shevrin, H. and Dickman, S. (1980). The psychological unconscious: a necessary assumption for all psychological theory? *American Psychologist, 35*, 421-34.

Shiffrin, R.M. and Schneider, W. (1977). Controlled and automatic human information processing: II. Perceptual learning, automatic attending, and a general theory. *Psychological Review, 84*, 127-90.

Shils, E. (1975). *Center and periphery: studies in macrosociology*. Chicago: University of Chicago Press.

Shiner, L.E. (1975). Tradition/modernity: an ideal type gone astray. *Comparative studies in society and history, 19*, 245-53.

Shklar, J. (1969). *Men and citizens: a study of Rousseau's social theory*. Cambridge: Cambridge University Press.

References

Shweder, R.A. and Bourne, E.J. (1982). Does the concept of the person vary cross-culturally? In A.J. Marsella and G.M. White (Eds.), *Cultural conceptions of mental health and therapy*. Boston: D. Reidel.

Silverman, L. (1976). Psychoanalytic theory: "The reports of my death are greatly exaggerated." *American Psychologist, 31*, 621-37.

Singer, J.L (1979). Affect and imagination in play and fantasy. In C.E. Izard (Ed.), *Emotions in personality and psychopathology: an introduction*. New York: Plenum Press.

Singer, M. (1968). Culture. In D. Sills (Ed.), *International encyclopedia of the social sciences*, Vol.4. New York: Free Press.

Skinner, B.F. (1953). *Science and human behavior*. New York: Free Press.

Skinner, B.F. (1971). *Beyond freedom and dignity*. Middlesex: Penguin Books.

Skinner, B.F. (1974). *About behaviorism*. New York: Vintage Books.

Skocpol, T. (1979). *States and social revolutions: a comparative analysis of France, Russia, and China*. Cambridge: Cambridge University Press.

Smelser, N.J. and Smelser, W.T. (1963). *Personality and social systems*. New York: Wiley.

Smith, E.A. (1983). Anthropological applications of optimal foraging theory: a critical review. *American Anthropologist, 24*, 625-51.

Snyder, C.R. and Smith, T.W. (1982). Symptoms as self-handicapping strategies: the virtues of old wine in a new bottle. In G. Weary and H. Mirels (Eds.), *Integrations of clinical and social psychology*. New York: Oxford University Press.

Solomon, R. (1971). *Mao's revolution and the Chinese political culture*. Berkeley: University of California Press.

Solomon, R.L. (1980). The opponent-process theory of acquired motivation. *American Psychologist, 35*, 691-712.

Sorokin, P. (1947). *Society, culture, and personality*. New York: Harper and Brothers.

Spielberger, C.D. (1979). *Understanding stress and anxiety*. New York: Harper and Row.

Spindler, G.D. (1955). *Sociocultural and psychological processes in Menomini acculturation*. Berkeley: University of California Press.

Spindler, G.D., Ed. (1978). *The making of psychological anthropology*. Berkeley: University of California Press.

Spiro, M.E. (1952). Ghosts, Ifaluk, and teleological functionalism. *American Anthropologist, 63*, 820-4.

Spiro, M.E. (1961). Social systems, personality, and functional analysis. In B. Kaplan (Ed.), *Studying personality cross-culturally*. Evanston, Illinois: Row, Peterson.

Spiro, M.E. (1965). *Context and meaning in cultural anthropology*. New York: Free Press.

Spruiell, V. (1975). Narcissistic transformations in adolescence. *International Journal of Psychoanalysis, 4*, 518-36.

Sroufe, L.A. and Waters, E. (1977). Attachment as an organizational construct. *Child Development, 48*, 1184-99.

425

References

Stanner, W.E. (1958). The dreaming. In W.A. Lessa and E.Z. Vogt (Eds.), *Reader in comparative religion: an anthropological approach*. New York: Harper and Row, 1972.

Steinbruner, J. (1974). *The cybernetic theory of decision: new dimensions of political analysis*. Princeton, New Jersey: Princeton University Press.

Stent, G.S., Ed. (1978). *Morality as a biological phenomenon: the presuppositions of sociobiological research*. Berkeley: University of California Press.

Sternberg, R.J. (1979). The nature of mental abilities. *American Psychologist, 34,* 214-30.

Sternberg, S. (1975). Memory scanning: new findings and current controversies. *Quarterly Journal of Experimental Psychology, 27,* 1-32.

Steward, J. (1955). *Theory of culture change: the methodology of multilinear evolution*. Urbana: University of Illinois Press.

Steward, J. (1968). Cultural ecology. In D. Sills (Ed.), *International encyclopedia of the social sciences,* Vol.4. New York: Free Press.

Stone, M.H. (1981). *The borderline syndromes: constitution, personality, and adaptation*. New York: McGraw-Hill.

Stotland, E., Sherman, S.E., and Shaver, K.G. (1971). *Empathy and birth order*. Lincoln: University of Nebraska Press.

Straus, A.S. (1977). Northern Cheyenne ethnopsychology. *Ethnos, 5,* 326-57.

Straus, A.S. (1982). The structure of the self in Northern Cheyenne culture. In B. Lee (Ed.), *Psychosocial theories of the self*. New York: Plenum Press.

Sullivan, B.J. (1979). Adjustment in diabetic adolescent girls: II. Adjustment, self-esteem, and depression in diabetic adolescent girls. *Psychosomatic Medicine, 41,* 127-38.

Sullivan, H.S. (1953). *The interpersonal theory of psychiatry*. New York: W.W. Norton.

Swanson, G.E. (1960). *The birth of the gods: the origin of primitive beliefs*. Ann Arbor: University of Michigan Press.

Swann, W.B. and Reid, S.J. (1981). Acquiring self-knowledge: the search for feedback that fits. *Journal of Personality and Social Psychology, 41,* 1119-28.

Taylor, S.E. and Crocker, J. (1980). Schematic bases of social information processing. In E.T. Higgins, P.M. Herman, and M.P. Zanna (Eds.), *Social cognition: the Ontario symposium*. Hillsdale, New Jersey: Lawrence Erlbaum.

Thomas, D.L., Gecas, V., Weigert, A., and Rooney, E. (1974). *Family, socialization, and the adolescent*. Lexington, Massachusetts: Heath.

Tilly, C. (1978). *From mobilization to revolution*. Reading, Massachusetts: Addison-Wesley.

Tinbergen, N. (1951). *The study of instinct*. New York: Oxford University Press.

Tipps, D. (1973). Modernization theory and the comparative study of societies: a critical perspective. *Comparative Studies in History and Society, 15,* 199-226.

Tizard, B. and Hodges, J. (1978). The effect of early institutional rearing on the development of eight-year-old children. *Journal of Child Psychology and Psychiatry, 19,* 99-118.

426

References

Tolman, E.C. (1948). Cognitive maps in rats and men. *Psychological Review, 55,* 189-208.

Tolman, E.C. (1951). *Behavior and psychological man.* Berkeley: University of California Press.

Tönnies, F. (1957). *Community and society.* New York: Harper and Row.

Trevarthen, C. (1977). Descriptive analyses of infant communicative behavior. In H.R. Schaffer (Ed.), *Studies in mother-infant interaction.* New York: Academic Press.

Triandis, H.C. (1972). *The analysis of subjective culture.* New York: Wiley.

Triandis, H.C., Ed. (1980). *The handbook of cross-cultural psychology,* 6 vols. Boston: Allyn and Bacon.

Trivers, R. (1971). The evolution of reciprocal altruism. *Quarterly Review of Biology, 46,* 35-57.

Trivers, R.L. and Hare, H. (1976). Haplodiploidy and the evolution of the social insects. *Science,* 249-63.

Tulving, E. (1972). Episodic and semantic memory. In E. Tulving and W. Donaldson (Eds.), *Organization of memory.* New York: Academic Press.

Turk, D.C. and Salovey, P. (in press). Cognitive structures, cognitive processes, and cognitive-behavior modification: I. Client issues. *Cognitive Therapy and Research.*

Turner, V.W. (1967). *A forest of symbols: aspects of Ndembu ritual.* Ithaca, New York: Cornell University Press.

Turner, V.W. (1969). *The ritual process.* Chicago: Aldine.

Tylor, E.E. (1958). *The origins of culture.* New York: Harper and Row.

Unger, R.M. (1975). *Knowledge and politics.* New York: Free Press.

Vaillant, G. (1977). *Adaptation to Life.* Boston: Little, Brown.

van der Waals, H. (1965). Problems of narcissism. *Bulletin of the Menninger Clinic, 29,* 293-311.

van Gennep, A. (1908). *The rites of passage.* M.B. Vizedom and G.L. Caffee (Trans.). Chicago: University of Chicago Press.

Vygotsky, L.S. (1978). *Mind and society: the development of higher psychological processes.* Cambridge: Harvard University Press.

Wachtel, P.L. (1977). *Psychoanalysis and behavior therapy: toward an integration.* New York: Basic Books.

Wachtel, P.L. (1982). *Resistance: psychodynamic and behavioral approaches.* New York: Plenum Press.

Waelder, R. (1936). The principle of multiple function. *Psychoanalytic Quarterly, 5,* 45-62.

Wallace, A.F.C. (1956). Revitalization movements. *American Anthropologist, 58,* 264-81.

Wallace, A.F.C. (1961). *Culture and personality.* New York: Random House.

Wallace, A.F.C. (1966). *Religion: an anthropological view.* New York: Random House.

Wallace, A.F.C. (1972). Paradigmatic processes in culture change. *American Anthropologist, 74,* 467-78.

427

References

Wallace, A.F.C. (1980). Review of "Cultural Materialism." *American Anthropologist*, 82, 423-6.

Wallerstein, I. (1974). *The modern world-system: capitalist agriculture and the origins of the European world-economy in the sixteenth century.* New York: Academic Press.

Wallerstein, I. (1980). *The modern world-system II: mercantilism and the consolidation of the European world economy, 1600-1750.* New York: Academic Press.

Warner, W.L. (1937). *A black civilization: a social study of an Australian tribe.* New York: Harper and Row.

Watson, J. (1925). *Behaviorism.* New York: W.W. Norton, 1970.

Watson, M.W. and Fischer, K.W. (1977). A developmental sequence of agent use in late infancy. *Child Development, 48,* 828-36.

Weber, M. (1946). *From Max Weber: essays in sociology,* H. Gerth and C.W. Mills (Eds.). New York: Oxford University Press.

Weber, M. (1947). *The theory of social and economic organization.* New York: Free Press.

Weber, M. (1949). *The methodology of the social sciences.* E.A. Shils and H.A. Finch (Trans. and Eds.). New York: Free Press.

Weber, M. (1958). *The Protestant ethic and the spirit of capitalism.* New York: Scribner's.

Wegner, D.M. and Vallacher, R.R., Eds. (1980). *The self in social psychology.* New York: International Universities Press.

Weinberg, N.M., Gold, P.E., and Sternberg, D.B. (1984). Epinephrine enables Pavlovian fear conditioning under anesthesia. *Science, 223,* 605-7.

Weinstein, F. and Platt, G. (1969). *The wish to be free: society, psyche, and value change.* Berkeley: University of California Press.

Weinstein, F. (1973). *Psychoanalytic sociology: an essay on the interpretation of historical data and the phenomena of collective behavior.* Baltimore: Johns Hopkins Press.

Werner, E. (1979). *Cross-cultural child development: a view from the planet earth.* Monterey, California: Brooks/Cole.

Werner, H. (1947). The concept of development from a comparative and organismic point of view. In D.B. Harris (Ed.), *The concept of development.* Minneapolis: University of Minnesota Press.

Werner, O. (1973). Structural anthropology. In J.J. Honigmann (Ed.), *Handbook of social and cultural anthropology.* Chicago: Rand-McNally.

Westen, D. (1984a). Cultural materialism: food for thought or bum steer? *Current Anthropology, 25,* 639-53.

Westen, D. (1984b). The superego: heir to the Oedipus complex or successor to a different throne? Unpublished manuscript.

Westen, D. (1984c). On the relation between narcissism and egocentrism. Unpublished manuscript.

Westen, D. (1984d). Information processing and transference in psychotherapy. Unpublished manuscript.

Wheelis, A. (1958). *The quest for identity.* New York: W.W. Norton.

References

Whitaker, C.S., Jr. (1967). A dysrhythmic process of political change. *World Politics, 19,* 190-217.

White, L. (1949). *The evolution of culture: the development of culture to the fall of Rome.* New York: McGraw-Hill.

White, L. (1949). *The science of culture.* New York: Grove.

White, R.W. (1959). Motivation reconsidered: the concept of competence. *Psychological Review, 66,* 297-333.

White, R.W. (1960). Competence and the psychosexual stages of development. In N. Jones (Ed.), *Nebraska Symposium on Motivation.* Lincoln, Nebraska: University of Nebraska Press.

White, R.W. (1963). *Ego and reality in psychoanalytic theory: a proposal regarding independent ego energies.* Psychological Issues, Monograph 11, Vol.3, No.3.

White, R.K. (1972). The pro-us illusion and the black-top image. In B.T. King and E. McGinnies (Eds.), *Attitudes, conflict, and social change.* New York: Academic Press.

Whiting, B. (1950). *Paiute sorcery.* Viking Fund Publications in Anthropology, No.15.

Whiting, B. and Whiting, J.W.M. (1975). *Children of six cultures: a psychocultural analysis.* Cambridge: Harvard University Press.

Whiting, J.W.M. (1959). Sorcery, sin and the superego. In N. Jones (Ed.), *Nebraska Symposium on Motivation.* Lincoln: University of Nebraska Press.

Whiting, J.W.M. and Child, I.L. (1953). *Child training and personality.* New Haven: Yale University Press.

Whiting, J.W.M., Kluckhohn, R., and Anthony, A. (1958). The function of male initiation ceremonies at puberty. In E.E. Maccoby, T.M. Newcomb, and E.L. Hartley (Eds.), *Readings in social psychology.* New York: Henry Holt and Company.

Whiting, J.W.M. and Whiting, B.B. (1973). Altruistic and egoistic behavior in six cultures. In L. Nader and T. Maretzki (Eds.), *Cultural illness and health.* Washington, D.C.: American Anthropological Association.

Wicklund, R.A. (1975). Objective self-awareness. In L. Berkowitz (Ed.), *Advances in experimental social psychology,* Vol. 8. New York: Academic Press.

Wicklund, R.A. and Frey, D. (1981). Cognitive consistency: motivational versus nonmotivational perspectives. In J.P. Forgas (Ed.), *Social cognition: perspectives on everyday understanding.* New York: Academic Press.

Wiley, R. (1979). *The self-concept,* Vol. 2. Lincoln: University of Nebraska Press.

Williams, G.C. (1966). *Adaptation and natural selection: a critique of some current evolutionary thought.* Princeton: Princeton University Press.

Wilson, B.R. (1966). *Religion in secular society.* London: Watts.

Wilson, E.O. (1978). *On human nature.* New York: Bantam Books.

Wilson, W.R. (1975). *Unobtrusive induction of positive attitudes.* Unpublished doctoral dissertation, University of Michigan.

Winnicott, D. (1971). *Playing and reality.* New York: Basic Books.

Witkin, H.A. and Berry, J.W. (1975). Psychological differentiation in cross-cultural perspective. *Journal of Cross-Cultural Psychology, 6,* 4-87.

References

Wolf, E. (1966). *Peasants*. Englewood Cliffs, New Jersey: Prentice-Hall.

Wolf, E. (1969). *Peasant wars of the twentieth century*. New York: Harper and Row.

Wolff, P.H. (1960). *The developmental psychologies of Jean Piaget and psychoanalysis. Psychological Issues*, Monograph 5, Vol.1.

Wolin, S. (1968). Paradigms and political theories. In P. King and B.C. Parekh (Eds.), *Politics and experience*. Cambridge: Cambridge University Press.

Wolpe, J. (1974). *The practice of behavior therapy*. New York: Pergamon Press.

Wynne-Edwards, V.C. (1962). *Animal disperson in relation to social behavior*. Edinburgh: Oliver and Boyd.

Young, F.W. (1962). The function of male initiation ceremonies: a cross-cultural test of an alternative hypothesis. *American Journal of Sociology, 67,* 379-96.

Young, F.W. (1965). *Initiation ceremonies: a cross-cultural study of status dramatization*. New York: Bobbs-Merrill.

Zajonc, R.B. (1968). Attitudinal effects of mere exposure. *Journal of Personality and Social Psychology Monograph*, Vol. 9.

Zajonc, R. (1980). Feeling and thinking: preferences need no inferences. *American Psychologist, 35,* 151-75.

Zajonc, R. (1984). On the primacy of affect. *American Psychologist, 39,* 117-23.

Zajonc, R., Pietromonaco, P., and Bargh, J. (1982). Independence and interaction of affect and cognition. In M.S. Clark and S.T. Fiske (Eds.), *Affect and cognition: the 17th annual Carnegie Symposium on cognition*. Hillsdale, New Jersey: Lawrence Erlbaum.

Zillman, D. (1978). Attribution and misattribution of excitatory reactions. In J.H. Harvey, W. Ickes, and R.F. Kidd (Eds.), *New directions in attribution research*, Vol. 2. Hillsdale, N.J: Lawrence Erlbaum.

Index

431

Index

Campbell, D., 101n, 153, 218, 253, 294, 306
Cantor, N., 12, 13, 20, 60, 102, 111-12
capitalism, 191-2, 348, 353-4, 389
Carneiro, R., 201n, 268
character, 119, 123, 125
charisma, 192, 279, 356, 372, 377, 383-5
Cheyenne, 315-17, 323
Child, I., 290-3, 327-8
child abuse, 113-14
Christie, R., 388
Clark, M., 65, 76, 182
class, 212, 216, 218, 231, 234-7, 265
cognition (*see also* information processing), 29, 53, 59-64, 71-2, 173, 183-4; and culture, 230, 240, 308, 345n; unconscious, 200
cognitive development, 168, 170n
cognitive dissonance, 19, 35
cognitive-evaluative mismatch, 43, 47, 53, 64, 80, 83, 125, 220, 308; and cognition, 71; and depression, 84-90; hierarchical organization, 59-63; and morality, 147-8; and motivation, 97, 100; and self-esteem, 76, 112-13; and stress, 92
cognitive psychology, 59-60, 96
cognitive social learning theory, 3, 12-15, 18, 49, 67, 77, 115-16, 291; and emotion, 22-3, 29; moral autonomy, 178; moral development, 145-8, 171-2; motivation, 57; and psychotherapy, 184
cognitive therapy, 26, 84-8, 184
Cohen, P., 249
Cole, M., 312-13, 345n
collective consciousness, 193, 218, 224, 249, 351
collective representations, *see* schema, collective
collectivism, 241, 384
Collins, A., 40, 59, 78
Comaroff, J., 252
communitarian collectivism, 245, 263, 265-6, 271, 275, 280-1, 392; and personality, 311-29, 349-50, 359-60, 364-5, 368, 379, 381, 383, 384, 390; *see also* primary communitarian collectivism, secondary communitarian collectivism
competence, 99, 150, 181; and modernization, 346; *see also* self-efficacy
compromise-formation, 32, 47, 58, 60, 81, 138, 239; cultural, 226, 230-2, 248-9, 294, 302
conditioning (*see also* reinforcement), 9-11, 25-8, 40, 50, 71, 75-6, 295; and morality, 161, 167, 171-2; and psychotherapy, 81; and unconscious emotion, 68-9, 80
configurations, *see* culture pattern

conflict-free ego sphere, 124
context of discovery, 181
context of justification, 181
control mechanism (*see also* coping, defense mechanism), 24, 33, 35, 89, 124, 184, 369; cultural, 220-4, 239, 247, 292, 299-309, 363-4, 379; and ego processes, 115; hierarchical organization, 116-17; routinization, 47, 119, 224; style, 119
Coombs, G., 204-5
Coon, C., 244
coping (*see also* control mechanism, stress and coping): hierarchical organization, 42, 62-3, 116-17; response to affect, 33, 34, 38; style, 119
Craig, D., 325
cross-cultural psychology, 297-8
cultural integration, 367-8, 383; disintegration, 305, 356-60, 367-8, 379, 384; disintegration in Java, 360-5
cultural relativism, 195-6, 237-40
cultural selection, 232-3, 280, 306-9
culture ideal, 219, 224-9, 233, 239, 249, 360-7; and ego ideal, 300-1, 349, 356; evolution, 241, 245-6, 256, 259-60, 263, 268, 311, 326
culture pattern, 196, 212, 216, 237n, 288-9
culture real, 219-29, 244, 360-7; evolution of, 268, 275, 279-80

Darley, J., 35
Darwin, C., 33, 101n, 280n, 293-4
Dawkins, R., 107
de Laguna, 314-16
decision models, 203-6, 303-4, 307
defense mechanism (*see also* control mechanism), 7, 8, 30, 32, 45, 116-17n, 117-18, 291; cultural, 222, 228, 239-40, 305; hierarchical organization, 42, 122; and motivation, 50; response to affect, 33, 38, 46, 52; and stress, 93; style, 119
Denich, B., 203-4
d'Entreves, A., 273
dependencia theory, 330
depression, 27, 84-91, 113-14, 122
Deutsch, K., 33, 350
developmental lines, 48, 51, 123, 183
differentiation, 175, 177, 310-11; in infancy, 155-6, 160-1; of self-schemas from ideal self, 165; social-structural, 258, 313; symbolic/cultural, 245, 250-5, 313-29
Dinka, 321-4
Dollard, J., 22, 31-2
Doob, L., 335-6
Douglas, M., 45, 223-4, 308, 319, 323, 368-9, 379, 381, 383

432

Index

Index

Index

learned helplessness, 88, 113
Lee, D., 252-3, 300, 316, 318
Lerner, D., 332, 334-8, 351
LeVine, R., 218-19, 226-7, 253, 288-9, 292-6, 307, 348, 387
Lévi-Strauss, C., 197-201, 211, 214, 248-9, 254, 266, 281, 301-2, 319, 325, 390
Lévy-Bruhl, L., 313
Lewis, M., 157, 319
libido, 5, 101, 102, 129-30, 133; *see also* psychosexual development
Lienhardt, G., 321-4
Lifton, R., 109, 342, 246, 358, 377-80, 383, 385
Lindemann, E., 43, 126
Linton, R., 217, 224, 289-90
Little, B., 12, 81
Locke, J., 275, 278-9
Loevinger, J., 103, 136, 150-3, 173, 281
Loftus, E., 40, 59, 78
Luckmann, T., 269, 304, 342, 347
Lukes, S., 231
Luther, M., 273-4

McClelland, D., 296, 301, 336-8, 340
Maccoby, E., 160, 165
McFall, 62
Machiavelli, N., 273-4; Machiavellianism, 388
MacIntyre, A., 269-70, 273-4
Madsen, M., 387
Mahler, M., 159-62, 163
malevolent transformation, 171
Malinowski, B., 197, 233, 249-50, 285, 323
Maring, 203n, 220-2, 324
Markus, H., 13, 111-12
Marris, P., 383
Marshall, L., 254
Marx, K., 189, 291-3, 201-2, 207, 208, 210, 212, 216, 234, 241-3, 266, 290, 296, 338, 391; civil and political society, 217, 242-3; Marxism, 218, 231, 236-7, 263, 279, 347, 360; Marxist anthropology, 233; and modernization, 344, 348, 353-4; and religion, 226; structural Marxism, 233
Maslach, C., 50, 82, 85
Maslow, A., 98-9, 151, 170
mastery, *see* competence
material, 191, 217; conditions, 201, 207; cultural materialism, 206-10; interests, 201, 235; Marxian materialism, 208; materialism, 210, 225, 337; vs. ideal, 210-12
Mauss, M., 256, 316-17
Mead, M., 196, 288, 350-1
meaning-system, *see* structures of meaning
Meichenbaum, D., 13, 85

member-needs, 217-19, 228, 233, 239, 367-8; and class, 235-6
mental processing, 61n, 76n
Merton, R., 227, 229, 230, 241, 357
Meyer, D., 78
Migdal, J., 330, 350
Milgram, S., 32
Mill, J., 277
Miller, N., 22, 31-2
misattribution, *see* attribution
Mischel, W., 12-16, 20, 36, 60, 81, 111, 117-18, 145-8
Mitchel, V., 3
mode of production, 191, 210
modeling, 12, 71, 82, 146-8; and identification, 165-7
modernization, 191, 330-4, 355-8, 367, 384-5; approaches to psychodynamics, 334-45; and ego ideal, 346-54, 386-90; and identity, 361, 366
Moore, B., 248, 262, 360n
moral autonomy, *see* autonomy
moral development, 136, 158; cognitive-developmental theory, 140-6; psychoanalytic theory, 136-40, 146; social learning theory, 145-8
morality, 105-7, 142-4, 241-2, 391-3; and culture, 267; and individuated collectivism, 278; moral judgment, 163; moral philosophy, 269-79, 391-3; moral psychology, 105, 154, 178, *see also* moral development; peasant, 260
motives, 97-8, 100, 107; *see also* cognitive-evaluative mismatch, needs
Motley, M., 78-9, 182
mourning, *see* grieving
multiple functions, 230, 249; mutlifunctionalism, 230, 234
multiple loyalties, 217-19, 222
Munroe, R.H., 294, 388
Munroe, R.L., 294, 388
Mussen, P., 389
myth, 198-9, 293, 301, 307; communitarian collectivism, 247-50

narcissism, 104, 110, 131-5, 154, 159, 163n, 168, 267, 286; and collectivism, 267, 384; and culture, 241; pathological, 131, 169, 279, 358, 384
nationalism, 236-7, 300, 366, 384-5
Ndembu, 216, 222, 247-8, 255, 264-5, 308
needs, 99, 217
network of association, *see* associational networks
Nietzsche, F., 122, 140, 277-9, 391
Nisbett, R., 51-2, 79, 166, 182-3
Nuer, 251

435

Index

Index